Understanding Employment Relations

Understanding Employment Relations

Derek Rollinson and Tony Dundon

**McGraw-Hill
Higher Education**

London Boston Burr Ridge, IL Dubuque, IA Madison, WI New York San Francisco
St. Louis Bangkok Bogotá Caracas Kuala Lumpur Lisbon Madrid Mexico City
Milan Montreal New Delhi Santiago Seoul Singapore Sydney Taipei Toronto

Understanding Employment Relations
Derek Rollinson and Tony Dundon
ISBN-13 978 0077114862
ISBN-10 0-07-711486-8

McGraw-Hill
Higher Education

Published by McGraw-Hill Education
Shoppenhangers Road
Maidenhead
Berkshire
SL6 2QL
Telephone: 44 (0) 1628 502 500
Fax: 44 (0) 1628 770 224
Website: www.mcgraw-hill.co.uk

British Library Cataloguing in Publication Data
A catalogue record for this book is available from the British Library

Library of Congress Cataloging in Publication Data
The Library of Congress data for this book has been applied for from the Library of Congress

Commissioning Editor: Rachel Gear
Editorial Assistant: Karen Harlow
Marketing Manager: Alice Duijser
Production Editor: James Bishop

Text design by Hard Lines
Cover design by Paul Fielding Ltd.
Typeset by Wearset Ltd, Boldon, Tyne and Wear
Printed and bound in Spain by Mateu Cromo Artes Graficas SA, Madrid

ISBN-13 978 0077114862
ISBN-10 0-07-711486-8

Dedication

To my wife Victoria, whose tolerance and help enabled this book to be written, and my daughter Sara, who kept my feet on the floor.
Derek Rollinson

To my wife Diane, and children Liam and Kate, who have offered so much support and encouragement during the writing of this book.
Tony Dundon

Brief table of contents

Detailed table of contents

Preface

About this book

This book deals with employment relations in Great Britain. It has been written to make it suitable for students and lecturers of employment relations, personnel management and human resource management, and in particular, for students with no prior exposure to this subject. However, it also gives access to some of the more advanced knowledge in the area, which makes it of use to those who wish to commence studying the subject at a higher level. More specifically, the book is directed at final year undergraduate and postgraduate students taking these subjects as part of a first degree, diploma or masters degree. The book has also been written for use on programmes that are recognised as meeting the professional standards for employee relations as set out by the Chartered Institute of Personnel and Development (CIPD). An essential part of these professional standards is for students to acquire a range of skills and competences in the area, and there are several components of the book that facilitate this. These are:

- *integration chapters*, which explain the connections between processes and themes
- dedicated *skills-based chapters*, such as Chapter 6, which covers discipline and grievance handling skills, and Chapter 10, which covers negotiating skills
- *pause for reflection exercises*
- *case studies*
- *margin notes*
- *review* and *discussion questions*.

In addition, an online learning centre accompanies the book (www.mcgraw-hill.co.uk/textbooks/rollinson), containing extra resources for both lecturers and students. These include additional teaching materials, assignments and skills exercises. The way that the book provides coverage of CIPD's professional standards is summarised in Table M1.

Not so very long ago this book would have used the expression 'Industrial Relations', rather than 'Employment Relations' in its title. Indeed, as you will see when you read Chapter 1 of the book, industrial relations is a subject area from which employment relations traces its origins. However, without going into matters in great detail at this stage, industrial relations and employment relations have analytical and conceptual differences in terms of their underlying philosophies and assumptions. Industrial relations is almost exclusively focused on the ways that rules and regulations in employment are made and modified, often by placing heavy emphasis on the role of collective bargaining as a central process in managing workplace conflict. This means that industrial relations has a strong tendency to restrict itself to considering only large, unionised settings, and there are very few industrial relations texts that consider small firms or the non-union setting. While employment relations also addresses the nature of conflict in employment, it is much more eclectic in its approach. For example, it considers informal as well as formal workplace relations; it embraces the social, economic and psychological dynamics of workplace relations, and includes processes and outcomes in both small and large, union and non-union organisations. It also recognises that as well as having opposing

Employee relations management in context	The parties in employee relations	Employee relations processes	Outcomes	Employee relations skills
Understanding employment relations				
(*1.1*) Chapters 1 and 2 (*1.2*) Chapter 2 (*1.3*) Chapters 2 and 5 (*1.4*) Chapter 5 and Integration 1 (*1.5*) Chapter 5	(*2.1*) Chapter 3 (*2.2*) Chapters 4 and 8 (*2.3*) Chapter 5	(*3.1*) Chapter 8 (*3.2*) Chapter 5 (*3.3*) Chapter 3 (*3.4*) Chapter 9 (*3.5*) Chapter 11 (*3.6*) Chapter 5	(*4.1*) Chapters 6–12 (*4.2*) Integrations 2, 3 and 4	(*5.1*) Chapter 10 (*5.2*) Chapter 9 (*5.3*) Chapter 6 (*5.4*) Chapter 6 (*5.5*) Chapter 7 (*5.6*) Chapters 8 and 10
Note Numbers in parentheses and italics refer to the CIPD indicative content topics.				

Table M1 CIPD professional standards for employee relations
Source: adapted from: CIPD Professional Standards for Employee Relations, www.cipd.co.uk (April 2006).

interests, the parties usually have interests in common; otherwise they would have no incentive for the relationship to continue. Employment relations also has an abiding interest in many of the changes that have occurred in the past two decades, some of which have had a strong influence on the ways that employment relationships are made and modified. For example, the globalisation of trade has resulted in a more unstable and volatile environment in which firms have to operate, which in turn means that firms themselves have to change more frequently. There has also been a vast increase in the amount of legislation affecting employment, which gives an additional reason for firms to make internal adjustments. Moreover, the structure of industry itself has changed in significant ways, as has the nature and composition of the labour market in Great Britain. Perhaps most important of all, working people could well have different aspirations in terms of the rewards and obligations they expect from paid employment. Therefore, employment relations also gives consideration to implicit and informal contracts – for example, to the psychological contract and whether this is satisfied for employees, or alternatively violated in some way because of changes in contextual factors or employer actions. It is for these reasons that the term 'employment relations' has eclipsed 'industrial relations'. Indeed, the title of the well-respected Workplace Industrial Relations Survey, now in its fourth cycle, has been changed to Workplace Employment Relations Survey. The study of employment relations therefore requires that we acknowledge the complex and dynamic nature of the relationship between employers and employees. It also requires that we recognise that there are both formal and informal aspects of the relationship, and that, as well as having tangible physical and economic dimensions, the relationship also has psychological and social dimensions, which are equally important in small and large firms, and in unionised and non-unionised settings.

Using the book

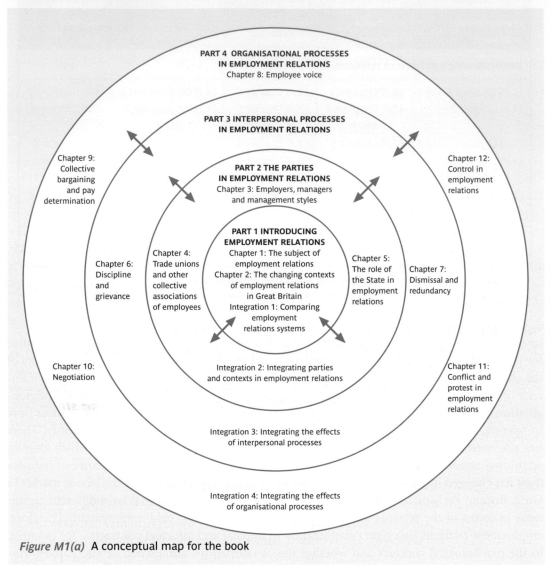

Figure M1(a) A conceptual map for the book

The structure of the book

The above diagram, which indicates the contents of the book, has two main uses. As can be seen, while the book is divided into four main parts, it is important to note that straddling the boundaries of each part there are a pair of double-headed arrows. These reflect the idea that the issues or topics covered in different chapters are all interconnected in some way. Thus the first use for the diagram is to emphasise that the reality of employment relations is often highly complex and varied.

The second use for the diagram, which is somewhat simpler, is as a navigational aid to help the reader steer him or herself through the book. For this reason it will reappear in a slightly modified form in the short introductions that precede the four parts into which the book is divided. Each of these parts deals with topics that are focused on a particular facet of employment relations, and are briefly described in what follows.

Part 1 *Introducing employment relations*

This section contains two chapters that are introductory in nature. The first gives a general introduction to the subject of employment relations, and this is based on the assumption that the reader has no prior exposure to the subject. The second chapter deals with effects of the surrounding environment on employment relations, and explains how the changes in the surrounding contexts have influenced the nature of British employment relations. These two chapters are followed by the first of the four integrative chapters in the book. This extends the discussion given in Chapter 2, by demonstrating how the characteristics of employment relations in three additional countries reflect the influence of certain inbuilt features, such as national cultures, laws and economic conditions.

Part 2 *The parties in employment relations*

This section contains three chapters, each of which is focused on one of the main parties in employment relations. These are: employers and managers and management styles (Chapter 3); trade unions and employee associations (Chapter 4); and the State (Chapter 5). At its end, the section has a short integrative chapter (Integration 2), which traces some of the ways in which the actions of these parties are interconnected and influenced by wider environmental factors. It also shows that the behaviour of any two of these parties can have an impact on the behaviour of the third.

Part 3 *Interpersonal processes in employment relations*

The two chapters in this section both deal with what could most conveniently be described as interpersonal process. These are: discipline and grievance (Chapter 6); and dismissal and redundancy (Chapter 7). They are followed by an integrative chapter (Integration 3) that traces links between the ways in which the conduct of these processes can affect the employment relations climate in a firm. It also draws attention to the idea that the way in which any of these processes is conducted is strongly connected to other processes and outcomes in employment relations.

Part 4 *Organisational processes in employment relations*

The chapters in this section deal with five important organisational level processes: employee voice (Chapter 8); collective bargaining and pay determination (Chapter 9); negotiation (Chapter 10); conflict and protest behaviour (Chapter 11); and control in employment relations (Chapter 12). These are followed by the fourth integrative chapter (Integration 4), which explains how the processes are interconnected; how conduct of these processes can have an impact on the employment relations climate of an organisation; and also how the ways in which they are conducted can impact on other processes and outcomes.

How to use the book
General

There is considerable variation between lecturers in terms of what they consider to be the necessary minimum coverage for a particular topic. They also differ in terms of the amount of time they have available for instruction. However, in the interests of providing a text that can be used by the widest possible number of lecturers, this book has purposely been made comprehensive in terms of the number of theories and concepts covered in each chapter. Indeed, some chapters will contain far more information than a lecturer wishes to use. For this reason chapters have been written in a way that allows (if necessary) some of the material to be omitted. Therefore, lecturers should not hesitate to be selective about the concepts and theories they use from each chapter.

For the most part chapters in the book deal with separate topics, and each one has a clear set of learning outcomes that can be met by covering its contents. Therefore, providing the general structure of the book is followed, it is not vital to use the chapters in the order in which they appear. The material reflects teaching styles that have now become more common in higher education in Great Britain. It is also cognisant of the professional standards required by CIPD, which place an emphasis on *learning* and *applying knowledge* to real-world situations. Both of these mean that there is now less emphasis on formal, in-class instruction, and students are required to take increased responsibility for aspects of their own learning outside the classroom. For this reason periods of instruction often have a stronger focus on checking that learning has taken place, and applying the skills and concepts through exercises and/or case studies. To facilitate this, the book has been written as a complete vehicle of instruction in its own right, rather than just background reading. Each chapter contains a full explanation of the concepts and theories it contains, together with associated exercises and/or case studies that can be used to apply the material. There are two main reasons for doing this. First, to produce a text in which students and instructors have confidence. Second, the aim has been to *eliminate the need for an additional workbook to support the text*. This latter point reflects the difficulty of persuading students to buy *any* book, let alone an additional one, at a time when their income has been progressively reduced by cutbacks in funding.

Activities featured in the text

A set of **Learning Outcomes** is given at the start of each chapter, and these tell the reader what he or she should be able to understand or accomplish, after covering the chapter's contents. To some extent, these can also be used by students to measure their own progress.

A small number of **Pause for Reflection** exercises are included in each chapter. These are very short exercises that confront the reader with questions that encourage the application of concepts and theories covered in the text, but in a way that prompts the person to draw on his or her own learning and experiences. While these are primarily designed to be an aid to learning, which allows students to complete exercises outside the classroom, they can, if required, be used for classroom discussion. The text also provides **Margin Notes**, which define new concepts as they are introduced, and these are also brought together at the end of the book in a **Glossary**.

From Chapter 3 onwards each chapter contains a number of short **Case Studies,** which give students the opportunity to apply a single concept or theory. In addition, the online learning centre contains supplementary cases, which bring together several concepts or theories. Most cases are drawn from real-life situations, some from the authors' own experiences of encountering these conditions within an organisational context, when collecting research data. Others were reported to the authors by students or colleagues and were subsequently written up into cases. Although primarily intended for in-class use, the longer cases can also be used as material around which assignments or examination questions can be based.

Exhibit boxes will also be found in most chapters. These are not case studies in the accepted meaning of the expression, although they can be used to illustrate a point or to stimulate discussion in applying skills and knowledge. They are real-world examples of the application of concepts or theories covered in the text, and sometimes they supplement a point already made in the chapter. Their main use is to emphasise the idea that theories and concepts in employment relations are not abstract pieces of knowledge constructed for the amusement of academics, but things that find real-world applications in organisations.

Summary Points will also be found at the end of each major section of a chapter. Each one consists of a list of bulleted points that re-emphasise concepts, theories, ideas and themes contained in the section.

At the end of each chapter there is a block of **Review and Discussion Questions**. These can be used for a final review of its contents, or to re-emphasise its major points. They can also be used for separate tutorials, or as a check on learning. Finally, for those who may wish to delve deeper into a particular topic or issue, each chapter also contains a short list of **Further Reading** at its end.

List of abbreviations

ACAS	Advisory, Conciliation and Arbitration Service
ACOP	Approved Code of Practice
AEEU	Amalgamated Engineering and Electrical Union
AEU	Amalgamated Engineering Union
AFL-CIO	American Federation of Labor – Congress of Industrial Organisations
ASE	Amalgamated Society of Engineers
BA	British Airways
BDA	British Dental Association
BMA	British Medical Association
BPR	Business Process Re-engineering
BT	British Telecom
CAB	Citizens Advice Bureau
CAC	Central Arbitration Committee
CBI	Confederation of British Industry
CCT	Compulsory Competitive Tendering
CEHR	Commission for Equality and Human Rights
CIPD	Chartered Institute of Personnel and Development
CMI	Chartered Management Institute
CPSA	Civil and Public Servants Association
CRE	Commission for Racial Equality
CWU	Communication Workers Union
DRC	Disability Rights Commissioner
DTI	Department of Trade and Industry
EAT	Employment Appeals Tribunal
ECC	European Consultative Council
EEF	Engineering Employers Federation
EIRO	European Industrial Relations Observatory
EOC	Equal Opportunities Commission
ESOP	Employee Share Ownership Plan
ETUC	European Trades Union Confederation
ETUI-REHS	European Trade Union Institute for Research, Education and Health and Safety
EU	European Union
EWC	European Works Council
FDR	Federal Republic of Germany
GCHQ	Government Communications Headquarters
GDR	German Democratic Republic
GMB	General, Municipal and Boilermakers Union (now just called the GMB Union)
GPMU	Graphical, Paper and Media Union
HPWS	High Performance Work Systems
HRIS	Human Resource Information Systems
HRM	Human Resource Management
HSC	Health and Safety Commission
HSE	Health and Safety Executive

IBM	International Business Machines
ICE	Information and Consultation of Employees Regulations, 2004
ICI	Imperial Chemical Industries
ICT	Information and Communication Technology
ILO	International Labour Organisation
IPA	Involvement and Participation Association
IPRP	Individual Performance Related Pay
IRS	Industrial Relations Services
JIT	Just In Time Management
JSSC	Joint Shop Steward Committee
JWC	Joint Works Council
LPC	Low Pay Commission
LSC	Learning and Skills Council
MBO	Management By Objectives
MSF	Manufacturing, Science and Finance Union
NASUWT	National Association of Schoolmasters and Union of Women Teachers
NFU	National Farmers Union
NHS	National Heath Service
NLRB	National Labour Relations Board
NMW	National Minimum Wage
NUT	National Union of Teachers
PBR	Payment By Results
PCSU	Public and Commercial Services Union
PFI	Private Finance Initiative
POEU	Post Office Engineering Union
PRB	Pay Review Body
PRP	Profit Related Pay
QWL	Quality of Working Life
RCN	Royal College of Nursing
RSA	Royal Society for the Encouragement of Arts, Manufactures and Commerce
SAYE	Save As You Earn
SCoR	Society and College of Radiographers
SME	Small to Medium Sized Enterprise
SNB	Special Negotiating Body
TEC	Training and Enterprise Council
TGWU	Transport and General Workers Union
TINA LEA	This Is Not A Legally Enforceable Agreement
TUC	Trades Union Congress
TULRCA	Trade Union and Labour Relations (Consolidation) Act, 1992
TUPE	Transfer of Undertakings (Protection of Employment) Regulations
UCW	Union of Communication Workers
ULR	Union Learning Representatives
UNICE	Union of Industrial and Employers' Confederations of Europe
UNISON	The public service union
USA	United States of America
USDAW	Union of Shop, Distributive and Allied Workers
WERS	Workplace Employment Relations Survey

Guided tour

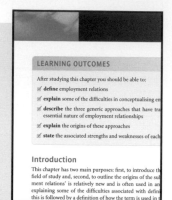

Learning outcomes

Each chapter opens with a set of learning outcomes, summarising what students should learn from each chapter.

Pause for reflection boxes

Throughout the book these quick activities ask students to consider their own ideas on the topics presented.

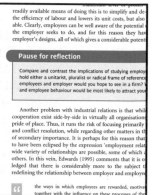

Margin notes

Key terms are highlighted throughout the chapter and definitions provided in the margin so they can be found quickly and easily.

Case studies

There are a number of case studies throughout the text which place concepts into a real-life context and increase students' understanding.

Summary point boxes

These briefly review and reinforce the main topics students have just covered to ensure they have acquired a solid understanding of the key concepts.

Summary points
- The social exchange perspective argues that the emp... than a simple economic or legal exchange.
- Five shared features of the social exchange situation c... employment relationships. These are: the exchange c... evaluations of fairness; unvoiced expectations and ob... unequal power of the parties.
- These features are largely responsible for the prevale... continually surface in the employment relationship.
- A recent expression of social exchange as applied to t... the psychological contract.

An overview and integration of the th...

As noted earlier, none of the three perspectives given above... are all different frames of reference that can be used to vie... reason, they should not be regarded as competing viewpoints... For ease of comparison in what follows, their major featu... where, because it is now an important conceptualisation in it... column.

An obvious conclusion that can be drawn from this com... picture of the complexity of the employment relationship is... these perspectives, and this can be illustrated by considering...

Exhibit boxes

These real world examples illustrate points and stimulate discussion of main topics.

The statement should cover the following:
1 The identities of the employer and employee.
2 Date of commencement of employment, and whether any previo... as continuous.
3 The job title, nature of work (but not necessarily a full job descrip... with an indication of whether there could be a requirement to wor...
4 The rate of remuneration (including overtime rates) or methods by...
5 Whether paid weekly, monthly, or at some other interval.
6 Hours of work and normal working hours.
7 Holidays, rights to holidays, and pay on termination.
8 Provision for sickness and injury and entitlements to pay.
9 Pensions rights.
10 Entitlement to receive notice of termination of employment and o...
11 Disciplinary rules that apply.
12 The person to whom application can be made of a dissatisfactio... raise any other grievance.
13 The procedure to be followed on any such application.
14 Whether a contracting-out certificate is in force under Social Secur...
15 If the contract is for a fixed period, the date of its expiry.
16 Any terms of collective agreements that affect work conditions.

The intention of legislation is that the document should reduce the s... it is not in itself a contract, nor is it conclusive proof of all of its terms... ment of what the employer believed the major terms to be at the time... required that the document spell out in explicit detail all the informati... to other documents which contain the details, and to which access can...

Exhibit 1.1 Written particulars of terms and conditions of employ...

controversial is the fact that the sole author of the rules is inva...

Figures and tables

Each chapter provides a number of figures and tables to illustrate and summarise ideas.

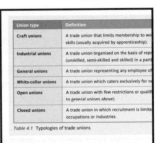

Union type	Definition
Craft unions	A trade union that limits membership to wo... skills (usually acquired by apprenticeship).
Industrial unions	A trade union organised on the basis of repo... (unskilled, semi-skilled and skilled) in a part...
General unions	A trade union representing any employee of...
White-collar unions	A trade union which caters exclusively for n...
Open unions	A trade union with few restrictions or quali... to general unions above).
Closed unions	A trade union in which recruitment is limite... occupations or industries

Table 4.1 Typologies of trade unions

Although the first three types shown at the top of Table 4.1... there are a number of shortcomings. First, because there are... entry to salaried and clerical employees, for completeness W... be added. However, the biggest problem is that the techno... these union categories were once based have changed out of al... the original craft unions now represent unskilled and semi-... unions have their own white-collar or clerical membership se... of union mergers over the last two decades. Thus, it would be...

Review and discussion questions

These end-of-chapter questions encourage students to review and apply the knowledge they have acquired from that chapter.

Review and discussion que...
1 Describe each of the four environmen...
2 In your own words briefly explain w... different employment relations proce...
3 In what way does European social pol...
4 Briefly describe how the changing co... relations processes and outcomes.
5 Explain key differences between nume...
6 Given that flexibility is something o... might there be for employees with flex...
7 What is meant by blurred organisatio... for employment relations processes an...
8 How does the current political and le... of 10 or 15 years ago?
9 Briefly define the terms 'union substit...
10 Explain how technology has changed... tion.

Further reading

This annotated list acts as a useful resource for students who wish to increase their knowledge of a particular topic.

Further reading

Baldry, C. (2003) 'Employment relations in the... Relations, Law and Practice, 4th edn, B. Tow... changes in technology over the last decade,... many organisations have impacted on employ...

Bryson, A. and R. Gomez (2005) 'Why Have W... Membership in Britain', British Journal of Ind... ant article that explains the rise and extent of... been union members, using data from the Bri...

Dundon, T. and A. Wilkinson (2003) 'Emplo... Employment Relations, Law and Practice, 4th... chapter devoted specifically to employment... prises in Britain.

Ewing, K. (2003) 'Industrial relations and the la... trial Relations in Transition, P. Ackers and... thoughtful essay that examines the impact of t... tions, and in particular the implications for vo...

Forth, J., H. Bewley and A. Bryson (2006) Sma... 2004 Workplace Employment Relations Surve... Routledge. Similar to the 'first findings' boo...

Online Learning Centre (OLC)

After completing each chapter, log on to the supporting Online Learning Centre website. Take advantage of the study tools offered to reinforce the material you have read in the text, and to develop your knowledge in a fun and effective way. These resources are designed to make your learning easier and to act as a useful revision tool for exams and tests – we hope you find them useful!

Resources for students include:

- *Chapter outlines*
- *Hints for completing exercises and using case studies*
- *Additional case studies*
- *Multiple choice questions and answers*

Also available for lecturers:

- *Chapter outlines*
- *Assessment materials*
- *Case studies*
- *PowerPoint slides*
- *Additional questions*
- *Teaching notes*

Details of this online content are correct at the time of going to press and may be subject to change.

Lecturers: customise content for your courses using the McGraw-Hill Primis Content Centre

Now it's incredibly easy to create a flexible, customised solution for your course, using content from both US and European McGraw-Hill Education textbooks, content from our Professional list including Harvard Business Press titles, as well as a selection of over 9000 cases from Harvard, Insead and Darden. In addition, we can incorporate your own material and course notes.

For more information, please contact your local rep, who will discuss the right delivery options for your custom publication – including printed readers, e-Books and CD-Roms. To see what McGraw-Hill content you can choose from, visit ***www.primisonline.com***.

Study skills

Open University Press publishes guides to study, research and exam skills to help undergraduate and postgraduate students through their university studies.

Visit *www.openup.co.uk/sg/* to see the full selection of study skills titles, and get a **£2 discount** by entering the promotional code **study** when buying online!

Computing skills

If you'd like to brush up on your computing skills, we have a range of titles covering MS Office applications such as Word, Excel, PowerPoint, Access and more.

Get a £2 discount on these titles by entering the promotional code **app** when ordering online at *www.mcgraw-hill.co.uk/app.*

Acknowledgements

Authors' acknowledgements

We are grateful to The Department of Trade and Industry for permission to use Figure 4.1, H. Grainger and H. Holt, from *Trade Union Membership 2004, Employment Market Analysis and Research*, April 2005.

In addition, we would like to extend our grateful thanks to the following, who have helped in the completion of this book: Wally Russell, European Employee Relations Manager, Hewlett Packard, who provided details of Hewlett Packard's information and consultation forum; Alan Roe, Amicus officer, who provided details of partnership and collective bargaining agreements; and John Forth, WERS 2004 Information and Advice Service, for timely details and help with the interpretation of WERS data.

Publisher's acknowledgements

Our thanks go to the following reviewers for their comments at various stages in the text's development:

Richard Beresford – Oxford Brookes University
Bob Mason – University of Ulster
Peter Prowse – University of Bradford
Brian Critchley – London Metropolitan University
Jereme Snook – Nottingham Trent University
Geoffrey Wood – University of Sheffield
Edward Lugsden – Newcastle University
Steve Fleetwood – Lancaster University

PART 1

Introducing employment relations

Part contents

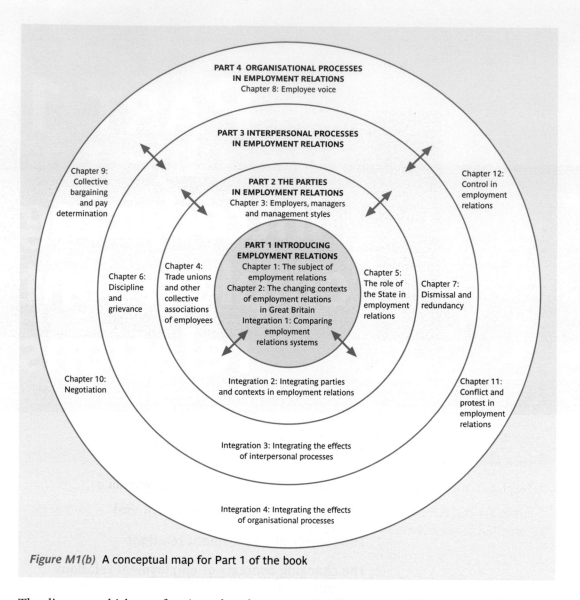

Figure M1(b) A conceptual map for Part 1 of the book

The diagram, which was first introduced on page xii, tells you that this part of the book contains three chapters. Two of these are introductory in nature. The first introduces the subject of employment relations and the second describes the contexts of employment relations in Great Britain. These are followed by an integrative chapter, which compares employment relations in three additional countries.

Chapter 1

The subject of employment relations

LEARNING OUTCOMES

After studying this chapter you should be able to:

- ☑ **define** employment relations
- ☑ **explain** some of the difficulties in conceptualising employment relationships
- ☑ **describe** the three generic approaches that have traditionally been used to portray the essential nature of employment relationships
- ☑ **explain** the origins of these approaches
- ☑ **state** the associated strengths and weaknesses of each approach.

Introduction

This chapter has two main purposes: first, to introduce the reader to employment relations as a field of study and, second, to outline the origins of the subject. Because the expression 'employment relations' is relatively new and is often used in an imprecise way, the chapter starts by explaining some of the difficulties associated with defining an employment relationship, and this is followed by a definition of how the term is used in this book.

Employment relations can trace its origins to three separate, but interconnected, streams of thought, each of which is taken by its advocates to represent the very essence of what is meant by the term 'an employment relationship'. The next part of the chapter considers each of these in turn and explains its origins, how it conceptualises the employment relationship, and the strengths and weaknesses of the approach. Finally, the chapter closes with a section that integrates these three perspectives into a more comprehensive view of employment relations;

a view that embraces all three approaches but is, of necessity, broader than any one of them when used on its own.

Employment relations: towards a definition

There is considerable debate about what constitutes an employment relationship, and what can be taken to be its most important characteristics. To some extent this problem exists because there are several different ways in which the relationship can be conceptualised, and these will be discussed presently. For the present, however, it can be noted that most employment relationships are replete with potential ambiguities and contradictions. For example, although workers and managers have some objectives in common, there are others in which their interests can be diametrically opposed, which means that the employment relationship is one in which antagonisms and cooperation can exist side-by-side (Edwards, 2003). To give a simple if somewhat obvious example: employers often desire profit maximisation, but at the same time employees want an equitable share in the profits from their labours. Having said this, even where conflicts of this type exist, one can argue that there is some scope for them to be reconciled. For instance, one route to profitability is to engage the commitment and cooperation of labour, which can go some way towards satisfying employee desires for employment security, social status and identity. However, a lasting reconciliation of this type still usually requires some form of employee cooperation, if not compliance. One of the things that stands in the way of this is that the balance of power in the workplace is normally tilted heavily in favour of management (Blyton and Turnbull, 2004). For this reason, employees often have a perceived need to erect and maintain enduring checks and balances on management power.

Even without these things, current conditions have made it much harder to be specific about the nature of the employment relationship. For instance, one school of thought draws attention to the idea that the whole nature of work within modern organisations has undergone such a radical change that traditional conceptions of employment are now obsolete (Gallie and White, 1998). According to this viewpoint employers increasingly demand more flexible and accommodative modes of production and service delivery from employees and, to achieve this, nonstandard patterns of work such as part-time, temporary and casual employment have become far more commonplace, all of which has resulted in a major reconfiguration of the labour market in most industrialised economies. An allied argument by Rubery *et al.* (2001) points to widespread changes in work structures, in which traditional boundaries between workers and their employing organisations have become increasingly blurred by such practices as complex multi-employer networking, public–private partnerships, commercial alliances and franchising systems, all of which have serious implications for the legal and socially constructed image of the employment relationship. To quote:

> the notion of a clearly defined employer–employee relationship becomes difficult to uphold under conditions where the employee is working in project teams, or on a site alongside employees from other organisations, where responsibilities for performance and for health and safety are not clearly defined, or involve organisations other than the employer.
>
> (Rubery *et al.*, 2001: 1)

Given that the factors noted above are increasingly prevalent in today's conditions, any definition of employment relations is likely to be controversial. Accordingly, a rather broad definition of the subject is adopted for this book. This defines employment relations as:

> " a field of study that deals with the formal and informal relationship between an organisation and its employees. This embraces the potentially wide range of inter-actions and processes by which the parties to the relationship adjust to the needs, wants and expectations of each other in the employment situation. "

A number of important points, to which the reader is asked to pay special attention, flow from this definition:

- The definition embraces both formal and informal aspects of the relationship.
- Since the definition embraces processes of adjustment and (by implication) change, an employment relationship is not something static and unchanging, but an extremely dynamic state of affairs.
- The definition points to the idea that the parties to the relationship each have their own needs, wants and expectations, which means that there is always some potential for conflict in the relationship.
- Strictly speaking, the definition is based on what is technically called a **reification**. That is, it treats an abstract idea (an organisation) as something that is tangible and real, in the same way that a person or persons (employees) are tangible and real. However, since this has by now become a common reflection of the way that people conceive of (and refer to) the world, it is meaningful to retain it as part of the definition.

reification
To treat an abstract idea as something that actually exists.

Alternative conceptions of the employment relationship

Historically, a number of different perspectives on the nature of the employment relationship have emerged. None of these is inherently right or wrong. Rather, they are different **paradigms** that can be used to view the same phenomenon, and each tends to be accepted by a particular community of interest. Within each of these paradigms there are also different schools of thought that emphasise particular facets of the relationship, and to try to cover them all would be well beyond the scope of this chapter. For this reason, only the mainstream approaches will be described and this will include an explanation of the factors prompting the emergence of each particular view, together with a note of its strengths and weaknesses.

paradigm
An example or model, which is used as a standard and expresses the prevailing framework of theories and concepts.

Pause for reflection

Before you go on to read about it, try to define what you understand by the expression the *legal conception of the employment relationship*. What do you feel could be the particular strengths of what you have described? Are there any potential weaknesses?

The legal conception of the employment relationship

Theoretically, although this is by far the most straightforward view of what constitutes an employment relationship, it is probably the weakest of all theoretical perspectives. It views the *contract of employment*

A legal agreement in which an offer of employment is made by an employer, and accepted by the employee.

relationship between employer and employee as a contract: the **contract of employment**. This is generally taken to be the cornerstone of British labour law (Kahn-Freund, 1967) and there are three major assumptions underpinning the nature of the contract, that:

- the relationship is an individual one, made between two parties of equal bargaining strength

- it consists of a promise to work (or to be available for work) in return for which payment is promised

- since there has been a free exchange of promises, the two parties have reciprocal, but different rights and obligations (Kahn-Freund, 1977).

The idea of a contract of employment dates from reforms to master–servant legislation that took place in the latter half of the nineteenth century, and was prompted by pressures exerted by early trade unions. Although this removed many impediments to genuine freedom of contract, some of the prior concepts remain, and there are still some important ways in which the idea of a master–servant relationship persist, which effectively gives the employer a great deal of power to decide, unilaterally, what the terms of the contract should be (Hepple, 1983). For this reason there is a strong element of unreality in the notion that a person who accepts an offer of employment is fully conversant with all the terms and details it contains. Indeed, it has been powerfully argued that the contract is not even an agreement about terms and conditions, but simply an agreement to enter into a relationship, the terms and conditions of which have yet to emerge (Honeyball, 1989).

The idea of a contract of employment has both economic and legal implications (Davis and Freedland, 1983). In economic terms it forms the basis of wages, holidays and other fringe benefits that are not necessarily delineated by law in an explicit way. In addition, because it also covers matters that go beyond the simple economic exchange of rewards for service, the contract also influences factors such as how employees are managed in order to meet market demands and the performance of the firm (Clark, 1994). As such, there are a number of difficulties inherent in the very idea of a contract, two of which arise in its underpinning assumptions. The first of these is the assumption that the contract is an individual one. This implies that each employee has a personal contract with the employing organisation, which can be called into question by the reality of most work situations. These contain a number of very powerful forces that induce people to abandon a great deal of their individuality. For example, people are normally brought together into groups and departments, which inevitably means that they develop a sense of collective identity about some matters. In addition, it is probably not convenient for an employer to treat employees in a totally individual way, and there are usually rules of the workplace that apply to everyone. As such, many issues in employment are virtually certain to have a collective element.

Second, there is the matter of an imbalance of power in the relationship, about which the employment contract is notoriously silent. This is underpinned by an assumption that the parties enter into the relationship of their own free will and that either party can refuse to do so. In a practical sense, however, even this can be questioned. Cohen (1988) alludes to the dilemma between free in theory and forced in practice by citing the example of an unemployed, unskilled worker faced with the choice of taking a hazardous job, or no job at all.

> To infer from the fact that John was free to do other things, that he was therefore not forced to take a hazardous job, is to employ a fake account of what it is to be forced to do something. When a person is forced to do something he has no reasonable or acceptable alternative course. He need not have an alternative at all.
>
> (Cohen, 1988: 245)

Kahn-Freund (in Davis and Freedland, 1983) further takes issue with the idea of employee freedom in the contract of employment by noting:

> In its operation it is a condition of subordination, however much that submission and the subordination may be concealed by that indispensable figment of the legal mind known as the contract of employment.
>
> (Kahn-Freund in Davis and Freedland, 1983: 18)

Terms which make up the contract

Whether or not an offer of employment is made in writing, in strict legal terms someone who accepts an offer has entered into a binding contract of service. When this happens, the terms and conditions under which both parties can later be deemed to have honoured the contract will have been fixed. While these terms come from a variety of sources, for simplicity they can be grouped under six headings, a brief explanation of which is given in what follows.

Expressly agreed terms

These are the specifics of what has been agreed and most of them are, or should be, stated in any written offer of employment that is made. In addition, the Employment Rights Act (1996) requires that within two months of taking up an appointment, employees (other than the small minority who fall into certain excluded categories) should be given a written statement of particulars of employment, which covers certain minimum details (see Exhibit 1.1).

Collectively incorporated terms

Where trade unions negotiate terms and conditions of employment, parts of collective agreements can become incorporated into the contract of each individual. This is usually acknowledged in any offer of employment by noting that pay, hours, holidays and other substantive terms are fixed and varied from time to time in negotiations between the employer and recognised trade unions.

Legislative terms

There are also a number of terms and conditions arising in legislation, which are swept up into the contract and become binding on almost all employees. Many of them are aimed at preventing unfair discrimination, or to ensure compliance with minimum wage legislation and health and safety provisions.

Works and organisational rules

These are one of the most controversial inclusions in the contract, because they sometimes only exist in an informal way. They can also vary from place to place and it can sometimes be difficult to determine whether they are part of the contract. Where they are written down, especially if they are brought to the attention of employees, perhaps by giving them a rule book or posting the rules as notices, they are likely to become contractual terms. What makes them

The statement should cover the following:

1 The identities of the employer and employee.

2 Date of commencement of employment, and whether any previous service with the employer counts as continuous.

3 The job title, nature of work (but not necessarily a full job description) and normal location, together with an indication of whether there could be a requirement to work elsewhere.

4 The rate of remuneration (including overtime rates) or methods by which it is calculated.

5 Whether paid weekly, monthly, or at some other interval.

6 Hours of work and normal working hours.

7 Holidays, rights to holidays, and pay on termination.

8 Provision for sickness and injury and entitlements to pay.

9 Pension rights.

10 Entitlement to receive notice of termination of employment and obligation to give notice.

11 Disciplinary rules that apply.

12 The person to whom application can be made of a dissatisfaction with any disciplinary action, or to raise any other grievance.

13 The procedure to be followed on any such application.

14 Whether a contracting-out certificate is in force under Social Security Pensions provisions.

15 If the contract is for a fixed period, the date of its expiry.

16 Any terms of collective agreements that affect work conditions.

The intention of legislation is that the document should reduce the scope for future ambiguity. However, it is not in itself a contract, nor is it conclusive proof of all of its terms and conditions. Rather, it is a statement of what the employer believed the major terms to be at the time the contract was made. Neither is it required that the document spell out in explicit detail all the information. It can simply refer the employee to other documents which contain the details, and to which access can be gained on request.

Exhibit 1.1 Written particulars of terms and conditions of employment

controversial is the fact that the sole author of the rules is invariably the employer. Moreover, a prospective employee is hardly likely to be shown, or made aware of, the rules as part of the selection process and, because there has been no opportunity to assent or dissent, the terms are effectively imposed in silence. Since the law usually gives an employer a great deal of scope in varying these rules, this part of the contract can be somewhat open-ended (Honeyball, 1989), and this tends to negate the idea that the contract is an agreement made between two equally well-informed parties.

Custom and practice rules

In some situations, local or workplace customs and practices govern the conduct of the parties in much the same way as written agreements (Brown, 1972). Bonus payment rates, notice periods, disciplinary penalties, and speed and conditions of work are all matters that can be decided by local custom, and this can become part of the contract.

Terms implied by common law

In addition to the foregoing, there are a number of implied terms arising in common law that get incorporated into all contracts of employment. Most of them have been handed down from the master–servant conception of employment, and those affecting the employer are regarded as duties that a reasonable employer owes to his employees, for instance to:

- pay wages and salaries (and backdated increases) promptly
- not make unauthorised deductions from pay

- reimburse employees' expenditure on the employer's behalf
- (in certain circumstances) provide work for the employee
- provide a safe system of work
- obey the law and not to require employees to break the law
- (in certain specified circumstances) allow time off from work (not necessarily with pay), for example, for trade union, and certain public, duties.

Those incumbent on the employee are to:

- work and cooperate
- obey reasonable and lawful instructions
- perform competently and proficiently
- take reasonable care and avoid damaging the employer's property
- be trustworthy, honest and behave with integrity.

Since the law regards these obligations as fundamental, it has been argued that this results in a situation where employees are virtually forced to give a very general and diffuse degree of obedience and loyalty, which is seldom reciprocated by the employer (Fox, 1985). The problem is that legislation is often so complex and incomprehensible that laymen lack knowledge of their common-law rights, whereas employers usually have personnel or other specialists to advise them, which gives them a far greater capability to assert their rights in common law (Hyman, 1975). A recent example of this is the passage of the Employment Relations Act (1999) which, among other things, contains a provision for statutory union recognition. Although it is not widespread, there are some employers who are so anxious to avoid recognising trade unions that they have sought the advice of management consultancy and law firms who specialise in circumventing union recognition (Gall, 2004).

floor of rights concept

The idea that individual rights established by law are no more than a fall-back position that can be resorted to if all else fails.

For the above reasons individual labour law really needs to be seen as little more than what one prominent lawyer has described as a **floor of rights** (Wedderburn, 1980), in which the law is something to fall back on, if all else fails. This is the position taken by most trade unions, who tend to see the rights conferred by individual labour law as something they have already achieved (and in many cases exceeded) by collective bargaining. Or, to quote from the doyen of British labour lawyers:

 trade unions are a more effective force in redressing the imbalance of power inherent in the contract than the law has, or ever could be.

(Kahn-Freund, 1977: 10)

Finally, there are difficulties that exist because of the changing nature of organisational structures and rules. The fast growing use by employers of non-standard forms of work have made it increasingly difficult for the courts to decide whether some employees have the protection of a contract of employment. For example, in the case of agency workers or employees based elsewhere than on an employer's main site, it is sometimes unclear who the employer actually is (Rubery *et al.*, 2004).

For all these criticisms, contracting between employer and employee undeniably takes place, and so the legal perspective has a role in conceptualising the employment relationship.

However, the legal perspective is incapable of expressing the complexity, subtlety and potential unevenness of the relationship. As noted earlier, one way in which employees can resolve this is by collectivising and using the agency of a trade union to remove some of the ambiguities and inherent inequalities in the relationship. For this reason it is relevant to consider the industrial relations conception of the employment relationship, which is covered next.

Summary points

■ The legal conception of the employment relationship is that a contract of employment exists between employer and employee.

■ This is underpinned by three major assumptions: it is made by two parties of equal bargaining strength; it consists of a promise to work, for which payment is promised; the two parties have reciprocal, but different rights.

■ The contract is made up of terms originating from one or more of six sources: expressly agreed terms; collectively incorporated terms; legislative terms; works or organisational rules; custom and practice; terms implied in common law.

■ While contracting of some sort inevitably takes place between employer and employee, the contract is notoriously silent about some of the terms and conditions that it contains.

Pause for reflection

Before you go on to read about it, what do you understand the meaning of the term 'industrial relations perspective' to be? How is it likely to differ from the legal conception of the employment relationship and is it likely to have any particular strengths or weaknesses?

The industrial relations perspective

The industrial relations perspective, which came into prominence in the four decades following the end of the Second World War, was a response to the conditions of its time. This was a period in which full employment gave rising affluence and aspirations in the working population of Great Britain, together with a rapid and sustained growth of trade union membership.

unitarist perspective

A frame of reference in which an organisation is seen as one large family, all on the same side and pulling together in the same direction, and in which conflict is seen as deviant behaviour.

This was in sharp contrast with conditions prior to the war, which were characterised by long periods of economic depression, high unemployment and distinctly **unitarist** management perspectives, in which employees who challenged what many managers saw as their prerogatives, were often invited to put up or shut up. Problematically, while economic conditions changed considerably after the war, there were certain fundamental weaknesses in the British economy – notably, declining competitiveness compared to other industrialised nations. In 1968 therefore, the government of the day established a Royal Commission (the Donovan Commission) to investigate what in some quarters had come to be seen as the exercise of power without responsibility by trade unions, and from then until the mid-1980s industrial relations came into its own as an area of academic study.

It is important to point out, however, that industrial relations is not a single approach, but one that draws on a number of academic disciplines, such as history, economics, the law, politics, sociology and psychology (Ackers and Wilkinson, 2003). It is also a subject that contains a number of distinctly different schools of thought, each of which has its own concerns. Nevertheless, the mainstream view is that industrial relations is concerned with:

> the making and administering of rules which regulate the employment relationship; regardless of whether these are seen as formal or informal. structured or unstructured.
>
> (Bain and Clegg, 1974: 95)

Since rules cannot sensibly be understood in isolation from the parties to rule making, of necessity this has traditionally embraced the study of trade unions, management, employer associations, and government and its agencies (Clegg, 1979). Although this results in an approach that has a much stronger recognition of some of the vagueness and ambiguity in industrial behaviour, it nonetheless contains a number of difficulties.

The antecedents of the approach are firmly rooted in the institutions of job regulation, and ever since the seminal, pioneering work of Webb and Webb (1897), this has come down to an almost exclusive focus on collective bargaining; a process that has been described as the 'institutionalisation of conflict' (Flanders, 1965). In essence, this expresses the idea that the collectivisation of labour is a means of counterbalancing unequal power in the employment relationship, allowing employees, through their representatives, to speak with one voice. Indeed, the prominence of industrial relations ideas in academic and industrial circles owes much to a widespread acceptance of the **pluralist perspective**, in which collective bargaining came to be seen as the most practical method of reducing tensions between the parties, primarily by regulating the terms and conditions of employment (Donovan Commission, 1968). One problem, of course, is that this facility is denied to employees in non-union firms and, while in theoretical terms collective representation can occur in other ways than through a trade union, there is very little evidence of any sustainable alternative system (McLoughlin and Gourlay, 1994; Towers, 1997). For this reason, industrial relations has devoted scant attention to the non-union situation. Indeed, it is remarkably silent about how rules could be made and modified where employees are not collectivised, and so pronounced is this silence that it is all too easy to assume that a non-union organisation is an aberration, or even that organisations of this type are all so similar that it is not worth the effort of studying them (Wilkinson, 1999). In some respects this is one of the most severe criticisms of the industrial relations perspective. Even in the early 1980s, when trade unions were at their zenith in the UK with approximately 13 million members, **trade union density** was only slightly over 55 per cent. As a result, industrial relations has always had some tendency to ignore completely a sizeable proportion of the working population. These days, where density is nearer to 30 per cent, the omission is arguably untenable.

Here it is worth mentioning that as well as the unitarist and pluralist frames of reference on industrial relations, there is an additional approach, which goes much further than pluralism. This is the **radical perspective**, the origins of which are derived

pluralist perspective
A frame of reference in which an organisation is seen as a collection of different groups, all with their own legitimate aims to pursue, and so a degree of conflict is a normal state of affairs.

trade union density
The proportion of potential members who are actually in membership of trade unions.

radical perspective
One that argues that employment relations mirrors the inequalities of social class, property ownership and political ideology in wider society.

from the work of Karl Marx (1894) to whom organisational conflicts were simply a manifestation of inherent conflicts in society as a whole – that is, between the interests of those who own the means of production, and those who simply work in enterprises. While space precludes an extensive discussion of this stream of theory, it can be noted that Marx's ideas were 're-discovered' somewhat later and re-surfaced in the guise of what is now known as **labour process theory** (Braverman, 1974). Essentially, this argues that in the capitalist mode of production, the employer has a vested interest in taking control over the labour process – the set of operations that actually transforms raw materials into finished, saleable products – in order to extract the maximum level of profits from employees' efforts. The most readily available means of doing this is to simplify and de-skill work, which not only increases the efficiency of labour and lowers its unit costs, but also makes workers more easily replaceable. Clearly, employees can be well aware of the potential repercussions for themselves of what the employer seeks to do, and for this reason they have a vested interest in resisting the employer's designs, all of which gives a considerable potential for conflict.

---

labour process theory

A neo-Marxist perspective that focuses on employer attempts to control the labour process, and employee attempts to exercise counter-control in return.

Pause for reflection

Compare and contrast the implications of studying employment relations if you, as a student, hold a unitarist, pluralist or radical frame of reference. What sort of relationship between employees and employer would you hope to see in a firm? What particular aspects of employer and employee behaviour would be most likely to attract your attention?

Another problem with industrial relations is that while it recognises that antagonism and cooperation exist side-by-side in virtually all organisations, it is the first of these that receives pride of place. Thus, it runs the risk of focusing primarily on the institutions of job regulation and conflict resolution, while regarding other matters in the employment relationship as being of secondary importance. It is perhaps for this reason that the term 'industrial relations' tends to have been eclipsed by the expression 'employment relations', which accepts that a very wide variety of relationships are possible, some of which are inherently more conflictual than others. In this vein, Edwards (1995) comments that it is only recently that texts have acknowledged that there is considerably more to the subject than analysis has hitherto revealed, redefining the relationship between employer and employee as:

> the ways in which employees are rewarded, motivated, trained and disciplined, together with the influence on these processes of the major institutions involved, namely management, trade unions and the state.

(Edwards, 1995: 3)

It should not be overlooked, however, that a traditional industrial-relations perspective contains a number of important features, some of which can help considerably in understanding the complexities of managing, even in a non-unionised relationship. It goes well beyond the legal definition of the employment contract and also alerts us to the idea expressed by Dunlop (1958) that industrial relations is a sub-system which mirrors conditions in wider society, in which a set of rules based on societal norms, power and authority, and political and legal structures shapes the behaviour of the actors involved. Additionally, it reminds us that the employment relationship is not a static system of consequences and actions, but something that is dynamic and always in motion (Hyman, 1975). Features such as freedom, conflict, power and authority and legitimacy are, therefore, not permanent states but dynamic frontiers of control (Goodrich, 1975) that transcend both time and space. In order to capture some of this dynamic complexity, the discussion will shortly consider a third perspective (social exchange), which can help to build an analytical framework that is more theoretically robust. Before doing so, however, it is important to consider another development which, although it started out as an offshoot of industrial relations research, is now widely accepted as something that is so different, that it has effectively become a new approach in its own right.

The human resource management (HRM) perspective

Across the last two decades, the term 'human resource management' (HRM) has become commonplace as a shorthand expression to describe a different (to industrial relations) approach to managing the employment relationship. The term originated in the USA in the early 1980s, where a number of influential analysts drew the conclusion that in the highly volatile business environment of the late twentieth century, successful organisations would be those that could compete on the basis of rapid innovation and quality, together with an ability to cope with change, all of which would require a particular type of employment relationship. While there is no universally accepted definition of HRM, most accounts argue that its core principles are inherently unitarist, with policies and practices driven by the needs of the business. In the eyes of commentators such as Hendry and Pettigrew (1990) this results in four key characteristics:

- A strong emphasis on planning the use of human resources
- Coherent employment policies that are underpinned by a distinct philosophy
- The machinery of human resource activities is matched with a clearly stated business strategy
- A view of people (employees) as a strategic resource for gaining competitive advantage.

soft HRM
An approach that views employees as valued assets, the appropriate use of which can lead to competitive advantage for an organisation.

hard HRM
An approach focused on bottom-line considerations in which employees are viewed in much the same way as other resources that can be used or disposed of as necessary.

These, however, are very general principles and in practice it is now widely accepted that there are a number of variants, the extremes of which are **soft HRM** and **hard HRM** (Storey, 2001). The soft version is said to stress the word *human*, and is underpinned by ideas associated with the human-relations movement. Here, employees are viewed as valued assets, the appropriate use of which leads to a distinct competitive advantage for the organisation. According to this view, an organisation has (or should have) policies and practices that are geared to producing innovative, resourceful human beings. Thus there is a high emphasis on eliciting a degree of commitment to organisational goals, perhaps by devoting attention to communication and employee involvement (Sisson and Storey, 2000).

In hard HRM the emphasis is on employees as a *resource*. Human-resource policies and practices are primarily driven by bottom-line considerations and are geared to achieving the strategic objectives of the organisation (Formbrun *et al.*, 1984). This can mean that humans are regarded in much the same way as any other resource – for example, land or machinery – which in turn implies a less humanistic approach, and a close watch on effort and headcount. Clearly, therefore, HRM can reflect two diametrically opposed sets of policies and practices and, while the evidence suggests that most organisations articulate the philosophy of soft HRM, in practice the hard version is more frequently encountered (Truss *et al.*, 1997). The theoretical importance of HRM is that it could be used as a substitute for a traditional industrial relations approach. Indeed, from early on in its development a number of writers such as Wickens (1987) argued that HRM is effectively a new model for industrial relations. Moreover, industrial relations scholars such as Edwards (2003) point out that since HRM is a way of managing the employment relationship, it needs to be included in the study of industrial relations. Accordingly, Guest (1995) outlines four different approaches to managing the employment relationship:

1 *Traditional collectivism:* the use of an industrial relations approach, with no emphasis on HRM

2 *New realism:* the use of both industrial relations and HRM approaches in tandem, with high priority given to both

3 *Individualised HRM:* the HRM approach substitutes for the traditional industrial relations approach

4 *The black hole:* which uses neither HRM nor industrial relations.

In more recent work by Guest and Conway (1999) a large sample of organisations was surveyed, approximately 40 per cent of which were unionised. Of these, approximately half had a high usage of HRM practices, which leads to the conclusion that industrial relations and HRM are not mutually exclusive, but can exist side-by-side. This is consistent with other evidence, which suggests that the take-up of HRM has mostly been in organisations that previously relied on a traditional industrial relations approach. Interestingly, in non-union organisations a slightly lower percentage of firms made extensive use of HRM practices. However, in the past two decades there has been a very favourable climate for organisations that wish to work without trade unions, and it has been very difficult for unions to halt the spread of non-unionism. Accordingly, there is more than a possibility that some unionised firms have used HRM practices as a tactic to marginalise collectivised employment relations, by substituting individual reward packages, and using so-called 'joint employee' voice mechanisms such as works councils (Dundon, 2002a; Lloyd, 2001). Thus, in non-union companies these practices could well be used to give an appearance of providing some of the collective features of industrial relations in a situation where there is no intention of recognising trade unions. For this reason, where a reference is made to industrial relations in this book, this should be taken to embrace the use of certain elements of the HRM approach.

Summary points

- The mainstream industrial relations perspective is strongly focused on the rules that regulate the employment relationship.

- It assumes that conflicts of interest between employer and employees are virtually inevitable and that these are best resolved by constructing rules that regulate the employment relationship through collective bargaining mechanisms.

- While it gives a richer account of the complex nature of employment relationships (than the legal perspective), it has a tendency to overstate the prevalence of conflict.

- Because its major focus is on the institutions of collective bargaining (notably trade unions), it gives a less than satisfactory account of relationships in organisations where trade unions are not recognised.
- The study of human resource management (HRM) which has eclipsed other, more traditional approaches for managing the employment relationship, can be viewed as a sub-paradigm of the industrial relations perspective.

Pause for reflection

Before you go on to read about it, what do you understand the meaning of the social exchange perspective to be? What do you feel might be involved in social exchange as opposed to purely economic exchange as a way of conceptualising the employment relationship?

The social exchange perspective

Social exchange theory (Blau, 1964) has a long pedigree of use in both industrial and employment relations. It takes a very broad, but in many ways more penetrating, view of interpersonal relationships, which recognises that the employment relationship is full of inherent ambiguities (Blau, 1964). Although it acknowledges an economic dimension to the relationship, it goes much further by recognising that the parties to the relationship normally expect that it will continue well into the future. Therefore, exchange conditions are not static, but are deemed to have dynamic properties. Because the relationship is also replete with unspecified obligations and expectations, this draws attention to the complexity of the exchange. There are five shared properties that can be used to characterise social exchange relationships, all of which can give rise to a number of problems and issues that keep surfacing in the employment relationship. These are described in what follows.

Costs and benefits

Social exchange theory acknowledges that the basic motivation for an individual to enter a relationship is the rewards that he/she expects to gain. The problem is that a relationship brings not only benefits to the parties, but also costs. For example, while an employee gains salary and other benefits, he/she also forgoes self-determination. Similarly, although a firm gains the benefits of employee effort, it incurs the cost of wages. Because both parties incur costs, they feel that the other one is under some obligation to provide benefits in return. Similarly, anyone who acquires benefits feels (or should feel) an obligation to incur costs. However, it is seldom the case that everything is specified before the commencement of the relationship and this brings us to the second property.

Unvoiced expectations and obligations

Social exchange involves a host of unspecific and unvoiced expectations and obligations. Although people obviously weigh up the costs and benefits when a relationship commences, they also have expectations that the relationship will continue to remain in balance, which means that they expect that the perceived cost–benefit ratio should never be less favourable than it was at the outset. For this reason, if their costs rise, workers tend to have expectations that benefits will increase accordingly. Similarly, if conditions in the environment force a change in the organisation, the employer can feel that employees are obliged to accommodate themselves to this. As noted above, both parties tend to perceive that the other one is under an obligation to comply with these expectations, but seldom, if ever, are these perceived obligations spelt out at the start of the relationship, and this brings us to the third property.

Fairness

Even if the terms of the exchange are only formulated subconsciously, each party to the relationship is aware that he/she has a ratio of costs to benefits. Indeed, if either of them perceives that the cost–benefit ratio is heavily weighted in favour of the other party, he/she is likely to feel that the exchange is unfair, and it is doubtful if that party would willingly enter into the relationship. Problematically, there are no absolute standards of fairness and people tend to define it in a very personal and subjective way; the minimum criterion is usually that costs incurred are matched by the benefits received. Indeed, because the objectives of employers and workers will quite often differ in both substance and content, this illustrates why there is an undercurrent of both *conflict* and *cooperation* within the employment relationship.

An allied matter that often results in evaluations of fairness is **equity**. Because there are no absolute standards of fairness, the expectations of individuals and groups are usually linked to their particular circumstances. This inevitably means that fairness is evaluated in comparison with some other individual or group: that is, they compare their own balance of costs and benefits with what is assumed to be the balance of another individual or group. Comparison groups are usually selected from those that are perceived to be broadly similar, and in close proximity; for example from within the same firm or locality (Gartrell, 1982). If an individual or group perceives that it is under-rewarded in comparison to the reference group, it feels a sense of **relative deprivation**, which often leads to behaviour to redress the imbalance.

equity
The idea that people should be treated with parity to each other in terms of the personal costs they incur, and benefits they accrue from work.

relative deprivation
Feelings of deprivation that arise when one individual or group feels that it has been unfairly treated in comparison to another individual or group.

Trust

No one can know for certain whether the other party will honour his/her obligations and so each party has to take it on trust that this will happen. The problem is that if we trust someone whose behaviour cannot be controlled, we are more vulnerable to their actions and that person has a potential power advantage (Zand, 1972). Nevertheless, trust is the essential lubricant of all on-going relationships and this is as true in the employment relationship as elsewhere. For example, trust is necessary between trade unions and management in order to be able to reach agreements, and for day-to-day activities to be completed smoothly, trust is necessary between a workgroup and their supervisor. However, it is important to realise that there are subtle and crucial ways in which the design of an organisation makes a trusting relationship more or less likely to occur, a lucid explanation of which is given by Fox (1974) in his concept of institutionalised trust. If, for example, jobs are designed to give people very little discretion in what they do, and their behaviour is heavily supervised, they often interpret this as a signal that they are not trusted. Since trust tends to beget trust in return, and mistrust to beget mistrust, it is hardly surprising to find that where job design results in low-discretion work roles, the organisation is often one that has a correspondingly low degree of trust in its employment-relations processes.

power

The capacity of an individual or group to modify the conduct of other individuals or groups in a manner which they desire, without having to modify their own conduct in a manner which they do not desire.

authority

Power conferred on an individual or group as a legitimate part of the person or group's role.

Unequal power

Social-exchange theory explicitly assumes that there is always an imbalance of power in a relationship, and the party that is least able to withstand the severing of the relationship is the one who is potentially at a power disadvantage. Authority, which is the most usual claim to power in organisations, is simply a special way in which power can manifest itself, and is also one of the most prominent issues in employment relations. For example, it is commonplace for a trade union to claim that it has the authority of its members to act in a certain way, and for managers to dispute this. Similarly, management often claims that it has the legitimate authority to make certain decisions without reference to employees, and in return the workforce or its union will assert that management is exceeding its authority. Management has its own rationale to legitimise its authority, and since this is considered in detail in Chapter 3, it will not be explored here. However, any legitimisation of management authority by employees is a matter of social convention and norms more than anything else. Most people are socialised from an early age into accepting that employment involves a degree of direction and control, and that failure to accept the situation inevitably results in sanctions of some sort (Fox, 1971). Like most things, however, there are boundaries to this acceptance, and where these boundaries lie often depends on how much authority management claims. For this reason the ways in which boundaries are established, and sometimes contested, is also one of the most important topics in employment relations.

An imbalance of power is, of course, the most obvious explanation for the collectivisation of employees and, needless to say, the idea of unequal power has implications for the capabilities of the parties to vary the terms of exchange to their own advantage. However, it needs to be recognised that power can be utilised in both overt and covert ways. For example, evidence clearly demonstrates that trade unions have been an enduring check on the use of unfettered employer power.

individualism

A philosophical stance that reflects the idea that each employee should be treated as an individual in the employment relationship.

collectivism

A philosophical stance that recognises that some issues in the employment relationship are best dealt with on a collective basis.

A final issue, which in strict terms is not really one of the shared properties of social exchange, but is nevertheless very important, is that of individualism and collectivism. Because there have been strong moves in the UK to individualise the employment relationship and to de-emphasise its collective aspects, this is currently a very important issue in employment relations. Whether this move has been part of a concerted strategy to weaken the power of trade unions, or more a way of trying to improve productivity by a greater emphasis on individual incentives is still a matter of some debate. Suffice it to say that, although this emphasis is in line with a unitarist and legal view of the employment relationship, as was noted when discussing the contract of employment, it can be argued that many things in the employment relationship are essentially collective in nature.

The psychological contract: an expression of social exchange

A concept that reflects the social exchange view of the employment relationship is that of the psychological contract. Its origins can be traced to ideas put forward by Argyris (1960), who describes it as something that is embedded in the perceptions of both parties to the relationship. The potential importance of the psychological contract was first expressed in a clear way by

Schein (1980), and more recently there has been a significant reawakening of interest in its application to the employment relationship (Guest *et al.*, 1996; Guest and Conway, 1997).

Schein draws attention to the idea that in the employment relationship there are really three types of contract. The formal contract, which deals largely with economic aspects of the exchange, and is reflected in the legal concept of a contract of employment. In addition, there is an informal contract, some of the components of which are derived from wider social norms about how people should treat each other, while others are more specific to a particular organisation: for example, how much give and take there will be about timekeeping and working late.

The third type of contract, the psychological contract, has contents that are seldom, if ever, explicitly stated. These largely consist of the unvoiced expectations and obligations of the parties, neither of whom could be consciously aware of their expectations until they are not met. Therefore, the psychological contract reflects intangible needs, wants and expectations that can vary widely and its details can be very difficult to specify. Nevertheless, some idea of what it might embrace can be seen in Table 1.1.

All three of these contracts have an impact on the nature and shape of the relationship between employer and employee. For the relationship to come into existence the formal contract has to be seen by both parties as acceptable. By putting in place convenient variations through which the parties accommodate to or oppose each other, the informal contract acts a lubricant to the formal one. Finally, the psychological contract goes to the very heart of the exchange by expressing the emotional aspects of the relationship, such as fairness and trust. Crucially, should either party perceive that the other one is failing to honour his/her part of the implied bargain, this will lead predictably to similar behaviour in return.

formal contract
The formally agreed terms of the employment relationship, i.e. the legal concept as reflected in the contract of employment.

informal contract
A less formal expression of the employment relationship that reflects a degree of give and take between the parties.

psychological contract
An (unvoiced) set of expectations that the parties have of each other, together with the obligations that they feel towards each other.

Employee expectations	Employer expectations
■ Working conditions will be safe and as pleasant as possible	■ Acceptance of main values of the organisation
■ Jobs will be interesting and satisfying	■ Diligence and conscientiousness in pursuit of objectives important to the organisation
■ Reasonable efforts to provide job security	■ To avoid abusing the trust and goodwill of superiors
■ Involvement or consultation in decisions that affect them	■ To have concern for the reputation of the organisation
■ Equality of opportunity and fairness in selection and promotion	■ Loyalty and willingness to tolerate a degree of inconvenience for the good of the organisation
■ Opportunities for personal development and progression	■ Trustworthiness and honesty
■ To be treated with consideration and respect	■ To conform to accepted norms of behaviour in the organisation
■ Fair and equitable remuneration	■ Consideration for others

Table 1.1 The psychological contract – possible expectations of employees and employers
Source: adapted from Dundon and Rollinson (2004)

Summary points

- The social exchange perspective argues that the employment relationship is much more than a simple economic or legal exchange.
- Five shared features of the social exchange situation can be used to characterise and analyse employment relationships. These are: the exchange of social costs and benefits; subjective evaluations of fairness; unvoiced expectations and obligations; trust (or lack thereof); the unequal power of the parties.
- These features are largely responsible for the prevalence of certain themes and issues that continually surface in the employment relationship.
- A recent expression of social exchange as applied to the employment relationship is that of the psychological contract.

An overview and integration of the three perspectives

As noted earlier, none of the three perspectives given above is inherently right or wrong; they are all different frames of reference that can be used to view the same phenomena. For this reason, they should not be regarded as competing viewpoints, but complementary sets of ideas. For ease of comparison in what follows, their major features are summarised in Table 1.2 where, because it is now an important conceptualisation in its own right, HRM is given its own column.

An obvious conclusion that can be drawn from this comparison is that, if a comprehensive picture of the complexity of the employment relationship is desired, it is vital to consider all of these perspectives, and this can be illustrated by considering the use of the legal view in isolation. Although this draws attention to the idea that contracting of some sort inevitably takes place between employer and employees, it can be notoriously unspecific about the precise details of the exchange, or more to the point, what people involved believe the precise details are. People do not simply trade rewards for effort, they trade performances. Each person's performance includes expectations about what the other party is perceived to have promised to deliver, as well as felt obligations to deliver something in return. In addition, both of them are likely to have perceptions of whether the other person has honoured his/her part of the bargain, together with emotional reactions to what is perceived. These subjective features are all most effectively addressed by supplementing the legal perspective with a social exchange viewpoint.

Similar dangers exist if an exclusive industrial relations perspective is adopted. While this has the strength of recognising that the wage–work bargain can, at times, be very one-sided and potentially conflictual, this is only a potential for conflict, and is probably not conflict about everything. Here the problem is that the industrial relations view tends to oversensitise us to the presence of conflict, and at times can prompt us to ignore situations where no conflict exists. Moreover, it directs a strong focus on the institutions of conflict resolution and rule-making as an 'end in themselves', rather than the 'means to an end' that shapes the dynamics of behaviour in the employment relationship. This can blind us to other, less formal and diverse methods that are used to modify the processes of employment relations.

Finally, there are also attendant risks in relying too strongly on a social exchange perspective. While it alerts us to the idea that perceptions and emotions have a huge impact on how the world of work is subjectively experienced, there is always a danger that these factors will be

	Legal conception	Industrial relations	Human resource management	Social exchange and psychological contract
Assumed type of employment relationship	Contractual: the contract of employment	Within parameters established by statute, the parties are free to establish their own arrangements	Needs, wants and expectations of employees deemed to be of secondary importance to needs of the enterprise	Formal, informal and psychological contracts acknowledged to exist
Frame of reference adopted	Neutral, but basically unitarist because elements are weighted in favour of employer	Pluralist	Unitarist	Pluralist
Nature of rights and obligations (costs and benefits) established	Reciprocal, explicit and legally prescribed	Negotiated rules govern rights and obligations	Imposed by employer	Some are specified, others assumed to exist in perceptions of actors
Conception of fairness at work	Weighted in favour of employer	Collectively determined	Imposed by employer	Subjective (perceptual)
Emphasis on trust	Since rights and obligations specified, trust considered unnecessary	The emphasis on negotiated rules that govern rights implies an attempt to remove the necessity for trust	Mutuality assumed in the relationship, i.e. what is good for the business is good for the employee	Recognition that trust and mistrust are dynamic and evolving aspects of the relationship
Acknowledgement of power inequalities	Assumption of equality	High inequalities assumed to exist	Power inequalities legitimised	Power inequalities acknowledged to exist
Individualistic or collectivist	Individualistic	Collectivist	Individualistic	Individualism and collectivism not discrete characteristics, but can be mutually inclusive
Extent that conflicts of interest assumed to be present in relationship	No assumption	Assumed to be endemic	Assumption of no conflicts of interest	High
Methods of conflict resolution envisaged	If necessary, recourse to the law	Collective bargaining and joint consultation	None, or at most good communication	Likely to incorporate mechanisms for employee voice

Table 1.2 Comparison of alternative conceptions of the employment relationship

given pride of place, and other things will be ignored. In particular, it can sometimes prompt us to ignore the idea that there are often legal and contractual obligations that place severe constraints on what the parties are free to agree as part of an exchange.

For these reasons the approach adopted in this book is to take all three perspectives into account wherever possible. Clearly, this is not possible about everything, and in the case of some topics covered in the book, legal or industrial relations considerations dominate everything else. Where this is the case the reader will be alerted to the point in the particular chapter in which the topic is covered. In the meantime it is important to summarise some of the more important differences between employment relations and the traditional legal and industrial relations perspectives and how, in general, these differences will be handled throughout the book.

First, it is important to recognise that we are in an era where the world of work is constrained by legal influences to an extent that would have been considered unprecedented two or three decades ago. Wherever paid employment exists, the law takes the view that there are contracts of employment, and so an employment relationship devoid of any legal considerations would be illegal, and probably could not exist. This in no way negates what has been said earlier about the shortcomings of the legal view in terms of being able to express the richness, subtlety and complexity of the employment relationship. What it does mean, however, is that in order to make up the deficiency, an employment relations perspective involves supplementing the legal view with a social exchange perspective and in particular, the idea of a psychological contract.

Second, as noted earlier, the radical perspective on industrial relations places a strong emphasis on the ways in which wider social factors such as class, property ownership, political ideologies and economic variables all become part and parcel of events within an organisation. Employment relations does not underrate the importance of these matters and, as will be seen in the next chapter in the book, it is firmly acknowledged that factors outside an organisation have a bearing on the nature of the relationship between an organisation and its employees. However, because they are not under the complete control of either employers or employees in conducting their relationship, in employment relations these factors are usually given far less prominence. For this reason they tend to be viewed less as an integral part of employment relations when matters within a firm are being considered, and more as 'influences' that constrain and limit the nature of the relationship between the two parties.

Third, as noted earlier, industrial relations is based on the assumption that there are fundamental differences of interests between employers and employees. In employment relations, however, the relationship is conceived of as something that has similarities to any other continuing relationship between two parties. Alongside differences in interests, there are also interests in common; otherwise there would be no incentive for the parties to continue the relationship. Therefore, although employment relations is often concerned with exploring conflicting interests and how they can affect the nature of the employment relationship, they are regarded more simply as just one of a whole host of factors that can influence its nature. This is also reflected throughout this book.

Fourth, like industrial relations, employment relations also has a strong interest in institutions and rules. However, these are not its primary focus. The first and foremost concern is with the nature of the relationship between an organisation and its employees in a wider sense. Although the parties themselves, the rules that they construct, and the processes that they use for rule making and administration are clearly all of interest, these things tend to be viewed more as characteristics of the relationship. At the risk of oversimplifying matters, this difference between the two subjects can perhaps most easily be grasped by contrasting their positions on the rules that regulate the employment relationship. In employment relations both formal and informal rules tend to be regarded as things that emerge from the relationship, and are thus a reflection of the type of relationship that exists. Conversely, in industrial relations there is a far stronger tendency to see the relationship itself as an outcome of the rules. In other words, it is the rules themselves that define how the two parties will relate to each other. Having said this, although the difference is a fairly accurate reflection of the two perspectives, a note of caution should be sounded. Neither of them sees matters in quite such stark terms, and both acknowledge that rules and relationships interact, so that rules affect relationships and vice versa.

Finally, another important difference is that employment relations has a somewhat stronger focus on management as an influential player in the relationship. Although traditional industrial relations has always acknowledged the importance of management's role, for many years trade unions received the lion's share of attention in the subject. However, because the prime focus of employment relations is on the relationship between an organisation and its employees, it is necessary to acknowledge that managers are key players shaping the nature of this relationship. Indeed, in current conditions, where there has been a huge increase in the number of firms in which employees are not represented by trade unions, it might well be the case that managers are the most influential party. This does not mean, as is asserted by some writers such as Marchington and Parker (1990), that the subject has 'a focus on management alone'; rather, that employment relations is equally interested in any party that is influential in shaping the relationship. Nevertheless, because management action is considered important in employment relations, this is perhaps one reason why employment relations has (wrongly) become associated with the human resource management (HRM) or new industrial relations approach. Because HRM also has a concern with the relationship between an organisation and its employees, it has one point in common with employment relations; but one point in common does not mean that they are the same thing. Since some of the practices associated with this approach will be covered later in the book, an extensive discussion would be out of place here, and for the present it is sufficient to note that HRM is almost exclusively focused on the needs and interests of management, as opposed to analysis of their actions. It also contains an assumption that the interests of managers and employees can be co-aligned sufficiently for any differences to become negligible, or at least to be glossed over. Employment relations makes no such assumption. In addition, HRM is highly prescriptive, and somewhat one-sided in favour of managers about what it considers to be the desirable terms of a relationship. Employment relations is much more wary of making prescriptions about relationships. Instead it studies their nature, and acknowledges that a wide variety of relationships are possible, some of which are inherently more conflictual than others.

❓ Review and discussion questions

1 Define employment relations and, in the light of current working arrangements prevalent in many organisations, outline potential difficulties in defining what constitutes an employment relationship.

2 Describe the main features of the legal conception of the employment relationship and state what you see as its major strengths and weaknesses.

3 Describe the main features of the industrial relations perspective on what constitutes an employment relationship, together with what you see as the major strengths and weaknesses of this view.

4 In what ways does the social exchange perspective on the employment relationship differ from the legal and industrial relations perspectives? Are there any particular advantages or disadvantages in viewing the employment relationship from this perspective?

5 What is the psychological contract and how is it likely to differ from other contracts that an organisation might have with its employees?

Further reading

Ackers, P. and A. Wilkinson (eds) (2003) *Understanding Work and Employment: Industrial Relations in Transition*, Oxford University Press, Oxford. A useful book of readings, which gives a well-rounded picture of changes taking place in the world of work, and how these impact on employment relations in organisations.

Blau, P. (1964) *Exchange and Power in Social Life*, Wiley, New York. A classic statement of the theory of social exchange which, despite its apparent age, is truly timeless in its scope and content.

Braverman, H. (1974) *Labor and Monopoly Capital: The Degradation of Work in the Twentieth Century*, Monthly Review Press, New York. A book that can be a rather turgid and jargonistic read in places, but gives a sound appreciation of one of the more prominent neo-Marxist approaches to industrial relations.

Cappelli, P., L. Bassi, H. Katz, D. Knoke, P. Osterman and M. Useem (1997) *Change at Work*, Oxford University Press, Oxford. A very readable text that gives an extensive explanation of many of the changes now taking place in the world of work, and how these have an impact on employment relations.

Clark, I. (1994) 'The employment relationship and contractual regulation', in *Human Resource Management: A Contemporary Perspective*, I. Beardwell and L. Holden (eds), Pitman, London. A penetrating chapter that examines developments in the contract of employment.

Dundon, T. and D.J. Rollinson (2004) *Employment Relations in Non-Union Firms*, Routledge, London.

Edwards, P.K. (ed.) (2003) *Industrial Relations: Theory and Practice*, 2nd edn, Blackwell, Oxford. A book of readings, which gives an excellent introduction to current thinking in the field of industrial relations.

Gall, G. (2004) 'British employer resistance to trade union recognition', *Human Resource Management Journal*, 14 (2), pp. 36–53. A useful article that gives a penetrating overview of some of the tactics adopted by employers to avoid recognising trade unions.

Gallie, D., M. White, Y. Cheng and M. Tomlinson (1998) *Restructuring the Employment Relationship*, Clarendon, Oxford. A penetrating account of many of the changes now taking place in the world of work, and how these impact on the relationship between organisations and their employees.

Guest, D. and N. Conway (2002) 'Communicating the psychological contract: an employer perspective', *Human Resource Management Journal*, 12 (2), pp. 22–38. A useful account of how employers convey their expectations of what they consider to be the implicit obligations of employees in the psychological contract.

Kelly, J. (1998) *Rethinking Industrial Relations: Mobilisation, Collectivism and Long Waves*, Routledge, London. An interesting re-conceptualisation of what prompts workers to unionise, with a strong emphasis on theorising.

Rousseau, D. (1995) *Psychological Contracts in Organisations: Understanding the Written and Unwritten Agreements*, Sage, London. An easy-to-read book that deals with concept of psychological contracts in organisations.

Rubery, J., J. Earnshaw, M. Marchington, F. Lee-Cooke and S. Vincent (2001) 'Changing organisational forms and the employment relationship', *The Future of Work, Working Paper No. 4*, ESRC, London. A very useful paper which addresses the matter of the changing nature of organisations, and how this has very strong implications for the nature of their relationships with employees.

Turner, T. and D. D'Art (eds) (2002) *Industrial Relations in the New Economy*, Blackhall Press, Dublin. A useful book of readings that documents how changes currently being implemented in organisations are changing the nature of industrial relations in firms.

Chapter 2

The changing contexts of employment relations in Great Britain

Introduction

At the push of button a venture capitalist in Hong Kong can move millions of dollars around the world, the consequence of which could have a huge impact on the lives of thousands of employees in hundreds of different companies. While this is a dramatic example of the way that an event outside an organisation can have repercussions on people inside it, there are many other ways that matters inside a firm are affected by environmental factors. Explaining these effects can be a difficult and complex task, particularly in the case of employment relations.

Some of the external factors can be rather unspecific in terms of their effects, some can act in combination with other internal influences, while other contextual factors have indirect and less obvious consequences that are hard to quantify. Thus, any description or explanation is always open to criticism, either for being too simple, or for being incomplete. Nonetheless, as is pointed out by Blyton and Turnbull (2004: 88), a full understanding of employment relations can only be obtained if broader contextual factors are incorporated into the framework for analysis.

The chapter commences by presenting an explanatory model which identifies a number of broad contextual factors that can influence the nature of employment relations in an organisation. Since this book is mainly concerned with employment relations in Great Britain, the greater part of the chapter is concerned with applying this model to the British situation. Here it can be noted that most changes in employment relations tend to be evolutionary, rather than revolutionary, and therefore with certain factors it is necessary to give a historical view to illustrate how things have changed.

The contexts of employment relations: an explanatory model

Employment relations is part of a wider societal system, and there are a host of environmental factors that can affect factors inside a firm (Grimshaw and Rubery, 2003). One way of inspecting these broad contextual influences is to use the PEST framework shown in Fig. 2.1. Before explaining this framework, however, it is first necessary to sound a cautionary note. Since Fig. 2.1 is the first explanatory diagram of this type in the book, it is important to point out that it is only a simplified representation of what is a more complex reality. Therefore, the reader is asked to remember that, while models of this type can aid understanding, they are of necessity incomplete, and can never fully capture the richness and complexity of the real-world situation.

Employment relations: processes and outcomes

*employment relations –
processes and outcomes*

The dynamic interactions between employees and an organisation that are concerned with the economic, social, psychological and legal exchanges associated with paid employment.

This is shown at the centre of the model. It is seldom a static or uniform state of affairs, but varies considerably in both type and character from one organisation to another. This reflects the idea that the employment relationship is the result of dynamic interactions between an organisation and its employees, and concerns the economic, social, psychological and legal exchanges that are associated with paid employment. For example, in a small family-run business the employment relationship might be characterised by a high degree of informality, with very few formal rules and policies. Interactions between employees and managers may be based on informal communication, pay may be determined by a few key family members, the firm may well be non-union and the owner-manager works alongside employees doing the same or a very similar job on a daily basis, thereby engendering close working relationships. In contrast, the relationship in a large multinational corporation will probably be completely different. Interactions between managers and employees are likely to be much more formal and prescribed, and might well take place via a European Works Council (EWC), in which employees meet and consult with co-workers and managers from different countries. Pay might be determined by senior managers setting targets for employees to achieve, or through collective bargaining with a trade union, and day-to-day interactions between employees and managers will be based on a team or departmental identity. For these reasons the employment relationship can vary considerably, and even similar contextual circumstances can give rise to different employee relations processes and outcomes in different firms.

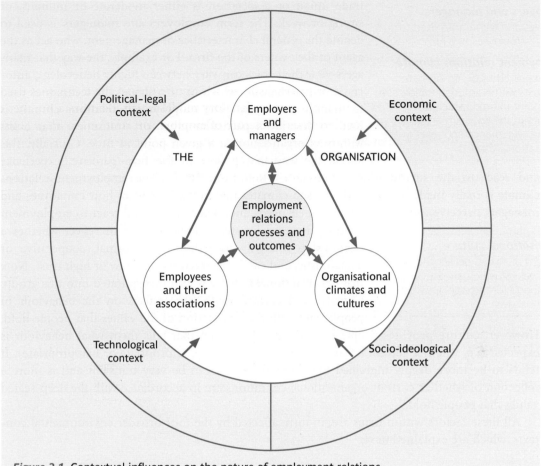

Figure 2.1 Contextual influences on the nature of employment relations

Organisational factors

The employment relationship at the centre of Fig. 2.1 is shown as being influenced by three major groups of factors within a firm. Note, however, that these factors are connected by double-headed arrows, which means that they are likely to affect each other in a highly interactive way. Two of these factors represent the principle actors (or stakeholders) who have a vested interest in how employment relations processes are made and modified. **Employees and their associations** embraces two important features. First, whether employees are organised as a collective group (for example, in a trade union) in order to influence the nature of employment relations processes and rules. This is by no means inevitable, and these days there are an increasing number of organisations that do not recognise trade unions. Moreover, even in non-union firms it is sometimes the case that employees belong to an in-house collective organisation that organises them – i.e. a staff association or employee forum of some sort. Second, where employees are collectivised, the nature of the collective organisation can be an important influence; for example, whether the

employees and their associations

Whether employees mobilise as a collective group, and the characteristics of that collective group.

employers and managers
The roles and techniques used to manage employees in a firm.

employment relations climate
A particular ethos or atmosphere that exists within an organisation at a given point in time, which is reflected in the way its members perceive, experience and react to the organisational context.

trade union or association is either moderate or militant, or strong or weak. The term **employers and managers** is used to denote the general characteristics of management, who act as the agent of the owners of the firm. For example, the way that managers view their roles can vary between highly benevolent, autocratic or paternalistic, which in turn shapes the techniques used to manage employees. The **employment relations climate** is used to describe a particular ethos or atmosphere that exists within an organisation at a given point in time. Crucially, this affects the way that people in the firm perceive, experience and react to the surrounding organisation (Rollinson, 2005). The employment relations climate is really made up of a series of sub-climates that are indicative of how employees and managers perceive each other, express their needs and expectations, and react to employment

organisational culture
A system of shared beliefs and deep-seated values, which are a prescription for the ways in which people behave.

relations issues. Climates, therefore, tend to reflect whether a relationship is highly formalised or informal, cooperative or antagonistic, and can be characterised by low or high trust. Note that **organisational culture** is also incorporated into this group. Climates and cultures both have effects on the behaviour of people, and both are a reflection of the values that people hold.

However, culture provides people with a code of conduct that tells them what behaviour is expected (i.e. whether certain behaviours are right or wrong, appropriate or inappropriate). It tends to be more deeply ingrained than climate, which can be very transient and is more a reflection of whether current organisational conditions are in accordance with the deep-seated values that people hold.

All these factors within firms are, in turn, affected by the four broader environmental contexts, which are explained next.

Wider environmental contexts

The **political-legal context** refers to the extent to which the State plays a role in employment

political-legal context
The extent to which the government plays a role in employment relations, directly and/or indirectly.

relations, which can occur in one of two ways. Where *direct intervention* takes place, the government or one of its agencies plays an active and on-going role in determining certain aspects of the employment relationship. Examples include the use of incomes policies in Britain in the 1970s or, later in the 1980s and 1990s, the privatisation of public utilities and the injection of free-market principles into the public services. Direct legal intervention also includes employment laws that require the parties (employers, employees and trade unions) to modify their relationship to conform with certain standards, such as health and safety obligations and laws covering the national minimum wage and statutory trade union recognition.

Indirect intervention is rather different. It occurs when the State passes a law or seeks to promote a particular public policy objective, both of which can affect employment relations policies and work rules. Examples include the government's work–life balance objective that encourages companies to adopt more family-friendly policies for employees, or by promoting more cooperative employment relations through union–management partnerships. There is, for example, a designated partnership fund administered by the Department of Trade and Industry (DTI) to help promote public policy in that direction.

economic context

The overall state of the economy in which an organisation operates, for example whether it is buoyant or recessionary.

socio-ideological context

The behavioural norms and cultural values in a society which can influence the nature of the relationship between a firm and its employees.

The **economic context** is used to denote the key characteristics of a country's economy, such as whether it is buoyant or recessionary. Key economic dimensions include global economic pressures, international currency fluctuations, labour market conditions such as employment and unemployment, wage costs, and changes to consumer tastes and demands. The third wider environmental context in Fig. 2.1, the **socio-ideological context**, describes the behavioural norms and cultural values in a society, particularly those that can influence the nature of the relationship between a firm and its employees. Four important social values include: (i) whether deference to authority is considered normal; (ii) whether trade unions are regarded as legitimate social partners in workplace decisions, or viewed as interfering in management's right to manage; (iii) whether there are certain ethical labour standards that should prevail, for instance whether the use of child labour is permitted, or there are minimum wage protections; and (iv), whether health and welfare issues are important employment-related concerns: say, smoking in the workplace. These examples vary quite significantly from one country to another and from one firm to the next. For instance, child labour is a common occurrence in less-developed countries, and while trade unions have a long history in British employment relations, many commentators argue that their role is more embedded and legitimate in other European countries, such as Sweden or Germany.

The need to accommodate to different social values by changing our behaviour can sometimes become very obvious if we travel outside our native country. In addition, it is important to note that the culture of an organisation needs to be compatible with the culture or region in which it is located. If this is not the case, people can find that expected patterns of behaviour in the enterprise clash with what they have been brought up to regard as acceptable and normal, about which more will be said in the next chapter (Integration 1).

technological context

The choices made by firms about the technology that they use in their activities, which affects employee job tasks, skills and competences.

The **technological context** reflects the choices made by firms about the technology that they use in their activities. This can have very far-reaching effects on employment relations, and in particular, technology can influence not only *what* tasks employees perform, but also *how* they perform them (Child, 1972). Technological innovation can make some jobs redundant, provide management with new and more sophisticated forms of employee control and surveillance, and yet at the same time create new jobs that require additional employee skills and competences. For these reasons, the technological context has significant implications for the social relations that shape an organisation's employment relations climate (Fox, 1985: 13).

Pause for reflection

Under each of the PEST contextual factors described above (i.e. Political-legal, Economic, Socio-ideological, and Technological), list what you think are main employment relationship influences for McDonald's.

In essence the PEST model is only an analytical tool and it will reappear in the next chapter (Integration 1) to compare contextual factors in three additional countries to show how employment relations can be influenced by different environmental contexts. In the meantime, and to set the scene for the remainder of the book, it is more important to describe changes in the main contextual factors in Great Britain. An understanding of these environmental changes is important, because later in the chapter we will consider how these changes have impacted on each of the three groups of factors within firms; namely, the impact on *employees and their associations*; *employers and managers*; and *organisational climates and cultures*.

Summary points

- The employment relations system in a firm is affected by conditions in its wider environment.
- This wider environment can be viewed through the PEST framework, which gives a simplified conceptual model that describes the range of contextual factors. These are:
  - the political-legal context
  - the economic context
  - the socio-ideological context
  - the technological context.

The changing nature of employment relations contexts in Great Britain
The political-legal context

A detailed description of the current political-legal context in Great Britain will be given in Chapter 5, in which the role of the State in employment relations is considered in greater depth. However, for the sake of completeness, and because this context has proved to be highly influential in shaping the nature of employment relations in Britain, it should also be considered in outline here.

voluntarist system
A system of employment relations that operates with minimal legal intervention, where the parties determine for themselves the main terms and conditions of employment.

juridification
The extent to which legislation influences employment relations processes and outcomes.

Employment relations in Great Britain has always been viewed as a **voluntarist system**, in which the parties (management, employees and unions) are left to seek their own salvation in terms of agreeing the details of the employment relationship. However, the principle of voluntarist employment relations came into question during the 1960s and 1970s, when Britain's economic performance seriously declined in comparison to other industrialised nations. From this era onwards political and legal **juridification** has changed the face of employment relations in Britain, and the State has become increasingly active in passing laws that influence the relations between an organisation and its employees.

Here it is important to recognise that the government is the only institution that has the capability to make new laws or abolish old ones and, in so doing, it effectively establishes the rules of the game. From 1979 onwards the government abandoned the principle of non-intervention and employment law became a central plank in its attempts to reform employment relations. Successive Conservative governments adopted a strongly anti-union stance and introduced, on average, an item of statutory legislation every two years, much of which was aimed at curbing trade union activities in some way (Ackers *et al.*, 1996). The net effect of these laws has been to shift the balance of power firmly to the advantage of employers. The political ideology underpinning this legislation was one that argued that these steps were necessary to weaken trade unions in order to free the market, and subsequent legislation enabled employers to counter industrial action and to promote a more individualistic (rather than collective) dimension to employment relations. Indeed, the Conservative government's approach to employment relations with its own employees reinforced this philosophy, when, in 1989, it banned trade union membership for workers employed at the Government Communications Headquarters (GCHQ) (McLoughlin and Gourlay, 1994).

The election of a 'New Labour' government in 1997 led to further political and legal changes. Faced with the unpalatable extremes of Thatcherism in Great Britain and Communism in the former Soviet Bloc, the newly elected Blair government offered a new approach based on the so-called *Third Way* (Giddens, 2000). As with many political ideologies however, it is easier to describe what the Third Way is not, rather than what it is. In general, it eschews a return to 'old' Labour values of nationalisation, public spending, high taxation and a union–government relationship determined over 'beer and sandwiches' at Downing Street; nor

'Third Way'

A political ideology in which government charts a path between state regulation and free-market forces. Its core values include support for competitive markets, innovation, skills, fairness and equity.

is it a continuance of Thatcherite free-market enterprise. Rather, the metaphor of the **Third Way** seems to be derived from two paths that are purposely avoided, in favour of an alternative (third) path in which government mediates between the rules imposed by State institutions on the one hand, and the exploitative character of unregulated market forces on the other (Callinicos, 2001). Therefore, any definition is bound to be somewhat imprecise, but having said this, there seem to be five core pillars that underpin the Third Way project: competitive markets, innovation, skills, fairness and equity (Blyton and Turnbull, 2004).

Nevertheless, there is considerable debate about the extent of political change prompted by this political ideology. For some commentators the Third Way is little more than a continuation of Thatcherite neo-liberal free-market principles (Callinicos, 2001). For example, 'New Labour' continues to privatise public-sector jobs, the labour market remains fundamentally unequal for many women and part-time workers, and for millions who are subject to precarious forms of employment. In addition, while there is a raft of associated legal rights that protect individual workers – for example family-friendly workplace policies and minimum wage protection – the restrictions on trade union behaviour remain on the statute book. As Ewing (2003) argues, for the most part, employment contracts are now underwritten by individual employment laws rather than regulated through voluntary collective agreements.

Many of the changes in the political and legal context that affect employment relations have

European Social Policy

A set of regulations that provide rights for workers which are comparable across EU member states, and which embrace rights on working hours, employee voice, redundancy, health and safety, and maternity and paternity leave.

arisen from developments at the European Union level (Green, 2001). **European Social Policy** sets out regulations on matters such as working hours, equal pay, redundancy, employee protection during company takeovers and transfers, maternity and paternity leave, and consultation rights. These matters are enshrined in the Social Chapter of the Maastricht treaty, from which the Conservative government obtained an opt-out in 1991. However, the newly elected Labour government in 1997

adopted an obligation to conform to the Social Chapter, and since then it has become an increasingly significant way in which the political-legal context has affected employment relations. The government argues that many of the individual worker laws, such as the national minimum wage and rights for part-time workers, serve to rectify the injustices of a previous political era. However, European legislation has its critics. For example, many British employers argue that these European-led statutes are restrictive and burdensome, and that they impose severe constraints on management's 'right to manage'. Furthermore, some leading trade unions are suspicious of European social policy on the grounds that it could undermine collective union organisation, and some of them go so far as to argue that European legislation could discourage workers from joining trade unions because protective rights are established without union bargaining (Towers, 2003).

European legislation is seldom transposed into domestic legislation in a verbatim way, because each member state has the scope to adapt policy and legislation to suit its own national customs and practices. In simple terms, EU legislation can be transposed in one of four ways (Marchington and Wilkinson, 2005a).

1 *Directives:* these represent the main instrument from which EU policy is eventually transferred into domestic legislation. While directives are binding on member states, their requirements tend to be defined in general terms, and so member states can adapt the principle objectives to suit national customs and laws.

2 *Regulations:* these tend to take immediate effect in a member state and are often technical and legal instructions of compliance.

3 *Directions:* these apply to specific member states who may have been called to account for breach of certain EU directives and laws.

4 *Framework agreements:* the European social partners, who are effectively the main employer and union confederations (European Trade Union Confederation, ETUC; and Union of Industrial and Employers' Confederations of Europe, UNICE) can initiate negotiations themselves and issue a framework agreement on certain issues. Once agreed and adopted, a framework agreement substitutes as legislation.

Summary points

- Political and legal aspects surrounding employment relations have changed more since 1980 than in any other post-war period.

- After 1980 Conservative governments were extremely hostile to trade unionism and as a result the balance of power in employment relations was shifted firmly into the hands of employers, and away from workers and unions.

- Since 1997 the Labour government has continued with many free-market principles such as privatisation, but at the same time has introduced several important worker rights and protections. As a result, British employment relations remains a voluntarist system, albeit one with important legal interventions in many areas, such as the minimum wage protections and trade union recognition rights.

- European Social Policy has been at the vanguard of new rights and worker protections, the objective being to create a more even playing field in terms of employment relations across EU member states.

The economic context

The economic environment has undergone far-reaching changes, all of which can influence the nature of British employment relations. Following the Second World War, full employment resulted in rising affluence and aspirations in the working population. However, there were certain fundamental weaknesses in the British economy, notably declining competitiveness that fuelled a growing skills deficit compared with other market economies. By the 1980s decline had firmly set in, and manufacturing industry was particularly hard hit, with many regions in the UK plagued with high unemployment. While these recessionary effects have had a lasting impact on British employment relations, economic growth since 1997 has largely exceeded most forecasts. For example, inflation has remained relatively low and, with the growth of a new service sector, unemployment has declined. Two particularly important context changes that are important to employment relations include *globalisation* and the changing *composition of the workforce*.

Globalisation

In simplest of terms, **globalisation** refers to the idea that many organisations now seek to produce goods and/or services to meet the demands of a 'one-world' market economy (Rollinson, 2005). According to Boxall and Purcell (2003: 100), globalisation refers to a whole series of interrelated market developments. For instance, the takeover of Manchester United Football Club by the American business tycoon, Malcolm Glazer, who has apparently little interest in soccer, is testimony to the global reaches of corporate investors.

globalisation

A series of interrelated economic developments, in which organisations seek to produce goods and services for a one-world market economy.

This implies that there are few restrictions that impede an organisation's trading capacity, or hinder the spread of shareholder capitalism.

Pause for reflection

In what ways, and for what reasons, do you think the concept of globalisation in employment relations can be questioned?

It is important to remember that it is often employees, rather than shareholders, who feel the brunt of global economic changes (Ghoshal, 2005). For example, if investors are dissatisfied with the performance of a company or its management, they can move their assets virtually instantaneously. In contrast, most employees find it much harder to obtain new jobs, or to exit from a relationship in which so much time and skill has been invested. In this respect, global economic factors potentially transcend almost all forms of employment (Giles, 2000). Some economic changes have a significant effect on the way we all conduct many of our everyday activities. For example, most banking and finance services are now available over the Internet, accessible from almost anywhere in the world, no matter where the bank is actually located. Similarly, thousands of people are employed in call centres situated in different parts of the globe, irrespective of the customers' exact location, and budget airlines such as Ryanair utilise technology and agency labour in different countries to provide what they regard as a rapid and flexible service. Moreover, it is quite common for designer clothing manufacturers, such as Nike and The Gap, to produce many of their products in low-wage economies, with subsequent employment and unemployment consequences in both the domestic and host-country market (Eaton, 2000). Globalisation can even impact on the employment conditions of workers employed in local supermarkets. For example, the US retailer Wal-Mart has taken over Asda, the German-owned Lidel and Aldi retail chains have significantly increased the number of outlets in Great Britain, and Tesco has now established stores in several other European countries.

Even with these trends, however, the true extent of global economic change is questionable (Blyton and Turnbull, 2004). First, globalisation is not really a new phenomenon, and many of Britain's larger companies have been operating in international markets for decades. Consequently, while the character and pace of global economic pressures might have changed over time, these pressures are not homogenous, but are highly variable across different industries, and influence employment relations processes in different organisations in very different ways. Thus for some organisations, the main issue may be one of evolving adaptation, rather than coping with a fundamental transformation in the nature of global economic pressures. In other words, while globalisation is itself a real phenomenon, its impact on employment relations is not universal.

A second problem is that of definition, because there can be important differences between a genuinely 'one-world' global market, and what simply comes down to the power of a few large multinational and transnational organisations. Some of these large corporations continue to occupy a dominant place in the market in particular countries, and thus have important effects on employment and unemployment in the national and local, rather than the global, marketplace (Hirst and Thompson, 1996). Thus, although larger corporations might use the language of global competition to justify their actions, these actions are very localised because of certain industry standards and levels of competition.

multinational organisation
One that is managed from the firm's country of origin, in which goods and services are produced in overseas subsidiaries to cater for the demands of overseas markets.

transnational organisation
One that operates simultaneously in different international markets producing similar and different goods and services through independent subsidiaries.

While these criticisms may be significant as academic arguments, the effects of global economic factors on employment relations tend to be more practical and real. With the increasing use of new technologies and new ways of working, global economic activity can shape the fabric of employment for millions of people. For example, the sense of security and insecurity of a workforce, or the ability or inability of trade unions to mobilise workers collectively, are all influenced in some way by world economic events, and details of these effects will be illustrated in the next section of the chapter.

The changing composition of the workforce

One of the most visible economic impacts is evident in the structure and composition of the British labour market. In the 1900s the population of Great Britain was approximately 38 million people, whereas it is currently close to 60 million, a 56 per cent increase, of which 28 million make up the workforce. With associated economic changes across this period, the proportion of women who now work has also increased substantially. In 1900, for example, 29 per cent of the workforce was female, whereas the current figure is 46 per cent (Lindsay, 2003). Other changes include earnings, working and leisure time. For example, average weekly hours worked fell from 53 hours per week at the beginning of the twentieth century, to 42 hours at the beginning of the twenty-first century.

These and other changes have been brought about by wider economic pressures. As shown in Fig. 2.2, there has been a sharp increase in service sector jobs, with a significant reduction in

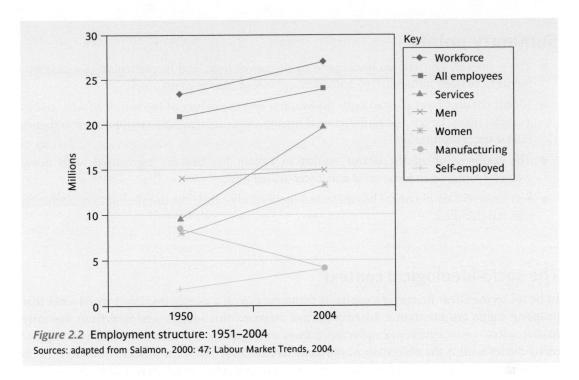

Figure 2.2 Employment structure: 1951–2004
Sources: adapted from Salamon, 2000: 47; Labour Market Trends, 2004.

manufacturing employment. In addition, the pace of change in female employment has been much more significant than it has been for men. After Sweden and Denmark, Britain currently has one of the highest female labour market participation rates in the European Union (Labour Market Trends, 2004). However, when viewed in more detail, the labour market is highly segmented. For example, compared to most male occupations, many of the jobs taken by women tend to be part-time and of a temporary nature. In addition, women in full-time employment earn only about 80 per cent of the salary of men in equivalent full-time occupations (Office for National Statistics, 2004). About half of all women work in service sector jobs, such as catering, cleaning and personal contract services, and these are often lower-paid and lower-skilled occupations, with little access to trade union membership. According to the Low Pay Commission (Annual Report, 2005), the main beneficiaries of the increase in the national minimum wage are women, part-time workers, some minority ethnic groups and younger workers. Thus, reference to the female participation rate on its own can hide other important labour market changes, many of which reflect a disproportionate distribution in the quality and security of work for millions of women (Grimshaw and Rubery, 2003).

In part, explanations for the increased participation of women in employment can be accounted for by wider changes in the economy (Millward *et al.*, 2000). For example, the proportion of jobs in manufacturing industry, once regarded as the mainstream of British employment relations with high levels of unionisation and formalised employment relationships, has fallen quite substantially. Indeed, over the course of the twentieth century, employment in manufacturing industry has decreased from 28 to 14 per cent of all employees (Lindsay, 2003). In the 1950s only about 9 million people worked in service sector occupations and the current figure is now over 20 million (Labour Market Trends, 2004). Furthermore, there are one-third fewer workers employed in public services now than there were in the early 1980s. This reduction in public-sector employment illustrates the connections between economic changes and political developments with the privatisation of whole industries (Millward *et al.*, 2000).

Summary points

- The economic context has undergone significant change, and in particular, two developments have been influential: *globalisation* and *labour market composition*.

- Global changes have affected both the location and the nature of thousands of jobs, and as a result, many larger and multinational organisations increasingly conduct their activities in low-wage economies.

- The composition of the labour market in Britain has become segmented, with many women employed in lower-paid and lower-skilled jobs.

- Service sector employment has increased significantly, while the number of manufacturing jobs has declined.

The socio-ideological context

In broad terms Great Britain is a capitalist democracy, with a deeply ingrained social tenet that property rights are sacrosanct. In employment relations this idea is inherited from the early master–servant conception of employment, from which springs the idea that accepting employment carries with it the obligation of obedient service (Fox, 1985). In modern contracts this is embodied in the *implied contractual terms* that were explained in Chapter 1: for instance, the duties of obedience, trust and honesty in employment. In the aftermath of the Second World War there was a belief that stronger members of a society should protect the weak. For this reason the government of the day constructed the Welfare State, which included the National Health Service (NHS). It nationalised key industries to operate as a public good rather than for private profit, and widened access to education and social welfare provision. In addition, post-war full employment and the growth of trade union membership largely saw the demise of the deferential society, which resulted in aspirations of security, affluence and basic living standards.

However, throughout the 1980s and 1990s the economic and political changes described above negated many of the social developments of earlier decades, and increased the gap between the 'haves and have-nots'. Following 18 years of neo-liberal economic policies, the ideological values of private profit and entrepreneurship are more prevalent in Britain now than they were two decades ago. Many organisations are now smaller businesses, in which employers adopt a hostile or, at best, a neutral response to the idea of unionisation. Changes to broad social values also tend to be reflected in government policy, and 'New Labour' continues to promote greater market choice and flexibility, albeit with important individual worker protections built in to the social and economic fabric of society. Consequently, in the twenty-first century, Britain is (theoretically at least) more of a **meritocracy** that is guided by those who believe that the basic principles of a free-market society are superior to its alternatives.

meritocracy
A social and economic system in which advancement is based on ability or achievement.

Summary points

- Social and ideological values are strongly connected to changes in the economic and political-legal contexts.

- Broader social values and norms are also reflected in individual attitudes; for example, whether workers desire (or not) union membership.

- Social norms can also reflect employer ideologies and hostility towards employee collective representation.

The technological context

There is a strong connection between technology and some of the economic changes described above, and it is no coincidence that the decline in manufacturing industry has occurred during periods of rapid technological innovation (Towers, 2003). Indeed, technology in general, and in particular the use of information and communication technologies (ICT), have transformed almost every aspect of employment.

As explained earlier, the word 'technology' can be used to embrace not only *what* tasks employees perform, but also *how* these tasks are undertaken. In addition, the use of various technologies denotes the choices that employers make about how people are managed. Significantly therefore, technology in the workplace is seldom a matter of new hardware or software, but tends to be part and parcel of new ways of managing people, such as just-in-time management (JIT), business process re-engineering (BPR) methods or more flexible organisational structures.

Pause for reflection

List what you think have been the main technological context changes in the last decade that relate to employment relations.

In many situations, technological change has streamlined workers' tasks, increased productivity and in some cases empowered employees in their jobs (Baldry, 2003). In employment relations terms, technology has altered the way employees are managed, with increasingly invasive forms of surveillance and control over almost every part of a worker's job. It is fair to say that technological change of one sort or another has affected practically all sectors of economic activity, from manufacturing, finance and banking to the way McDonald's makes its burgers. Indeed, most people are touched by technology in some way in their everyday lives, both as customers and workers. Some of these technological developments have had an impact on health and safety at work. For example, the amount of time workers spend in front of computer screens or using various computer-aided technologies can have adverse health effects. Indeed, it was the adverse health effects of increased computer usage that prompted trade union campaigns to improve safety conditions, which eventually led to the introduction of the 1992 European Display Screen Regulations (Baldry, 2003).

Summary points

- The technological context not only affects the tasks workers perform, but also how they perform them.
- This provides employers with a greater degree of control over what and how employee tasks are performed.
- Technology has also affected workplace health, safety and well-being, particularly in terms of the increased use of computer-related work activities.

The impact of contexts at organisational level

The broader contextual changes discussed above do not exist in a vacuum; they affect people and organisations in very different ways. In this section some of the effects of these wider environmental changes are considered in more detail. It will be recalled that Fig. 2.1 shows that changes in the environment impact on one or more of the three factors at an organisational level (*employees and their associations; employers and managers; organisational climates and cultures*), and these in turn influence employment relations processes and associated outcomes. Because it is never easy to trace the impact of environmental changes with any great precision, it is important to stress two very important points. First, it is seldom the case that an internal change can be attributed to something in one environmental context alone. Rather, it usually occurs because one of the parties in employment relations feels that it is necessary to respond in some way to changes in several contexts together. Second, and to complicate matters even more, as Fig. 2.1 shows, there are interactions between the internal factors within firms. For instance, a change in the stance of *employers and managers* to some external change is likely to prompt a response by *employees and trade unions*. For example, a change initiated by management because of an external economic condition may produce either a supportive or antagonistic response by workers and unions, depending on the issue and extent of change desired by management. In turn, these internal responses to external contexts can impact on *organisational climates and cultures*. This makes for a very complex situation, and in the interests of simplicity, each of the three factors at the organisational level will be dealt with separately, by drawing on some of the evidence about broader contextual influences described thus far in the chapter.

Employees and their associations

One of the most dramatic changes that has occurred across the past three decades is the declining prominence and influence of trade unions. In 1980, for example, approximately 50 per cent of the working population were trade union members. This had shrunk to 29 per cent by 2004 (Labour Market Trends, 2004). To a large extent much of this can be accounted for by changes in the *economic context*, with very different effects in different industrial sectors (Millward *et al.*, 2000). For example, the proportion of jobs in manufacturing industry, which had hitherto been the mainstay of unionisation and formalised employment relationships, had fallen substantially. As previously noted, across the past half-century employment in manufacturing industry decreased from 28 to 14 per cent of all employees (Lindsay, 2003). In the 1950s for instance, only about 9 million people worked in service sector occupations, whereas the current figure is now over 20 million (Labour Market Trends, 2004).

In terms of the effects on trade union membership, the trend was further exacerbated by changes in the *political-legal context*, not least the anti-trade union laws passed by the previous Conservative governments. In addition, *political-legal* changes also brought about a decline in public-sector employment, which had previously been an area of high unionisation. For example, there are one-third fewer workers employed in public services now than there were in the early 1980s, a reduction that is mostly due to the privatisation of whole industries, such as gas and telecommunications, together with the outsourcing of other public sector functions to private enterprises (Millward *et al.*, 2000). The situation regarding union decline in Britain is so severe that the majority of those in the labour force are now classified as **never-members**: that is, a majority of the working population in Britain have never experienced union membership, and are unlikely ever to join a trade union during their working lives (Bryson and Gomez, 2005). The extent of this change is illustrated in Fig. 2.3 below.

never-members

Employees who have no experience of a unionised relationship.

To some extent it is possible that part of this decline in unionisation can be attributed to a loss of confidence in trade unions by employees, or a least a shift to more individualistic *socio-ideological* values in the working population, a trend that was identified as early as 1990 (Phelps Brown, 1990). The net result is a far lower level of trade union representation at the workplace in British industry, which is evidenced by the fact that the number of employment-related complaints handled by the Citizens Advice Bureaux (CAB) has more than quadrupled over the past 25 years (from 140 000 complaints in 1975 to over 600 000 in 2002) (Abbott, 2004).

The *technological context* has also had an impact on employees and their associations because it has provided managers with new methods of workplace surveillance; a matter that will be explored in greater detail in Chapter 12. Although there are legal restrictions, such as the Data Protection Act and the Human Rights Act that limit what employers can do in terms of technological surveillance, managers tend to regard the right to control workers' activities as their fundamental prerogative (Findlay and McKinlay, 2003). The capability to do this has been vastly increased by the use of surveillance techniques that are both *covert* and *intensive* in nature. For instance, in call centres electronic surveillance is often used to scrutinise employee effort and behaviour, and even to monitor employee telephone conversations with customers. However, workers are seldom passive recipients of this type of control, and in some cases they respond in

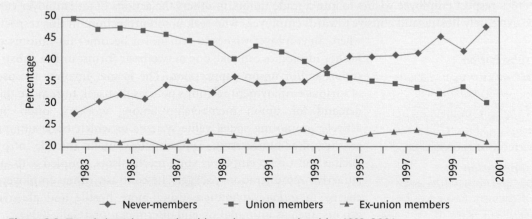

Figure 2.3 Trends in union membership and never-membership: 1983–2001
Source: adapted from Bryson and Gomez, 2005: 68.

individual and collective ways that challenge the legitimacy of management's surveillance techniques. Above all, worker reactions show that managerial attempts to control effort and protect property often conflict with the employees' expectations of privacy (Findlay and McKinlay, 2003: 317).

Technology has always had an impact on trade unions (Greene, 2003). Indeed, unions have a long history of bargaining about the introduction of new technology because of its impact on workers. However, a more recent development concerns the way that unions have adapted to technology to further their own aims. For example, over half of all TUC-affiliated unions now use the Internet to publicise their objectives and highlight issues of concern to their members. Most of them communicate internally through email to a greater extent than ever before, and this may reduce the time taken to respond to member concerns (Baldry, 2003). The Internet has also made it possible for unions to establish international alliances and solidarity pacts with workers in other countries. A noteworthy example of this was the Liverpool Dockers dispute, that ran from September 1995 to December 1997. The dispute generated more attention through its own Internet network (www.labournet.net) than was ever reported in the British media, and provided a highly effective way of coordinating three separate days of work stoppages in 27 countries. This dispute illustrates an enhanced capacity for technology to be used to mobilise trade union activity across the globe (Carter *et al.*, 2003: 302).

Employers and managers

As a backdrop to many of the changes that are described below, perhaps the first thing to be noted is that the impact of the *political-legal context* has been extremely strong across the past three decades. As described earlier, from the 1980s onwards there was a sustained assault by the government on trade unionism, and a concomitant support for non-collective forms of employee representation (Ackers *et al.*, 1996). The effect of this was to send two clear signals to managers: first, that henceforth non-unionism was to be considered as the preferred form of employment relations and, second, that management should legitimately be the party with the upper hand in the employment relationship. While this describes a distinct change in the *socio-ideological* context, it does not automatically mean that all managers became more aggressive or macho. Nevertheless, it was probably strong enough – even in the face of opposition from some workforces – to imbue management with a far greater sense of self-confidence in pushing through a whole series of other changes. Suffice it to say that, while the managers of some companies respect employee wishes to join a trade union, in others the actions of an employer can be extremely hostile and abusive towards employees who seek union protection. In this respect, where an employer wishes to remain (or become) un-unionised his/her ideologies can take one of two basic forms: **union substitution** and/or **union suppression**. The former involves the use of various employment relations policies that seek to remove the demand for union membership among workers, often by actively promoting social value systems in which trade unions are viewed as unnecessary. Typical polices might include introducing non-union employee voice mechanisms, coupled with an attractive remuneration package. In contrast, other employers engage in *union suppression*, using more hostile and abusive actions, such as intimidation and discrimination (Gall, 2004).

Various economic pressures have led managers to search for more flexible and responsive ways of using labour. This can have

union substitution

Non-union employment relations policies that seek to remove the demand for union membership among workers. Typical strategies include non-union voice and attractive remuneration packages.

union suppression

Aggressive and hostile managerial actions designed to resist possible union membership and recognition. Typical strategies include intimidation and discrimination.

a huge impact on how organisations are structured, and has important implications for employment patterns within firms. A model that explains some of these initiatives is that of Atkinson's flexible firm (Atkinson, 1984a; 1984b; Atkinson and Meager, 1986), which is shown in Fig. 2.4.

The flexible firm concept, which results in an ideal-type model, describes what would happen if all the characteristics that are described below were present together. While it has been criticised since its inception in the early 1980s (Proctor and Ackroyd, 2006), its main features remain largely unchanged. It argues that in today's fast-moving business environment, firms have a need to address two major issues. The first is to be able to alter products and production methods in order to cater for changes in customer tastes, and to take advantage of new technologies. A second issue is the need to be able to respond rapidly to changes (either upwards or downwards) in the level of demand for products and services. To address these issues the organisation needs to be flexible in two different ways. Rapid adjustment of products and processes requires it to have *functional flexibility*, whereas coping with changes in the level of output requires *numeric flexibility*. The key to achieving these is to structure the workforce into two main groups. The first group consists of a permanent core workforce of highly skilled, and to some extent multi-skilled, workers, which gives the firm a high degree of **functional flex-**

functional flexibility

An organisation's capability to vary what is done and how it is done.

ibility and enables it to adapt its products and services more rapidly through skill acquisition by existing employees. To ensure that this core group can deliver the required flexibility, the firm has a vested interest in providing training and retraining

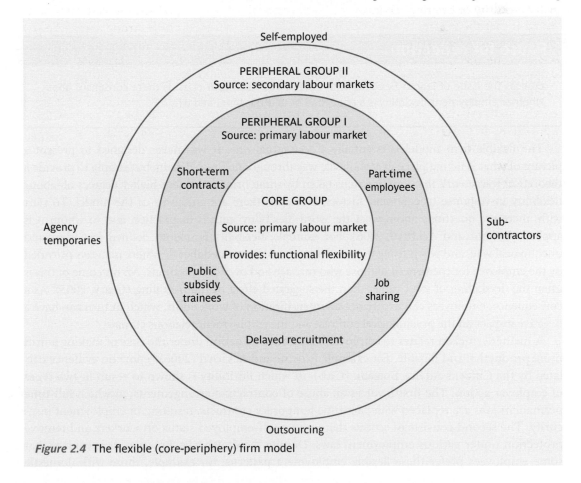

Figure 2.4 The flexible (core-periphery) firm model

as necessary, and the firm seeks to retain this group of employees with an attractive package of rewards and a degree of employment security.

numeric flexibility
An organisation's capability to match the size of its workforce with its required output levels.

To obtain **numeric flexibility**, employers need to be able to change the number of people employed and/or the hours that they work. This is achieved by having up to three peripheral sub-groups of workers. The first (peripheral group I), is drawn from the firm's internal labour market and consists of employees with skills which are important to the firm, but skills which, by their nature, are general and easily imported at short notice. These employees may have a degree of permanence in their employment, but do not enjoy the same reward package or degree of employment security as those workers in the core group, so this first peripheral sub-group also consists of occupations that can be filled by part-time workers, whose hours can quickly be adjusted upwards if necessary.

The second sub-group (peripheral group II), consists of workers who are drawn from the external labour market and enter the firm from time to time to give an additional degree of numeric flexibility, and they tend to be employed on a short-term and casual basis, to meet output demands. Many of these workers enter the firm in this way in the hope their temporary employment contracts will be made permanent some time in the future. In addition to these two peripheral sub-groups, there are other categories of workers who are completely external to the firm. These can be workers supplied in the short term by agency companies, are self-employed, or are part of an outsourced organisation performing non-core business activities, such as security or catering services.

Pause for reflection

Discuss the issue of labour flexibility with other students in your class. Is there consensus about whether employment flexibility is a good, bad or neutral thing, and why?

The flexible firm model is essentially a conceptual one. It was never designed to present a picture of what is taking place in a wholesale way throughout Great Britain, but simply to provide a theoretical framework that explains steps taken by some firms to achieve higher degrees of labour flexibility in response to economic factors. However, there are criticisms of the model. To start with, there are questions about what the word 'flexibility' means in practice, and to whom it is applied (Proctor and Ackroyd, 2006). For example, flexibility is seldom defined in a clear and unequivocal way, and when using the word it tends to be assumed that flexibility is always provided by the employee for the benefit of those who manage and own organisations. An outcome of this is often the de-skilling of jobs, rather than the suggested effect of multi-skilling (Geary, 2003). As a consequence, employees can experience an intensification of work effort, which in turn can have a negative impact on the psychological contract and the employment relations climate.

A further criticism relates to employer behaviour and action under the ruse of making a firm more productive and flexible. For example Proctor and Ackroyd (2006) report on evidence collated by the Citizens Advice Bureaux (CAB), in which flexibility is shown to result in two types of employer action. The first involves an abuse of contractual arrangements, in which full-time permanent jobs are replaced with part-time temporary contracts, resulting in employment insecurity. The second consists of actions that impose self-employed status on workers and remove protection under various employment laws. Despite the drawbacks, however, it is evident that some employees prefer these flexible employment patterns; for example, those with domestic care responsibilities, those who prefer more leisure time, or students who want to work weekends or in the evening while studying full-time.

A third criticism of the model is that it is predicated on a single and exclusive employer relationship (Rubery *et al.*, 2004), which fails to capture the fact that these days many firms are embedded in complex inter-firm economic networks. This often means that employees from one firm can be physically located at, and actually work for, another organisation, often for quite lengthy periods of time. Such inter-organisational working patterns can be quite common where firms are involved in supply-chain relationships that utilise outsourcing arrangements or are dependent on the supply of agency workers to meet business fluctuations or seasonal demand (Grimshaw *et al.*, 2004). Indeed, the number of workers whose employment is of a temporary nature has increased in Britain – from around 1.2 million employees in 1992, rising to 1.7 million in 1997 – and currently stands at around 1.4 million (Summerfield and Gill, 2005). Employees on some sort of fixed-term contract account for almost 50 per cent of the labour force, with a marked increase in agency temping, from 7 per cent of all forms of temporary employment in 1992 to 16 per cent by 2004 (see Fig. 2.5).

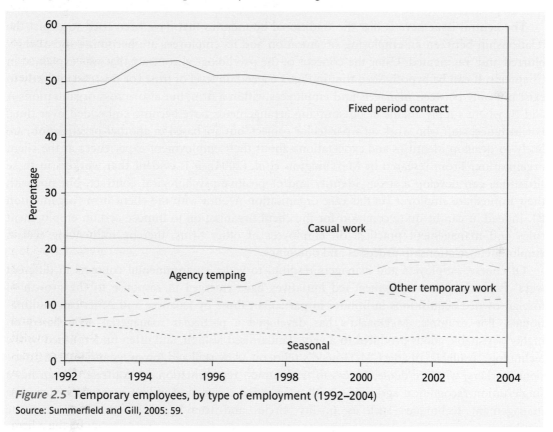

Figure 2.5 Temporary employees, by type of employment (1992–2004)
Source: Summerfield and Gill, 2005: 59.

The implication of all this is that, as organisational forms change in terms of their structure, shape and character, the social relations within and between firms are likely to change as well. This is depicted in simplified form in Fig. 2.6, which illustrates the idea that there can be influences that extend beyond the boundaries of a single employee–employer relationship. In Fig. 2.6 for example, the employment relationship is essentially influenced and modified by a series of network relations that take place both inside and between different firms: that is, networks that have largely come about because of changes in the *economic context*.

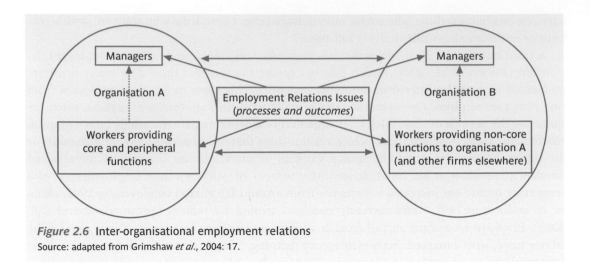

Figure 2.6 Inter-organisational employment relations
Source: adapted from Grimshaw *et al.*, 2004: 17.

The central issue here is that the traditional boundaries that have been used to depict the relationship between an employing organisation and its employees are becoming increasingly blurred and fragmented. Using the concept of the psychological contract that was explained in Chapter 1, it can be hypothesised that in Fig. 2.6 a certain level of trust (or mistrust) is likely to exist not only between managers and employees within a firm, but also across organisations A and B, where supply chains or outsourcing arrangements have become embedded over time. For instance, staff who work on a particular project, but are based in another organisation, are likely to develop identities and expectations about their employment experiences at the client organisation. From research by Marchington *et al.* (2004), it is evident that workers in these situations can develop a strong identity and/or positive psychological contract, but not with their immediate employer (in this case organisation A), but with the client firm (organisation B). Indeed, it can be quite common for the client organisation to impose certain employment rules and management practices on employees of other firms, thereby influencing certain employment relationship processes and outcomes.

Of course, employers and managers respond to wider environmental contexts in different ways. For example, management-led initiatives have emerged in response to the growth of foreign-owned acquisitions in Britain; in particular, those by Japanese and American multinationals. For example, McDonald's has developed a particular managerial style based on highly perishable goods produced in a very standardised fashion, and often underpinned by the technology available. In effect, McDonald's relies on a low-skill and low-wage model using transient workers, who are denied access to trade union representation. In contrast, Nissan has a single-union recognition agreement, with a no-strike clause, and utilises a variety of Japanese management techniques such as quality circles and team-based structures to motivate employees.

Another management-led reaction to the phenomenon of globalisation is the ruthless search for new methods of cutting the costs of labour. To some extent this is associated with countries such as Taiwan, Malaysia and China, together with some of the new EU accession states, as economies with cheap and abundant labour. Thus, labour costs in these countries become the benchmarks for what managers in Great Britain try to achieve. In reality, however, Great Britain is also a low-wage economy relative to other 'advanced' economic nations. For example, of all G7 nations (Great Britain, Germany, Japan, America, France, Canada,

Italy), Britain is ranked sixth in terms of its relative wage levels – Italy is seventh (Blyton and Turnbull, 2004: 53).

Organisational climates and cultures

An indirect way in which organisational climates and cultures have been affected is through the impact of changes emanating in both *economic* and *socio-ideological contexts* of the environment over the last two decades, mainly because these things have prompted a shift in social values. For instance, there are now more women in paid employment, and increasing numbers of people who are engaged in precarious and temporary forms of work. Coupled to this there has been a decrease in the time spent in paid employment over a person's lifetime, with increased life expectancy among the population resulting in longer retirement, while younger people remain in education for greater periods of time. The net effect of this is a tendency for people to enter employment later and leave earlier, with increased demand for leisure and travel often occurring during retirement.

Some of these changes are reflected in the disposable incomes and lifestyles that people expect from paid employment. For example, the number of people who own their own homes has increased by 88 per cent since the 1970s (Summerfield and Gill, 2005). More people now travel to work in private cars than a generation ago, and a greater proportion of earnings is spent on non-essential items – such as travel abroad, recreation and communications – than on food or shelter. Nonetheless, there remains considerable social and economic inequality in Great Britain, with around three-quarters of adults believing that the gap between those on high and low incomes is too large (Summerfield and Gill, 2005). Indeed, one of the most striking features of Great Britain in the twenty-first century is the matter of unequal wealth: roughly 1 per cent of the population are in possession of one-quarter of Great Britain's wealth, with 50 per cent of the population sharing between them only 6 per cent of the country's wealth (Office for National Statistics, 2004). A striking phenomenon associated with this is the distribution of occupational earnings, with the average salary for a company director or chief executive being almost eighteen times that for some of the lowest-paid jobs (see Table 2.1). The effect of these factors in many organisations is the prevalence of a climate characterised by strong 'them and us' attitudes between workers and managers (Kelly and Kelly, 1991; D'Art and Turner, 1999). Indeed, organisational climates are considerably poorer in workplaces where managers actively discourage possible unionisation (Kersley *et al.*, 2006: 283).

Sad to say, the evidence suggests that there is also a widespread disenchantment with the state of society, which verges on alienation. For example, fewer people actually vote for political parties than did a decade ago, only one-third of the population believe that people 'help each other out' (Office for National Statistics, 2003), and the proportion of people who volunteer for local community activities has declined from 60 per cent in 2002 to just over 50 per cent of the population now (Summerfield and Gill, 2005).

These broad *socio-ideological* developments all have an impact on organisational cultures and climates. For example, a larger number of household occupants are now dependent on employment to maintain their ever-challenging and evolving lifestyles and, although people seem to expect more demanding and interesting work, at the same time many of them also face insecure and precarious forms of employment. Problematically, the declining influence of trade unions in the workplace has resulted in a situation in which few people feel able to challenge or resist employer actions. One sign of this is that the number of working days lost through industrial disputes has fallen dramatically in the last three decades. In some quarters this

	Numbers employed	£ Average annual salary	£ Average gross weekly pay
Highest paid			
Directors and chief executives of major organisations	48 000	162 026	3103
Financial managers and chartered secretaries	187 000	72 124	1381
Medical practitioners	84 000	67 895	1300
Senior officials in national government	n/a	63 928	1224
Managers in mining and energy	7000	59 893	1147
Aircraft pilots and flight engineers	9000	56 206	1076
Management consultants, actuaries, economists, statisticians	66 000	51 770	991
Solicitors and lawyers, judges and coroners	62 000	49 970	957
Police officers (inspectors and above)	19 000	47 020	900
Personnel, training and industrial relations managers	72 000	45 641	874
Lowest paid			
Cleaners, domestics	105 000	12 492	239
Childminders and related occupations	8000	12 408	237
Hotel porters	n/a	12 299	235
Hairdressers, barbers	18 000	11 552	221
Kitchen and catering assistants	82 000	11 408	218
Waiters, waitresses	22 000	11 156	213
Bar staff	26 000	11 094	212
Retail cashiers and check-out operators	27 000	10 734	205
Launderers, dry cleaners, pressers	13 000	10 629	203
Leisure and theme park attendants	n/a	10 405	199

Note
n/a = Not known.
Average weekly hours not known.

Table 2.1 Highest and lowest paid occupations in Great Britain, 2004
Source: calculated from: Office for National Statistics, 2004 (on-line); Summerfield and Gill, 2005: 70.

is often portrayed as an indication that there now exists a more cooperative employment relations climate with a contented workforce. However, a reduction in industrial disputes is far from being a foolproof indicator of cooperative organisational climates or increased employee commitment (Edwards, 2003). Indeed, there are distinct signs that discontent and mistrust can be manifest in other ways. For example, survey evidence indicates that the number of employees who believe that managers seek to 'get the better of workers' increased from 53 per cent in 1985 to 64 per cent in 1995. Similarly, employees tend to believe that 'big business will inevitably benefit owners at the expense of workers' (Kelly, 1998). Overall, workers' perceptions about the general state of employee–management relations have shown little change over time, with around half (51 per cent) of employees reporting a more negative experience of employment relations than their managers (Kersley *et al.*, 2006: 278). It is probably no exaggeration to suggest therefore that employment relations climates can be highly volatile in many organisations.

Another way in which climates and cultures have been affected is by the responses of employers and managers to the *economic* environment. As noted earlier, in recent times the boundaries between organisations have become blurred by the increasing use of outsourcing arrangements (see Fig. 2.6). Here tensions can emerge if employees are moved from organisation A and then re-employed by organisation B as outsourced workers. Conflicts can arise between managers and workers, or among workers employed on very different terms and conditions, especially if some groups of employees are doing the same job. This is a common situation in many parts of the public sector and among local authorities, as a result of *political and legal* changes that introduced compulsory competitive tendering (CCT) initiatives. With these arrangements non-core business activities are effectively privatised, and employees, even though they continue to do the same jobs as before, are transferred to new organisations under the Transfer of Undertakings Regulations. It is not uncommon to find there are climatic repercussions of these developments on matters such as remuneration, employee voice, career development, skills, and contractual and legal status. Some pertinent examples of these are given in Exhibit 2.1.

There have also been climatic repercussions from changes that have emanated in the *technological context*. As a managerial tool technology has affected employment relationships in several ways, two of which are particularly noteworthy. First, **human resource information systems (HRIS)** are used to store, manipulate and analyse information about how people are managed in an organisation (Kavanagh *et al.*, 1990: 29), and this provides management with the tools to evaluate individual employee effort, or alter work teams according to employee skill profiles and competence levels. These information systems are often used to set individual performance targets, catalogue employee skills and competences, and extend merit-based remuneration systems across whole organisations. In this way standard pay rates and grading structures determined by job tenure have been fundamentally altered (Baldry, 2003).

human resource information systems (HRIS)
The use of a range of computer packages that store, manipulate and analyse information related to how people are managed in an organisation.

Second, technology has prompted a resurgence in the use of Taylorist and scientific management techniques. Such managerial strategies can lead to a low trust climate, because every minute detail of an employee's job task is subject to technological control and managerial scrutiny (Warhurst and Thompson, 1998). Examples here range from the production of cars and washing machines, to the way McDonald's produces burgers, or how employees in a call centre deal with customers over the telephone.

Even when outsourced services do perform well, tensions arise that can have a bad effect on public services . . . particularly where 'retrained' (i.e. public-sector) and 'transferred' (i.e. outsourced) staff work alongside one another in the same building. One staff group gets a performance bonus; the other does not. One cadre of managers races around in leased cars while others still have years outstanding on their car loans. (*Sunday Times*, 15 September 2002)

Motorola Ltd v (1) *Davidson* (2) *Melville Craig Group Ltd*
An agency worker employed at Motorola for two years claimed unfair dismissal against the agency and the client firm (Motorola) . . . Motorola appealed against Mr Davidson's successful claim of unfair dismissal by arguing that the legal power to control is the key issue in determining who was the employer, and that this resided with the agency, not Motorola. The appeal was unsuccessful. The Employment Appeal Tribunal decided that Motorola's practical, as opposed to legal, power to control agency workers constituted it as the employer. Hence, the 'non-legal' employer, Motorola, was held to be responsible for unfair dismissal compensation.

Exhibit 2.1 The blurring of organisational boundaries and employment relations
Source: adapted from Grimshaw *et al.*, 2004: 9–20.

Employment relations: processes and outcomes

Although there are several general characteristics of British employment relations, it is also important to note that processes and outcomes in British firms are astonishingly diverse. For this reason, the characteristics set out in what follows should not be interpreted as a picture of conditions that exist everywhere. Having said this, there are some general characteristics that should be noted. First, in spirit at least, British employment relations remains essentially voluntarist in principle, and the parties have a large degree of freedom to agree and modify the terms and conditions of the relationship. However, much of the anti-union legislation from the Thatcher era remains on the statute books, as do several important worker protection laws from the 1970s relating to health and safety at work. At the same time, newer developments have emerged that seek to restrict the worse excesses of employer power and abusive behaviour in employment relations, while also satisfying company needs for competitiveness and flexibility. Consequently, the huge volume of legislation that now exists means that the outcome of employment relations processes is heavily influenced by employment laws.

Second, beyond this there is almost certainly a sharp divide between unionised and non-union workplaces. As was noted earlier, the size and influence of British trade unions have declined severely in the last three decades (Kersley *et al.*, 2006). Thus although some degree of joint determination of the employment relationship is not unknown in non-union organisations, the highly collective systems of employment relations that were commonplace in earlier times are now probably confined to large, unionised organisations and to the public sector. As a result, many employment relations issues are now handled in smaller, non-union workplaces in private-sector organisations: for example, in hotels, restaurants, call centres and finance and insurance companies. Indeed, almost 40 per cent of all jobs exist in private-sector service firms, while some 94 per cent of all private sector firms have fewer than 250 employees (Dundon and Wilkinson, 2003; Forth *et al.*, 2006). The outcomes are that there are now probably more people in Britain than not, who have never experienced a unionised relationship during their whole working lives. Moreover, whatever their size, newer firms that set up on greenfield sites tend to adopt very different employment relations policies and practices than older, more traditional organisations (Gunnigle *et al.*, 2001). Around 80 per cent of employees in small to medium-sized firms have their pay set unilaterally by management (Forth *et al.*, 2006: ix), with many workers employed on a temporary or agency basis.

It is almost certainly the case that smaller, non-unionised firms have the greatest diversity in employment relations processes and outcomes. At one extreme some of them have processes and outcomes that mirror the formality found in larger unionised firms. In others, however, managers are likely to be more concerned with maintaining their assumed prerogatives and, at best, they will consult with employees rather than negotiate with them: that is, management informs employees about its proposals and listens, but still reserves the right to act as it pleases. At the other extreme are firms in which managers have taken even stronger steps: for example, by withdrawing from recognition of trade unions altogether. To some extent other changes at enterprise level have facilitated similar outcomes by breaking down prior patterns of collectivism and promoting a more individualistic ethos associated with 'human resource management' techniques. For example, individual merit as a basis of payment and multi-skilling have both become more widespread. The use of either could have some effect in weakening the traditional basis of collective solidarity that is rooted in occupational groupings.

In Britain the major structural changes in industry have resulted in less certain employment relations outcomes. Recessionary pressures coupled with changes in the composition of the labour force have resulted in a situation where prior aspirations of job security are not so easily met. These feelings are likely to have been reinforced by the strategies adopted by firms to seek greater flexibility in the use of labour in order to meet increased competitive pressures. Moreover, managers have largely been able to get their own way by forcing through change thanks to the increased power put into their hands by the twin weapons of economic recession and the legal assault on trade unions. In consequence, although it is by no means unknown (witness the industrial action in British Airways in August 2005), any adversarial stance by employees is far less prevalent now than a decade ago.

Conclusions

The overriding themes of this chapter are twofold. First, that organisations are not sealed off from the rest of the world, but are subject to a host of forces that emanate from their environments. Second, that since an organisation cannot exert control over its environment, it has little choice but to respond by adapting itself to changing environmental circumstances.

The chapter commenced with a simplified model that identifies four major groups of contextual factors that influence and shape the general nature of employment relations within firms. These are: the *political-legal context*, the *economic context*, the *socio-ideological context* and the *technological context*. The model also identified three factors within organisations that tend to be the direct recipients of these influences: *employees and their associations, employers and managers,* and *organisational climates and cultures*, all of which interact to give rise to very diverse *processes and outcomes* in employment relations. Needless to say, what happens in the environment does not necessarily impact on employment relations in the same way, or to the same extent, in all organisations. Certain issues are likely to be more significant in some firms than in others, and relations between managers and workers will evolve and change over time and space.

The chapter then reviewed the extent of some of the main changes in the wider environmental in Great Britain. These included: *political and legal* changes over the past two decades; the *economic pressures* of globalisation and changing labour force composition; evolving *socio-ideological values*; and *technological* forms of control and surveillance. From this, the chapter then traced the impacts on matters within organisations, commenting on how these factors influence managerial and employee responses, which in turn shape the general characteristics of employment relations in British firms. Note, however, that it goes no further than describing matters in Great Britain, which is by no means the end of the story. The general characteristics of any system of employment relations are those that are most applicable to the particular circumstances of a country – for example, its political values and its national culture, which tend to change more slowly. For this reason the next chapter (Integration 1) uses the broad conceptual model given at the start of this chapter, and applies it to three additional countries (the USA, Germany and Japan) to illustrate how employment relations processes and outcomes can take on a very different set of characteristics elsewhere.

? Review and discussion questions

1 Describe each of the four environmental contexts.

2 In your own words briefly explain why environmental contexts are likely to lead to very different employment relations processes and outcomes for different organisations.

3 In what way does European social policy affect employment relations?

4 Briefly describe how the changing composition of the workforce can affect employment relations processes and outcomes.

5 Explain key differences between numeric flexibility and functional flexibility.

6 Given that flexibility is something of a watchword in many organisations, what benefits might there be for employees with flexible and atypical forms of employment?

7 What is meant by blurred organisational boundaries, and what implications does this have for employment relations processes and outcomes?

8 How does the current political and legal context for employment relations differ from that of 10 or 15 years ago?

9 Briefly define the terms 'union substitution' and 'union suppression'.

10 Explain how technology has changed the face of trade union organisation and representation.

Further reading

Baldry, C. (2003) 'Employment relations in the information society', in *Handbook of Employment Relations, Law and Practice*, 4th edn, B. Towers (ed.), London, Kogan Page. A review of the changes in technology over the last decade, explaining how some of the technologies used by many organisations have impacted on employment relations.

Bryson, A. and R. Gomez (2005) 'Why Have Workers Stopped Joining Unions? The Rise in Never-Membership in Britain', *British Journal of Industrial Relations*, Vol. 41 (1), pp. 67–92. An important article that explains the rise and extent of people in the British labour force who have never been union members, using data from the British Social Attitudes Surveys.

Dundon, T. and A. Wilkinson (2003) 'Employment relations in small firms', in *Handbook of Employment Relations, Law and Practice*, 4th edn, B. Towers (ed.), London, Kogan Page. A book chapter devoted specifically to employment relations issues in small and medium-sized enterprises in Britain.

Ewing, K. (2003) 'Industrial relations and the law', in *Understanding Work and Employment: Industrial Relations in Transition*, P. Ackers and A. Wilkinson (eds), Oxford University Press. A thoughtful essay that examines the impact of the law on the changing nature of employment relations, and in particular the implications for voluntarist employment relations.

Forth, J., H. Bewley and A. Bryson (2006) *Small and Medium-sized Enterprises: Findings from the 2004 Workplace Employment Relations Survey*, London, Department of Trade and Industry/Routledge. Similar to the 'first findings' booklet for WERS 2004, this pamphlet describes the context and changes to employment relations specifically in smaller firms in Great Britain. Available from: http://www.ecdti.co.uk/.

Gallie, D., M. White, Y. Cheng and M. Tomlinson (1998) *Restructuring the Employment Relationship*, Oxford University Press. A penetrating account of many of the changes now taking place in the world of work, and how these impact on the relationship between organisations and their employees.

Kersley, B., C. Alpin, J. Forth, A. Bryson, H. Bewley, J. Dix and S. Oxenbridge (2005) *Inside the Workplace: First Findings from the 2004 Workplace Employment Relations Survey*, London, Department of Trade and Industry/Routledge. A pamphlet that provides a summary of main key findings from the 2004 WERS survey, summarising key changes to employment relations contexts. Available from: http://www.ecdti.co.uk/.

Kersley, B., C. Alpin, J. Forth, A. Bryson, H. Bewley, J. Dix and S. Oxenbridge (2006) *Inside the Workplace: Findings from the 2004 Workplace Employment Relations Survey*, London, Routledge. The complete and latest WERS sourcebook, reporting on major changes and continuities in employment relations contexts and practices in Great Britain.

Lindsay, C. (2003) 'A century of labour market change: 1900–2000', *Labour Market Trends (Special Feature)*, London, Office for National Statistics. A study of some of the major labour market changes that have occurred in Britain over the course of the last century.

Marchington, M., D. Grimshaw, J. Rubery and H. Willmott (eds) (2004) *Fragmenting Work: Blurring Organisational Boundaries and Disordering Hierarchies*, Oxford University Press. A research monograph that presents both theoretical and empirical case study data on the impact of changing organisational forms, and the implications for how the study of employment relations is approached.

Millward, N., A. Bryson and J. Forth (2000) *All Change at Work? British Employment Relations 1980–1998, as portrayed by the Workplace Industrial Relations Series*, London, Routledge. A comprehensive survey about employment relations changes, including a summary review of trends in general environment contexts applicable to the world of work.

Proctor, S. and S. Ackroyd (2006) 'Flexibility', in *Contemporary Human Resource Management: Text and Cases*, 2nd edn, T. Redman and A. Wilkinson (eds), London, Prentice Hall. A good review and critique of the concept of the flexible firm.

Comparing employment relations systems

Introduction

This is the first of four Integration chapters in this book, all of which have the objective of demonstrating the interconnected nature of certain themes and processes in employment relations. Thus, each integration chapter focuses on a number of processes described in preceding chapters, and explains how they either are interconnected or differ in terms of the associated outcomes. For this first Integration chapter, the purpose is to demonstrate how contextual factors can have very different employment relations outcomes in different countries. This is done by expanding on two points made at the end of Chapter 2: first, that the general characteristics of a country's employment relations system are those that match its particular circumstances; and second, that these characteristics are not only a response to changing contextual factors, but also reflect certain inbuilt features such as national cultures, which change more slowly.

Because it can be very difficult to illustrate these points when discussion is restricted to a single country, as was the case in Chapter 2, this chapter adopts a comparative perspective. It applies the conceptual model given at the start of Chapter 2 to three additional countries: United States, Germany and Japan. These have purposely been selected for two reasons. First, to illustrate the effects of contextual factors in countries where they are very different in nature, and, second, because in the particular countries chosen, there has been (or is likely to be in the future) a tendency to import some of their employment relations practices into Great Britain. For example, human resource management, which is now widely used in Great Britain, originated in America. Similarly, there is still much talk among British managers of the desirability of adopting certain Japanese work practices, such as high performance work systems (HPWS). Finally, Germany has a well-developed system of employee participation and involvement, some elements of which are similar to recently introduced employee information and consultation rights now adopted in Great Britain as a result of European Directives.

As in the previous chapter the analysis starts on the periphery of the model, and briefly describes the nature of the environmental contexts for each country. It then traces the impact of these contexts on the three factors within firms, namely; *employees and their associations*, *employers and managers*, and *organisational climates and cultures*. The chapter concludes with a brief overview of the employment relations processes and outcomes in the three countries, which for completeness compares them all with the influence of the contextual factors in Great Britain that were reviewed in Chapter 2.

The environmental contexts of the USA, Germany and Japan
The political – legal contexts

Although the national government of the United States has minimal direct involvement in employment relations, the political and legal context has a strong influence owing to the effects of legislation. The National Labor Relations (Wagner) Act of 1935 gives employees the legal right to organise collectively, and requires employers to bargain in 'good faith'. If a properly supervised ballot of employees (conducted by the National Labor Relations Board, or NLRB) is won, a firm cannot refuse to recognise a trade union for bargaining purposes. Note, however, that, while there is legal support for trade unions and collective bargaining, this is often something of a double-edged sword. For example, there is nothing to prevent a firm from moving its operations to another location in the United States, where another recognition ballot may be more difficult for the trade union to win. Indeed, one common response by American managers to NLRB union certification ballots is to employ the services of union-busting consultants, in the hope of defeating possible union recognition. Part of the employer's anti-union armoury in America is the 'captive audience tactic'. This effectively means that the employer has an advantage, because he/she can speak to employees during working time on a daily basis, in the hope of discrediting a union-recognition campaign (Logan, 2001). Furthermore, if conditions change over time, an employer can use the legislation to force another ballot on continued recognition. If this reveals there is little support for recognition or that management have 'persuaded' employees away from union bargaining, it can legally be withdrawn. In addition to the above, each state usually has its own labour laws specifying minimum wages and limitations on working hours. Thus, in many American firms, the political and legal context can lead to managerial counter-strategies of union avoidance (Gall, 2004), which in turn, can influence the character of the prevailing organisational climate and culture.

In Germany, because there is a clear legal framework within which the parties must operate, there is also complete abstention from any direct intervention by the government. For instance, there are federal laws that regulate labour standards, hours of work, sick pay, dismissal protection, discrimination and health and safety, and German employment relations is based on a legally enshrined dual structure of representation. At the macro level (either nationally or for specific industrial groupings) collective bargaining between trade unions and employers associations sets the major conditions of employment. The rights to collective bargaining are not subject to detailed legislation, but are nevertheless enshrined in law and, once fixed, collective agreements have the force of law and contain an explicit peace obligation (Grahl and Teague, 2004). In addition, in all firms employing five or more people, employees have a right to seats on a works council, which deals with a large number of matters that affect the relationship between an organisation and its employees. Unless it is by prior agreement, works councils are forbidden by law from negotiating about anything that is already regulated by collective bargaining, but have statutory participation rights in many areas of management decision making. As a quid pro quo, works councils are not permitted to resort to industrial action, and in the event of a serious disagreement they must first exhaust internal disputes procedures before taking the matter before an industrial court for adjudication. Since 1978 employees have also had a right to a number of seats on the supervisory board of a firm. Here it should be explained that German firms have a two-tier system of boards of directors. The higher (supervisory) board meets about four times each year, and in turn appoints (but cannot interfere with the workings of) the executive board which is responsible for policy making, and the day-to-day running of the enterprise.

Traditionally the Japanese government, through the Ministry of International Trade and Industry, has promoted a highly cooperative legislative framework for employment relations. For example, the Labour Standards Law (1947) and the Trade Union Law (1947) provide for equality in collective bargaining for both workers and employers (Matsuura et al., 2003). Furthermore, the Japanese constitution guarantees workers the right to organise collectively, and it goes much further by establishing rights for trade unions that are over and above what may be found in many other countries. The Japanese employment relations system is therefore designed so that the parties (workers, unions, management and the State) have little need for anything other than the very minimum of intervention. Unlike the union-busting tactics and strategies evident in America, what legal intervention that does exist in Japan also tends to be very much supported and viewed as part of the social fabric of society, and in the same way labour law also protects the autonomy of 'enterprise unions' from employer interference (Kuwahara, 1987). In addition, there are central and local labour relations commissions. These are State agencies that provide conciliation and mediation services in the very rare event that disputes cannot be resolved by the parties involved.

The economic contexts

For many years America had a relatively low rate of inflation, and modest but consistent economic growth. Like most industrialised countries, however, it has had its economic problems, many of which are associated with globalisation. Although it has always been heavily engaged in international trade, its prosperity was relatively independent of exports. However, over the past three decades its domestic markets have faced increasingly stiff competition from imported goods, especially those from the Far East. This has resulted in strong recessionary pressures, rising unemployment, and a great deal of change in firms to try to regain a competitive edge.

For some time now there has been a trend for fewer people to be employed in manufacturing, with new jobs mostly confined to the service sector, many of which are low-paid, part-time and undertaken by women and immigrant labour entering the US from South America.

For the four decades immediately following the Second World War, what was then West Germany experienced an era of unprecedented prosperity. Sustained economic growth and low price inflation gave a situation that was viewed as something of an economic miracle, but since then Germany has been beset with economic problems. To some extent these were associated with the same issue facing other industrialised nations: globalisation. In the case of Germany, however, these problems were overshadowed by economic difficulties inherent in the task of re-unifiying West Germany (formally the Federal Republic of Germany (FDR)) and East Germany (the German Democratic Republic (GDR)). This process commenced in 1990 with the dismemberment of the former Soviet Union (USSR) and its satellite states. Realising that living standards in the GDR were much lower than in West Germany, there was a commitment from the outset to equalising conditions such as wage rates and social security provisions, and the problems facing Germany in this matter were and are formidable. In the GDR industry was grossly uncompetitive compared to the West. Much of what it had produced prior to reunification was exported to the Soviet Union or its satellites, but after reunification these markets dried up and there was little demand for its outputs. Moreover, labour usage was based on a set of highly inflexible practices, and compared to West Germany, East German labour was highly unproductive, one estimate suggesting that actual labour costs were as much as 55 per cent higher (Tuselman and Heise, 2000). Small to medium-sized enterprises (SMEs), which accounted for two-thirds of all employment in the East, were particularly hard hit and many went into liquidation (Grahl and Teague, 2004). Thus, in the years after reunification imports into the GDR vastly exceeded exports and this, together with the need to finance social expenditure to maintain income levels or finance unemployment, resulted in a huge drain on the economic resources of West Germany.

Japan's economy is second in size only to America, and until the early 1970s it enjoyed extremely low price inflation, and had economic growth rates that averaged 10 per cent each year. For the next two decades its performance started to decline, and economic growth averaged only 5 per cent per year. Since the early 1990s the Japanese economy has been erratic, alternating between periods of recession and extremely low growth. As a result, by 2002 unemployment had risen to nearly 6 per cent, as many Japanese firms faced stiffer international competition (Benson and Debroux, 2003). One response was to move into lower value-added products, many of which were made outside Japan (Ornatowski, 1998). This, it is estimated, resulted in a consequent loss of 1 million Japanese jobs.

The socio-ideological contexts

Perhaps the most outstanding social value held in America is that it is probably the most fiercely capitalist country in the world. It is a nation in which individualism is a strongly held social value (Hofstede, 2001), and Americans have a passionate belief that their society is, and should remain, a meritocracy. As such, although it is nowhere near as much a class-based society as Great Britain, it is perhaps the most strongly achievement-oriented society in the world (McClelland, 1961).

Germans have a strong sense of national identity, which gives a correspondingly strong sense of community (Fox, 1974). Moreover, since Germany epitomises a thorough absorption of the Protestant work ethic (Weber, 1976), competence, diligence and hard work are all highly valued attributes. While these remain strong social and ideological tenets of German society, they are of course not homogeneous. The reunification of East and West Germany has meant there has been a fusion of former communist values with deeply ingrained capitalist traditions in the West. This has led to rising expectations for higher incomes and affluence among former East German workers, with consequent concerns among West German workers about how the demands of a reunified Germany will be met and who bears the cost. To some extent, therefore, the solid tradition of community identity has been watered down in Germany as a result of political factors and global economic pressures.

Perhaps because it only emerged from being a feudal society a little over a century ago, Japan is somewhat unique for an industrialised country. One legacy of feudalism is that Japan is what is technically called a **gerontocracy**, in which age is respected and regarded as synonymous with wisdom, which spills over into workplace relations. A second characteristic of the Japanese value system is that individualism is comparatively rare, and another is that being similar to, and interdependent with, others is positively valued. Indeed, personal identity is far less derived from being an individual than from being a member of a group (the Japanese), and this results in a highly collective spirit. Hand in hand with this goes a fairly pronounced tendency towards the avoidance of uncertainty. People feel threatened by ambiguous situations, risk taking is discouraged, and uncertainty and its associated stress are combated by hard work, career stability and intolerance of deviancy (Hofstede, 2001). For these reasons it is hardly surprising to find that some of the features of Japanese industrial society have, in the past, placed a strong emphasis on cohesion and cooperation. For example, there tended to be close ties between business and the stable political system. Indeed, many large firms were members of corporate groupings, in which banks and firms were near to being partners. In addition, although Japanese firms were ruthlessly competitive abroad, there was very little real competition between firms in the same industry, which gave very orderly internal markets. Finally, most firms had a line-up of exclusive suppliers, which fostered stability and loyalty between them and was a visible expression of the 'one big family' philosophy (Matsuura *et al.*, 2003; Schaede, 2004).

gerontocracy
Government by and respect for older people in society.

The technological contexts

Like Great Britain, America, Germany and Japan are all highly industrialised countries, and there is a strong similarity in terms of their technological contexts. In addition, across the past two decades all of them have experienced the effects of globalised economic pressures and have had to adopt new technologies in response to these pressures. Having said this, however, there are differences between the technological contexts of each country. Japan and Germany have been in the vanguard of technological innovation to a much greater extent than Great Britain or the USA, and to some extent this is connected to political factors and the choices made by managers. For example, the German government has invested much more heavily in the skills and vocational training of workers than has been the case in Britain, so that there exists a significant *skills gap* between these two countries. Similarly, Japanese employers have encouraged employee training and retraining so that companies are at the cutting edge of new technological innovations, whereas in America there is a reliance on individuals investing in their own training.

The effects of contexts at organisational level
Employees and their associations

In the last half-century there has been a progressive decline in the size and influence of American trade unions. For instance, in 1955 approximately 35 per cent of workers were trade union members, but by 2003 this had fallen to 13 per cent. Unlike Great Britain, where there is a politicised trade union movement (British unions actually formed the Labour Party to pursue working-class interests on a political front), American unions have few, if any, wider social or political objectives. Indeed, the Taft-Hartley Act of 1947 explicitly forbids the expenditure of union funds on political activities. There are two distinct types of unionisation in America: 'business unionism' and 'union organising'. By far the most prevalent form is the **business unionism** approach, which is almost exclusively concerned with parochial bread-and-butter issues. The vast size and diversity of America makes it virtually impossible for national bargaining to take place for whole industries, and where it exists, union organisation rests on a very well-developed system of 'locals', who deal with employers. Agreements are very detailed, are legally enforceable and in the workplace trade unions largely devote themselves to policing the agreements to see that they are scrupulously observed. In contrast is the newer **union organising** model, which instead of focusing on immediate bread-and-butter issues such as pay and contract negotiation, seeks to recruit members and leave in place self-reliant workplace union activists. The idea is also related to the concept of a community of union members, based on either occupation, social status or in some cases even ethnicity. Specific union-organising examples include the 'Justice for Janitors' campaign, which sought to raise awareness of the perceived second-class-citizenship status faced by many janitors, or the representation of thousands of immigrant workers in regional parts of America, such as Los Angeles (Bronfenbrenner *et al.*, 1998; Milkman, 2000). It is also noteworthy that the two forms of American unionism have resulted in some significant tensions among unions so that in 2005 some of America's traditional unions decided to leave the movement's national federation, the AFL-CIO. Needless to say, there are also sharp differences between unionised and non-unionised firms in America, and these are more easily explained later, when describing employers and managers.

German trade unions and employee associations are organised along broad industry lines, with one trade union for each industry, or group of industries. They are very large, and have stable, highly bureaucratised patterns of centralised authority. Unions in West Germany were reconstructed by the occupying powers shortly after the end of the Second World War as **industrial unions**, representing all workers in a given industry or group of industries. With slight modifications, some of which have been brought about by mergers, this pattern has been maintained after the reunification of Germany. At present, there are only eight trade unions, and bargaining about basic terms and conditions takes place with employers' federations, either nationally or regionally. Since trade unions are essentially national bodies, they concern themselves with a wide range of matters beyond the simple bread-and-butter issues of pay and conditions, and act as pressure groups on government. The German system of **co-determination** means that trade unions are regarded as important social partners, who

---

business unionism
A type of unionism that is non-idealistic and which strictly confines itself to the improvement of wages and working conditions.

organising unionism
A type of trade unionism that focuses strongly on recruiting and training members, with the aim of leaving in place a strong, self-reliant cadre of workplace activists.

industrial union
A trade union organised on the basis of representing all grades of workers in a particular industry.

co-determination
A system based on legal rights for workers (at enterprise level) and unions (at national level) to participate in decision making.

works councils

A joint council of workers and management, established in Germany under the Federal Works Constitution Acts (1952 and 1972) as a vehicle of co-determination.

consult with employer associations and the government about most aspects of social and economic policy. At workplace level the pivotal institution is the works council rather than national trade unions. **Works councils** consist of managers and elected employees, and have statutory participation rights in a wide range of management decisions. Although in practice it is often shop stewards who are elected as works council representatives, they represent constituencies of employees and do not act as officials of the trade union.

The past decade has been a difficult one for German trade unions, in which membership has fallen from 36 per cent of the workforce in the early 1990s (before reunification) to 28 per cent in 2003. To some extent this has occurred because of a loss of jobs in what were previously highly unionised industries, coupled with an inability on the part of unions to successfully recruit in newer industries (Grahl and Teague, 2004). However, there is also another possible reason for union decline. In Soviet East Germany, although they were officially independent, trade unions were widely perceived by workers to be part of the communist party apparatus. As such, they were viewed with suspicion, and many employees opted out of membership on reunification of Germany.

There are said to be three 'pillars' that support Japanese-style employment relations (Whittaker, 1990). These are the application of the principles of:

- enterprise-based unions
- egalitarian management
- lifetime employment (or as it is sometimes known, a 'living guarantee').

All of these will be explained in due course in what follows, but taking the first of them: in Japan an **enterprise union** is a trade union where membership is restricted to the employees of a

enterprise union

A union in which membership is restricted to employees of a particular firm.

particular firm, even though such unions are often affiliated to an industry federation. All permanent employees, except those at the very top, are members of the same union, and the Japanese believe that this way of doing things is far more able to deal with situations that are specific to the firm, than is a system that relies on external unions. Since only permanent employees become union members, a relatively small proportion of the Japanese workforce is unionised. For example, small firms, which employ about 88 per cent of all Japanese workers, seldom have permanent employees (Kuwahara, 1987). In Japan trade union density is about 25 per cent of the workforce, but unions tend to operate mainly in larger firms; for example, less than 10 per cent of employees in businesses with fewer than 100 workers are trade union members.

American management has long held a deeply ingrained hostility towards the very idea of trade unionism (Wheeler, 1987). Indeed, many managers will go to great lengths to avoid the incursion of trade unions, including using the services of overtly hostile union-busting consultants where the political and legal context allows for such action (Logan, 2001). In non-union firms management often determines the terms of the employment relationship unilaterally. In addition to deploying union-avoidance tactics noted earlier, management often employs a strategy of making things just that little bit better than in unionised firms to lower the incentive for workers to join unions (Wheeler, 1987; Fiorito et al., 1987). Other managerial responses include introducing a whole range of individualised human resource management policies in an attempt to engender high levels of worker motivation, job satisfaction and organisational commitment.

German managers tend to be standard bearers of some of the national values and ideologies outlined earlier. The factory system, which developed in Germany in the late nineteenth century, has left a strong legacy of paternalism. For example, many managers see the sharing of influence in works councils as one way to achieve the ideal of a community of interests. Prior to reunification most large German firms tended to compete internationally on a non-price basis, using a high-wage, high-productivity, high-skills and high-reinvestment strategy. A fundamental part of these strategies was the use of corporate governance systems that focused strongly on the interests of the internal stakeholders of the firm (Edwards, 2004). It was probably this, as much as anything else, that gave firms the stability and cooperation in employment relations that enabled them to operate as 'communities of interest'. However, since reunification, which roughly coincided with an era of increased global competition, matters have changed considerably. Although larger firms were able to benefit from a surge in exports, SMEs began to suffer from stagnant domestic markets, and their managers came to view Germany's centralised bargaining system as something that is too closely aligned with the interests of large firms. Since then, managers in SMEs, and in particular those in the former GDR, seem to have successfully pursued a policy of negotiating exemptions from national agreements in works councils, in order to obtain increased flexibility in work organisation and wages (Tuselman and Heise, 2000).

Japanese employers tend to have a strong paternalistic approach to managing which, to some extent, could be a legacy of the feudal origins of industry. From this has sprung the second of the three pillars of Japanese-style employment: the use of egalitarian management. For example, there are few status distinctions between managers and their subordinates, and this is seen as an essential part of the Japanese way of managing. In addition, payment systems based on seniority – something that is associated with the third of the three pillars of Japanese employment: lifetime employment – have traditionally been commonplace. These emphasise length of service, age or education as the primary basis for pay or promotion, rather than merit. However, there are now strong pressures to introduce performance-based pay and evaluation schemes to replace seniority as the basis for rewards, primarily with the aim of giving higher levels of labour flexibility in firms (Benson and Debroux, 2003).

Climates and cultures

Since American trade unions are almost as fiercely devoted to the free enterprise system as employers, part of their philosophy of business unionism is the idea that 'what is good for the company is good for its employees'. In addition, American managers are also much more willing to use a wide range of applied behavioural science techniques to try to improve cultures and climates. The origins of this seem to lie in claims made in the 1970s that there was widespread discontent and alienation among American workers (Lawler, 1975), from which sprang what became known as the 'quality of working life' (QWL) movement. More recent evidence suggests that things have not changed greatly since the 1970s, and American workers still seem to lack trust in their managers (Mercer Consulting, 2005). Nevertheless, perhaps because of their different educational backgrounds, American managers seem to be willing to make more use of such techniques as job enrichment and job enlargement to try and promote cooperative climates.

quality of working life (QWL) movement
A campaign that concerns itself with measures to improve the experience of working life for American workers, often by placing emphasis on such matters as job design and the use of participative management techniques.

In Germany the sense of community derived from wider social values and ideologies has its effects within organisations.

Managers and employees usually have a very positive approach to each other, and in works councils there is a great deal of cooperation, which extends to discussing matters of mutual interest that go well beyond those normally covered in collective bargaining.

Wider social values also have their effects in Japan, notably in larger firms where there is a strong sense of everyone being a member of the same big family, or a 'community of fate'. In general managers and employees have relatively high levels of trust, because both share ownership of problems and strive together to overcome them. Indeed, since the desirable Japanese state of affairs is where everybody sees the firm as a family, the endemic conflict and adversarial relationships found in some Western organisations are less prevalent in many Japanese firms.

Employee relations processes and outcomes

America can be viewed as having two employment relations systems: the union and non-union (Kochan *et al.*, 1986). In unionised firms negotiations usually cover a wide range of benefits such as medical insurance and pensions, as well as pay and conditions, and this is one of the reasons why American unions have little need to pursue these things on a political front – for example, by pressing for social legislation. Agreements tend to be complex and highly detailed, and most run for between one and four years. They are legally enforceable, are assumed to contain a no-strike clause and, strictly speaking, unless it can be demonstrated that the agreement has been broken, industrial action is illegal. Bargaining relationships are often very professional, if somewhat competitive in nature. Moreover, the 'business unionism' approach of American trade unions has, in the past, resulted in them being willing to engage in **concession bargaining**, in which some of the benefits obtained during earlier, more prosperous times, have been sacrificed in order to save a firm from going out of existence in recession (Dworkin *et al.*, 1988). In non-union firms, as noted earlier, management usually determines the terms of the relationship unilaterally. It is also commonplace, in union as well as non-union workplaces, to use applied behavioural science techniques that seek to influence organisational climates in a way that makes the relationship a cooperative one. However, climates and cultures in America are somewhat less supportive of harmony than in Germany and Japan, and so employment relations processes and outcomes are often far less cooperative. This is because managers have a strong belief in their right to manage, and as American industry is not heavily unionised, employers are very much the dominant party in employment relations. Thus, partly by inclination, and perhaps partly to stay within the law, managers in unionised firms tend to adopt individualised human resource management strategies as a way to woo employees away from union influence (Barbash, 1988).

Although Germany has experienced a number of post-reunification tensions, processes and outcomes are still very much a product of the system of co-determination, in which shared influence and the idea of the enterprise as a community remain strong principles supported by managers and workers. Employee representation at board level and on works councils not only ensures effective communication between managers and employees, but also gives employees an active role in determining many of the features of the employment relationship. For example, works councils determine company rules, such as disciplinary policy, work methods, new technology and payment systems. Moreover, they tend to be seen by both employees and managers as a highly effective method of working out or modifying the terms of the relation-

---

concession bargaining

A practice used in America, where, because a negotiated contract is legally enforceable, the employer needs to engage in bargaining with a trade union to be able to obtain concessions over matters such as wage rates in order to vary the contract during a recession.

ship. Therefore, unlike in many other countries where new technology is seen as a threat or destroyer of jobs, in Germany it is not. Rather it tends to be viewed as a potential benefit, the impact of which depends less on what it is, and more on how it is introduced.

Japanese employment relations practices are a personification of the national culture (Abegglen and Salk, 1985). Large Japanese companies have a tradition of recruiting permanent employees direct from school or university, and they are expected to remain there with guaranteed employment for the rest of their working lives. However, the lifetime employment principle – the third of the three pillars of Japanese-style employment – does not, and never has applied to everyone. It exists only in large companies, and even in large firms only about 30 per cent of the workforce is employed on a contract of this type. For example, temporary workers, subcontractors, seasonal workers and part-time employees are all excluded. Nevertheless, although even large firms are more restrictive about the size of their permanent workforces, they still tend to view some form of permanent employment as a fundamental part of what they offer to employees, and it is unlikely to be abandoned completely. Most training is within the firm, and for the firm, and it usually includes a measure of normative instruction to promote what are seen to be the proper attitudes and values. Thus, it encourages identifying with the organisation, and to some extent the families of employees are looked upon as peripheral members of the firm. However, if, on some occasion, the interests of the family and firm do not coincide, the firm is expected to come first. Differences in wages and fringe benefits between managers and workers are usually quite modest compared to Western standards, although with economic pressures to promote greater workforce flexibility, this is slowly being eroded. Nevertheless, Japanese companies tend to look upon themselves as employing the whole man (or woman), not just paying the market price for a job, and for this reason permanent employees are seen as a valuable resource worthy of a training investment. In consequence, there is still an assumption that the longer a person has been with the firm, the greater is his/her range of skills, and this is reflected in pay. Paternalism still runs strong, and responsibility for the personal welfare of employees is seen to be very much part of a supervisor's role. There is also a strong alignment between employer and trade union about almost everything, especially those things that affect the firm's competitive advantage. Working conditions and security are seen to be strongly linked with company success, and thus enterprise unions cooperate strongly with management. Above all, in order not to damage the spirit of community, when grievances occur they are much more likely to be settled informally, rather than through a formal procedure. Work rules and union–management agreements are very comprehensive in Japan, so that the rights and obligations of employee and employer are permanently fixed in order to avoid future ambiguity and misunderstandings.

Therefore, in both Japan and Germany, employment relations processes and outcomes tend to be more cooperative than in America or Great Britain. To a large extent, these divergent employment relations outcomes stem from their distinctive cultures. Social values in both Japan and Germany support a paternalistic outlook towards employees and, although this manifests itself through very different processes, in each country managers and employees both have a strong sense of common identity. In Germany social values promote the idea of the firm as a community of interest, or a society in miniature, whereas in Japan there is more of a sense of the firm as a family. This gives some clue as to why cooperative processes in each country take a somewhat different form. As well as the obvious differences in size between a community and a family, there are important differences in the way that each one tends to regulate the conduct of its members. Communities usually evolve formal rules of conduct (laws), whereas families tend to operate much more informally. In Germany the State has provided a legislative framework that is highly formalised, and which facilitates the sharing of decisions in a way that suits the German national character. Japan has its own methods of shared decision making, and again these fit comfortably with its social values of teamwork, togetherness and belonging.

The major features of contexts and outcomes for each country are summarised in Table I1.1, which for comparative purposes, also includes the major features of Great Britain from Chapter 2. As can be seen, although the foregoing descriptions are only in outline form, each country's contextual circumstances can have a strong impact on relationships within firms, and each nation has its own unique brand of employment relations.

	Great Britain	America	Germany	Japan
Political-legal context	Little direct intervention. Laws framed to protect individual employee rights, but also to restrict trade union activities	No direct intervention. Laws framed to protect trade unions and collective bargaining, but often circumvented by employers	No direct intervention. Laws framed to promote system of co-determination at enterprise level	Non-interventionist, but some law to protect independence of unions
Economic context	Turbulent due to effects of global economy, but currently a fairly stable economy	As Great Britain	Fairly buoyant and prosperous, but large economic problems due to reunification	As Great Britain
Socio-ideological context	Increasingly individualistic and meritocratic, but with some collective ideals still present	Highly individualistic, with strong belief in free enterprise system	Medium individualism, but cohesive/collective sense of national identity	Low individualism and a group-based sense of cohesion
Technological context	Medium technology-based society	Medium technology-based society	High technology-based society	High technology-based society
Employees and their associations	Independent trade unions, but smaller and less influential than in past	Business unionism with unions in severe decline	National trade unions who have no official representation role at enterprise level	Enterprise trade unions
Employers and managers	Increasingly assertive about their rights to manage, with an increase in the use of individual HR practices	Widespread hostility to trade unions. Widespread use of individual HR practices	Some residual traces of paternalism	Paternalistic
Organisational climates and cultures	Highly variable from hostile to benign	As Great Britain	Strong ethos of the firm as a community of interests	Strong ethos of the firm as a family
Employment relations processes and outcomes	Where unions recognised, variation from social partnership to adversarial processes	Unilateral regulation by management in non-union firms; where unions recognised, highly competitive	Constitutional and cooperative	Flexible and highly cooperative

Table I1.1 Major contextual circumstances and employment relations outcomes in Great Britain, America, Germany and Japan

Further reading

Abegglen, J.C. and G.J. Salk (1985) *Kaisha: The Japanese Corporation*, New York, Basic Books. A classic account of the Japanese industrial system, which contains some interesting observations on its origins and characteristics.

Addison, J., L. Bellman, C. Schnabel and W. Joachim (2004) 'The reform of the German Works Constitution Act: a critical assessment', *Industrial Relations* 42 (2), pp. 292–420. An interesting review of changes in the operation of works councils in German industrial relations.

Bennett, R. (1997) *Employee Relations,* 2nd edn, London, Pitman. The book contains brief, but useful, descriptions of employment relations in America and Japan.

Dore, R.P. (1973) *British Factory – Japanese Factory: The Origins of National Diversity in Industrial Relations*, London, Allen and Unwin. A classic comparative study that gives an explicit comparison of the similarities and differences between British and Japanese firms.

Jacoby, S.M. (2005) *The Embedded Corporation: Corporate Governance and Employment Relations in Japan and the United States*, Princeton NJ, Princeton University Press. A very interesting book, which compares recent changes in Japan and America. It shows how, despite global economic pressures, two of the three central pillars of Japanese industrial organisation have remained largely intact.

Lawler, J.J. (1990) *Unionisation and Deunionisation: Strategy, Tactics and Outcomes*, Columbia, SC, University of South Carolina Press. A useful book that explores some of the reasons for the decline in American trade unions.

Moody, K. (1988) *An Injury to All: The Decline of American Unionism*, New York, Verso. An early and interesting account of the decline of American trade unions.

Rogers, J. and W. Streeck (eds) (1995) *Works Councils: Consultation, Representation and Cooperation in Industrial Relations*, Chicago Ill, University of Chicago Press. A penetrating exploration of the strengths and weaknesses of German works councils.

Visser, J. and J. van Ruysseveldt (1996) 'Robust corporatism still? Industrial relations in Germany', in J. van Russeveldt and J. Visser (eds), *Industrial Relations in Europe: Traditions and Transitions*, London, Sage. A useful paper that explores and documents changes in employment relations in Germany post reunification.

PART 2

The parties in employment relations

Part contents

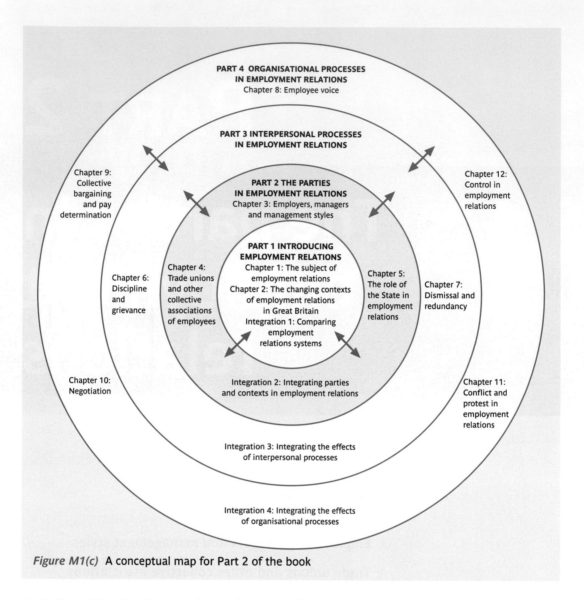

Figure M1(c) A conceptual map for Part 2 of the book

As indicated by the diagram above, this part of the book consists of four chapters. Three of them deal with the main parties that interact in employment relations: employers and managers; trade unions and collective employee associations; and the State. These chapters are followed by the second integrative chapter in the book, which traces some of the main influences that the three parties have on each other, and how they are all influenced by the contexts of employment relations in Great Britain.

Chapter 3

Employers, managers and management styles

Introduction

This chapter focuses on one of the two parties directly involved in employment relations at organisational level: the employer and the employer's agent, management. Because the word 'management' can have two different meanings, the chapter starts by defining the way in which it is used here – to distinguish a group of people within an organisation. This is followed by a description of the way that the structure of the modern enterprise gives rise to management positions, together with some of the associated employment relations processes and outcomes.

Management's role in employment relations is then discussed, its claims to authority are examined, and some of the available methods that are commonly used to influence employee behaviour are noted. Flowing from this, the all important topic of management's behavioural style is examined, and a number of different ways of categorising styles are given. The implications of style are then briefly explored, with particular reference to corporate governance policy and employment relations. The chapter concludes by briefly examining management style in non-union firms.

Pause for reflection

Working together with other students in your class, briefly define what you take the word 'management' to mean.

Management defined

The word 'management' can be used in two different ways: first, to distinguish those members of the organisation who usually have some formal authority over other employees and, second, to describe a set of activities that are concerned with running an organisation. In employment relations, the term is more often used in the first way, and the same convention will be followed here, to refer to either **line management** or **staff management**.

Line management usually involves the responsibility for achieving one or more objectives, and in addition, these days line managers often have employment relations responsibilities to attend to. However, the term 'management' also encompasses staff managers: those people who, while they do not necessarily have subordinates, are still designated as part of management. Normally, these people are specialists who advise other managers, or make decisions on their behalf; in employment relations for example, this would include personnel or human resource specialists. For clarity, wherever it is necessary to refer to the activity of management, the word **managing** will be used.

line management
Members of an organisation who normally have formal authority over other employees.

staff management
Those managers in specialist roles who advise line managers, or act on their behalf.

managing
The activity of running an organisation (or part thereof), included in which is the responsibility for achieving one or more objectives.

Management in the modern enterprise

The emergence of management as a distinct group of people in organisations is largely attributable to two phenomena, both of which are associated with the development of the modern form of industrial organisation. Apart from small firms and sole proprietors, the days have long since passed when the people who run organisations are those who actually own them. The size and complexity of the modern enterprise usually results in ownership being divorced from actually running a firm, a task that is normally undertaken by managers who act as the agents of the ultimate owners, i.e. shareholders. Appropriately, this is generally referred to as the **agency function of management**, which broadly means that management has a duty of stewardship – that is, to protect and advance share-

agency function of management
The responsibility of management to safeguard and advance shareholder interests.

holder interests. These days both public and private sector organisations are large and complex, and size and complexity usually mean that planning, coordinating and controlling the activities of an organisation becomes a formidable task, the main remedy for which is to structure the organisation (Child, 1984). Size usually gives rise to two characteristics of structure that make structures more complex and elaborate: **horizontal differentiation** and **vertical differentiation**. Since both of these can have some impact on employment relations they will be considered separately.

horizontal differentiation
The division of an organisation's overall task into different activities.

vertical differentiation
The establishment of a hierarchy of authority in an organisation.

Horizontal differentiation

Most large organisations are differentiated into specialised departments and functions, for instance, production, marketing, finance, research and development and so on. Although these functions perform their own specialist tasks, in an ideal world they should all mesh together to achieve objectives that are set for the whole organisation. However, in practice organisations do not exist in an ideal world, and each function operates in its own sub-environment, which has its own set of constraints (Lawrence and Lorsch, 1967). For example, customer and competitor pressures usually have a stronger impact on marketing departments than elsewhere, and trade union and supplier problems can have effects on the production function. A consequence of this is that each function looks inwards to some extent, to focus on its own problems and tasks. Indeed, the more specialist and differentiated its task, the greater is the tendency for a function to develop its own outlook and values, and for the objectives of the department to displace the overall goals for the organisation (Wilson, 1966). The structural remedy for this is to assign specific responsibility for achieving objectives to an individual rather than to the department as a whole. Thus someone (a manager) is placed over the department and charged with meeting objectives.

Pause for reflection

Bearing in mind that horizontal differentiation can result in different 'world views' in different organisational functions, what particular employment relations problems might this give rise to?

One of the most notable problems this can give rise to in employment relations is that different informal practices can spring up throughout an organisation and, needless to say, informal management processes tend to be the norm in many smaller firms. Therefore, the role of managing tends to be quite diverse, even within a single organisation, and more will be said of this later when dealing with management styles. In larger organisations, if corporate objectives are not met, it is managers who tend to bear the brunt, and come under the most immediate pressure from above. However, because their subordinates can sometimes be one of the most powerful constraints on meeting objectives, managers have a very real incentive to make their own informal agreements with employees. While informality can have its positive side, and is highly valued by many managers because an informal deal can sometimes be a useful way of making adjustments to working practices (Terry, 1977) from an organisational point of view, this sort of thing can quickly get out of hand and lead to serious problems. For example, concessions granted in one department can be quoted as a precedent by employees in another.

Case study 3.1: **The shift-pay incident**

Throughout the 1960s and 1970s increased attention was paid to acoustic and thermal insulation, and asbestos was a widely used building material. However, somewhat later in time the health hazards of certain types of asbestos became fully recognised, and to conform with new health and safety legislation, many firms with premises that contained asbestos had to have it removed. One such case that had interesting employment relations implications took place in one of Britain's largest companies, which discovered that it had a large number of buildings containing asbestos, some of which were used by both employees and the general public. Accordingly, plans were made to remove the material, but due to the inherent health hazards of doing so, it was necessary to close the building completely while work took place. To try to minimize the disruptive effects, contractors worked 24 hours around the clock to remove the material, and the renovation of each building needed between two and five days. Legislation also required that while the work was in progress, and for a short time afterwards, chemists would be in attendance around the clock to monitor the atmosphere for the presence of asbestos fibres. This was a highly specialist task, which contractors could not perform for themselves, but fortunately, the organisation had a small chemical laboratory with chemists qualified to do the work, who were also able to sign the required documentation that gave premises a 'clean bill of health' when jobs were completed.

Shortly after the first job was completed the employee representative (departmental steward) of the chemists approached his laboratory manager, to claim the payment of shift allowances for chemists involved in this work. The organisation had a comprehensive set of nationally negotiated pay agreements, one of which contained a provision for shift pay. However, according to the wording of the agreement, shift payments could only be made where the nature of a job involved shift working as a permanent duty. After consulting with the Human Resources Department, the laboratory manager explained this to the steward, and stated that he was unable to authorise shift allowances. The steward then reported this to his members and shortly afterwards informed the manager that the chemists would refuse to work around the clock, and in addition reserved their right to inform both the contractors and the Health and Safety Executive, which would probably result in 'closure orders' on the buildings concerned.

This placed the manager in a difficult position. If he authorised shift payments, this would probably be spotted by the salaries department, who would refuse payment. In addition, his own superior had told him to stand firm on the matter, lest it be used as a precedent by other groups who also had occasionally to work around the clock when emergencies occurred. Indeed, other managers, including his boss, made it clear that they would hold him responsible for any loss of business or disruption that resulted from closed premises.

If you were the laboratory manager how would you go about resolving this situation?

In large complex organisations, another important consequence of horizontal differentiation is the existence of line and staff management roles side by side. In employment relations an important group of specialists are the personnel or human resources staff of an organisation. These days there is an increasing tendency for human resource specialists to regard their work as a profession in its own right. Indeed, in some firms they advise and formulate employment relations policies and strategies, which line managers then implement at shopfloor and office levels. Like all professions, they often lay claim to a monopoly of expertise and knowledge, asserting that their role in managing people is vital to organisational success. However, as noted above, line managers also have objectives to achieve, and their subordinates perform tasks that can be crucial to achieving these objectives. Consequently, they can also claim a responsibility for evolving and implementing employment relations practices appropriate to their own areas, and this can bring them into conflict with human resource specialists. For instance, line managers can come to feel that personnel specialists should not exercise too much influence over policy, and that they (the line managers), are better placed to handle employment relations matters with their staff. Indeed, this can even lead to an element of subterfuge and secrecy creeping into the way these things are handled, and make the fragmentation problems outlined above much worse.

Vertical differentiation

Within all organisations, and usually within their departments and functions, there is a hierarchy of authority that goes hand in hand with differences in the scope of decision making. Managers lower down are more involved in the day-to-day operations of the enterprise, and general managers at the very top are usually concerned with policy and corporate strategy. Rewards get larger as the hierarchy is ascended, and higher-level strategic decisions are made that affect subordinates elsewhere in the organisation. In many firms, those below the level of supervisor can have little or no input into overall strategic matters, and this can result in them feeling a need to challenge decisions that are perceived to affect them adversely. Since they have little or no power as individuals, one way in which they can do this is to act in concert, by joining trade unions, which are covered in the next chapter. Indeed, this effect can also spread within the management hierarchy itself. For example, in some organisations junior and middle-level managers can be excluded from all but the most trivial of decisions, which makes them little more than a sub-group of employees. If they come to see themselves in this way, they too can start to see advantages in collectivising to protect their own interests, and this has been advanced as a major reason for the growth in managerial unionism (Poole *et al.*, 2005).

Employers associations

In addition to managers as the agents of owners, there is also another potentially significant party that is strongly connected to the process of managing. This is an **employers association**,

---

employers association

An organisation of employers that exists for the purpose of regulating relations between employers and employees, or trade unions.

---

which is an organisation of employers, whether temporary or permanent, whose main purpose includes the regulation of relations between employers and employees, or trade unions. Like trade unions, employer associations are defined in law, registered with the Certification Officer, and their size and influence varies considerably. Some, such as the Engineering Employers Federation (EEF) and the National Farmers Union (NFU), are very large, having memberships of over 5000 and 127 000 respectively. Others, however, are much smaller, mainly because their members are mostly drawn from industries that are themselves very small. Here, for the purposes of discussion, it is important to distinguish between employers associations and trade associations, because the latter tend to restrict their activities to commercial matters, whereas the former exist primarily to deal with employment relations.

Across the past two decades the number of employers associations has declined severely, from over 1350 in 1968 to 85 in 2005 (Annual Report of the Certification Officer, 2005). Like trade unions, which will be covered separately in the next chapter, employers associations perform a number of broad functions for member firms, four of which are by far the most important:

1 *Direct negotiation with trade unions about collective agreements about pay and conditions of service*: at one time this was their major activity and in some respects it is still an important one for some employers, especially where multi-employer or industry collective bargaining

exists. For example, small firms, whether unionised or not, seldom have the time or resources to engage in an extensive round of wage negotiations. Thus, they often peg their own wage rates to trends negotiated by their respective association. This is particularly important in industries that are made up of a large number of small firms, because it effectively puts them all in the same boat, so far as labour costs are concerned.

2 *Assisting members in the resolution of disputes*: again this can be an important function for some firms. For instance, in engineering the EEF provides a conciliation and arbitration facility for its members as the final step in a disputes procedure, or in individual grievance matters.

3 *Provision of advisory services on employment relations matters*: this can be particularly useful for small employers, who might well be unable to afford the services of a human resource specialist in the organisation to keep them abreast of changes in the law.

4 *Representation of their members' views and interests to government and other agencies*: in other words, a political lobbying function.

Summary points

- The emergence of management as a distinct group in organisations is associated with the separation of ownership from day-to-day control.

- Due to the increased size and complexity of most modern organisations, their activities are normally structured into a pattern of horizontal and vertical differentiation.

- Although horizontal and vertical differentiation gives advantages in terms of the control of activities, it can also give rise to a number of problems in employment relations.

- In many smaller firms, the function of management is often very different from that of the large organisation, and there is a tendency for informal practices to dominate.

- Employers associations exist as a party that can influence employment relations, by providing advice and guidance to employers and managers on various employment relations matters.

The management role in employment relations

Although some managers would argue that they too are only employees, most would also assert that, because they are given control of resources and made responsible for their efficient and effective utilisation, this makes them different from other workers. Whichever way we look at things, the people who are managed are part of the resources of an organisation. Therefore, to some extent it is the manager who will be held responsible for the conduct of employment relations. However, it is all too easy for academics to forget that managers have other things to attend to than employment relations, and this is particularly the case in the light of **delayering** and **downsizing** initiatives that have increased across the past two decades. These steps have resulted in a wave of employee discontent, because employees feel that the organisation they work for treats them as a commodity, rather than as human beings who deserve consideration (Thornhill *et al.*, 1997). Moreover, as a result of delayering there are now fewer supervisors

delayering
A reduction in the number of functional levels in an organisation's hierarchy, usually by removing one or more levels of supervision and/or middle management.

downsizing
A reduction in the number of people employed by an organisation or in the scale of its activities, theoretically to attain the appropriate size for its volume of business.

and managers to attend to employee discontent (Morris, J.R. *et al.*, 1999). For instance, a recent survey of members of the Chartered Management Institute (CMI) revealed that the vast majority of British managers have experienced a decline in their involvement in handling employment relations matters (Poole *et al.*, 2005). In consequence, so far as employment relations is concerned, time pressures probably mean that management involvement is restricted to 'fire-fighting', or simply trying to ensure that the part of the organisation for which they are responsible runs smoothly. For this reason, effective employment relations is more likely to be seen by managers as a means to an end, rather than an end in itself. Nevertheless, an important implication of the view that subordinates are resources is that management is likely to lay claim to a right to command their actions, or to use a phrase which is common in employment relations, they will feel that the right to command is part of the **managerial prerogative**. Management behaviour can often be a reflection of the ferocity with which these claimed prerogatives are asserted or defended. Thus, it is important to have some understanding of the arguments that can be used to assert the prerogatives in the first place.

managerial prerogative
Rghts and functions that managers assert are exclusively theirs.

property rights argument
That managers are the agents of the ultimate owners of the business, and therefore have the delegated authority of the owners to make decisions on their behalf.

One basis for asserting the right to command has been called the **'property rights'** argument. As noted earlier, while the ultimate property rights in a business belong to its owners, in the modern enterprise the owners are usually shareholders, who have no part in the day-to-day running of the firm. Thus, managers deem themselves to be agents who exercise these rights and argue that they have delegated shareholder authority to do so (Storey, 1983). While the idea is a very old one, whose roots are lost in history, it is still prevalent and most managers tend to assert that the managerial role is one of stewardship, and that the interests of the owners should take precedence over all other groups in the enterprise.

professional manager argument
That management is a profession that has emerged as an occupational group which has a monopoly of the skills, knowledge and expertise necessary to conduct the affairs of an organisation.

In recent years however, an additional and somewhat different claim to authority has been asserted; the so-called **'professional manager'** argument. These days organised groups of managers, such as the Chartered Management Institute (CMI) and the Chartered Institute of Personnel and Development (CIPD) suggest that the occupation of managing should be regarded as a profession, because management has emerged as an occupational group that has unique skills, knowledge and expertise. For this reason, managers argue that they, and they alone, have the necessary competence to conduct the affairs of the enterprise and to make decisions about the best use of its resources (Salamon, 2000).

Whichever argument is the most prevalent – and probably both are used to some extent – they give rise to a very powerful set of ideologies and values which can lead management to take the view that its role in employment relations is legitimately that of the dominant party, a view which is likely to be reinforced by the authority conferred on managers by organisational structure. However, and as will be seen in the next chapter, if there is a trade union presence in an organisation, the union also has a source of authority: that which is conferred on it by its members. Wherever there are separate sources of authority in an organisation there is the attendant risk of conflict: in this case, conflict that arises from a clash of ideologies about the legitimisation of authority. For instance, managers might assume that any change they propose should automatically be adopted and implemented by employees, whereas trade unions could see things somewhat differently. They might be prepared to agree only to those changes that benefit their members, or at least to those that have no adverse affect on their interests. While the subject of power and politics is far too extensive to cover here, it can be noted that authority is only a special form of power, and wherever power exists, the use of politics as a means to acquire and exercise it is seldom far away. As a result, both sides can engage in political behaviour to try to enhance their own power relative to the other. For example, under the guise of keeping all employees well informed, managers sometimes seek to undermine trade union authority by communicating directly with the workforce about matters which are normally handled collectively with trade union representatives. Similarly, trade unions can deliberately 'misunderstand' management in order to mobilise bias in their members. All of this can mean

frame of reference
A 'world view' that influences how a specific state of affairs is perceived by its holder, and, by implication, how he/she reacts to the situation.

that the two parties approach the same issue in fundamentally different ways, and with quite different frames of reference, which in turn means that a dialogue between them is difficult because they simply do not see the same issue in the same way. For these reasons management ideology and the behavioural style to which it gives rise can be a major factor which influences the nature of a firm's employment relations. Style is a topic that will be covered in greater depth presently, but before doing so it is important to stress that, other than simply asserting a right to be obeyed, there are ways in which management can influence the behaviour of employees. For example, structure, technology and job design (or rather its assumed motivational effects) can all be used in this way. So important are these that it is worthwhile considering them all separately.

Pause for reflection

Together with other students in your class, consider the potential effects of structure, technology and job design on employees, and answer the questions below:

1 How could structure shape the behaviour of employees into something that is acceptable to management?
2 How could technology shape the behaviour of employees into something that is acceptable to management?
3 How could the design of jobs shape the behaviour of employees into something that is acceptable to management?

Organisational structure

As was noted earlier, the modern business organisation tends to be heavily structured into a pattern of horizontally and vertically differentiated parts. Although structure itself does not completely determine human behaviour, it is seldom appreciated how much it establishes predictable behavioural patterns. For example, it specifies roles and rules that lay down the activities undertaken by employees. These details are often incorporated into job descriptions, works rules and operational procedures that are enshrined in contracts of employment, which gives a large measure of control over employee behaviour. These features also shape behaviour in other, more subtle ways. Differences in authority not only map out the formal authority of managers to reward some behaviour and punish that which is prohibited; differences in power also have psychological effects. They establish embedded rules of conduct which legitimise management power so that those lower down cooperate in their own subjugation. Thus pursuing management's will comes to be seen as organisational common sense (Weick, 2001).

Technology

Technology is generally taken to denote the means by which tasks are accomplished. It is something that is usually considered to be a management choice, and can have a huge effect on the capability to influence employee behaviour and employment relations outcomes. For this reason, what is chosen is unlikely to be solely dictated by considerations of rational economic efficiency, but can often owe as much to management's desire to control people's activities as anything else (Child, 1972). A fairly obvious example of this is the machine-paced nature of work on a mass-production line, where the speed at which the line moves dictates how much effort employees have to expend. Using mass production methods also de-skills work, which not only lowers labour costs, but also makes labour more easily replaced. Employees can, of course, be well aware of this and, if a change in technology has too dramatic an effect, its introduction may very well be opposed. Thus, it is no coincidence that the most highly organised and cohesive union organisations are often found in the mass-production industries.

Job design and motivation

Another way in which management can attempt to influence the efficiency and effectiveness of employees is to design jobs with an eye to their perceived motivational outcomes. How to get the most willing work performance from employees has long been a concern of management, and across the years there have been a whole string of theories about what motivates employees. The oldest of all, the so-called 'scientific management' approach (Taylor, 1911), while basically a theory and method of job design that involves simplification and specialisation of tasks, nevertheless contains the assumption that employees are primarily motivated by money – an idea which is a lot older than the theory itself. Somewhat later, and arising out of what became known as the Hawthorne Experiments in the General Electric Company in America, it was discovered that social interaction between people in a working environment could be a source of motivation (Roethlisberger and Dixon, 1939). The implication is that if people are responsive to the social milieu rather than just to the carrot-and-stick techniques of scientific management, more effective and efficient work performance can be obtained by meeting their needs. Later still, a stream of theory emerged which emphasised the needs of human beings to use their inherent capacities and skills in a mature and productive way. Examples here are Maslow's hierarchy of human needs (Maslow, 1970), McGregor's theory X and theory Y (McGregor, 1960), Herzberg's theory of hygiene factors and motivators (Herzberg, 1966), or more recently Pfeffer's Best Practice HRM theory (Pfeffer, 1998), which suggests that workers perform better when certain human resource policies and practices such as sophisticated recruitment, contingent pay and employee involvement are bundled together. Broadly speaking, the implications of these theories are that jobs should be designed to permit a degree of autonomy and challenge, which results in a more productive workforce because people find work meaningful and self-fulfilling. In addition, there are other approaches to work motivation. Unlike the above theories, which emphasise a universal set of motivators, later approaches assume that individuals make highly complex mental judgements about the nature of their work. For example, Vroom's valence expectancy theory views work motivation as a function of an individual's perception that by behaving in a certain way it will lead to particular outcomes. Thus, if the outcomes are valued enough, the motivation to produce them is increased (Vroom, 1964).

Since human motivation is extremely complex, it is unlikely that any of these theories is more than a partial explanation. However, most of them have received some support from research, and if their principles are applied in appropriate circumstances, they can give

Case study 3.2: **Motivation and job design at work**

An example of an experiment in the use of job enrichment techniques to influence employee behaviour took place several years ago in a large manufacturing firm. It involved sales representatives, who, although having a high degree of job satisfaction, were given very little discretion over the way they operated. The company was carrying out a number of job-enrichment studies at the time, and despite the company's products being fully competitive, sales showed no improvement over those for previous years, so the representatives were seen as a suitable group for the changed work conditions. The changes were generated by managers above the supervisors of the sales representatives, and were introduced gradually.

In the changed situation sales representatives were allowed to pass on or request information at their own discretion, instead of writing a report on every customer call. They were also allowed to determine calling frequencies, how to deal with defective or surplus stock, request calls from the technical service department, and if they were satisfied it would not prejudice the company's position, to settle customer complaints by payments of up to £100. They were also given a 10 per cent discretion on the prices of most of the products sold.

As a matter of deliberate policy, and to avoid any artificial effect resulting from knowing they were under observation, representatives whose jobs were enriched were not informed that they were part of an experiment. For comparison a control group, which was not subject to the changes and also kept in ignorance of its role in the experiment was used.

What do you feel would be the likely results of these changes?

---

management some capability to influence the behaviour of employees. For example, techniques such as job rotation or enlargement can be used to remove some of the monotony of performing a single repetitive task. Similarly, jobs can be enriched by using employee participation schemes to give a measure of autonomy and satisfaction.

Although motivation theory can be a useful tool, it is important to realise that there are limitations on the freedom with which these techniques can be used by management. To start with, both the task itself and the technology used clearly impose some limitations. In addition, choice is likely to be influenced to some extent by worker and union responses to management action, or by management's own values. Indeed, management can be just as much a captive of its own ideologies and values as anyone else; in particular those about what it is that motivates employees. For example, managers who assume that employees are only likely to be motivated by money are probably more likely to apply a scientific management philosophy, and reserve to themselves all planning and directing as strictly part of their prerogatives. Conversely, managers who feel that intrinsic motivation is more important are likely to incline towards enlarged and enriched jobs.

A somewhat new twist to the story is that in today's conditions, where management is searching for even more effectiveness and efficiency from employees, enlargement and enrichment techniques have witnessed something of a renaissance under the guise of **empowerment**, but for other reasons. It will be remembered that, in Chapter 2, it was noted that there is an increasing tendency to move towards a flexible multi-skilled workforce, and almost by definition, a multi-skilled, highly flexible workforce has enlarged and possibly enriched jobs. However, the reason for these changes is normally to keep labour costs to a minimum rather than to make jobs more intrinsically satisfying. There has been a tremendous amount of work

empowerment

Giving people the authority to make decisions in their own area of operations, without the approval of senior management.

redesign of this type, and economic factors have enabled management to reassert its power to push these changes through, often with little or no concern for whether they are viewed favourably by employees. Therefore, it would be unwise to assume that, just because jobs have changed in a way that could make them more interesting, those who perform the jobs are more highly motivated as a result; indeed, what evidence there is tends to indicate the reverse (Cunningham and Hyman, 1999). Nor would it be safe to assume that people are unaware that they are probably doing more work for the same money. Thus, while job design is one way in which managers can attempt to improve efficiency and effectiveness, a lot will depend on how the changes are brought about. Changes that are forced on employees, even if they do result in jobs which are potentially more satisfying, could, in the long run, have an effect which is exactly opposite to the one predicted by the motivational theories. A great deal is bound to depend upon the way management goes about these things, or to put matters another way, management's style of behaviour. This is such an important topic for employment relations that it deserves separate consideration, which follows next.

Summary points

- Because managers have many matters other than employment relations to which they need to attend, effective employment relations tends to be seen by them as a means to an end, rather than an end in itself.

- Managers tend to use one or both of two arguments to justify their 'right to command': the 'property rights' argument and the 'professional manager' argument.

- The use of either argument can sometimes lead to a clash of ideologies in an organisation.

- Other than asserting its assumed 'right to be obeyed', management has other ways of influencing employee behaviour, by using some combination of: structure, technology and job design.

Pause for reflection

Working together with other students in your class, briefly define what you take the expression 'management style' to mean.

Management style

The expression **management style** has a particular meaning in employment relations. This is quite different from the way it is used in other subjects such as organisational behaviour, where it is most often employed to distinguish between different leadership styles – for example, democratic/participative versus autocratic. In employment relations, style is used in a more global way to refer to a manager's preferred approach to handling employment relations, which reflects the way that he/she exercises authority over subordinates.

management style

A manager's preferred approach to handling employment relations matters with employees, which reflects the way that he/she exercises authority over subordinates.

While managers have a variety of ways of influencing the actions of employees, they are also likely to inject their own ideas, values and beliefs into the processes used to manage people in organisations, and the origins of these ideas and beliefs often lie in the extent to which they perceive that they have a legitimate right to exercise authority over employee actions. However, because there are a variety of constraints that can exercise a mediating influence on style, a particular style should not be taken as an infallible indication of the way managers will behave in all circumstances; rather it is a manager's preferred way of doing things. Two simple examples will serve to illustrate the point. In the 1960s and much of the 1970s, when managers in certain industries had to deal with powerful and highly unionised workforces, they adopted a style of behaviour that involved a great deal of consultation and negotiation with employees and their representatives. In those very same firms, in the recession of the 1980s, the idea of managerial prerogatives emerged – or possibly re-emerged – as a dominant line of thinking, and gave rise to what has been dubbed confrontational 'macho' management. This represents a situation where the underlying style, or preferred way of doing things, lay dormant, and could only emerge when conditions were ripe. In contrast, there are organisations where, because management actions were based on entirely different philosophies, the recession produced little or no change in their behaviour, and consultation and negotiation continued in a relatively unaltered way. This perhaps reflects the idea that in employment relations as in other matters, management is sometimes less concerned with short-term gains than with safeguarding the long-term security of the firm. Just as they have a need to seek external stability by responding to market environments, some managers have attempted to build up systems of jointly agreed rules with the workforce to ensure long-term internal predictability and security.

However, the concept of management style in employment relations needs to be used with some care, as visible behaviour can sometimes be a poor indicator of the underlying style. One problem that arises is that managers are individuals, and by definition individuals are unique. Potentially, therefore, there are as many different styles as there are managers. Clearly this is not very helpful in trying to understand the implications of different styles, and it is easier if we have a simpler scheme to classify different style types. There have been a number of studies over the years that have catalogued style types, all of which point towards very distinctive patterns of behaviour that can be expected from managers.

The original scheme for describing style was devised by Alan Fox (1966) who drew a fundamental distinction between two contrasting management frames of reference, that were encountered in Chapter 1: unitarist and pluralist. Managers with a unitarist frame of reference make the assumption that an organisation is basically an integrated and harmonious whole. These managers are likely to see any conflict in the organisation as unnecessary, unnatural, and probably the result of otherwise loyal employees having been led astray. Exhibit 3.1 gives an example of the unitarist way of thinking. Conversely, with pluralist managers, the organisation is assumed to consist of a number of competing groups, all of whom legitimately have different interests to pursue. As such, there is always some potential for conflict to exist, and more important, such conflict can have a positive function if it is harnessed and managed though effective employment relations institutions and procedures. For instance, as long as it is controlled and managed in an orderly way, conflict can generate more creative solutions to problems, and can therefore have potential benefits.

However, Purcell and Sisson (1983), who later elaborated Fox's scheme, pointed out that it has some inherent problems, because there are different shades of unitarism and pluralism, that can both exist within the same organisation. For example, personnel specialists might well hold pluralist views, while line managers might hold a unitarist frame of reference. Moreover, they point out that Fox's scheme essentially describes attitudes and values of individual managers, whereas style is a more useful tool to describe an overall approach to employment relations.

We deplore the use of the terms 'industrial relations' and 'labour relations'. We prefer 'human relations', by which we mean a recognition of the essential human dignity of the individual.

An employee, at whatever level, must be made to feel that he is not merely a number on a pay-roll, but a recognised member of a team: that he is part of the company and an important part; and 'company', not in the sense of some inanimate thing possessing no soul, but rather in the sense of a goodly fellowship.

We reject the idea that amongst the employees of a company there are 'two sides' meaning the executive directors and managers on the one hand and the weekly paid employees on the other. Executive directors are just as much employees of the company as anyone else. We are all on the same side, members of the same team. We make no secret of our belief that any employee, from executive director to office boy, who does less than his best, while drawing his full salary or wages, is morally indistinguishable from a thief who helps himself to the petty cash.

We recognise that the tone of any organisation depends primarily on one man, on the executive head of it: on his philosophy, on his outlook, on the standards which he sets, on his example: in short on his leadership.

Exhibit 3.1 Management ideology
Source: Reddish, 1967.

Starting from these observations Purcell and Ahlstrand (1993) developed a scheme of six management styles (seven if we allow for two sub-types that are both variants of a single category), which were mapped onto two dimensions of employment relations: **individualism** and **collectivism**. These dimensions can be expressed as continua, along which the different styles can be located. This is shown in Fig. 3.1.

individualism dimension

Reflects the extent to which an organisation treats employees as important individual members of an organisation.

collectivism dimension

Reflects the extent to which an organisation endorses the idea that employees should be involved as a collective group in decisions that affect them.

Considering the dimension of *individualism* first: this expresses the extent to which employees as individuals are regarded as an important resource for the organisation. At the bottom of this dimension are *traditionalists*, who tend to be anti-union, because unions are seen to interfere with management's perceived right to manage. These firms often adopt a cost-minimization approach, in which employees are viewed simply as one of the overhead costs of the business. Typically they receive low pay, little or no training and have poor working conditions. Examples can be found in some small firms, and in the hotel and catering sector. At the other extreme, in the top left-hand cell of Fig. 3.1, where there is a strong focus on employee development, the authors locate the style of *sophisticated human relations*. These firms are more non-union than anti-union, but differ from traditionalists in a very important way. Rather than adopt an openly hostile stance, a number of tactics are used to keep unions out of the organisation. For example, by the use of careful selection and training methods, offering superior conditions of service and higher pay, management attempts to create a set of conditions in which employees see no benefits in collectivising. These companies put a strong emphasis on making the most of individual employees as organisational resources. Usually this will involve playing down any opposing distinctions between management and employee interests, and in addition employees are given a great deal of encouragement and help to expand their talents and work capabilities, and rewards systems are often designed to encourage individual contributions to the organisation. Examples of firms of this type are Marks and Spencer and IBM.

In the middle of the continuum is what the authors identify as a *paternalist* style. While there is little emphasis on employee development and career progression, these firms nevertheless have a strong ethos of care underpinned by unitarist values. Examples might include some of the building societies and banks that emerged at the turn of the nineteenth century, favouring their own internal staff associations as a way to avoid unionisation.

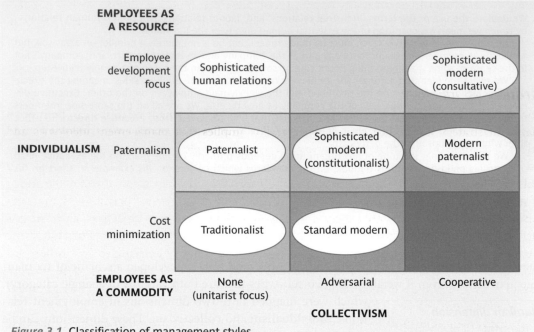

Figure 3.1 Classification of management styles
Source: adapted from Purcell and Ahlstrand, 1993.

Turning now to the *collectivist* dimension: this reflects the extent to which an organisation endorses the idea that employees should be involved in decisions that affect them. Purcell and Ahlstrand stress that because there are other methods, such as joint consultation, this does not necessarily mean recognising trade unions. Nevertheless, where a firm is unionised, trade unions are the most readily available mechanism for employees to participate in decision making. In the middle column in Fig. 3.1 are firms who tend to have an adversarial focus. At the bottom are *standard modern* firms, who recognise trade unions, although managers tend to view employment relations as a matter of fire fighting, which is characterised by pragmatic and opportunist behaviours. Accordingly, the more dominant party (management or employees) at any particular point in time tends to be the one who holds the balance of power, and an example of this is reputed to be British Aerospace. Above this are seen *sophisticated modern (constitutionalists)*, where union recognition is reluctantly conceded, and agreements are usually framed to draw clear distinctions between issues that are bargainable, and those that are reserved for management discretion. Although the frontier of control between management and workforce on these matters is somewhat movable over time, it tends to remain fixed for long periods, and a notable example of this type is the Ford Motor Company.

In the top right-hand cell of Fig. 3.1 are *sophisticated modern (consultors)*, among whom there is often found a willingness to share some power with trade unions, because their role is seen as one that helps to foster an employee development and cooperative focus. Here the aim is to minimize and manage inherent conflicts, and mechanisms of cooperation and joint determination are strongly emphasised, possibly as partnership, and these often contain provision for lengthy and extensive consultation procedures. Examples include large manufacturing and processing facilities, for example, ICI, and some Japanese car plants in Britain, such as Nissan.

Finally, in the cell located half-way down the right-hand side, are *modern paternalists*. These are firms that have a cooperative focus, but are nevertheless paternalistic in that they have a strong sense of social responsibility. Examples of these can be found among former Quaker employers, such as Cadbury's and Unilever, or among professional and skilled employees in newer, high technology sectors of the economy.

Management style: some implications
Strategy vs. ideology

The Purcell and Ahlstrand scheme suggests that style in employment relations can be more a matter of strategy and policy choice, whereas Fox implies that management ideologies and values determine the way that authority is exercised over employees, and that this in turn gives rise to the policies and strategies in employment relations (see Fig. 3.2(a)). Purcell and Ahlstrand, on the other hand, accord far less prominence to ideology as the direct determinant of management behaviour. They argue that management also develops policies and strategies for the roles that employees are expected to play in achieving business objectives, and that it is these that largely determine style (see Fig. 3.2(b)). To put matters more bluntly, Fox argues that a manager's way of exercising authority over employees is largely determined by his/her personal preferences, whereas Purcell and Ahlstrand imply that style is more likely to be a reflection of the organisation's human resource strategies. For this reason it is pertinent to comment briefly on which of the two is likely to be the case.

At the present time, because the evidence is mixed, it would be unwise to opt for either view in a definitive way. On the one hand, there are firms who for a long time have had highly developed employment relations policies and strategies, which are translated into definite patterns of behaviour that their managers are expected to observe in dealing with employees. For example, as noted above, non-union employers, such as Marks and Spencer or IBM, both lean very strongly towards a sophisticated human relations approach to employment relations: an

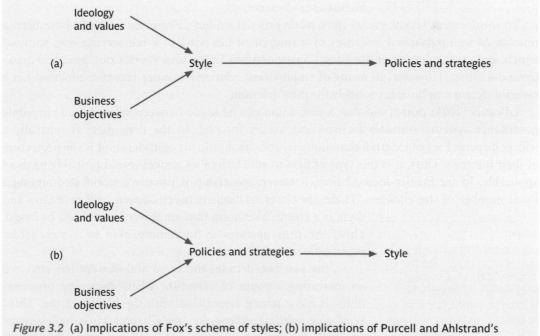

Figure 3.2 (a) Implications of Fox's scheme of styles; (b) implications of Purcell and Ahlstrand's scheme of styles

approach that has a strategic emphasis on eliciting employee commitment while simultaneously avoiding trade unions. However, the influence of ideology should not be discounted completely, if only because a unitarist frame of reference still runs very deep in British management (Poole *et al.*, 2005). Therefore, it seems more likely that in certain circumstances strategy will have the most prominent role in shaping style, but in other circumstances ideology has the major impact, for example, in small, owner-managed firms. Thus, in summary, it seems probable that managers have a pragmatic appreciation of whether, at a particular time and place, a free rein can be given to their ideologies and values, or whether the need to develop policies must take precedence.

The implications of corporate governance for style

One of the ways in which an organisation's policies and strategies could have a strong impact on management styles is in terms of its system of corporate governance. In broad terms this can be defined as the enhancement of corporate performance by ensuring the accountability of management to shareholders and other stakeholders (Keasey and Wright, 1997). The dominant theory in this area is the principal–agent (P–A) model (Jensen and Meckling, 1976), which starts from the assumption that the divorce of ownership from control in large corporations provides an incentive for managers (the agents) to act in a self-interested and opportunistic manner, and to prevent this happening, the owners (principals) should invest in formal corporate governance mechanisms. This, of course, is simply a polite way of saying that, because shareholding results in a delegation of responsibility from the owners to management, the central role of corporate governance is to restrain the self-serving inclinations of executives.

corporate governance
The enhancement of corporate performance via the supervision or monitoring of management performance to ensure the accountability of management to shareholders and other stakeholders (Keasey and Wright, 1997).

principal–agent (P–A) model
A theory of corporate governance which explains the need to protect the organisation from the potentially harmful effects of the divorce of ownership from control.

To some extent recent events have made this self-evident. For instance, there have been a number of well-publicised instances of management behaving in a self-serving way, some of which, such as the demise of the giant US corporations Enron and WorldCom, have had disastrous outcomes. However, in terms of employment relations, a more recent model that has a rather different emphasis is probably the most relevant.

Edwards (2004) points out that a distinction can be made between two types of corporate governance systems: outsider focused and insider focused. In the first, there is normally a widely dispersed set of external shareholders, and the dominant consideration is the protection of their interests. Thus, it is this type of firm to which the P–A model would probably be most applicable. In the insider-focused firm, however, ownership is usually concentrated among a small number of shareholders. There are closer relations between owners and managers and there is a greater likelihood that employee 'voices' will be heard. Thus, the firm operates as something akin to a stakeholder organisation.

stakeholder
People or groups with an interest in the activities of an organisation and the outcomes of those activities . . . they are identified as people who have an interest in the organisation, whether or not the organisation has an interest in them (Donaldson and Preston, 1995: 67).

In the past two decades the word stakeholder has attracted an increasing amount of attention when discussing organisations. It has a strong association with the notion of the 'Third Way' as a political philosophy (see Chapter 2). Indeed, anyone who followed the run-up to the 1997 UK general election could not avoid becoming aware that New Labour had incorporated the concept into its manifesto vocabulary, and that it had embraced the idea of the stakeholder organisation. In organisational terms, stakeholders can be defined as:

> " people or groups with an interest in the activities of an organisation and the out-comes of those activities ... they are identified as people who have an interest in the organisation, whether or not the organisation has an interest in them.
>
> (Donaldson and Preston, 1995: 67) "

There is nothing new about the idea that organisations have stakeholders, and in academic circles the term has been in use for some time. However, Donaldson and Preston (1995) point out that the word has been used in three different ways. First, *descriptively*, to advance the idea that there are many groups of people who have a vested interest in the actions of an organisa-tion. Second, in an *instrumental* way, usually by academic researchers to explore the idea that there is a link between organisational performance and the interests of a wide constituency of stakeholders. Finally, there is what Donaldson and Preston call the *normative* use, which is essentially a moral and philosophical argument that firms should be managed in a way that takes due account of the interests of all stakeholders. Currently it is this use that dominates the debate, and it is in sharp contrast to the traditional corporate governance view that, since share-holders are the owners of the business, the primary (if not sole) consideration should be to maximise their return. One of the most visible signs that this view is taking root in Britain was the appearance in 1995 of a report entitled *Tomorrow's Company* (RSA, 1995). This strongly advocates a style of corporate governance that is fast becoming known as a stakeholder management perspective, the key attribute of which is a simultaneous attention to the legitimate interests of all appropriate stakeholders, including employees. While a strong rearguard action is being fought by traditional-ists, there are encouraging signs that the report has had some impact. For instance, to explore ways of implementing the report's proposals, a permanent 'think tank', The Centre for Tomorrow's Companies, now exists.

stakeholder management perspective
Simultaneous attention to the legitimate interests of all appropriate stakeholders of an organisation.

Nevertheless, the stakeholder approach is not straightforward. In legal terms, the directors of a company owe a primary duty to protect the interests of shareholders and, while this does not prevent other interests being considered as well, it still leaves the problem of defining whose interests should legitimately be considered (Mitchell *et al.*, 1997). The most interesting and comprehensive approach to this matter is to adopt what can be described as the potential harms and benefits approach. Using this concept, relevant stakeholders are defined as 'those who potentially benefit or are potentially harmed by the actions of an organisation' (Donaldson and Preston, 1995). Although this would include a wide spectrum of groups – for example, anything between the wider environment and creditors – it would clearly embrace employees.

potential harms and benefits approach
Defining stakeholders as anyone who potentially benefits or is potentially harmed by the activities of an organisation.

Although this approach might seem somewhat alien, particularly in Great Britain, where a legal duty to protect the interests of shareholders is placed on the directors of an organisation, it is not unknown elsewhere. For example, Lubatkin *et al.* (2005) give a penetrating comparison of corporate governance practices in America, Sweden and France. They point out that those used in Sweden are based on social norms and cultures that promote a long-term view, which pays attention to a wide range of stakeholders, including employees. Clearly, therefore, to the extent that an organisation adopts a stakeholder approach to corporate governance, and irrespective of whether or not the firm recognises trade unions, there could be an impact on management styles. For instance, since a firm of this type would clearly need to know what employees perceive their interests to be, it seems likely that attention would be paid to providing opportunities for employees to voice their concerns.

Summary points

- The expression 'management style' refers to management's preferred approach to handling employment relations; in particular, the way management exercises its authority over subordinates.
- Different schemes of categorising management styles have been used. These include: Fox's (1966) scheme, which traces the ideological roots of style; Purcell and Sisson's (1983) scheme, which is an amplification of Fox's ideas, using an increased number of style types; and Purcell and Ahlstrand's (1993) scheme, which focuses on the strategic implications of style.
- Management style could conceivably be influenced by the nature of the corporate governance system of a firm.

Pause for reflection

From what you have read so far, what would you expect management styles to be like in non-union firms?

Management style and the non-union firm

So far in this chapter management style has been portrayed in a rather one-sided way, in which one of the essential features of style is whether management recognise or avoid trade unions. For example, in the Purcell and Ahlstrand (1993) scheme, only firms with traditionalist or sophisticated human relations styles are assumed to be non-union. One problem with this is that it tends to present matters in terms of an 'either/or' scenario, in which management styles in the non-union firm are assumed to be one or other of two extreme types: that is, those with a sophisticated human relations style are 'good' non-union employers, while traditionalists represent the 'bad or ugly' face of non-unionism (Guest and Hoque, 1994). This is almost certainly a gross oversimplification, and the evidence suggests that there are many smaller non-union firms who cannot accurately be described in this way (Lewis *et al.*, 2003). Therefore, since employment relations in small and non-union organisations has been a neglected area of study for some time (Wilkinson, 1999), it is necessary to look at the matter of management style in non-union firms in a more explicit way.

In addressing this neglected issue, McLoughlin and Gourlay (1994) review the dimensions of management style used by Purcell and Sisson (1983) and Purcell and Ahlstrand (1993), and apply a revised scheme to the non-union situation. This uses two dimensions to depict the four non-union style types, shown in Fig. 3.3.

The first dimension is that of *individualism* and *collectivism*, which is used in much the same way as the words are used in the Purcell and Ahlstrand (1993) scheme. Here, individualism rep-

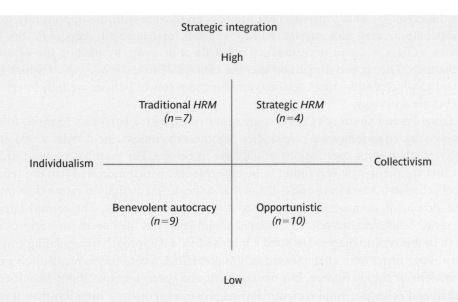

Strategic integration

High

Traditional *HRM* (n=7)	Strategic *HRM* (n=4)

Individualism ——————————————————— Collectivism

Benevolent autocracy (n=9)	Opportunistic (n=10)

Low

Traditional HRM	Benevolent autocracy
Employees viewed as central to achieving the goals and objectives of the firm. A proactive HR strategy is used, together with individualisation of the relationship. Managers point to the irrelevance of trade unions, which is redolent of a 'union avoidance' approach and results in some tendency for a low demand for trade unions on the part of employees. Mostly a unilateral approach by management to making and modification of the terms of the relationship, with some tendency towards 'them and us' in the relationship	Close, friendly and informal contact between employees and managers. High employee skills tend to give a degree of labour-market independence from the employer, which can influence the degree of unilateral regulation by management and the degree of informality in regulation. Managerial preferences tend to be for high degrees of individualisation to foster close links with and between employees, together with high trust relations
Strategic HRM	**Opportunist**
Trade union recognition for some or all parts of the workforce. This gives some element of joint regulation, but probably limits are placed on trade union demands, by carefully framing agreements to distinguish between negotiable and non-negotiable areas. Fairly high degree of formality in regulating the relationship	Fragmentation of policies and practices and a lack of formalisation. Minimalist HR strategy, with little development of employees, who are essentially seen as a 'cost that must be contained'. Some degree of collective regulation, perhaps as a hangover from earlier times when unions were recognised. Strong element of 'them and us' in the relationship

Figure 3.3 Management styles in non-union organisations
Source: adapted from McLoughlin and Gourlay (1994).

resents the extent to which management provides employees with the opportunity to develop their capabilities, and collectivism reflects whether management recognises the right of employees to have a say in decisions that affect them at work, by making use of non-union voice channels. The second dimension uses the concept of *strategic integration*, which expresses the extent to which employment relations and human resource policies are fully integrated with overall business strategy.

McLoughlin and Gourlay's (1994) study commenced with a survey of 30 firms, from which three were selected as follow-up case studies. Significantly, management styles were found to be more diverse than prior speculations would have us believe. For example, in one-third of their sample, management style was found to be *opportunistic*, which indicated that the remnants of prior collective structures were evident, and that strategic fragmentation rather than integration was the dominant managerial approach to employment relations. The second largest non-union style, *benevolent autocracy*, displayed a similarly low degree of strategic integration, although in this type managers favoured a more individual approach to regulating employment relations. Four firms were characterised as *strategic HRM*, where union recognition existed for some sections of the workforce, but management was more selective about how it combined individual and collective employment relations processes. Finally, a little less than one-quarter of McLoughlin and Gourlay's non-union sample displayed a *traditional HRM* style, in which both individualism and strategic integration were high, thus indicating a more concerted union-avoidance approach.

While the McLoughlin and Gourlay study shows that non-union management styles can be extremely diverse, there are a number of shortcomings in their research methodology. First, it can be misleading to suggest that the dimensions, individualism and collectivism, are somehow mutually exclusive (Bacon and Storey, 1993). Rather, both can exist simultaneously within an organisation, and an important feature that distinguishes a particular non-union style is where the balance between the two is struck (Peetz, 2002). For instance, individualism could imply a high-trust situation, based on notions of a *relational* psychological contract between employees and line managers (see Chapter 1). At the same time however, an organisation could use collective-type processes that reinforce more formal and *transactional* relationships (see Chapter 1). Perhaps the most important limitation concerns the way that the data were collected. For example, to assess strategic integration, a survey method was used, and this typically relies on asking managers to recall certain information about their organisation when responding to closed questionnaire items. However, just because managers say that certain human resource policies exist at an organisational level, it is not safe to assume that these policies translate into actual practice lower down (Purcell, 1999). As explained earlier in the chapter, local or departmental managers often have an incentive to make their own informal arrangements with employees, which means that their preferred approach can differ somewhat from formal organisational policy. In other words, there is a need to establish whether policy objectives actually result in appropriate action.

In approaching the same matter from a different direction, Dundon and Rollinson (2004) incorporated the concept of *managerial intent* into their framework for evaluating non-union managerial style. In addition to the dimensions described above, this involved gaining a deeper and somewhat richer picture of the motives, practices and actions of local managers at workplace level, if only because the *inaction* of managers can be an important indication of their preferred approach (Marchington and Parker, 1990). In their study, Dundon and Rollinson (2004) investigated four different non-union firms in some detail, not only by speaking to managers, but also by assessing employee perceptions of management style. Two of the case studies were SMEs and two were much larger organisations. One of the smaller firms and one of the larger cases were subsidiaries of different American-owned multinationals. In categorising non-union styles in a more extensive way, this study not only uncovered managerial motives and intentions with respect to remaining non-union, but also identified several intermediary factors that influenced management styles: for instance, market pressures, managerial ideologies and the prevailing organisational climate.

In the smallest organisation (120 employees, in five separate locations), management style was found to be not just opportunistic, but also *exploitative*. All decisions were made by the chief executive, who regarded employment relations issues as irksome and annoying. Groups of employees would find their employment contracts terminated as a way of bypassing statutory employment rights, such as unfair dismissal or redundancy, only to be re-employed on fresh contracts a few weeks later. Trade unions were considered abhorrent, mainly because they were regarded as an impediment to the chief executive exercising his personal whims. Moreover, management style was shaped by a commercial imperative to drive down labour costs, and in achieving this goal, employees were treated as a disposable commodity. Thus, while the firm displayed many of the same opportunistic-style characteristics as in the McLoughlin and Gourlay scheme, there were also other managerial characteristics which led to its classification as an *exploitative autocracy*. In the second SME (130 employees on two sites), management style closely resembled the dimensions of a *benevolent autocracy*. Once again this was traced to the personal values and philosophies of a dominant manager, the operations director, whose motives and actions to avoid the incursion of a trade union were shaped by his prior experiences in an unionised company. However, his benevolent approach meant that workers experienced more palatable employment conditions, and many of them viewed him as a likeable and charismatic person, who took the time and effort to balance employee needs and wants with those of the organisation.

Turning now to the larger non-union companies in the sample: one of these (2800 employees across numerous sites) had recently de-recognised the trade unions, and this seemed to have been prompted by the perceived need to free management's hands to restructure the firm in response to highly competitive market conditions. According to the McLoughlin and Gourlay style dimensions, the firm could have been classified as *traditional HRM*, because there was a new emphasis on individualism, and a centrally designed strategic response to employment relations and market pressures. However, this category would not have captured the influence of managerial intent. At a deeper level of analysis, policy and strategy was highly fragmented across the organisation, and several line managers actively circumvented new HR policies because these were perceived to restrict their freedom to 'do things their own way'. Consequently, strategic integration and policy application were very erratic. For example, there was a high degree of employment insecurity that could be traced to the criteria used for redundancy selection, which were interpreted differently by line managers on several occasions. Ultimately, therefore, management style was more a case *manipulative regulation* than traditional HRM (Dundon and Rollinson, 2004).

The final organisation (3500 employees across numerous sites) was the only one in which management style could be classified as *strategic HRM*, and the firm displayed similar characteristics to those of a *sophisticated paternalist*. Significantly, style was strongly influenced by the need to follow closely certain policy objectives set at the American corporate headquarters, indicating the influence of foreign ownership in shaping style. In this firm employees were viewed as assets: there was a definite attempt to cultivate a climate of informality, establish friendly working relations and engineer a positive psychological contract. To this end management consciously substituted other features to counter any possible demand from employees for union representation. For example, employees enjoyed an attractive employment package in terms of wages and other benefits. The firm also had an extensive range of non-union employee voice mechanisms, and local managers and team leaders were encouraged to involve employees with an emphasis on 'fun at work'. Taken together, the approach translated into a more caring management style; and even though the intention was to avoid unions through sophisticated union-substitution techniques, employees were reasonably well treated, and this showed.

The important feature that emerges from the research is that far from being the same everywhere, there is likely to be a huge amount of diversity in management styles in both non-union and smaller firms, and this could range from the exploitative to the sophisticated. Indeed, within smaller organisations, it is possible that much depends on the preferences and ideologies of founding owners. Furthermore, since SMEs are characterised by informality in their processes and relationships between people, this could well be a function of size as much as anything else. In contrast, among larger multinational, non-union organisations, there is the added effect of complex corporate structures, some of which can influence management styles because of the customs and practices which are imported into subsidiaries, which may or may not include strategies to avoid trade union recognition. The Dundon and Rollinson study provides some evidence that factors which influence non-union styles include a combination of: the ideologies of managers and founding owners, market pressures, organisational structure, size, and ownership. For this reason, non-union management styles are almost certainly far more varied than traditional 'ideal types' suggest, and so it is desirable to avoid sweeping generalisations about style that are intended to embrace both large and small organisations, or union and non-union firms.

Conclusions

There seems little doubt that management occupies a dominant position in the modern enterprise, and when viewed in the light of the declining size and influence of trade unions, the significance of its role in employment relations will continue for the foreseeable future. Management has a number of ways at its disposal of shaping employee behaviour, and when taken together, these give managers a huge capability to influence employment relations processes and outcomes. As a result, the matter of management style can be all-important.

There are two divergent views on management style, and both have rather different implications. The first locates the origins of style in terms of the values and ideologies of managers, and these in turn give rise to an imperative to behave in a preferred way. The second implies that style is something that is selected as a matter of conscious choice, and reflects a set of options about the most appropriate way of managing employment relations, either by recognising or avoiding trade unions. These divergent views have important implications for the study of employment relations. For instance, an ideologically driven style, particularly if it veers towards unitarism, is likely to have a highly significant effect on management's approach to handling the processes described in Chapters 6 to 12. The disciplinary regime in an organisation could be very harsh, grievances could be regarded as an affront to managerial authority, and employee voice could be virtually non-existent. In an extreme case, it could also be expected that the processes of bargaining and negotiation might be conducted by managers through a frame of reference that is perhaps best expressed by the statement 'the answer's no – now what's the question'? In contrast, management style can be viewed more as a matter of conscious choice, and therefore the employment relations implications would be rather different. For instance, employees and unions might be regarded as valuable partners who can contribute in a positive way towards organisational effectiveness, either though genuine employee voice or collective bargaining processes. These matters will be considered in Chapters 8 and 9.

❓ Review and discussion questions

1 Distinguish between line managers and staff managers.

2 How do you account for the emergence of management as a distinct group in organisations?

3 What do the terms 'horizontal differentiation' and 'vertical differentiation' refer to in terms of the structure of an organisation?

4 What employment relations problems and issues can be associated with horizontal and vertical differentiation?

5 In what way is management likely to view its role in employment relations in an organisation?

6 On what basis can managers assert that they have a 'right to be obeyed' by employees?

7 What methods, other than asserting a 'right to be obeyed', do managers have at their disposal to shape employee behaviour?

8 What is 'management style' in employment relations? Describe two schemes for categorising management styles.

9 In what ways and why could management style be influenced by a firm's corporate governance policy?

10 What sort of management styles would you expect to encounter in a non-union firm?

Further reading

Donaldson, T. and L.E. Preston (1995) 'The stakeholder theory of the corporation: concepts, evidence and implications', *Academy of Management Review*, Vol. 20 (1), pp. 65–91. A useful paper that examines stakeholder theory and by implication, exposes some of the woolly thinking in this area.

Dundon, T. and D. Rollinson (2004) *Employment Relations in Non-Union Firms*, Routledge, London. As the title suggests, the book reports a research study that explores employment relations in non-union firms. Among other things it gives a detailed picture of management styles in non-union firms, that illustrates the wide variety of styles that exist.

Keasey, K. and M. Wright (eds) (1997) *Corporate Governance: Responsibilities, Risks and Remuneration*, Wiley, Chichester. A standard text on corporate governance.

McLoughlin, I. and S. Gourlay (1994) *Enterprise Without Unions: Industrial Relations in the Non-Union Firm*, Open University Press, Buckingham. The book reports what was perhaps the first rigorous attempt to explore employment relations in non-union firms in Great Britain.

Mitchell, R.K., B.R. Angle and D.J. Wood (1997) 'Towards a theory of stakeholder, identification and salience: defining the principles of who and what really counts', *Academy of Management Review*, Vol. 22 (4), pp. 853–886. A useful paper that gives a good introduction to the thorny problem of identifying the relevant stakeholders of an organisation.

Poole, M., R. Mansfield, J. Gould-Williams and P. Mendes (2005) 'British managers' attitudes and behaviour in industrial relations: a twenty-year study', *British Journal of Industrial Relations*, Vol. 43 (1), pp. 117–134. Poole and his colleagues have regularly conducted surveys of members of the Chartered Management Institute at ten-year intervals, across the past twenty years. This paper reports the results of the latest survey and gives interesting insights into current management attitudes to employment relations.

Purcell, J. and B. Ahlstrand (1993) *Strategy and Style in Employee Relations*, Oxford University Press, Oxford. A useful book giving the authors' ideas on the relationship between strategy and management style.

Purcell, J. and K. Sisson (1983) 'Strategies and practice in industrial relations', in *Industrial Relations in Britain*, G.S. Bain (ed.), Blackwell, Oxford. While it is really only an amplification of an earlier scheme by Fox (1966), this was the first real attempt to explore the wide diversity of management styles at work in employment relations. Well worth reading.

Chapter 4

Trade unions and other collective associations of employees

Introduction

Like the previous chapter, this also deals with one of the parties in employment relations; in this case, collective employee associations. Because these associations vary in both type and character, it would be near impossible to state with certainty how many employees belong to them, and the only reliable figures are for those that are registered, either as a trade union or as a professional association. Moreover, not all employees join unions or other collective associations, although there are some general trends. For example, collectivisation is more common in larger organisations, and unionisation is noticeably higher in the public sector than in private-sector firms. Traditionally, collective representation has been more prevalent with manual workers than clerical or salaried staff, and also more common with men than women. However, there are some exceptions to these trends. For instance, there are many small enterprises in Britain where employees are not represented by a collective association, and some large employers such as Marks and Spencer and IBM have purposely avoided unionisation by forming their own in-house associations.

For the above reasons this chapter deals with trade unions as well as other collective associations. Because trade unions are by far the most significant type of collective association the chapter starts by defining them, and this is followed by a description of their origins, purpose and functions. The next section of the chapter examines trade union membership in Great Britain and, since there has been a decline in the size and influence of trade unions, this is followed by a section that examines a number of union-renewal strategies. As there is now a legal mechanism in Great Britain through which an employer can be required to recognise a trade union, the provisions for statutory trade-union recognition are outlined. Following this, the chapter then considers the all-important topic of workplace trade unionism, and explains how union organisation at this level can differ significantly from unions at the national level. Finally, the chapter examines other types of collective employee associations and non-union mechanisms for worker representation.

Trade unions in Great Britain
Defining trade unions

In employment relations, **trade unions** are by far the most significant form of collective employee association. In legal terms a trade union is defined as:

> an organisation (whether temporary or permanent), which consists wholly or mainly of workers . . . whose principle purposes include the regulation of relations between workers . . . and employers or employers' associations
>
> (Trade Union and Labour Relations (Consolidation) Act 1992, Part 1)

Clearly this is a very broad definition, and there are several different types of trade union. Historically, the traditional way of distinguishing between these types was on the basis of those employees that they normally represent, and this is shown in Table 4.1.

Pause for reflection

After studying the different types of trade unions given in Table 4.1, what advantages and disadvantages do you think there might be with using such a classification scheme?

Although the first three types shown at the top of Table 4.1 are appealing for their simplicity, there are a number of shortcomings. First, because there are a number of unions who restrict entry to salaried and clerical employees, for completeness *white-collar unions* would need to

Union type	Definition
Craft unions	A trade union that limits membership to workers possessing definable craft skills (usually acquired by apprenticeship)
Industrial unions	A trade union organised on the basis of representing all grades of worker (unskilled, semi-skilled and skilled) in a particular industry
General unions	A trade union representing any employee of any grade in any industry
White-collar unions	A trade union which caters exclusively for non-manual workers
Open unions	A trade union with few restrictions or qualifications for membership (similar to general unions above)
Closed unions	A trade union in which recruitment is limited to workers of specific occupations or industries

Table 4.1 Typologies of trade unions

be added. However, the biggest problem is that the technologies and industries on which these union categories were once based have changed out of all recognition. As a result, most of the original craft unions now represent unskilled and semi-skilled workers, and virtually all unions have their own white-collar or clerical membership sections, often because of the scale of union mergers over the last two decades. Thus, it would be virtually impossible to find any trade union in Great Britain that exactly matched the original specification. For this reason other classifications have been suggested: for instance, the *open* and *closed union* distinction, shown at the foot of Table 4.1. In addition, some employee associations have evolved from what were once regarded as occupational or professional bodies, to what are now accepted as independent trade unions that are both registered with the Certification Officer and affiliated to the TUC, and carry out the same collective functions as other unions. One example is the Society and College of Radiographers (SCoR), representing members in the NHS and private medical care. Thus, a case could be made that there are also 'professional-type' union categories.

Summary points

■ The broad legal definition of a trade union reflects a primary purpose of regulating relations between workers and employers.

■ One way of classifying different types of trade unions is according to the type of employees that they represent.

■ Most classifications of this type have now been adapted to reflect the idea that almost all unions now represent more heterogeneous groups of workers.

Origins and development

Trade unions are largely a consequence of the factory system, which developed in the industrial revolution. In its current form British trade unionism has, therefore, emerged from a complex interaction of social, legal and economic factors. For instance, until 1825, when the Combination Acts of 1799 and 1800 were replaced with the Combination Laws, most trade union activities were illegal, and until then, all that working people were allowed to do in terms of collective action was to form mutual benefit or friendly societies (Pelling, 1987). With the repeal of the Combination Acts however, trade unions were allowed to come out into the open, but since industrial action was legally deemed to be an act that involved criminal conspiracy, they could not pursue their objectives in a free way (Hawkins, 1981). These early unions were very locally based, and almost exclusively confined to craft workers, hence one of the classification types given above. However, in 1851 the first forerunner of a national trade union as we know things today was formed. This was the Amalgamated Society of Engineers (ASE), from which developed the Amalgamated Engineering Union (AEU) and which, after a series of union mergers, is now called Amicus. Its unique feature was a structure known as *new model unionism*, which was based on a system of national union officials with layers of local representatives at branch and workplace levels. This system has been adopted and replicated by many other British unions, with union officials employed full time on trade union activities.

One of the major strengths of the original craft unions was their control of the apprenticeship system, which gave craftsmen the ability to regulate the number of workers in a particular trade, thus protecting their market value. This meant that craft workers were not as vulnerable in recessionary periods as unskilled workers. Thus, following a severe economic recession in the 1880s, labourers and unskilled workers recognised that they too could achieve gains from organising into large numbers along the same lines as craft workers. As a result, a number of unions emerged that have grown into what are the largest British general unions today; for example, the Transport and General Workers Union (TGWU). By the late nineteenth century, embryonic unions of non-manual workers also began to appear, hence the additional union classifications described in Table 4.1. These were mainly in public-sector occupations such as schoolteaching and local government, and later private-sector occupations such as clerks and draughtsmen.

From their inception, trade unions faced laws which were hostile to their very existence. Indeed, prior to the Union Act of 1871 and the Conspiracy and Protection of Property Act 1875, there was an assumption in law that two or more people combining to organise a dispute constituted an act of criminal conspiracy, and even when the laws of 1871 and 1875 were passed, and the assumption of criminal conspiracy was removed, trade unions were still subject to the severe weight of the law: this time for civil conspiracy, i.e. inducing their members to breach their individual contracts of employment. It was not until the passing of the Trades Disputes Act of 1906 that the civil-conspiracy restraint was completely removed, which gave trade unions immunity in respect of pursuing a trade dispute.

Trades Union Congress
A federal body for the coordination and cooperation of member unions in Britain.

European Trades Union Confederation (ETUC)
A pan-European federal body to promote and coordinate the interests of trade unions across European countries.

The Trade Union Congress and the European Trades Union Confederation

No account of trade union development would be complete without some mention of the British **Trades Union Congress** (TUC), and also its more recent pan-European association, the **European Trades Union Confederation** (ETUC). The TUC, which was formed in 1868, is a national body that exists to coordinate the activities of member unions in Britain, and not, as is sometimes assumed, a body which has senior or automatic authority over all trade unions. Like trade unions themselves, the TUC has its origins in local grassroots organisations, trades councils, which were formed to coordinate union activities in cities throughout Great Britain. Because the legal climate in the nineteenth century was extremely hostile to trade unions, the TUC became a vehicle to pursue legislative reform. In 1871 it formed a parliamentary committee, from which emerged the Independent Labour Party in 1893. In 1906 it set up a Labour Representation Committee, and 29 parliamentary seats were won in that year's election. The committee subsequently changed its name and became what is today's Labour Party.

trades councils
Local bodies formed to coordinate union activities in cities throughout Britain.

Since the 1980s the TUC's relationship with government has changed considerably. The Thatcher government abolished many of the tripartite bodies in which the TUC had a voice: for instance, the Industrial Training Boards. Because of the historical links between the TUC and the Labour Party, it is closer to the Labour government than to other political parties. The TUC has 67 affiliated member unions which represent the interests of 6.5 million workers, or about 90 per cent of all trade union members in Britain. On behalf of its affiliate unions, it promotes a number of economic, social and public policy objectives, by:

- coordinating common policies for British trade unions
- lobbying the Government to implement policies that will benefit all workers
- conducting economic and social campaigns
- representing the interests of working people on public bodies
- representing the interests of British workers at an international level (including the European Union and the United Nations employment body, the International Labour Organisation)
- conducting research on employment-related issues
- providing training and education for union representatives
- helping unions to avoid clashes with each other.

(Source: adapted from: http://www.tuc.org.uk/the_tuc/about_role.cfm).

The European Trades Union Confederation (ETUC) is a pan-European federal body that promotes and coordinates the interests of trade unions across European countries. It was first established in 1973 in response to growing economic and political forces developing across Europe, in particular the power of multinational companies. It currently has 76 member organisations in 34 countries, which, when combined, represent the interests of over 60 million workers (www.etuc.org/r/13). In April 2005 the European Trade Union Institute for Research, Education and Health and Safety (ETUI-REHS) was formed as part of the ETUC, to provide support and expertise to affiliated members in three areas of employment relations: research, education, and health and safety. The incumbent general secretary of the ETUC is John Monks, the former general secretary of the British TUC, and its purpose is similar to that of the British TUC, but at a European level. However, there is one important exception to this. Together with its employers' counterpart (the Union of Industrial and Employers' Confederations of Europe, UNICE), the ETUC and UNICE can affect European legislation, and ultimately regulations that then apply in Great Britain. That is, at a European level the ETUC and UNICE can negotiate a *framework agreement*, and once such an agreement is made and adopted by the European Council of Ministers, this agreement can substitute for legislation. Thus, the ETUC can have a significant influence on employment legislation in Britain.

Summary points

- In their early formative years, trade unions faced laws that were extremely hostile to their very existence.

- While early unions were locally based, and mostly confined to craft workers, the emergence of New Model Unions eventually resulted in the basic structure for most large trade unions today.

- The TUC is a federal body for the coordination and cooperation of member unions. It pursues a broad set of economic, social, legal and political objectives.

- The ETUC is a counterpart to the TUC that pursues a range of similar objectives, but at the European level.

The purpose and functions of British unions

Trade union purpose

In simple terms, a trade union exists to protect and improve the working lives of its members, and it is this that gives rise to the expression **trade union purpose**. However, because the concerns of one union can be very different to those of another, there is seldom an all-embracing or single purpose. Flanders (1970: 14) explains the complexity of trade union purpose by using the metaphor of a double-edged sword. One edge of the sword represents the pursuit of a *vested interest* – for example, recruiting new members and improving the pay and employ-ment conditions of workers. Of necessity, these interests may well take precedence over increasing the profits of a company. The other edge of the sword concerns what is known as the *sword of justice* effect. This is the social purpose of trade unions: for instance, campaigning for the rights and protections of those more vulnerable in society, irrespective of whether they are union members or not. Historically, the sword of justice card was played successfully by unions in campaigning to abolish child labour and penal laws. More recent examples would include anti-racist campaigns or the rights of immigrant workers.

> **trade union purpose**
> To protect and improve the interests of union members, vis-à-vis those of management or the employing organisation.

The functions of trade unions

The **functions of trade unions** refer to the methods used to achieve their aims, which can vary considerably from one union to another. Some, for example, may rely on collective bargaining to advance and protect their members' interests, whereas others may seek to change employ-ment laws through political lobbying. Some unions favour a *partnership* arrangement with employers as the best means to achieve their purpose, while others eschew the very idea of cooperating with management. However, while it is sufficient to note that there are many ways in which even very similar aims can be pursued, there are four broad classifications that help explain the diversity of union functions.

The first of these is that of **economic regulation**, which broadly consists of securing the highest possible real wages for their members in order to counteract the vulnerability of individuals in the labour market (Hyman, 2001). On average, the hourly rate of

> **functions of trade unions**
> The means used by trade unions to achieve their aims.

> **economic regulation**
> The trade union function of securing the highest possible real wages for its members.

pay for a trade union member is 17 per cent greater than the hourly rate paid to non-union members (Grainger and Holt, 2005: 9). Although this implies that trade unions may adversely affect the level of profits in a firm, there is plenty of evidence to show that trade unions are in fact associated with better firm performance and productivity (Nolan and Marginson, 1988). For example, a trade union can actually help to raise the calibre of management, by ensuring that organisational change is appropriate and robust (Cameron, 1987). Moreover, evidence of a direct causal link between the existence of a trade union and its mark-up on wages is almost impossible to verify given the range of other variables that can affect profits; for instance, global trade patterns, international currency fluctuations or investment in new technology (Metcalf, 2005).

job regulation
The trade union function of being one of the joint authors of the rules and procedures that govern employment in a firm.

A second union function is **job regulation** (Hyman, 2001). In addition to some of the functions of collective bargaining, which are described more fully in Chapter 10, job regulation allows union representatives to become joint authors of the rules and procedures that govern employment in a firm; for example, rules that specify working hours, equal opportunities or health and safety obligations. This regulatory function can also occur in more informal ways through the day-to-day communications that exist between union stewards and management. Thus, job regulation can improve the general employment relations climate or psychological contract of workers, and has for some time served as a vehicle for industrial democracy (Flanders, 1970).

power holding
The trade union function of acquiring power relative to management, so that it is capable of taking retaliatory action in pursuing its objectives.

wider social change
The trade union function that involves engaging in activities to bring about changes in wider society, often by political lobbying.

A third function is that of **power holding**. Regardless of whether it pursues militant or moderate objectives, a trade union cannot ignore the fact that it is an association based on a collective worker identity, and that this identity is quite distinct from the interests of management. Thus, a trade union's credibility and persuasiveness is ultimately underpinned by its potential capability to take retaliatory action in pursuing its aims. As Hyman (2001: 4) observes, unions are first and foremost power agencies for workers.

Finally, as unions exist within a political and social framework, **wider social change** has been a function of many unions since their earliest days (Jackson, 1982). For this reason, one of their important functions has become that of political lobbying and using pressure tactics, usually to try and persuade the government of the day to legislate in a way that benefits all employees. Examples of this would include pressing for various employment laws in Britain, such as health and safety legislation in the 1970s, or union support for the national minimum wage and statutory trade union recognition in the late 1990s.

Summary points

- The purpose of trade unions is to protect and advance the interests of their members (workers).

- How unions go about protecting and advancing membership interests relates to the functions of unions.

- Trade union functions differ from one union to another, and also change within a single union over time, although four broad functional classifications include: *economic regulation, job regulation, power holding* and *wider social change*.

The structure of British trade unions

The term trade union structure tends to be applied to the trade union movement as a whole,

trade union structure
The groups of workers represented by a particular union.

and is usually taken as a reflection of which unions represent certain groups of workers: for example, which union represents printers, bricklayers or nurses. In this sense structure can also reflect how a union represents the interests of its members, which is strongly connected to the origin and evolution of particular unions. As previously noted, craft unions of skilled workers unionised first. They had the basic aim of preserving better conditions for themselves, which to some extent was achieved by controlling the apprenticeship system. The unskilled who came next had no craft lines on which to organise themselves, and had to rely more on size and industrial muscle for their bargaining power.

However, while history is important in understanding the way that trade unionism is structured today, the political and economic changes that have occurred over the past three decades are perhaps more relevant. These changes have altered membership boundaries, with union mergers and amalgamations resulting in fewer unions, as shown in Table 4.2. One of the main reasons for the wave of union merger activity was for defensive reasons; for example, as their respective memberships have fallen, unions have joined forces to minimize the burden on union finances. At the same time, mergers have given a potential increase in bargaining power for the new (and larger) trade union (see Table 4.3).

However, these changes do not necessarily make life easier for trade unions, and a prime example is the changes that have taken place in what were originally craft unions in the engineering industry. In the 1920s increasing mechanisation gave rise to an influx of semi-skilled workers. Strictly speaking, because they had not served an apprenticeship, these workers were not eligible to join craft unions. However, to protect their territory, the unions changed their rules to admit semi-skilled employees into membership. Later on in the Second World War, when much semi-skilled work was work done by female labour, the unions had to change their rules again to admit women. More recently, in 2002, Amicus was created from a merger between the Amalgamated Engineering and Electrical Union (AEEU) and the Manufacturing, Science and Finance Union (MSF). Thus, in a little over a half a century, what was a closed, craft union confined to the engineering industry now has members across diverse industries and occupations, such as engineering, higher education, and insurance and financial institutions.

Year	Total number of unions	Total of registered members (millions)
1980	467	12.6
1985	391	10.8
1990	306	9.8
1995	260	8.0
2000	221	7.8
2005	186	7.5

Table 4.2 Number of British trade unions, 1980–2005
Source: adapted from Certification Officer's Annual Reports *(number of total registered members)*.

Trade union	Membership
UNISON: the public service union[a]	1.3 million
Amicus: the union[a]	935 321
Transport and General Workers' Union (TGWU)	816 986
GMB	600 016
Royal College of Nursing of the United Kingdom (RCN)	372 506
Union of Shop, Distributive and Allied Workers (USDAW)	331 703
National Union of Teachers (NUT)	324 284
National Association of Schoolmasters and Union of Women Teachers (NASUWT)	304 762
Public and Commercial Services Union (PCSU)[a]	295 063
Communication Workers Union (CWU)[a]	258 696

Note
(a) union created from merger or amalgamation.

Table 4.3 The largest ten unions in Britain, by membership size
Source: adapted from Certification Officer, Annual Report 2004–2005 (2005).

Another example is the Post Office Engineering Union (POEU). This would also have been classified as a closed, craft union two decades ago, with its membership confined to skilled occupations in the nationalised Post Office. However, in response to the commercial separation and privatisation of British Telecom from the Post Office, the POEU merged with the clerical employees union to form what could be described as an industrial-type union (then the telecoms section of the Civil and Public Servants Association, CPSA). Another merger followed shortly afterwards with postal workers, represented by the then Union of Communication Workers (UCW), to form what is now the Communication Workers Union (CWU). Thus, in a little over two decades the CWU has come to represent manual and clerical employees, skilled and non-skilled workers not only in the former large utilities such as BT and the Post Office, but also in smaller companies created after the privatisation of BT in areas as diverse as telecommunications, call centres and banking.

Pause for reflection

What advantages and disadvantages do you think there are for two or more unions merging?

Trade union government

As noted above, the term 'trade union structure' denotes patterns of organisation in the whole trade union movement. Trade union government, however, describes the internal manage-

trade union government
The internal management and decision-making processes of an individual trade union.

ment and decision-making processes of an individual trade union. As a result of the mergers and amalgamations described above, large trade unions tend to have memberships drawn from a wide range of occupations in a variety of industries, and these people are often dispersed throughout the whole of Great Britain. For this reason, most British trade unions adopt a federal system of government, the

geographic federalism

A form of union government which gives a degree of decision-making autonomy to districts or regions.

occupational federalism

A form of union government which gives a degree of decision-making autonomy to the union's different occupational groups.

geo-occupational federalism

A more complex form of union government in which geographic and occupational autonomy exist together.

simplest form of which is based on **geographic federalism**. This gives an element of decision-making autonomy to districts or regions. Alternatively, unions can choose to organise along the lines of **occupational federalism**, which gives a degree of autonomy to different occupational groups. The most complex system of all is a **geo-occupational federal structure**, where both geographic and occupational federalism exist together. With some variation most of the larger unions follow this principle; for example the GMB, Amicus, TGWU and UNISON, the public services union.

Pause for reflection

Having considered the purpose and functions of trade unions, and how they are structured, do you think they are democratic bodies? Why/why not?

Democracy and representativeness

Because trade unions are often large and diverse, there is sometimes a disparity between national policies and actions, and the expectations of rank-and-file members. The overall direction of activities for all unions is invariably in the hands of a small number of officials who, although they are lay representatives, can hold quite different views from the average member. Thus, a question which is often raised about trade union government, is whether it is genuinely democratic. To some extent the whole question can be traced back to Michels' (1915) famous **iron law of oligarchy**: a theorem which predicts that social actors (such as union activists) become incorporated into the higher echelons of an organisation. One implication of this is that union leaders will become detached from those whom they are supposed to represent, and may well end up siding with management rather than the rank-and-file membership.

iron law of oligarchy

A theory which predicts that union officials are likely to become incorporated into the ranks of management and further their own interests, rather than pursuing membership concerns.

One difficulty in applying Michels' theory is that the word 'democracy' can be interpreted in a very fluid way. What research does exist seems to show support for Michels' theory in a situation where union strength is weak in relation to that of management, but with the reverse being the case where union structures are strong and robust (Geary and Roche, 2003; Oxenbridge and Brown, 2004). It is unlikely, therefore, that the validity of Michels' ideas will ever be uncovered, and in any event, the essential question about union democracy often comes down to what it is taken to mean. If the criterion of democracy is whether or not rank-and-file members have an adequate opportunity to elect those who direct matters on their behalf, the answer must be an unequivocal 'yes'; unions are democratic bodies. Most trade unions have an impeccable record in terms of conducting elections, and ballots for national leaders are often supervised by independent bodies, such as the Electoral Reform Society. Even though the proportion of members voting in elections is usually very low, this in no way detracts from the democratic nature of the election, because members are given the opportunity to take part in the selection process.

A more important criterion however, is whether rank-and-file members have the chance of participating in national policy in the first place. In most unions it is not the national leadership that is the supreme policy-making body, but the **national delegate conference** comprised of lay representatives. These conferences take place every one or two years, and the national leadership merely oversees the implementation of policy between conferences. At branch meetings rank-and-file members invariably have the opportunity to instruct their conference delegates on how to vote on motions that establish policy. Again, although attendance at these meetings is often low, the opportunity to shape policy is readily presented. So, by either criterion, trade unions must be regarded as democratic bodies.

national delegate conference
The supreme policy-making body of a trade union, which is comprised of lay representatives.

Summary points

- A trade union's structure can be based on either geographic or occupational lines, or a combination of both.
- The expression 'trade union government' refers to the decision-making powers of a trade union, which can occur at branch, regional and national levels.
- A question often raised is whether trade unions are democratic bodies. Judged by different criteria, the answer is 'yes'.

Trade union membership in Britain
The changing face of British unions

As noted in Chapter 2, trade union membership in Britain has undergone significant decline. At its zenith in 1979, approximately 13 million people were members of trade unions, which equated to a union density figure of around 54 per cent of the working population. Today, only around 29 per cent of the workforce is unionised, which equates to three in ten workers (see Fig. 4.1). Moreover, predications for the future suggest that union membership will decline even further in the next decade, possibly to around 20 per cent of the working population (Metcalf, 2005).

However, broad trends such as these tend to disguise important variations. For example, density is highest in Northern Ireland and Wales, and lowest in the South-east of England (Grainger and Holt, 2005). In private services it is only about 17 per cent, but in the public sector it is relatively high at 57 per cent (Grainger and Holt, 2005). Significantly, trade union density in manufacturing industry, which was once regarded as the heartland of unionisation, is now below the national average, at 27 per cent. In 2004 aggregate union density for women overtook that of men for the first time ever, largely because a greater proportion of women work in the public sector (Grainger and Holt, 2005). In small firms only 7 per cent of employees are unionised (Forth *et al.*, 2006: 46), suggesting considerable variation in the incidence of 'never-members' between large and small organisations (Bryson and Gomez, 2005). For example, around 71 per cent of employees who work in small and medium-sized firms have 'never' been a union member, compared with 55 per cent of those employed in larger organisations (Forth *et al.*, 2006: 47). Overall, the occupations with the highest propensity to unionise these days are not miners, dockers or steel workers, but teachers and nurses, with an average density for their occupations of 48 per cent, whereas employees in sales have the lowest union density of all occupations, at 11 per cent (Metcalf, 2005).

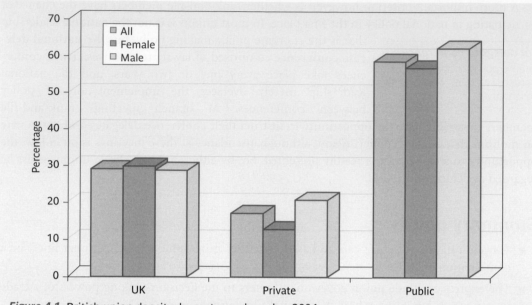

Figure 4.1 British union density, by sector and gender, 2004
Source: H. Grainger and H. Holt, *Trade Union Membership 2004*, Employment Market Analysis and Research, April 2005, DTI, London. Reproduced with the kind permission of the Department of Trade and Industry (DTI).

Explaining the growth and decline of trade union membership is, however, more complicated than simply describing recent trends, and it is to some of the explanatory models that the chapter turns next.

Explaining trade union membership

One of the most comprehensive explanations of factors affecting union membership is provided by Bain and Price (1983), who identify three major groups of variables that can influence union membership. These are shown in Fig. 4.2.

The first group, *contextual variables*, consists of factors such as the composition of the workforce, management ideologies, the role of the government and wider social values. Where management's prevailing ideology is anti-union, this tends to result in opposition to unions gaining recognition in a firm. In addition, because it is more difficult for unions to organise and recruit part-time or casual employees, workforce composition can also be an important variable. Important too is the role of the State, which can alter the general contextual milieu that influences trade union membership. For example, legislation and public policy in the 1980s actively sought to undermine collectivism, while in the late 1990s the Labour government introduced statutory trade union recognition provisions, which offer some protection to workers who want to join a union. Finally, social values are important, in that, if individuals have little interest in unionisation, this could adversely affect membership. For example, the prevalence of the 'never-member' across all sectors (with the exception of public services) provides some evidence to suggest that individual employees have simply lost their appetite for union membership (Metcalf, 2005; Bryson and Gomez, 2005).

The second group of factors consists of *business cycle variables*. For example, as the real price of goods rises, employees tend to unionise to protect their standards of living and, when real wages rise, people tend to give the credit to trade unions, which reinforces the predisposition of

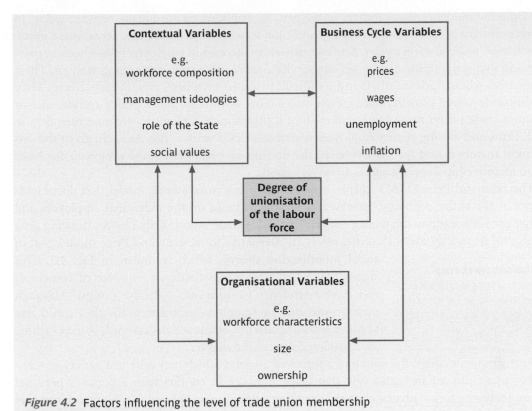

Figure 4.2 Factors influencing the level of trade union membership
Source: adapted from Bain and Price (1983).

people to join. Other related economic factors are unemployment, employment and inflation. If people are in work and perceive unemployment as a threat, they may join a trade union for defensive reasons. However, if they work for an anti-union employer, and fear that membership might be used against them, there can be a tendency in the reverse direction.

The final group of factors includes *organisational variables*, such as the concentration of ownership into large and foreign-owned firms, organisational size, or the use of agency labour that is associated with outsourcing strategies. For example, unionisation is much more common in larger organisations, and with the possible exception of the public sector, unionisation is usually much lower among a workforce that is predominantly female, or has large numbers of atypical and peripheral employees.

These groups of variables are all interconnected, and it is not so much that any one or two of them are more significant than the others, but that they all interact and play a part in influencing aggregate union membership. For example, the role of the State is likely to affect the general climate of employment relations, which in turn can influence the extent to which management is either supportive or hostile to unionisation. Likewise, how employers respond to the prospect of unionisation or to wage demands will spill over and shape the general perceptions and attitudes of individual workers. Bain and Price conclude that, since the Second World War, these variables have had different effects in different sectors of the economy, and this has resulted in a tremendous impact on the capability of trade unions to increase in size after a period of membership loss. For instance, in the public service and the manufacturing sector where trade union growth has traditionally been greatest, economic factors and favourable public policies towards trade unionism combined in the years to 1980 to give a major expansion.

While the model explains matters in the past, its implications are equally relevant today. In the recessionary periods since 1980 the greatest job losses have been in those areas where union growth took place in earlier years. Any compensatory increase in employment has been in part-time and atypical employment in private services, more often than not among women. These are all areas where trade unions found it difficult to attract members, even in earlier years when conditions favoured growth. Indeed, even with a more favourable public policy agenda, such as statutory trade union recognition, unions find it increasingly difficult to organise members in small firms and among agency employees where casualised work is rife. As such, given the loss of union members and the persistence of the non-union organisation, the prognosis for trade union membership does not appear to be very good.

The Bain and Price (1983) scheme is essentially a macro-economic model that documents factors in the wider economy. However, it fails to focus in on the individual employees and his/her possible motives for joining (or not joining) a trade union. Kelly (1998), drawing on a number of American social theorists, offers an alternative to the Bain and Price model, that of

social mobilisation theory

A theory which argues that when people experience an injustice or grievance, they have a tendency to form into collective groups.

social mobilisation theory, which is shown in Fig. 4.3. This argues that when people experience an injustice of some sort they have a tendency to form into collective groups. Although these groups may be trade unions, theoretically they could also be other sorts of collective employee associations, some of which are considered later in the chapter.

At the model's core is the notion of a *perceived injustice*, which may arise in a variety of ways. Management can act in such a way that work rules are in conflict with a person's personal values, there can be an adverse change to existing rules, or new policies can be introduced that undermine declared employee rights. For example, managers may pressure employees to 'opt out' of working-time regulations, or violate an employee's psychological contract by introducing new policies that are detrimental to workers. Furthermore, a sense of injustice may also evolve when employees adopt a view that they have the power to change things for the better (i.e. personal efficacy).

Encountering this perceived injustice then sets in motion a series of other events, which could potentially transform an individual issue into a collective matter. For this to happen however, *social identification* would need to occur, in which individuals align themselves with other like-minded individuals. This process of social identification is one in which trade unions can play a part; for example, by promoting an issue among a wider constituency of workers. A

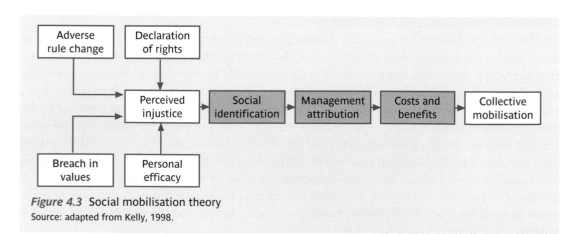

Figure 4.3 Social mobilisation theory
Source: adapted from Kelly, 1998.

union or other collective employee association can also be the vehicle that ensures that this stage occurs, by actively *attributing* blame to management for the injustice. Where this happens employees then engage in an on-going process of *cost–benefit analysis*. In its simplest form this might consist of setting the cost of paying membership subscriptions against the benefits – for example, the potential strength of collective muscle to counter an injustice – that accrue from joining a union. If all of the above stages are encountered, Kelly predicts that the final stage of the process – some form of *collectivisation* – will occur. Theoretically, collectivisation can take a number of forms: for example, joining a union or other collective employee association, registering a grievance with management or, in extreme circumstances, some form of protest behaviour.

Here it is important to point out that the Bain and Price model and Kelly's model of social mobilisation are not in opposition. Rather, they seek to explain the phenomenon of union membership from slightly different perspectives, and so they are complementary. Whereas Bain and Price use econometric analysis of a large set of data, Kelly utilises social movement concepts to focus on inter-personal processes, and this is reinforced by evidence which indicates that employees become more active in their union when they perceive that an injustice exists in the workplace (Johnson and Jarley, 2004).

Summary points

- Trade union membership has declined significantly over the last three decades and there are currently just over 7 million members in Great Britain, which equates to a union density level of 29 per cent.

- Union membership is also more common in the public rather than private sector, and the occupations with the greatest propensity to unionise include teachers and nurses.

- 'Never-membership', that is, people in employment who have never been and are unlikely to be a union member, is now more common across all industrial sectors with the exception of public services.

- Two models can be used to describe the changing patterns of union membership:
  - the *Bain and Price Model*, which includes macro-level variables such as Context Factors, Business Cycle Fluctuations and Organisational Factors
  - the *Social Mobilisation Model* which incorporates interpersonal processes of injustice, identification and attribution in explaining possible collectivisation in employment relations.

Trade union renewal strategies

Somewhat prophetically, Phelps Brown (1990) described the extent of trade union decline as the most profound 'counter revolution of our time'. By this he referred to a sea change in attitude, so significant that it was likely to permanently recast the way that economic and social relations are conducted at the workplace. Fifteen years later it has become obvious, at least in terms of size, that the trade union movement is running just to stand still (Gall, 2005). Consequently, the function and character of many unions has changed and adapted. Some, for example, have embarked on a strategy of cooperation with employers, mostly through partnership agreements, while others have adopted new organising and recruitment methods to help boost their legitimacy with members (Coats, 2005). Others have disappeared altogether owing to union mergers and amalgamations, and only a few have remained steadfast in terms of their militant traditions (Kelly and Willman, 2004). Given the extent of union decline and the rise of the 'never-member', it is apparent that the mere availability of a collective body does not mean that employees will flock to join it. For this reason it is important to ask whether unions have engaged in activities to try to make themselves more attractive, both to existing and potential members. In this section a number of contemporary union strategies are examined, and since these vary considerably, only some of the main initiatives will be described.

Underpinning any union renewal strategy is a fundamental question: are unions still useful for workers? This issue was first addressed in a seminal study by Olson (1965), who analysed the activities of voluntary associations, and pointed out that there is an inherent paradox for collective associations such as trade unions. While the addition of a single member adds very little to the collective strength of the organisation, the benefits obtained by anyone who joins are strongly related to the number of people who are already members. However, there are costs as well as benefits associated with union membership; for instance, a person who joins has to pay subscriptions and observe the association's rules. Importantly, if a firm is already highly unionised, it is likely that all employees (not just trade union members) would reap the benefits

free rider

A person who receives the benefits of union membership, but who avoids any associated costs by not joining the union.

of increases negotiated by the union, and in this situation an individual's most rational course of action would be to become a **free rider** – someone who takes the benefits of membership but avoids its costs by not joining. For this reason, even though the addition of a single individual adds little to its strength, a trade union has a vested interest in pulling all employees into membership. It is this basic task that lies at the heart of all union-revival strategies, and four general approaches that seek to achieve this can be identified: *union restructuring*; engaging in *partnership*; adopting a *servicing union approach*; and developing an *organising model of unionism*.

In *union restructuring* the aim is to bring about a more effective use of resources, and in the

closed shop

An arrangement in which union membership is a condition of employment.

past, trade unions could achieve this by increasing their membership base by engaging in a **closed shop** arrangement with management, thereby making union membership a condition of employment. However, as a result of employment legislation introduced in the 1980s, the closed shop is virtually illegal in Great Britain, and so some unions have turned to *mergers* and *amalgamations* as a way of restructuring to increase size (see Table 4.2). While this does not increase total union membership in Great Britain, it can increase a newly merged union's potential bargaining power with employers, and therefore its utility to prospective members. However, most union mergers have been for defensive reasons to minimize the burdens on union resources, rather than as a renewal strategy *per se*.

Another strategy is to adopt a *partnership* approach, which in general terms involves greater cooperation between union and management (Guest and Peccei, 2001). As a method of union renewal, partnership relations tend to be defined by three overarching characteristics: i) an emphasis on consultative structures; ii) the involvement of employees and union officials in formulating and implementing management plans; and iii), a respect by the parties for each other's interests (Haynes and Allen, 2001). Indeed, in some partnership agreements, unions have learnt to consult and negotiate with management alongside other non-union employee representatives, something that would have been unthinkable a few years ago (Ackers *et al.*, 2005).

However, 'partnership' is a very imprecise term and can exist in many forms. Some unions have signed up to a new cooperative relationship because the alternative might have been de-recognition (Coats, 2005). Another form is what has been termed *de facto* partnership in which, although the relationship is not formally called 'partnership', it has all the main ingredients such as: cooperation, satisfaction of mutual and separate interests, and dialogue and consultation. In effect, therefore, *de facto* partnership formalises what was previously an informal relationship (Ackers *et al.*, 2005).

The impact of partnership as a form of union renewal is difficult to judge. There has certainly been a growth in the number of partnership agreements in Great Britain, and the TUC and Labour government both strongly endorse the principle (Coats, 2005). It is possible, therefore, that the popularity of partnership owes more to its formal endorsement by government, than as a conscious union-centred revival strategy. Moreover, it is evident that many union–management relationships have had characteristics that are similar to partnership for a considerable time, even though they did not use this grand title (Oxenbridge and Brown, 2004). Nonetheless, partnership can have disadvantages as well as advantages. For example, there is evidence showing that in partnership companies employee wage increases have been lower and job losses higher than in non-partnership firms in the same sector (Kelly, 2005). A corollary to this is that an over-reliance on partnership could result in further union decline and weakness, because unions lose their capacity to resist unpalatable management plans or wage cuts when the relationship is based solely on cooperative dimensions (Kelly, 1998).

A third renewal approach is to adopt what has become known as the **servicing model of unionism**. In this the parent union offers a range of professional services that act as incentives for people to join: for example, giving individual protection in grievance, discipline and redundancy situations, and offering a professional negotiating service to individuals where collective bargaining does not exist. Other features of the servicing approach include the provision of ancillary benefits such as legal and financial services, which many trade unions now provide, but only to their members.

servicing unionism

The provision of a range of professional membership services by the parent union, such as the representation of members' interests and legal advice.

organising unionism

A type of trade unionism that focuses strongly on recruiting and training members, with the aim of leaving in place a strong, self-reliant cadre of workplace activists.

The final strategy is one that has attracted an increasing amount of attention, and is based on adopting the **organising model of unionism**. Here, the union's objective is to empower workers directly, by providing the structures for them to determine their own agendas. This is underpinned by a belief that a union's attractiveness is enhanced through activism at the workplace. Accordingly, it focuses on providing training for local leaders, who can then recruit new members. This model is strongly endorsed by several of Britain's largest unions, and more directly by the TUC, which now has a dedicated *Organising Academy*. Organising marks a shift away from the idea that unions should simply provide a servicing function, towards one that emphasises fostering local and self-dependent workplace unions (Heery, 1998). Indeed, the *Organising Academy* provides the training and expertise to encourage union activists to be more innovative in addressing the needs of particular employees, such as women or ethnic minorities (Heery *et al.*, 2000). In this way it is hoped that they may be better equipped to recruit and train workers to represent their own interests, rather than depend upon a parent union. The idea of organising unionism draws on initiatives used in the USA and Australia (Heery *et al.*, 2000), and in outline, organising and servicing unionism are contrasted in Table 4.4.

These different union renewal strategies are often contrasted as alternative approaches. However, one criticism is that the different strategies are so diverse they are incompatible and

Servicing unionism	Organising unionism
Union solves members' problems	Members own their problems and decide how best to solve them
Union tells members	Members tell union
Existence dependent upon management recognition	Existence relies on workers at the workplace
Cold selling of the idea of membership	Identify natural leaders based in the workplace
Union provides ancillary services (e.g. insurance)	Workers empowered and trained to take initiative
Recruitment of new members a separate activity	Recruitment integral to all activities
Low membership participation in union activities	Active membership participation in all union activities
Union officer-led agenda	Workplace member-led agenda

Table 4.4 Servicing and organising unionism contrasted
Source: adapted from Blyton and Turnbull, 2004.

send contradictory messages to potential members and employers (Heery, 1998). For example, most of the larger unions and the TUC have endorsed a strategy of union–management *partnership* since the early 1990s, yet at the same time seem to support the simultaneous use of more assertive *union-organising* approaches. *Union organising* has also been criticised as being too centralised in Britain, with the bulk of policy determined by national union leaders and the TUC's Organising Academy. Perhaps the most significant barrier to these union revival options is the fact that a large proportion of the working population are now 'never-members', and there is a strong indication that these generations of workers will never encounter a unionised relationship during their working lives (Bryson and Gomez, 2005).

Notwithstanding the extensive academic debate about these renewal strategies, it is clear that they have not reversed the decline in aggregate union density. However, one possible impact is that they may have altered the form and character of trade unions (Fairbrother and Yates, 2003). Furthermore, it is still possible that alternative strategies could exist side-by-side, according to the nature of a given workplace or occupational group (Charlwood, 2004). Indeed, the TUC has noted that when faced with a 'bad employer', partnership is unlikely to work (Hyman, 2001: 111), but in other situations, when faced with intense global economic pressures or under conditions of high-performance work systems, partnership could add considerable value to employees, unions and employers (Heery *et al.*, 2004: 19). Similarly, in situations where management is reluctant to recognise a union, employees could find the organising model more attractive in seeking to counterbalance the actions of an employer (Johnson and Jarley, 2004). In contrast, it appears that the *servicing model* of unionism is overly dependent upon full-time union officers providing a representative function to members, or what Fletcher and Hurd (1998) describe as 'stale unionism' that is desperately in need of revision and modernisation.

Pause for reflection

Given what you have read thus far in the chapter, why do think workers join trade unions, especially why do people join during a period of membership decline?

Case study 4.1: **The union-membership dilemma**

Assume you have just completed your studies and have now graduated. Also assume you have been successful in your application to work for the TUC as a development and research officer. In your first week you are appointed to a new membership task force, the purpose of which is to evaluate recent data on union membership in Britain, and make recommendations to the General Council about the possible response options that could be adopted by the trade union movement.

Your task force is presented with the following data about union membership in Britain.

Union member	Pay determined by collective bargaining		
	Yes	No	Total
Yes	5.5m	1.6m	7.1m
No	3.3m	14.0m	17.3m
Total	8.8m	15.6m	24.4m

Source: adapted from Metcalf, 2005: 23.

The above shows there are 8.8 million workers whose pay is determined by collective bargaining. Of these, only 5.5 million are actual union members. The other 3.3 million either work in companies that are part of an industry-wide collective agreement, or are individual free riders who take the benefits of union membership but do not join.

Of the 15.6 million workers whose pay is not set by collective bargaining, 1.6 million are union members, which could be explained by management in these firms having downgraded collective negotiation to joint consultation.

Your task force quickly identifies that the 17.3 million workers who are not members represent the best hope of recovery, and in particular, the 14 million workers who do not enjoy any of the benefits that can accrue from collective negotiation. However, you also have to make considered recommendations for each of the other groups of workers (members and non-members), and how best the trade union movement could respond in a way that helps boost membership and credibility.

The question as to which of these renewal options is likely to be the most appropriate depends on the answer to an even more basic question: why do people join unions?

Some evidence to answer this question is given in Table 4.5, which documents the reasons given by those people who had recently joined a trade union (Waddington and Whitston, 1997). One of the more noticeable features that emerges from Table 4.5 is that the top three reasons all relate to what can conveniently be described as the collective utility of unions. For example, three-quarters of respondents said they joined a union because they wanted support for a problem, and one-third because they sought improvements in pay and conditions of employment. It may also be noted that some of the features of a servicing union model figure less prominently: for example, only about 6 per cent of respondents list professional services as a reason for joining, with just 3.5 per cent joining for financial benefits offered by the union. In addition, the data lend support to some of the ideas reflected in *social mobilisation theory*; for example, that people have a sense of collective identity, from which has grown an apparent 'belief' in unionism, albeit for very instrumental reasons.

Reasons for union joining	%
Support for a problem	72.1
Improvements in pay and conditions	36.4
Belief in trade unions	16.2
Free legal advice	15.1
Most people at work are union members	13.8
Professional services	6.2
Training and education	5.0
Industrial benefits	4.4
Financial services	3.5
Other reason	6.9
	N = 10 823

Table 4.5 Why workers join trade unions
Source: adapted from Waddington and Whitston, 1997.

Summary points

- Trade unions serve a range of useful functions for employees, including providing individual services and collective support mechanism.

- Four union renewal strategies can be identified: *union restructuring*; *partnership*; *servicing unionism*; and *organising unionism*.

- While these renewal strategies may have altered the form and character of some unions, overall they have not reversed the decline in union membership.

- The reasons why people join unions include both collective protection and membership services.

Statutory trade union recognition

In view of its intentions to legislate for trade union recognition rights, the fortunes of British trade unions were given a positive boost with the election of a Labour government in 1997. The idea of statutory union recognition is not new in British employment relations, and in the 1970s attempts were made to legislate on this matter, only to be repealed by the Conservative government in the 1980s.

Nevertheless, provisions for statutory trade union recognition were reintroduced in Britain through the Employment Relations Act 1999, and subsequently incorporated into Schedule A1 of the Trade Union and Labour Relations (Consolidation) Act 1992. **Trade union recognition** is an arrangement in which an employer agrees that one or more trade unions will represent the interests of some or all of the employees in the organisation, for the purpose of collective bargaining. Unless otherwise agreed by the parties, the legislation defines collective bargaining as 'negotiations over hours of work, holidays and pay', the latter including pensions (Lewis and Sargeant, 2004). In practice, once recognition is obtained, it is

trade union recognition

An arrangement in which an employer agrees that one or more trade unions will represent the interests of some or all of the employees in the organisation, for the purpose of collective bargaining.

also extended to representational rights in individual issues such as grievance and discipline. It should be noted that recognition can be enacted in one of two ways: either voluntarily, or via legal means – for example, following a declaration issued by the Central Arbitration Committee (CAC). It is not the intention here to describe every detail of the statutory trade union recognition provisions, but to draw general inferences about what these details might mean for the parties in British employment relations. To this end Exhibit 4.1 gives a summary of some of the main statutory trade union recognition provisions.

As might be expected, the initial response from employer groups was to oppose the 1999 Act, suggesting instead that voluntary arrangements best serve the needs of industry. Although trade unions endorsed the principle of statutory recognition, they were somewhat disappointed with the detail of the legislation, arguing that it did not go far enough (Smith and Morton, 2001), and in particular voiced four specific concerns. First, unions were disappointed that the provisions of the Act were confined to workplaces with over 21 employees, thereby excluding an estimated 8 million workers employed in smaller firms (Dickens and Hall, 2003). Crucially, given that trade union membership is currently only just over 7 million people, the legislation was felt to exclude a significant pool of potential members.

Second, concerns were voiced about balloting requirements. Here, the legislation requires a trade union to do more than win a straightforward majority; it has to ensure that at least 40 per cent of those eligible to vote do so, and vote in favour of union recognition. This could be difficult where ballots are conducted by postal methods, because these tend to have low returns.

Third, trade unions envisaged difficulties in defining groups of employees who would be

bargaining unit
A group of employees covered by a negotiated collective agreement.

covered by any future collective agreements. In this matter an appropriate **bargaining unit** has to be established, but doing this is far from straightforward. For example, the unit can be influenced by management; by the characteristics of a workforce; or determined by the way an organisation is structured in terms of its location or number of plants. Nevertheless, the Employment Relations Act 2004 further clarifies what is meant by an 'appropriate' bargaining unit for trade union recognition (see Exhibit 4.1).

Finally, for some unions, the legislation can be extremely difficult to apply in practice, especially in smaller firms who have never before experienced a union presence (Dundon, 2002b). Indeed, there are also concerns that in the longer-term statutory recognition laws could result in an American-style system, in which employers vigorously campaign against union recognition, or even use loopholes in the law to avoid union certification (Logan, 2001).

The impact of statutory trade union recognition in Britain

Setting aside longer-term consequences, for which, as yet, there is no evidence, it appears that the impact of union recognition legislation has been broadly positive. One reason for this is that the

shadow legal effect
An indirect outcome of statutory trade union legislation, which has led employers and unions to agree new *voluntary* recognition arrangements.

legislation itself has produced what has come to be known as a **shadow legal effect**. This means that employers and unions have managed to agree to recognition on a *voluntary* basis, rather than have statutory provisions imposed (Wood *et al.*, 2003). For example, out of a total of 1730 new recognition agreements recorded between June 2000 and July 2006, only 296 were the direct result of accepted CAC applications (Gall, 2005; CAC, 2006). However, despite these initial encouraging signs, the decline in union membership does not seem to have been reversed. Nor has the legislation resulted in more workers being covered by collective bargaining, which

- In the legislation trade union recognition is for the purpose of collective bargaining (on pay, hours and holidays). The provisions were introduced in the Employment Relations Act 1999; further amended in the Employment Relations Act 2004; and subsequently incorporated into Schedule A1 of the Trade Union and Labour Relations (Consolidation) Act 1992.
- A request for recognition can be made to an employer by an independent certified trade union.
- The request must be in writing and identify the union and bargaining unit to which the request applies.
- The rules concerning statutory trade union recognition apply to organisations that employ 21 or more workers (although the bargaining unit can be less than 21).
- If, following a written request by a union, there is no response from the employer after 10 working days, or the employer is unwilling to negotiate, the union can refer the matter to the Central Arbitration Committee (CAC).
- When the matter is referred to the CAC, then two issues will be decided:
  1) whether the proposed bargaining unit is appropriate
  2) whether the union has the support or not of a majority of employees in the bargaining unit.
- In deciding whether a proposed bargaining unit is appropriate, the CAC must consider the union proposal first. If it decides this is appropriate, then that is satisfactory. An employer's proposal can only be considered in respect of whether the union's proposed bargaining unit is appropriate or not.
- The CAC must consider the following with respect to whether a bargaining unit is appropriate:
  – the views of the employer and the union
  – existing bargaining arrangements (local and national)
  – the objective of avoiding small and fragmented bargaining units within an organisation
  – the characteristics of workers in the proposed bargaining unit
  – the location of workers in the proposed bargaining unit.
- A bargaining unit can include more than one employer, where there is evidence that multiple employers are really one and the same (e.g. standardisation of contracts, unitary management structure across different employers etc.).
- If the CAC accepts the proposal from a union, then it is obliged to help the parties reach an agreement within 20 days of its acceptance, or longer if the CAC specifies.
- Once a bargaining unit is decided, then the CAC has to be satisfied that the union has majority support from employees in the bargaining unit in order to proceed further.
- If the union can show a majority of employees in the bargaining unit are union members, then the CAC must issue a declaration that the union is to be recognised for the purpose of collective bargaining.
- There are three conditions to be met for the CAC to conduct a ballot rather than make a recognition declaration:
  1) the CAC believes a ballot is in the interests of good industrial relations
  2) a significant number of employees in the bargaining unit indicate to the CAC they do not seek union membership for collective bargaining purposes
  3) union membership evidence leads the CAC to doubt the extent of membership in the bargaining unit; such evidence may relate to the circumstances in which membership came about, or length of union membership.
- Employers must comply with three duties should a ballot be conducted:
  1) to cooperate with the union and any independent person(s) appointed to conduct the ballot
  2) to provide the union with access to employees so it can seek support
  3) to provide to the CAC within 10 working days the names and home addresses of employees connected to the bargaining unit.
- The cost of the ballot will be shared equally by both parties.
- The CAC will issue a declaration for recognition when the following is satisfied:
  a) a majority of those who vote support union recognition, and
  b) at least 40 per cent of those employees in the bargaining unit support recognition.
- If there has been a change in the bargaining unit, such as organisational restructuring or a substantial change in the number of people employed, either party may apply to the CAC regarding the appropriateness of the bargaining unit.
- An employer can apply to the CAC to de-recognise a union 3 years after the CAC's original recognition declaration, provided that:
  – the size of the workforce is less than 21 employees
  – there is no longer a majority of employees who support collective bargaining
  – the rate of union membership has fallen below 50 per cent of those in the bargaining unit
  – the way the organisation does business or the structure of the organisation has changed substantially.
- Once a recognition agreement has been reached, or CAC declaration issued, it then becomes a legally enforceable contract.

Exhibit 4.1 Summary of statutory trade union recognition provisions

Source: adapted from Lewis and Sargeant, 2004.

has remained static at around 40 per cent of the labour force. While some employers have entered into a new form of dialogue with unions, this seems to be based more on consultation than actual negotiation (Moore *et al.*, 2005). Furthermore, recent survey evidence suggests that recognition attempts have been confined to those sectors where union membership has traditionally been strongest, such as manufacturing, or recognition was limited to selected sections of an organisation's workforce (Blanden *et al.*, 2005). This could well indicate that initially, unions requested recognition from employers who were more likely to concede agreements voluntarily, thus leaving a hard core of less supportive managers who are unlikely to grant recognition without a fight.

With this in mind, Gall (2005) suggests that the impact of statutory trade union recognition has led to three types of emerging union–management relationship. The first, *partnership*, implies a degree of cooperation between management and unions, based on satisfying each party's mutual as well as separate interests, and about 20 per cent of reported recognition agreements are estimated to fall within this category. The second type, *business as usual*, describes employers who agree to union recognition, but at the same time frustrate negotiations. Since 2001 there have been approximately 150 cases that fall into this group, an example of which is provided in Exhibit 4.2. Finally, about 8 per cent of all new recognition agreements fall into the category of *continued conflict*, which indicates a continuation of previous employee–management conflicts after formally granting union recognition. According to Gall (2005), it could be the case that these conflicts have emerged because of heightened union and worker expectations following recognition, and that these might well disappear as new collectivised relationships become embedded over time.

Richmond Mirrors is a London-based mirror manufacturer. The company's reaction to union recognition legislation probably typifies some of the strategies employers use to frustrate the impact of the law.

The Central Arbitration Committee (CAC) decided that a request for union recognition from the company's employees and the GMB union was valid, and ruled accordingly. However, three weeks after the CAC's ruling, and following the company's acceptance of a method for collective bargaining, Richmond Mirrors returned to the CAC and argued that the bargaining unit defined in the original ruling no longer existed because the company had been reorganised following a takeover of Richmond Mirrors and another mirror manufacturer, Bluebird, by a third company, Ardengate. The CAC therefore had to agree that the original bargaining unit had ceased to exist in the form it was originally presented, and subsequently ruled in favour of the firm.

According to the GMB union official involved in the case: 'This case means that a small firm can close down once union recognition has been agreed and thereby avoid the establishment of bargaining rights.'

Exhibit 4.2 Union recognition and 'business as usual'
Source: adapted from Pickard, 2005: 33.

Summary points

- Trade union recognition means that an employer recognises one or more unions for the purpose of collective bargaining.

- Statutory trade union recognition provisions were reintroduced in Britain in the summer of 2000 through the Employment Relations Act 1999, and apply to enterprises that employ over 21 workers.

- A request for recognition has to be made in writing by an independent trade union, either to the employer or to the Central Arbitration Committee (CAC).

- The *shadow legal effect* of the legislation has resulted in several unions and employers entering into new 'voluntary' recognition agreements.

Workplace trade unionism

To most employees, the real trade union is not some remote national institution, but the organisation found at the workplace (Goldthorpe *et al.*, 1968). At this level employees are in face-to-face contact with their union; they can shape its actions and therefore determine what particular issues it pursues. More important, if there is any possibility of a clash between rank-and-file worker interests and those of the national union, workplace representatives can usually be persuaded to promote the interests of local members (Darlington, 1998). For these reasons workplace trade unionism can often be totally different in its nature from that of national union bodies. Other than for a few dedicated activists, wider social or political matters tend to be of little concern and there is often a fair measure of parochialism. For reasons which will be explained presently, there is sometimes a degree of detachment from the national trade union.

Most workplace trade unions make use of a lay representative system of some sort. This includes a number of different roles performed by workers who are elected by fellow union members to represent their interests. The key role is that of the **shop steward**, a general term used to describe lay representatives elected by specific groups of members in the workplace. However, the term is not universal: in what was the Graphical, Paper and Media Union (GPMU, now merged with Amicus), the 'father or mother of the chapel' was used, while in some white collar unions they are called 'office representatives'. As part of the workplace representative system, there are also **health and safety representatives**, who have legal rights to inspect workplaces on behalf of union members, and **union learning representatives** (ULR), a new category of lay union representative who can advise union members on their training needs and make representations to management, underpinned by legal rights to do so.

The main representative role, which includes assisting members in discipline or grievance cases, is typically performed by the shop steward. This is not a popular job, and is often only filled out of a sense of desperation by some individual who cannot tolerate the disorganisation which results from ineffective or non-existent occupancy of the role (Moore, 1980). In addition, because the job can be a difficult one to fill, shop stewards come in many varieties. One distinction that has been drawn is between leader and populist stewards (Batstone *et al.*, 1977). **Leader stewards** are those who are politically and ideologically committed to trade union principles, and seek to influence the opinions and actions of the membership (Darlington, 2002). In contrast, **populist stewards** are often more content to let their constituents lead them by the nose. In practice, however, shop steward activities tend to gyrate between a number of overlapping roles, and which one is occupied at a particular time varies according to the demands of the situation (Pedler, 1973).

In large enterprises stewards will usually be part of a union structure. In most British trade unions the branch is traditionally the fundamental unit of organisation, and union constitutions

---

shop steward

A general (but not universal) term used to describe a representative accredited with management by the trade union, who is elected by a specific group of members to represent their interests.

health and safety representatives

Union representatives at the workplace who have, among other things, the legal right to inspect the workplace on behalf of union members.

union learning representatives

Union representatives at the workplace who have legal rights to advise union members on their training needs, and make representations to management.

leader stewards

Union stewards who tend to be politically and ideologically committed to trade union principles, and who seek to influence the opinions and actions of the membership accordingly.

populist stewards

Stewards who ae content to let their constituents dictate how they act in representing member interests.

endow it with certain sovereign rights. Within certain specified limits it is usually allowed to formulate its own policies, choose its own approach to the issues that it deals with, discipline its own members, and make and ratify agreements in its own name. It may, for example, enter into a *partnership* agreement with management, pursue more *militant* objectives or adopt an *adversarial* stance with an employer, even in contrast to national union objectives (Dundon, 1998). Where there is no workplace branch, or in smaller firms, there will commonly be a hierarchy of stewards at a workplace level. In multi-plant firms there may well be a group of shop stewards from a number of different unions and locations, who determine policy through a Joint Shop Steward Committee (JSSC), sometimes also known as a Combine Committee (see Fig. 4.4). Such a body is often chaired by a full-time union **convenor**: someone who is a lay officer of the workplace union, appointed from among accredited shop stewards, and released from work tasks to perform union duties.

convenor
A lay officer of the workplace union appointed from among accredited shop stewards.

Survey evidence shows that union stewards are present in around 38 per cent of unionised workplaces, a decline from 53 per cent in 1980 (Millward *et al.*, 2000; Kersley *et al.*, 2006: 123). What this means is that around 77 per cent of all union members in Great Britain have access to a workplace union representative (Kersley *et al.*, 2006: 123). In contrast, there are only 5 per cent of establishments with a stand-alone 'non-union' employee representative (Kersley *et al.*, 2006: 125). Evidence also shows that union stewards spend a lot more time representing their members' interests than do their non-union counterparts. For example, about 40 per cent of union stewards spend over five hours each week on union duties, whereas the corresponding figure for non-union employee representatives is only one in seven (Kersley *et al.*, 2005). Public-sector shop stewards also tend to spend more time representing member concerns than do stewards in the private sector (Kersley *et al.*, 2005).

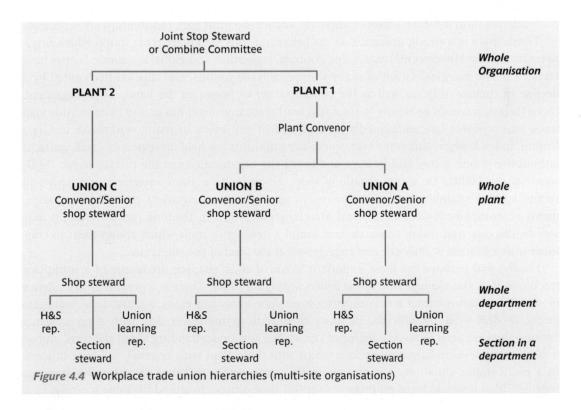

Figure 4.4 Workplace trade union hierarchies (multi-site organisations)

The type of issues that stewards deal with on behalf of their members fall into four broad categories (Kersley *et al.*, 2005). The most common issues are those concerning *terms and conditions* of employment, which embraces pay, hours of work, holidays and pension entitlements. The second category, *staffing issues*, are those where issues such as training, performance appraisals and staffing levels are the focus of attention. The third category, *welfare issues*, embraces matters such as health and safety, absence or equal opportunities. Finally, the category of *disputes* embraces discipline and grievance handling. Significantly, trade union stewards seem to be more likely than their non-union counterparts to have spent time dealing with *terms and conditions* and *disputes*-related issues (Kersley *et al.*, 2005). As can be seen therefore, the union steward role at the level of the enterprise is often a busy one that deals with a wide range of substantive issues, within a sophisticated hierarchical structure.

Structure is one thing, but the use to which it is put can be altogether different, and this gives rise to four important considerations that can shape the nature of workplace unionism. First, the *nature of existing collective agreements* will play an important part. Nationally negotiated agreements which are framed very tightly leave little room for local variation, and this can restrict the scope of a workplace union (Boraston *et al.*, 1975).

Second, *national trade union policies* can also be influential in this respect. They can be framed in a way that either restrains or facilitates the autonomy of local stewards. Indeed, there can sometimes be tensions between local shop stewards, who are elected or selected by their co-workers, and full-time union officers, who are appointed as an official of the union (Dundon, 1998). The full-time official has an allegiance to the wider union and its policies, rather than to a specific group of members, whereas workplace stewards are subject to direct pressure from the rank-and-file members that they represent. For this reason, and irrespective of wider union policies, they are likely to feel that they are far more competent to define the interests of their members than any full-time officer (Batstone *et al.*, 1977). However, it would be comparatively rare to find that workplace activists shun full-time officers completely, and for the most part, relationships are very close.

Third, there is a strong influence on the behaviour of a workplace trade union which originates from its *environmental context*. For example, legislation and global economic factors have resulted in the marginalisation of many workplace trade unions, and this has been aided by a decline in membership, as well as the concentration of power in the hands of management. Nevertheless, it would be wrong to infer that workplace unionism has ceased to exist. Although trade union power has undoubtedly been diluted, it still exists in many workplaces in Great Britain. Indeed, where this is the case, workplace unionism has held up reasonably well, particularly in the public sector and in large and multi-site organisations in the private sector (Millward *et al.*, 2000). In some situations shop stewards have been extremely pro-active in recruiting new members and participating in new union–management partnership arrangements at workplace level (Godfrey and Marchington, 1996). In the long run therefore, it may well be the case that union stewards have found a new set of tools which allows them to continue with a process of dialogue and engagement at the level of the enterprise.

Finally, and perhaps the most important factor of all in shaping the nature of a workplace trade union, is the *management of the employing organisation*. There is a great deal of evidence to show that autonomous and competent workplace unionism exists because local managers prefer to deal with lay officials. In many organisations managers deal with shop stewards because they are seen to have a degree of knowledge and understanding about the firm, and so it is easier to develop bargaining relationships with them than with external, full-time officers. In a multi-union situation, it is also easier for management to bring several union stewards together, than it would be to get three or four full-time officers to attend the same meeting.

Summary points

- The nature of trade unionism at the workplace can be very different from that of a national trade union.
- Most workplace unions make use of a shop steward system of elected lay representatives.
- Shop steward roles are wide and varied, and an important distinction can be made between *leader* and *populist* stewards.
- The number of workplace union representatives has fallen in Britain, but on average, shop stewards spend more time representing their members' interests than do their non-union employee representative counterparts.
- Four broad factors influence the nature of workplace trade unionism, including:
  - *the nature of existing collective agreements*
  - *national trade union policies*
  - *environmental context factors*
  - *management in the employing organisation.*

Non-union institutions for worker representation

Although trade unions are by far the most significant associations representing the interests of employees, there are other collective institutions that are part and parcel of British employment relations. While these bodies can be very different from trade unions in terms of their aims and purposes, they can still be influential in representing the interests of some groups of workers, and as Ackers *et al.* (2005) point out, it would be remiss to discount their roles before examining the evidence. Non-union employee associations can be either wholly *voluntary*, or in some cases they exist in a *state-regulated* form arising from legislation. Within each type there is inevitably bound to be a great deal of variation, and so in what follows, a number of general descriptions are given.

Professional associations

One accepted definition of a professional association is:

> any organisation which directly aims at the improvement of any aspects of professional practice: for example by providing a qualification, by controlling conduct, by coordinating technical information, by pressing for better conditions of employment.
>
> (Millerson, 1964: 33)

The official aims of most of these voluntary bodies are derived from a bygone era when their members were largely fee earners in independent practice. Their major function was to control the supply of labour and coordinate the activities performed by an association's members, as a form of labour cartel (Prandy *et al.*, 1983). However, these days many professionals are in paid employment, and some of the more significant professional associations retain a high degree of power and influence over the working conditions and remuneration received by their members.

For example, the Law Society regulates the conduct and entry of people into the legal profession; and in the health service, the British Medical Association (BMA) and British Dental Association (BDA) function as the collective association for doctors and dentists. These associations effectively use many of the same methods as trade unions in advancing their members' interests. Indeed, the BMA is registered as a trade union, even though it does not use the word in its title, and neither is it affiliated to the TUC.

Since the function of many professional associations is to endorse a level of competence and certify formal qualifications, they can, to some extent, control the number of new entrants into a profession. This gives them a very powerful means of keeping the market value of their members' services high which, interestingly, was the very same function used by some of the early craft unions in Britain. Thus it is with some logic that professional associations have been dubbed 'the craft unions of a different social group' (Bain *et al.*, 1973).

Staff associations

The term **staff association** is usually applied to in-house collective associations that cater for particular employees (mainly salaried staff), who all work for the same employer. However, some care is needed in using this term. For example, in certain parts of the civil service and NHS, the term is used to describe independent trade unions that represent particular grades of employees. Nevertheless, as the name implies, they usually cater for only salaried staff, and associations of this type are found in organisations such as banks, building societies and insurance companies (Prandy *et al.*, 1983).

staff association

A voluntary in-house collective association that caters for particular employees, mainly salaried staff, who all work for the same employer.

In trade union circles the term 'staff association' is often used in a highly pejorative way. For example, it is frequently asserted that by their very nature they are under the control of the employer, and lack the independence to represent their members' interests (Morrell and Smith, 1971). However, most associations would hotly dispute this and in practice, things are slightly more complicated. For example, some staff associations are registered as trade unions and to achieve this they have to satisfy the government's Certification Officer about their independence from the employer. Nevertheless, it is probably fair to say that an in-house staff association can hardly be expected to be as independent as an externally based trade union, especially where it is not registered with the Certification Officer. The most penetrating observation of their activities comes from a study of white-collar unions, in which staff associations were also examined (Bain, 1970). The majority were formed at the initiative of the employer, usually as a response to avoid trade unionism in the company, and only one was found to be genuinely independent. Perhaps of greater significance is what staff associations actually do, or rather do not do. For example, most do not engage in negotiating with management over pay or other conditions of employment, and most exist only as an information and consultation conduit with management (Bain, 1970).

Non-union mechanisms of worker representation

In non-union firms employees are unlikely to have the elaborate representation structures that can be found in unionised organisations. However, given the extent of union decline noted earlier, it is not surprising that many non-union firms seek to put in place mechanisms that give a facility for employees to be informed and consulted about matters that affect them. These methods are considered in greater detail in Chapter 8, which deals with employee voice, and are

internal employee forum
A management-initiated employee body, such as a company committee.

external (third party) association
An institution that articulates the concerns of employees to management and/or represents their interests in a court of law. One example is the Citizens Advice Bureaux (CAB).

mentioned here for the sake of completeness. One method used is an **internal employee forum** of some sort, such as a company committee. For the most part these are management-initiated bodies which are (nominally) voluntary in nature. However, they can also exist as a result of state regulation, for example to conform with the 2004 Information and Consultation of Employees (ICE) regulations. A second type includes **external (third party) associations**, which articulate the concerns of employees to management and/or represent the interests of workers in a court of law. An example of an external (third party) association is the Citizens Advice Bureaux (CAB). Strictly speaking, this is not a collective association of employees, in which membership is available to workers. Rather, it is an agency that as a last resort can be used by a worker to represent his/her interests.

Clearly, these non-union mechanisms for worker representation are very different from trade unions or staff associations. To start with, they have little direct access to management decision makers, and occupy the role of an outsider group which seeks to exert pressure on management. At best, their role might only be complementary to that of a collective association, and a more distant one at that: for example, by providing advice to individual employees or by seeking to expose bad management practice, mainly by assisting an employee at a legal hearing.

Summary points

■ In addition to trade unions, there are other collective institutions and non-union representative mechanisms that are part and parcel of British employment relations.

■ Professional associations are bodies that regulate the supply of labour and the activities of professional employees, and who often act as qualifying associations.

■ Staff associations are voluntary in-house employee associations that represent the interests of particular employees, usually in a single organisation.

■ In practice, non-union mechanisms for worker representation exist, either as a management-initiated practice, or because of state regulations to inform and consult employees.

Case study 4.2: Identifying the nature of collective associations

Consider the two firms described below. In each case try to identify what you feel would be some of the main characteristics of the collective employee association that might emerge.

TG Metal Inc

TG Metal is a long-established light engineering company that employs approximately 2000 workers on three sites, all of which are within two miles of each other. The company designs and manufactures engineering products for the shipping industry. There are separate trade unions for clerical and manual workers, and all employees below the level of departmental manager are normally members. Pay and conditions are negotiated at company level, and over the years unions and management have negotiated a comprehensive set of agreements covering most aspects of employment. TG Metal is considered to be a good employer in the local area, and pays slightly above average market rates of pay, with additional benefits such as generous holidays and pension arrangements as a result of negotiated agreements. The trade unions are given full facilities to operate within the different plants, and have developed stable systems of shopfloor and office representation, including a company-wide Joint Shop Stewards Committee (JSSC). In addition, each plant has its own joint union–management consultative committee, composed of management and union stewards, which meets four times per year. However, the committees can meet more frequently than this, and often do so to deal with matters arising in a particular plant. Indeed, over the past few years it has been common for management to call additional meetings to explore solutions to issues that arise, such as new product designs and safety regulations in the shipping industry. At company level wages are negotiated centrally with all unions together on a bi-annual basis. There was a one-week strike over new shift working patterns at one of the sites about six years ago, but otherwise there has been no other major dispute at the company. Summary statistics for each of the three plants at TG Metal are as follows:

	Plant A	Plant B	Plant C
Total no. of employees	700	450	850
Managerial staff (non-union)	9	5	14
Non-manual employees			
Clerical	12	7	32
Technical	31	51	38
Supervisory	11	6	16
Manual employees			
Production craftsmen	17	16	12
Maintenance craftsmen	12	14	21
Semi-skilled production	602	347	706
Ancillary (canteen etc.)	6	4	11

Burlington and Leigh Mutual Society (BLMS)

BLMS is a large building society employing about 1000 people, located in the north of England. It has a large headquarters with 650 people, and 32 branch outlets of varying size, from 5 employees in the smallest to 15 in the largest, with an average number of 10 employees per branch. BLMS has been trading for over 120 years, and recognised a staff association for its employees 100 years ago. It has what BLMS calls a 'Staff–management Dialogue Forum', which meets quarterly to discuss staff-welfare issues and other matters of mutual interest, including the running of the BLMS Staff Social Club. Pay, holidays and other service conditions are fixed by management, but prior consultation with the staff association usually takes place before any announcement is made. BLMS have a good reputation for providing high levels of customer care, and although pay is regarded as below average for junior members of staff, employment is considered secure. BLMS values employee loyalty, and staff are rewarded for long service and diligence to the customer. The typical breakdown of staff for an average branch employing 10 employees is as follows:

Branch manager	1
Assistant manager	1
Back-office clerical assistants	2
Customer advisers	6

There are approximately 650 staff at head office, made up as follows:

Directors	5
Senior managers	17
Investment managers	121
Clerical and branch support staff	488
Porters, security and maintenance staff	19

Conclusions

This chapter has dealt with the roles and functions of collective employee associations. While trade unions are by far the most significant of these bodies, staff associations and professional associations also exist to represent the interests of some employees. Of necessity the chapter has dealt with trade unions and other collective associations in isolation, but this is not how matters occur in the real world. To some extent, this is reflected in sections of the chapter that dealt with *trade union renewal strategies, statutory union recognition*, and *workplace trade unionism*. These all show that trade unions respond to, and react with, environmental factors such as the state, economic conditions and the actions of management. Therefore, the importance of trade unions in British employment relations can only be comprehended if there is some recognition of the ways in which they represent employee interests, and how they respond to the challenges they face in contemporary society.

Successive chapters in the book will consider some of these challenges in more detail. For example, some of the methods of employee voice covered in Chapter 8 take place in collective ways, which means that union activities will be reconsidered again. In Chapters 9 and 10 the processes of bargaining and negotiation are examined, and these are strongly connected with the functions of trade unions. It is also important to bear in mind that these functions are not always collective in nature, in the sense that they involve large numbers of employees acting in unison. Thus, in Chapters 6 and 7, the individual processes of discipline, grievance and redundancy are covered, and the reader should bear in mind that in many of these cases, the individual employee would normally be represented by his/her trade union in these matters.

Finally, it should be noted that the role of management and of the government of the day both have a strong influence on trade union behaviour. Reflecting this, there is a very clear link between this chapter and the preceding one, and also with the one that follows, which focuses on the role of the State.

❓ Review and discussion questions

1 In what ways do trade unions differ from other collective employee associations, such as staff associations and professional associations?

2 Briefly explain why there are problems with the conventional classifications of trade unions given in Table 4.1.

3 Explain what is meant by the terms trade union *purpose* and trade union *function*.

4 Describe three general functions of a trade union.

5 What factors can be used to help explain the changing patterns of trade union membership in Britain?

6 To what extent has statutory trade union recognition legislation had an impact on trade unions and on employment relations in a wider sense?

7 In what ways have trade unions responded to the decline in their membership?

8 What factors may influence the nature of a trade union at the workplace?

Further reading

Bain, G.S. and R. Price (1983) 'Union growth: dimensions, determinants and destiny', in *Industrial Relations in Britain*, G.S. Bain (ed.), Blackwell, Oxford. A seminal study charting factors that affect union growth and decline.

Blanden, J., S. Machin and J. Van Reenen (2005) *Have Unions Turned The Corner? New Evidence on Recent Trends in Union Recognition in UK Firms*, Centre for Economic Performance Discussion Paper No. 685, London School of Economics. (http://cep.lse.ac.uk/pubs/download/dp0685.pdf).

Bryson, A. and R. Gomez (2005) 'Why Have Workers Stopped Joining Unions? The Rise in Never-Membership in Britain', *British Journal of Industrial Relations*, Vol. 41 (1), pp. 67–92. An important article that explains the rise and extent of people in the British labour force who have never been union members, using data from the British Social Attitudes Surveys.

Coats, D. (2005) *Raising Lazarus: The Future of Organised Labour*, Fabian Society Pamphlet No. 618, London. A very readable paper that sets out the case for union renewal with both workers and employers, not through militant and confrontational action, but by means of independent and cooperative approaches.

Forth, J., H. Bewley and A. Bryson (2006) *Small and Medium-sized Enterprises: Findings from the 2004 Workplace Employment Relations Survey*, London, Department of Trade and Industry/Routledge. A booklet of the 2004 WERS survey, with some interesting findings on union membership in smaller firms. Available from: http://www.ecdti.co.uk/.

Grainger, H. and H. Holt (2005) *Trade Union Membership 2004*, Employment Market Analysis and Research, Department of Trade and Industry, London. (http://www.dti.gov.uk/er/emar/trade.htm). A government publication by the DTI that uses Labour Force Survey data to analyse the latest trends in union membership in Britain.

Heery, E., G. Healy, and P. Taylor (2004) 'Representation at work: themes and issues', in *The Future of Worker Representation*, G. Healy, E. Heery, P. Taylor and W. Brown (eds), Palgrave Macmillan, Basingstoke. A book chapter that is highly recommended. It provides a comprehensive review of different union-renewal strategies, the theoretical perspectives from which they are drawn, and a summary of responses and debates from the academic literature.

Heery, E., M. Simms, D. Simpson, R. Delbridge and J. Salmon (2000) 'Organising unionism comes to the UK', *Employee Relations*, Vol. 22 (1), pp. 38–57. An empirical paper that examines the use of union organising approaches by British unions and the TUC.

Hyman, R. (2001) *Understanding European Trade Unionism: between market, class and society*, Sage, London. A very thoughtful and articulate review of different union functions and purposes. Chapter 5 is well worth a read for the history and current identity crisis in British trade unions.

Kelly, J. (2005) 'Social partnership agreements in Britain', in *Partnership and Modernisation in Employment Relations*, M. Stuart and M. Martinez Lucio (eds), Routledge, London. A chapter worth reading for its rebuttal of the value of partnership for employees and unions. It uses empirical evidence to show that partnership companies often shed more jobs and pay workers less than non-partnership organisations.

Metcalf, D. (2005) *British Unions: Resurgence or Perdition?*, Provocation Series (Vol. 1, No 1), The Work Foundation, London. A provocative paper that reviews union membership in Britain. It argues that unless union evolve and respond in new and innovative ways, they are on the road to extinction. (http://theworkfoundation.com/pdf/British_Unions.pdf).

Waddington, J. and C. Whitston (1997) 'Why do people join unions in a period of membership decline?', *British Journal of Industrial Relations*, Vol. 35 (4), pp. 515–546. An empirical paper that reports on a large-scale survey of employees who had recently joined a trade union, providing evidence on the reasons why people joined.

Wood, S., S. Moore and K. Ewing (2003) 'The impact of trade union recognition under the Employment Relations Act 2000–2002', in *Representing Workers: Trade Union Recognition and Membership in Britain*, H. Gospel and S. Wood (eds), Routledge, London. A comprehensive review of the statutory union-recognition procedures, using empirical evidence to illustrate the broadly positive impact of the law in the UK.

Chapter 5

The role of the State in employment relations

LEARNING OUTCOMES

After studying this chapter you should be able to:

☑ **define** the State and its role in employment relations

☑ **describe** the different political philosophies associated with legal intervention by the State in employment relations

☑ **analyse** the changing nature of State intervention in British employment relations

☑ **explain** how employment legislation can influence one or more of the parties to an employment relationship

☑ **describe** the major State institutions of employment regulation in Great Britain, including the effects of the European Union.

Introduction

Managers and employees (and their collective associations), who were discussed respectively in the previous two chapters, are the parties that interact directly in employment relations. There is however, a third important player, *the State*, which in addition to the government of the day, includes all those agencies such as the civil service, the police, the judiciary and military, who carry out its will. Despite globalisation and the spread of international business, employment relations systems are usually deeply embedded in national rather than global institutions. Governments of all nation-states pass laws that influence how managers, workers and unions interact with each another, and in so doing shape the 'rules of the game'.

It is important to understand why the State feels compelled to become involved in employment relations in this way, and how this impacts on the behaviour of employees and managers, and the chapter starts by defining the State and outlines its means of intervention. This is followed by a section that examines the changing roles played by governments of different political persuasions in Great Britain, where it will be seen that enacting legislation – sometimes by transposing European regulations – has become the main vehicle of State intervention. This is followed by an outline scheme that explains how these rules and regulations influence one or more aspects of the employment relationship, and the chapter closes with an explanation of how the law operates in practice.

The role of the State in employment relations
The State defined

The State can be a difficult body to define, because there are many different institutions and government departments that can influence employment relations outcomes. For example, the army and police have been deployed during particular strikes, and the courts have passed judgements which have changed the day-to-day relationships between managers, employees and unions. In addition, the government also confers extensive powers on some of its institutions, such as the Equal Opportunities Commission (EOC) and the Advisory, Conciliation and Arbitration Service (ACAS). Given the extent of political influence and power, one of the earliest descriptions of the State described it as 'all government institutions which hold a monopoly on the legitimate use of force' (Weber, 1919). These days however, more explicit definitions are used, and in employment relations terms, **'the State'** is normally taken to mean the elected government of the day, together with all other agencies that carry out the will of government and implement its policies and legislation (Gospel and Palmer, 1993).

the State
The elected government of the day, together with all other agencies that carry out its will and implement its policies and legislation.

> ## Pause for reflection
>
> You may recall that in Chapter 2, a traditional view of British employment relations describes it as 'voluntarist'. Given this, would you say the State in Great Britain adopts a low or high interventionist approach to employment relations matters?

Until the 1950s there was probably no other industrialised country in world where the State was less interventionist in terms of its employment relations laws than in Britain (Kahn-Freund, 1965). However, the pace of State intervention has accelerated significantly since the end of the Second World War: first during the 1960s and 1970s; then in the 1980s; and further interventions by the State during the new millennium have altered the employment relations landscape in Britain even more. As a result it is now probably fair to say that individual employment laws, rather than voluntary collective bargaining agreements, regulate working conditions in Britain (Ewing, 2003), all of which has a huge impact on the behaviour of managers, trade unions and employees.

The objectives of the State in employment relations

In broad terms, it is often reasoned that the State's objective in intervening in employment relations is to achieve economic and social goals for the nation as a whole. One of the prime tasks of government is to manage the economy so that it is prosperous, and this means it has to try to achieve four broad economic policy objectives, each one of which can easily conflict with the others:

1 To maintain high levels of employment
2 To ensure price stability
3 To maintain a balance of payment surplus
4 To protect the exchange rate

While the actual government of the day is, by definition, a transient body, the above objectives are broadly similar for most political parties. However, each of the main political parties tends to have very different views about what are the most appropriate ways of achieving these aims, and these views reflect distinctly different philosophies about the way in which society should be ordered. For this reason, a government's objective for employment relations is not only directed at the economic and social ends it seeks to achieve, but is also an expression of its political ideology about the desirable nature of society.

In Britain there has long been an affinity between the trade union movement and the *Labour Party*, who at one time saw themselves as two different wings (industrial and political) of the same working-class movement. Thus, organised labour traditionally had a voice in formulating Labour Party policy, even though it was rarely a decisive one. In contrast, the British *Conservative Party* sees itself as the champion of free enterprise and the market economy, and it has equally strong ties with private business. These connections usually take place through strong personal and business networks, which deliver a considerable amount of financial support to the party. Many of these donations are hard to identify, and tend to be channelled via groups such as the Centre for Policy Studies or The Economic League, which are all known to be conduits for private-industry contributions to the Conservative Party (LRD, 1985a). Although the third force in British politics, the *Liberal Democrats*, receives some donations from private enterprise (LRD, 1985b), to a large extent the party is purposely non-aligned with either side of industry.

It is important to recognise that these differences in affiliation go well beyond financial support, and reflect the prevailing ideologies of governments. Although the current Labour government is regarded as more pro-business than earlier labour administrations, it has its own distinctive approach to employment legislation. For example, it has sought to promote a culture of competitiveness and partnership, which is underpinned by a floor of legal rights for workers. In contrast, former Conservative governments not only removed many hard-fought-for legal rights, but also aggressively attacked the trade union movement by passing laws to curb union activities. However, since enacting legislation is just one way in which the State can intervene in employment relations, it is important to consider other possible methods that it has at its disposal.

The scope and methods of State intervention

One of the earliest frameworks to capture the scope and extent of State involvement was provided by Armstrong (1969), who described several potential methods, each of which can influ-

employer, paymaster and buyer of goods (the State)

By virtue of its role as an employer, the State is able to intervene in employment relations in both public and private sectors of the economy by setting standards of responsible employment practice.

ence employment relations processes and outcomes. The first is related to the State's role as an **employer, paymaster and buyer of goods**. Around 20 per cent of the British workforce is funded either directly or indirectly by the State (Office for National Statistics, 2005). This covers many millions of workers – for example, people in the National Health Service (NHS), the civil service, local government and school teachers and fire fighters. A long-held principle in Great Britain is that in this role the State should act as a responsible employer, thereby sending signals to the private sector about how people should be treated at work. In return for this, public sector employees and trade unions accepted a reciprocal obligation to try and avoid conflict in employment relations (Winchester, 1983). Indeed, the origins of this philosophy are much older and go back to 1891, when the Fair Wages Resolution of the House of Commons was passed, in which the principle was established that government contracts would not automatically be awarded to the lowest bidder – a move designed to ensure that unscrupulous private employers were not at an automatic cost advantage. The idea of the State as a responsible employer also resulted in a degree of encouragement for trade union membership in the public sector, which is perhaps why union membership has remained healthy among many public-sector workers.

incomes regulator (the State)

An employment relations role adopted by the State, in which it seeks to control prices and wages, either through direct intervention or in its management of the economy.

A second means by which the State is able to intervene in employment relations is through its role as an **incomes regulator**. Since the end of the Second World War governments of both political persuasions have felt a need to regulate prices and wage increases, with the aim of controlling inflation. For example, in the 1970s the government consulted with employers and unions in an attempt to set acceptable incomes policies for the country. While the Conservative governments of the 1980s publicly rejected the very idea of market controls, they nonetheless set prices and wages in less visible ways: for instance, by manipulating interest rates, public spending and the money supply, they effectively regulated the rate of real-wage increases for public-sector workers.

manpower manager (the State)

An employment relations role adopted by the State, in which it promotes effective manpower utilisation.

Another way of intervention by the State is as a **manpower manager**, in order to promote effective manpower utilisation; for example, by providing return-to-work incentives, or by operating employment exchanges to link those seeking work with those who have employment to offer. In this role the State has also taken steps to encourage labour mobility: for example, by passing legislation which ensures that people made unemployed receive minimum redundancy payments, or providing training such as the new apprentice schemes introduced in the late 1990s to help address Britain's skills shortage.

protector (the State)

An employment relations role adopted by the State, in which it establishes and monitors minimum standards through its agencies.

A fourth and equally important role is the State as a **protector** of minimum standards in employment. These standards have existed in different ways since the beginning of the twentieth century: for example, in 1920 the Employment of Women and Young Persons and Children Act established basic standards on health and safety. In the 1970s a great deal of protective legislation was introduced for unfair dismissal, race discrimination and equal pay. The scope of protective intervention also saw the creation of specialist State agencies, such as the Equal Opportunities Commission (EOC) and the Health and Safety Executive (HSE). In the new millennium, the scope has widened even further with the introduction of minimum wage legislation and the establishment of the Low Pay Commission (LPC).

Finally, perhaps the most visible method of intervention in employment relations by the State is in its role as a **rule maker**. This involves direct promulgation of legislation, and according to Kahn-Freund (1965), the law in this respect has three main functions. First, it has an *auxiliary* function, which encourages good employment relations by specifying sanctions that can be taken against those who flout the rules. An example would be the Codes of Practice issued by ACAS that define good employment practices and procedures.

rule maker (the State)
An employment relations role adopted by the State, in which it enacts legislation to create auxiliary, restrictive and regulatory rules of conformity for the parties in employment relations.

An organisation that fails to observe these Codes of Practice can be called to account in a court of law. There is also the *restrictive* function of the law, in which the State outlaws certain practices, such as child labour or racial discrimination in employment. Finally, there is the *regulative* function, in which the State establishes minimum standards for all citizens: for example, the national minimum wage.

It is important to note that the extent of these interventions varies over time, and often depends on the political ideologies of the government of the day. For example, the role of the State as *an employer* diminished greatly between 1980 and 1997, when public-sector employment declined year on year and whole industries were sold off through privatisation. However, since 1998 things have changed and public-sector employment has grown every year (Office for National Statistics, 2005). Moreover, the role of the State as a *protector* and *rule maker* has grown considerably since the election of the Labour government in 1997, with its support for European-led employee rights. In order to appreciate the variation in State intervention, and the way it has changed across the years, it is necessary to examine changes in the political philosophies of governments, and this is considered next.

Summary points

- In employment relations 'the State' is taken to mean the elected government and all other State agencies that carry out government policy and legislation.

- The objectives for State intervention tend to reflect the political priorities of government in terms of its economic and social goals for society as a whole.

- There are several ways in which the State can intervene in employment relations, including:
  - as an employer, paymaster and buyer
  - as an incomes regulator
  - as a manpower manager
  - as a protector
  - as a rule maker.

The changing nature of State intervention

Until the beginning of the last century the prevailing belief in Great Britain was that employers and employees were the best judges of what form their relationship should take. For the most part therefore, the State officially abstained from direct intervention in employment relations. However, this does not mean that it completely ruled out interventionist policies. Rather, it decided what aspects of the employment relationship were appropriate for intervention, and whether this should be of a direct or indirect nature. Since then, what has changed more than anything else is the definition of what constitutes an appropriate area for State intervention, and this in turn reflects very different government approaches towards employment relations. In explaining the changing nature of State intervention over time, Crouch (1982) considers two related variables: the existence of certain *dominant politico-economic philosophies*, and the development of *strong, autonomous trade unions* in a society. The way that these two variables interact can be plotted to give four characteristic patterns of State intervention, which are shown in Fig. 5.1.

corporatism
A state of affairs in which centralised economic activity dominates society, trade unions are relatively weak and subordinated by State control.

market individualism
A level of State intervention in employment relations synonymous with weak, unregulated trade unions and laissez-faire economic philosophies, in which the State supports ruling class interests and severely curtails trade union power.

Except for a very brief period in wartime, full **corporatism** has never really existed in Great Britain and is of little concern here. Suffice it to say that the corporate state is one that is associated with totalitarian regimes, and if trade unions are allowed to exist, they can become incorporated into the State apparatus. For Great Britain the story really starts with **market individualism**. This was the situation in Great Britain until the late nineteenth century. Trade unions were very weak and undeveloped, and the dominant economic philosophy was laissez-faire: a belief that market competition would encourage the strongest to rise and prosper. This, in turn, gave legitimacy to the existence of social inequalities. The employment relationship tended to be seen as an extension of the master and servant relationship and, while the

State avoided direct involvement in employment relations, its laws reinforced the social values of the ruling class, the most sacred of which were their property rights. Crucially, trade unions were only just inside the law and operated in a precarious way, which gave employers a free hand to be

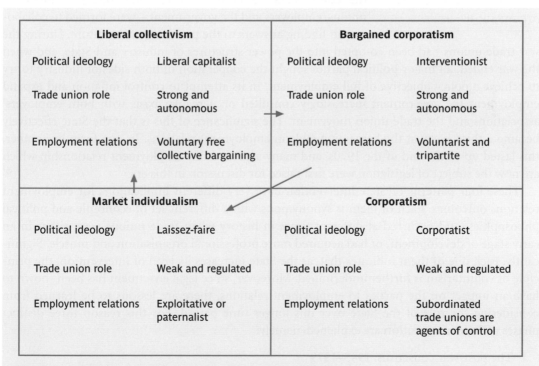

Figure 5.1 Variations of political intervention in employment relations
Source: adapted from Crouch, 1982.

highly exploitative. As Crouch points out, the whole thing subordinated workers to the control and authority of the owner, which at best was paternalistic, and most of the time was downright repressive. Thus, it was inherently unstable, and employees had a strong incentive to collectivise in order to redress their disadvantaged position.

The subsequent growth in union membership and a higher degree of professional organisation in union activities prompted the State to change its stance to one most easily described as *liberal collectivism*. In this the government philosophy remained essentially capitalist, although at the same time it recognised that there are competing interests in the employment relationship, and trade unions were afforded a greater role in articulating employee concerns. Realising that unions had a power resource at their disposal, namely their members, the State's role came to be seen as that of supporting a framework that encouraged the parties to find ways of voluntarily reconciling their differences. Under **liberal collectivism** therefore, it was possible for employees and unions to challenge managerial domination in a limited way, and in one form or another, this state of affairs continued for over half a century.

Shortly after the end of the Second World War a further development started to appear. This was **bargained corporatism**, in which there was a greater recognition of a plurality of interests in industry. While employment relations was considered to be mostly voluntarist at an organisational level, at a national level there was a strong emphasis on planning the future prosperity of the nation. Thus a number of tripartite bodies – involving unions, employers and the government – were formed to collaborate in finding answers to the problems of the future. During the war trade unions had been co-opted into the power structures of industry and State, and when the war ended, all major political parties sought the cooperation of both sides of industry to try to achieve a policy objective of full employment. In its attempt to control inflation and expand employment the government increasingly consulted on a regular basis with both employers' associations and the trade union movement. The significance of this is that the State effectively became a third party at the bargaining table in employment relations. In one form or another, this lasted up to the end of the 1970s, and many aspects of the employment relationship which are now the subject of legislation were first raised for discussion in this era.

These four patterns of State intervention have very different implications for employment relations outcomes. Each of them is synonymous with a different set of economic and political philosophies, and occurred at different times in history when trade unions were either in an early stage of development, or had acquired more professional organisation and muscle. Significantly, each one of them indicates that, as the State increases its level of intervention, the principle of voluntarism is further undermined. Moreover, since legal enactment has been shown to have an impact on the parties to employment relations, there are lessons to be learned from considering the role of the State over this longer time period. For this reason three distinct phases of State intervention are explained, namely:

1 The post-war consensus: 1945–1979

2 A return to market individualism: 1979–1997

3 The 'Third Way' agenda: post-1997

---

liberal collectivism

A level of State intervention in employment relations synonymous with the emergence of stronger and more autonomous trade unions under a liberal capitalist philosophy, in which the outcome is a legislative framework that encourages the legitimate interests of both parties.

bargained corporatism

A level of State intervention in employment relations synonymous with the existence of strong, autonomous trade unions and an interventionist philosophy on the part of the State, which involves the creation of tripartite national bodies who consult on a broad range of economic and social matters.

The post-war consensus: 1945–1979

While it is not the intention to provide a history lesson, a consideration of government approaches over a longer time period is necessary to understand the changing nature of State intervention. From the end of the Second World War governments of different political persuasions adapted broadly similar Keynesian economic objectives designed to manage the demand side of the economy in several ways. These included:

Keynesian (economics)

A macro-economic theory which concentrates on managing the demand side of the economy through government fiscal policies, with the aim of achieving full employment, price stability and a balance of payments equilibrium.

demand side (economics)

A macro-economic approach which seeks to stimulate the demand for goods in an economy, which is presumed to lead to an increase in employment and economic growth.

- the aim of achieving full employment and price stability
- stimulating economic demand through fiscal expenditure (and, where appropriate, lowering taxation)
- ensuring that the State should be a model employer
- supporting a voluntarist approach to employment relations
- supporting collective bargaining and trade union representation
- a commitment to involving the social partners in the formation of State policy (i.e. the TUC, employer associations and the government).

While the government of the day changed between Conservative and Labour during this period, all governments had a common purpose in terms of economic management and employment relations (Kessler and Bayliss, 1998). This era can be characterised as being similar to that of *bargained corporatism*, as described by Crouch. The role of the State was regarded as that of providing a general framework, which would enable the parties to engage in constructive dialogue. The full extent of the legislation during this period is beyond the scope of this chapter, although there are several developments that point towards a consensus-building approach on the part of the State, and these are briefly summarised in Table 5.1.

First, protective-type laws were enacted which not only gave employees legal rights at work, but also specified the obligations employers had towards their workers. For example, shortly after the war, powers were given to Wages Councils to protect workers in so-called 'sweated trades'. Thus, the legislation in 1946 and 1959 enabled Wages Councils not only to set basic pay rates for workers, but also to cover matters such as overtime pay and holidays. Other protective-type laws passed in this period are extremely significant for the conduct and behaviour of employment relations today. For example, the Race Relations Act 1976, the Sex Discrimination Act 1975 and the Equal Pay Act 1970 placed a statutory obligation on employers to outlaw discriminatory practices in employment (see Table 5.1).

Second, auxiliary-type legislation during the 1970s provided a role for ACAS as a State agency that helped the parties settle disputes through mediation. In addition, the State established tripartite bodies in which the TUC, employers' associations and the government consulted about a broad range of economic and social objectives. From this emerged a 'social contract', in which trade unions agreed to give assistance to the government in resolving some of the country's economic problems, and in return for union support, the government delivered a number of reforms to promote social and economic equality; the so-called 'social wage'.

However, the period was also plagued with economic and employment relations tensions, and the philosophy of *bargained corporatism* came under scrutiny. Despite the government's 'social contract' with the trade union movement, unemployment and wage demands continued to rise. The public sector came to be seen as the major culprit in what was continuing economic

Legislation	Matters covered
Wages Councils Act 1946 and 1959	■ Renamed Industrial Trade Boards, then Wages Councils ■ Extended their powers beyond the setting of basic pay, to include overtime pay and holidays
Prevention of Crime Act 1953	■ Contained clauses relating to the conduct of pickets during strikes
Industrial Training Act 1964	■ Established industrial tribunals as courts to deal with employment relations matters
Trade Disputes Act 1965	■ Provided union members with protection from employer threats when contemplating strike action
Equal Pay Act 1970 and 1975	■ Provisions to ensure equal pay for work of equal value ■ Allowed women to take a claim for pay discrimination to a tribunal
Industrial Relations Act 1971	■ Reduced trade union immunity during disputes by defining certain union practices and actions as unfair ■ Powers for Secretary of State to order a 'cooling-off' period if a dispute was likely to damage the economy ■ Statutory provisions for trade union recognition ■ Introduced an employee's right to claim unfair dismissal
Trade Union and Labour Relations Act 1974	■ Repealed most of the 1971 Industrial Relations Act provisions ■ Re-defined trade union immunities with respect to strikes and industrial disputes
Health and Safety at Work Act 1974	■ Introduced statutory obligations on employers and employees with respect to health and safety in the workplace ■ Provided statutory rights for trade union health and safety committee ■ Established the Health and Safety Commission (HSC) and Health and Safety Executive (HSE)
Employment Protection (Consolidation) Act 1975 and 1978	■ Established tripartite employment relations processes (i.e. including TUC, CBI and government) ■ Outlined the statutory role and provisions of ACAS ■ Entitlement to written particulars of employment contract ■ Time off work for public duties ■ Time off work for trade union duties
Sex Discrimination Act 1975	■ Provisions to outlaw sexual discrimination in employment practices (i.e. recruitment, pensions, promotion, training) ■ Established the Equal Opportunities Commission (EOC)
Race Relations Act 1976	■ Provisions to outlaw racial discrimination in employment practices (i.e. recruitment, promotion, training) ■ Established the Commission for Racial Equality (CRE)

Table 5.1 Major legislation during the period 1945–1979

instability and rising inflation, which in turn fuelled aspirations in private industry, the effect of which was a wave of major private-sector disputes, most of which resulted in significant wage rises (Thomson and Beaumont, 1978). This prompted an eruption in the public sector, which culminated in widespread industrial action; the so-called *1978–1979 Winter of Discontent*. On the back of this the Conservative government led by Margaret Thatcher came to power in 1979 with promises to 'roll back the frontiers of the State' and to curb trade union power.

A return to market individualism: 1979 – 1997

Between 1979 and 1997 successive Conservative governments systematically dismantled the consensus-building approach of the previous three decades. As a result, out went the Keynesian economic policies of the past, and in came monetarism, an economic theory based on the philosophies of *market individualism* described earlier in Fig. 5.1. The government argued that there was a natural level of unemployment, and for the market to operate effectively, supply-side constraints had to be removed, such as price controls or restrictive labour practices (Keegan, 1984). The most significant supply-side constraint was perceived to be trade unionism, and a number of radical policy objectives were adopted, which included:

monetarism

A right-wing economic theory which argues that self-regulation through market forces is the most efficient way to control inflation. In this trade unions are deemed to be a supply-side constraint, and so their activities need to be systematically weakened and curbed by the State.

supply side (economics)

A set of macro-economic policies designed to eradicate presumed market constraints in managing prices, income, employment and economic growth.

- the private sector, not the State, being viewed as the best model employer
- abandoning the objective of full employment, and instead seeking to combat inflation by controlling the money supply (prices and wages)
- abolishing the tripartite employment relations system (i.e. excluding the TUC and CBI from government policy formulation)
- the privatisation of nationalised industries to enable them to compete in a free-market environment
- weakening trade unions so that the market could operate freely.

Several strategies underpinned the government's approach to employment relations during this period. The first was an outright attack on the public sector (Seifert and Ironside, 2001), because in the eyes of the government, these workers were responsible for a wave of strikes during the so-called 'Winter of Discontent' of 1978–1979. As a result, the government immediately sought efficiencies in wages and labour utilisation among teachers, local government workers, the civil service and in nationalised industries. One of the more enduring aspects of the government's approach in this respect was the privatisation of whole industries, such as British Telecom, British Gas, British Airways and British Rail. In what remained of the public sector, a range of free-market initiatives were also introduced, which further destabilised public sector employment; for example, Compulsory Competitive Tendering (CCT) allowed private-sector contractors to bid for local authority work. Consequently, it was no longer deemed a responsibility of the State to be a model employer, but instead the private sector was promoted as a shining example for a new era of non-union employment relations.

Second, and perhaps the most visible strategy of the State, was to weaken trade unionism, and in this respect the government practised what it preached, when in 1989 it outlawed trade union membership at the Government Communications Headquarters (GCHQ). Overall, the government adopted what can be described as a 'step-by-step ratchet approach' to legal intervention. Significantly, this stands in stark contrast to the wholesale legal reform of previous governments (1945–1979). For example, the ill-fated Industrial Relations Act of 1971 set out to completely reform collective labour law, and had it succeeded in its aims, it would have imposed on British industrial relations many of the features of the American system: that is, collective agreements would have become legally enforceable unless they included, among other things, a specific disclaimer clause to the contrary (Weekes *et al.*, 1975). This wholesale legal approach of previous governments enabled unions (and employers) to coordinate their opposition against the 1971 Industrial Relations Act, whereas since 1979 such resistance has been considerably more difficult as the government passed, on average, one major piece of statutory legislation every two years (Ackers *et al.*, 1996).

It was this 'drip-drip' approach to legal reform during the 1979–1997 era which made it more difficult to mobilise a counter-offensive, especially for the trade unions. For example, the employment laws of 1980, 1982, 1984, 1988 and 1990 restricted union activities and the capability of employees to take industrial action (see Table 5.2). The 1982 Employment Act limited the scope for trade unions to claim immunity from prosecution during disputes; the 1988 Act forced unions to elect their leaders by postal ballot; and the 1990 Employment Act made unions legally responsible for the actions of their members. Even after a decade of systematic legal intervention the government's attack on trade unionism never abated. For instance, the 1993 Trade Union Reform and Employment Rights Act placed further restrictions on union activities: a Commissioner with powers to assist individual union members to take their union to court was established; written permission had to be obtained from every union member to have their union subscriptions deducted from their salaries; and additional procedures were applied to any union that wanted to engage in lawful industrial action (see Table 5.2).

Finally, in line with the philosophy of *market individualism*, laws were passed which limited or removed individual employee protections, and this in turn provided employers with a greater degree of freedom to alter the employment relationship. For example, the Employment Act 1982 made it easier for an employer to dismiss workers, because the qualifying period to claim unfair dismissal was increased from one to two years' continuous employment (see Table 5.2). In addition, changed Industrial Tribunal Regulations in 1984 placed new burdens of proof on employees when claiming unfair dismissal. Moreover, Conservative governments took little interest in the development of individual rights derived from the European social model. In 1989 the government refused to sign the *Social Charter* on fundamental rights for workers under the Maastricht Treaty (1992), and in so doing excluded British workers from a set of employment rights available to employees in all other European member states (Collins, 2001). In summing up the effect of these radical State interventions at the time, one commentator remarked that 'if it were not for the Clean Air Act, the government would reintroduce child chimney sweeps' (Keegan, 1991).

The 'Third Way' agenda: post-1997

The election of the Labour government in 1997 marked a further shift in the direction of the State's intervention policies for employment relations. Speaking at the TUC's annual conference shortly before the election in 1997, Tony Blair summed up the values of the Labour government vis-à-vis trade unions as 'fairness not favours'. The approach was labelled

Legislation	Matters covered
Employment Act 1980	■ Employers able to take legal action against individual employees who were believed to be engaged in unlawful industrial action ■ Removed immunity for those engaging in secondary industrial action
Employment Act 1982	■ Disputes could only relate 'wholly or mainly' to terms and conditions of employment or bargaining machinery ■ Definition of a trade dispute revised, so that immunity for unions narrowed ■ The qualifying period for an individual to claim unfair dismissal extended from 1 to 2 years' continuous employment ■ Industrial action to compel union membership or trade union recognition made unlawful ■ Rescinded 'fair wages' resolutions of House of Commons (1891 onwards) which obliged government contractors to observe terms and conditions no less favourable than those agreed by trade unions and employers in a locality
Trade Union Act 1984	■ Political fund ballots to be conducted at least once every ten years if a union seeks to pursue political objectives ■ Introduced secret ballots for election of union executive council members ■ Trade union liability for damages established, enabling unions to be sued for unlawful industrial action
Industrial Tribunal Regulations 1985	■ Burden of proof about the 'reasonableness' of unfair dismissal placed equally on employer and employee, and no longer solely on employer
Wages Act 1986	■ Powers for wage councils to set wage levels for workers under 21 years of age abolished ■ Truck Acts (1831–1840) rescinded to allow employers to make cashless wage payments and deductions from an individual's salary
Sex Discrimination Act 1986	■ Extended range of areas to protect individuals from discrimination in: dismissal, promotion or demotion, retirement and training ■ Amended Equal Pay Act 1970, under same provisions
Employment Act 1988	■ Industrial action to enforce union membership made unlawful ■ Commissioner for Trade Union Rights established, with powers to support individual union members who: want to prevent industrial action by union where there has been no ballot; inspect union accounts; or pursue a grievance against the union in a court of law ■ Requirement for unions to elect leaders (general secretaries/presidents) by secret ballot *continued*

Table 5.2 Major legislation during the period 1979–1996

Legislation	Matters covered
Employment Act 1990	■ Trade unions made liable for all industrial action, unless measures taken to repudiate the action ■ Legal right for employers to dismiss an individual engaged in unofficial industrial action, with no right to claim unfair dismissal ■ Industrial action in support of other employees dismissed for taking unofficial industrial action made illegal
Trade Union Reform and Employment Rights Act 1993	■ Established a Commissioner for Protection Against Unlawful Industrial Action. The Commissioner to assist members of the public in the High Court who attempt to prevent unlawful industrial action ■ Introduced legal provisions to ensure ballots for industrial action; ballots to use postal methods ■ Requirement of union to give employer seven days' written notice prior to commencement of official industrial action ■ Requirement for trade unions to obtain written permission from individual members to have union subscriptions deducted from their salaries

Table 5.2 Continued

a 'Third Way' agenda, in which it is assumed that the State has a responsibility not only to promote economic competitiveness and labour market flexibility, but also to support social justice at the workplace, and in this respect, a number of policy objectives were adopted:

■ Improve competitiveness and innovation in industry by encouraging partnership, flexibility and high performance in industry

■ Improve employee skills and adaptability

■ Promote a policy for work–life balance

■ Establish a floor of individual employee rights (rather than general immunities for trade unions) by supporting the European social model.

One of the first steps, which signalled a new era of State intervention, was the government's adoption of the *Social Charter* for workers' rights, as contained in the Maastricht Treaty, which was signed in 1998 (the Conservative government had refused to sign this a decade earlier). The net result was that individual workers in Britain could now expect support and protection for twelve fundamental employment rights (see Exhibit 5.1). In addition, the ban on trade union membership at GCHQ was revoked, and a Low Pay Commission created to investigate and report on a national minimum wage (DTI, 2002).

national minimum wage

A statutory minimum rate of pay for all workers and trainees in Britain, which is changed periodically on recommendations from an independent Low Pay Commission.

Some of the main legal interventions establishing these fundamental rights in British law are summarised in Table 5.3, and one of the first laws passed was the National Minimum Wage Act (1998), which established a legal right to a **national minimum wage** for all workers (see Table 5.3). Significantly, the minimum hourly rate was set at a level calculated to avoid damaging the competitive standing of British industry, especially for

- Freedom of movement between EU member states
- Adequate protection for remuneration and employment
- Improvement to working conditions
- Adequate social security and social protection
- The right to join or not to join a trade union (freedom of association)
- Adequate and on-going vocational and job-based training
- Equality of treatment for men and women
- Rights to information, consultation and participation in workplace issues
- Adequate heath and safety at work
- Protection of children and young people at work
- Protection against age discrimination in employment (access for elderly people to labour market participation)
- Protection against disability discrimination in employment (access for disabled people for labour market participation)

Exhibit 5.1 Fundamental rights for workers under the Social Charter of the Maastricht Treaty
Source: adapted from Rose, 2004.

smaller firms who are more constrained by tight labour costs (Metcalf, 1999). Arguably the most significant legal intervention by the State since 1997 was the passing of the Employment Relations Act 1999, which provided for the first time in Britain a set of new rights and obligations in employment: for instance, new maternity and paternity rights; statutory mechanisms for trade union recognition; a renewed role for ACAS; and a reduction in the qualifying period from two years to one year for an employee to be able to claim unfair dismissal (Wedderburn, 2001).

Subsequent legislation in 2002 and 2004 extended further the philosophy of balancing social justice for employees while encouraging competitiveness and flexibility. For example, the 2002 Employment Act required employers to 'seriously consider' the option of flexible working arrangements for employees with childcare responsibilities, established the right to extended (unpaid) maternity leave, and set out the legal status for trade union learning representatives to be able to bargain about employee skills and training needs (see Table 5.3). Among other things, the 2004 Employment Relations Act also clarified the definition of a bargaining unit for the purposes of collective bargaining and trade union recognition, and the Pensions Act 2004 established the requirement for substantial change to a company's pension to be first approved (following consultation) by representatives of the scheme's members (i.e. with employee representatives).

In addition to the legislation summarised in Table 5.3, the practice of making greater use of *statutory instruments* has been adopted by the State. These deal with the many employment regulations contained in European directives: for example, the 1998 Working Time Regulations which set maximum working hours, rest periods and holidays for employees (Böheim and Taylor, 2003). Other regulations include comparable rights for part-time and fixed-term employees with those of full-time workers. Additional regulations are those that confer rights on people in employment who are over 65 years of age, to give protection against unfair dismissal and provide for redundancy payments (Dickens *et al.*, 2005).

Legislation	Matters covered
National Minimum Wage Act 1998	■ Established a statutory basis for the Low Pay Commission ■ Set the first national minimum wage rate
Public Interest Disclosure Act 1998	■ Employee protection from dismissal established for disclosing information that is deemed to be in the public interest, for example, health and safety concerns or an employer failing to comply with legal requirements
Employment Relations Act 1999	■ Reduction in qualifying period to claim unfair dismissal from 2 to 1 year's service ■ 18 weeks' maternity leave ■ Statutory right to unpaid parental leave of 3 months for all employees ■ Statutory trade union recognition provisions ■ Restricted employer discrimination on the basis of union or non-union membership ■ Revised the role and duties of ACAS
Learning and Skills Act 2000	■ Established the Learning and Skills Council (LSC) for post-16 education and training (excludes higher education)
Employment Act 2002	■ Revised maternity leave provisions of 6 months' paid and 6 months' unpaid for mothers (2 weeks' paid paternity leave for fathers) ■ Sets out minimum standards for organisational discipline and grievance procedures ■ Rights for fixed-term workers ■ Obligation for employers to 'seriously consider' requests from parent employees for flexible working arrangements ■ Statutory roles, duties and time off with pay for trade union learning representatives
Pensions Act 2004	■ Requires an employer to consult about pension scheme changes with pension scheme member representatives, including employee and/or union representatives
Employment Relations Act 2004	■ Clarifies and defines an 'appropriate bargaining unit' for the purpose of collective bargaining for trade union recognition ■ Provides rights of access for the purpose of trade union recognition ballots ■ Provides employee protection from detrimental action in circumstances relating to union membership ■ Outlaws the practice of employer offering inducements not to be a member of a trade union ■ Rights for employees to be accompanied by a trade union officer or fellow worker at non-trivial disciplinary and grievance hearings

continued

Table 5.3 Major legislation during the period since 1997

Legislation	Matters covered
Transfer of Undertakings (Protection of Employment) Regulations 2006	■ Provisions have been widened to cover cases where services are outsourced, insourced or assigned to a new contractor, where such service provision is provided on an 'on-going' basis ■ The regulations do not apply to 'one-off' service provisions ■ There is a duty on the old employer (the transferor) to supply information about employees being transferred to the new employer (the transferee employer) ■ Provisions clarify the ability of employers and employees to agree to modify employment contracts where a transfer occurs ■ Provisions specify that it is unfair for an employer to dismiss employees for reasons connected with a transfer ■ Employee representatives of the employees affected have the right to be informed and consulted about a prospective transfer

Table 5.3 Continued

Pause for reflection

In your own words, explain whether the Labour government's approach to employment relations intervention is fundamentally different from that of the previous era of market individualism (1979–1996), or are there any strong similarities?

Despite these legal interventions since 1997, there are a number of criticisms of the government's approach to employment regulation in Britain. First, in practical terms, it has been found that many employees simply cannot afford to take unpaid maternity leave, and some employers still treat part-time workers less favourably than their full-time counterparts (Houston and Marks, 2003). A result of this is that many employees find they work excessively long hours, despite regulations to the contrary (DTI, 2004). A second criticism is from the trade union movement, which feels 'let down' by the Labour government (Wood *et al.*, 2003). The main concern here is that many of the anti-union laws of the previous Conservative government remain on the statute books, particularly those that affect ballots and industrial action. Finally, it has been argued that the Labour government's 'Third Way' agenda is simply an extension of Conservative neo-liberal ideologies which underpins market individualism (Callinicos, 2001). For example, privatisation, labour market flexibility, compulsory competitive tendering and the outsourcing of many public-sector jobs all remain a central plank of the Labour government's employment relations agenda. For this reason, it has been argued that Labour's attempt to balance the needs of business efficiency with employee justice has meant that the government has 'annoyed everyone and protected only the few' (Gennard, 2002). Arguably, Labour's claim to promoting 'fairness at work' is questionable, as the government has had a consistent record of opposing some of the major employment law interventions at a European level, such as the protected rights to working time and information and consultation.

Notwithstanding these concerns, it needs to be recognised that the role of the State in employment relations is now very different from what it was in the past. There now exist very different employment rights in Britain, such as the national minimum wage, extended paternity leave, statutory union representation and employee consultation. Indeed, given the plethora of European regulations that will require transposing into British law in the decades ahead, future developments of this type are virtually inevitable. Therefore, the next section explains how such regulations are transposed, and how employment law operates in Great Britain.

Summary points

■ Variations in State intervention can be assessed according to two variables: *dominant politico-economic ideologies* and the *role of trade unions*, and these give rise to four characteristic patterns of State intervention:
- Corporatism
- Market individualism
- Liberal collectivism
- Bargained corporatism.

■ From the above scheme, three distinct phases of State intervention can be described in Britain:
- The period 1945–1979 – voluntary consensus
- The period 1979–1997 – a resurgence in market individualism
- Post-1997 to the present – a Third-Way agenda, based on balancing market competition and individual social justice.

The law in employment relations

An overview of sources

The laws that influence employment relations come from a number of different sources, and a fundamental distinction that can be made is between *criminal* and *civil* law. **Criminal law** deals with unlawful acts that are offences against the public at large: for example, theft of an employer's property by an employee, or an employer's wilful neglect of the health and safety of its employees. In contrast, **civil law** deals with the rights of private citizens, and their conduct towards each other (a corporation being regarded as an individual person in the eyes of the law). The most significant laws affecting employment relations are civil laws, although there are elements of criminal law which have some relevance.

The most important source of civil law is **statute law**, which comes into existence when the government of the day introduces legislation in Parliament, which is passed by both houses and receives royal assent. Sometimes, however, an Act makes provision for a government minister to modify or update the details of a law through a **statutory instrument**. In addition,

criminal law
Deals with unlawful acts that are offences against the public at large.

civil law
Deals with the rights of private citizens and their conduct towards each other.

statute laws
Laws that are passed by Parliament and have received royal assent.

statutory instrument
A device used by a minister of the government to change or update legislation that already exists.

European law
Directives and regulations passed by the European Parliament, which are then transposed into British statute law.

common law
Laws that arise from legal decisions made in a court of law or an employment tribunal.

European law has increasingly had a major impact in Britain, and the most important sources are *European directives*. For convenience, *statutory instruments* and *European Law* can be regarded as part of statute law.

Another important source of law in employment relations is **common law**, which results from decisions made by judges and by tribunals, which then creates binding precedents on judgements in subsequent cases.

Pause for reflection

In your own words, briefly define each of the six sources of law that can affect employment relations in Britain.

A typology of employment relations law

In law, employees and organisations are both treated as individuals in their own right, and either one can be taken to law in a criminal prosecution or a civil lawsuit. While the laws affecting employment relations are diverse, they all have one thing in common: they all serve to regulate relationships of some sort. Thus they can all be placed into one or more of five categories according to the relationships that they influence. These are shown in Fig. 5.2.

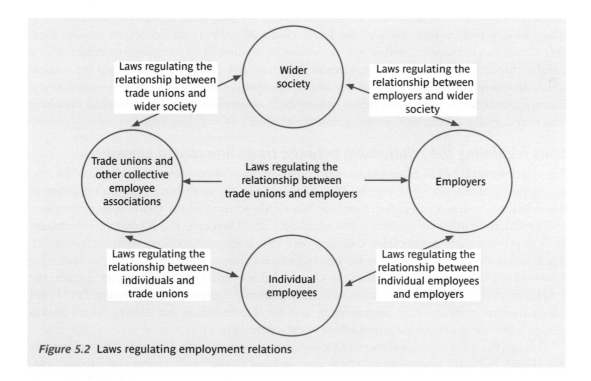

Figure 5.2 Laws regulating employment relations

Laws regulating the relationship between individual employees and employers

In Chapter 1 it was explained that the law assumes that the relationship between an employee and his/her employer is an individual one. For that reason, the main body of law that is relevant here is that affecting the contract of employment. Examples include the Health and Safety at Work Act (1974); Race Relations Act (1976); Employment Protection (Consolidation) Act (1987); the Employment Acts of 1980, 1988, 1999, 2002 and 2004; and the Transfer of Undertaking (Protection of Employment) Regulations, 1981, 1998 and 2004.

Because the contract of employment can never be so specific that it details every possible contingency for the future, the laws in this area have been subject to considerable on-going amendment. One example is the Transfer of Undertakings (Protection of Employment) Regulations (TUPE), which was introduced in Britain as a result of the European Acquired Rights Directive. Its purpose is to protect the rights and conditions of workers should a company merge or change ownership. Problematically, the original Directive failed to define a transfer, and so a number of contradictory court rulings appeared (see Case 5.1). Thus, in 2006 the government had to clarify the issue by amending the original law with a revised set of TUPE Regulations. The effect of TUPE is to preserve the continuity of employment conditions for those employees who may be transferred to a new employer when a relevant transfer or service provision occurs. With the exception of some occupational pension rights, this effectively means that, when the jobs of employees are transferred to a different employer, their terms and conditions remain the same. However, the regulations do not prohibit the old or new employer varying employment conditions with the employees' (or their representatives') agreement (DTI, 2006).

Laws regulating the relationship between individuals and their trade unions

In this area there exist legal provisions that define the obligations of trade unions towards their members. Most of these have been introduced since 1979, and were arguably designed to frustrate union activities. For example, the Trade Union Act (1984) forced unions to elect their executive councils by postal ballot, and to confirm by a ballot of all members the existence of a political fund. In addition, the Employment Relations Act (1988) made it illegal for a trade union to discipline its members for breaching the union's rules. This act also established a Commissioner for Trade Union Rights, whose main objective is to assist individual members who may consider taking legal action against their union.

Laws regulating the relationship between trade unions and employers

The relationship between trade unions and employers has always been constrained by the law, usually to the disadvantage of unions. This is because the law accords a paramount position to the individual contract of employment, and takes little account of the fact that many employment relations matters are essentially collective in nature. Therefore, much labour law in Britain aims to prevent trade unions from cutting across what is deemed to be an individual contract. Again this is an area in which there has been significant change since 1979, and most laws have remained on the statute book under the current Labour government. Examples include the Employment Act (1980) which makes secondary picketing illegal; the Employment Act (1982) which outlaws a closed-shop arrangement; and the Trade Union Act (1984), which makes unions liable for unofficial industrial action by their members.

Perhaps the most significant piece of legislation in this area originates in the Trades Disputes Act (1906), the main provisions of which were updated in the Trade Union and Labour Rela-

Case study 5.1: **Contradictory TUPE legal interpretations**

Brookes v *Borough Care Services Ltd* and *CLS Care Services Ltd* [IRLR 636, 1998]
In this case Wigan Council decided to transfer the running of care homes for the elderly to the voluntary sector. There were 335 employees who worked for a company established by Wigan Council, CLS Ltd. A transfer occurred by transferring the shares of CLS Ltd, along with the same directors, to Borough Care Services Ltd. The court ruled that since there had been no change as to who the employer was, in this case the directors, there had not been a transfer.

Suzën v *Zehnacker Gebäudereinigung* [IRLR 255, 1997]
In this case a school transferred a cleaning contract from one contractor to another, and Suzën was not offered work with the new contractor, claiming her employment should have been protected by the TUPE regulations. The European Court of Justice (ECJ) ruled that as there was no transfer of an 'entity', which includes assets and/or a majority of a workforce and their skills, but only those of an 'activity' (i.e. the cleaning of a school), there had been no transfer. The ruling meant there was considerable uncertainty as to whether the TUPE regulations apply in cases which involve a transfer of only labour-intensive activities.

ECM Ltd v *Cox* [IRLR 559, 1999]
However, in another case there was a change of contractor who ran a car-delivery contract. In this case there was no transfer of tangible assets or employees or their skills, but the Court of Appeal upheld that there was a transfer, implying that labour-only activities do fall under TUPE. The court ruled that the employer could not escape TUPE by failing to take on the previous contractor's workforce.

Questions

1 For each case above, describe the reason for the court's judgement.

2 Explain why these three cases seem to provide contradictory interpretations of the TUPE regulations.

---

tions (Consolidation) Act (1992) (TULRCA). This Act stipulates that while employees engaging in industrial action are in breach of their contracts of employment, and the trade union involved in organising the action is, in effect, inducing a breach of contract, they are granted a degree of (**trade union**) **immunity** from prosecution. For a trade union to qualify for the immunity certain conditions have to be met, and these are known as the *Golden Formula* (see Exhibit 5.2). To this end, Section 219(1)a of the TULRCA states that as long as industrial action taken is in contemplation or furtherance of a **trade dispute** (defined as a dispute between workers and their employing organisation), then a union is protected from legal prosecution for inducing its members to breach their employment contracts. However, interpreting what is, and what is not, a legitimate trade dispute can be quite complex. For example, when UNISON members at University College Hospital in London voted overwhelmingly in favour of strike action in 1999, the Court of Appeal held that the intended dispute would not be legal, because employees were seeking employment guarantees

trade union immunity

A convention that protects a trade union from prosecution for inducing its members to breach their individual employment contracts when engaging in strike or other similar industrial action.

trade dispute

A dispute between workers and their employing organisation, which complies with Section 219(1)a of the TULRCA 1992 (i.e. the *Golden Formula*).

A trade dispute is defined as a dispute between workers and the employing organisation, and which relates wholly or mainly to one or more of the following:

■ Terms and conditions of employment, including physical conditions and the reasonableness of an employer's instructions about work

■ The engagement or non-engagement, or termination or suspension of employment, or the duties of one or more workers

■ The allocation of work or the duties of employment between workers or groups of workers

■ Matters of discipline

■ The membership or non-membership of a trade union, excluding compulsory conditions of union membership (i.e. to enforce a closed shop)

■ Facilities for trade union representatives and officials

■ The machinery for negotiation or consultation, or other arrangements relating to the above matters

Exhibit 5.2 The meanings of a trade dispute (the 'Golden Formula')
Source: adapted from Lewis and Sargeant, 2004: 261.

in a new hospital that would be created in the government's Private Finance Initiative (PFI). Here the court held that the dispute was not concerned with the terms and conditions of employees at the existing NHS Trust, but was in fact connected with the future employment conditions of prospective employees, who would work in the new hospital when it opened. Therefore the industrial action was deemed to be outside the conditions specified in the *Golden Formula* (Lewis and Sargeant, 2004).

In many ways the UNISON example is indicative of the way that the goalposts have been moved by the State in order to make it more difficult for a union to sanction or organise industrial action. In addition to the 'Golden Formula' summarised in Exhibit 5.2, there are many other legal hurdles a union must overcome. For example, it must ballot its members; it must ensure the employer agrees to the wording on the ballot paper; and following the result of a ballot, it must provide the employer with at least seven days' written notice prior to the commencement of any industrial action. Failure to comply with these conditions could result in a union's finances being sequestrated by the courts, and needless to say there are nowhere near as many reciprocal obligations on an employer who decides to lock out workers, close a factory or move part of its operations to another part of the world.

Laws regulating the relationship between trade unions and wider society

For the most part the law in this area is aimed at ensuring that the actions of trade unions do not affect the well-being of society at large. Therefore, it is an area in which certain aspects of criminal law are relevant. For example, the Conspiracy and Protection of Property Act (1875) contained clauses pertaining to the orderly conduct of pickets during industrial disputes. Similarly, public order measures during strike action were introduced in the Prevention of Crime Act (1953); the Criminal Law Act (1977); and in the Public Order Act (1986). In addition, the powers of the police to tackle public disorder were strengthened after the miners' strike of 1985–1986, and the TULRCA (1992) lists potential criminal actions when pickets use abusive or threatening behaviour or obstruct the police in their duties (Lewis and Sargeant, 2004). Arising from this legislation there is now a government *Code of Practice on Picketing*, which gives guidelines recommending that the number of pickets at a workplace entrance or exit should not normally exceed six.

Laws regulating the relationship between employers and wider society

The legislation in this area falls mainly into two categories. First, there is a huge volume of company law which regulates the activities of firms as corporate entities, some of which is part of the field of criminal law and designed to protect shareholders against fraud or malpractice. Second, there are laws which regulate to some extent the responsibilities of organisations towards the general public. For example, Section 3 of the Health and Safety at Work Act (1974) imposes a duty on employers to ensure that members of the public are not at risk: for instance, a person entering a hospital or shopping at a local supermarket. In other commercial activities there can be strong employment relations implications: for example, when there is a company merger or takeover, the TUPE regulations mean that contractual employment conditions may have to be transferred to the new owner.

Pause for reflection

Review the legislation summarised in Tables 5.1, 5.2 and 5.3, and then identify at least two specific laws that regulate each of the five relationships described in the model in Fig. 5.2.

How the law operates

This section briefly describes how the various courts and institutions deal with employment law cases in England and Wales (Northern Ireland and Scotland have a slightly different legal system). The British legal system has a hierarchical structure, shown in Fig. 5.3, and the general principle is that attempts are always made to resolve a case at the lowest level possible. Only when a decision is not accepted by the parties, or it is beyond the jurisdiction of a lower-level court, does it pass to the next one.

The key institutions of employment relations law

Criminal cases involve prosecution by an agency of the State such as the police or one of the various employment relations commissions. For example, health and safety violations can be brought by the Health and Safety Executive (HSE) and dealt with in a magistrates' or crown court, and can result in prohibition orders, fines or plant closure if they are ignored. Prosecutions can also be brought by the police for obstruction, assault, and public-order offences that may occur during industrial disputes.

criminal case

A legal prosecution brought to either the magistrates' or crown court by an agency of the State, such as the police or one of the various employment relations commissions.

employment tribunal

A legal court that adjudicates on employment law cases.

Civil cases are progressed through one of two general routes that deal with cases brought by individual employees or organisations. An employment tribunal is a legal court that adjudicates almost exclusively on employment relations cases. Tribunals were first established as 'industrial tribunals' under the Industrial Training Act (1964). Since then their legal jurisdiction has been greatly extended, and their name was changed to 'employment tribunals' in the Employment Rights (Dispute Resolution) Act (1998). From their inception they were designed to be less threatening than other British courts, mainly because cases are brought by individual employees, who often lack the detailed knowledge of how the British legal system works. Employment tribunal cases are heard by three members: a legally qualified chairperson appointed by the Lord Chancellor, plus two lay

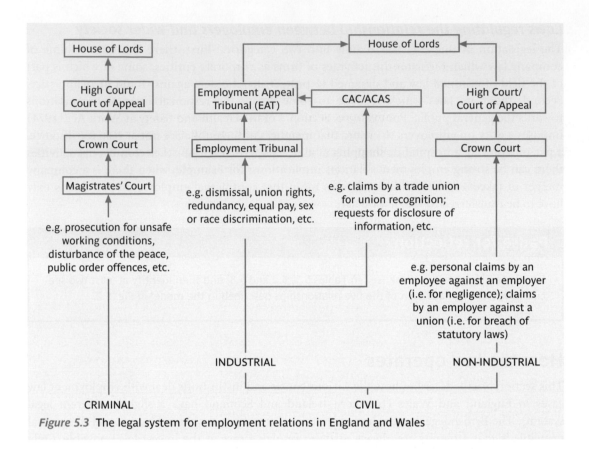

Figure 5.3 The legal system for employment relations in England and Wales

members – one nominated from employers' associations and the other selected from a panel nominated by the TUC. While the two lay members of the tribunal are required to have expertise in workplace employment relations issues, they are not legally qualified. Nor are they repre-

employment appeals tribunal
A higher legal court that deals with appeals from employment tribunals.

sentatives of their nominating organisation. Employment tribunals are bound by the decisions of higher courts, such as the *high court* and **employment appeals tribunal (EAT)**. The latter hears appeals on points of law from tribunals, or on matters arising from a decision of the Certification Officer. They are composed of a high court judge, and up to four people nominated by the TUC and the CBI. The parties can be represented by anyone of their choosing, and for the employee this often includes a trade union officer, a union-appointed solicitor, or the Citizens Advice Bureau (CAB).

non-industrial civil courts
Courts that deal with an array of other employment-related matters, such as claims of negligence against an employer or injunctions seeking to restrain union action.

Non-industrial civil courts deal with a vast array of issues: for example, claims for compensation for injury resulting from an allegation of negligence would be handled in this way. It is also the route that would be used by an employer seeking to restrain a trade union from taking industrial action, and in these situations employers typically go directly to the high court.

The Advisory, Conciliation and Arbitration Service (ACAS)

The Advisory, Conciliation and Arbitration Service (ACAS) is an independent body established by Parliament in 1975, and has its origins in the passing of the Industrial Relations Act (1971), when both trade unions and employers called for an independent conciliation and arbitration service to be established. It has a general duty to improve employment relations by advising employers, unions and individuals on their rights and obligations, and its functions are to help settle any potential or on-going industrial disputes (ACAS, 2005b).

However, ACAS has a whole series of other related responsibilities which merit attention. As its name indicates, conciliation is one of the most important functions of ACAS. Where a collective dispute exists or is likely to exist, ACAS can provide advice and assistance to help bring about a resolution, either at the request of one or more parties, or of its own volition. In around 94 per cent of the collective disputes using the services of ACAS, conciliation has been successfully used to bring about a resolution (Lewis and Sargeant, 2004). ACAS also offers conciliation in cases where individual employees have complained to an employment tribunal. Indeed, ACAS is automatically informed of these cases and, in the interests of expediency, must try to settle them before they are heard by a tribunal.

conciliation
Advice and assistance to help resolve a collective or individual dispute.

A second service is that of mediation: a process in which a potential solution to a dispute is recommended by ACAS to the parties. With mediation, however, the parties still carry on negotiating in order to work out the details of a settlement. Arbitration is another important ACAS service, in which an arbitrator is appointed to set the terms of a settlement. Arbitration has to be at the request of at least one party, and at the express consent of both. Here it should be noted that ACAS is obliged to first consider whether the dispute may be settled through conciliation or mediation, before moving to arbitration. It does not arbitrate itself, since this would affect its ability to conciliate. Rather, it appoints an arbitrator or arbitration panel.

mediation
A process in which the mediator recommends a potential solution to a dispute for the parties to consider.

arbitration
A process in which an arbitrator or arbitration panel is appointed to set the terms of a settlement to a dispute.

In addition to these highly visible activities, ACAS provides a range of *advisory services* for both employers and trade unions, and again these are highly valued by both parties. ACAS produces *Approved Codes of Practice (ACOP)*, which can substitute as *statutory instruments*, and conformance with them can be taken into account during a case at an employment tribunal; for example, in relation to an organisation's dismissal or grievance procedures. ACAS also undertakes inquiries and investigations in an attempt to improve employment relations in specific industries or firms. Finally, it also undertakes a good deal of *research*, either directly or commissioned from others, to provide commentaries on new and current issues relating to the nature of British employment relations.

Pause for reflection

In your own words, briefly distinguish between the functions of 'conciliation, mediation and arbitration' in employment relations.

The Central Arbitration Committee (CAC)

In addition to arbitration requests received directly from the parties to a dispute, cases can also be referred to the *Central Arbitration Committee (CAC)* from ACAS. The CAC is comprised of members appointed by the Secretary of State following consultations with ACAS. It has a legal chairperson, industry practitioners and academic experts drawn from the field of employment relations and personnel management. Like ACAS, the CAC is an independent body and is not subject to directions from a government minister (Lewis and Sargeant, 2004). It has a statutory obligation to make decisions in a number of specific areas: for example, where an employer fails to disclose information to a recognised trade union for the purpose of collective bargaining; to adjudicate in disputes concerning the establishment of a European Works Council; to establish the procedure or instigate a ballot on receipt of a request for trade union recognition; and to establish arrangements in relation to the Information and Consultation of Employees (ICE) Regulations, 2004. No court can overturn a CAC decision, unless there has been an error in law or it has exceeded its legal jurisdiction (Lewis and Sargeant, 2004).

Other State institutions

In addition to the courts of law involved in administering justice in employment law cases, there are a number of other State institutions that have an on-going role concerning the conduct and outcomes in employment relations.

The Certification Officer

The *Certification Officer* is responsible for maintaining a list of trade unions and employers associations. However, the powers of the Certification Officer extend far beyond the compilation of lists. The Employment Relations Act (1999) conferred powers on the Certification Officer to be able to act as an alternative to the courts where trade union members complained about a union breaching its rules. The Certification Officer also scrutinises union political activities; issues a certificate of union independence; oversees their rules and accounts; and handles disputes that may arise following a union merger or amalgamation. Appeals against the decisions of the Certification Officer can be made to the EAT, and only on questions of law or fact (Lewis and Sargeant, 2004).

The Equal Opportunities Commission (EOC), the Commission for Racial Equality (CRE) and the Disability Rights Commissioner (DRC)

These State agencies are closely related, and a number of British laws are affected by their activities: for example, discrimination in recruitment, selection, disability or religious belief. It is perhaps because of the overlap in their respective remit that the government plans to merge these agencies into a single statutory body in 2007: the Commission for Equality and Human Rights. While an individual or a trade union can bring a complaint to each of these bodies, it is only the relevant commission itself that can instigate legal proceedings where there have been pressures to discriminate (Lewis and Sargeant, 2004: 65). The EOC, CRE and DRC issue their own *Approved Codes of Practice*, which can be cited as examples of good practice in a case at an employment tribunal. Each of these State agencies has the power to investigate matters pertaining to their respective areas and, where necessary, issue non-compliance notices with penalties or initiate legal proceedings at an employment tribunal.

Health and Safety Executive (HSE) and the Health and Safety Commission (HSC)

These two State agencies are closely related and were established under the Health and Safety at Work Act (1974). The HSC is charged with carrying out research, providing advice, information and training in relation to health and safety at work, and submitting proposed regulations to the Secretary of State. The HSE exists to effect proposals and policy established by the HSC, and has an inspectorate to encourage good practice and enforce the law (Lewis and Sargeant, 2004). The legal powers of enforcing officers are quite extensive, ranging from entering an organisation to inspect its premises to the serving of a prohibition notice which, in serious cases, may mean the immediate closure of a company's premises. An employer can appeal to an employment tribunal against a prohibition notice.

Learning and Skills Council (LSC)

The *Learning and Skills Council* is charged with elevating the skills of all post-16-year-olds. It replaced the former Training and Enterprise Councils (TECs) in 2001, and is regionally based across Britain. While part of its remit is concerned with schools and sixth-form colleges, it is also responsible for encouraging work-based training programmes and establishing links between industry and education providers to help alleviate Britain's skills deficit. The LSC works toward the achievement of key learning targets set by government, and its aim is to improve both efficiency and skill levels across industry.

The Low Pay Commission (LPC)

A *Low Pay Commission* was established in Britain as a result of the National Minimum Wage Act (1998). Under the legislation the Secretary of State can refer matters to the LPC for consideration and review, and this body has been primarily responsible for recommending the national minimum wage rates for the UK. While it does not have a direct intervention role, the Inland Revenue is charged with ensuring that workers are paid according to the national minimum wage, with legal remedies determined at an employment tribunal.

Summary points

- Six principle sources of employment relations law exist: *criminal laws*; *civil laws*; *statutory laws*; *statutory instruments*; *European laws*; and *common laws*.
- These laws can regulate one of five aspects of the employment relationship:
  1 relations between employees and employers
  2 relations between individual employees and trade unions
  3 relations between trade unions and employers
  4 relations between trade unions and wider society, and
  5 relations between employers and wider society.
- In Britain, the law operates through a hierarchical court structure, as follows:
  - Employment Tribunal
  - Employment Appeal tribunal
  - High Court
  - House of Lords.
- In addition to the courts, there are a number of other State institutions that can regulate employment relations, such as ACAS, the CAC, EOC or the HSE.

Conclusions

By virtue of its law-making powers, the State is able to exert a significant influence on the relationship between an organisation and its employees. Indeed, legal intervention by the State has been a continually unfolding process, which has changed direction according to the political ideologies and philosophies of those in power. At the present time, the government has sought to pacify business concerns by supporting a number of free-market principles, but at the same time, it has embraced the spirit of fairness and social justice through a European-style social model, albeit with a degree of questioned acceptance.

Since the State is an influential player, its actions have clear implications for some of the topics already covered in the book, and those that will follow in subsequent chapters. For example, the rights of employees as defined by the contract of employment, which was explained in Chapter 1, have been extended and enhanced. Similarly, the role of trade unions has been legitimised with statutory union-recognition procedures, as explained in Chapter 4. Furthermore, the topics of discipline and grievance, redundancy and employee voice, which will be covered in Chapters 6 to 8, are also heavily influenced by important legal interventions. Finally, there are also legal aspects to the topics of collective bargaining, negotiation and conflict, and these will be covered in Chapters 9 to 11.

Review and discussion questions

1 How would you define the role of the State in employment relations?

2 Identify at least four specific ways in which the State can intervene and influence employment relations matters, other than by legal means.

3 How would you explain the variation in government approaches to employment relations intervention?

4 Distinguish between Keynesian and monetarist economic philosophies of the State.

5 Outline the main criticisms of the government's approach to employment relations intervention in the years 1949 to 1979.

6 How would you characterise the State's approach with regard to employment law intervention since 1997?

7 What are the six main sources of employment relations law in Britain?

8 Identify, and explain, some of the main laws that affect the relationship between a trade union and employers.

9 How does the law operate for employment relations matters in Britain?

10 In your own words, describe the functions and roles of ACAS and the CAC.

Further reading

Collins, H. (2001) 'Regulating the employment relationship for competitiveness', *Industrial Law Journal*, Vol. 30, pp. 17–47. A very readable analysis of the post-1997 Labour government's objectivities towards State intervention and the idea of social justice.

Crouch, C. (1982) *The Politics of Industrial Relations*, Fontana, London. Despite its date this is a penetrating and highly readable analysis of the growth of government intervention in employment relations in post-war Britain.

Dickens, L., M. Hall and S. Wood (2005) 'Review of research into the impact of employment relations legislation', *Employment Relations Research Series No. 45*, Department of Trade and Industry, London. An extensive review and summary of the main research studies that have sought to assess the impact of employment laws introduced by the post-1997 Labour government. Available from the DTI website: http://www.dti.gov.uk/er/errs_45.pdf.

DTI (2006) *Employment Rights on the Transfer of an Undertaking: A Guide to the 2006 TUPE Regulations for Employees, Employers and Representatives*, DTI, London. A useful and practical guide which explains the main provisions of the updated 2006 TUPE regulations.

Houston, D. and G. Marks (2003) 'The role of planning and workplace support in returning to work after maternity leave', *British Journal of Industrial Relations*, Vol. 41 (2), pp. 197–214. An empirically based research article which reports on limitations arising from government intervention in the area of extended maternity leave.

Lewis, D. and M. Sargeant (2004) *Essentials of Employment Law, 8th edn*, CIPD Publishing, London. A valuable resource guide with a comprehensive and practical coverage of numerous British employment laws.

Metcalf, D. (1999) 'The British national minimum wage', *British Journal of Industrial Relations*, Vol. 37, pp. 171–201. A paper that presents a concise and analytical review of national minimum wage in Britain.

Wedderburn, Lord (1986) *The Worker and the Law, 3rd edn*, Penguin, Harmondsworth. A seminal study that, despite its age, is highly recommended for its insightful and analytical coverage of the sources and philosophies of labour law, and especially for its extensive coverage of the topics of voluntarism versus state intervention.

Integrating parties and contexts in employment relations

2

Introduction

The purpose of these integrative chapters is to convey something of the dynamic and real nature of employment relations, and to show how many of the topics covered in the book are interconnected. In this, the second of these integrative chapters, the aim is more modest. It traces the ways in which contextual factors in employment relations can influence the three main parties, that is: *employers and managers; trade unions and other collective associations of employees;* and the *State.*

Each of the preceding three chapters dealt with one of these parties separately; however, they do not exist in isolation, but within a wider environment. Perhaps more important, they are interconnected in ways in which the actions of any one of them can affect the behaviour of the others. There are many different ways in which these links could be explained, but the simplest and most convenient is to consider the three parties in pairs, and trace some of the known linkages between them. To do this it is necessary for the State and its interventionist activities (which were described in Chapter 5) and the political-legal context of the environment (covered in Chapter 2) to be treated as the same thing, because employment relations laws can only be passed or modified by the government of the day. Nevertheless, for completeness, it is also necessary to trace the effects of other contexts (*economic, socio-ideological and technological*) on employers and managers and trade unions, and so these effects are treated separately. The interconnecting linkages are shown in Fig. I1, and there are two particular features of this model that should be noted. First, the State can exert some influence over environmental contexts, but this is not the case for either trade unions or employers and managers, who are only shown as connected by one-way influence arrows. Second, in some cases the parties are capable of influencing each other, and where this is the case, they are connected by double-headed arrows.

The effects of environmental contexts on the parties
The influences on employers and managers

The *economic context,* which embraces key features of the domestic and global economy such as labour market conditions, unemployment and international trade, is never far from the minds of employers and managers. As such, it tends to be a constant source of influence. However, its precise impact can be more apparent than real in some cases. Even though not engaged in international trade themselves, many managers tend to assume that globalisation is such a powerful and all-pervasive phenomenon that addressing it requires their urgent and sometimes drastic attention. For this reason, managers of firms often assume that economic pressures are always so pressing that it is necessary to conduct a near-continuous search for cheaper, more flexible

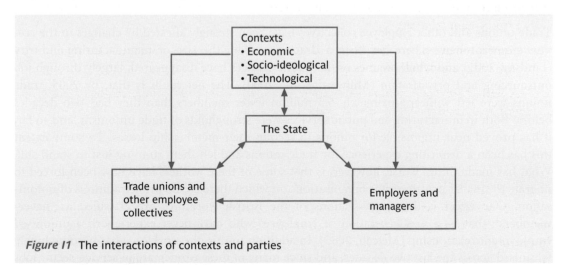

Figure I1 The interactions of contexts and parties

and productive ways of using employees. In some cases this has led to the adoption of 'flexible firm' techniques, such as core and periphery labour strategies (Atkinson and Meager, 1986). For similar reasons there has also been an increased use of temporary and atypical workforces, many of which have been sourced from external agency contractors but work alongside (core) employees in an organisation. These factors help explain why the boundaries between an employer and employee have become increasingly blurred and fragmented. One effect has been the displacement of what used to be more secure employment, as jobs are either outsourced to an external agency firm, or production facilities are moved to cheaper overseas markets, with consequences for employment levels in Great Britain.

The *socio-ideological context* of the environment is broadly reflective of the behavioural and cultural norms of Great Britain, and so far as this is concerned, British employers and managers retain many of their unitarist ideologies. In addition, many organisations are now small businesses, in which owner-managers have their own preferred styles of managing that are based on very informal practices. Even though the anti-union repressiveness of the 1980s and early 1990s has diminished, there is still a strong attempt by many managers to safeguard their perceived prerogatives. In these firms management is still probably confident enough to feel that it retains the upper hand in pushing through changes in work organisation, and even where employers and managers are tolerant of trade unions, it may well be because they feel that they can, if they wish, engage in union substitution and/or union suppression strategies at some other time.

The *technological context*, which reflects the choices that firms make about the technology that they use, has always been a highly influential factor. It can destroy some jobs and create others, and makes some work infinitely more controllable than before. New technology has been used to streamline work organisation, increase productivity and cut costs, while also providing managers with additional tools for job control and employee surveillance (Baldry, 2003). Since managers tend to regard the 'right to control' as one of their most sacred prerogatives (Findlay and McKinlay, 2003), the ability to do this has probably been welcomed with open arms. Moreover, new technology has facilitated the development of human resource information systems (HRIS), which has prompted a resurgence in the use of Taylorist scientific management techniques (Warhurst and Thompson, 1998).

The influences on trade unions and other collective employee associations

Trade unions and other employee collectives have been strongly affected by changes in the *economic* environment. There has been a dramatic fall in the size of manufacturing industry (Lindsay, 2003) and whole swathes of the public services have disappeared, largely through job outsourcing and privatisation (Millward *et al.*, 2000). The net result is that, by 2005, trade unions were left with approximately 6.5 million fewer members than they had two decades before. Both manufacturing and public services were strongholds of trade unionism, and so far, it has proved near impossible for unions to recoup their membership losses. To some extent this has been a dispiriting experience for trade unions and left them running just to stand still. What has made things worse, however, is that some of these workers have now been forced to migrate to smaller private-sector organisations, in which there are no prior traditions of unionisation. One effect is that large sections of the British workforce are classified as 'never-members': that is, a new generation of employees who have never experienced a unionised employment relationship (Metcalf, 2005). In addition to this, the workforce has become highly feminised across the last two decades, and since many of these women are in service-sector jobs that are low paid and low skilled, it is harder for unions to attract them into membership because of the fragmented nature of their jobs.

There has also been an important impact from the broader *socio-ideological context*. It is possible that part of the decline in trade union membership is attributable to a loss of endearment to trade unions, or because of a shift towards an individualistic ethos on the part of the working population of Great Britain (Phelps Brown, 1990). Nobody completely knows the truth of this, but it is known that the number of trade union representatives at workplace level now tends to be much lower than before, and many work-related complaints are now handled by bodies such as the Citizens Advice Bureaux, because of a permanent union absence in many workplaces (Abbot, 2004). Thus, apart from the public sector, the highly collectivised employment relations common in earlier years is now confined to large organisations, and a great deal of the employment relations in the country is handled in small, non-unionised companies (Dundon and Wilkinson, 2003). From what we know of non-union companies there is often a strong tendency for managers to protect what they see as their legitimate managerial prerogatives. Therefore, although managers will sometimes consult employees, many try to avoid negotiating, which again makes it hard for a collective body to make inroads and recruit new members.

So far as the *technological context* is concerned, trade unions have responded and adapted to the effects of new technology on their members' jobs, from as far back as the late nineteenth century. In the 1960s, for example, when new technologies led to a decline in manufacturing jobs, trade unions were very much occupied in dealing with the effects on employee jobs and their terms and conditions. Later, when management embarked on its numerous searches for more flexible, innovative and productive ways of working, the introduction of another wave of new technology found trade unions negotiating on these matters. For unions themselves, technology has enabled them to campaign on behalf of their members in different ways – for example, using the Internet to establish international solidarity alliances, or simply responding to member concerns more effectively through email communications.

The influences on the State

As will be seen shortly, the State is not so much a recipient of influences, but something that can have an impact both on the environment, via laws and policies, and also on other parties in employment relations, such as employers and managers, employees and unions. There is an exception to this, because the British government is heavily influenced by the European Union. However, as European law has to pass through the British parliamentary system, the EU can conveniently be treated as part of the State. In addition there are other influences of which the State in Great Britain needs to take account, and some of these originate in the contexts of employment relations.

As was noted in Chapter 5, irrespective of the political party that forms the government of the day, the State is often pre-occupied with trying to achieve a number of broad economic and social policy objectives. Underpinning these objectives, political parties have their own distinct philosophies and ideologies, which reflect their employment relations priorities and aims for the nature of wider society. The *economic context* tends to set limits on the extent to which these are achievable, and for this reason, the State has to organise its priorities according to domestic and global economic pressures. One way that it can do this is to influence the economy and labour market, through taxation policies, unemployment benefits or retraining initiatives. However, the *political* system in Great Britain is such that no party can govern unless it has a majority in Parliament and to achieve this, it needs to appeal to the widest possible public constituency. Arguably, it was for this reason that the policies of 'New Labour', elected in 1997, were much more business-friendly than those of earlier Labour governments. This was dubbed the 'Third Way agenda', and while it set aside the economic dogma of previous (Conservative) administrations, it stopped short of a return to former (old) Labour party values by eschewing nationalisation, high taxation and high public spending. Thus the promise of 'fairness but not favours' to the trade union movement was in many ways the presentation of a new economic and social agenda, designed almost exclusively to get elected at all costs after three decades in the political wilderness. Although it might seem cynical to portray matters in this way, the Labour party felt the need to re-align itself more closely with the mainstream *socio-ideological* values of the vast majority of working people: namely the electorate. In short, therefore, like any astute newspaper it listened to its readership, and reflected the readership's own values back, as being synonymous with the aims of New Labour.

The effects of the State
The influences on employers and managers

Employment relations in Great Britain are now influenced by government legislation to a much greater extent than ever before, and the State has become what is probably the most influential of all the parties in employment relations. Not only does it constrain the freedom of the other two parties to regulate the details of the employment relationship, but the rules of the game are now set out in more highly detailed and prescribed ways. Over the past quarter-century, State intervention has influenced employers and managers in two main waves.

First, much of the legislation enacted by Conservative governments between 1979 and 1997 was aimed at curbing trade union activities, and shifting the balance of power firmly towards employers (Ackers *et al.*, 1996; McIlroy, 1995). This wave of intervention gave a very strong signal to employers that, in the government's eyes, managers should legitimately hold the upper hand in employment relations, and that, henceforth, non-unionism would be the preferred form of employment relations. Although this was by no means sufficient to turn all employers into anti-union managers, it engendered a greater degree of confidence in themselves as managers to be able to alter the employment relationship into something that was more favourable to the employer. Included in this was the use of strategies to either marginalise unions, or substitute and suppress union representation completely.

The second wave occurred shortly after the election of the Labour government in 1997, and since then State intervention has had a new emphasis. Not only did it seek to promote social justice for many disenfranchised employees, it combined this with a distinctly 'business-friendly' economic agenda (Metcalf, 1999). There was also strong support for a European-style social model, and employers had to accommodate a whole raft of new individual employment rights (Rose, 2004). However, and to the disappointment of trade unions, the State was noticeably silent about the repeal of the anti-union laws of the previous (Conservative) administration (Wood *et al.*, 2003). For some commentators, therefore, the influence of the State under 'New Labour' appeared to be a watered-down extension of Conservative policies under another name, and as such, maintained a high degree of managerial freedom and power (Callanicos, 2001). Nevertheless, for others, it has meant that the actions and behaviours of employers are now regulated to a greater extent by legislation than by voluntary bargaining, thereby restraining managerial actions and protecting employees (Ewing, 2003), and in broad terms this is how matters have remained since 1997.

Where then does this leave employers and managers in terms of being under the influence of the State? Because this influence is exerted through legislation, managers have little choice but to comply. However, they probably continue to receive many of the messages that they want to receive, and are probably not unhappy with them. The anti-union legislation of the previous government is still in place, which leaves managers comparatively free of trade unions, and although there are provisions for compulsory trade union recognition in place, it is still too early to tell whether these will be that salvation that trade unions hope for. True, there have been considerable advances in terms of individual employment rights, some of which originate from the EU, but as things stand, these do not seem to be an undue worry to managers. Indeed, many employers are linked to powerful lobbying organisations that can help ensure that managerial values are incorporated into any proposed legislation, and will result in watered-down laws. Overall, therefore, employers and managers not only seem to have retained the things that they want from the legislation of a prior era, they have become willing recipients of further influence from the State.

The influences on trade unions and other collective employee associations

In broad terms, trade unions and other collective associations have always had to bear the brunt of State influence, and as with employers, one of the main sources of influence has been legislation. However, the main thrust of this has produced effects in the opposite direction to those experienced by most employers and managers.

Although the climate for trade unions and their activities was extremely hostile before the election of the new Labour government in 1997, since then it has been more positive. Broadly speaking, the State seems to have striven hard to find a new (and possibly slightly modified) place in the world for British trade unions, and if anything typifies this, it is a single piece of legislation. This was the introduction of provisions for statutory trade union recognition in the Employment Relations Act 1999, as explained in Chapters 4 and 5. Although trade unions expressed disappointment with the detail of the recognition legislation, arguing that it did not go far enough and excluded an estimated 8 million people employed in smaller firms (Dickens and Hall, 2003), the legislation appears to have led to a number of new voluntary recognition agreements in organisations that had previously been non-unionised (Gall, 2004). In addition, the Employment Relations Act 2002 has led to a new and potentially re-energised role for trade unions. Specifically, the 2002 Act placed the activities of Union Learning Representatives (ULR) on a statutory footing. Thus unions are now able to advise their members (and enter into dialogue with management) about possible training needs; a move that signals another role for trade unions in the British workplace.

Much the same can be said with respect to another landmark piece of legislation. This was the Information and Consultation Regulations 2004 (ICE), which are described later in Chapter 8. These reflect State philosophies about ensuring that all employees, regardless of union recognition, are informed and consulted by the management of an employing organisation. To one author at least, this is an important step that might ultimately turn out to be as significant as the right not to be unfairly dismissed or discriminated against in employment (Sisson, 2002).

Overall, although the State now exerts just as much influence on trade unions as ever, the philosophy underpinning it is now considerably less antagonistic towards unions than before. While they by no means get their own way about everything, trade unions have probably benefited considerably from the present regime. Perhaps as important, and in line with the spirit of consultation promoted in other areas, the State is now more willing – in conjunction with employer and manager representatives – to admit trade unions into a dialogue about future legislation. It is worth noting that both trade unions and management are perfectly capable of exerting (or at least attempting to exert) a modicum of influence on the State in return. For example, the British TUC is a member of the European Trade Union Confederation (ETUC), which promotes and coordinates the interests of trade unions in Europe. At a European level the ETUC, in conjunction with its employers' counterpart, the Union of Industrial and Employers Confederations of Europe (UNICE), can come together to negotiate a framework agreement. Once adopted by the European Council of Ministers, the agreement can substitute for legislation, and ultimately become part of the regulations that apply in Great Britain.

The effects of trade unions on management and employers

The influences that trade unions can exert on managers and employers can be many and varied. Indeed, it is not so much a case of trade unions seeking to exert influence, but that this is their *raison d'être* for existence. They influence wages, working conditions, health and safety, discipline and grievance, and also seek to improve the general well-being of people in employment. Similarly, although managers have many other things to attend to in their respective organisations, they too seek to influence the actions of trade unions, which can sometimes include the design of policies and practices that try to avoid having to deal with unions.

The processes and procedures through which these influences are exerted are covered in subsequent chapters of the book, and since each one of them can be a complex story in its own right, space precludes covering them here. Nevertheless, it is worth noting that, even if a firm does not recognise a trade union, there is a silent implication that a union will someday seek recognition, and this in itself can be a source of influence that leads to a range of manoeuvres to try and stay union-free. Indeed, even if a firm recognises a trade union and is willing to allow it to exert influence, this influence is likely to be limited. This will be explained in more detail in a later chapter, when the concept of a 'frontier of control' is explained. In basic terms this sets boundaries on the freedom of action that management and trade union can exercise in the employment relationship, and this will show that the nature of the struggle between the two main protagonists in employment relations can take on a very dynamic, fluid and rapidly shifting character.

Further reading

Dickens, L., M. Hall and S. Wood (2005) 'Review of research into the impact of employment relations legislation', *Employment Relations Research Series No. 45*, Department of Trade and Industry, London. An extensive review and summary of the main research studies that have sought to assess the impact of employment laws introduced by the post-1997 Labour government.

Dundon, T. and D.J. Rollinson (2004) *Employment Relations in Non-Union Firms*, Routledge, London. As the title suggests, the book reports a research study that explores employment relations in non-union firms. Among other things it gives a detailed picture of management styles in non-union firms, that illustrates the wide variety of styles that exist.

Gallie, D., M. White, Y. Cheng and M. Tomlinson (1998) *Restructuring the Employment Relationship*, Clarendon, Oxford. A penetrating account of many of the changes now taking place in the world of work, and how these impact on the relationship between organisations and their employees.

Hyman, R. (2001) *Understanding European trade unionism: between market, class and society*, Sage, London. A very thoughtful and articulate review of different union functions and purposes. Chapter 5 is well worth a read for the history and current identity crisis in British trade unions.

Poole, M., R. Mansfield, J. Gould-Williams and P. Mendes (2005) 'British managers' attitudes and behaviour in industrial relations: a twenty-year study', *British Journal of Industrial Relations*, 43 (1), pp. 117–134. Poole and his colleagues have regularly conducted surveys of members of the Chartered Management Institute at ten-year intervals, across the past twenty years. This paper reports the results of the latest survey and gives interesting insights into current management attitudes to employment relations.

Wood, S., S. Moore and K. Ewing (2003) 'The impact of trade union recognition under the Employment Relations Act 2000–2002', in *Representing Workers: Trade Union Recognition and Membership in Britain*, H. Gospel and S. Wood (eds), Routledge, London. A comprehensive review of the statutory union recognition procedures, using empirical evidence to illustrate the broadly positive impact of the law in the UK.

PART 3

Interpersonal processes in employment relations

Part contents

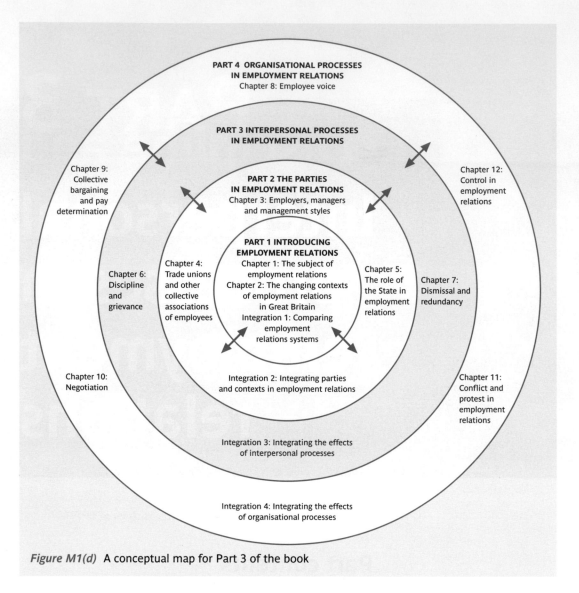

Figure M1(d) A conceptual map for Part 3 of the book

As indicated by the diagram above, this part of the book consists of three chapters, all of which focus on interpersonal processes in employment relations. The first, Chapter 6, examines discipline and grievance and the second, Chapter 7, focuses on dismissal and redundancy. These are followed by the third integrative chapter in the book, which traces some of the main effects that these processes can exert on the employment relations climate of an organisation.

Chapter **6**

Discipline and grievance

LEARNING OUTCOMES

After studying this chapter you should be able to:

- ☑ **distinguish** between discipline and grievance and the criteria that can be used to evaluate the effectiveness of discipline and grievance procedures

- ☑ **explain** the legal imperatives to have formal processes for handling discipline and grievance

- ☑ in outline, **describe** schemes for the effective handling of discipline and grievance in organisations

- ☑ **describe** factors that can influence the effective handling of discipline and grievance.

Introduction

This chapter deals with two important individual issues, the handling of which can have a strong influence on employment relations in organisations. However, although at first sight they appear to have similarities and are often bracketed together, most organisations try to keep discipline and grievance apart. Therefore, in order to direct the reader's attention to the idea that there are a number of conceptual and practical differences between discipline and grievance, the chapter starts by defining each process. The remainder of the chapter then examines each process separately, first, by exploring its aims; second, by considering the legal implications of each process; third, by describing a scheme for effective handling of each one; and finally, by describing the effects of some of the factors that can influence effectiveness.

Discipline and grievance: a theoretical perspective

Although discipline and grievance can be described in many different ways, a precise, well-respected and widely adopted definition of **discipline** is:

> Some action taken against an individual who fails to conform to the rules of an organisation of which he or she is a member.
>
> (Wheeler, 1976)

In the case of **grievance** there are also many different ways in which the process can be described, but by far the most comprehensive definition is given by the International Labour Organisation, which is as timely as ever. This is:

> with respect to conditions of employment where a situation appears contrary to the provisions of collective agreements, the individual contract, work rules, laws or regulations or custom and practice.
>
> (ILO, 1965)

Both of these definitions point to an apparent similarity between the processes. This is that if one party to the employment situation fails to abide by the rules of the relationship, the other party can bring a procedure into play to attempt to get the offending party to adjust his/her behaviour; managers can use disciplinary procedures, and employees can use grievance mechanisms. This does not necessarily mean that the procedure is a formalised one, and in the early stages of both discipline and grievance informal methods are quite common.

Nevertheless, once procedures are entered matters can become formalised very quickly, and this gives rise to another apparent similarity. Because formal processing of disciplinary and grievance matters usually consists of hearings which are quasi-judicial and quasi-legalistic in nature, both processes are often bracketed together and referred to as 'complementary' faces of industrial justice. This, however, can be extremely misleading and it is not safe to assume that, because they appear to be similar, the two processes are directed at anywhere near the same ends. In reality there is no overarching theory, be it justice or something else, that can be used to encompass both discipline and grievance. They are two different processes, which in practical terms exist for distinctly different purposes. However, because it is appealing in its simplicity, the **two faces of justice** concept is still widely quoted and for this reason it is important to examine it in greater depth. The theory posits that organisations can be likened to societies in miniature. Just as societies have rules of behaviour for their members, and use formalised legal procedures to establish whether the rules have been breached, grievance and discipline are taken to be the organisational equivalents of these processes. However, this comparison can be extremely misleading when some of the features of the two processes are examined further.

two faces of justice concept
That discipline and grievance are both processes that afford opportunities for the parties in employment relations (employer and employee) to obtain justice, ultimately by ensuring that the other party can be forced to observe the terms and conditions of the relationship.

Criteria of justice

Discipline has a superficial resemblance to a society's system of criminal justice, and the current guide to good practice (ACAS, 2003a) reinforces this idea. This stresses that people should not be accused or arraigned until the matter has been investigated, and that in arraignment, evidence should be presented to substantiate any allegation. It is also considered important that a process of considered judgement should precede the imposition of any sanction, and there should be a right of appeal against the judgement. However, there are huge problems in comparing wider society and organisations in this way. Criminal laws exist to protect all of society's members. Nominally, they are drawn up in public (in Parliament) and society has an opportunity to choose the lawmakers every five years. Imperfect as this system is, it contains features that are largely absent in organisations. Here, management is the lawmaker. While managers sometimes draft organisational rules in consultation with trade unions, for the most part management drafts its laws in private, and these are largely designed to protect their own interests, rather than those of all of the members of the organisation. Thus, it is hardly surprising that discipline has been called a 'very private system of justice' (Henry, 1987). Grievance has no similarity to this whatsoever, and the concept of justice is much more akin to that used in civil law. This is apparent in the definition given earlier, where the words *appears contrary to the provisions of* are used. As was noted in Chapter 1, the employment relationship is full of obligations that are implied rather than specific, and for this reason the parties often have expectations of each other that are unstated. Indeed, employees' expectations of management are often the result of a lack of explicit rules, and there are often no definite rules or criteria against which it can be judged whether an employee has been wronged by some action of management.

Capabilities to control behaviour

Discipline is much more a method of control than grievance. For instance, in most organisations there are rules of behaviour that employees are expected to follow, and their actions are monitored by supervisors. Grievance, however, has little claim to being a system that can control management's behaviour. More often than not it deals with situations where there are no prior rules to govern a manager's actions. Therefore, the only thing that can be asserted with any certainty is that something unanticipated has happened, which at best is saying that there should have been a rule in the first place. Consequently, it is less concerned with bringing management's behaviour into line with predetermined rules, and more to do with providing an opportunity for employees to question what a manager's behaviour *should* be in the future. As such it is essentially part of a rule-making system, rather than a system of behavioural control.

Different effectiveness criteria

Although the idea of using discipline to control behaviour can be viewed as unethical, this at least gives one clear criterion against which the effectiveness of the process can be evaluated – i.e. does it result in changed employee behaviour? Since grievance is essentially a way for employees to express a concern to management, which may result in future rule modification, evaluating of effectiveness can be far more difficult. Effectiveness can only really be evaluated in terms of whether both parties are satisfied with the outcomes and rules that result. However, employees and managers are likely to have different conceptions of what constitutes a fair rule of behaviour in the first place, all of which can make the handling of grievance a highly problematic affair. Indeed, as is discussed in Chapter 2, this can be even more difficult in situations where employees are employed by one organisation, but located at another firm as an agency contractor (Grimshaw *et al.*, 2004).

As can be seen, therefore, discipline and grievance are very different in a number of important ways. For this reason the remainder of the chapter will deal with them separately, and in a very practical and skills-based way. An employee is not likely to enjoy being disciplined, and no manager is likely to enjoy a subordinate saying that he or she is so dissatisfied with management that grievance procedures will be invoked. Nevertheless, this does happen, and perhaps the major consideration should be to try to ensure that, when it does, there is mutual satisfaction with the outcome and the way matters have been handled; or at least, that dissatisfactions are minimized as far as is possible.

Summary points

- In theoretical terms discipline and grievance are often portrayed as complementary processes for the administration of organisational justice.
- However, this is a misleading idea and in practice, discipline and grievance have: different criteria of justice; different capabilities to control future behaviour of employees and managers; and different criteria of effectiveness.

Case study 6.1: **The scrap bin incident**

You are the newly appointed manager of the Service Department of Terrondel Ltd, an organisation which manufactures a wide range of domestic appliances. Your department services and rebuilds appliances that have been returned from dealers as imperfect, and also rectifies faults on those that have been rejected by inspection on the production line. This morning when you came into work, you found a note from the Production Manager referring to one of your subordinates, Gerry Green. This instructs you to look into what has happened with a view to disciplinary action.

On leaving work at the end of the night shift, Mr Green was approached by a security guard who ordered him into the office, and instructed him to turn out the contents of the small duffel bag he was carrying. Mr Green at first declined, at which the guard snatched the bag and emptied its contents onto a table. Among the contents were two small items of decorative trim from a washing machine. When this was pointed out to Mr Green, he protested that there was nothing wrong. The items had been removed from the scrap bin, and it was normal practice for people in the department to retrieve these components for their own use. Nevertheless, the security guard reported the matter to the night superintendent, who instructed Gerry to report to your office at 2.00 p.m. this afternoon. He also telephoned the production manager, which resulted in the note you received.

You know that there are explicit company rules about removing things from the premises, but suspect that they have not been strictly enforced in the past. Perhaps more important, you were approached by the shop steward first thing this morning, who told you that what had happened had also been reported to him by Mr. Green. Although as yet you have no idea what he will say, the steward has made an appointment to see you about the matter at 10.30 this morning.

Questions

1 If you were the shop steward, what concept of justice would you be emphasising most, and what outcome would you be seeking as a 'just' solution?

2 In your role as the manager, what conception of justice might you be emphasising, and what outcome would you be seeking as a 'just' solution?

> Although studying at a university or college is not the same as being an employee in an organisation, universities and colleges have rules that students are expected to observe. Consider your own institution and answer the questions below.
>
> 1 Is there anything that corresponds to a disciplinary procedure that can be used to bring to a student's attention that he/she has broken an institutional rule?
> 2 What is this procedure called, and how does it operate?

Discipline
General considerations

Perhaps the most pragmatic way to view discipline is as a process that aims to adjust employee behaviour. While this is fully in accord with current thinking (ACAS, 2003a), it gives rise to two questions: what aspects of behaviour does it seek to regulate, and how does it try to do this? It is probably safe to say that the aspect of behaviour that it ideally seeks to regulate is an employee's mental processes, so that he or she willingly behaves in a way that is deemed to be acceptable to management. The question of how it seeks to do this is much more complex, and is connected with the philosophy that underpins disciplinary action. Here there is a whole range of philosophies that could be at work, but for the sake of simplicity the three main perspectives can be expressed along the continuum shown in Fig. 6.1.

punishment approach (to discipline)
An 'eye for an eye' and 'tooth for a tooth' philosophy, which emphasises taking retribution for having transgressed an organisational rule.

deterrence approach (to discipline)
The use of disciplinary action to provide an unpleasant consequence following a rule transgression, to deter an employee from future transgressions of the same nature.

rehabilitation approach (to discipline)
The use of the disciplinary process to show an employee that certain behaviour is unacceptable, with the aim that in the future she or he will voluntarily adopt patterns of behaviour that are acceptable.

Punishment, which is used here in the everyday sense of the word, has little to do with shaping future behaviour. It is more concerned with taking retribution against an employee for having broken a rule; an 'eye for an eye' and 'tooth for a tooth' philosophy. **Deterrence** is only a short way from punishment. It uses disciplinary action as an unpleasant consequence that follows a rule transgression, and in so doing it is hoped that the employee will be persuaded to avoid transgressing again. **Rehabilitation** uses the disciplinary process to show an employee that certain behaviour is unacceptable, with the aim that in the future she or he will voluntarily adopt patterns of behaviour that are acceptable. The important thing to note, however, is that the philosophy at work it is likely to have a strong impact on how

Punishment	Deterrence	Rehabilitation
Disciplinary action as retribution for rule transgression	Disciplinary action to highlight the aversive consequence of further rule transgression	Disciplinary action as correctional training

Figure 6.1 Alternative philosophies of discipline

disciplinary issues are handled, and as will be seen later, this has strong implications for the success of the process in terms of modifying future behaviour. To illustrate this only the two extremes of the continuum will be considered.

Space precludes an extensive technical discussion of the use of punishment, but it is important to note that, psychologically, it is a well-established way of shaping behaviour. However, to do this successfully requires that extremely stringent conditions are observed. These are difficult to achieve in practice, even in a well-designed psychological experiment, and within the confines of disciplinary procedures it is near impossible to do so. Perhaps more important, unless these conditions are met, even mild punishment is likely to give rise to emotional reactions (Kadzin, 1986), and these can set up forces that actually resist conformity (Beyer and Trice, 1984). Thus, the use of punishment can quickly become a self-defeating action, and in consequence, the rehabilitation approach currently receives the strongest endorsement in guides to good practice. In this there are different stages and, as sanctions become progressively more severe for repeated transgressions, an employee is given every chance to modify his/her behaviour. Nevertheless, it is important to note that aversive stimuli such as rebukes and other sanctions are regularly used, and these are delivered after a transgression has taken place. Thus, even where a manager's philosophy is truly correctional, unless very great care is taken about *how* matters are handled, it is almost certain that the recipient will interpret the sanction as a punishment. So, it could be argued that even a genuinely rehabilitative approach is based on a highly illogical premise: that if an employee is treated in a progressively harsher way for repeated transgressions, his/her behaviour will get progressively better (Redeker, 1983).

Codes of practice and the legal implications

It is now a legal requirement that all organisations should have procedures for handling disciplinary matters, and while there is a wide range of sanctions that can be used in the process, the law gives most employees a statutory right not to be dismissed for unfair reasons. Thus, a fair and effective disciplinary procedure is as vital to management as it is to employees. Wherever possible it is advisable that the procedure should conform as closely as possible to the code of practice formulated by the Advisory Conciliation and Arbitration Service (ACAS, 2003a). This code can be cited as evidence in a case to an employment tribunal, and recommends the use of the rehabilitation approach. In broad terms, it sets out the principles that should be observed by sound procedures, and these are summarised in Exhibit 6.1.

The code does not lay down universal procedures, but recognises that they need to be tailored to the circumstances of each organisation. For example, it notes that in SMEs it is not always practicable to adopt all of the steps set out in the guide to good practice, and that where an employee contests the fairness of dismissal at an employment tribunal, account will be taken of an organisation's size and administrative resources in deciding whether the employer has acted reasonably. To this end the code lays down a **statutory minimum procedure** that must be followed by all organisations who contemplate dismissing an employee, or imposing a disciplinary penalty that goes beyond suspension on full pay, or a warning; otherwise the dismissal is liable to be automatically ruled unfair by an employment tribunal. These are shown in Exhibit 6.2.

statutory minimum procedure (discipline)
A set of stages that must be followed by all organisations which contemplate dismissing an employee, or imposing a disciplinary penalty that goes beyond suspension on full pay, or a warning.

The code of practice places a strong emphasis on establishing rules of conduct and publicising them, and in the event that they need to be modified, involving employees (and where

Good disciplinary procedures should:

- be put in writing
- say to whom they apply
- be non-discriminatory
- allow for matters to be handled without undue delay
- allow for information to be kept confidential
- tell employees what disciplinary action might be taken
- say what levels of management have the authority to take disciplinary action
- require employees to be informed of the complaints against them and supporting evidence before a meeting
- give employees a chance to have their say before management reaches a decision
- provide employees with the right to be accompanied
- provide that no employee is dismissed for a first breach of discipline, except in cases of gross misconduct
- require management to investigate fully before any disciplinary action is taken
- ensure that employees are given an explanation for any sanction
- allow employees to appeal against a decision.

Exhibit 6.1 Sound disciplinary procedures

Source: adapted from ACAS (2003a).

This applies to disciplinary action short of dismissal (excluding oral and written warnings and suspensions on full pay) based on either conduct or capability. It also apples to dismissals (except for constructive dismissals) including dismissals on the basis of conduct, capability, expiry of a fixed-term contract, redundancy and retirement, The procedure (of which the following is a summary) is set out in full in Schedule 2 to the Employment Act 2002.

Step 1: Statement of grounds for action and invitation to meeting

- The employer must set out in writing the employee's alleged conduct or characteristics, or other circumstances, which lead them to contemplate dismissal or taking disciplinary action against the employee.
- The employer must send the statement or a copy of it to the employee and invite the employee to attend a meeting to discuss the matter.

Step 2: The meeting

- The meeting must take place before action is taken, except in the case where the disciplinary action consists of suspension.
- The meeting must not take place unless: (i) the employer has informed the employee of the basis for the meeting, including in the statement under Step 1 the ground or grounds for dismissal/discipline; and (ii), the employee has had a reasonable opportunity to consider their response to that information.
- The employee must take all reasonable steps to attend the meeting.
- After the meeting, the employer must inform the employee of their decision and notify them of the right to appeal against the decision if they are not satisfied with it.
- Employees have the right to be accompanied at the meeting.

Step 3: Appeal

- If the employee wishes to appeal, they must inform the employer.
- If the employee informs the employer of their wish to appeal, the employer must invite them to attend a further meeting.
- The employee must take all reasonable steps to attend the meeting.
- The appeal meeting need not take place before the dismissal or disciplinary action takes effect.
- Where reasonably practicable, the appeal should be dealt with by a more senior manager than attended the first meeting (unless the most senior manager attended that meeting).
- After the appeal meeting, the employer must inform the employee of their final decision.
- Employees have the right to be accompanied at the appeal meeting.

Exhibit 6.2 Standard statutory dismissal and disciplinary procedure

Source: adapted from ACAS (2003a).

minor misconduct
Transgression of one of the rules of employment established by the employer.

gross misconduct
Transgression of one of the rules of employment established by the employer, which constitutes a serious breach of contractual terms and results in a fundamental breakdown in the employment relationship.

necessary, their representatives) so that they are clearly understood. More important, it distinguishes between two degrees of seriousness in rule transgression: **minor misconduct** and **gross misconduct**. The first of these embraces transgression of rules that are established by the employer to give a safe and efficient workplace. Where a rule of this type is broken it would not normally result in a serious penalty for a first offence. Nevertheless, since most employers take behaviour of this type seriously enough to want to avoid further transgressions, repeated rule breaking by an employee could result in more severe penalties. Because gross misconduct constitutes a serious breach of contractual terms, and is potentially something that results in a fundamental breakdown in the employment relationship, it can result in dismissal for the first offence. However, it should be noted that the dividing line between minor and gross misconduct is something that varies considerably according to organisational circumstances. For instance, a first incident of smoking in a no-smoking office might be dealt with as a case of mild misconduct, but the same behaviour where there is a risk of explosion, might well be viewed as gross misconduct. As such, it is difficult to give hard and fast rules about what behaviour falls into each category. Nevertheless, some of the transgressions that can be regarded as disciplinary offences are given in what follows.

Pause for reflection

Working together with other students in your class, carefully consider the disciplinary procedure you identified in the previous Pause for Reflection exercise, and answer the questions below.

1 What types of student transgressions is it designed to deal with?
2 Classify these offences into minor misconduct and gross misconduct.
3 Are there any sanctions that could be taken against students for proven rule transgressions?

Incapacity

This is the inability of an employee to perform the job for which she or he has been employed, and can be for reasons of lack of skill, qualifications, inefficient or ineffective work performance, or poor health. Because poor health is not necessarily something for which an employee can be held to blame, these days many organisations have a **capability procedure**, a variant of the disciplinary procedure, which is primarily designed to uncover reasons for an employee's incapacity. If this turns out to be for reasons of poor health, it is usually incumbent on management to establish that the employee's state of health noticeably affects performance, and where dismissal seems to be the only option, to demonstrate that suitable alternative work is not available.

capability procedure
A variant of disciplinary procedures that is primarily designed to uncover reasons for an employee's incapacity to perform the job for which he/she was employed.

Misconduct

Transgressions of this type can encompass a wide range of behaviours, such as unauthorised absence, poor timekeeping, fighting, drinking, swearing, harassment or victimisation, insolence or rudeness, misuse of organisational facilities (e.g. email and Internet), and wilful disobedience. Some transgressions of this type fall into the category of gross misconduct, and are dismissable offences for a single occurrence. However, if dismissal occurs, the onus is usually on the employer to show that dismissal is fair in the circumstances. In the case of drinking, for example, it is not the act of drinking, but its effect on work performance that counts, and bad language could be contested, because it is sometimes part of the working culture of certain groups of employees.

Breach of statutory duty

In certain circumstances this can also be classified as gross misconduct, usually because the employer could not reasonably continue to employ the person in their designated job without breaking the law. For example, where a driver loses his/her licence for some reason.

Other substantial reasons

Because employment tribunals consider whether an employer has acted reasonably towards an employee, this is potentially a catch-all reason. For example, it may be evoked as a reason by an unscrupulous employer where an employee refuses to agree to impossible changes that a manager imposes unilaterally. As was noted in Chapter 1, the employment contract is an individual one. Strictly speaking, therefore, any change needs to be deemed reasonable and should preferably occur with the consent of both parties. Thus, if one party (management) unilaterally imposes a change which cannot reasonably be met by the other party (employee), a claim can be made that the contract has been broken, and that constructive dismissal has taken place. It should be noted that constructive and unfair dismissal is a very technical aspect of employment law, and as every individual case differs, there is no golden rule to define the fairness or reasonableness of an employer's actions. Employment tribunals are required to assess whether an employer's decision falls within a range of responses that a reasonable employer could have taken in similar circumstances (Lewis and Sargeant, 2004: 163).

Although the Code of Practice purposely avoids laying down a universal set of steps for anything other than the statutory minimum procedure, a specimen set of stages can be inferred. These are shown in Fig. 6.2, which illustrates an extensive six-stage procedure.

A number of points should be noted with respect to Fig. 6.2. The ACAS Code of Practice gives an employee the right to be accompanied at a disciplinary hearing by a work companion, or his/her trade union representative. Although this could occur at the very first stage of the procedure where an informal warning might be given for minor misconduct, this stage tends to be conducted informally. From then onwards, however, matters become much more formal, and although a supervisor conducts the proceedings and, where necessary, issues a formal verbal warning, most employees would probably prefer to be represented by their trade union (Guest and Conway, 2004). Also note that the employee has a right of appeal against the sanction for this stage.

In the interests of fairness and justice these appeals are normally heard by successively higher levels of management, and in organisations that recognise trade unions the employee is normally represented by successively higher levels in the trade union hierarchy. Where the employee is disciplined for repetition of an earlier transgression, because the sanction could be heavier, the use of higher levels of management and union is also quite commonplace. For the ultimate sanction, dismissal, the employee's only appeal is to an employment tribunal, and it should be noted that dismissal can occur for repeated occurrences of minor misconduct.

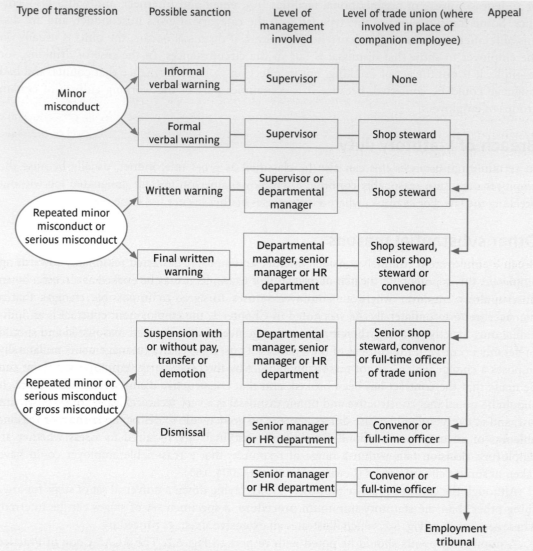

Figure 6.2 Outline stages of disciplinary procedure

Summary points

- Managers differ in their philosophies towards the use of discipline in terms of the following: as a punishment for wrongdoing; as a deterrent to future rule breaking; or as a rehabilitative process.

- The ACAS (2003) Code of Practice sets out a number of principles that should be observed in formulating and applying disciplinary procedures, and also establishes a statutory minimum procedure that should be followed for using disciplinary penalties that go beyond warnings or suspension on full pay.

- The Code of Practice recognises two degrees of seriousness in rule transgressions: minor misconduct and gross misconduct.

An outline scheme for effective handling of discipline

Effectiveness is defined here as handling that results in future willing observance by an employee of an organisational rule of conduct. To be effective, disciplinary handling must be fair and just; not simply because there are legal implications if it is not, but also because these are important aims in their own right. To be seen as fair and just, effectiveness also means being systematic and consistent in the way issues are handled from the outset; otherwise everything from then on can be called into question. Because early stages in a disciplinary procedure are usually handled by first-line supervisors, what follows is largely directed at this level of management, and the scheme is shown in Fig. 6.3.

In the initial stages it is crucial that the issue is viewed as one that is only *potentially* a disciplinary matter. This means that the process should be one of tentative exploration, in which the aim is to reach a *decision* about whether or not to enter disciplinary procedures.

Awareness and clarification

When first becoming aware of an issue it is important to avoid falling into the trap of assuming a proven case. Indeed, since the aim of discipline is to encourage an improvement in behaviour, the first step is to clarify whether or not a case exists. Answering the four questions shown in Fig. 6.3 can be a useful step, and from these it should be possible to decide whether or not a potential infringement of rules has occurred. To do this, it is obviously necessary to know what the rules are, and how they are applied in practice. Moreover, it is important to take note of any **custom and practice arrangements** that condone what has happened. These things should all be taken into account before deciding whether or not matters will be taken further, and if after having done so it is decided that a problem or issue exists, in fairness and justice the next step is to see the person concerned.

custom and practice arrangements
Unwritten and informal workplace rules that regulate work and employment.

Preparation

Although it is advisable not to make the initial interview too formal and intimidating, to ensure that it serves its purpose of clarifying matters it is important that it is pre-planned to some extent. It needs to be held somewhere that is free from interruption, and big enough to accommodate all those who need to be present. These people (e.g. the individual concerned, his/her representative and witnesses) should all be notified. It is also advisable to make some enquiries about the contextual circumstances surrounding the situation: for example, are there any current employment relations matters or problems that could escalate as a result of any action that is decided, or is the problem itself part of a wider employment relations issue?

An important note of caution is warranted here. It can be tempting to look at the past record of the person involved to see whether he/she has a history of disciplinary offences. However, it needs to be remembered that the purpose of seeing the person is essentially exploratory and tentative. It is therefore inadvisable to look into the past because, if disciplinary action does eventually occur, it can result in accusations that the individual's past record caused matters to be viewed in a biased way.

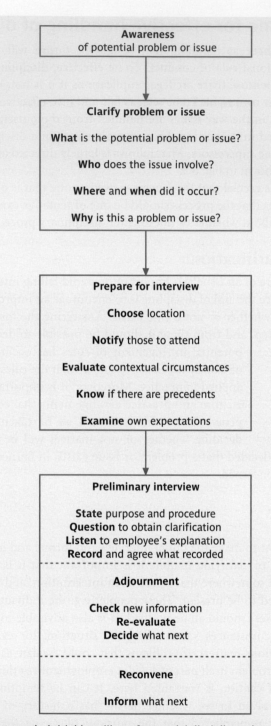

Figure 6.3 Outline of stages in initial handling of potential disciplinary issue

The interview

In fairness to the employee concerned, and in the interests of getting to the root of the matter, it is helpful to put the person at ease with an opening statement that outlines the purpose of the interview, and how it will be conducted. In a non-threatening way it should be made clear that, while the interview is not a disciplinary hearing but a fact-finding meeting, depending on its outcome there is a potential for matters to progress into disciplinary procedures. The purpose of other people being present should also be explained. At this point the facts (as they are known at this stage) should be stated, and fairness and justice dictate that the employee should be given a chance to state his/her version of matters. Since the aim is to clarify and gain further information, witnesses called by either the employee or supervisor can often shed further light on matters, and in the interests of clarity, what they and the employee say should, if necessary, be examined and confirmed. Indeed, only through intelligent questioning is it likely that the matter can be fully explored. Throughout the interview the most important skill that is needed is listening, and this seldom happens of its own accord. For this reason it can be useful if the person conducting the meeting summarises what has emerged at fairly frequent intervals, which can help both parties to listen attentively. It is also important that a record be kept of what is said at the meeting, and that the record is agreed by both parties.

At the end of the interview it may be the case that there is some difference between the way the employee and supervisor perceive the situation. If so, it is important that the supervisor avoids trying to force her/his perceptions of the matter on the employee. Conversely, it is possible that a conclusion is reached that there is no case to answer. In this eventuality it should be remembered that the experience will almost certainly have been a harrowing one for the employee. Thus, an honest admission at this stage that matters were not as they originally appeared can do a great deal to win his/her respect, and improve future relationships.

In a situation where there appears to be a difference in perceptions, it is important to avoid making a hasty decision, and it may be prudent to call an adjournment lasting long enough to enable further investigations to be made. If this is done, the matter should not be left hanging in mid-air, but a definite time, date and venue should be fixed for reconvening the meeting. The adjournment should be used constructively, to review outstanding issues from the interview: for example, the real status of the rule which it is claimed has been broken. It can also be useful to look into the circumstances surrounding the case, particularly if any mitigating reasons have been raised. Having done this, the next important thing to do is to decide whether a case still exists, and if so what it is. Whichever of these applies, the fairest place to say so will be at the reconvened interview.

Where it is decided that the matter needs to be handled through disciplinary procedures, it is now fair to examine the employee's past record. Indeed, it can be important to do so. If there have been previous incidents of the same nature, it may well be that procedures dictate that matters should now be handled at a level above that of the supervisor. In these circumstances more senior levels of management such as the departmental head or a human resource specialist should be consulted. However, these people need to be selected with a great deal of care. The next level of management upwards would almost certainly be the one who has to deal with the matter if a sanction is taken, and it must be remembered that the employee might well decide to appeal against the sanction. Thus, it is important to avoid a situation in which a future judge of the issue has become an unwitting party to the sanction.

Where the supervisor can pursue the matter further, it is vital that any action taken is both consistent and fair. Checking with other supervisors, managers and human resource specialists could be useful, particularly if there are circumstances that might mitigate the normal penalty in some way. Again, however, and for the reasons given above, any consultation needs to be done with a great deal of care. It is also important to plan the conduct of the reconvened interview, and many of the points made earlier about clarity with respect to its aims and objectives also apply.

The reconvened interview

The basic purpose of this is twofold: to conclude the investigation, and to take any action that is deemed necessary. The structure of this meeting will be similar to the previous one and it should open with a statement of how things stood at the adjournment of the first interview. Any new information that has come to light should be presented, and once again the employee should be given the opportunity to raise questions, and state his/her point of view. When this has been done, the interview should be brought to an end by the supervisor stating what conclusions have been reached, and what action it is proposed to take. If this does not involve a sanction, but simply consists of a warning that the employee's conduct must improve, it is important that the person be told:

- what should be achieved
- whether that standard is normal
- whether help can be expected from management in meeting that standard (i.e. training)
- the time scale over which the improvement is to take place.

It is clearly much better if the employee understands the reasons for what has happened, and that if an improvement is made matters will go no further. Where he/she does not agree with the outcome, and irrespective of whether a sanction has been imposed, fairness and justice dictate that the employee be informed of any rights of appeal against the decision, and how to proceed.

Factors affecting the effective handling of discipline

The list of things that can interfere with the effective handling of discipline is potentially endless. Some of these result from misuse of procedures, and others from human fallibility. Indeed, some are not actually concerned with the handling itself, but may be the result of contextual circumstances that play a part in shaping handling styles. There is only space to describe some of the more prominent factors here, and for convenience these can be grouped under four general headings given by Rollinson (1992), which are shown in Fig. 6.4.

Contextual factors

Clearly unless there are **substantive rules of behaviour** that proscribe certain employee behaviours, it is hard to demonstrate that a transgression has occurred. What is perhaps more important is to recognise that it is managers who largely determine these rules, and their *attitudes and ideologies* can play a part in how they are framed. For example, some managers can jealously guard what they perceive as their legitimate prerogatives (Klass and Wheeler, 1990), and one problem that can arise is where a manager uses the process to establish a new rule that reinforces his or her authority. Problems can also arise because managers have a tendency to link an

substantive rules of behaviour
Rules that are normally found in employee handbooks and disciplinary procedures that proscribe certain actions on the part of employees.

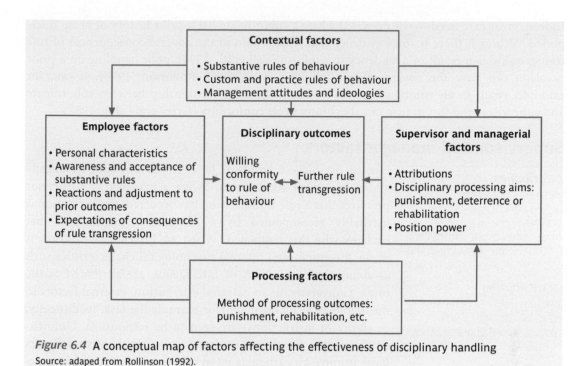

Figure 6.4 A conceptual map of factors affecting the effectiveness of disciplinary handling
Source: adaped from Rollinson (1992).

employee's observance of formal rules with vaguer expectations, such as having a willing and cooperative attitude. Thus, an employee who is found guilty of breaking a minor rule can sometimes be subject to a sanction that is out of all proportion, simply because he/she is also judged guilty of not conforming to a particular manager's behavioural expectations.

Another problem can arise from informal *custom and practice* arrangements, which play a strong part in determining whether formal rules are observed in practice (Terry, 1977). Substantive rules can easily get out of date, and those who formulate them need to ensure that they are explicit, realistic, and above all acceptable. It is probably as well to remember that if everybody is breaking a rule, it is probably high time it was changed anyway. Under no circumstances should the disciplinary process be used as a matter of convenience to resurrect a long-dead rule that has remained unenforced for some time. Rather, notice should be served that the rule is to be reintroduced, and that future observance is required. Finally there is the all-important problem of communicating the rules and, where appropriate, agreeing them with the recognised trade unions. Instead of making vague assumptions that employees know the rules, or at best posting them on a noticeboard, it would arguably be more cost-effective to devote some attention to explaining rules, and the reasons why they exist. Unfortunately, rather than informing people beforehand, the disciplinary process is sometimes abused by using it as a way of teaching people the rules after they have been broken.

Employee factors

Awareness of rules does not guarantee their acceptance. While there is some evidence that *personal characteristics* can influence an individual's willingness to flout substantive rules (Hogan and Hogan, 1989), great care needs to be exercised in branding people in this way. To make these judgements and then use the process to try to bring people into line can lead to a charge of victimisation, and quickly escalate what is an individual matter into a collective dispute.

Indeed, great care needs to be exercised where a subordinate has a prior history of being disciplined. Although there is some evidence that anticipation of the adverse consequences of rule transgression can result in a tendency to conform (Ball *et al.*, 1994), poor handling on a prior occasion can have the reverse effect (Rollinson *et al.*, 1997; Rollinson, 1997). It can, for example, result in an emotional reaction which affects the relationship between subordinate and supervisor, and this in turn can affect future rule conformity (Greer and Labig, 1987).

Supervisor and manager factors

causal attribution
A special type of perception in which, when observing a certain pattern of behaviour in another person, the observer also attributes a cause for the person behaving in this way.

internal attribution
The cause of a person's behaviour is assumed to be connected with his/her psychological characteristics, e.g. personality, etc.

external attribution
The cause of a person's behaviour is assumed to be connected with a factor in his/her environment.

One of the biggest problems here lies in what are technically known as causal attributions. When a manager or supervisor perceives that a rule transgression has occurred, the perception is inevitably accompanied by a judgement (attribution) that explains why this happened. When an internal attribution is made, the employee's internal psychological characteristics such as ability, aptitude, effort or intelligence, are attributed as the cause. Conversely, in an external attribution, external factors in the employee's environment (for example the task, its difficulty, or clarity of instructions) are seen to be responsible. Unfortunately, people are all too ready to assume that internal factors have prompted a particular act of behaviour, and external factors tend to be ignored (Mitchell and Wood, 1980). Clearly this problem is much more likely where vague expectations about the right attitudes are linked to overt behaviours, but the important point is that internal attributions have been shown to be much more likely to attract severe disciplinary actions (Bemmels, 1991), and this is something against which supervisors and managers need to be on their guard.

position power
The degree of freedom of action in a supervisor or manager's role.

Another factor of some importance is that of the supervisor's position power, where evidence suggests that there is a greater tendency to use disciplinary procedures where position power is high. Conversely, where managerial freedom of action is constrained by the presence of a trade union, managers can be much more wary of using disciplinary procedures (Klass *et al.*, 1999; Rollinson, 2000).

Issue-handling factors

This can perhaps be the most crucial aspect in terms of obtaining rule observance. It is not easy to shape employee attitudes in a way that gives conformity to rules, and the use of discipline is not something that is likely to endear a supervisor to an employee. Thus, methods of handling which emphasise a corrective or problem-solving approach, rather than those that have even a hint of being punitive, can be highly important (Rollinson *et al.*, 1997). For example, non-threatening methods, which explain to an employee why he/she may have erred, are less likely to result in resentment and emotional reactions (Rollinson, 1997).

Summary points

- Disciplinary handling is effective where it achieves the outcome of an employee willingly conforming to an organisational rule of conduct that he/she has transgressed in the past.
- To be effective, disciplinary handling should ideally adopt a rehabilitative approach.
- The disciplinary handling process can be divided into a number of stages: awareness and clarification; preparation for an exploratory interview with the employee; the interview itself (which, if necessary, can be suspended to allow collection of further relevant information); a reconvened interview.
- Many factors can influence the effectiveness of disciplinary handling. These include: contextual factors; employee factors; managerial or supervisory factors; and issue-handling factors.

Case study 6.2: **The night shift supervisor**

You are Tony Edwards, Customer Enquiries Manager for Gasco Plc, an organisation that supplies gaseous fuel to a wide variety of customers. Under its public liability provisions Gasco is required to have a bank of telephones manned around the clock, so that customers can make contact in the case of emergency. Some three months ago you appointed James Kerr as night shift supervisor. Kerr is 27, and has all the signs of being a sharp, intelligent and conscientious man. However, when you arrived for work this morning you found a note on your desk from a night shift supervisor in another department, the computer room. This was in a sealed envelope marked 'Confidential'.

The computer room supervisor reported that he had tried to see Kerr the previous night at about 3.40 a.m., to inform him of a temporary malfunction which would have affected the capability of telephone operators to access customer records on the computer. He had first gone to Kerr's office, and although the telephone operators were working normally, Kerr was not there. On enquiring of his whereabouts, an operator told him that Kerr was looking for the duty technician, as there was some trouble in accessing customer records on the computer. The computer supervisor thought no more of it, but on the way back to his own department had noticed a light on in another office. He looked through the window in the door, and saw Kerr apparently asleep. Kerr was aroused, apologised and left almost immediately. The computer supervisor also reported that there were rumours among his own staff that Kerr had been seen asleep on several other occasions.

You telephoned the computer department manager, who stated that his night shift supervisor is a fair man, and not given to exaggeration. Therefore you telephoned his night shift supervisor at home, and he confirmed everything that he had put in the note, and added that he had also recorded the information in the incident book which he is obliged to complete at the end of every shift. You thanked him, came back to your office, and wrote to Kerr asking him to come in and see you at 5.00 p.m.

How are you going to handle this situation?

Pause for reflection

Having considered earlier whether your university or college has anything similar to a disciplinary procedure for students, now consider the following questions in relation to 'grievance' at your institution:

1 Is there anything that corresponds to a grievance procedure that allows a student to make a formal complaint, or express a dissatisfaction?
2 What is this procedure called, and how does it operate?

Grievance

The scope of grievance

In British employment relations the term 'grievance' is often used in a very unspecific way, that embraces both individual and collective matters. Unfortunately, this lack of clarity tends to blur the distinction between grievances, which are essentially individual matters, and disputes, which are collective in nature. Despite this, and as is noted in what follows, individual grievances sometimes turn out to have implications for larger numbers of employees. Thus, grievance procedures are sometimes purposely framed in a way that permits an issue to pass directly from being a (individual) grievance to become a (collective) dispute, which is then handled by collective bargaining machinery (see Chapter 9). An even more confusing matter is that some writers distinguish between complaints and grievances. For example, Torrington *et al.* (2002) argue that the former are dissatisfactions brought to the attention of a supervisor or shop steward, while grievances are dissatisfactions that are formally presented. Unfortunately this implies that complaints are merely issues that are raised, while grievances are those that are formally pursued. However, there is a great deal of support for the idea that a grievance which is dealt with informally, and as close as possible to its point of origin, has the best chance of being resolved to the satisfaction of both parties. Indeed, formal procedures usually recognise this by specifying that a grievant and his/her superior should have made every attempt to resolve the matter directly between themselves, before recourse is made to the formal process. Therefore, so far as this chapter is concerned a grievance is taken to be an expression of a dissatisfaction by an individual, and how this issue is initially raised, or for that matter how it is subsequently handled, is considered to be of less significance than the fact that it exists in the first place. No distinction is made between complaints and grievances, and the discussion covers any situation where an individual considers it important enough to voice a dissatisfaction to her/his immediate superior with the aim of resolving it.

The legal implications of grievance

As with discipline, there are legal implications if an organisation does not have fair and just procedures for the resolution of grievances. The same Code of Practice (ACAS, 2003a) that covers disciplinary procedures also deals with grievance, and specifies a statutory minimum procedure that should be followed. However, there are important features that make grievances different from discipline. First, in large organisations it is fairly common for a number of different but separate procedures to exist side-by-side. These are used to deal with particular types of

grading appeals procedure

A procedure that enables an employee to contest the pay grade for his/her role.

equal pay (for work of equal value) procedure

A procedure that enables an employee to contest the pay grade for his/her job on the grounds that it entails duties and responsibilities equal to some other organisational role.

bullying and harassment procedures

A procedure that enables an employee to formally complain about bullying or harassment to which he/she believes that he or she has been subjected.

whistle-blower procedure

A procedure that enables an employee to formally complain (as per the provisions of the Public Interest Disclosure Act of 1998) about bullying or harassment to which the individual believes he or she has been subject, subsequent to having made public his/her concerns about unethical or unfair organisational practices.

employee dissatisfaction, examples of which are: grading appeals; equal pay (for work of equal value); bullying and harassment; and so-called whistle-blowing procedures.

Second, as noted earlier, in some organisations individual grievances and collective disputes are initially dealt with through the same procedure, and disputes tend to involve groups, or a whole workforce. However, in certain circumstances an individual grievance can develop into a collective dispute, and where separate procedures for grievances and disputes exist, it is regarded as useful practice for the two procedures to be linked so that an issue can, if necessary, pass from one to the other.

Third, there are a number of situations which could put an organisation at a distinct legal disadvantage if it does not have a grievance procedure. For example, there is a considerable body of legislation designed to prevent sexual and racial discrimination in employment, and after passing through a grievance procedure, an employee who still feels personally aggrieved in this respect has the right of access to an employment tribunal. However, if an organisation has no grievance procedure through which an employee could try to resolve an issue of this type, it would clearly be liable to face legal penalties if a case reaches a tribunal. In addition, there is the matter of constructive dismissal. For instance, consider the situation where the management of a firm has attempted to impose a complete and radical revision of an employee's job. If the employee has been given no opportunity or facility to raise the issue as a grievance and to work out a mutually satisfactory resolution with management, she or he might decide to leave and claim constructive dismissal at an employment tribunal. In these circumstances it could be construed that the lack of a formal procedure for handling matters of this type had forced the employee's hand, and this could sway matters in her or his favour in the eyes of a tribunal.

Effectiveness in grievance handling

Here it is important to note a point made in the Code of Practice; that the aim of a grievance procedure is to *settle* or *resolve* a grievance. Grievance is not simply the reverse of discipline, and often there are no explicit rules for management behaviour that make an issue clear-cut. Therefore, the simple criterion of rule observance used for discipline is not an appropriate one to judge the effectiveness of grievance, and after Briggs (1981), two criteria are used here:

1 *Conflict management*: does the process enable peaceful settlement of dissatisfactions without recourse to other protest behaviours, i.e. individual action such as absenteeism or quitting, or escalation in which the individual seeks group level support?

2 *Agreement clarification*: does the process permit clarification (and where appropriate re-definition) of the terms of the reward–effort bargain in a way that ensures both parties have satisfaction with the outcomes?

At first sight these aims might seem stringent, but there is no reason why a well-constructed grievance process should not be capable of meeting them. Having said this, it is extremely important that the procedure puts boundaries on what it can and cannot deal with. Collective matters, which are more appropriately handled through disputes procedures, are an example of those that should normally be outside the individual grievance process. Therefore, grievance procedures need to be tailored even more closely to the specific needs of an organisation than do those for discipline. Furthermore, it is correspondingly more difficult to generalise about the features necessary for an ideal procedure. Nevertheless, a model that illustrates the principles involved is given in Fig. 6.5, and this also covers the necessary steps in statutory minimum procedure, as laid down in the ACAS Code of practice.

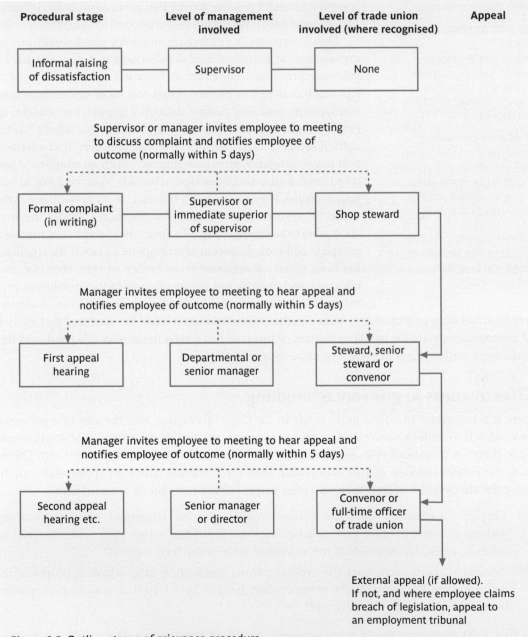

Figure 6.5 Outline stages of grievance procedure

The first thing to note is that the employee initially raises the dissatisfaction with the supervisor in an informal way. Because this is an attempt by an employee and his/her immediate supervisor or manager to resolve matters between themselves, strictly speaking, the formal procedure has not yet been invoked. This reflects a cardinal principle of natural justice: that is, that if an employee is dissatisfied with his/her supervisor's conduct, the supervisor should be the first to hear of it, and have an opportunity to remedy the situation. The importance of the informal nature of this first step is well recognised, and in practice, many grievance procedures prohibit entering subsequent formal stages until this has occurred. It can also be noted that in all the steps that follow this stage, the employee has the right to be accompanied by a companion (work colleague) or a trade union representative. In Great Britain, the owner of a grievance is the individual concerned, and so there is nothing inevitable about trade union involvement. Moreover, unlike discipline, where most employees value trade union involvement, with grievance the majority seem to have a high degree of faith in management to show fairness and justice (Guest and Conway, 2004).

After the first informal step matters become much more specific to the organisation. Clearly if at any stage the employee receives an answer to satisfy his/her concerns, the grievance no longer exists, and the procedure automatically terminates. Usually at least one level of appeal exists, and the number of appeals allowed can sometimes be equivalent to the number of levels in the management hierarchy. However, where formal negotiating machinery exists, a joint committee of management and trade union will sometimes hear the final appeal, and some procedures allow the case to be heard outside the organisation in front of an independent third party as the final stage. For instance, in organisations that are members of an employer's association, it is sometimes the association that provides the final stage. Although eventual recourse to an external and independent judge is by no means universal, it can do much to encourage fair and just decisions earlier on.

Summary points

- A grievance is an individual complaint or dissatisfaction brought to the attention of management by an employee, with a view to resolution or removal of the dissatisfaction.

- Organisations are now required to have procedures in place for this purpose, and many large organisations have multiple grievance procedures that operate in parallel, for the resolution of specific categories of employee dissatisfaction.

- Effective handling of grievances should ideally achieve two outcomes: (i) peaceful resolution of employee dissatisfactions without recourse to other individual or collective protest behaviours; and where necessary, (ii) clarification or redefinition of the terms of the rewards–effort bargain.

An outline scheme for effective grievance handling

For the process to be effective, fairness, justice and systematic handling are just as necessary in grievance as they are in discipline. Moreover, the initial (informal) stage can often be the most crucial one. While this stage will almost inevitably be handled by a junior manager or supervisor, in terms of its potential after-effects, there is an important difference to the parallel stage in discipline. Even where a supervisor is scrupulously fair and just, in discipline she or he can hardly expect that the process will result in a better relationship with the employee. Grievance, on the other hand, presents a positive opportunity to build good working relationships. This does not mean that the supervisor has to give ground on every occasion; rather that people usually prefer to work for someone who is perceived to be fair and understanding. The handling of an employee's dissatisfaction in an appropriate way is an unrivalled opportunity for a supervisor or manager to demonstrate that he/she possesses these attributes. Accordingly, the first stage of a grievance should be regarded as essentially tentative and exploratory, and a scheme for effective handling is shown in Fig. 6.6.

Depending on the nature of the issue about which the employee expresses a dissatisfaction, some managers and supervisors have a tendency to feel that their authority is threatened. The most serious threat is usually experienced when an employee challenges the fairness of work duties that have been allocated (Hook *et al.*, 1996). However, it is important to remember

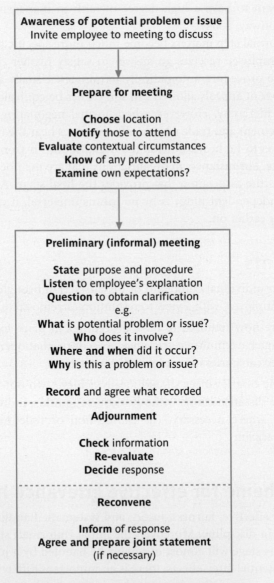

Figure 6.6 Outline of stages in initial handling of potential grievance issue

that unless the dissatisfaction is brought to the supervisor's attention and dealt with, it could fester beneath the surface and become a far more serious issue. It can therefore be beneficial for a supervisor to curb any feelings of defensiveness or annoyance that the dissatisfaction has been raised, and in order for the true nature and origin of the dissatisfaction to emerge in clear and unambiguous terms, it is crucial that the first informal approach is handled in an open-minded way. Because the employee has to inform the supervisor about these things, it is difficult to plan the detailed conduct of the initial interview beforehand. Nevertheless, details such as deciding where any meeting is to be held, and notifying those who have a need to be present, obviously need prior attention. Similarly, some thought should be given to any surrounding circumstances: for example, whether there are any current problems that might be associated with the issue, or indeed, whether the issue itself is part of a wider employment relations matter.

The interview

In a grievance situation it is unlikely that a full awareness of the nature of a dissatisfaction can emerge until this very first stage has taken place. It is important to note that the employee may well feel what he or she has to say challenges the supervisor's judgement in some way, and this can make it difficult for either party to clearly articulate matters. However, the issue is hardly likely to be capable of resolution unless the full details emerge, and in this respect supervisors and managers have an active part to play in helping employees to state their case. Thus, an opening statement which outlines the purpose of the meeting, and how it will be conducted, often helps in this matter. Indeed, it might be wise to state at this stage that the meeting is being held at the employee's request, and that she/he has full rein to explain the nature of the complaint. In the interests of obtaining clarity and openness, questioning may be required. However, questioning does not mean interrogation, and it is crucial that it should be done in a way that leaves no impression that there is an attempt to sweep the matter under the carpet. Thus, the skills of attentive listening and summarising are also important.

At the end of the meeting the supervisor may be able to make a decision that removes the dissatisfaction. If this is not the case, it is vital that the supervisor does nothing to force his/her perceptions on the employee. The meeting should be brought to an end by summarising where matters stand, and if there seems to be a possibility that the dissatisfaction could be resolved by seeking higher authority, then the meeting should not be closed, but adjourned, and a date and venue fixed for it to be for reconvened. In these circumstances perhaps the most suitable way to bring matters to a close is to agree to draw up a concise but accurate statement of the matter, by presenting the complaint as a formal one in writing. Here it needs to be remembered that setting out a grievance in writing can be a daunting task, particularly if the grievant's first language is not English. In these circumstances the employee should receive assistance in formulating a written grievance, as recommended under the Disability Discrimination Act (1995).

Notwithstanding what is said above, for some issues the supervisor might feel that he/she cannot (or will not) give ground. Where this happens it would be normal for the supervisor to effectively withdraw from the case by advising the employee of his/her rights of appeal. Thus, the supervisor's immediate superior will probably become involved.

Pause for reflection

Working together with other students in your class carefully consider the grievance procedure you identified in the previous Pause for Reflection exercise, and answer the questions below.

1 What type of student complaint or dissatisfaction is it designed to deal with?
2 Does the procedure have an initial, informal stage?
3 If a student invokes the procedure and matters are not settled to his/her satisfaction, is any appeal stage provided for?
4 To whom would it be necessary to make this appeal?

Factors affecting the effectiveness of grievance handling

As with discipline there are factors that can affect the successful use of grievance procedures, and in the interests of consistency, these can be grouped under the same four headings used for discipline in Fig. 6.4 earlier. Note, however, that because the factors at work in discipline and grievance can be very different, it is only the main headings from Fig. 6.4 which identify groups of factors that can be used.

Contextual factors

Having a grievance procedure is one thing; whether employees know that it exists and that it can be used to resolve their dissatisfactions can be something altogether different. Grievances can be extremely rare in some organisations, and it has been suggested that this is because few people would wish to risk antagonizing a superior by questioning her or his judgement (Torrington *et al.*, 2002). However, it can be extremely dangerous to assume that a low number of grievances means that there are few dissatisfactions: it might well mean that the employment relations climate is so threatening that nobody dares question management's judgement. Indeed, there is a stream of evidence which shows that there are many employees who experience unfair or unjust treatment, but nevertheless remain silent for fear of managerial retribution (Boroff and Lewin, 1997; Lewin and Boroff, 1996). Therefore, to make grievance procedures effective, employees must not be made to feel guilty if they seek to have dissatisfactions remedied. Rather, higher managers should ensure that appropriate *rules and procedures* exist, that their existence is advertised, and that lower-level managers understand how to operate the procedures (Swann, 1981). Indeed, it could be as well to remember the old adage that if a firm has to announce, and then keep on announcing, that it has an open-door policy, it probably needs to be questioned whether the doors are really open (Beck and Beck, 1986). In addition, it should be noted that *custom and practice* rules also play a crucial role in the raising of grievances. These influence the traditions of workgroups, which could affect the willingness of their members to contest supervisory decisions. It is important, therefore, that senior managers avoid the automatic assumption that a supervisor who appears to handle a high number of grievances is ineffective. It could very well be a sign of the reverse.

With grievance the *ideologies and attitudes of managers* can be just as influential as in discipline. It is their actions that usually give rise to employee dissatisfactions in the first place and, perhaps more important, ideologies and attitudes can influence the way that employee dissatisfactions are dealt with. For example, managers who hold a unitarist frame of reference are much more likely to make arbitrary and frequent changes that give rise to employee dissatisfactions and, problematically, unitarist managers are almost certainly those who are most likely to consider that employees have no justification for feeling aggrieved.

Just as management ideologies and attitudes can be important, so can those of a *trade union*. While there is nothing inevitable about trade union involvement in a grievance issue, where it occurs it may well have some connection with two important characteristics of employment relations. The first of these is the *nature of workplace representation*, where in some organisations employees are actively encouraged to pursue grievances by their representatives (Bemmels *et al.*, 1991; Dalton and Todor, 1981). However, even where this happens it should not prompt defensive reactions, or the assumption that stewards are troublemakers. Bringing matters out into the open clearly lowers any tendency for things to lie hidden beneath the surface, and erupt in more disruptive ways and in the long run stewards may well be performing a valuable service.

The second characteristic, *employment relations climate*, is much more intangible, but can be an extremely important factor in grievance handling. There is a considerable body of evidence to show that hostile climates are associated with high rates of grievance activity and low morale in employees (Norsworthy and Zabala, 1985). Unfortunately, however, in these circumstances it is often the climate itself that seems to give rise to grievance-handling methods that are of low effectiveness. For example, grievances are unlikely to be handled informally, and those that are not upheld at early stages are then doggedly pursued through all the successive levels of appeal in the procedure. In consequence, therefore, rather than being a problem to be solved, both trade union and management use grievances as an opportunity to score points, and tend to see matters in terms of winning or losing.

Employee factors

A factor that can be extremely important in the raising of grievances is that of *employee perceptions*. Dissatisfactions often arise where a person makes a comparison between his/her own efforts and rewards, and the efforts and rewards that others receive. Indeed, the perceived degree of inequity, together with the extent to which a supervisor is considered to have used fair methods in allocating rewards and effort, have both been shown to affect the likelihood of using grievance processes (Barrett-Howard and Tyler, 1986; Fogler *et al.*, 1983). In addition, just as supervisors make *attributional judgements* in disciplinary cases, in the grievance situation employees are likely to attribute motives to supervisors for their actions. For example, if an employee makes an internal attribution and assumes that internal factors such as attitude, personality or mood are the reason why a supervisor allocated a particularly unpleasant task, the person is much more likely to interpret the action as a personal punishment and retaliate by either using grievance procedures (Gordon and Bowlby, 1985), leaving the organisation, or even remaining but engaging in antagonistic behaviour such as absenteeism and poor work performance (Frone, 2000).

Managerial and supervisory factors

There is some evidence that certain management and supervisory styles are associated with higher rates of grievance activity among employees. For example, managers who do not adequately explain or justify changes to employees are much more likely to attract grievances as retaliatory action. Moreover, how a supervisor reacts to prior grievances can give rise to even more dissatisfactions. There is, for example, a stream of evidence to show that if an employee successfully pursues a grievance, there is a tendency for the supervisor to retaliate in some way at the next opportunity (Colquitt *et al.*, 2001; Masterson *et al.*, 2000; Olson-Buchanan, 1996)

Issue-handling factors

The importance of handling dissatisfactions quickly, and at the lowest possible managerial level, is well supported by both managers and trade unions. Indeed, one of the very first studies of grievance handling shows that this has huge benefits, not the least of which is a more cooperative employment relations climate (Turner and Robinson, 1972). This, as was noted earlier, is likely to have an effect on the subsequent rate of grievance activity.

Summary points

- Fairness, justice and systematic methods are all required for the effective handling of grievances.

- Arguably the most important stage in the grievance process is the first (informal) one, which should be approached as a fact-finding exercise to uncover the full extent of an employee's dissatisfaction.

- The handling process can be divided into a number of stages: awareness seeking; preparation for a meeting with the employee to discuss the issue; a preliminary (informal) meeting, which, if necessary, can be adjourned to collect further information; a reconvened meeting and (if more formal stages of the procedure are to be entered) preparation of a joint statement of the grievance.

- Many factors can influence whether grievance handling is effective, and for convenience these can be grouped together as: contextual factors; employee factors; supervisor factors; issue-handling factors.

Conclusions

Despite their apparently straightforward nature, in practice, discipline and grievance issues can be extremely complex to handle, and there are a large number of factors – not the least of which are the skills and competences of supervisors and managers – that can influence whether the processes work effectively. It is the early stages of procedures that are often the most crucial, and these are often left to supervisors to handle, many of whom are untrained and ill-equipped to do so. Nevertheless, discipline and grievance processes go to the very heart of the employment relationship, and in the future both are likely to influence the on-going employment relations climate in organisations. For this reason, organisations have strong incentives to develop and use sound processes and practices for handling issues of this type, and providing sensible, consistent methods are used, it is possible for these matters to be handled effectively.

Review and discussion questions

1 Define discipline and grievance.

2 Explain what is meant by the 'two faces of justice' concept with respect to discipline and grievance.

3 Explain three criteria that differentiate between discipline and grievance, and state which of these cast doubt on the 'two faces of justice' assertion.

4 Define and distinguish between punishment, deterrence and rehabilitation as different approaches to application of discipline in organisations.

5 To what extent is it a legal requirement for an organisation to have formal, written disciplinary procedures?

6 Explain how contextual factors in an organisation can impact on the effectiveness of its disciplinary procedures.

7 To what extent is it a legal requirement for an organisation to have formal, written grievance procedures?

8 State the criteria against which the effectiveness of an organisation's grievance procedures can be judged.

9 Explain how contextual factors in an organisation can impact on the effectiveness of its grievance procedures.

10 Explain why the first (informal) stages of disciplinary and grievance procedures can often be the most crucial ones in terms of achieving effectiveness of the processes.

Further reading

ACAS (2003) Code of Practice 1: *Disciplinary and Grievance Procedures*, Advisory Conciliation and Arbitration Service, London.

Boswell, W.R. and J.B. Olson-Buchanan (2004) 'Experiencing mistreatment at work: the role of grievance filing, nature of mistreatment and employee withdrawal', *Academy of Management Journal*, Vol. 47 (1), pp. 129–139. The paper reports an empirical investigation of employees who have used grievance procedures and the eventual outcomes of doing so.

Fenley, A. (1998) 'Models, styles and metaphors: understanding the management of discipline', *Employee Relations*, Vol. 20 (4), pp. 349–371. A useful theoretical examination of the use of discipline in organisations, which gives a critique of policies and practices in its use.

Hook, C.M., D.J. Rollinson, M. Foot and J. Handley (1996) 'Supervisor and manager styles in handling discipline and grievance: part one – comparing styles in handling discipline and grievance', *Personnel Review*. Vol. 25 (3), pp. 20–34. A useful paper that explores and compares the handling styles of managers in discipline and grievance. Surprisingly, handling styles tend to be quite different for discipline than for grievance.

Larwood, L., P. Rand and A. Der Hovanessian (1979) 'Sex differences in response to simulated employee discipline cases', *Personnel Psychology* Vol. 32 (3), pp. 529–550. A fascinating study of sex bias in disciplinary judgements. Because women are in many cases evaluated as less competent than men, they seem to attract more internal attributions to explain their rule transgressions, and are thus more likely to attract severe sanctions.

Lewin, D. and R.B. Peterson (1999) 'Behavioural outcomes of grievance activity', *Industrial Relations*, Vol. 38 (4), pp. 554–576. An informative paper that reports a longitudinal empirical study comparing people who raise grievances with those who do not, together with the outcomes for them and their supervisors.

Rees, W.D. (1997) 'The disciplinary pyramid and its importance', *Industrial and Commercial Training*, Vol. 29 (1), pp. 4–9. A paper with a somewhat managerial approach to discipline, but which draws attention to some of the skills needed to use it effectively.

Rollinson, D.J. (1997) 'More than a rap on the knuckles', *Croner Reference Book for Employers Magazine*, June, pp. 10–13. An easy-to-read article, reporting some of the results of an empirical study that investigates employee perceptions of the disciplinary handling styles of managers. In many cases management's handling of discipline was found to be so poor that many employees had ongoing tendencies to transgress in the future.

Rollinson, D.J., J. Handley, C. Hook and M. Foot (1997) 'The disciplinary experience and its effects on behaviour: an exploratory study, *Work, Employment and Society*, Vol. 11 (2), pp. 283–311. The paper reports an exploratory study of management handling styles for disciplinary issues. In many cases these were so poor that employees had continuing tendencies to transgress rules in the future.

Thomson, A.W.J. and V.V. Murray (1976) *Grievance Procedures*, Saxon House, Farnborough. A comprehensive study of the operation of grievance procedures and mechanisms in a sample of British firms. Gives valuable insights into the ways in which managers and shop stewards view and use procedures to resolve dissatisfactions.

Trevino, L.K. (1992) 'The social effects of punishment in organisations: a justice perspective', *Academy of Management Review*, Vol. 17 (3), pp. 647–676. A conceptual article which gives, with the aid of a model, a large number of propositions about the likely effects of using punishments in the disciplinary situation.

Dismissal and redundancy

Introduction

This chapter deals with two important issues: dismissal and redundancy. Both are heavily regulated by statute law, and both can have a strong impact on the employment relations climate and psychological contracts within an organisation. Since employees can be dismissed for disciplinary offences, this means there is a clear connection between one of the topics (discipline) covered in the previous chapter. Therefore, the first part of this chapter starts with a definition of dismissal, then distinguishes between different categories of dismissal, and closes with a review of the remedies for unfair dismissal that can be sought by an employee.

The second topic, redundancy, is what is normally classified as one of the 'fair' reasons for dismissal. It starts by defining redundancy, and this is followed with a discussion of the efficacy of having formal redundancy policies and procedures. The main provisions of statute law and its effects on redundancy handling are explained, and the chapter closes by setting out a comprehensive procedure for handling redundancy.

Dismissal

For the purposes of this chapter, dismissal is defined somewhat loosely as the termination of a

dismissal

The termination of a contract of employment.

contract of employment. Perhaps the first thing that needs to be recognised is that, while huge advances have been made in the past two decades in giving individual employees an increased level of employment protection, in absolute terms there is nothing in statute law that stands in the way of an employer dismissing an employee for any reason. Indeed, should an employee be dismissed in circumstances that are unfair or unjust, ultimately all that the law can do is to make it more expensive for the employer. Nevertheless, one of the basic principles expressed in the original Redundancy Payments Act (1965) was that employees should enjoy a level of irremovability from their jobs, and from this has followed a progressive refinement of circumstances in which the dismissal of an employee can be considered to be fair and just. In line with these developments, many of which are now enshrined in statute law, there are a number of general categories into which dismissal can be grouped:

- Dismissal for automatically fair reasons
- Dismissal which is for potentially fair reasons
- Dismissal which is for automatically unfair reasons
- Wrongful dismissal
- Unfair dismissal
- Constructive dismissal.

Pause for reflection

Together with other students in your class examine the six categories into which dismissals can be grouped. What do you feel are the merits of having an elaborated classification system such as this?

Before describing these it is important to point out that the dividing line between the categories is sometimes less to do with the conduct for which a person is dismissed, than with the way dismissal is handled. Even with the most blatant piece of misconduct by an employee, unless matters are handled fairly, a case of potentially fair dismissal can quickly become unfair, because the law in Great Britain is not only concerned with *what* is done, but *how* it is done. For this reason the law encourages organisations to have formal disciplinary procedures to evaluate employee rule transgressions. In addition, to try to ensure that fairness and justice are dispensed to employees who are judged guilty of serious transgressions, employers are required to follow the Standard Statutory Dismissal Procedure given in the ACAS Code of Practice on Discipline and Grievance (2003a), which is shown as Exhibit 6.2 in the previous chapter. It is also relevant to note that legal principles tend to be subject to constant revision. Thus, what falls into one category rather than another can be subject to revision due to the development of case law.

Dismissal for automatically fair reasons

As opposed to the majority of countries in Europe, where employees are assumed by the law to have merely suspended their contracts of employment if they take part in industrial action, in

Great Britain they are assumed to have broken their contracts. Thus, irrespective of whether there has been a ballot for industrial action, or whether notice has been given to the employer of such action, it is perfectly legal for the employer to dismiss striking workers. However, where this occurs, there can be no element of selectivity about dismissals. If the employer dismisses any of those who took industrial action, they must all be dismissed, and it is near impracticable for an employer to dismiss a whole workforce. Nevertheless, this sometime happens, and the employer can, if he or she desires, selectively re-employ dismissed employees on whatever terms he or she chooses, providing this takes place three months from the date of dismissal.

Dismissal for potentially fair reasons

There are a wide variety of reasons where a dismissal can be considered to be potentially fair. These are:

- lack of capability, skill, qualification or poor work performance
- misconduct
- redundancy
- where continued employment would contravene a statutory duty or restriction
- some other substantial reason.

All of these, with the exception of redundancy – which will be considered in detail later – were discussed in Chapter 6, which deals with discipline and grievance handling. Some of them can ultimately result in the decision to dismiss an employee and if this happens, the individual concerned could contest the fairness of the decision. Providing the employee's complaint is received within three months of the date of termination, the case will eventually be heard by an employment tribunal. However, if both employee and employer agree, the merits of the case can arbitrated under the ACAS Arbitration Scheme.

When dealing with cases of this type an employment tribunal is required to examine whether:

1 dismissal was for an admissible reason (see list above), and was fair in terms of equity of treatment with other employees

2 the offence, or the employee's past record, justified dismissal as a reasonable response in the circumstances

3 the employer followed proper and adequate procedures before arriving at the decision to dismiss.

Assuming that the reason for the employer seeking dismissal was for an admissible reason, the two main questions to be addressed by a tribunal are numbers 2 and 3. With respect to number 3, the most desirable and equitable course of action is for the employer to have followed the Standard Statutory Dismissal Procedure (Denton, 2005). However, it is surprising just how many cases are taken to employment tribunals for ajudication in which there are procedural defects. For example, a study for the DTI (Earnshaw, 1997) shows that in nearly 40 per cent of claims employment tribunals find in favour of the employee because there are procedural discrepancies. Typical failings include the lack of opportunity for employees to give an explanation of their conduct; the fact that dismissals occurred without any prior disciplinary hearing; and that procedures did not comply with the firm's own rules.

Cases where dismissal is for lack of capability, skills, or poor work performance are often those where an employee challenges the fairness of the employer's decision to dismiss, and where this happens, the employer is usually required to justify the employee's lack of suitability. One of the more common misconceptions in this area is that dismissal for prolonged ill health can be a sufficient and valid reason for dismissal, particularly if it means that an employee cannot discharge the terms of his or her contract of employment. In addition, cases of sickness absence are often felt by employers to be similarly foolproof. However, these cases are seldom clear-cut, and each one needs to be considered on its own merits. To this end Duggan (1999) argues that an employer should always seek medical evidence before making a decision on whether or not to dismiss. It is also worth noting that the legislation on disability discrimination makes it necessary for employers to exercise a great deal of caution in dismissing disabled people. For example, it is probably worthwhile considering whether changes could be made in the workplace that would allow a disabled person to carry on working. Indeed, in the interests of equity and justice, it might well be necessary for an employer to tolerate a higher than normal level of absence in someone who is disabled.

Pause for reflection

Together with other students in your class, try to identify where a dismissal could automatically be classified as unfair.

Dismissals that are automatically unfair

Before discussing dismissals that fall into this category, it is necessary to acquaint the reader with an important practice in British legislation. The basis of employment protections afforded to employees is laid down in the Employment Rights Act (1996). However, from time to time the State uncovers an important omission in these rights, and they are extended; not by reworking a whole piece of legislation, but with the use of a statutory instrument that updates legislation that already exists (see Chapter 5). In the interests of presenting a picture that is easily understood, this chapter largely confines itself to dealing with only the basic principles of the law on employment rights, and additional rights granted by statutory instruments are mostly ignored. Nevertheless, the use of statutory instruments to update the law must be acknowledged, and that this gives an important element of fluidity in the employment rights that an employee can claim.

As the number of individual employment rights has increased, there has been an expansion in the number of 'inadmissible' reasons to dismiss an employee. This has given rise to an important difference between cases in which a dismissal is automatically unfair, and those where unfair dismissal has to be proved. Where the unfairness of a dismissal actually has to be adjudicated by a tribunal, an employee must have at least one year's continuous service with an organisation before he or she is able to make a complaint. If automatically unfair grounds for dismissal exist, however, there is no length of service requirement; the employee has been dismissed because he or she exercised a right to something already granted by a statute law. These are rights:

- to pregnancy or maternity leave
- to parental leave, paternity leave, adoption leave, or time off to care for dependants
- to representational rights, including acting as a workplace representative, safety representative, learning representative, pension trustee, trade union officer, or taking part, or proposing to take part, in a lawful union activity

- to join or refuse to join a trade union
- to protection from discrimination (unless objectively justified) on the grounds of sex, race, disability, sexual orientation, religion or political belief (in Northern Ireland only)
- from dismissal on the grounds of being a part-time or fixed-term employee
- from dismissal for refusing to work on Sundays (retail workers only)
- from dismissal for taking part in official industrial action (organised and approved by a trade union executive) during the first eight weeks that the action takes place
- from dismissal for exercising a statutory trade union right, including observing working-time regulations, annual leave entitlement, the national minimum wage, or transfer of undertakings (TUPE) regulations
- from dismissal without the use of the Standard Statutory Dismissal Procedure.

Dismissals that are contestable

According to research undertaken by the DTI, well over 1 million employees are subject to dismissal of some sort in Great Britain each year. If an individual feels that he or she has been treated unfairly, either because of the reason given for dismissal or because of the way that dismissal came about, the person can complain to an employment tribunal. Clearly not everyone does this, but it is estimated that somewhere between 5 and 10 per cent of employees who qualify to do so eventually bring claims of this nature to a tribunal (DTI, 1999).

In Great Britain there are three forms of dismissal complaint that can be made, and for all of them the employee is required to have one year's continuous service with the employer. First, **wrongful dismissal**, in which an individual complains that the way he or she was dismissed constituted a breach of his or her contract of employment. Second, **constructive dismissal**, where a person feels forced to resign, as a direct result of his or her employer's actions. Third, **unfair dismissal**, which is the most common complaint, and is a situation in which it is claimed that the act of dismissal fell short of reasonable treatment, as laid down by the Employment Rights Act (1996).

wrongful dismissal

A claim by an individual that the way he or she was dismissed constitutes a breach of his/her contract of employment.

constructive dismissal

A claim by an individual that he or she was forced to resign as a direct result of his or her employer's actions.

unfair dismissal

A claim by an individual that the circumstances of his or her dismissal fell short of reasonable treatment as laid down by the Employment Rights Act (1996).

Wrongful dismissal

There is a long-standing common-law right to damages for an employee who has been wrongfully dismissed. However, claims of this type can sometimes be expensive to pursue, because only claims for £25 000 or less are dealt with by employment tribunals, while those above this figure are taken to a county court. Since all wrongful dismissal cases are effectively allegations that the terms of the contract of employment have been breached, they are only appropriate in selected circumstances: for instance, where an employee has not been given adequate notice, or has been denied access to the organisation's disciplinary procedure. It is relatively easy for an employer to defend a case of this type by showing that the contract of employment was lawfully terminated for good cause: for example, by showing that the employee had effectively repudiated the terms of the contract by committing an act of gross misconduct, neglect of duty or insubordination.

Somewhat more simply, the employer can avoid the claim by giving the employee the correct period of notice (or payment in lieu). In the case of a fixed-term contract (and in the absence of a clause that allows it to be brought to an end early) the case can be avoided by allowing the employee to work out the contract. Table 7.1 shows the statutory minimum periods of notice to which employees are entitled as per the Employment Rights Act (1996).

An employee has six years in which to bring a claim for wrongful dismissal, and in successful cases, damages are designed to put the employee in the situation that he or she would have been in if employment had continued. Thus, wages for the notice period, commission and even the value of fringe benefits such as a company car can be awarded. However, should the employee find another job during what would have been the notice period, pay can be deducted. Moreover, the employee is under a positive duty to minimize his or her losses by seeking new employment.

Constructive dismissal

This is judged to have occurred when the behaviour of management forces an employee to resign, and usually this is because the manager showed a clear intent not to be bound by the terms of the contract of employment, which left the employee with no choice but to resign. Note that because it is the employee who has resigned, employment tribunals are required to examine the circumstances that led to the resignation. This tends to make cases harder for employees to win, and easier for employers to defend, if only because a tribunal is required to establish that dismissal actually took place before ever considering the reasonableness of the employer's behaviour. This can be very difficult to uncover, and effectively places the burden of proof on the employee to show that he or she was forced into resignation. To do this it is not sufficient to show that the employer behaved in a capricious or offhand way. There usually has to be something much more specific that the employer did that went to the very heart of the employment contract. For example, the use of violence, demotion of the employee, a reduction in pay, a significant change in duties or of work location, might all be examples that could result in a win for the employee.

Length of service	Length of notice
after 4 weeks	1 week
over 4 weeks but less than 2 years	2 weeks
over 2 years but less than 3 years	3 weeks
over 3 years but less than 4 years	4 weeks
over 4 years but less than 5 years	5 weeks
over 5 years but less than 6 years	6 weeks
over 6 years but less than 7 years	7 weeks
over 7 years but less than 8 years	8 weeks
over 8 years but less than 9 years	9 weeks
over 9 years but less than 10 years	10 weeks
over 10 years but less than 11 years	11 weeks
over 11 years but less than 12 years	12 weeks
over 12 years	12 weeks

Table 7.1 Statutory minimum notice periods

Unfair dismissal

Claims of this type are the most common of those that are made in respect to termination of employment. Roughly 40 000 claims each year are made to employment tribunals, although fewer than a third of them actually result in a full tribunal case, and in many instances ACAS attempts to help the parties to reach agreement. Indeed, copies of papers lodged with tribunals are sent automatically to ACAS with a view to conciliation under the ACAS Arbitration Scheme, and many are settled in this way without the necessity of a full tribunal hearing. Unfair dismissal is a claim by an employee that a protection conferred by the Employment Rights Act (1996) has been breached: a protection that gives all employees the right not to be unfairly dismissed. However, there are certain excluded categories of employees: for example, those who have less than one year's continuous employment with the firm; employees with fixed-term contracts of more than one year who have explicitly waived their rights in writing; employees who normally work outside Great Britain; and those who are past normal retirement age (or a default age of 65), although with the introduction of legislation to outlaw age discrimination, it seems likely that this provision could be removed.

The position with people on fixed-term contacts is particularly interesting. A large number of employees who work in these circumstances fail to realise that they have a right to claim unfair dismissal if their contracts of employment are not renewed in a fairly automatic way. An employer can avoid a claim of this type by getting the employee to sign an express exclusion waiver at the time the person is employed. However, there is a widespread practice of simply terminating the person's employment in silence at the end of the contractual period, and the employee in his or her ignorance simply departs.

Where it has been established that an employee is not excluded from claiming unfair dismissal for some other reason such as redundancy, he or she next needs to prove that dismissal has actually taken place. Usually this is quite clear in the surrounding circumstances, but where there is some dispute about the matter, the onus is always placed on the employee to show that termination of employment has actually occurred. For the purposes of an unfair dismissal case three circumstances of dismissal are acknowledged:

1 The employer simply terminates the contract, with or without notice, by effectively telling the employee to quit.

2 The employer terminates a fixed-term contract without it being renewed.

3 Constructive dismissal, where an employee terminates the contract with or without notice, because of the employer's conduct.

In the face of a claim for unfair dismissal, an employment tribunal focuses on two separate but connected questions: (i) whether the reason for dismissal was one that is classed by the law as legitimate; and (ii) whether the employer acted in a reasonable way in dismissing the employee for this reason. If the answer to the first is 'No', clearly the employee has won his or her case. However, when it comes to evaluating the reasonableness of the dismissal, things tend to be much more neutral.

Written statement of reasons for dismissal

Dismissed employees who have completed one year's continuous service are entitled by the Employment Rights Act (1966) to receive, on request (orally or in writing), a statement of reasons for dismissal. Where an employee is dismissed during pregnancy, maternity or

> ### Case study 7.1: **Mohammed Al-Hudoun**
>
> Until he was dismissed, Dr Mohammed Al-Hudoun was employed as a senior registrar by the South Clayshire Regional Health Authority, where it was normal practice to allow a registrar three attempts at passing the examination of the Royal College of Surgeons. Success in this examination would have qualified him to apply for a consultant's post when one became vacant somewhere in the National Health Service, but not automatic promotion, and he would have to wait for a vacancy to arise. However, Dr Al-Hudoun failed the examination at the third take, and was subsequently dismissed. He immediately claimed that the dismissal was unfair on the grounds that he had had insufficient training to pass the examination, and appealed to an employment tribunal. Evidence was given to the tribunal by the Royal College of Surgeons, who stated that in their opinion Dr Al-Hudoun's training had been adequate.
>
> What do you feel will be the outcome for Dr Al-Hudoun?

adoption leave, there is an entitlement to a written statement regardless of length of service, and whether or not a request is made.

Remedies for unfair dismissal

In the event that an employee is successful in his or her claim for unfair dismissal, there are three alternative remedies: reinstatement, re-engagement and compensation. In **reinstatement** the employee gets his or her original job back, with all prior conditions restored, with additional financial compensation to reflect any time spent out of work. **Re-engagement** results in suitable alternative employment with the original employer, plus compensation for time spent unemployed.

It has been argued that, although reinstatement or re-engagement were always intended to be the primary remedies for unfair dismissal, successful claims are almost always settled by compensation, which means that the system seriously fails people (Lewis, 1981). However, there is a pragmatic consideration in this matter. An employment tribunal cannot compel an employer to re-employ a dismissed individual and, unless he or she requests either reinstatement or re-engagement, the option is never considered. Consequently, only a tiny proportion of successful claims (about 1.5 per cent) result in either of these options.

The level of **compensation** received consists of the sum of four different awards, each of which is assessed separately: the *basic award*; the *compensatory award*; the *additional award*; and the *special award*.

The *basic award* is calculated according to a scale in which the amount is varied according to age and length of service (see Table 7.2). This gives a figure that is the same as for compensation for redundancy. Since the maximum number of weeks for which the award can be made is 20, this means that the current maximum award is £5600, which can be reduced where the tribunal takes the view that the employee contributed to his or her own dismissal. Note, however, that notice (or pay in lieu of notice) is also given.

The terms of the *compensatory award* are intended to provide recompense for any financial loss suffered. Most employees are entitled to be considered for this, and it would embrace

---

reinstatement

A remedy for unfair dismissal in which the employee gets his or her original job back, with all prior conditions restored, and with additional financial compensation to reflect any time spent out of work.

re-engagement

A remedy for unfair dismissal in which suitable alternative employment with the original employer is given, plus compensation for time spent unemployed.

compensation (unfair dismissal)

A remedy which consists of the sum of four different awards.

Age band	Assumed maximum weekly wage	Maximum reckonable years of service
over 18 but under 22 – half of a week's pay 22 and over but under 41 – one week's pay 41 and over but under 65 – one and a half weeks' pay	£280 per week	20 years
Notes (i) Where the normal retirement age for the job is 65 and the employee is within twelve months of that age, the statutory redundancy entitlement is reduced by one-twelfth for each complete month after the employee's 64th birthday. (ii) An employer who intends to dismiss an employee to whom a pension payment is due under an occupational pension scheme not more than 90 weeks after the dismissal, may offset part of the pension payment against the redundancy payment.		

Table 7.2 Calculation of basic award for unfair dismissal and redundancy compensation

matters such as lost earnings, including commission and fringe benefits. Theoretically, this could be a substantial sum of money in the case of a senior employee, but there is a ceiling on the award that is something in the order of £13 000, and this can also be reduced if the employee is considered to have contributed to his or her own dismissal.

The two further awards are only made in particular circumstances. The *additional award* is only made where a tribunal has ordered reinstatement or re-engagement, and the employer has refused to comply. This could result in additional compensation of between 13 and 26 weeks pay at a maximum of £280 per week. However, if the dismissal was for reasons of sex or race discrimination, 52 weeks' pay would normally be awarded. A *special award* is made where dismissal was for a reason that is *automatically unfair*; for instance, for dismissing a trade union representative for performing his or her duties, and the size of this award depends on whether reinstatement or re-engagement has been requested. Where it was requested by the employee, but is refused by the tribunal, the award could be up to an additional 104 weeks' pay. If, however, reinstatement or re-engagement was also ordered by the tribunal and the employer refuses to comply, the award could be as high as an additional 156 weeks' pay.

Summary points

- Dismissal consists of the termination of an employee's contract of employment.
- It can occur for a number of reasons, which can be grouped into the following categories: dismissal for automatically fair reasons; dismissal for potentially fair reasons; dismissal which is for automatically unfair reasons; wrongful dismissal; unfair dismissal; constructive dismissal.
- Where an employee contests the reason for dismissal, or the manner in which dismissal was carried out, he or she can make a claim to an employment tribunal that the dismissal has been unfair.
- An employment tribunal can grant one of three remedies in a successful case brought by an employee: reinstatement; re-engagement; or compensation.

Redundancy and redundancy-handling: background

In the past, many traditional industries such as coal, iron and steel and shipbuilding went through periods of severe decline, and as a result, redundancies were quite common. In the late 1980s redundancies in these industries were running at about half a million each year. However, by the late 1990s the number had declined to about 200 000 redundancies annually (Terryn, 1999) and these days the basis on which redundancies are made has changed. The phenomenon is now far more closely associated with cost-cutting, and new names such as 'downsizing', 'rightsizing' and 'delayering' have been invented to gloss over the task of labour shedding. Indeed, so pronounced is this effect that the announcement of redundancy in a firm can often result in a rise in its share price, because this is interpreted by the stock market as an indication that its profits will shortly rise due to lower labour costs (Cameron, 1994). Firms who did this in the past may well have become leaner and fitter in the process. However, redundancy can have a huge detrimental effect on psychological contracts (Caulkin, 1995), and people who have experienced redundancy are likely to continue to feel insecure in future employment (Gregg and Wadsworth, 1995). Moreover, there is often a hidden cost that many organisations fail to consider: that of the enduring psychological effects on employees who survive a redundancy programme. These effects can mean that a leaner and fitter workforce also has lowered organisational commitment and loyalty, and a feeling of insecurity that can quickly lead to a desire to leave the organisation (Allen *et al.*, 2001). For these reasons, redundancy is a matter that an organisation needs to handle with a great deal of care and attention, and it is hardly surprising that carefully drafted legislation exists to encourage firms to approach matters in this way.

Redundancy: definitions

In a situation where an employer proposes to make 20 or more people redundant over 90 days or less, redundancy is defined as:

> dismissal for a reason not related to the individual concerned, or for a number of reasons all of which are not so related.
>
> ACAS (2005a)

In employment law using the word 'redundancy' has two different purposes: (i) to establish an entitlement to redundancy compensation; and (ii) to establish rights to consultation. For the purposes of establishing an entitlement to compensation, as per the Employment Rights Act (1996), redundancy is confined to situations where employees are dismissed because:

- the employer has ceased, or intends to cease, to carry on the business for the purposes of which the employee was so employed
- the employer has ceased, or intends to cease, to carry on the business in the place where the employee was so employed
- the requirements of the business for employees to carry out work of a particular kind has ceased or diminished or is expected to cease or diminish
- the requirements of the business for employees to carry out work of a particular kind, in the place where they were so employed, has ceased or diminished or are expected to cease or diminish.

Since there is also a need to follow proper procedures when making even a single person redundant, the ACAS guide to Redundancy Handling cautions:

> If an employer is thinking of dismissing an employee on the grounds of redundancy, they must follow a standard dismissal procedure. This involves writing to the employee, setting out the reasons for the dismissal; meeting with the employee to discuss the dismissal; and, where necessary, holding an appeal.
>
> ACAS (2005a)

Reasons for redundancy
The causal factors

Across the years redundancy has been associated with a number of main causes, which can be reduced to four that have a direct impact on the extent to which it becomes a common phenomenon. These are: *structural decline and change in industry*; *economic changes*; *technology*; and *work reorganisation*, which will briefly be considered in turn.

Starting in the mid-1950s a great deal of redundancy was associated with *structural decline and change* in British industry. For the most part this involved older, less efficient and technologically outdated manufacturing industries, which suffered from either a rapidly declining demand for their outputs, or an inability to compete with foreign competitors. Although this 'shake-out' in industry is now largely a historical phenomenon, there are still examples of it taking place. For example, deep-mined coal extraction is now nearly defunct in Great Britain; fishing which was once a thriving industry has now declined because of the near exhaustion of fish stocks; and iron steel production and shipbuilding are shadows of their former selves.

Another cause for redundancy has periodically been *declining levels of economic activity*, either in whole industries, or in particular organisations. Recently this has been associated with globalisation, but although the globalisation of world trade is real enough, to use it as an excuse for every case of redundancy is probably a gross overstatement. What is probably just as important are the huge pressures for amalgamations and mergers of organisations, because when two firms amalgamate, there are winners and losers, and in the reorganisation that follows, parts of the prior firms disappear.

A great deal of redundancy has also been prompted by waves of *technological change*, which has had very far-reaching effects. Technology not only affects the quantity of labour that is required, it has a dramatic impact on the composition of a workforce, and the jobs that it does. For example, few jobs these days need the brawn that at one time was supplied by men. Thus, female workers are now as commonplace in most jobs as men. In addition, the use of other technologies, and in particular the use of electronic information and communications technology (ICT), has revolutionised many jobs. To use but one example, electronic point-of-sale readers on supermarket checkouts have greatly simplified cash handling and warehousing activities.

Finally, and as was pointed out earlier, *work reorganisation* has been used extensively to obtain a more efficient use of plant and machinery, and to bring about a more concentrated use of labour. This is only the latest in a long line of developments and has probably done as much as anything else to give rise to the most recent wave of redundancies.

The important thing to note, however, and as portrayed in Fig. 7.1, is that there are often cumulative effects from all of these factors, so that redundancy sometimes seems to have a momentum of its own. In today's conditions the management of an organisation probably has no choice but to keep a wary eye on the environment, in order to avoid becoming one of yesterday's casualties. As

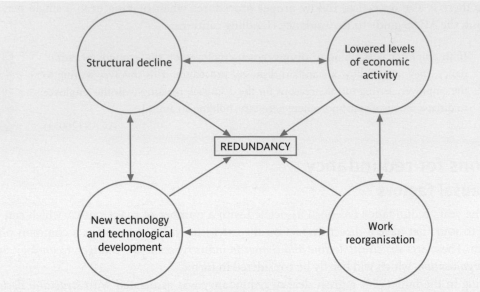

Figure 7.1 The interconnected nature of factors potentially giving rise to redundancies

well as trying to equip itself to produce the goods and services that customers want, a firm tries to keep ahead of the game by using new technologies, and more efficient and effective work methods. Because this takes place against a backdrop of competitors who are all trying to do the same thing, it takes a comparatively short time for redundancy to come to be seen as a panacea by many firms.

Pause for reflection

Working in pairs with another student in your class, imagine that you are both trade union officers in a firm that has just announced that it is about to make a considerable number of employees redundant. The managing director gives his reasons why the firm suddenly finds itself in this situation, and both of you are mandated by the trade union to make an initial response. What will your responses be in each case if the reasons given by the MD were respectively:

1 aggressive competitor activity has reduced demand for the firm's products
2 re-equipping with new technology has reduced staffing requirements
3 reorganisation and using new work methods has resulted in greater efficiency in the production process, and so fewer staff are required?

The legal framework to redundancy

There are three main provisions in the legal framework that affects redundancy:

1 Compensation for redundant employees
2 Protection against unfair dismissal and rights to time off from work to search for new jobs
3 Employee and trade union rights to consultation with management prior to the occurrence of redundancies.

These will be considered in turn.

Redundancy compensation

Provision for this has existed for some years, and the intention of the original Redundancy Payments Act (1965) was twofold: first, to give redundant employees a measure of compensation for the loss of a job, and second, to foster mobility of labour.

In the 1960s some of the redundancy programmes taking place were in very large, traditional firms that were often major employers in a town or locality. As a result, considerable numbers of people were released together, and there was little prospect of them finding replacement jobs. It is all very well telling workers to look further afield for new employment, but this is hardly possible without the resources to finance a move of location. Thus, one of the aims of the 1965 Act was to promote labour mobility, by giving redundant workers the wherewithal to finance a move of location. Until 1986, when the practice was abolished, the State took a positive part in this process by reimbursing part of a firm's redundancy costs from the State-administered Redundancy Fund. This was built up from contributions levied on all employers, but since 1986 employers have had to find compensation from their own resources.

To qualify for a redundancy payment, the individual concerned must be an employee of the firm with at least two years' continuous service after the age of 18. He or she must also be a person whose employment is terminated in what qualifies as a redundancy situation (see definition earlier). Compensation is made on a scale that varies according to age and length of service, and the basis for calculating compensation is described in Table 7.2 shown earlier.

There are certain groups of workers who are excluded from receiving redundancy payments:

- Those who would reach the age of 65 before the date of dismissal
- Those who work for a company with a normal retirement age of less than 65, who have reached that age
- Merchant seamen, former registered dock workers engaged in dock work covered by other arrangements, and share fishermen
- Crown servants, members of the armed forces or police services
- Those on fixed-term contracts of at least two years' service who have waived their rights to redundancy
- Apprentices who have not become employees at the end of their training
- A domestic servant who is a member of the employer's immediate family.

In addition, there are other circumstances that can affect whether an individual qualifies for a redundancy payment. For example, within limits, an employer has the right to expect a certain amount of adaptability, flexibility, relocation and change in duties (to either part-time or full-time) in a reorganisation. Should an employee refuse to give this cooperation, the person could wind up being disqualified from claiming a redundancy payment. In addition, if the employer finds a position for a redundant employee in another firm, and then by mutual agreement dismisses the individual, this would not count as a redundancy situation, and there would be no right to compensation. Moreover, where management gives advanced notice of impending redundancies, and an employee of his or her own volition finds a job elsewhere and resigns, there is no right to redundancy compensation, because management had not specified to whom or when redundancy would be applied. Indeed, even though a programme of redundancy might be in progress, if an employer can show that a particular individual is dismissed for misconduct or some other misdemeanour, he or she has no right to redundancy compensation. Finally, an employee who refuses a reasonable offer of suitable alternative employment would

short-time working
An employee receives less than a week's pay for a particular week.

layoff
An employee receives no pay at all for a period of time, although still technically an employee of the organisation.

bumping (redundancy)
For reasons of operational convenience, and with the consent of the two employees, a potential redundancy in one individual's role is transferred to another employee's role.

not be entitled to redundancy compensation, providing of course that it can be shown to be a reasonable alternative.

However, if an employee has been working under short-time or layoff conditions for four consecutive weeks, or for any six weeks out of the last thirteen, he or she has a right to terminate the contract of employment (with notice) and claim a redundancy payment. In addition, there are certain practices that are allowed to try to safeguard as many jobs as possible in a redundancy situation. For example, with the consent of the employees concerned, a potential redundancy in one part of an organisation can sometimes be transferred to a person elsewhere in the organisation. This practice is sometimes known as bumping, the main provision being that one of these two jobs has to permanently disappear.

Unfair dismissal protection and rights to time off to look for work

Employees often feel particularly vulnerable where a redundancy programme is in progress, and the law gives them protection from unfair selection for redundancy. In basic terms the protections provided are identical to the rights concerning 'automatically unfair' dismissal given earlier in the chapter.

Employees who are given notice that they will be made redundant, and have been continuously employed in the organisation for at least two years, qualify for a statutory entitlement to a reasonable amount of (paid) time off to look for another job, or to arrange training. This time off must be allowed before the employee's notice expires, but what is a reasonable amount of time off is somewhat more contentious, and in current legislation is only two days.

Consultation rights

Where an employer proposes to dismiss 20 or more employees as redundant at one establishment over a period of 90 days or less, there is a statutory duty to consult representatives of recognised independent trade unions. If no trade union is recognised, other elected representatives of employees affected must be consulted. The employer also has a statutory duty to notify the Department of Trade and Industry of these redundancies.

Employee representatives may be elected solely for the purpose of consultation about specific redundancies, or they could be part of an existing consultative body. However, employers

Case study 7.2: **Mr Kunz**

Mr Kunz was 53, and had defective eyesight. He was selected for redundancy by managers at Sugco, when the firm reduced its staffing levels on the introduction of a more highly automated production process. The selection criteria used to choose people for redundancy included employee assessments of competence and potential, and on both evaluations Mr Kunz scored poorly because of his visual impairment, although managers at Sugco admitted he was a willing worker, and had it not been for the introduction of the automated line he would not have been made redundant. After discussing the matter with his trade union Mr Kunz then took his case to an employment tribunal.

What do you feel would be the likely outcome for Mr Kunz?

are required to consult with the appropriate representatives of any employees who may be affected (directly or indirectly) by the proposed dismissals. It can be noted that the ACAS guide to redundancy handling explicitly states that consultation should include ways of avoiding the dismissals, reducing the number of employees to be dismissed, and mitigating the circumstances of dismissals.

Pause for reflection

Working with other students in your class, try to identify a full range of steps that could be taken by a firm that is faced with having to make people redundant to avoid dismissals, reduce the number of employees to be dismissed, or mitigate the circumstances of dismissals.

Moreover, the employer must consult *with a view to reaching agreement* with appropriate representatives on these issues, and this duty applies even where employees volunteer for redundancy. Failure to comply with these consultation requirements could lead to a claim for compensation, and result in the employer being ordered to pay a **protective award**, equivalent in size to a normal week's pay for the employees, for up to 90 days.

protective award (redundancy)
An award made to a group of employees in recognition of the fact that their employer failed to observe the statutory right for employees to be consulted about proposed redundancies.

It is recommended that consultation should begin in good time and be completed before any redundancy notices are actually issued. It must begin:

- at least 30 days before the first dismissal takes effect if between 20 and 99 employees are to be made redundant at one establishment over a period of 90 days or less
- at least 90 days before the first dismissal takes effect if 100 or more employees are to be made redundant at one establishment over a period of 90 days or less.

In order to allow appropriate representatives to play a full and constructive part in the consultation process, employers have a statutory duty to disclose in writing the following information concerning redundancies:

- The reasons for the proposed redundancies
- The numbers and descriptions of employees it is proposed to dismiss as redundant
- The total number of employees of any such description employed at the establishment in question
- The proposed way in which employees will be selected for redundancy
- How the dismissals are to be carried out, taking account of any agreed procedure, including the period over which the dismissals are to take effect
- The method of calculating the amount of redundancy payments to be made to those who are to be dismissed.

While the above still applies, the whole matter of consultation rights has recently been changed with the introduction of the Information and Consultation of Employees (ICE) Regulations (2004), which give employees important new rights. These include the right to be kept informed about the economic situation of the business, and to be informed and consulted about employment prospects and decisions that could lead to substantial changes in work organisation or contractual relations, including redundancies. Although it is still too early to predict whether this new legislation will have a significant effect on redundancy consultation, it seems likely that this could be the case, particularly in small firms. Since this legislation has been designed to have an impact on information and communication in firms in a wider set of circumstances than redundancy, it is covered in the next chapter, which deals with the important topic of Employee Voice.

Redundancy handling

One of the things that makes redundancy difficult to handle effectively is that it is a situation which is heavily laden with emotions and strong feelings. When faced with the prospect of losing their jobs employees can feel anger, or a sense of being betrayed by management can prevail. To some extent this is inevitable because as individuals, much of our self-identity comes from the work roles we occupy. Perhaps more important, many people regard working for a living as contributing to being a full and productive member of society. For these reasons, redundancy is a situation that needs to be handled with a great deal of care and sympathy. Although management will have the objective of reducing staffing levels, it needs to be remembered that the business will still need to operate smoothly and effectively in the post-redundancy situation. Moreover, a poorly handled redundancy situation can not only result in employment relations conflict, it can generate a considerable amount of bad publicity for an organisation. Accordingly, the goodwill and morale of the remaining employees is all important, and this is only likely to be forthcoming where workers feel that they have been treated in a fair, equitable and sympathetic way.

Clearly, however, the onus for behaving appropriately does not rest with management alone, and there is a similar responsibility for trade union and other employee representatives. The aim of trade unions will be primarily that of protecting the interests of their members; normally by minimizing job losses. However, as the law stands, an employer has a clear right to dismiss for reasons of redundancy, and this means that somewhere in the proceedings, discussing job losses will become inevitable. Unfortunately, some trade unions have a long-held prejudice against negotiating job losses, although in the interests of securing the best deal for those who are to be made redundant, pragmatic considerations often override this traditional view. Another problem for trade unions could be that certain employees could be only too eager to be made redundant, particularly if the level of redundancy compensation is relatively generous.

ad hoc approach (redundancy)
There are no formally established arrangements for handling redundancy, and practice is varied according to the circumstances of each redundancy situation.

redundancy policy
Sets out the approach that will be adopted by management, if and when it is faced with having to make redundancies.

redundancy agreement
Sets out a procedure that will be followed when redundancies need to be considered, with the contents of such a procedure being the subject of prior negotiation and agreement between trade union and management.

Redundancy policy and procedures

A redundancy exercise can be approached in three ways. First, by using an **ad hoc approach**, in which there are no formally established arrangements, and practice is varied according to the circumstances of each redundancy situation. Second, by having a **redundancy policy** that sets out management's approach, if and when it is faced with making people redundant. Third, by having a formal **redundancy agreement**, which sets out a procedure that will be followed when redundancies need to be considered, with the contents of the procedure resulting from prior negotiation and agreement between trade unions and management.

There have long been arguments that organisations should have redundancy agreements. For instance, some time ago Mumford (1975) argued strongly that a redundancy policy and procedure is essential if destructive employment relations is to be avoided, and more recently, best-practice people management procedures advocate incorporating explicit policies on employment security (Pfeffer, 1998). Advice such as this is fully in accordance with the stance adopted by ACAS in its advisory booklet on redundancy handling (ACAS, 2005a). Indeed, ACAS stresses that there are many advantages to be gained from negotiating redundancy agreements, particularly where they can be agreed in advance, at a time when redundancies are not envisaged, because this allows the parties to focus on long-term considerations, rather than becoming preoccupied with immediate issues.

Nonetheless, there can often be considerable problems involved in negotiating agreements of this type. To start with, it is a pointless exercise unless there is a trade union or some other collective employee association in existence, with whom the arrangements can be agreed. The problem here is that these days many organisations simply do not recognise trade unions. Second, management's willingness to discuss the matter can all too easily start rumours that redundancies are just round the corner. Third, trade unions can be wary of joining management in discussing the topic, lest it creates an impression that the union has accepted the principle of future redundancies. Fourth, there can also be problems with managers, some of whom might feel that having an agreement in advance commits them to a level of redundancy compensation that might not be affordable in the future. Finally, managers in small, non-union firms probably have an inbuilt tendency to do things in an informal way, and might be reluctant to have too many formal procedures in place.

Nevertheless, where they are seen as appropriate, there is much to be said for a formal redundancy agreement, and an example of a comprehensive agreement of this type is shown in Exhibit 7.1.

Redundancy handling: a staged approach

In outline, Fig. 7.2 shows the stages in a redundancy exercise. Here it must be stressed that what follows is not a case study, but more in the nature of a guided exploration of a redundancy programme that highlights activities that tend to occur at different stages. You should try to grasp the idea that certain events and activities need to be addressed at different stages, and you will probably need to refer back to Fig. 7.2 fairly frequently.

Background

For the purposes of explanation, it is assumed here that the organisation concerned has a pre-existing redundancy agreement, negotiated between management and trade unions. Also that it has a Joint Works Council (JWC), composed of equal numbers of trade union and management members. Before going further, it is necessary to direct attention to an important feature of Fig. 7.2. It will be noted that consultation and negotiation play a pivotal role in the middle phase of the exercise, which makes it appear as though both processes are the same thing, whereas there is an important difference between the two. Although there is a legal obligation on the employer to consult with trade unions and/or employees, with a view to reaching agreement, this is not necessarily negotiation, about which you will read more in Chapter 10. It only

Background

The policy of Compco is to ensure, so far as is possible, the security of employment of its employees, by the use of careful forward planning. Nevertheless, it is recognised that staffing needs can be affected by the nature of competitive conditions, technical developments and other organisational requirements. Therefore, Compco and its recognised Trade Unions agree that the current and future employment prospects of its workforce can best be achieved by seeking to maintain the company's efficiency and profitability. In the event that staffing requirements are affected by as yet unforeseen events, Compco, in consultation with its recognised Trade Unions, undertakes to attempt to minimize the effects on its employees by identifying alternative employment for surplus staff, and if and when compulsory redundancy seems inevitable, to handle redundancies in the most fair, consistent and sympathetic manner possible, with all reasonable steps being taken to minimize hardship to the employees concerned.

To these ends Compco agrees to undertake to:

1 Keep Trade Union side members of the Works Council fully informed on a regular basis about staffing requirements and any implications that these have on staffing levels in the company.

2 In the event that the need for staffing reductions is identified, Trade Union side members of the Works Council will be informed, and sufficient time provided for consultation prior to redundancies taking effect.

3 For the purposes of consultation, members of the Works Council will, at the time notice is given of the redundancies, receive the following information:

- The reasons for the proposed redundancies
- The numbers and descriptions of employees it is proposed to dismiss as redundant
- The total numbers of employees of such descriptions employed at the establishment(s) in question
- The way in which it is proposed that the employees will be selected for redundancy
- How the dismissals will be carried out, including the period over which the dismissals are to take effect
- The methods to be used to calculate the amount of redundancy compensation to be made to those who are dismissed.

4 Trade Union side members of the Works Council will also be acquainted with the methods by which it is envisaged that individual employees will be selected for redundancy. At all times fair, consistent, objective and non-discriminatory methods will be applied to this task, and in the event that there is a disagreement about the way in which a named individual is selected for redundancy, the matter will be handled as a matter of urgency through Compco's Grievance Procedure.

5 Employees selected for redundancy will be eligible for time off to look for work, training or new employment. In the first instance this will be restricted to two days' leave, taken by mutual arrangement. Where appropriate, additional training will be provided by Compco to those employees made redundant, in the form of counselling, financial advice, guidance on job seeking and interviews.

6 As a guide to severance payments, these will be as per the provisions of the Employment Rights Act 1996, which are updated annually. For each year of service, up to a maximum of 20 years, these entitle employees to:

- for each year of service at age 18 or over, but under 22: half a week's pay
- for each year of service at age 22, but under 41: one week's pay
- for each year of service at age 41, but under 65: one and one half weeks' pay

NOTE: where the normal retirement age for a job is 65 and the employee is within 12 months of that age, the severance payment is reduced by one-twelfth for each complete month after the employee's 64th birthday.

7 Employees made redundant also qualify for notice, or pay in lieu of notice. In addition to the severance payment, additional payment will be made for commission, outstanding accrued holidays and any time off in lieu owing.

8 This agreement will be reviewed or renewed not less than once every two years, and may be cancelled by either the Trade Union or Management side of the Works Council by giving three months' notice to withdraw from being bound by its provisions.

Signed (Chair of the Management Side, Compco Works Council).................................. Date....................

Signed (Chair of the Trade Union Side, Compco Works Council)................................... Date....................

Exhibit 7.1 Compco's redundancy agreement

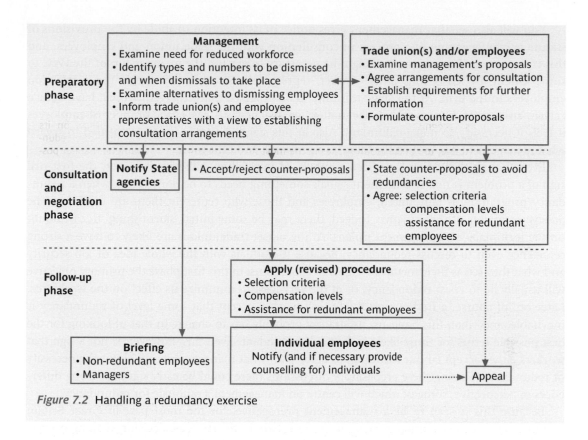

Figure 7.2 Handling a redundancy exercise

obliges management to engage in a joint consultative process, and strictly speaking, this means that the two parties consider each other's point of view, before management makes the final decision, which of course establishes a clear imbalance of power in management's favour. Having said this, it is worth noting that a redundancy agreement already exists, and this can be taken as a reason for optimism. It probably means, for example, that management and trade union have a fairly healthy working relationship, otherwise they would not have been able to construct an agreement of this type in the past. It is also indicative that a level of trust exists between the parties, which in turn means that if necessary, the terms of the agreement are likely to be able to be varied to inject a certain degree of flexibility and room for manoeuvre into the proceedings. With these points in mind the progress of the redundancy exercise can be explained by considering the different phases of Fig. 7.2 in turn.

The preparatory phase (see Figure 7.2)

This commences when management first tables its proposals for redundancies in the firm, probably at a meeting of the JWC. In doing this management is effectively signalling its intention to seek a change in the *status quo*, and until this happens, the trade union could legitimately regard steps to do anything more concrete as a blatant case of bad faith. It is highly unlikely that any group of managers would actually want to dispense with part of a workforce, and so redundancy would probably be seen as a last resort. Indeed, there may well be a measure of embarrassment for having to go to these lengths. However, having grasped the nettle, management will have its own ideas about what is necessary to rescue the situation, and will want to pursue these ideas as the remedy.

You will also see that management gives notice of its intention to abide by the provisions of statute law by engaging in a process of consultation with the trade union and employees, and this is important. For example, it might be necessary to expand the membership of the JWC to some extent by co-opting other worker representatives, who can speak for non-union employees in the firm. At this stage it is only to be expected that management will have done a certain amount of 'homework' on the matter, for instance to arrive at the number of employees it feels it necessary to make redundant. Also at this stage, the trade union is entitled to regard what management has 'put on the table' as a proposal, and little more.

Even though there may have been rumours of impending cutbacks, however, the first real sign of a problem is that management signals something needs to be done. Thus, when a redundancy programme is announced, employees and those who represent them are unlikely to be passive recipients of the initiative. Indeed, there may be some initial 'skirmishing' to cast doubt on the legitimacy of management's plans. At the outset trade unions are likely to have a strong reluctance even to discuss redundancy, because it conflicts with the whole idea of job security and what they see as their members' rights to a job. Thus, in this first phase the primary objective will usually be to resist redundancy, or at the very least to minimize its effect on the workforce. Later on, of course, a trade union might well have to accept that some level of redundancy is inevitable, and when this happens, its strategy probably has to change to that of looking for the best possible terms for those likely to be made redundant. Even this, however, is not a sign that workers either accept labour shedding, or agree with what management says about the necessity of redundancy. During these preparatory discussions there could be early signs of strong differences in perspective, some of which will centre on management's rationale for redundancy.

Because this is seen to be a management prerogative, for the most part in Great Britain employees are unaccustomed to being invited to share in the strategic decision-making process with management. Instead, the workforce is simply required to do its job until something dramatic happens, such as a crisis that prompts a perception on the part of management that heavy labour-shedding is necessary. This crisis can sometimes produce a dramatic change in attitudes on management's part, and managers want the cooperation and goodwill of employees, and for them to willingly adopt management's solution to the problem. In response this can result in a good deal of acrimony on the part of the workforce, and attempts to push the blame back where they believe it belongs. For instance, if the reason management gives for the necessity for redundancies is that the whole industry is in decline, it might well invite the retort that these things do not happen overnight and, since management claims to be 'in control', it was they who should have seen things coming, and done something. An even harsher trade union response could be forthcoming to the argument that 'more aggressive competitor activity' was the root of the problem. Here the retort might be that management has been derelict in its duty to keep a watch on competitors. Where the introduction of new technology is given as a reason to justify redundancies, this can sometimes be interpreted as a lightly veiled threat that everyone will end up working much harder for the same, or even less, money. The predictable reaction to this might be actually to resist the redundancies, and a similar response might be given to proposals for work reorganisation.

Having vented their spleen, however, some of this indignation is likely to subside, and representatives will probably realise that they need time to assimilate the information, and produce a more sober response. At this stage, there would be little more that could take place, beyond setting up a special meeting of the JWC in the near future. However, to calm things down, and as a sign of goodwill, management would probably concede that the statutory consultation period would not be considered to have started until this further meeting had taken place. This gives the trade union time to request certain, more detailed information to which it is legally entitled, and also to consult those of its members who are likely to be affected, in order to take their views at first hand.

Between the closing of this meeting and the start of the next one, it is almost certain that there will be meetings of a less formal and public nature. These would probably take place between senior trade union and management figures, and be concerned with obtaining clarification of management's proposals. There would also be some gentle probing to identify what could become the sticking points in the next phase.

The consultation and negotiation phase (see Figure 7.2)

At this stage in the proceedings, the main priority of the trade union and/or employees is likely to be to protect jobs. To this end, it is virtually certain to make proposals concerned with avoiding, or at least minimizing, compulsory redundancies. There are a number of questions or suggestions that the trade union might make here, for example:

- What plans are there to take advantage of natural wastage in the firm?
- To what extent has recruitment of permanent staff in the firm been restricted?
- To what extent has the use of temporary staff been reduced?
- Have plans been made to retire all employees at normal retiring age?
- Have plans been put in place to fill any existing vacancies from exiting employees?
- Has overtime working been reduced to an absolute minimum?
- Has the use of short-time working been considered as an option?
- To what extent has retraining or redeployment of employees for different work for which there is a requirement, at either the same site or different sites, been considered?

It might well be the case that management has already explored some of these options, and this has been allowed for in its proposals about the numbers and types of employees who would be dismissed. However, in guides to good practice, giving employees the opportunity to discuss matters such as these is seen to be one of the main benefits of the consultation exercise. Moreover, in order to convince employees that no constructive suggestion will be left unexplored, this is something that management should be prepared to discuss. Therefore, it is well worthwhile giving this matter an extensive airing, which could take considerable time. When this discussion has been completed, however, it is likely that a milestone in the process will have been reached, because by now, it should be possible to reach agreement on the magnitude of the problem: that is, how many employees of each particular type will need to be made redundant.

Pause for reflection

Working with other students in your class, try to identify a set of fair, objective and consistent criteria that could be used to select people to be made redundant. Try to ensure that those that you select would be likely to be acceptable to managers, trade unions and employees in a firm.

From here onwards there is likely to be a great deal of detailed discussion about how the actual redundancies will be handled. Perhaps the first matter to be resolved is the *selection criteria* that will be used to select individual candidates for redundancy. These need to be objective, fair and capable of being applied consistently. It is as well to remember that certain criteria, such as pregnancy, sex, race, disability, religion, trade union membership and more recently, age, are all potentially discriminatory in nature, and because they can give rise to claims for 'unfair selection for redundancy', they need to be avoided. One criterion, which seems to be beloved of trade unions because of its (apparently) objective nature, is the 'last in, first out' (LIFO) principle. Unfortunately, while this protects those with seniority, it can also lead to a highly unbalanced workforce. Therefore, managers will usually try to ensure that the employees selected are those who have the least value to the firm, and opt for selection criteria such as: low skills and experience; poor work performance; poor attendance; high absenteeism, high sickness, or poor disciplinary record. The problem with many of these is that an element of subjectivity can creep into their use, and trade unions can be very wary of passing too much power into the hands of management, lest the criteria used be manipulated to settle old scores.

One criterion that permits an element of self-selection to be used is that of *voluntary severance*. In this volunteers for dismissal are sought, which is clearly less controversial than making people compulsorily redundant. To encourage volunteers, it is normal to offer an incentive of enhanced severance pay, above the less generous statutory level of compensation, and it usually involves setting a cut-off date for volunteering, after which compensation would revert to the statutory level. However, from an organisation's perspective this could be a more expensive way of making people redundant and, for this reason, management might be reluctant to use it. Moreover, since it can result in a highly unbalanced workforce, management usually reserves the right to say 'no' to some of those who apply.

Another uncontroversial, but expensive, option is to encourage early retirement, and in some cases it has occasionally led to firms giving additional years of pensionable service to those willing to exit in this way. In the past, particularly where there were few prospects of obtaining new employment, there were usually some employees who actively sought this way out. Nowadays, however, with the widespread public recognition that pensions have become devalued, it is perhaps unlikely that volunteers would be so readily forthcoming.

Another matter that would need to receive some consideration in this phase would be *assistance to redundant employees*. As noted above, an employer is required to inform the Department of Trade and Industry where more than ten employees are to be made redundant, and in addition, grant redundant workers reasonable time off to seek new work and/or retraining. Beyond this there are a number of steps that employers can take to provide help for employees, such as:

- giving State agencies facilities on-site to advise employees on job opportunities, retraining schemes and unemployment benefits
- commissioning employment agencies to actively seek work for those made redundant
- using their own internal contacts to try to obtain new work for ex-employees
- providing help and guidance to ex-employees to set up their own businesses
- providing financial guidance on coping with unemployment
- providing an element of training in matters such as being interviewed and making written applications for new jobs
- counselling those who are psychologically traumatised by being made redundant.

An additional issue that requires some thought is that of an *appeals procedure*. In some respects this is one of the most crucial matters that needs to be resolved because, no matter how much care and attention has been devoted to trying to identify fair and objective selection criteria, there could well be individuals who feel that these have been misapplied, or are unfair to them. While this is not likely to come to light until the next phase, it needs to be available when needed and it is worthwhile considering the matter beforehand. The aim of any appeals procedure is to resolve the matter in a speedy and demonstrably fair way, and there are two particular ways that this could be done. First, the person concerned could be referred to the grievance procedure to make a complaint. This has some advantages, in that management and trade union representatives are likely to be familiar with the procedures. However, the problem is that, while grievance mechanisms are designed to be scrupulously fair, they usually have several levels of appeal, and sometimes a final appeal outside the organisation. As such, they tend to be slow, and could be too unwieldy to operate in a highly charged situation such as redundancy handling.

Second, a small ad hoc committee of managers and representatives (or even just a single senior manager) could be deputed to hear these appeals. This poses less of a risk to delaying the redundancy exercise. However, where this committee consists only of a single person, it is important that he or she should not only be fair and impartial, but also be seen to be fair and impartial.

The follow-up phase (see Figure 7.2)

In this phase the decisions made in the previous phase are implemented. That is:

- criteria for selecting people for redundancy are applied, and those targeted for dismissal identified
- the compensation that individuals will receive (including notice, or payment in lieu of notice) will be identified
- arrangements for offering assistance to individuals will be put in place; where possible, including offers of alternative work within the firm and a four-weeks' statutory trial period, together with details of any change in the contract of employment that is involved if the offer is subsequently accepted.

Fairness and openness then dictate that the people targeted should be informed individually because, if this is not done, people will be unable to decide whether they wish to appeal. Setting aside the matter of appeals, informing employees of their likely fate clearly needs to be done in a sensitive and sympathetic way. There is probably no such thing as a 'good' time to tell someone that their employment is to be terminated, but to shy away, or put off telling them until everyone else knows, is cruel and can lead to misunderstandings, rumours and distrust. The task needs to be undertaken as soon as the time is ripe and, preferably, everyone affected should be told on the same day. Needless to say, no matter how tempting it is to try to let people down lightly, nothing should be said that holds out a false hope of re-employment in the future.

As well as informing employees who are to be made redundant, there are two other groups that need to be kept informed. The first are employees who have also gone through the redundancy exercise, who now need to know formally that it is over. These employees can vary in their reactions anywhere from relief to guilt. While relief is understandable, it is seldom recognised that survivors of a redundancy exercise can have acute feelings of guilt for having survived, while others have been dismissed. Moreover, they can also feel highly apprehensive that the whole matter might be repeated in the future (Ebadan and Winstanley, 1997). Therefore, there can often be a clear case for drawing a line under the episode, by briefing employees with an optimistic look to the future.

The second group that needs to be briefed are managers in the organisation, some of whom might have had to inform employees of their redundancy, or these days might themselves be made redundant. Indeed, this group should have been kept well informed from the start, because it is to them that employees probably turn first to resolve their queries. However, there is a particular reason for briefing managers who have been on the sharp end of handling redundancy. They are one of the most strongly affected groups of survivors in an organisation who, because they have had to make others redundant, often have subliminal fears that what they have done to others, could be done to them (Kets de Vries and Balazs, 1997). For this reason they are often highly apprehensive, and there can be a particularly strong case for briefings or forward-looking discussions that engender a more optimistic view.

Summary points

- The most widely cited reasons for redundancy are:
  - structural decline and change in industry
  - economic change
  - technology
  - work reorganisation

- There are three main legal provisions in the law affecting redundancy, which regulate:
  - compensation for redundant employees
  - protection against unfair dismissal and time off from work to search for new employment
  - employee or trade union rights to consultation with management

- Redundancy can be handled by one of three main approaches:
  - ad hoc
  - by having a redundancy policy
  - using a formal redundancy agreement

- A redundancy procedure tends to fall into three main stages:
  - a preparatory phase, in which management announces and sets out its plans
  - a consultation/negotiation phase
  - a follow-up phase where the redundancies are implemented.

Conclusions

This chapter has reviewed the topics of dismissal and redundancy, and since employees are sometimes – but not always – dismissed as a result of being disciplined at work, there is a clear connection between this chapter and the one that precedes it. However, not all dismissals occur as a result of the disciplinary process. They can take place in a wide variety of circumstances, some of which are potentially less fair than others in the eyes of the law, and give grounds for an employee to contest the fairness of what has happened. However, in legal terms, what is common to all dismissals is that, because they all involve the termination of an employee's contract of employment, they are individual matters and, technically, this is true even in the case of redundancy. Nevertheless, what is different with redundancy is that it is almost always handled in a collective way up to a certain stage in the proceedings. Therefore, its pivotal process is arguably the consultation and negotiation that takes place between managers and the representatives of employees, and this gives it very strong connections with two other chapters that appear later in this book: Chapter 9, which covers collective bargaining; and Chapter 10, which deals with negotiation. It is also important to note that, because redundancy has this dual (individual and collective) aspect, it can have a strong impact on the employment relations climate in an organisation, and the same is true of dismissal, and disciplinary and grievance handling. Therefore, the next chapter, Integration 3, brings Chapters 6 and 7 together to trace links between the operation of the processes that they cover and employment relations climates.

? Review and discussion questions

1 Define dismissal.

2 Name six different categories into which dismissals can be grouped.

3 State five different potentially fair reasons for dismissal.

4 State the reasons why a dismissal could be regarded as automatically unfair by an employment tribunal.

5 What categories of dismissal could be contested by an employee?

6 What three remedies are there for a person who successfully pursues a case for unfair dismissal?

7 Define and explain the definition of redundancy given in your text.

8 What are the four main factors that are said to cause redundancy?

9 What are the three main provisions in the legal framework that affects redundancy?

10 Beyond informing people that a programme of redundancy is envisaged in a firm, what additional and more specific information does the employer have a statutory obligation to disclose to a trade union and/or employee representatives?

Further reading

ACAS (2005) *Advisory Booklet – Redundancy Handling*, Advisory Conciliation and Arbitration Service, London. http://www.acas.org.uk/publications/b08.html. A very useful booklet, giving a thorough overview of practice, and a comprehensive review of the law as it affects redundancy handling.

Allen, T.D., D.M. Freeman, J.E.A. Russell, R.C. Reizenstein and J.O. Rentz (2001) 'Survivor reactions to organisational downsizing: does time ease the pain?', *Journal of Occupational and Organisational Psychology*, Vol. 74 (2), pp. 154–164. The paper reports an interesting study of downsizing, with particular attention to the survivors of redundancy, and how long it takes them to get over feelings of resentment and anxiety.

Duggan, M. (1999) *Unfair Dismissal: Law, Practice and Guidance*, CLT Professional Publishing, Welwyn Garden City. The book gives a thorough review of the law as it affects the matter of unfair dismissal.

IDS (2005) *Managing Redundancy*, Human Resource Studies Plus No. 797, Income Data Services, May. An excellent booklet that reviews the matter of redundancy handling, and also contains a number of interesting case studies of firms giving details of how they handled recent redundancy situations, together with notable features of their redundancy agreements.

Torrington, D., L. Hall and S. Taylor (2002) *Human Resource Management*, Chapter 14, pp. 224–240, Financial Times, Prentice Hall, London. One of the authors of this book is a member of employment tribunals, and this makes for an interesting and highly informative chapter.

Integrating the effects of interpersonal processes

Introduction

In this, the third integrative chapter in the book, the aim is to show that there are strong interconnections between the interpersonal processes described in the two preceding chapters. Both of these chapters dealt with processes that affect people in an organisation, and even though redundancy is mostly handled collectively, it is individuals who experience the outcomes. While these processes almost certainly have some impact on each other, these are not the links that are explored in this chapter. Rather, the aim is to show that all four processes can have an impact on what is a very important employment relations outcome: the state of an organisation's employment relations climate.

Employment relations climate is a variable that was briefly mentioned in Chapter 2, and with this in mind this chapter commences with a more considered explanation of its importance in employment relations. Following this, each topic covered in the previous two chapters (*discipline*, *grievance*, *dismissal*, and *redundancy*) is reviewed to trace the links between the way it is handled in an organisation and its effects on the employment relations climate. As with most complex social systems, however, there can also be links in the reverse direction. Therefore, some attention is directed to ways in which employment relations climate could have recursive effects on how the four processes are likely to be affected by climate.

Employment relations climate

For the sake of clarity, perhaps the first thing that needs to be noted is that culture, which currently tends to be the more fashionable topic, is not the same thing as climate; although at least one authority in the area argues that climate and culture tap similar phenomena, but from different methodological perspectives (Denison, 1996). However, one thing that links the concepts of culture and climate is the importance accorded to values. Values are a fundamental part of any culture and to some extent a culture is what gives people their values. Climate, however, is much more a reflection of whether current organisational conditions are in accordance with the values that people hold (Nicholson, 1979), and in the words of Koys and DeCotis (1991) climate is an experienced-based, multi-dimensional and perceptual phenomenon that has the capacity to influence behaviour. From this, climate is defined as:

> a characteristic ethos or atmosphere within an organisation at a given point in time, which is reflected in the way its members perceive, experience and react to the organisational context.
>
> (Rollinson, 2005: 563)

Climate is essentially an experienced state of affairs, therefore, and can be thought of as the way that people describe an organisation to themselves, and interpret what they find (James and Jones, 1974; Jones and James, 1979). Nevertheless, because it is wrapped up with experiences, it affects attitudes, which in turn has behavioural implications (Schneider, 1983). Its explanatory importance is that many of the factors that influence the nature of the employment relationship act through the prevailing climate, and this can alter the behaviour of one or more of the parties in some way. For instance, an autocratic management style, or an absence of employee voice opportunities, could result in an antagonistic climate that makes for 'them and us' attitudes between employer and employees. After Rim and Mannheim (1979) employment relations climate is taken to be a reflection of the way that employees and managers see each other, and this takes account of the idea that, once formed, climates can be extremely resistant to modification. This means that, when one party perceives that the other behaves towards them in a certain way, the recipient tends to respond accordingly, which in turn evokes perceptions and behaviour in return. Thus, climate can quickly become a self-fulfilling prophecy (Biasatti and Martin, 1979) and, if, for example, the climate is harmonious, issues tend to be approached by both sides in a joint problem-solving way (Harbison and Coleman, 1951) whereas if it is hostile, this can result in an extremely frosty atmosphere, where each side tries to undermine the other.

Although the very expression 'employment relations climate' implies that it is an organisation-wide phenomenon, it needs to be recognised that it arises in individual feelings and experiences, and this means that it is strongly connected with individual mental processes (Kozlowski and Doherty, 1989). It is necessary to distinguish between both climate at the individual level and climate at the group level, but at the same time acknowledge that the two levels are strongly connected. The individual effect is normally referred to as *psychological climate* (Koys and DeCotis, 1991), which is a reflection of how a person reacts to his or her surroundings or experiences. *Organisational climate* (of which employment relations climate is simply a sub-climate) is a social phenomenon that affects the behaviour of groups, or even a whole organisation. However, climates are not just the sum of individual feelings. Where a group of people are exposed to the same milieu, they share their interpretations, and what emerges is a degree of shared consensus about the characteristics of the climate, which, although they might be slightly different, have enough in common to make them recognisable to the whole group.

Therefore, whichever way we view it, climate is almost completely determined by factors associated with people, and if employees perceive that managers are not to be trusted and tend to behave in this way towards them, they will probably look for evidence to confirm their assumptions. When managers become aware of this, they will then look for opportunities to behave the same way in return, and relations can deteriorate very quickly. It may be recalled that, in Chapter 4, social mobilisation theory explained the processes that can lead to employees becoming aggrieved when management is perceived to have reneged on a right or expectation in employment, and in what follows, the ways that the interpersonal processes explained in the previous two chapters can affect climate will be examined in terms of their potential effects on both *psychological* and *organisational* climates. Where there is some likelihood that there could be effects in the reverse direction, this will also be noted.

The effects of interpersonal processes
Discipline

There are two main ways in which discipline and disciplinary handling can influence employment relations climate. The first is associated with an individual's experience of having been disciplined. In some circumstances, notably where a manager has used a rehabilitative approach, there are usually few adverse effects, but in others, for example, where a manager has used a punitive approach, the employee can find the event so unfair and demoralizing that there are profound emotional reactions. The second way in which there can be an impact on climate occurs more as a result of social effects. Here there is a considerable body of evidence to show that, when a member of a workgroup undergoes a harrowing or stressful experience, he or she receives a huge amount of social support from colleagues (Homans, 1950). When this first happens, it is probably designed to do little more than comfort or soothe the person, but later it also tends to affect a group's sense of injustice, and this can have an adverse effect on employment relations climate.

Considering first the direct effects on the individual, there is a stream of evidence to show that some managers guard what they perceive to be their legitimate prerogatives so closely that they are prone to using the disciplinary process as a way of establishing a new rule where one has not existed before (Klass and Wheeler, 1990). Worse still, managers sometimes have vague expectations that employees should always have willing, cooperative attitudes and accordingly, they tend to use disciplinary sanctions for the mildest transgression. There is also a strong stream of evidence from attribution theory to show that, when making a judgement about what could be a case of poor behaviour, some managers are all too ready to assume the worst. For example, instead of carefully questioning an employee to determine whether the apparent rule transgression was prompted by something such as the difficulty of a task, or the lack of clarity in instructions, they assume that it was the employee's personality or attitude that was the root of the problem. In other words, they automatically assume that what the employee did was tantamount to a personal fault, and ignore the possibility that it could have been caused by something in the employee's surroundings that gave rise to the problem in the first place.

Above all, there is what seems to be an ever-present problem of management handling styles. Here the evidence is that punitive styles are extremely commonplace. These give an employee no opportunity to explain his or her behaviour, and can be disastrous in terms of the effects on climate (Rollinson *et al.*, 1997). For this reason, a very strong case can be made for using a rehabilitative approach for disciplinary handling: an approach which involves handling a case in a careful, non-threatening way so that the employee sees that the diagnosis of his or her behaviour is not only fair, but accurate. However, it is surprising just how many disciplined employees report that their disciplinary hearing lasted no longer than two minutes, and that the manager concerned seemed to have his or her mind made up about guilt and punishment before the hearing even started (Rollinson, 1997). In the light of this it is perhaps unsurprising that many employees have a highly cynical perspective on the prospects for justice in the disciplinary situation. There are, of course, likely to be additional effects from this impact on climate. To start with, it is almost bound to sour the relationship between the employee and his or her manager, which in turn is likely to have an adverse effect on the state of the psychological contract. Moreover, another outcome could well be that there are effects in the reverse direction. For instance, if someone perceives that they have been badly treated in a disciplinary hearing, the resentment that this causes can then result in a tendency to flout disciplinary rules in the future (Greer and Labig, 1987; Rollinson *et al.*, 1997).

Considering now the group effects, the emotional support that fellow employees give to those that are disciplined are so well known that they probably need no further elaboration. Neither is it necessary to state that, even where this occurs when there are feelings in the workgroup that the employee had some guilt in the matter, an element of 'them and us' can appear in attitudes. These, of course, are symptomatic of a more adverse employment relations climate in their own right.

Grievance

Grievance and grievance handling can have effects on employment relations climate in similar ways to discipline. First there can be effects because employees have been exposed directly to grievance procedures that were handled in an insensitive way. Second, there are situations where employees make a positive attempt to air their dissatisfactions, but are unable to obtain an opportunity to have the grievance heard. Third, there can be an indirect impact on the prevailing climate because of social effects, and these will be considered in turn.

It is never easy for an employee to articulate a dissatisfaction to a manager, if only because he or she might have fears that the manager could feel challenged or threatened in some way and retaliate. It is for this reason that it is widely recommended that the first stage of the proceedings should be treated as the most important one, and conducted in a very informal way. Unfortunately, however, there is often a tendency for managers to forget the necessity of putting employees at their ease, and to be over-formal in their approach. Even worse, managers are sometimes confronted with a dissatisfaction that they simply do not have the authority to resolve without consulting higher management. Therefore, they simply wait (albeit politely) until the employee has finished speaking, and then disallow the grievance, because they fear that they will appear indecisive if they approach their superior. Another problem is that managers are seldom the proficient actors that they think they are, and this sometimes leaves an employee with the impression that the grievance was only heard to allow him or her to 'let off steam'. Consequently, the whole event can come to be seen as an exercise in hypocrisy, which can lead to a worsened employment relations climate.

Let us turn now to the situation where an employee finds it difficult to obtain an airing for a grievance. The aim of a grievance procedure is, of course, to *resolve* or *settle* a dissatisfaction: preferably in a peaceful way, that avoids recourse to other protest behaviour; and if necessary, to clarify the issue to the satisfaction of the two parties. Therefore, managers should not shrink from procedures, but welcome them as an opportunity to build good working relations. However, many managers either feel that handling a grievance is an irksome task, or that an attempt to raise a dissatisfaction is a threat to their authority (Hook *et al.*, 1996). For this reason grievances can be rare in some organisations, because many employees shy away from raising them in case it antagonizes the manager (Torrington *et al.*, 2002). Indeed, it is a matter of empirical record that many employees experience unfair and unjust treatment, but feel that they have little alternative but to suffer in silence for fear of a management backlash (Boroff and Lewin, 1997; Lewin and Boroff, 1996). This appears to be particularly prevalent in small firms, where prevailing styles are set in the mould of a founding owner, or the members of a close family who run the business. Even worse, where an individual eventually obtains a hearing and it is successful, matters can sometimes lead to a climate of mistrust. There is, for example, a stream of evidence which shows that, if an employee successfully pursues a grievance, the manager concerned seeks an opportunity to retaliate in some way at the next opportunity (Klass and DiNisi, 1989; Colquitt *et al.*, 2001; Masterson *et al.*, 2000; Klass *et al.*, 1991; Olson-Buchanan, 1996). Clearly outcomes such as this can have very unpleasant repercussions on employment relations climate.

In terms of the indirect social effects on employment relations climate, there is something of an inbuilt impetus for these things to happen in unionised organisations, because dealing with members' problems is a central part of the union representative's role. Therefore, although it is grievants who actually have the dissatisfactions, it is often workplace stewards, particularly those who seek to expand union membership, who play a major part in encouraging employees to pursue them through formal mechanisms (Bemmels *et al.*, 1991).

Finally, as with many things, there can also be recursive effects, in which employment relations climate has an influence on tendencies to pursue grievances in a formal way. One of these has already been mentioned above, where it is noted that union representatives can play some part in encouraging employees to pursue grievances formally. In addition, there is a stream of evidence that makes a positive connection between the existence of a hostile employment relations climate and a high rate of grievance activity in an organisation (Norsworthy and Zabala, 1985).

Dismissal

Because someone loses his or her livelihood when dismissed, it is an action that can clearly have significant climatic repercussions. As with the processes discussed above, the climatic conditions can come about in two main ways: either because of an emotional impact on the person dismissed; or because a wider social support engenders sympathy among workers. Perhaps the most important thing to note, however, is that because the law acknowledges that there are circumstances in which dismissal can be blatantly unfair, it purposely sets out to give employees protection: for example, in the circumstances where it is automatically unfair to dismiss an employee. These are circumstances in which it is only to be expected that there will be a climatic impact. With this in mind, it is convenient to comment briefly on the likely climatic implications of each of the six categories into which individual dismissals can be grouped, which are given in Chapter 7.

Except for perhaps one notable exception, dismissals for *automatically fair reasons* are perhaps the least likely of all to have a climatic impact on an individual employee. In these circumstances the dismissal would be a collective one, in which an employer decided to exercise his legal right to dismiss all striking workers. However, a legal right is very different to a moral right, and should an employer dismiss all striking workers, there is a risk of reprisals from those who feel aggrieved at their dismissal. In addition, although rare, attempts at selective re-engagement are not unknown, and in doing so the employer would have automatically escalated matters to a wider climatic level. Thus, if the dismissed workers decided to picket the site, or stage public demonstrations in some other way, a extremely hostile climate would be almost certain to be engendered.

If dismissal takes place for *potentially fair reasons*, there is virtually unlimited scope for poor climatic conditions to arise. However, much, of course, depends on the specific grounds for dismissal, and on the extent to which the dismissed individual sees them in the same light as the employer. In this matter there is always a potential for wide differences in perception to arise, particularly about the seriousness of the transgression that resulted in the employee's dismissal. For instance, the seriousness of offences such as lack of capability, lack of skill, or misconduct are, in some cases, little more than a matter of opinion. Therefore, they are particularly prone to perceptions that enable someone to rationalise him/herself as a victim. Perhaps most difficult of all are cases where someone has been dismissed for prolonged ill-health, or sickness absence. Here the individual concerned is likely to experience feelings of being treated unfairly, and there could also be considerable social support for the way that the person has been treated, which is likely to result in much wider climate repercussions.

Those dismissals that can be classified as *automatically unfair*, are probably those that are most likely to have severe and widely experienced climatic effects, simply because they effectively result in the flouting of an employment protection that has already been granted by statute law. Moreover, some of these things are now near to being considered basic human rights, the removal of which would be likely to engender such indignation that adverse climates would arise, both for individual reasons, and from social and collective effects.

Finally, certain dismissals are contestable, notably: *wrongful dismissal*; *constructive dismissal*; and *unfair dismissal*. If contested, however, the case normally has to be heard in a court of law. This is a very public process, and is stressful enough to require the person involved to steel him/herself up to undergo it. Therefore, in itself this is likely to have climatic effects at the individual level, and in addition, when the person's colleagues realise that the individual feels so incensed about the matter that he or she is prepared to 'put up a fight', the climatic conditions can spread much more widely.

Redundancy

For those who are likely to be affected directly, redundancy also contains the implied threat of a loss of livelihood, and so it is another situation where there could be significant climatic repercussions. Redundancy is widely acknowledged to be a highly charged, emotive affair, in which feelings can run high, and employees can feel betrayed by management. Moreover, it is a situation in which blame stories abound, and management are often perceived as incompetent, or derelict in their duty for having allowed the enterprise to deteriorate to the point where employees face the prospect of unemployment. In these circumstances it is very difficult for managers to engender even the smallest amount of goodwill and cooperation in the workforce, because at the outset, management tends to be seen by employees as the 'villain of the piece'. Significantly, however, while there will usually be some individuals who have stronger feelings than others, redundancy is a situation in which those most affected are not singled out for individual treatment, but are represented by others and spoken for with 'one voice'. Thus, from the outset, there is likely to be a strong element of collective cohesion, the end product of which is the emergence of an identifiable employment relations climate. In addition, there are important employee protections in redundancy handling, which are underpinned by a solid basis of statute law, which prescribes what should happen, and the order in which it should happen. Accordingly, those who have to handle the matter on behalf of employees, are likely to be on their guard to ensure that these rights are respected, and at the least this means that the beginnings of a mild ethos of 'them and us' will probably be present: highly fertile ground in which an adverse climate can flourish.

However, it should not be assumed from this that a hostile climate will necessarily emerge. Much depends on the way in which the redundancy situation is handled, and in particular, the way that management chooses to approach it. Therefore, whether or not a hostile climate develops is likely to depend on such things as: whether management's approach to consultation is flexible enough for employees to feel that they are not faced with a *fait accompli*; or whether management shows itself willing to do the maximum possible to make severance from the organisation a non-acrimonious experience. With these things in mind, the simplest way to predict the type of employment relations climate that could arise is to discuss some of the potential behaviours in a redundancy situation.

First, however, there is a general point that applies to all redundancy situations. While managers will probably have grasped the nettle of labour shedding with some reluctance, having done so they will understandably want to get the matter over with as soon as possible. Nevertheless, there are employee consultation rights that need to be observed, and in law these are expressed in a way that states that consultation should take place with a view to reaching agreement. If this practice is observed it can engender a more *conciliatory* climate, albeit one that is likely to be emotionally charged. However, there is a caveat in this matter. The role of employee representatives in consultation (trade union or otherwise) is concerned with safeguarding their members' interests; they are not there just to underwrite decisions already made by managers. This is important, because if managers regard representatives as a 'rubber stamp', this can quickly derail a conciliatory climate. Accordingly, it is important to remember that representatives might well see it as part of their role to cast doubt on the validity and feasibility of management's ideas about labour shedding. Therefore, the emerging climate could well turn out to be one that also has elements of an *oppositional* perspective on how to resolve the issue of redundancy.

Given that legislation specifically states that the method and number of people to be made redundant should be explored in consultation, this could also shape the emerging climate. It requires, for example, a discussion of a full range of steps that could be taken to minimize redundancies, and this is needed to avoid any impression that management is seeking to impose its plans. Here, it is important to recognise that a climate of *consultation* and *dialogue* is likely to exist alongside one of *opposition*. Moreover, when it comes to choosing criteria for identifying those people who will be selected for redundancy, there is likely to be an expectation that the criteria will be objective, fair and capable of being applied in a consistent way. However, there is a potential tension in this matter because some criteria, for example gender or age, are inherently discriminatory, and these would be avoided by trade unions at all costs. In addition, managers will often want to use criteria that retain the most useful employees and dispense with the least useful, whereas trade unions have a history of preferring the 'last in, first out' principle. Trade unions can also be expected to steer well clear of any criteria that are capable of being manipulated, so that, although the climate may well be *conciliatory*, and inclined towards *compromise*, it can also be *oppositional* and *conflictual*, and these aspects all depend on how entrenched are the positions of the parties on these issues.

If a hostile climate is to be avoided, it is useful wherever possible to make the greatest use of voluntary severance, even if this means paying enhanced redundancy compensation. It is relatively uncontroversial, and allows people to retain their dignity when dismissed, and since both are ways of maintaining a *cordial* climate, the same can be said about early retirement. Because it can do much to build a positive employment relations climate for the future, it is also helpful to ensure that when people depart, they do so with benefit of the maximum help that the firm can provide in the way of finding new jobs.

Finally, until a redundancy situation is well behind them, there will probably be a number of apprehensive and insecure people remaining in the organisation (Ebadan and Winstanley, 1997). It is also probable that the climate that emerges out of a redundancy situation will shape employment relations in the organisation for some time to come. Whether the climate is *poor*, *conflictual* or *conciliatory*, however, will probably depend on how matters have been handled by management, and the subsequent responses and positions taken by employees and unions.

Conclusions and review

Depending on the way each one is handled, discipline, grievance, dismissal, and redundancy all have the potential to engender an adverse employment relations climate. Initially, this would probably emerge as what is identified earlier as an individual psychological climate, and arise as a reaction to what an employee has experienced in undergoing the process. However, it is not inevitable that matters will stop at this, because people interact with each other in a work setting, and share their experiences. Thus, if work colleagues sympathise with an employee who has been through one of these processes, they can give a measure of social support, and the resentment felt by one person is likely to be taken up by the others, as a collective response to management. With some of the processes there is also a potential for recently emerged adverse climate conditions to result in additional effects. For example, in the case of discipline, an adverse psychological climate can prompt a future tendency to flout organisational rules, and with grievance, where someone tries to raise a dissatisfaction, but fails to obtain a grievance hearing, the climate can promote a degree of cynicism about the prospects of obtaining justice in the organisation. Furthermore, in situations involving redundancy or dismissal, collective reactions by employees can emerge, and these in turn shape the climate experienced by employees and managers in an organisation.

What has not been mentioned so far however, is the potential impact of a poor climate on another facet of interpersonal relations: the psychological contract. This, it will be recalled from Chapter 1, is a set of unvoiced expectations and felt obligations about the ways in which employee and manager should behave towards each other. When a climate deteriorates at the individual level because a process has been poorly handled, what tends to happen is that poor climatic conditions prompt the individual to feel that the manager has breached his or her side of the psychological contract, and this in turn provides the employee with the emotional energy to resist honouring the contract in return.

The remaining chapters in the book all cover organisational-level processes that can have their own impact on employment relations climate, notably: employee voice, collective bargaining, negotiation, conflict and protest, and control. Therefore, a return to the matter of climates will be made in the last integrative chapter in the book, where the impact of these processes on climate is traced. For the present the effects and linkages traced in this chapter are brought together and summarised in Fig. I2 below.

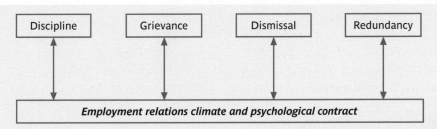

Figure I2 The effects of discipline, grievance, dismissal and redundancy on employment relations climate

PART 4

Organisational processes in employment relations

Part contents

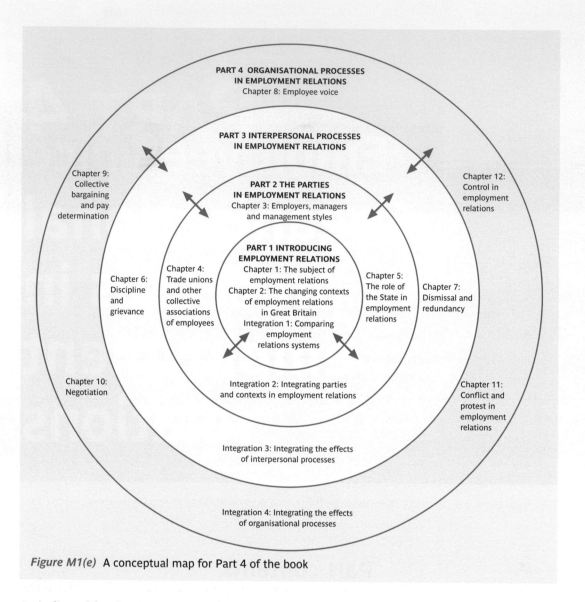

Figure M1(e) A conceptual map for Part 4 of the book

As indicated by the diagram above, this part of the book consists of six chapters, all of which focus on organisational level processes in employment relations. The first, Chapter 8, examines employee voice, the second, Chapter 9, focuses on collective bargaining and pay determination, the third, Chapter 10, on the allied process of negotiation, the fourth (Chapter 11) examines the topic of conflict and protest in employment relations, and the fifth (Chapter 12) the topic of control in employment relations. These are followed by the final integrative chapter in the book, which traces some of the main effects that these processes can exert on each other, and on the employment relations climate of an organisation.

Chapter 8

Employee voice

LEARNING OUTCOMES

After studying this chapter you should be able to:

- ☑ **explain** the different concepts used to describe the term 'employee voice'

- ☑ **identify** and **explain** the different purpose of employee voice according to the viewpoints of the main employment relations stakeholders

- ☑ **evaluate** the extent to which different employee voice schemes are used in practice, including an explanation of the key differences between union and non-union voice arrangements

- ☑ **explain** worker rights and employer obligations with respect to the key legal influences in the area of employee voice

- ☑ **analyse** the potential outcomes of employee voice for the stakeholders involved.

Introduction

The term 'employee voice' is becoming more popular in employment relations. Over the past few decades the practices of employee voice have taken many different forms, often with different names that describe what can appear to be the same type of process. For instance, in the 1970s employee voice found favour in notions of worker *participation*, typically (though not exclusively) via trade union channels of representation. In the 1980s and 1990s, however, the term *worker participation* was replaced with what came to be known as *employee involvement*, and more recent developments use the term *partnership*. As we shall see later, it is important to unravel the concept of employee voice more thoroughly, in order to understand the variety of mechanisms used. For this reason, the chapter commences by distinguishing between worker *participation* and *employee involvement*, and then explains the context of employee voice in Britain.

Because the stakeholders to an employment relationship view the purpose of employee voice differently, there can be differences in the perceived utility of voice, and this is explained next. Following this, a four-dimensional framework that can be used to evaluate the extent to which employees have a say in matters that affect them at work is given, together with a review of the evidence concerning the type of mechanisms that are used in practice.

The chapter then considers the growing influence of European developments in the area, and reviews some of the suggested outcomes of employee voice. The chapter concludes with a note that, while (for the most part) employee voice remains shallow in terms of the extent to which it allows employees a say in matters that affect them, there are significant legal developments in the offing, some of which are likely to influence management choice for employee voice in the years ahead.

Defining employee voice

The literature on employee voice can often be confusing. Some authors use terms such as *involvement*, *participation*, *empowerment* or *consultation* without fully acknowledging any distinctions between them. In one company, the term 'involvement' may be used to identify certain practices that in another firm are regarded as 'participatory' (Marchington, 2005). In addition, terminology can be further complicated depending on whether or not there is a trade union presence in a firm. For example, some non-union companies prefer the terms 'empowerment' or 'communications', even when referring to representative bodies such as works councils or joint consultative committees. Therefore, it is necessary to be clear how the term is used and, after Boxall and Purcell, employee voice is defined as:

> a whole variety of processes and structures which enable, and at times empower, employees, directly and indirectly, to contribute to decision-making in the firm.
>
> Boxall and Purcell (2003: 162)

Clearly this is a very broad definition and for this reason, it is necessary to be precise about some of the terms used to describe different forms of voice. One of these is worker *participation*, which means something very different from *employee involvement*, even though the two terms tend to be used interchangeably by some commentators. Indeed, many managers often use the term *participation* when they are in fact describing a form of *communication*.

Participation embraces a set of mechanisms that are generally considered to be extensive in terms of how much influence employees (or their representatives) actually have. **Participation** is usually regarded as a more extensive form of voice, because it tends to incorporate a greater share of power in decisions made jointly with management. In other words, workers (often through their elected representatives) take part in the making of decisions that management normally reserves for itself (Farnham and Pimlott, 1987). In contrast, **employee involvement** is regarded as a weaker form of voice, primarily because it relates to a set of practices used by management to solicit employee ideas, in the hope that this will bring about a degree of employee commitment, while at the same time preserving management's right to make decisions. The idea here is that involvement will harness employee cooperation in achieving management objectives, which is a far cry from sharing power (Farnham and Pimlott, 1987).

participation

The sharing of power between employees (or their representatives) and management, in the making of joint decisions.

employee involvement

The soliciting of employee views, opinions and ideas to harness the talents and cooperation of employees, but without the sharing of power in an eventual decision-making outcome.

From the above it can be noted that there is an important difference between involving employees and allowing them to participate in decisions, and the reader is urged to keep this in mind later in the chapter, when reviewing the types of voice practices used by organisations.

Pause for reflection

In view of the effects of management ideologies given in Chapter 3, and given that there are different terms associated with employee voice which are outlined above, what meaning do you feel that managers would attribute to the term 'employee voice'?

The changing context for employee voice

In one form or another, employee voice has been high on the employment relations agenda for a long time, although the pressures for particular voice mechanisms have changed considerably over the past half century. Shortly after the Second World War rising economic prosperity, together with higher levels of awareness and education in the working population, helped to fuel rising aspirations for greater participation at the workplace, and by the 1960s and 1970s, when trade union power was at its greatest, there was an increased willingness to question traditional patterns of deference in industry. Thus politicians and managers alike sought to involve

Bullock Committee

A government inquiry consisting of employers, trade unions and consumer groups set up to identify how plans for worker directors could be implemented in Britain.

workers. A landmark event here was a 1970s parliamentary committee of inquiry, known as the **Bullock Committee** after its chairman, Lord Bullock. In part the inquiry was union-initiated, but included members from both sides of industry and was charged with examining the whole question of industrial democracy (Bullock, 1977). At that time several countries in Europe had made provision for some form of worker participation in decision making, the most notable example being Germany. In the UK the prevailing mood of the government of the day was that some move in this direction had become inevitable. Thus, the terms of reference for the Bullock Committee were quite explicit: to identify how some form of worker representation on the boards of directors of firms *could* best be achieved; not (it can be noted) *whether* it should occur. In anticipation of this, a number of voluntary experiments with worker representatives on the boards of directors took place, namely in the Post Office and the British Steel Corporation. However, the eventual findings of the Bullock Report were controversial, and a minority report was published by its employer members, who condemned its recommendations as too collectivist in nature (Brannen, 1983). Given this opposition from employers to the very idea of worker directors, further moves in this direction were abandoned when a new Conservative government was elected in 1979.

However, this did not mean that discussion on employee voice disappeared in employment relations. Indeed, the term has become more popular in recent years in the light of developments originating in the European Union, of which more will be said later. Nevertheless, it can be noted that participatory voice is seldom an aim of British management, and in practice, managers usually aim for a form of employee involvement that is highly defensive of managerial prerogative, and can often be used to enhance managerial control as much as anything else. Indeed, one writer has wryly observed that, when conditions are severe enough for managers to have a strong need for employee cooperation, they tend to rediscover employee voice, only to forget it very quickly when the emergency has passed (Ramsay, 1977).

This does not, of course, mean that involving employees is harmful or that it fails to benefit workers. Giving employees a say in matters that affect them at work can ameliorate the degradation and alienation associated with many jobs. What is different, however, is that during the

1980s and 1990s the objective for employee voice became much more management-led, and stressed a direct form of *employee involvement*. It has been argued that this emphasis on voice through *involvement* (rather than participation), would improve the commercial standing of an organisation by tapping into employee ideas and creativity.

From the start of the new millennium public policy in the area of employee voice has begun to change even more. The British government promoted polices for voice through initiatives such as Fairness at Work and Partnership, often stimulated by European Social Policy. These policies seek to promote a more cooperative employment relations climate by encouraging greater mutuality and understanding, rather than employment relations based on adversarial principles. Thus, the policy agenda of the British government is now more supportive of European Social Policy, and more sympathetic to trade union recognition as well as individual worker rights for information sharing (Ewing, 2003). The twenty-first century has ushered in a new environment for employee voice in terms of both legislative reforms and competitive pressures that influence managerial choice (Ackers *et al.*, 2005).

Summary points

- The context for employee voice has changed dramatically over the last half century.
- Shortly after the Second World War, interest in the idea of industrial democracy was commonplace, and in the 1960s and 1970s participation was often based on the assumption of continuing high levels of union membership.
- The 1980s and 1990s saw a shift to more management-led initiatives using *involvement* rather than participation.
- In the new millennium there has been a renewed regulatory drive for employee voice, emanating from *European Social Policy* initiatives.

Differences in the purpose and utility of employee voice

Because the parties in industry have their own views as to the purpose and value of employee voice, the reasons why organisations move in this direction also differ. An early use of the concept of voice comes from a seminal study of commercial decline in the African railways by Hirschman (1970), who advocated voice in terms of its effect on loyalty towards a supplier. The argument here is that workers will be more loyal and committed to their employing organisation when they have a voice. This was developed further by Freeman and Medoff (1984), who suggested that voice would reduce labour turnover. For this reason it is important to note that employee voice has both consensual and conflictual dimensions. By allowing employees a voice facility it is argued that management can improve productivity by tapping into employee knowledge. At the same time the facility gives the opportunity to resolve potential conflicts as they arise, rather than having workers leave the organisation because of unvoiced dissatisfactions. However, it has also been noted that exit is not necessarily an alternative to voice and in a survey of non-union firms, Boroff and Lewin (1997) found that loyal employees who experienced unfair treatment tended to suffer in silence, rather than exit the organisation. In social exchange terms, this is a particularly important point as it may indicate a less than positive psychological contract, since employees are denied a voice while employers may fail to deliver what is expected by employees.

Another reason for employee voice is that it is assumed to bring commercial benefits to the organisation. This is part of what can be described as the high performance work system (HPWS) view, in which involving employees is seen to enhance the competitiveness of the firm (Pfeffer, 1998). This, of course, comes very close to saying that if voice adds commercial value, then it is acceptable; if it does not, then there is no case for it. However, even if there is no business case, there are other benefits that can be conceived for employee voice. For example, there is the argument that having a voice is a human right, an entitlement rather than a privilege (Towers, 1997). Budd (2004) suggests that because work is the single biggest influence in people's lives, there should be a balance in the employment relationship between efficiency *and* equity *and* voice. Therefore, although employers have a need to satisfy market demands, this does not mean that they should ignore the needs of employees for self-actualisation, autonomy and expression, as explained in terms of social exchange theory in Chapter 1. In other words, there need not be a contradiction between voice for enhanced competitiveness, and its purpose as an extension of democracy at the workplace.

Nonetheless, the parties to the employment relationship tend to see the utility of voice in very different ways. To this end, Table 8.1 summarises the contrasting purposes and possible outcomes of voice, as viewed by different stakeholders in employment relations (Dundon *et al.*, 2004). The first purpose for voice listed in Table 8.1 concerns the *articulation of individual dissatisfaction*. This views the value of voice in terms of the opportunity to rectify the problems or concerns of workers, which fits well with arguments advanced by Freeman and Medoff (1984) that voice is an alternative to exit. A second purpose starts from the premise of *collective representation*. In this view, collective voice is a countervailing source of power to managerial prerogative, typically via trade unions and collective bargaining. The thinking behind the recommendations of the Bullock Committee noted earlier support this purpose, as would the human-rights case that unions are a check and balance against unregulated managerial power. A third purpose in providing employees with a voice is that their ideas and suggestions can contribute to *management efficiency*: that is, a voice mechanism can help improve business performance by releasing the creative talents and knowledge of workers, and in so doing stimulate greater commitment and satisfaction. This would be comparable with the HPWS literature noted earlier. Finally, employee voice can be argued to build trust and mutuality in an employment relationship through *partnership*. This fits well with the theory that in employment relations there are important social and psychological exchanges between the stakeholders (Guest and Conway, 2002). In the UK context this has a strong resonance with the current British government's belief in promoting *partnership* between employees, management and unions as a way of engendering greater commitment and mutuality.

All of the purposes shown in Table 8.1 can be viewed as different starting blocks that influence different actors' approaches to the matter of employee voice. While the list is by no means exhaustive, it illustrates the idea that there can be considerable diversity in the views of the parties involved. For this reason, the stakeholders in employment relations are likely to behave differently, according to what they perceive their interests to be.

The purpose of voice	Perceived utility from voice	Mechanisms for employee voice	Range of perceived outcomes
Articulation of individual dissatisfaction	To rectify a problem with management or prevent deterioration in relations	Complaint to line manager; Grievance procedure; Speak-up programme	Exit – Loyalty
Collective representation	To provide a countervailing source of power to management	Union recognition; Collective bargaining; Industrial action	Partnership – Derecognition
Contribution to management efficiency	To seek improvements in work organisation, quality and productivity	Upward problem-solving groups; Quality circles; Suggestion schemes; Attitude surveys; Autonomous teams	Identity and commitment – Disillusionment and apathy – Improved performance
Demonstration of mutuality and partnership	To achieve long-term viability for the organisation and its employees	Partnership agreements; Joint consultative committees; Works councils	Significant influence over management decisions – Marginalisation and sweetheart deals

Table 8.1 Perceived differences in the purpose and utility of employee voice
Source: adapted from Dundon *et al.*, 2004: 1153.

Summary points

- The aims for employee voice have changed over time.
- There are now more legal developments affecting employee voice than a decade ago, in particular those that form part of the European employment policy agenda.
- The perceived utility of employee voice tends to be seen differently by different parties, with its purpose usually being related to one or more of the following: articulation of individual dissatisfaction; a collective form of representation; a contribution to management efficiency; to build mutuality and partnership.

A framework to evaluate employee voice

Since there can be wide differences in the perceived purpose of employee voice, and also whether it should be voice as involvement or voice as participation, it is necessary to have a way of evaluating the different forms it can take and the extent to which it facilitates employees having a say in matters that affect them. After Marchington and Wilkinson (2005b) a framework for doing this is to evaluate voice along four dimensions:

- The *depth* of employee voice
- The *scope* of employee voice

- The *level* at which voice occurs in an employing organisation
- The *form* of employee voice mechanisms.

These dimensions are explained in what follows and are brought together in Fig. 8.1.

Depth expresses the extent to which employees (or their representatives) share influence with management in decision making. Shallow voice occurs when employees or their representatives have very little or no say over management action, and in contrast, deep voice enables employees to contribute to the final decision-making outcome in some way.

depth (of employee voice)

The extent to which employees (or their representatives) share in decision-making outcomes with management.

scope (of employee voice)

The range of issues or matters on which employees (or their representatives) have a say.

The second dimension, scope of voice, is conceptually distinct from the previous one, but in practical terms tends to be connected. This expresses the range of issues addressed within a particular voice mechanism, and a process which is narrow in scope allows management to define certain matters as totally reserved for their consideration or to ensure that only minor issues are available for employee input (e.g. the colour of the paint in a staff restroom). In contrast, employee voice that has a wide scope would have few restrictions or reserved issues, with employees or their representatives having an input into more senior and strategic matters (e.g. new technology or even corporate investment plans). As can be seen in Fig. 8.1, a move from a narrow to wider scope of issues is accompanied by a tendency for depth to increase as well.

level (of employee voice)

The hierarchical level in an organisation at which a voice mechanism takes place.

The level of employee voice concerns the hierarchical level in an organisation at which a voice mechanism takes place. This can be extremely important, and ranges between a high (e.g. corporate headquarters) to low level (e.g. team or individual task level). As can be seen in Fig. 8.1, in practical terms, the level at

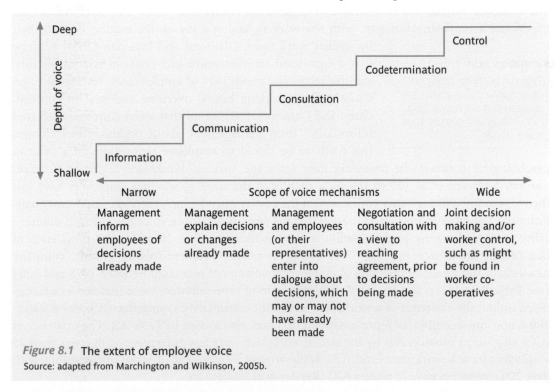

Figure 8.1 The extent of employee voice
Source: adapted from Marchington and Wilkinson, 2005b.

which voice occurs is also connected to depth and scope, since more strategic organisational matters are unlikely to be considered at a low level.

form (of employee voice)
The type of method used, which can be direct and/or indirect in nature.

direct voice
Where contact is between individuals or small groups of employees and their immediate manager.

indirect voice
Where contact is between management and an employee intermediary, such as a shop steward or other employee representative, who acts as the agent for a larger group of workers.

The final dimension, form, expresses the actual methods used to facilitate voice. This can be by *direct* and/or *indirect* methods. Direct voice methods, such as individual appraisals, bring managers and workers into contact with one another, although they can also involve small groups of workers with their immediate manager: for example, task-based mechanisms that deal with specific team, work or quality issues. Indirect voice methods are those in which representatives, such as union stewards or non-union employee representatives, deal with management on behalf of employees. For matters which affect the whole organisation, it would be a practical impossibility for the whole workforce to engage in individual processes. Therefore, the linkage between level and form is an important one. By their very nature direct methods almost inevitably limit the issues that are dealt with to task- or work-related matters and take place at lower levels in the hierarchy. It is perhaps for this reason that low-level direct methods are strongly favoured by managers, but viewed with some suspicion by shop stewards, who tend to favour indirect methods at a higher level which they see as giving them greater access to management decision makers. There are also forms of financial involvement and participation, such as share-ownership schemes, and these will be explained shortly.

Employee voice in practice

The evidence on the use of different voice schemes shows that many employees in Britain experience a representation gap, with few workers having a say on the matters beyond their immediate work tasks. Diamond and Freeman (2001: 6) show that a significant representation gap exists in relation to substantive terms and conditions of employment: for instance, on issues such as working hours, overtime and pay. In contrast, Guest and Conway (2002) found that when employees received information from management about organisational change, this tends to be linked to employee perceptions of a positive psychological contract. In reviewing data from the various *Workplace Employee Relations Surveys*, Millward *et al.* (2000) devote a chapter to the issue of whether employees have lost their voice, and although they conclude that the answer must be 'no', there are important qualifications. The most important of these is that the *form* of employee voice has changed dramatically, from *indirect* to predominantly *direct* mechanisms. For example, the prevalence of face-to-face workforce meetings, the use of employee problem-solving groups, company newsletters and financial methods of employee involvement increased between 1998 and 2004 (see Table 8.2). It can also be noted that 'any' form of representative voice (defined as a recognised union, the existence of a workplace-level joint consultative committee (JCC) or a stand-alone non-union employee representatives) declined, also shown in Table 8.2. The existence of JCCs also varies considerably by the size of workplace: very few enterprises with fewer than 25 employees have a workplace-level JCC, while around 59 per cent of those organisations with over 200 employees have in place a JCC (Kersley *et al.*, 2006: 126).

representation gap
The difference between how much influence employees say they have over management decisions, and how much influence they say they would like to have.

	% of all workplaces	
	1998	2004
Face-to-face meetings between management and employees	85	91
Suggestion schemes	31	30
Regular newsletters	40	45
Problem-solving groups (e.g. quality circles)	28	36
Use of one or more employee share ownership schemes	15	21
Workplace-level joint consultative committee (JCC)	28	14
Any form of representative voice[1]	57	49

Note

(1) Representative voice is defined as the existence of: a recognised trade union; any JCC; union or stand-alone non-union employee representatives (Kersley *et al.*, 2006: 132).

Table 8.2 The use of different voice mechanisms in practice: 1998–2004

Source: Kersley *et al.*, 2006: 94; 127; 135; 191 (all workplaces with ten or more employees). The advice of the WERS 2004 Information and Advice Service (www.wers2004.info) is acknowledged in the compilation of the above figures.

In what follows, the evidence is presented in relation to four clusters of voice practices: *communications, problem-solving voice, representative voice* and *financial participation*. Although each cluster includes a set of voice mechanisms that could potentially overlap, they are listed separately because, conceptually at least, they are complementary. In discussing these clusters the numeric is supplemented with additional analysis concerning the *depth* and *scope* of employee voice.

Communications

In order to be able to manage its employment relationship, a flow of information is vital for an organisation, and good communication is often a precursor to deeper forms of employee voice. For this reason there is a very real sense in which the communication of information can be thought of as the life blood of a firm and an essential component of a psychological contract. However, all too frequently the very existence of problems is attributed to misunderstandings or inadequate communications, and from this it is but a short step to portraying improved communication as a panacea for all employment relations difficulties. However, no matter how much integrity and openness lie behind its telling, nothing in the world will transform an unpalatable message into a palatable one. Nor will an unlimited amount of effective communicating remove the basic differences that exist between employees and managers. For this reason it is better to regard effective communication as a process which allows the differences between employees and managers to surface and be dealt with. Ideally, it will perhaps go further by helping employees and managers to understand better each other's expectations, needs and wants.

The actual use of communication techniques has increased substantially in recent years, covering such arrangements as written memos or regular newsletters to staff, with over 90 per cent of workplaces reporting some form of face-to-face communications with employees (Kersley *et al.*, 2006: 135). More recent developments in this area include the use of information communication technologies (ICT) for employee voice, incorporating company intranets, electronic bulletin boards and emails (Marchington *et al.*, 2001; Kersley *et al.*, 2006: 135). However, while it may have a vital role to play in employment relations, it could be argued that, as an employee voice strategy, communications tend to be limited to methods that are shallow in depth and narrow in scope. Indeed, it is probably inaccurate to label **one-way communication** as a form of employee voice at all, since it does not allow workers to have a say, and its popularity in recent years may be more to do with its usefulness for managers, than as a genuine form of employee voice. An example of this in recent years has been the growth of so-called **two-way communications**, such as face-to-face meetings between employees and supervisors. Managers often refer to such arrangements as 'involvement' or 'participation' but at best they are really nothing more than effective communications. Even worse, senior managers of organisations sometimes assert that, because they have developed effective communication techniques, this amounts to an advanced form of employee voice. The main criticisms here are that management inevitably controls what (and when) information will be passed to employees, and its objectivity is likely to be in some doubt since the information communicated is invariably selected by management. Furthermore, many line managers and supervisors responsible for disseminating company information lack effective people-management skills. In this respect the media is replete with cases in which job losses and factory relocations have been announced publicly before management have actually communicated the message to workers.

one-way communication

A direct form of voice where information is disseminated from management to employees.

two-way communication

A direct form of voice in which information is exchanged between management and employees.

Problem-solving voice

The second cluster of voice methods includes **upward problem-solving** and **autonomous teamworking** mechanisms. While there are a number of variants of these, they typically include small group methods such as teamworking, quality circles and employee focus groups that identify work-based problems and make improvement suggestions to management. In addition, more individualised problem-solving mechanisms exist in the form of suggestions schemes and employee surveys. The key distinction between these mechanisms and what is normally labelled 'communication' is that in the former there tends to be some element of upward communication from employees to management, whereas communication channels typically only involve downward flows of information from management to workers.

upward problem-solving

Voice mechanisms that allow employees (either individually or in small groups) to suggest solutions to management about work and/or quality issues.

autonomous teamworking

Employees working in groups who meet the criteria of: working alongside each another; taking responsibility for their job tasks; deciding how their tasks are to be accomplished; appointing their own team leader from among the members of the group.

While they are often portrayed in an upbeat and uncritical way, conceptually team- and task-based structures are the most imprecise of all problem-solving voice mechanisms. Usually they involve small groups of up to twelve employees, who meet on a regular basis under the guidance of a group leader. However, it is often unclear whether they meet voluntarily, during (paid) working hours, or are coerced into searching for solutions to problems that may have been identified by management. Since many of these problem-solving groups tend to deal mostly with immediate, work-related matters, they are essentially a method of direct involvement. Moreover, they can be very narrow in scope and shallow in depth, and have little to do with the sharing of power or decision making in an organisation. For one author, these methods are merely *partial* or *pseudo participation,* because they fall short of allowing employees a full voice while at the same time leaving the power structures of an organisation untouched (Pateman, 1970).

In addition, other studies argue that far from providing employees with a say on work-related matters, the effects of problem-solving methods can be positively malevolent. For example, the feedback provided in response to an attitude survey is essentially based on a managerial agenda, which is reflected in the questions asked in a survey. Furthermore, in organisations where quality circles have been introduced, the take-up and enthusiasm among employees has often been found wanting, which has led to the claim that problem-solving groups result in a form of peer pressure and surveillance that strengthens managerial control (Barker, 1993). For example, the pressure to conform to group norms and meet production targets is often policed by co-workers, with management effectively monitoring employee effort and engagement from the sidelines (Geary and Dobbins, 2001). The net effect of this can be increased stress levels, as more work-related responsibilities are devolved to employee groups.

Of course, these criticisms do not mean that employees dislike group-based voice schemes, or that they have no benefit. Where teamworking or quality circles work well, it is more than possible that they could foster a degree of bottom-up decision making on particular problems and issues, and this could release some of the creative talents of employees that may engender a more positive psychological exchange (Strauss, 1998). The Human Relations and Quality of Working Life movements in the 1970s showed that a participative work environment, which gives some degree of autonomy to workers, can lead to a more cooperative employment relations climate. More recently, quantitative analysis has shown that employees are satisfied in their job when they experience voice mechanisms that are deep and embedded into the organisational decision-making processes (Cox *et al.*, 2006). Furthermore, even though employees in smaller firms do not have access to the same formal voice mechanisms that exists in many larger workplaces, they are actually more content with their level of voice than workers in larger firms (Forth *et al.*, 2006: 55–56).

Representative voice

The third cluster, indirect voice arrangements, embraces those in which management inform, consult and/or negotiate with employee representatives who are agents acting on behalf of a larger groups of employees. These mechanisms are often associated with trade union consultation and collective bargaining, although non-union representative systems have increased in recent years. For this reason, union and non-union situations will be reviewed separately.

Union-centred representative voice

In organisations that recognise them, the very existence of a trade union means that there is a definite voice mechanism, usually via collective bargaining and/or joint consultation. However, the existence of a *de facto* voice arrangement is not the same as effective or extensive voice, and the decline in union membership over the past three decades raises some doubts about the efficacy of a single union channel for employee voice (Terry, 2003: 274). Indeed, it has been observed that in some situations union forms of representation are little more than a 'hollow shell' (Charlwood, 2003), and that even where union structures exist, they can be ineffective and marginal to other direct voice arrangements.

The WERS data show that union recognition has declined quite substantially over the past two decades, with just 30 per cent of all workplaces recognising a trade union in 2004, and while

collective bargaining
A process in which the representatives of recognised trade unions and employers negotiate, consult and communicate to agree the procedural and substantive terms and conditions of employment.

joint consultation
A voice process that can be direct or indirect and one in which management and employees (or their representatives) discuss and consider each other's views prior to management making a final decision.

collective bargaining covered 70 per cent of employees in 1984, this was down to 39 per cent by 2004 (Cully *et al.*, 1999; Kersley *et al.*, 2006). Joint consultation has declined even further, with just 14 per cent of establishments reporting the existence of a workplace-level joint consultative committee (Kersley *et al.*, 2006: 127). Therefore, it is evident that British managers tend to be less favourably disposed towards unions as a voice channel. Nevertheless, trade unions are important actors in the employment relationship, and for this reason union voice will be considered in relation to collective bargaining and then a more recent and parallel process, namely partnership.

Since the next chapter will deal with the theory and practice of collective bargaining it is not the intention to present a detailed picture here. Suffice it to say that it is perhaps the most extensive form of voice in relation to the analytical framework described earlier, albeit a method that has experienced the most decline. It serves at least three functions: *economic, governmental* and *decision-making* (Chamberlain and Kuhn, 1965). The first of these, the *economic* function, represents the popular view of the process: that is, one which is used to determine the substantive terms on which employees will continue to supply their labour. However, the *governmental* function draws attention to the idea that collective bargaining is essentially a political and power-centred process. It comes about because the two parties are mutually dependent on each other, and through collective bargaining union representatives can veto, block or support changes brought to the table by management. This leads to the third function, that of *decision making*, which allows employees (through their elected representatives) to play a part in determining policies and actions which guide and rule their working lives.

Pause for reflection

In what ways could it be asserted that collective bargaining is a form of indirect employee voice?

In practice the extent to which all three functions are served together will clearly depend upon a number of factors: the size of union membership, availability of union officers and the willingness of representatives to share in the processes of managerial decision making. Managers will also have views on the legitimacy of collective bargaining as a form of voice. Nevertheless, when it takes place in good faith, it would not be exaggerating matters to assert that of all the voice mechanisms described in this chapter, collective bargaining is most likely to be the most extensive form of voice in terms of its *depth, scope* and *level*. Thus, it is with some validity that it has been argued to be an extremely practical form of industrial democracy (Clegg, 1974), and is by far the most favoured channel of employee voice for trade unions. Moreover, because the relationships built up in collective bargaining usually bring about a willingness to compromise, its potential as an effective indirect voice method for employees is much greater than other voice arrangements where commitment and enthusiasm may be lacking.

Partnership

Collective bargaining, as described above, is essentially an adversarial model of employment relations, where the gains accrued to one party are obtained at the expense of the other party; otherwise known as a zero-sum game. In contrast, *partnership* is claimed to be a positive-sum game, in which all the parties gain through a process of cooperation and mutual accommodation. Indeed, what is referred to as 'partnership' in the current UK context is known as 'mutual gains' in the US (Osterman *et al.*, 2001).

As with many employment relations developments, the concept of partnership is by no means a new one. The Involvement and Participation Association (IPA) was first established in 1896 as a voluntary body to promote consultation and partnership in industry, and is currently one of the leading advocates of partnership in the UK. Other voluntary bodies that seek to promote partnership in the UK include the Work Foundation (formerly the Industrial Society), the UK Work Organisation Network and the TUC's Partnership Institute. Membership of these associations is voluntary, although they consist of some of the leading UK employers and trade unions. While the aims and objectives of each body differ slightly, they all encourage projects that claim to improve organisational effectiveness through partnership and work–life balance initiatives. In practical terms, the most significant boost to the idea of partnership followed the election of a Labour government in 1997, which had an avowed policy of encouraging greater cooperation and involvement in employment relations. Indeed, around £20 million has been provided in seed funding to support separate projects under the DTI Partnership Fund.

partnership

A concept that is normally taken to imply cooperation (usually between management and trade unions) based on the satisfaction of mutual as well as separate interests.

However, the very term **partnership** remains ambiguous with no precise definition, and different interested parties tend to promote their own particular variants to suit their own ends. For example, the TUC stresses that partnership is a collective process, while other bodies such as the CBI and CIPD suggest that partnerships can and do exist between management and individual employees. Moreover, recent research also points towards the possibility of partnership in non-union as well as unionised settings (Ackers *et al.*, 2005). Both the IPA and TUC underwrite a number of very similar partnership principles (see Table 8.3), with the IPA endorsing a specific definition, as given by ACAS:

> " an interest based relationship – that is, a relationship based not simply on power and rights but on the satisfaction of mutual as well as separate interests.
>
> IPA (www.partnership-at-work.com) "

IPA partnership principles	TUC partnership principles
■ Recognition of employees' desire for security and the company's need to maximise flexibility	■ A shared commitment to the success of the enterprise
■ Sharing success within the company	■ Recognition of legitimate interests
■ Informing and consulting staff about issues at workplace and company level	■ Commitment to employment security
■ Effective representation of people's views within the organisation	■ A focus on the quality of working life
	■ Openness
	■ Adding value

Table 8.3 Principles of partnership
Source: www.partnership-at-work.com; TUC, 2001.

Notwithstanding these points there remains considerable disagreement surrounding partnership, with both advocates and critics having substantial differences. At one extreme are the advocates, such as Ackers and Payne (1998), Guest and Peccei (2001) and Haynes and Allen (2001), who argue that partnership can mediate longstanding tensions and contradictions in employment relations. For example, it is said that after two decades of membership decline, partnership could provide unions with a new lease of life and re-legitimise their role as the representative voice of workers. Advocates also argue that partnership could deliver more cooperative employment relations in return for management recognition of a union channel for employee voice. In addition, they also suggest that partnership can help employers manage in more flexible and customer-responsive ways, in return for which workers would obtain a degree of job security and share with management in decision-making processes. All of this, it is argued, would be likely to lead to a better employment relations climate characterised by higher trust and organisational innovation.

At the other extreme are the critics such as Taylor and Ramsay (1998), Danford *et al.* (2004) and Kelly (1998, 2005), all of whom question the legitimacy of partnership in a number of ways. First, as was noted in Chapter 1, the parties to the employment relationship do not enter it as true equals and, therefore, the very idea of partnership is rather false, because the balance of power tends to be tilted in management's favour.

Second, the critics suggest that partnership agreements can weaken rather than strengthen trade union participation. This not only occurs because of the unequal balance of power in employment relations but also, because of partnership, there is an attendant risk that shop stewards will be perceived to be a part of the management chain of command. The risk is that shop stewards endorse managerial change programmes which are not always perceived by workers to be in their best interests. Related to this is the critique that the outcome of negotiations in a partnership scheme can actually result in workers having to work harder than before, with the lion's share of any gains accruing to management. Finally, in comparing partnership and non-partnership companies in the same industrial sectors, Kelly (2005) shows that under partnership there are few significant gains in terms of employment security for workers or, indeed, profitability for employers. Consequently, the argument is advanced that unions could obtain a greater share of power by adopting more militant rather than cooperative strategies.

In between the extremes, there are those commentators who suggest there is more to partnership than straightforward gains or losses for either party (Roche and Geary, 2002; Oxenbridge and Brown, 2002; Martinez Lucio and Stuart, 2005). For example, in an empirical study Geary and Roche (2003) could find no support for the idea of a displacement of union representatives under partnership conditions, and claim that it is rash to suggest that unions become too cosy with management. In addition, it has been noted that partnership has a political dimension, which is more concerned with how the parties communicate and consult with each other. For this reason, viewing partnership as nothing more than a workplace process creates a vacuum that ignores other influences that shape the prospects for representative voice (Martinez Lucio and Stuart, 2005). Moreover, research by Oxenbridge and Brown (2004) shows that there are both *robust* and *shallow* forms of partnership. Under *robust* partnership unions obtain a greater degree of influence, while *shallow* partnerships provide few participatory channels. Of particular significance here are the conditions under which *robust* and *shallow* forms of partnership occur, and more often than not, the main factor is a willingness on management's part to concede some sharing of power. In other words, success is probably more dependent on certain contextual conditions being met – for example, the values of the parties and the informal and organic relationships that develop over time.

Pause for reflection

As a form of indirect voice, list the advantages and disadvantages of a partnership approach for both management and trade unions.

Non-union representative voice

Given the decline in union membership, and the possibility that partnership may be relevant in non-union settings, it can be argued that representative voice is no longer dependent on trade unionism. Indeed, it can be noted that indirect voice exists in other situations that do not involve unions, for instance in European Works Councils (EWCs) and non-union company committees. Moreover, in one study of employee voice and management choice (Marchington *et al.*, 2001) it was discovered that non-union consultative committees were more common than those that had been found in a similar study conducted by the same authors a decade earlier (Marchington *et al.*, 1992).

However, there is a regrettable tendency to view representative voice in comparison with its unionised counterpart. This can be somewhat problematic because it sometimes rejects out of hand the range of non-union voice schemes that may exist in an organisation, and dismisses them as shallow or ineffective, without fully evaluating the *scope, level* and *depth* of such voice mechanisms or considering the needs of non-union workers (Dundon *et al.*, 2005). As Ackers *et al.* (2005) remind us, some non-union employers, notably the retailer John Lewis, have developed deeper forms of voice than many union-centred channels. The main issue is the extent to which such arrangements provide for participatory voice, and here the evidence is disappointing. For example, only 5 per cent of British workplaces have facilities for 'stand-alone', non-union employee representatives: a figure that is comparable across both union and non-union establishments (Kersley *et al.*, 2006: 125). In addition to the incidence of non-union representative voice is the depth and scope of the actual mechanisms, and again the evidence is less than complementary. For example, in Gollan's (2002) study of News International it was found that the non-union Employee Consultative Council (ECC) lacked the ability to question managerial decisions. Similarly, Dundon and Rollinson (2004) show that the scope of a non-union works council was very shallow. In this case, not only was the works council's remit restricted to very minor issues, but employee representatives had to attend the meetings with management outside working time. Furthermore, there appeared to be a conscious strategy by management to marginalise and bypass employee representatives, thus excluding them from the decision-making process (Dundon and Rollinson, 2004: 103). In addition, other research has shown how non-union employers adopt a range of voice mechanisms that delay, stonewall and avoid union-centred forms of worker representation (Gall, 2004).

Pause for reflection

In what ways could it be argued that non-union voice is a strategy deployed by some employers to avoid union recognition?

Nevertheless, whether or not non-union voice is part of a union-avoidance strategy very much depends on the spirit in which management seek to engage with employees. Not all non-union firms are anti-union, and for some organisations, non-union employee representatives may be a valuable adjunct to direct communication channels. In other situations, however, non-union voice can be used to dampen down possible demands for unionisation. In this respect it can be noted that, while non-union employers in Britain prefer to manage without trade unions, they do not avoid unionisation in the characteristically aggressive fashion of many American union-busting organisations (Logan, 2001). On balance however, the evidence suggests that the *depth* and *scope* of non-union representative voice is at best variable, and at worst little more than a form of indirect employee *involvement*.

Financial participation

financial participation
Mechanisms that allow employees to share in the financial success of their organisation.

While the idea of profit sharing or other forms of financial participation is by no means a new one, encouragement for these initiatives was prompted by legislation in the 1980s. The idea is that employees participate in the success of a company by receiving financial rewards for their effort and input. Although methods of financial participation can vary considerably, three basic forms can be identified. In *profit sharing* there is some distribution of profits among employees, usually annually or twice yearly as a supplement to normal salary or wages. The second form is *employee share ownership schemes* (ESOPs), which distribute a proportion of profits as shares, either directly to employees or into a trust which holds them on their behalf. Finally, there are *profit-related pay* (PRP) schemes in which a set proportion of pay is made up of financial incentives.

Despite the way that these methods are generically referred to as 'financial participation', none would qualify as a form of employee voice as it is defined in this chapter. In share ownership, which nominally makes employees part owners of the enterprise, the total size of the employee shareholding is usually so small that employees would be unable to influence company decision making. Indeed, in many schemes of this type, the shares are non-voting anyway, which effectively makes financial participation little more than a very limited form of involvement.

The economic theory behind profit sharing is based on a monetarist ideology, in which financial participation is said to have macro-economic benefits in terms of reducing unemployment and inflation, while simultaneously increasing economic growth. It argues this will happen because wages are tied to profits, which will make employees more committed to the goals set by management. It further argues that for this to happen the direction of the enterprise must be left completely to management, with employees and trade unions being strictly excluded from organisational decision making. However, the whole theory has been hotly criticised by a number of writers who argue that these ideas completely ignore the human dynamics of employment relations and, therefore, schemes of this type are doomed to fail unless trade unions and/or employees are involved in decision making.

Summary points

- In practice, four distinct clusters of complementary practice can be found in firms: *communications, problem-solving voice, representative voice* and *financial participation*.
- Within each cluster some of the specific mechanisms used are likely to overlap and some mechanisms, for example teamworking and partnership, are ambiguous and difficult to define precisely.

- The current vogue is for partnership arrangements as an indirect form of employee voice, but evaluating what the respective parties may gain or lose under partnership is a contested point in employment relations.

- The day-to-day relations between the parties, which may be more informal than formal, strongly influence the efficacy of the mechanisms used.

European influences on employee voice

While Chapters 4 and 5 outline the statutory rights for trade union recognition, the law pertaining to employee voice and representational rights is not confined to trade union recognition alone. There is now a raft of European Directives and subsequent UK legislation that makes employment regulation an important topic in many organisations. For example, there are now legal regulations that require employers to inform and consult employees on matters such as collective redundancy, transfer of undertakings, pensions, health and safety and European Works Councils (EWCs). Although it is beyond the scope of this section to detail each and every European development in relation to employee voice, in what follows we briefly explain the role of EWCs as a form of indirect employee voice, and then consider a recent (and possibly more significant) development: the 2004 *Information and Consultation of Employees Regulations (ICE)*.

employment regulation
A set of rules and procedures governing the conduct of employment relations and the establishment of workers' rights that are determined by customs and/or legislation.

European Works Councils (EWCs)

A **European Works Council** is a joint consultative body for the purpose of sharing information and consulting with employee representatives on matters of transnational interest. The EWC Directive was passed by the EU Council of Ministers in 1994, although the (then) Conservative government in Great Britain opted out of the legislative requirements. With the election of a Labour government in 1997 this was reversed and the terms of the EWC Directive were transposed into UK law by the Transnational Information and Consultation of Employees Regulations in 1999. The qualifying criteria for an organisation affected by these regulations is that it should employ 1000 or more employees, with at least 150 of them being employed in two or more EU member states. Article 5 of the Directive stipulates that a request to set up an EWC should be the subject of negotiation between employee representatives and management, in what is known as a *special negotiating body* (SNB). However, management can voluntarily decide to opt for an EWC, as can employees by submitting a written request from 100 or more employees to management. In this respect Article 13 of the Directive is important, because it grants organisations an exemption from the main statutory requirements, providing the EWC is agreed by an SNB. Because it allows considerable latitude and even deviation from the legislation, as might be expected, this has been a favoured approach among managers.

European Works Council (EWC)
An employee forum/committee for the purposes of sharing information and consulting with management on matters of interest in a European community-scale company.

Article 13 (of the EWC Directive)
Refers to voluntary agreements made between management and the employee representatives of a European community-scale company to agree the purpose and function of an EWC, prior to the enactment of statutory provisions for such an EWC.

Evidence with respect to the extent of employee voice through EWCs is mixed. In terms of *coverage*, there are some

2169 multinational corporations with undertakings across the European Union that fall within EWC regulations. Only one-third of these actually have an EWC (see Table 8.4) and, by implication, this means there are more than 1400 multinational organisations who have yet to set up an EWC. In the UK the adoption rate for companies is 37 per cent and, while this seems low, it is comparable with other countries, many of whom have a long history of works councils at national level, for example, Germany, Denmark, France and Italy.

In terms of the *depth* of voice in EWCs, the evidence suggests a shallow outcome. For example, Wills (1999) shows that while many managers see benefits in having an EWC, they see its purpose as promoting a corporate message, rather than engaging with employee representatives in genuine dialogue. In some situations, information is only presented to an

Country	Number of companies with undertakings that fall under the EWC Directive	Number of companies with an EWC	% of EWCs implemented (rounded %)
Austria	45	16	35
Belgium	68	35	51
Czech Republic	8	0	0
Denmark	59	23	39
Finland	58	26	45
France	216	82	38
Germany	444	121	27
Greece	5	1	20
Hungary	12	1	8
Ireland	43	6	14
Italy	66	23	35
Japan	55	21	38
Luxembourg	5	2	40
Netherlands	135	50	37
Norway	19	13	68
Poland	8	0	0
Portugal	8	1	12
Spain	41	6	14
Sweden	117	55	47
Switzerland	104	37	35
UK	264	98	37
US	332	110	33
Other[1]	57	10	17
Total	2169	737	34

Note
(1) includes Australia, Bahrain, Canada, Croatia, Hong Kong, Israel, Malaysia, Russian Federation, Singapore, South Africa, South Korea, Taiwan, Turkey.

Table 8.4 Number of companies that fall under EWC regulations, by country of ownership
Source: Kerckhofs and Pas, 2004.

EWC *after* management have made a decision, thereby limiting the *depth* of any representative voice. In practical terms, it also seems likely that the *scope* of EWCs is confined to issues dealing with the implementation of change, rather than change-management decisions. Indeed, in some situations management will go to some lengths to avoid establishing an EWC. For example, Royle (2000: 185–187) found that the fast-food chain, McDonald's, transferred a number of restaurants into franchise ownership when faced with an employee request to establish a works council. The net effect was that these restaurants were no longer legally owned by McDonald's, and therefore did not fall within the regulations of the EWC Directive.

Employee information and consultation rights

A more immediate development for employee voice is contained in the Information and Consultation of Employees Regulations 2004 (ICE), which became effective in the UK in April 2005. These regulations transpose into UK law the 2002 European Directive on Employee Information and Consultation, and are based on an agreement made between the CBI, TUC and the British government. The ICE regulations are extensive, with 43 separate regulations and 2 schedules that provide additional interpretations of the regulations. A summary outline of the main ICE regulations is contained in Exhibit 8.1, and Fig. 8.2 charts the stages in setting up an information and consultation process. Given the extent and detail of the ICE regulations, the reader is advised to consult either the DTI or ACAS website where detailed guidance can be obtained. In this section some of the more salient issues associated with the introduction of these regulations will be explained.

The EU Directive itself required member states of the EU to establish a permanent and statutory framework for employees to receive information and to be consulted on matters affecting them at work. However, because the UK (together with the Republic of Ireland) has no existing statutory framework for employee voice, the ICE regulations will become effective in three stages in Great Britain:

- For undertakings with 150 or more employees, the regulations are effective from 6 April 2005.

- For undertakings with 100 or more employees, the effective date is 6 April 2007.

- For undertakings with 50 or more employees, 6 April 2008.

The ICE 2004 Regulations define information and consultation as follows:

> *Information* means data transmitted by the employer to: (a) the information and consultation representative; or (b), in case of a negotiated agreement, directly to employees.

> *Consultation* means the exchange of views and establishment of dialogue between: (a) the information and consultation representative and employer; or (b), in case of a negotiated agreement, the employees and employer.

The implications of these regulations are potentially far-reaching, both for employment relations generally, and for employee voice mechanism in particular. For the first time employees in Great Britain will have the legal right to be informed and consulted on a range of business and employment matters, should they wish. The *scope* of information and consultation relates to

- The regulations apply to undertakings in Great Britain with 50 or more employees. Equivalent legislation will be made in respect of Northern Ireland.
- The legal requirement to inform and consult employees is not automatic. A formal request has to be made by employees, or by an employer initiating the process (an employer notification).
- An employer must establish information and consultation procedures where a valid request has been made by employees.
- Such a request must be made in writing by 10% of employees in an undertaking (subject to a minimum of 15 and a maximum of 2500 employees).
- Where the employees making the request wish to remain anonymous, they can submit the request to an independent body (such as the Central Arbitration Committee).
- The employer would have the opportunity to organise a ballot of employees to endorse or reject the initial request.
- An employer can continue with pre-existing information and consultation arrangements, provided that such arrangements have been agreed prior to an employee written request and:
    i)   the agreement is in writing, including any collective agreements with trade unions;
    ii) the agreement covers all employees in the undertaking;
    iii) the agreement sets out how the employer is to provide the information and seek employee views for consultation; and
    iv) the arrangements have been agreed by the employees.
- If an employee request is to change a pre-existing agreement already in place in an undertaking, then 40% plus a majority of those voting must endorse the request. The employer is then obliged to reach a negotiated agreement with genuine employee representatives.
- Where fewer than 40% of employees endorse the request, the employer would be able to continue with pre-existing arrangements.
- The parties have 6 months to reach a negotiated agreement (extendable by agreement).
- Where a valid request (or employer notification) has been made, but no agreement reached, standard information and consultation provisions based on ICE Regulation 18 would apply.
- Where the standard information and consultation provisions apply, the employer shall arrange for a ballot to elect the employee representatives. Regulation 19 states that there shall be 1 representative per 50 employees, or part thereof, with a minimum of 2 and maximum of 25 representatives.
- Consultation should take place with a view to reaching agreement on decisions.
- Information must be given in such time, and in such fashion and with such content as are appropriate to enable the information and consultation representatives to conduct an adequate study and, where necessary, prepare for consultation.
- There are no prescriptive standard provisions and it is expected that these will vary from organisation to organisation. The standard provisions are based on Article 4 of the EU Directive. ICE Regulation 20 states that I&C representatives, once elected, must have the opportunity to meet with the employer and give their opinion on matters subject to consultation, with a view to reaching agreement. The employer must give a reasoned response to I&C representatives' views.
- Enforcement regulations do not apply to pre-existing agreements.
- A complaint regarding a negotiated agreement, or a failure to comply with standard provisions, must be brought to the CAC within 3 months of the alleged failure.
- Where the CAC upholds a complaint for failure to comply, the complainant may make an application to the Employment Appeal Tribunal (EAT). An appeal must be made within 42 days of the date on which written notification of the CAC declaration is sent.
- The maximum penalty for failing to comply with a declaration made by the CAC is £75 000.
- ICE Regulations 25 and 26 provide for the confidentiality of sensitive information given to I&C representatives.
- I&C representatives, and employees making a request, are protected against discrimination/unfair dismissal for exercising their rights under the ICE Regulations.
- I&C representatives are to be afforded paid time off to carry out their duties.

Exhibit 8.1 Information & consultation of employees (ICE) regulations 2004
Source: DTI, 2005.

three specific areas, and each area progressively increases the *depth* to which employees (and their representatives) should be informed and consulted, as follows:

1 Information pertaining to the economic situation of the organisation

2 Information *and* consultation on the structure and probable development of employment (including any threats to employment)

3 Information *and* consultation, *with* a view to reaching agreement, on decisions likely to lead to changes in work organisation or contractual relations.

---

trigger mechanism (in ICE regulations)

This sets out the initiation process to enact the legal rights for employees to be informed and consulted, which can occur either through a formal written request by employees, or by an employer notification to start the process and negotiate a new information and consultation agreement.

However, the requirement for an employer to inform and consult does not happen automatically. There is a **trigger mechanism** for these legal rights to be enacted, with three possible routes for initiating the process:

1 *Employee request* (ICE Regulation 7). An employer is obliged to initiate negotiations with employee representatives to establish an information and consultation arrangement when there is a valid request from at least 10 per cent of the workforce (subject to a minimum of 15 and maximum of 2500 employees). Anonymous requests can also be made by employees to the Central Arbitration Committee (CAC). However, if employees request a new I&C arrangement when a pre-existing agreement is already in place, then the employer may request a ballot of employees for the new request. Where a ballot is held, and 40 per cent of the workforce *plus* a majority of those voting endorse the request, the employer is obliged to negotiate a new information and consultation agreement.

2 *Pre-existing agreement* (ICE Regulations 8 and 9). Under Article 5 of the EU Directive, provision was made for employers to establish alternative information and consultation arrangements, similar to Article 13 Agreements under the EWC Directive cited earlier. In other words, employers can agree their own voluntary arrangements that may differ from any statutory model. The ICE 2004 Regulations provide for such voluntary agreements, providing they have been established prior to an employee request, and meet four criteria: i) that the agreement is in writing (including collective agreements with trade unions); ii) it covers all employees; iii) it sets out how the employer is to give information and seek employee views; and iv), it has been agreed by the employees concerned.

3 *Employer notification* (ICE Regulation 11). Employers may decide to initiate the process themselves. In this situation, the process would be the same as when employees trigger the process to request a new information and consultation agreement. An employer notification is not the same as setting up a pre-existing agreement.

Figure 8.2 below provides an overview of the processes to trigger the new legal rights to information and consultation under the ICE 2004 Regulations.

The *depth* to which the regulations provide employees (and their representatives) with a greater say is potentially far-reaching, but it is also contentious. For example, there are discrepancies between the ICE 2004 Regulations and the EU Directive in certain areas. The definitions for information and consultation cited above are not, strictly speaking, the same as those contained in the EU Employee Information and Consultation Directive. The ICE 2004 Regulations imply that *direct* forms of employee voice are acceptable, whereas (given the explicit

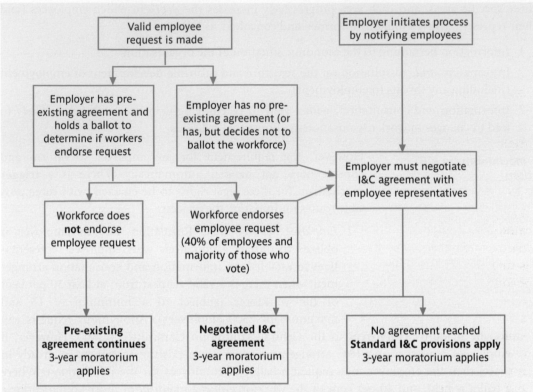

Figure 8.2 Process for setting up new information and consultation arrangements under the ICE 2004 Regulations
Source: DTI, 2005: 11.

reference to employee representatives), the 2002 European Directive from which the ICE Regulations are drawn, states that information and consultation should be of an *indirect* nature. To illustrate the difference, the 2002 European Directive defines information and consultation as follows:

> *Information* is the transmission, by the employer to employee representatives, of data in order to enable them to acquaint themselves with the subject-matter and to examine it.

> *Consultation* is the exchange of views and establishment of dialogue between the employees' representatives and the employer, with a view to reaching agreement.

Pause for reflection

Compare the text of the two sets of definitions cited above for *information* and *consultation* – the first from the ICE 2004 Regulations (see Exhibit 8.1, page 248), and the second from the EU Information and Consultation Directive. Are there any discrepancies between the two sets of definitions?

The explicit reference to *employee representatives* in the Directive is arguably a much clearer indication of *indirect* forms of information and consultation, whereas the UK ICE Regulations are more ambiguous and could be interpreted as allowing for *direct* methods, such as communication memos, quality circles or team-based voice mechanisms. Any definitive interpretation on this matter would, however, require a court decision should the ICE Regulations be challenged or questioned by a trade union, employee or a manager. However, in a European Court of Justice decision on collective redundancies (*Junk* v *Kuhnel)*, it was ruled that the term 'with a view to reaching agreement' is, in effect, an obligation to 'negotiate' (ECJ, 2005). Clearly the implication is that consultation could well be tantamount to bargaining between management and the employee information and consultation representatives.

Although there are other areas of debate with respect to the ICE Regulations, it is possible that these regulations may evolve as the norm rather than as a minimum floor of rights, with information and consultation replacing bargaining and negotiation. It is important to bear in mind that *consultation* and *collective bargaining* fulfil very different functions, and it is unlikely that non-union employee information and consultation representatives will be as experienced as union officers in terms of collective bargaining skills. It is also possible that trade unions may become marginalised, as these new legal rights apply to employees and employee representatives, not union shop stewards. The regulations might also be contentious because the rights to receive information and be consulted are not automatic, but have to be triggered. What this could mean is that in the absence of an independent trade union, employees who request these new rights might face managerial reprisals. Moreover, the *economic situation* of the organisation, and *decisions that will change work or contractual arrangements*, are the sorts of issues that many managers would regard as within their prerogatives, especially since there is an assumption that consultation means *reaching agreement* which, following the *Junk* v *Kuhnel* ruling, implies negotiation. The reaction of some employer groups suggests that such issues will remain highly contested. For example, the Institute of Directors (IOD) believes that managers should not be 'distracted by the manifestation of compulsory industrial democracy', and the whole idea of regulated information and consultation is 'alien to British workplaces' (Coats, 2004: 22).

Notwithstanding any possible ideological bias on the part of employers, the ICE Regulations are potentially wide in *scope* and *depth*, so much so that one author has suggested that they are as significant as the right not to be unfairly dismissed or discriminated against in employment (Sisson, 2002). However, given the variability of employer strategies for the emerging regulatory environment it is difficult to foresee a seismic shift in employment relations. One suggestion is the regulations might lead to 'legally prompted' forms of employee voice, in which employers devise their own voice arrangements rather than have a statutory model imposed (Hall and Terry, 2004). It has been further speculated that the ICE Regulations could provide a platform for union renewal, where trade unions present a case that they can provide a more effective (and independent) voice channel for employees. Yet another possible consequence is that the regulations will mean that employers do nothing more than tick the required compliance boxes, thus negating the intended *spirit* underpinning the legislation. In practical terms, it may even be that future cathartic events act as a catalyst to trigger these new legal rights. For instance, if workers experience job losses or organisational restructuring because of market pressures, they could come to realise that they could have had a say about these changes, had they triggered their rights to do so. One particular implication in this regard is how such issues will shape and influence employee expectations of a psychological contract, with the possibility that new demands for employee voice could be intensified.

It is likely that the practicalities of the new regulations will be more difficult to assess for those organisations that are partly unionised and have low union density. In all probability, highly unionised firms already have in place mechanisms that will suffice with little adjustment. Similarly, in completely non-union companies, management and employees have the opportunity to design and implement new works council structures that meet the new regulations and one case of this type, which concerns Hewlett Packard in the UK, is given in Exhibit 8.2. In a partial union membership situation, however, matters are likely to be more problematic, because it is unclear whether there would have to be duplicate union and non-union employee forums, particularly if existing union representatives find it unpalatable to represent the interests of non-members.

Scope and function

The HP Information & Consultative Forum (HPICF) is a joint consultative group representative of management and employees, established in a spirit of cooperation, openness and mutual trust and incorporates the *Information and Consultation of Employees Regulations 2004 (ICE)*, as of April 2005. The Forum will not replace other established methods of communication and consultation, e.g. employee focus groups, email communication, noticeboards etc.

The role of the HPICF is to establish and maintain a dialogue between management and employees so that the people working in HP can, through their representatives, be informed and consulted on key business issues. The HPICF is not a forum for negotiations, but where any substantial organisational or contractual changes are anticipated the company will consult with a view to reaching an agreement.

The Forum will discuss:

- HP UK Business Strategy, *including the competitive market place, the structure and probable development of the business, marketing strategies and broad employment trends*
- Financial Performance
- Operational Performance
- Customer Service
- Investment Plans, *including overall policy, impact on jobs, new working methods*
- Organisational Changes
- Legislation
- Health, Safety and Environment
- Diversity.

The Forum will also be the relevant body for HP-wide statutory consultations on:

- Collective Redundancies
- Transfers of Undertakings
- Workforce Agreements, *including working time and parental leave and any other legislation that provides for flexible implementation through negotiated collective agreements*
- Health and Safety
- Merger and Acquisition
- Pensions.

The employee representatives on the Forum will also nominate from among their members the UK representatives on HP's EWC as and when replacement representatives are required.

The Forum has been established to cover all employees of HP Ltd in the UK.

Membership of the Forum

The Forum will comprise 15 member representatives, as follows:

Management (×4), including:

- the UK Employee Relations Manager
- the UK Human Resource Manager
- two other management representatives.

Exhibit 8.2 Hewlett Packard Information and Consultation Forum (HPICF) agreement

Other management representatives may be invited to attend the Forum meetings from time to time or for specific agenda items.

Employee representatives (×11), including:

- 5 representatives from TSG
- 2 representatives from CSG
- 1 representative from PSG/IPG
- 2 representatives from Corporate Functions
- 1 representative from Finance and Administration (not business finance).

Additional employee representatives may be co-opted onto the Forum if it is felt necessary to ensure that all employees are effectively represented.

Role of employee representatives

It is the responsibility of employee representatives to respond to and comment on the information provided by management to the Forum. It is also their responsibility to raise issues of concern to their constituents at the Forum. Employee representatives will liaise with their constituents via email. Appropriate time and facilities, as agreed by the Forum, will be made available to employee representatives to discharge their responsibilities.

The employee representatives will be provided with the necessary information, in a reasonable time frame, to enable them to adequately study the information and to allow them to make an informed response to proposals from the company, subject to the confidentiality clause within this agreement.

Employee representatives will be provided with reasonable time and facilities to gather views from their constituents prior to the meeting and then to feed back to them post meeting.

Elections for employee representatives

- Employee representatives will be elected by a secret ballot of all employees within their respective constituencies.
- The election process will be organised and run by an appropriate independent agency.
- Employee representatives will be elected for a two-year period.
- All candidates must be employees with at least 12 months' company service.
- To stand for election an employee must be nominated by 10 fellow employees.
- Employee representatives will not suffer financial loss as a result of attending meetings of the Forum.

Protection for employee representatives

The company recognises that employee representatives on the Forum will make an important contribution to the success of the company. No employee representative will have their employment or conditions of employment adversely affected as a result of carrying out their duties for the Forum.

Operation of the Forum

Meetings

There will be four meetings per annum of the Forum, over one day.

Employee representatives will meet on their own for 2 hours. The management members of the Forum will then join them. The employee members of the Forum may meet on their own after the Forum meeting is concluded.

The Forum will be chaired by the UK Employee Relations Manager who will be responsible for all administrative work necessary to ensure the Forum's effectiveness.

The employee representatives will elect from among themselves a chair and a secretary. The chair and the secretary will be responsible for co-ordinating employee-side activity and for liaising with the Forum chair as regards minutes, meetings, agendas etc.

Agenda

An agreed agenda for each meeting will be circulated to all Forum members at least 2 weeks prior to the meeting. Items for inclusion on the agenda should be sent to the Forum chair/employee side chair/secretary at least four weeks before the meeting.

Minutes

Minutes of the meeting will be drafted within five working days of the meeting for agreement between the Forum chair and the employee chair/secretary. The agreed minutes will be published within ten working days of the meeting.

Exhibit 8.2 continued

Extraordinary meetings

Additional meetings of the Forum may be held in the event of major decisions or announcements, which significantly affect the interests of all employees and require statutory consultation. Such a meeting will be arranged between the Forum chair and the employee side chair/secretary.

Costs

HP will bear all reasonable costs of travel and accommodation associated with meetings of the Forum.

Training

In order to ensure the effective working of the Forum, appropriate training will be made available to all Forum members.

Confidentiality

Confidential information

Management may withhold any information from the Forum which it believes to be commercially sensitive. Should the company feel it necessary to withhold information on the grounds of confidentiality, it will give its reasons for doing so where it believes that giving reasons will not amount to a prejudicial disclosure or a disclosure which breaches statutory or regulatory rules.

Employee representative confidentiality

Members of the Forum shall not reveal any information expressly provided in confidence and will sign an undertaking to this effect at the first meeting of the Forum.

Period of confidentiality

Confidentiality remains binding even after such time as an individual ceases to be a member of the Forum or to be employed by HP.

Disputes

Any disputes arising from the operation of the Forum will be discussed in the first instance between the Forum chair and the employee chair, with the benefit of external advice if required. Disputes that may arise in relation to statutory requirements will be dealt with in accordance with the relevant legal procedures.

Review

The operation of the Forum will be reviewed every 2 years. Where there is a voluntary request for an amendment to the Forum rules within this period, the Forum chair will inform the company of the request and a meeting will be arranged to discuss the request. The result will be fed back via the Forum chair.

Exhibit 8.2 continued

Summary points

- There has been a growing volume of regulations in relation to employee voice.

- Evidence suggests that many EWCs are a platform for information and involvement, not participation.

- The European Employee Information and Consultation Directive, and subsequent ICE 2004 Regulations, provide new prospects for employee voice.

- However, some of the ICE 2004 Regulations may fall short of the initial EU Directive, while other aspects of the regulations are ambiguous.

Case study 8.1: **The dynamics of informal voice at CompuFix**

CompuFix started trading in 1997. It was set up initially by three friends all with a background in computer technology. It now employs 72 people and specialises in re-manufacturing and disposing of outdated computer equipment. Although employing only 72 people, the company has a global market presence and has contracts with some of the word's leading computer technology companies. Most of the employees are highly qualified technicians, and their technical expertise is the company's core asset. Employee voice at CompuFix is regarded as critical to commercial success, and the Managing Director claims to be an advocate of employee participation.

However, employee voice is not through formal mechanisms. Employees are expected to show a high level of responsibility in their work, and to this end are provided with considerable discretion in how they carry out their tasks. The MD explains that he expects employees to come up with new ideas to improve product efficiency, and work targets and appraisals are set with these objectives in mind. Quality and product-innovation meetings take place daily, involving technical specialists and teams of employees. In addition, the MD holds regular breakfast meetings with the objective of involving people in discussions about the business. The whole philosophy is aimed at getting people to make suggestions on how to do things better. There are also three or four social events each year, such as golf outings. The idea is that social bonding outside the workplace helps to support a more friendly climate. During such outings employees are given the opportunity to discuss any issues with the MD or other senior mangers of the company.

Overall, the aim is to provide employees with a voice, because the company wants employees to feel engaged and committed to their work. The MD believes this is better achieved by an informal and open culture than through more formalised voice mechanisms.

Questions for discussion

1 Imagine you have been asked by the MD of CompuFix for a brief report on the 2004 ICE Regulations. What are the key issues you would highlight from these regulations for CompuFix?

2 Can you envisage any difficulties for CompuFix in trying to maintain an informal approach to employee voice?

3 Would you describe the voice arrangements at CompuFix as constituting a form of employee participation or employee involvement, and why?

Theoretical outcomes of employee voice

voice outcomes
The potential organisational benefits arising from employees having a voice, which includes productivity measures, employee motivation and satisfaction levels, and lower labour turnover costs.

Over the past decade interest in the potential outcomes of employee voice has received considerable attention. Indeed, it has been asserted that employee voice is a crucial part of what is widely known as the high performance work system (HPWS) model. To this end a number of US and UK studies have sought to establish a link between organisations with extensive human resource polices (including employee voice) and better performance (Huselid, 1995). While the indicators of what performance actually is tend to vary, they are usually taken to mean some combination of increased productivity, employee motivation and satisfaction, and lower labour turnover costs.

However, as one study found, many organisations fail to keep satisfactory records or productivity data that would allow an independent assessment of these outcomes to be made

(Wilkinson *et al.*, 2004). In particular, there are three difficulties in assessing the voice–performance link. First, there are problems with how assessments are made. For example, claims that suggestion schemes save money because they release employees' creative talents and ideas fail to appreciate that these things could have been channelled through a different mechanism anyway. The second difficulty is that it is almost impossible to isolate the impact of just one employment relations process (e.g. giving employees a voice) from other variables that influence behavioural outcomes. For instance, where labour turnover decreases, it could have been influenced by job security, or the unavailability of other jobs in the labour market. Finally, there is often a lack of clarity about who is supposed to gain from the outcome: are the purpose and value of employee voice that of giving workers a greater say in organisational decisions, or is it intended that management should maintain control and protect their decision-making prerogative? Here it can be noted that it is often assumed in much of the extant literature that potential outcomes are those that benefit the organisation, and employee needs and wants are secondary.

It is also a leap of quantum proportions to suggest that if employees have a say on minor task-related matters there will somehow be a link to commitment or motivation. Indeed, it is by no means conclusive that a voice process which triggers motivation and commitment at lower levels also unlocks a more general type of commitment to management objectives as a whole. Nevertheless, management motives for introducing most schemes of employee voice are usually underpinned by an assumption that they will result in this type of outcome. However, since they are usually introduced in a way that removes very few of the features that create a *them and us* mindset in organisations, they may well be doomed to fail. Moreover, because of the arm's-length adversarial nature of employment relations, there is a longstanding assumption that worker participation will inevitably be *partial* and *shallow* (Hyman, 2003). This is because many union stewards can be too preoccupied with basic job controls, and managers tend to be concerned with protecting their prerogative. Thus, the requisite sharing of power that makes for effective employee voice is often absent. In this respect it is perhaps as well to remember the well-known, though often forgotten, adage, that for management to gain control they must first learn how to share it (Flanders, 1970: 172).

Summary points

- The past decade has seen a growing interest in the notion that employee voice can lead to improved organisational performance and increase employee motivation and commitment.
- While these are plausible and attractive claims, the evidence is not conclusive.
- To some extent, this can be because the parties conceptualise and interpret voice from very different starting points, as explained earlier in the chapter.
- Moreover, it appears that many employee voice schemes are 'bolted on' to other employment relations processes, giving them a limited shelf-life.

Conclusions

This chapter has explained and reviewed a whole series of processes concerned with whether employees have a voice at work, and from this a number of concluding comments can be made.

First, employee voice is not a unified concept, but one that can only be understood if we first understand the different elements within it. Here it can be noted that in terms of power sharing, legitimacy and managerial prerogative, there are important differences between employee *participation* and employee *involvement*. Participation involves sharing of power in the making of management decisions, while involvement is usually confined to seeking employee views to harness cooperation, but with little or no power sharing.

Second, it was also noted that the stakeholders in employment relations regard the purpose of voice in very different ways, according to their particular frames of reference. It can primarily be viewed as either: the *articulation of individual dissatisfaction*, as a form of *collective representation*, as a way to *improve efficiency*, or as a process to build *partnership*. None of these is inherently right or wrong. It is simply that different stakeholders in employment relations have prior conceptions about what employee voice is likely to deliver for them. For instance, management tends to favour improved efficiency and mutuality, whereas trade unions may initially conceive of voice as a form of collective representation and/or mutuality.

Third, the extent of employee voice can usefully be evaluated in relation to a fourfold classification scheme, namely: the *depth, scope, level* and *form* of employee voice. Evidence suggests that, in the main, the actual practices of employee voice have a shallow rather than deep orientation, together with a narrow rather than wide scope. Nevertheless, there are more recent developments such as the use of information technology and apparent growth in non-union forms of employee representation that give a considerable overlap between the range of voice mechanisms used.

Fourth, European initiatives have promoted a more regulatory environment for employee voice, especially in terms of *European Works Councils* and new employee rights contained in the 2004 *Information and Consultation of Employees Regulations (ICE)*. As such, for the first time, British workers in organisations that employ 50 or more employees will have a legal right to be informed and consulted in three core areas:

- The economic situation of the organisation
- Structure and probable development of employment (including any threats to employment)
- Decisions that will lead to changes in work organisation or contractual relations.

Fifth, the idea of *partnership* based on cooperation and commitment to business success is a recurring component in discussions about employee voice. However, there remains considerable disagreement about the practical outcomes of partnership, with *advocates* seeing it as a process that builds consensus, while *critics* see it as a way of marginalising and weakening independent union representation.

Sixth, the *outcomes* of employee voice tend to portrayed in terms of improved organisational performance and enhanced worker commitment and motivation. While it is plausible that providing workers with a say may encourage greater commitment and motivation, the evidence is inconclusive, and much seems to depend on the existence of conditions that could sustain and support voice.

Finally, it can be noted that while many of the employee voice mechanisms offered by employers centre on *involvement* rather than *participation*, there is a growing regulatory environment for information and consultation. Thus, in all probability management strategies for employee voice will be an area of considerable activity and interest in the years ahead.

Review and discussion questions

1 Explain key differences between the terms 'worker participation' and 'employee involvement'.

2 What is meant by direct and indirect forms of employee voice?

3 Do you think that the way employees express their voice to management should be of a direct or indirect nature? Provide a short justification to your answer.

4 Given that the parties to employment relations have different views on employee voice, in what ways are managers and trade unions likely to differ in their perceptions of the purposes of employee voice? What outcomes do you think each party will emphasise?

5 Should management fear the introduction of new regulations for employee voice, such as those contained in the 2004 Information and Consultation of Employees Regulations (ICE)? Explain and justify your answer.

6 Identify at least three difficulties with the claim that employee voice will improve organisational performance.

Further reading

Cox, A., S. Zagelmeyer and M. Marchington (2006) 'Embedding employee involvement and participation at work', *Human Resource Management Journal*, Vol. 16 (3), pp. 250–267. A quantitative article that shows a link between deeper employee voice practices and higher employee outcomes, such as job satisfaction.

DTI (2003) *High Performance Workplaces: Informing and Consulting Employees: Consultation Document*, July, Department of Trade and Industry, London. http://www.ecdti.co.uk/cgibin/perlcon.pl A government report that explains the results of a consultation exercise with interested bodies about the presumed benefits of employee voice.

Dundon, T., A. Wilkinson, M. Marchington and P. Ackers (2004) 'The meanings and purpose of employee voice', *International Journal of Human Resource Management*, Vol. 15 (6), pp. 1150–1171. An academic paper that reports empirical findings concerning the different meanings and managerial interpretations of the term 'employee voice'.

Geary, J. and A. Dobbins (2001) 'Teamworking: a new dynamic in the pursuit of management control', *Human Resource Management Journal*, Vol. 11 (1), pp. 3–23. An academic paper arguing, with evidence, that while the outcomes of teamworking may well lead to management control, it is not always the case that such control is harmful.

Guest, D. and R. Peccei (2001) 'Partnership at Work: mutuality and the balance of advantage', *British Journal of Industrial Relations*, Vol. 39 (2), pp. 207–236. A paper that seeks to capture the meaning of partnership, showing that there are mutual and beneficial outcomes to a partnership approach between management and unions.

Kelly, J. (2005) 'Social Partnership Agreements in Britain', in *Partnership and Modernisation in Employment Relations*, M. Stuart and M. Martinez Lucio (eds), London, Routledge. A book chapter that presents data on employment levels and profit among both partnership and non-partnership companies in paired industrial sectors. The argument is advanced that workers under partnership can be worse off, and it is suggested that unions should adopt a more militant rather than cooperative stance with employers.

Kersley, B., C. Alpin, J. Forth, A. Bryson, H. Bewley, J. Dix and S. Oxenbridge (2005) *Inside the Workplace: First Findings from the 2004 Workplace Employment Relations Survey*, London, Department of Trade and Industry. (http://www.dti.gov.uk/employment/research-evaluation/wers-2004/wers-2004/page25904.html). A pamphlet that provides key findings from the 2004 WERS survey, with particularly important insights into employee involvement and participation methods used in organisations.

Oxenbridge, S. and W. Brown (2002) 'The two faces of partnership and cooperative employer and trade union relationship', *Employee Relations*, Vol. 24 (3), pp. 262–277. This paper reports research findings showing that partnership and cooperative relations can be both robust and shallow. The implications suggest that partnership may alienate union members with union stewards being perceived to be too close to management.

Ramsay, H. (1977) 'Cycles of control: worker participation in sociological and historical perspective', *Sociology*, Vol. II, pp. 481–506. While trends and developments in employee voice have moved on considerably since Ramsay's paper in 1977, this is still one of the more influential conceptual writings on the topic. It takes issue with a view at the time that participation has evolved during phases of capitalism. Instead, Ramsay argues that worker participation is introduced by management when its authority is under threat.

Roche, W. and J. Geary (2002) 'Advocates, Critics and Union Involvement in Workplace Partnership: Irish Airports', *British Journal of Industrial Relations*, Vol. 40 (4), pp. 659–688. A paper that charts the path to partnership in the Irish Airports Authority. It demonstrates the depth and different levels at which partnership arrangements can provide access to management decision making for union representatives, as well as some pertinent pitfalls for those involved in the making of a partnership agreement.

Chapter 9

Collective bargaining and pay determination

LEARNING OUTCOMES

After studying this chapter you should be able to:

- ☑ **define** collective bargaining and explain its main purposes and functions

- ☑ **describe** the objectives and outcomes for the parties to a collective bargaining relationship

- ☑ **evaluate** the extent and variation in bargaining arrangements in Britain

- ☑ **describe** bargaining structures, scope and form, and assess how the dimensions of bargaining have changed over the last two decades

- ☑ **explain** the factors that have led to a shift from collective to individual-type wage payment systems in British industry

- ☑ **evaluate** the utility of different incentive-based wage payment systems

- ☑ **analyse** the legal implications associated with collective bargaining.

Introduction

Much of the literature on collective bargaining is anchored on two reference points. The first is the seminal work by Beatrice and Sydney Webb (1897), which first coined the term 'collective bargaining', describing the process as a 'trial of strength' between the parties (1897: 173). This alerts us to the notion that collective bargaining is both a conflictual and politically charged aspect of employment relations. The second point of reference is the Donovan Commission, a government inquiry which reported in 1968 on the conduct of relations between trade unions and employers and their associations. These early contributions have been highly influential, with much of the academic and practitioner literature returning to them time and time again to explain the evolution of collective bargaining in Britain. Up until the mid-1980s collective bargaining was comparatively widespread in Great Britain, but since trade union representation has declined, so too has collective bargaining diminished considerably.

The chapter commences with a definition of collective bargaining, together with an explanation of its main functions and purposes. This is followed by a consideration of the objectives of the parties. Next, the data concerning bargaining coverage in Britain are examined, together with an explanation of the different bargaining arrangements that exist. Since collective bargaining can exist in many forms, the chapter then presents a scheme that can be used to evaluate the nature of bargaining activity, and since most people associate collective bargaining with wage rates, the chapter directs its attention to the changing nature of pay determination in Britain, particularly to developments in individual-type remuneration strategies. Following this, some of the legal implications associated with collective bargaining will be examined, and finally, the potential outcomes of a collectively bargained employment relationship will be noted.

Defining collective bargaining
Towards a definition

Over one hundred years ago the Webbs (1897) noted that an individual employee is relatively powerless in comparison to an employing organisation, a logical conclusion of which was that employees banded together to act collectively in redressing this power imbalance. Accordingly, collective bargaining seeks to regulate the conduct and rules that govern employment relations, and is defined here as:

> a relationship in which the representatives of employees and employers negotiate, consult and communicate in order to agree the procedural and substantive terms of employment.

substantive rules
The terms of a collective agreement that refers to the exchange of effort for reward, for example, pay and hours of work.

procedural rules
The terms of a collective agreement that refers to the mechanisms to adjust substantive rules, such as when negotiations are conducted, and by whom.

The expression substantive rules has a very specific meaning, and refers to the main terms and conditions of employment, such as pay, hours of work or holiday entitlements. In contrast, procedural rules specify the arrangements adopted by the parties to modify substantive rules (for example, how and when negotiations are conducted, and by whom). They also provide guidance on the application and interpretation of substantive terms. In Great Britain, the way these rules have traditionally been derived is via trade union representation, which gives rise to a number of important features about collective bargaining.

First, a trade union becomes part of the structures and processes through which an organisation and its employees relate to each other, the purpose of which is to regulate the terms and conditions under which the relationship will continue. Thus collective bargaining derives *substantive rules* that define the exchange of effort for reward.

This implies that both parties have a vested interest in reaching agreement over the terms of the relationship, and while this does not mean that reaching agreement will always be easy, finding a way to continue the relationship is a definite aim, which makes having clearly defined *procedural rules* all the more important.

Second, the method most frequently used to agree the terms and conditions of employment is the process of negotiation. This will be dealt with in detail in the next chapter, and is not explored here. Nevertheless, it is important to stress that collective bargaining and negotiation are not the same thing. The term 'collective bargaining' essentially describes the nature of an employment relationship: a relationship that is based on collectively agreed rules. In contrast, negotiation is a process used to settle the specific terms within the relationship, and negotiation can exist in non-union firms between individuals, or be replaced by unilateral management decision making.

Third, in collective bargaining, employees are represented with one voice. Thus certain aspects of the relationship between an organisation and its employees are determined through an intermediary, typically a trade union or other collective employee association (e.g. a staff association). This, in turn, means that the bond between employer and employee inevitably becomes more remote and detached; what Hyman (2003) has referred to as an 'arm's-length' relationship.

The functions and purposes of collective bargaining

The classic view on the functions of collective bargaining is that its primary function is an economic one, in which trade unions influence the price and supply of labour. While it would be hard to deny that this does happen, to view things completely in these terms is to relegate collective bargaining to a purely economic transaction, whereas in the last two decades there has been an important shift in the attitudes of many trade unions in favour of bargaining over a range of other employment issues, such as employee skills and training and development opportunities for their members (Dundon and Eva, 1998). This wider purpose of collective bargaining was recognised some time ago by Flanders (1968), who draws attention to the idea that collective bargaining is a political process, the outcomes of which include a wide variety of rules that govern social as well as economic aspects of workplace relations. In Flanders' view, since the two parties become joint authors of *substantive* and *procedural* rules, the process can more accurately be described as a method of **joint regulation**. However, Flanders' viewpoint has its critics. For example, Fox (1975) criticises it for underplaying the economic purpose of collective bargaining by stating that:

joint regulation
The agreement of substantive and procedural rules between employers and employee representatives, the authorship of which can be attributed equally to both parties.

> It is as a bargaining agent that the union finds the major justification in the eyes of its members, and that issues of financial reward are still, whether for material or symbolic reasons or both, among its major bargaining preoccupations.
>
> (Fox, 1975: 157)

Pause for reflection

Do you think that collective bargaining fulfils mainly an economic or social process, and why?

What is perhaps more likely is that both of these arguments are true, and that collective bargaining tends to serve the purposes that those involved want it to serve. Thus it can fulfil either an economic or social purpose, or both simultaneously. This is expressed more clearly in Chamberlain and Kuhn's (1965) statement of the three different functions of collective bargaining.

economic function (collective bargaining)

Sets the price at which labour power is bought and sold.

government function (collective bargaining)

Establishes a set of rules or a constitution which becomes the foundation for an on-going relationship between management and employees.

decision-making function (collective bargaining)

Analogous to a system of industrial democracy, in which employees, through their representatives, participate in decisions that affect their interests.

First, the market or **economic function** fixes the price at which labour will be bought and sold, and is similar to the traditional economic purpose. Second, the **government function** is concerned with establishing a constitution, or rules of the game, which become the foundation of an on-going relationship between management and employees. In this respect collective bargaining can have a stabilising influence, because both management and employees prefer predictability. Therefore by setting the parameters of acceptable behaviour, collective bargaining provides a high degree of consistency in how the relationship is made and modified. Finally, the **decision-making function** gives a system of industrial democracy because employees, through their representatives, participate in making decisions on matters that affect their interests. This results in a process whereby workers and managers become bound together in a pattern of mutual accommodation.

Chamberlain and Kuhn (1965) stress that the three functions are stages of development. Thus, where the third exists, so will the first and second, and the nearer the relationship gets to the third stage, the more likely it is that decisions which were once regarded as the sole prerogative of management become the subject for negotiation. Clearly, where this happens, collective bargaining is capable of dealing with such a wide range of topics that it could virtually embrace everything in the employer–employee relationship. For this reason, it may be recalled that in Chapter 8, collective bargaining was identified as one of the deeper forms of employee voice.

However, a relationship which develops in this way is likely to encounter a number of tensions, and these depend on which issues can or cannot be negotiated. With some issues the relationship can be highly cooperative: for example, where the existence of an organisation is threatened by external market conditions, then both sides may find it prudent to collaborate in making changes that are necessary for survival. On other issues, however, such as the pay rate, a more conflictual approach can surface, and because there are always likely to be some conflictual elements in employment relations, the move towards joint decision making in collective bargaining is seldom complete. For example, this would require a willingness on the part of managers to negotiate about matters where decision making has traditionally been reserved for themselves. Similarly, it might require a trade union to play a part in implementing decisions, which would mean giving up its role in challenging management authority. Since past habits die hard, neither of these is an easy option for the two sides.

Summary points

■ Collective bargaining is a method in which the parties jointly agree the substantive and procedural terms and conditions of employment.

■ It can serve a number of functions and purposes, either separately or simultaneously (e.g. *economic, governmental* and *decision-making*).

■ Collective bargaining involves both *cooperation* and *conflict* in modifying the employment relationship.

The objectives of collective bargaining

The coexistence of conflict and cooperation in collective bargaining represents something of a paradox in employment relations. While collective bargaining usually indicates that there are underlying conflicts of interest between employer and employees, it also reflects a recognition that they have something in common, and thus a vested interest in finding ways of reconciling their differences. One way of viewing the objectives of the parties is by using the concept of a **frontier of control** (Goodrich, 1975). This illustrates the idea that there are boundaries on what can, or cannot, be achieved at any point in time, and is shown in Fig. 9.1. As collective

frontiers of control

A concept that describes the boundaries of either party's freedom of action to negotiate and bargain over certain issues.

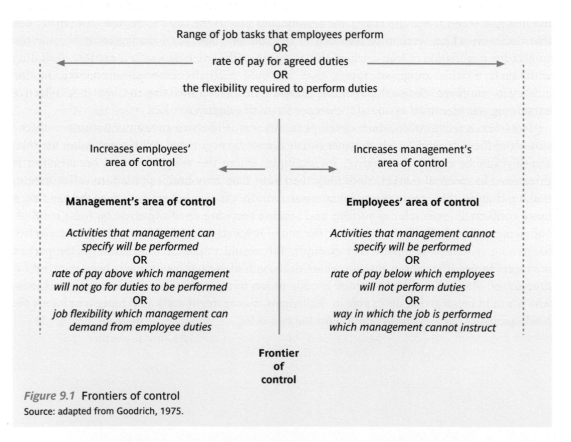

Figure 9.1 Frontiers of control
Source: adapted from Goodrich, 1975.

bargaining is concerned with fixing, ratifying or modifying some aspect of the employment relationship, frontiers can shift over time, depending on the issue and bargaining strength of the parties.

For simplicity, assume that as a result of some prior agreement, a certain amount of employee flexibility is required to perform certain work tasks. Also assume that a minimum level of pay has been agreed for performing these tasks, and that this gives management the freedom to alter the way in which the work is organised. These details are shown as the line down the centre of Fig. 9.1, which is the current *frontier of control*. Any shift of the line to the right would reduce the employees' area of control over the job, and correspondingly increase managerial discretion. A shift to the left would have the reverse effect. Clearly both parties have a vested interest in advancing their frontier of control, or at least preventing it being pushed back, and a number of important points should be noted.

First, frontiers are multiple, because control is usually sought over several aspects of a job at the same time. In the example above, the aim would probably be to exert control over *what* sort of flexibility management can demand, *how* the work is to be carried out, and the *pay rate*. Second, since certain aspects of the employment relationship have different degrees of importance attached to them by employees and managers, frontiers of control are situation-specific. Again using the example given in Fig. 9.1, in one workplace the rate of pay might be the dominant issue for employees, while an extension in managerial freedom to change work schedules can be the main issue for another employer. In this case the frontier is likely to be fixed at a point where, as long as employees are flexible, how they complete their work tasks is left for them to decide. Third, once established, frontiers might have to be defended. The ability to do this can ultimately depend on whether sanctions can be taken against the other party, as and when they attempt to encroach on territory. Thus, the balance of power between the parties can affect where frontiers lie, and this inevitably changes over time.

However, it should not be inferred that collective bargaining is simply a matter of one side grabbing territory in an opportunist way when they hold the balance of power, merely to relinquish it when power has passed to the other side. Indeed, in the long run, the most effective bargaining relationships are usually characterised by a degree of respect for the other party's territory (Huzzard, 2004). To start with, both sides must enter into the relationship with the aim of resolving their differences, and this means that they must bargain in good faith, with the aim of reaching an agreement that both accept as binding. Although this does not require the agreement to stand for ever, it does mean that it will be honoured for the foreseeable future, and stand until it is replaced by another agreement. In addition, to make agreements, and then make them stick, both sides must also have a minimum degree of organisation (Clegg, 1979). Management has many advantages relative to workers, and therefore it needs to give employees the freedom to organise themselves into a collective association which is genuinely independent of the employer (Thomas and Kumar, 1987). In this respect, the statutory union recognition procedures outlined in Chapter 4 can be seen as one attempt by the State to level the playing field for unorganised workers, in that an employer could be obliged to recognise and bargain with a union of the employees' choosing (Bogg, 2005). This implies that there are potential legal implications with collective bargaining, and these are explained later in the chapter.

Summary points

■ The parties to collective bargaining often have divergent objectives, some of which are inevitably conflictual in nature, while others will be based on mutual cooperation and accommodation.

■ These divergent objectives can be expressed by the concept of *frontiers of control.*

■ Frontiers of control are multi-dimensional, covering different issues, which tend to shift over time.

The extent of collective bargaining in Britain

While there remain various objectives for both employees and organisations in entering into a collective bargaining relationship, its extent in Great Britain has diminished considerably over the last two decades. **Collective bargaining coverage** refers to the total proportion of employees in the economy as a whole whose pay is influenced by collective bargaining, irrespective of the number of organisations that recognise trade unions.

collective bargaining coverage
The proportion of employees in the economy as a whole whose pay is influenced by collective bargaining.

The reason why the pay of individual workers can be influenced by collective bargaining without their employer necessarily recognising a trade union is an interesting one that merits a word of explanation. It comes about because there are some firms who are members of employers' associations and are therefore party to an industry-wide agreement, even though some of these firms do not recognise a union in their particular enterprise. In simple terms, there are employers who find it more efficient and convenient to pay the negotiated 'industry rate of pay'. As can be seen with reference to Table 9.1, the general coverage of collective pay determination in Britain has been in decline over the last two decades, falling from 70 per cent of all employees in 1984, to 39 per cent by 2004 (Millward *et al.*, 2000: 197; Kersley *et al.*, 2006: 187). Indeed, because bargaining is more common in larger enterprises, the proportion of firms who engage in any form of collective pay negotiation is much lower: at 22 per cent of all workplaces in Britain in 2004 (Kersley *et al.*, 2005: 19). As can be seen, it is in the private sector that organisations have experienced the sharpest decline, although there was a rise in coverage in the public sector in 2004, due to a new bargaining settlement for health-sector employees known as the Agenda for Change (Kersley *et al.*, 2005: 21). Bargaining coverage in union-recognised workplaces has experienced a modest (+1.4 per cent) average increase between 1998 and 2004 (see Table 9.1). The least coverage is in smaller firms, where collective bargaining is almost completely absent, and only 3 per cent of those working in SMEs have their pay and conditions determined through collective negotiation (Forth *et al.*, 2006: 58; EIRO, 2006).

Pause for reflection

What factors do you think explain the decline in collective bargaining coverage in Britain?

	Cell percentages				Percentages		
	Proportion of employees covered by collective bargaining				Average annual change		
	1984	1990	1998	2004	1984–1990	1990–1998	1998–2004
All workplaces	70	54	41	39	−2.9	−3.1	−0.7
Broad sector							
Private manufacturing	64	51	46	38	−2.6	−1.4	−2.6
Private services	40	33	23	21	−2.3	−4.2	−1.1
Public sector	95	78	66	77	−2.3	−2.0	+2.5
Any recognised unions	90	81	67	74	−1.3	−2.1	+1.4

Note
Base: all workplaces with 25 or more employees.

Table 9.1 Collective bargaining coverage in Britain, by broad sector and union recognition, 1984–2004
Source: adapted and calculated from: Millward *et al.*, 2000: 197; Kersley *et al.*, 2005: 19–21; Kersley *et al.*, 2006: 187.
Revised figures for 1998 and the figures for any recognised unions kindly calculated by the WERS 2004 Information and Advice Service (www.wers2004.info).

Several developments in management strategy, together with changes in the economy, shed some light on the overall decline in collective bargaining coverage. First, for collective bargaining to take place there has to be *trade union recognition*, and this in itself has declined substantially over the past two decades. Furthermore, even where union recognition exists, management have consistently restricted the role of trade unions by emphasising communication and consultation, rather than collective negotiation (Brown *et al.*, 1998). A second factor is associated with changes in the *structure of the labour market*. It is notoriously difficult for trade unions to organise and represent those employees who work in smaller firms, or in peripheral, casual and temporary occupations. A third explanation, about which more will be said later in the chapter, is the growth in *individualised pay determination* methods. For example, many employers now make use of a range of performance-related pay schemes that focus on individual and incentive-type remuneration for workers (Kessler and Purcell, 2003). Finally, *changes introduced in the public sector* removed around 2 million workers from national employer agreements. For instance, during the 1980s and early 1990s the government replaced collective bargaining with annual pay review bodies for many public-sector employees, such as school teachers. In addition, the decline in public sector bargaining was accentuated by the wholesale privatisations of several key public utilities, many of which had high union density and bargaining coverage. Moreover, the introduction of free-market principles, such as compulsory competitive tendering and the outsourcing of many jobs to smaller non-unionised firms, was another factor.

Variations in collective bargaining arrangements

Even though collective bargaining coverage has declined across it Britain, it is still important for over one-third of the working population, and there remains considerable diversity in the types of arrangements that exist. However, for simplicity, only three of the many different types of collective bargaining relationships will be described here. The first is

multi-employer bargaining

An arrangement in which bargaining takes place between one or more trade unions and an employers' association for a whole industry, with the terms of the agreement covering the majority of firms (or employee groups) in that industry.

multi-employer bargaining: an arrangement in which bargaining covers a whole industry or part thereof, and negotiations take place between one or more trade unions and an employers' association. The terms of the multi-employer agreement are then applied to a multitude of firms or specific occupational groups within a whole industry. Although multi-employer bargaining has diminished significantly in Britain, where it remains it is believed to have a strong utility for both employers and employees. For example, there are obvious cost advantages in allowing an employers' association to deal with several trade unions on behalf of firms in a particular industry. It can establish uniform and predictable labour costs, and lower the likelihood of different workplaces making parity or leapfrogging claims that undercut competitors on salary levels or working conditions (Sisson and Storey, 2000). Examples of these arrangements can be found in certain sectors of the economy: for instance, in electrical contracting, printing or in local government. Exhibit 9.1 below gives extracts from a multi-employer collective agreement for craft workers in local government in England and Wales.

single-table bargaining

An arrangement in which an employer negotiates with several recognised trade unions simultaneously.

single-union agreements

An arrangement in which an employer recognises just one trade union for the purpose of collective bargaining, for all the different categories of workers in the employing organisation.

A second type of bargaining is **single-table bargaining**, in which a single employer agrees to negotiate with a number of different trade unions that represent the interests of workgroups in the same firm, with bargaining taking place around the 'same table'. This arrangement can provide for a more efficient utilisation of resources and time, while not denying employees the opportunity to join a union of their choosing. Indeed, where unions can coordinate their actions and demands through single-table negotiation, this can give greater bargaining strength than when negotiating on their own.

A third type of bargaining relationship is a **single-union agreement**. In these situations an employer agrees to recognise and bargain with a particular trade union for all workers in the employing organisation: that is, for manual, white collar and in some situations managerial employees. In this situation, employers have a bad reputation for trying to 'cherry pick' what they believe will be the more moderate union, and then granting recognition to that union only. Examples of single-union agreements can be found among new entrants to particular markets: for instance, this approach was popular with Japanese car manufacturers, such as Nissan in Sunderland, who set up factories on greenfield sites in the 1980s.

The dimensions of collective bargaining

Since there can be wide variation in bargaining arrangements, it is also necessary to be able to evaluate with greater precision how bargaining is conducted. Therefore, in what follows a number of dimensions will be used to characterise the different arrangements that are found across British industry. These dimensions are similar to those used to describe employee voice in Chapter 8, and for collective bargaining they include the following:

- Bargaining level
- Bargaining units
- Bargaining form
- Bargaining scope.

PART 1: Principles and Implementation

The Joint Negotiating Committee (JNC) represents local authorities in England and Wales and other authorities of equivalent status and their craft and associated employees. Single-table bargaining will operate nationally. The national agreement will form the employee handbook known as the Red Book. A new National Agreement (Red Book) does not of itself alter existing local and provincial arrangements that differ from existing National Agreements.

The JNC is committed to the democratic control of services to the community. Our principle role is to reach agreement, based on our shared values, on a national scheme of pay and conditions. The JNC's guiding principles are to support and encourage:

a) high quality service delivered by a well trained, motivated workforce with security of employment. Local authorities are encouraged to provide training and development opportunities.

b) equal opportunities in employment; equality is a core principle which underpins both service delivery and employment relations

c) a flexible approach to providing services to the community

d) stable employment relations through negotiation and consultation between local authorities as employers and the recognised trade unions for employees.

The JNC has a strong commitment to joint negotiation and consultation, and to this end encourages employees to join and remain in recognised unions. Local authorities are encouraged to provide facilities to allow Trade Unions to organise effectively.

PART 2: Constitution

Scope:

The functions of the JNC shall relate to all craft and associated employees of local authorities in England and Wales.

Membership:

Membership of the JNC shall consist of 24 members, appointed as follows:

Local Government Association (LGA)	9	UCATT	6
Welsh Local Government Association	1	CSEU	1
N Ireland Local Government Association	1	GMB	2
National Association of Local Councils	1	TGWU	1
		MSF-AEEU	2
Total	12		12

Functions:

The functions of the JNC are as follows:

■ to negotiate collective agreements on pay and conditions and any other related matters the JNC agrees to negotiate on.

■ to urge all local authorities and recognised unions to apply national agreements.

■ to promote cooperation between employers and recognised unions.

■ to make advice available to local authorities, recognised unions and employees on employment relations issues.

■ to settle differences of interpretation and application of national agreements that cannot be resolved locally.

■ to assist where required in the resolution of disputes.

■ to undertake any activity incidental to the above.

Chair and Vice Chair

The JNC shall appoint from its members a Chair and Vice Chair. The Chair shall be held in alternate years by a member of the Employer's Side and a member of the Employees' Side.

Meetings

The annual meeting of the JNC shall be held during the month of October. Ordinary meetings shall be held as often as necessary. The Chair shall call a special meeting of the Committee if so requested by either side. The requisition and notice summoning the meeting shall state the nature of business proposed, and no other matters shall be discussed. The meeting shall take place within fourteen days of such a requisition being received.

Exhibit 9.1 Extracts from: National Negotiating Committee Agreement for Local Authority Craft and Associated Employees

Voting

The voting of the JNC and all sub-committees shall be by a show of hands, or as otherwise determined by the Committee. No resolution shall be regarded as carried unless approved by the majority of the members present and those voting on each side of the Committee.

Quorum

The quorum shall be one-third of the members of the JNC divided equally between the two sides. In the absence of a quorum the Chair shall declare the meeting closed and business under discussion shall be the first business to be discussed at the next meeting.

Amendment

The Constitution may be amended only with the assent of the Employers' associations and the recognised Trade Unions.

Arbitration

In the event of a dispute arising between the two sides, the dispute shall, if requested by either side, be referred for settlement by conciliation, mediation or arbitration. An arbitration award shall be accepted by both sides and shall be treated as though it were an agreement between the two sides.

Other Matters

The JNC or its sub-committees may invite the attendance of any person with special knowledge that would be of assistance. Such persons shall not have voting powers.

PART 3: Key National and Other Provisions

The key national provisions are dealt with nationally by the Committee. Other provisions may be modified locally, by negotiation between the relevant authority and the unions. A procedure for dealing with a failure to agree other local provisions is annexed to this agreement.

Key National Provisions

These cover the following: Equality; Official Conduct; Training and Development; Health, Safety and Welfare; Pay; Working Time; Leave; Part-Time Employees; Temporary Employees; Sickness; Maternity; Car Allowances; Reimbursement of Expenditure; Continuous Service; Notice to Terminate Employment; Grievance Procedures; Disciplinary Procedures; Trade Union Facilities; London Fringe Allowances. The detail of these provisions are annexed to this agreement.

Other Provisions

Other provisions that may be modified by local negotiation include the following: Working Arrangements; Travelling Time; Working Conditions; Training and Development; Sickness; Child Care; Car Allowances; Payments to Employees in the Event of Death or Permanent Disablement Arising from Assault.

National negotiators urge local parties to approach such local negotiations with an open mind and negotiate with a view to reaching agreement.

PART 4: Joint Advice

The JNC believes that public bodies such as local authorities should give a lead on good employment practices. The annex to Part 4 of this agreement covers guidance on good practice on the following: Equal Opportunities; Parental Leave Scheme; Maternity Scheme; Work–Life Balance Issues; Management of Health and Safety; Local Workforce Development Plans.

Agreement dated April 2005, and signed by both the Employer and Union Secretaries

Exhibit 9.1 Continued

Levels of bargaining

The **level of collective bargaining** refers to the organisational or industry level at which bargaining normally takes place, and this can exist at up to four levels:

- *National* (whole industry)
- *Organisational* (individual company)
- *Plant* level
- *Workplace* (department or workgroup level).

At a *national* level bargaining can occur on behalf of all firms in a particular industry (e.g. the engineering industry), while at an *organisational* level, it covers multiple plants and locations. At *plant* level collective bargaining covers workers at a particular site of a multi-plant organisation, while *workplace* bargaining takes place between management and a particular workgroup or department within a single workplace.

There can be considerable diversity in the way that *organisational level bargaining* is conducted. In multi-plant firms a distinction that can be drawn is between bargaining that is conducted at the organisational level covering all sites, and supplementary bargaining which occurs at the *plant* and *workplace* levels. Indeed, even where there is company-wide negotiation, some degree of supplementary bargaining at lower levels can become virtually inevitable, and this is often informal in nature. For example, these days the private sector is subject to a fairly rapid rate of change, and for this reason plant managers tend to feel that they need agreements that are specific to their particular workplace and local market conditions.

Perhaps more important are the preferences of managers in the employing organisation. Since the level at which agreements are made can crucially affect a trade union's ability to mobilise its members, management's choice of the bargaining level could well be prompted by strategic considerations. For example, multi-plant or company-wide bargaining enables management to separate the trade union from its major source of power – the workers. With this management can seek to create a set of 'divide-and-rule' conditions where better organised and more militant workers are marginalised, and moderate workplaces outvote those that are more inclined to take industrial action in pursuit of their objectives. Such divide-and-rule tactics can also exclude trade unions from senior corporate decision making, where unions might insist that higher-level matters become bargainable issues. Indeed, to justify their preferences management often argue that each workplace must be able to stand on its own feet financially.

A more intriguing development is that workplace bargaining may be an *illusion*. Just because negotiation takes place at the level of each plant, this does not mean that genuine bargaining occurs (Sisson and Marginson, 2003). In some organisations it has been shown that, while local managers sit at the negotiating table, they are guided by instructions from more senior managers at the corporate level. For example, there is evidence to suggest that situations like this occur quite frequently in larger multi-site organisations, where the real decisions about what can be agreed are made by senior head office managers who are at some distance from the actual negotiating table (Sisson and Storey, 2000). Other research has indicated that similar patterns also prevail in the public sector (especially among health trusts), where local managers are unable to exercise the required authority to make independent collective agreements (Kirkpatrick and Hoque, 2005). Furthermore, in smaller firms it has been noted that owner-managers, especially the founding family member of a firm, can exert considerable influence over the junior managers (also family members) who determine the employees' substantive employment conditions (Harney and Dundon, 2006).

Bargaining unit

bargaining unit
A group of employees covered by a negotiated collective agreement.

A **bargaining unit** is strongly related to the level at which bargaining occurs, and defines the group of employees on whose behalf bargaining takes place. For example, a bargaining unit could be as small as a workplace, or as large as a whole organisation with multiple plants. The most important point is that a bargaining unit is likely to have a bearing on which trade unions or other employee associations are involved, and for this reason, the selection of a bargaining unit also has strategic implications. If bargaining units are narrow, for example if there are separate units for white-collar, skilled and unskilled manual workers, management has the opportunity to use similar divide-and-rule tactics as those described above. However, if there are too many bargaining units, the negotiation (and subsequent renegotiation) of agreements can become a long-drawn-out affair for both management and employees.

Form of bargaining

bargaining form
The way in which collective agreements are recorded, whether formally or informally.

Because a bargaining unit can be large or small, the expression **bargaining form** denotes the way that collective agreements are recorded. Strictly speaking, although informal and unrecorded agreements can be made between local shop stewards and supervisors, it is more common for collective agreements to be formalised and highly detailed. The reason for this is because detailed and prescriptive agreements restrict the possibility of misinterpretation by either party. Thus, the form of bargaining is closely connected to the type of bargaining unit and its level. For example, where collective bargaining is conducted at a national or industry level, it is often the case that agreements resemble quasi-legal documents. This avoids ambiguity when the terms of the agreement have to be implemented at lower levels and by actors who were not involved in the making of the actual agreement (see Exhibit 9.1).

Pause for reflection

What advantages and disadvantages do you think there might be with both formal and informal forms of collective bargaining?

However, the implications of bargaining form can be much more complex than simply how an agreement is recorded. An important point here is the extent to which the bargaining relationship is based on formal or informal practices, which in turn has a bearing on the organisational climate. In this regard Purcell (1979) has commented on the importance of two characteristics of a bargaining relationship: formality and trust. Of the two, *trust* is by far the more important because it can engender cooperative relations, which in turn can result in more positive psychological contracts (Guest and Conway, 2002). For this reason, it is common to find that informal rules emerge at shopfloor level.

In contrast, very formalised bargaining can result in a pedantic and highly bureaucratised relationship, in which observing protocols and procedural rules becomes more important than anything else (Clegg, 1979). Arguably, too much *formality* can create a climate of mistrust, because the parties lack the flexibility to negotiate about new and emerging issues (Fox, 1974). Nevertheless, a degree of formality is often a prerequisite to effective bargaining, and an acknowledgement that there are rules to the game. It is not so much the formal writing-down of agreements that is important, but the effect that this has on the behaviour of the parties. For example, although a high degree of trust is often found in very informal arrangements, it is likely that these exist in the first place because of good interpersonal relationships between individual negotiators (Purcell, 1979). As these can quickly vanish if one of the main negotiators moves on to something else, some degree of formality is necessary to allow the bargaining relationship to transcend the effect of dominant personalities, and to survive changes in the occupancy of bargaining roles.

Bargaining scope

Bargaining scope defines the range of topics or issues that are the subject of negotiation for a

bargaining scope
The range of topics or issues which are the subject of negotiation for a given bargaining unit.

given bargaining unit, which can include both formal and informal bargaining forms. Theoretically, scope can vary between the extremes of a very narrow range of issues: for example, those which are confined to discussing lunch breaks or the quality of food in the company restaurant, to the other extreme where everything is negotiable. In Britain the *scope* of collective bargaining has narrowed considerably, with pay negotiation occurring in 61 per cent of unionised organisations, and in only 18 per cent of all workplaces (see Table 9.2). About half of all unionised workplaces negotiate over hours of work and holidays, and this is much lower for all enterprises in Great Britain. Bargaining is least likely to occur over staffing plans, training or staff selection, and in the absence of a trade union, on average bargaining only takes place on one of the twelve items in Table 9.2 (Kersley *et al.*, 2005: 22).

The narrowing of bargaining scope in Britain has not been smooth, evidenced by a shift from joint regulation including unions, to a greater use of unilateral managerial decision making in modifying employment conditions. Notwithstanding oversimplification, three discrete patterns can be noted in this respect. First, during the 1980s, with a growing political climate of anti-unionism and rising unemployment, managers became increasingly self-confident and assertive in defending their *frontier of control*. As a result, company 'affordability' and local 'market pressures' dominated pay negotiations, instead of previous union claims for 'wage comparability' and establishing a 'rate for the job'. This meant that the only issue that managers in unionised organisations bargained about was pay, and then very grudgingly. This was

Items subject to negotiation	% of workplaces	
	With recognised unions	All workplaces
Pay	61	18
Hours	53	16
Holidays	52	15
Pensions	36	10
Staff selection	9	3
Training	9	3
Grievance procedure	28	9
Disciplinary procedure	29	8
Staffing plans	7	3
Equal opportunities	15	5
Health and safety	15	5
Performance appraisal	14	4
N (*weighted*)	*1004*	*2007*

Note
Base: All workplaces with 10 or more employees.

Table 9.2 The scope of joint regulation on pay and non-pay items in Great Britain, 2004
Source: adapted from Kersley *et al.*, 2005: 22.

Case study 9.1: **Bargaining arrangements**

Consider the arrangements for bargaining in each of the following organisations:

Utility Co

Size (no. of employees)	8000
Managers	425
Salaried staff	3175
Manual ∎ skilled	4200
∎ unskilled	Nil
Number of Locations	Several locations covering a region of a former public utility with headquarters, retail outlets and 14 depots
Union Recognition	Four different unions represent all occupational groups nationally
Negotiating Committees	Three at national level, one for each of the following groups: ∎ managers ∎ white collar employees ∎ manual workers (including maintenance staff)
Nature of Agreements	Basic pay levels negotiated nationally. Individual performance-pay targets, and procedural agreements, subject to minor adjustments by local negotiation. Separate arrangements apply to each negotiating committee.

Car manufacturing

Size (no. of employees)	2500
Managers	130
Clerical/office staff	260
Manual ∎ skilled	1250
∎ unskilled	860
Number of Locations	One in North East: mass production of cars
Union Recognition	Single-union agreement for all employees
Negotiating Committees	One at organisational level, covering: ∎ clerical/office staff ∎ skilled manual ∎ unskilled manual ∎ supervisors/line managers
Nature of Agreements	The negotiating committee deals with a wide range of substantive and procedural agreements, including basic salary levels and productivity bargaining bonuses.

Road haulage

Size (no. of employees)	85
Managers	3
Clerical/office staff	8
Mechanics	4
Drivers	70
Number of Locations	One in the South West: independent road haulage and courier firm
Union Recognition	One local union branch looks after drivers and mechanics
Negotiating Committees	None
Nature of Agreements	Observes movement in industry-negotiated pay rates, and MD sets pay above this level to attract and retain suitable employees. Non-pay matters agreed on ad hoc basis between managers and shop stewards, who represent interests of all occupational groups.

followed by a second managerial offensive in the latter part of the 1980s and early 1990s, resulting in a wave of union de-recognition cases and the subsequent decimation of collective bargaining (Gall, 1998: 44). Consequently, collective negotiation was subsumed with newer forms of 'individual' performance-pay schemes that have fundamentally altered the pay determination landscape in both private- and public-sector organisations in Britain (Marsden and Belfield, 2005). Finally, in an era of social partnership and statutory trade union recognition, employers are arguably more subtle about how they determine pay rates. For example, many unions now have to concede new work structures, greater employee flexibility and individualised performance targets in order to secure a cost-of-living wage rise for their members (Brown *et al.*, 1998). Indeed, the idea of the high-performance work organisation, in which trade unions are only accepted if they add value to performance, is much more prevalent among private-sector companies (Ackers *et al.*, 2005). In addition, among public-sector organisations, the scope of collective bargaining has narrowed as a result of government initiatives, such as Pay Review Bodies (PRB) and performance-related pay schemes (Marsden and Belfield, 2005).

As the coverage and scope of collective bargaining has diminished, it is important to understand why organisations are now turning to management-led systems of employee remuneration, many of which eschew collective negotiation in favour of individualised incentive schemes. For this reason, the chapter next directs its attention to other systems of pay determination used by organisations in Britain.

Summary points

- There can be wide variations in how collective bargaining is structured in Britain, in terms of multi-employer, single-employer and workplace bargaining arrangements.

- The *coverage* of collective bargaining in Great Britain has declined substantially over the last two decades, and the dimensions that can be used to evaluate this decline include one or more of the following:
  a) Its *level*, by industry, company, or workplace
  b) Its *unit*, covering one or more groups of employees or trade unions
  c) Its *form*, including written and formal, or unwritten and informal agreements
  d) The *scope* of items that are negotiable.

- The determination of a bargaining unit and its level can be influenced by strategic management tactics, which can affect the bargaining strength of the parties.

- Of particular significance is the narrowing of bargaining scope, and the subsequent rise in individual and unilateral managerial methods for determining employee remuneration.

Pay determination in Britain
The shift from collective bargaining to individual remuneration

An organisation's wage payment system is the cornerstone of managerial strategies that seek to 'control and motivate' employees (Evans, 2003). In simple terms there are three broad ways in which pay can be set for employees: joint regulation through collective negotiation; unilaterally by management (with legal adjustment through the national minimum wage, where necessary); or unilaterally by workers themselves. Since the latter has never existed in Britain with any significance it will not be considered here. However, with the decline in union membership and the coverage of collective bargaining across British industry, it seems likely that pay determination through collective negotiation is progressively being replaced by unilateral management decision making.

reward system
The total of pay and non-pecuniary rewards that make up an employee's remuneration package.

incentive payment system
A system in which employee pay, either in whole or in part, is comprised of different monetary amounts determined by management evaluations of individual performance.

An organisation's employee **reward system** is more than simply pay rates, and tends to include a variety of non-pecuniary rewards such as subsidised meals, cars or private healthcare, as well as monetary benefits in terms of pensions and individual performance bonuses. Increasingly, organisations are moving away from collectively negotiated wage payments based on a 'rate for the job', and adopting newer **incentive payment systems** in which the remuneration of employees, either in whole or in part, includes performance benefits that are determined by managerial evaluations of the individual. Indeed, unilateral management decision making has become the most common method of setting employee pay levels in Britain, with 70 per cent of all workplaces determining pay in this way for at least some of their employees (Kersley *et al.*, 2005: 19). It is therefore important to consider these newer developments in pay determination, along with managerial and employee objectives for such reward packages.

Management and employee objectives

From management's point of view, individual employment relations processes tend to be underpinned by a distinct set of ideological motives. To start with, employers seem to have a preference for communicating directly with employees, rather than through a union or employee representative. As explained in Chapter 8, this gives managers a degree of freedom to manipulate and control the information that is disseminated. Second, many managers have an almost mystical belief in their abilities to motivate employees through incentivised employee reward systems. That is, incentive-based reward schemes are regarded as having a motivational effect on individuals, and higher individual rewards are believed to help recruit and retain better-quality employees. Allied to this is the belief that paying employees in this way can be a powerful tool to use to alter their behaviour. For example, bonuses and other incentives are believed to lead to a change in employee behaviours that are desired by management.

From the employees' perspective there are several potential objectives. First, in the absence of assistance from a trade union, many employees look to their immediate manager to provide a positive psychological contract in terms of a fulfilling and rewarding job, career advancement, and recognition from management for a job well done (Guest and Conway, 2002). This means that pay is the 'visible manifestation' of the expectations that underpin a positive psychological contract (Evans, 2003: 412). Second, workers are also concerned about pay levels because these affect their standard of living and relative purchasing power. Torrington *et al.* (2002: 563) suggest that the tradition of annually negotiated pay adjustment does little to reduce employee dissatisfaction. For example, depending on age, some employees might prefer to increase their leisure time, rather than receive an increase in basic pay. For other workers, however, the total reward package can be more important than the amount negotiated in a collective agreement. Moreover, given a choice, some might decide to opt for other benefits instead of an annually negotiated increase in basic salary: for example, additional pension benefits, health insurance or a car loan scheme. Finally, there are a large number of employees in Britain whose pay and conditions have 'never' been determined through collective negotiation, but set according to performance targets unilaterally determined by management. As noted earlier, only 3 per cent of employees in SMEs are party to a collective agreement, with the determination of pay and other conditions of employment almost wholly the prerogative of management, reflecting perhaps that conditions in smaller firms resemble more of a 'sweatshop' than a happy ship (Sisson, 1993). It is also possible that workers in smaller firms cherish the informal and close personal relationships that exist, while employees in other organisations may find that achieving performance targets set by management is a better reflection of their effort than an annually negotiated increase.

Recent developments in employee reward

Although the full range of pay determination methods is beyond the scope of this chapter, two generic categories are widely used to either complement or replace collective bargaining: *individual* and/or *group-based* methods. Before describing these, however, there is an important caveat to note. While these schemes for employee remuneration are presented separately, it is seldom the case that they substitute for collective bargaining completely, and in many unionised organisations they are often collectively negotiated, whereas in non-union firms unilateral management decision making tends to prevail.

Individual incentive reward practices

One incentive wage scheme is **payment by results (PBR)**. The philosophy underpinning this method is that managers assume workers are inherently idle, and are only motivated to work harder where there is a link between their efforts and the amount of pay they receive. Almost all PBR schemes have in common a focus on quantity and output, rather than quality or innovation, and a typical example is *piecework*, which can be found in sectors such as textiles, where negotiated agreements determine how much each individual employee is paid, often according to each 'piece they make'.

payment by results
A payment system in which employee pay is based on output and effort.

Another individual incentive scheme is **individual performance-related pay (IPRP)**, which is underpinned by the belief that workers are motivated by self-improvement, so that pay incentives are designed with this in mind: for example, employees are rewarded, either in whole or in part, according to an evaluation of total job performance (ACAS, 2003b). For the most part it is managers who assess employees, with criteria that reflect both physical output and other less tangible aspects of performance, such as customer satisfaction, desired behaviours or work innovation and creativity.

individual performance-related pay (IPRP)
A payment system designed to reward employees based on an evaluation of their whole job performance.

The reasons why many organisations have moved towards these reward schemes can be traced to three main factors. First, the political ideologies of the State, and in particular those government polices of the 1980s which sought to promote a more individualistic employment relations culture. A second reason for the use of individual incentive schemes in recent years has been the growing popularity of HRM among managers, of which a central tenet is individualism rather than collectivism. Finally, organisations have been continually searching for greater labour market flexibility, and to this end have adopted incentive-based pay methods as part of their strategies. These three factors have led to a widespread adoption of incentive-based remuneration schemes, and currently over 40 per cent of all workplaces in Great Britain utilise some form of performance-related pay, although these schemes are more prevalent in the private (44 per cent) than in the public sector (19 per cent) (Kersley *et al.*, 2006: 190).

IPRP schemes usually work by pegging different levels of monetary reward to different levels of performance. For example, employees who are graded as 'excellent' performers can receive an additional 5 per cent on top of their basic salaries; those rated as 'good or average' can receive an additional 2 per cent; while those rated 'below average' receive no additional pay, and may even face disciplinary action. The actual amount awarded is usually determined either by job evaluation, or by line-management appraisals of the individual employee. Thus, individually set performance criteria, which may or may not be the subject of union agreement, determine the level of reward received. Moreover, payment schemes of this type also send a very strong message to employees about the behaviours that management expect, such as working harder or displaying an increased awareness of customer and company needs. Although not covered here, other individual incentive methods include **competency-related pay** and **skill-related pay**. Unlike IPRP, the former is more futuristic, in that it sets individual pay (either wholly or in part) for the coming year according to a level of competence in certain job tasks. With *skill-related pay* a proportion of the employee's salary is allocated on the basis of acquired skills, and this is often determined by qualifications and/or training courses.

competency-related pay

Pay is set at a level, either in whole or in part, according to a level of competence exhibited in carrying out certain job tasks.

skill-related pay

Allocates a proportion of an employee's pay according to acquired skills and job qualifications.

Pause for reflection

> What problems or difficulties can you envisage with the introduction of individual incentive payment schemes in an organisation? Provide a short justification to your answer.

The evidence concerning the impact of individual incentive schemes is mixed. Some American studies suggest that performance incentives can be used as a lever to improve employee motivation and ultimately change organisational culture (Lawler, 2000). The argument here is that performance inducements have more of an impact on employee innovation and motivation, than does a straightforward pay-for-effort scheme. However, for a number of reasons, the use of these schemes in Britain has been the subject of considerable debate.

To start with, PBR schemes tend to produce very complicated and expensive wage payment systems, requiring dedicated personnel to evaluate and measure the rate paid for every job task. Consequently, how the rate for the job is determined can be a continuous bone of contention, especially when new technologies that speed up tasks without any compensatory increase in pay are introduced. Second, the claim that PBR leads to greater managerial control of employee effort is questionable. For example, employees themselves can choose whether to increase their earnings by increasing output, so that the control over production targets can be influenced as much by employees as by management. Third, in many cases IPRP schemes are no more than 'individually wrapped' standard packages, which merely create an impression that they are particular to each employee (Evans and Hudson, 1993). In practice, 'satisfactory' or 'average' performance grades tend to be awarded as the norm (Marsden *et al.*, 2000), the effect of which is that a perennial 'average' rating can become demotivating and, in the eyes of employees, managers are often seen to be shifting the goalposts by making it harder to achieve higher earnings. Fourth, there can be an inbuilt bias in the performance criteria used in many firms, which leads to accusations of favouritism, especially when performance indicators are determined by line managers using subjective measures, such as team effectiveness or a willingness to change. One effect of this is discrimination, especially if job evaluations and performance criteria are set by male managers for female employees (White and Druker, 2000). Finally, management's true intentions behind the introduction of incentive-based remuneration can be dubious, if not downright sinister. The argument here is that IPRP and PBR are not necessarily introduced as a way to motivate employees or reward individual performance, but rather as a tool with which to beat unions, and diminish the role of collective bargaining in favour of individual methods that are more easily controlled by management.

Group-based incentive reward practices

Like individual incentive schemes, there are several group-based methods that have risen in popularity among organisations, although only three will be described here: *gainsharing*; *profit-related pay* (PRP); and *employee-share ownership plans* (ESOPs). These are sometimes referred to as the 'people's form of capitalism', because in theory at least, they provide the opportunity for workers to share in the profits made by an organisation. Around one-third (37 per cent) of all trading-sector organisations in Britain use profit-related pay for their employees, and 21 per cent operate an employee-share plan (Kersley *et al.*, 2006: 191–192).

gainsharing
A group-based incentive payment scheme that links employee effort to productivity improvements and/or cost savings made by a defined group or team of employees in an organisation.

One group-based scheme to determine pay is **gainsharing**, in which output is directly linked to employee effort, and an element of the employees' remuneration is based on measured productivity improvements, or specific cost savings. Usually gainsharing rewards are paid to all members of a defined group or team involved in the scheme, and although schemes of this type have risen in popularity, they are more common in America than in Britain.

profit-related pay
A scheme in which part of an employee's salary is based on company profits.

A second type of group incentive scheme is **profit-related pay** (PRP), in which part of an employee's salary is based on company profits. In addition, and depending on government legislation, members of a profit-related pay scheme might also benefit from certain tax savings. While the financial dividends or bonuses are paid to individuals, most schemes of this type are designed for the whole workforce of an organisation, and many are negotiated where trade union recognition exists.

employee share ownership plans
These schemes provide the opportunity for employees to either purchase company shares through a dedicated company savings scheme, or receive a certain number of free shares each year as part of the salary package.

The final type of group-based wage payment system is an **employee share-ownership plan** (ESOP). These provide employees with the opportunity to either purchase company shares through a dedicated company savings scheme, or receive free shares as part of their salary package. The basic principle is that 'groups' of employees can receive different amounts of financial remuneration (plus some tax advantages) depending

Case study 9.2: **Incentive reward schemes at Beverage Co.**

Beverage Co. is a small to medium-sized company that employs 150 workers, making intermediary products for the food and drink industry. There is collective bargaining with the GMB union over pay and conditions for about 65 process operatives, while the remainder of its employees (white-collar, sales and call-centre staff) are non-unionised.

In the late 1990s Beverage Co. experienced a period of commercial uncertainty. It faced increasing international competition for food and drinks flavourings, which led to the loss of a few important export contracts. As a result of this, the company made ten production operatives redundant. This was the first time that Beverage Co. had ever experienced any form of job losses. The company has been owned by members of the same family for more than a century, and its approach to employment relations was informal and paternalistic. However, with increased market competition, the company's owners decided to distance Beverage Co. from its informal practices. Instead, they introduced a more strategic approach to employment relations, including new incentive wage payment systems for different groups of employees.

Anna is typical of most process operatives. Her basic salary is £200 per week, which is marginally lower than the going rate for the industry. However, with the introduction of a group gainsharing scheme negotiated by her union, the GMB, she regularly earns an additional £90 based on the output of her team. This is considerably less than what could be earned according to the gainsharing agreement, and this is because a team member has been absent on maternity leave without any cover. As a result, Anna and her colleagues have to work most Saturdays on overtime, and this adds another £120 to her wage packet. She is generally satisfied with her take-home pay, although she feels that she has very little say in the output targets that are set. Anna and her colleagues have recently been to see the shop steward to complain about the lack of cover for their absent team member on maternity leave.

Anna works on the adjacent shift to Seamus, who does exactly the same job. Like Anna, Seamus' team can earn additional pay through the gainsharing scheme. On average, Seamus earns around £245 in addition to his basic salary through the gainsharing bonus. His team consistently meet the agreed gainsharing targets, have a full complement of team members, and very rarely feel the need to work overtime.

Cathy works in the call centre which is non-unionised. Like her colleagues, she earns about £40 on top of her basic salary of £320 per week through the company's individual performance-pay scheme. Bonuses are made according to targets set unilaterally by management, which reflect the number of customer calls answered and the queries resolved. Brian is also a non-union employee, and works adjacent to the call centre in the admin office. Because he does not have direct customer contact, he is not allowed to join the performance-pay scheme. After complaining about this, the Chief Executive agreed that he and other admin staff could be paid a performance bonus based on attendance, timekeeping and the supervisor's evaluation of how well they perform. Brian is typical of other staff in this department, earning a bonus of between £30 and £50 each week, in addition to a basic salary of £275 per week. However, sometimes there is no performance award at all (e.g. if he has been absent for some reason).

James is an average-performing member of the sales function. His reward package is typical of most sales environments, which comprise a company car, a low basic salary supplemented with a performance bonus calculated on the volume of new customer sales in each quarter. James' performance for the last three quarters amounted to payments of £12 000, £7000 and £9000 respectively. In James' team is Sally, who joined Beverage Co. two years ago from a competitor firm, bringing with her several new contracts. These new Beverage Co. customers have earned Sally £42 000, £29 000 and £57 000 for each of her last three quarterly sales periods. Sally is considered a high flyer in the firm, and has recently been poached by another rival company, and is currently serving one month's notice before she leaves Beverage Co.

All workers and managers at Beverage Co. also receive profit-based pay, which is calculated as 3 per cent of company profits divided equally among all employees, and amounts to a one-off payment of £620 in the current year. In addition, employees are entitled to join a company share savings plan. Anna is typical of those employees who joined the scheme about four years ago. She has been saving £20 per week deducted from her salary, and with the tax incentive built into the scheme, she will have a sum of £5000 to purchase company share at a reduced rate in 12 months' time. Although company performance fluctuated in the first two years of the plan, over the 4-year period as a whole performance has increased, mainly because of the large customer contracts brought in by Sally about two years ago. When the share plan was last evaluated 6 months ago, it predicted that the typical savings value of £5000 will equate to £14 000-worth of shares at current market rates.

Questions

1 Describe each of the employee reward schemes in operation at Beverage Co.

2 For each of the schemes described in (1) above, how is the performance contribution of employees evaluated?

3 What issues are likely to emerge from each of the incentive schemes identified in (1) and (2) above?

4 Do you think a collectively negotiated reward system would benefit the non-union employees at Beverage Co?

on how well their organisation has performed (Pendleton, 2000). One of the more recent government-sponsored schemes of this type is the *Save as You Earn* (SAYE) share-ownership plan: a saving scheme administered by the company, in which employees save a specific amount deducted from their salaries, and at the end of a defined saving period (3, 5 or 7 years) they can purchase company shares, often at a reduced market value.

It is easy to see why schemes such as these appear attractive. To start with, there are potential tax advantages from operating these schemes, both for the company and its employees. Moreover, depending on overall company performance, they offer the potential for increased remuneration through bonus payments or share sales at some point in the future. Theoretically, they can act as a conduit for employees to gell together as part of a team, and feel more committed to the successes of the company in which they are employed. However, there are a number of criticisms of these methods.

First, with *gainsharing*, there is a potential for inter-group rivalry to counterbalance the advantages of redistributing the gains or savings among work groups, especially if some teams are rewarded differently from others. Second, with *profit* and *share-ownership plans*, employees have no input into management investment decisions, and these decisions are closely related to whether share prices go up or down. Third, there is some evidence to suggest that when schemes of this type are implemented, employees find themselves feeling insecure rather than more committed to the goals of the organisation (Marchington and Wilkinson, 2005a). This occurs because there is always a risk that long-term investment plans will depend on the (unforeseeable) success of the company. To put matters more bluntly, employees are asked to buy into these plans without ever fully knowing about future market fluctuations. Finally, the underpinning theory that some sort of profit incentive will make employees work harder is debatable to say the least (Pendleton, 2000). For example, there are simply too many other factors outside of management's control that influence whether share prices go up or down in the long-run (Robinson and Wilson, 2006). For these reasons many trade unions believe that group-based incentive rewards, particularly those controlled by management, have the potential to undermine gains achieved through other pay-determination methods, such as collective bargaining (Heery, 2000a).

Summary points

- There are a number of management and employee objectives for the use of incentive-based wages payment systems.

- Unilateral management decision making is by far the most common method used to determine employee reward in Great Britain.

- A number of individual and group-based incentive reward schemes exist, including *payment-by-results (PBR)*, *individual-performance-related pay (IPRP)*, *profit-related pay (PRP)*, *gainsharing*, and *employee share-ownership plans (ESOPs)*.

- Several factors affect the effectiveness of these different pay-determination methods, not least of which is the potential to undermine the gains employees have previously obtained from collective bargaining.

Legal aspects of collective bargaining

Earlier in this chapter it was noted that statutory trade union recognition means there are legal implications for collective bargaining. In fact, ever since the early nineteenth century there has been considerable government attention devoted to the legal (and non-legal) aspects of collective bargaining and pay determination. Indeed, the work of the Webbs (1987) and the Donovan Commission (1968) both provided a deeper understanding of the contours of collective bargaining, and generated considerable debate on the potential legal implications of collective

---

Donovan Commission

A Royal Commission (1965–1968) to review and make recommendations on the relations between trade unions and employers' associations in Great Britain.

custom and practice

Rules that result from an informal bargaining arrangement, which eventually become incorporated (implicitly) into the contract of employment.

---

agreements. Even though it reported as long ago as 1968, the **Donovan Commission** drew attention to the formal and informal aspects of collective bargaining mentioned earlier, and concluded that Britain had two systems of employment relations: the *formal* and *informal*. The former was said to exist at a national or industry level between trade unions and employers' associations, using formalised collective bargaining to produce agreements similar to those shown in Exhibit 9.1. However, and in addition to formal bargaining, a great deal of informal negotiation existed in many workplaces. With this emerged informal **custom and practice** rule-making between shop stewards and managers, which tended to adjust national agreements to reflect local conditions (Clegg, 1979). Indeed, where an informal practice becomes embedded over time, and condoned by management and workers, then it can effectively become a right that is incorporated (implicitly) into the contract of employment (Brown, 1972). Because of informal workplace bargaining, the Donovan Commission proposed that management needed to re-establish control by formalising the conduct of workplace bargaining. However, its proposals fell short of recommending legally binding collective agreements, and instead it endorsed the principle of voluntarily bargaining.

It is now widely recognised that the reforms of the Donovan Commission produced tensions of their own. It greatly encouraged the emergence of strong and autonomous workplace trade unionism (see Chapter 4), and this probably stood in the way of management reasserting control over labour costs and working practices (Ogden, 1981). What was more problematic was that, even if bargaining becomes more formalised, informal customs and practices quickly re-emerge (Terry, 1977), and this is linked to the legal status of trade unions and collective agreements. Since this has been discussed in Chapter 4 it will not be reconsidered here, other than to note that with the statutory recognition comes an obligation on an employer to bargain and negotiate with a trade union.

Collective bargaining and legal enforceability?

A legal obligation to bargain with a recognised trade union is not the same as a legally enforceable collective agreement, and in Britain the substantive and procedural aspects of an agreement are essentially up to the parties to agree. What this means, in legal terms, is that collective agreements are not legally enforceable, and it is commonplace for agreements to include the acronym 'TINA LEA' (*This Is Not A Legally Enforceable Agreement*). Nonetheless, the specific terms of a negotiated agreement as they apply to an individual have legal implications. For example, an agreement to reduce an employee's weekly working hours or increase his or her annual salary are substantive terms of employment, and these then become incorporated into the individual's contract of employment.

> ### Pause for reflection
>
> Before you read on, what reasons do you think there are 'for' and 'against' legally binding collective agreements?

It is apparent that many trade unions now favour the increased legal regulation of employment conditions, especially European-based rights for workers (Ewing, 2003). However, the law has stopped short of making collective agreements legally binding, and debate continues about whether this is a good or bad thing. To begin with, for an agreement to be legally enforceable, agreements would need to be explicit and comprehensive, so that the respective rights and obligations of management and employees are clear and fully understood. This, it is argued, would leave less room for ambiguity, and less potential for disagreement in interpreting and implementing them. However, it can also be argued that no agreement can be so comprehensive that it specifies every work detail made on a day-to-day basis, or at a future point in time. For this reason, some degree of informality is arguably necessary, simply to enable managers and employees to accommodate the myriad changes that are necessary on a daily basis.

The second argument in favour of making collective agreements legally binding is that trade unions would be forced to ensure that their members honoured agreements, which would reduce the possibility of unconstitutional industrial action. Against this it can be pointed out that various employment Acts, especially the anti-union legislation introduced during the 1980s, restrict how and when trade union members can pursue industrial action. However, even though this type of legislation remains on the British statute books, workers from time to time still take unofficial action, either in the heat of the moment or because an issue is important to them. An example of this was the strike at British Airways in August 2005, when BA staff engaged in unconstitutional strike action in support of dismissed workers in another company, Gate Gourmet, who supplied in-flight meals for BA. In practice therefore, it is unlikely that legally binding agreements would stop this sort of action completely.

Indeed, evidence from other countries where agreements are legally enforceable only reinforces the point. For example, despite the legal registration of workplace agreements in Australia, the number of days lost due to strike action was as much as four times higher than in Britain during the 1990s (Labour Market Trends, 2003; Lansbury and Wailes, 2004). It has also been shown that, because of the legal nature of Australian workplace agreements, managers in some organisations tend to implement individual HRM policies as a way of excluding trade unions, because Australian workplace agreements which include non-collective employment relations practices have a legal status (Campling and Gollan, 1999; Ellem, 2001). In addition, in Canada, the number of strike days per 1000 employees for the 1990s was as much as ten times higher than in Britain (Labour Market Trends, 2003), even though Canadian law requires that collective agreements specify a grievance procedure for handling disputes, and prohibit strike action during the term of a collective agreement. Consequently, collective agreements tend to be accompanied by high levels of litigation, and the amount of working time lost due to strike action has been reported as one of the main contemporary employment relations issues in Canada (Thompson and Taras, 2004).

A third argument for the legal enforceability of collective agreements is that it could promote long-term responsibility on both sides. For example, it would give predictability, and given the legal status of an agreement, would allow managers to get on with the job of managing the organisation, secure in the knowledge that a dispute would be less likely. Against this can be cited the experiences in other countries that are noted above. Under these systems, one party cannot technically invoke a sanction against the other party to bring about a change in the substantive conditions of employment during the life of an agreement: this is known as engaging in a **dispute of interest**. However, the parties do have the facility to engage in a **dispute of right**, because this consists of moving into dispute over a procedural matter relating to the terms of an agreement. Theoretically, the intention is that disputes of interest would be referred to arbitration or mediation within the lifespan of an agreed collective contract, although in practice such arrangements are difficult to enforce when stoppages are either very local or of short duration.

dispute of interest
A disagreement over the contents of a collective agreement, such as pay, pension entitlements or hours of work.

dispute of right
A disagreement over the interpretation of a collective agreement, such as the frequency of meetings for a negotiating committee or the facilities afforded to shop stewards to carry out their duties.

Finally, it should be noted that there are arguments that legal enforceability would actually bring disadvantages to both parties. For example, when agreements are negotiated voluntarily, they are binding in honour, and while reaching agreement can be difficult, when it is reached in this way it is held together by the strongest glue of all: honour. For this reason conflicts are usually handled professionally, and the system only tends to break down where one party perceives that the other is behaving unfairly. Arguably, if an agreement is made legally enforceable, it becomes fair game for litigation lawyers to look for, and exploit, the smallest loopholes in what has been agreed, rather than the negotiators searching for mutually beneficial solutions. Indeed, there is an even more significant drawback to legal enforceability, because it would apply to both sides. Thus in situations where change might be necessary, the *status quo* could be made legally enforceable until either employees or management agree otherwise. The result could be a very prolonged process of negotiation that could delay changes that might be necessary for survival.

Summary points

- Collective agreements are not legally binding under the British system of collective bargaining.
- Two legal implications for collective bargaining are: (a) changes to an individual's employment contract as a result of a negotiated agreement or a custom and practice rule; and (b), statutory trade union recognition.
- There exist several arguments both 'for' and 'against' the legal enforceability of collective agreements.

Outcomes of collective bargaining

The definition of collective bargaining given earlier in the chapter stressed that its purpose is to reach agreement on the rules that regulate employment conditions, mostly in unionised environments. Broadly speaking, rules can be of three types, each of which can have a very different impact on the employment relations climate in an organisation. For simplicity these are labelled as *informal dialogue, substantive agreements* and *procedural agreements*, each of which will be considered in turn.

Informal dialogue

Bargaining outcomes that promote a climate of informal dialogue often emerge from the existence of workplace *custom and practice* rules. In some situations these informal rules only result in very temporary agreements between union stewards and line managers, but on other matters they become a permanent feature of the employment relationship (Brown, 1972; Terry, 1977). In addition, because informal customs and practices are highly variable in nature, and very specific to the circumstances in which they are made, the outcomes depend on the context and issue. For example, supervisors may allow employees to leave early when a particular job is finished, and the employees concerned are paid for a full day's work. The point is that the precise outcome of a bargaining arrangement based on informal dialogue is often the result of the interactions between union representatives and line managers at shopfloor level.

Substantive agreements

These types of bargaining arrangements tend to result in very structured outcomes based on a transaction cost relationship between the two parties. Indeed, it can be said that substantive agreements tend to result in very formalised relationships, with agreements covering almost all aspects of the exchange of effort for rewards: for example, all forms of basic and performance remuneration, individual performance targets, hours of work and maternity and sick leave. Two types of substantive agreements have come to the fore in recent years. First, many employers now seek agreements that are more comprehensive and of a longer duration: for example, negotiated pay deals are often pegged to some external indicator such as the retail price index and run for two or three years. Second, in return for a comprehensive substantive agreement, employers often insist that certain managerial freedoms are built into the agreement, such as the ability to set employee performance targets and/or introduce incentive pay schemes that require greater employee flexibility. While substantive type relationships can result in more formalised and detailed employment relations climates, they also provide employers with a higher degree of predictability about future wage costs (Sisson and Storey, 2000).

Procedural agreements

Like substantive-type bargaining relationships, procedural agreements also result in highly for-malised and often prescriptive employment relations climates. Significantly, procedural agreements establish the machinery for the two sides to reconcile any differences, and have been likened to both 'treaties of peace, and devices for the avoidance of war' (Marsh, 1966). For this reason there is virtually a limitless scope for procedural agreements to deal with a whole range of issues. For example, procedural arrangements commonly exist for trade union recognition and shop steward facilities, grievance and disputes procedures, paternity and maternity leave, the use of agency staff, employee flexibility or how working methods will be changed by management in the future.

While procedural and substantive agreements are different, they are strongly connected. Indeed, it is probable that, when procedural arrangements are evident, this builds on pre-existing substantive agreements. For example, a (substantive) agreement on individual per-formance pay would probably also define the procedural rules as to how management set performance targets, or how an employee might appeal against a change to his or her work targets. Another way in which procedural and substantive bargaining can lead to related out-comes arises in the renegotiation of existing terms and conditions, shown in Fig. 9.2.

A procedural agreement about negotiating will sometimes specify that there are regular intervals at which trade union and management representatives will meet to consider matters of mutual interest; for example, during a monthly or quarterly joint negotiating committee. Where this is the case, a party wishing to bring about some alteration to an existing agreement (i.e. pay, holidays or hours) can table an agenda item and present a claim. It would also be during this type of forum where procedural arrangements can also be modified (i.e. to a disci-plinary rule or the methods by which an employee's grievance is resolved). Where negotiators meet on a more ad hoc basis, the way of seeking this alteration could be to lodge a collective grievance about a particular substantive term that currently exists.

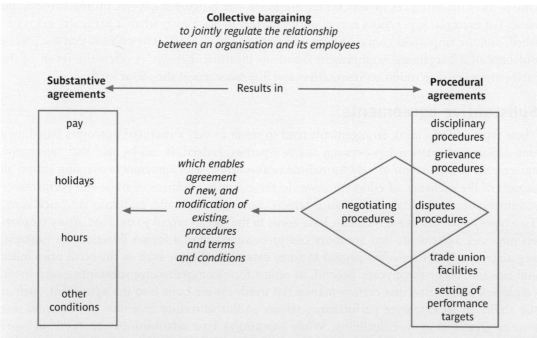

Figure 9.2 Relation of substantive and procedural bargaining agreements

Conclusions

This chapter has reviewed collective bargaining in contemporary employment relations, and because of the decline in collectively negotiated relationships in Britain, attention was directed to some of the recent developments in employee reward and pay determination. Since many organisations now place less emphasis on annual or bi-annual set-piece negotiations with trade unions, the methods used to regulate the employment relationship are now more connected with other employment relations processes. For example, the level of union membership in an organisation can affect the range of issues that are the subject of a collective agreement, and therefore the union strategies noted in Chapter 4 have a bearing in this regard. Similarly, the government of the day has views about collective bargaining, statutory union recognition, and the use of tax breaks that facilitate certain wage-payment systems. Thus, the role of the State and its stance on employment relations intervention covered in Chapter 5 is relevant. Furthermore, systems of corporate governance in the UK mean there is a connection to Chapter 3, especially in the light of changing attitudes and styles of management, which emphasise a preference for individualism and HRM rather than the joint regulation of employment conditions.

However, the strongest links with this chapter are with the topics covered in the following two chapters. While collective bargaining involves negotiation, it is not the same thing. Collective bargaining is essentially a relationship, and negotiation a process that takes place within this relationship, to which we return in the next chapter. After negotiation, Chapter 11 considers the matter of conflict, and in the eyes of some people, this is an inevitable by-product of collective bargaining and negotiation. For other people however, the absence of collective bargaining simply means that conflict and protest behaviours have become more subtle and embedded into an organisation's culture and climate.

❓ Review and discussion questions

1 With examples and using your own words, explain each of the three functions of collective bargaining.

2 What advantages do you think there are for management in having a collective bargaining relationship?

3 Why do you think the choice of a bargaining unit and its level is a strategic management issue?

4 Describe how bargaining form can affect the type of employment relationship in an organisation.

5 What are the parties likely to gain from a single-table bargaining relationship?

6 In your own words, briefly describe the arguments 'for' and 'against' the legal enforceability of collective agreements.

7 What factors have prompted the growth and use of individual incentive-based payment systems in Britain?

8 Explain why a group-based incentive payment scheme may weaken union influence in bargaining.

Further reading

Brown, W., S. Deakin, M. Hudson, C. Pratten and P. Ryan (1998) *The Individualisation of Employment Contracts in Britain*, Department of Trade and Industry Research Report No. 4, London. A research report commissioned by the British government. It evaluates the shift from collective to individual employment relations. Available from the DTI web site: http://www.dti.gov.uk/er/emar/dti3646.pdf.

EIRO (2006) *Employment relations in SMEs*, European Industrial Relations Observatory, April, http://www.eiro.eurofound.eu.int/2006/02/study/tn0602101s.html. A comparative study that reports some important trends concerning union coverage and bargaining activity in SME companies in 13 EU member states, showing that Britain has the lowest coverage of collective bargaining and lower industry average rates of pay for workers employed in smaller firms.

Evans, J. (2003) 'Pay', in *Employment Relations, 2nd edn*, G. Hollinshead, P. Nichols and S. Tailby (eds), London, Financial Times/Prentice Hall. A very readable chapter that reviews different pay determination methods, commenting on the shift from central to decentralised bargaining arrangements in Britain. It also locates pay determination within the context of the psychological contract.

Forth, J., H. Bewley and A. Bryson (2006) *Small and Medium-sized Enterprises: Findings from the 2004 Workplace Employment Relations Survey*, London, Department of Trade and Industry (http://www.dti.gov.uk/employment/research-evaluation/wers-2004/wers-2004/page25904.html). A very useful and informative booklet, contrasting SMEs with larger firms using the 2004 WERS results.

Kersley, B., C. Alpin, J. Forth, A. Bryson, H. Bewley, J. Dix and S. Oxenbridge (2005) *Inside the Workplace: First Findings from the 2004 Workplace Employment Relations Survey*, London, Department of Trade and Industry. (http://www.dti.gov.uk/employment/research-evaluation/wers-2004/wers-2004/page25904.html). A pamphlet that provides a summary of the main key findings from the 2004 WERS survey, with particularly important insights into the current state of collective bargaining and other pay determination methods in Great Britain.

Marsden, D. and R. Belfield (2005), 'Unions and performance-related pay: what chance of a procedural role?', in *Trade Unions: Resurgence or Demise?*, S. Fernie and D. Metcalf (eds), London, Routledge. A book chapter that reports empirical findings concerning performance-related pay for teachers. It provides interesting analysis on the implications for collective bargaining and union revitalisation strategies in the public sector.

Robinson, A. and N. Wilson (2006) 'Employee financial participation and productivity: An empirical reappraisal', *British Journal of Industrial Relations*, Vol. 44 (1), pp. 31–50. An empirical journal article that can be difficult to master, but is worth the effort. It assesses the route through which employee share ownership and profit-related pay might lead to productivity gains.

Chapter 10

Negotiation

Introduction

This chapter follows on from the previous one, where it was noted that in collective bargaining, negotiation is the dominant way of deciding the terms and conditions of employment. It was also pointed out in the previous chapter that there is a sense in which the topic of negotiation cannot be divorced from conflict in employment relations, and this is addressed in the next chapter. Therefore, the chapter starts by tracing this link. However, it should be noted that while most of the literature on negotiation is concerned with unionised settings, it is not exclusive to unionised relationships, and a 'negotiated order' can prevail in small and non-union companies through informal dialogue and customs and practices (Ram, 1994). For this reason, the chapter starts by examining negotiation from a theoretical perspective which stresses the importance of understanding the contexts in which negotiation takes place. Next, some of the important behavioural aspects of negotiation are described, and this is followed by considering the skills and practical stages for effective negotiation, namely: preparation, face-to-face negotiations, and post-negotiating activities.

Negotiation: a conceptual perspective and definition

Negotiation is not exclusive to a collective or unionised employment relationship. Indeed, an increase in the use of various human-resource management techniques, such as individualised remuneration and performance appraisals, has probably resulted in instances in which individual employees negotiate with their manager over a whole range of issues. In relationships that are regulated by collective bargaining, however, negotiation tends to make the prevailing climate very different, and it is this situation that occupies the lion's share of attention in the employment relations literature. In all employment relationships there is a basic and sometimes quite stark inequality of power, which arises because an employer's ability to withstand the loss of a single employee is far greater than the employee's ability to withstand the loss of his or her job. To counterbalance this inherent power inequality, employees can choose to be represented collectively, and in metaphorical terms, to speak with one voice.

From your reading of previous chapters, it should be apparent that in employment relations there is always the potential for conflict and disagreement between the parties, and this makes negotiation in employment relations somewhat different from other situations in which negotiation is used: for example, in a commercial situation. In a commercial negotiation for example, discussing any differences and trying to reconcile them is usually the first step in the process of both parties trying to achieve some gain. In employment relations, however, this first step is taken in the knowledge that either party has an alternative, and that the alternative has the potential to inflict harm. For example, given the consent of its members, a trade union can take sanctions against an employer, individual employees can leave the organisation, and management can reduce the size of its workforce by laying people off. This makes it quite different from traditional commercial negotiations where, for example, if a firm fails to find satisfactory terms for doing business with another firm, it has not actually been harmed. In business negotiations, both parties enter into a process of negotiation with the anticipation of gain and, if one withdraws, the outcome is that the other suffers a lost opportunity rather than experiencing some sort of harm.

In employment relations negotiations, the situation is fundamentally different, for two very important reasons. First, the very thing that brings employers and employees (or their unions) around the negotiating table is the knowledge that each one can suffer harm at the hands of the other party. This means that negotiation is a complex social process involving acts of *exchange*: that is, during negotiations one party may only achieve its desired objectives by accepting some or all of the desired objectives of the other party (Lewicki *et al.*, 2005). Second, the very fact that negotiations are in progress is in itself an admission that the parties have conflicting aims, and in many ways, the act of negotiating can be no less of an expression of conflict than a strike. It is therefore a gross oversimplification to think of negotiation as *peace*, and industrial action as *war*. They are simply different ways of pursuing the same end, which is finding an acceptable resolution to the differences between the two sides. In other words, negotiation and conflict are both processes of persuasion, in which one party attempts to get the other to see things their way. The only difference is that, while one uses the force of argument, the other uses the argument of force. Moreover, when negotiations are concluded it seldom means that conflict has been removed or that both parties have achieved all that they desire. Therefore, a concluded negotiation simply means that for the time being a situation has been reached where the major differences have either been resolved, or that one party has had to concede to certain terms and conditions as a result of either a lack of persuasion or a weaker bargaining position. In non-union situations this may mean that management have bypassed employee concerns and imposed their desired objectives on workers unilaterally. However, as will be seen in the next chapter, employees are not simply passive recipients of managerial actions, and conflict behaviour can manifest itself in ways other than the withdrawal of labour, many of which can involve tacit negotiation and persuasion. Therefore, how long a negotiated settlement persists tends to depend upon the type of differences that have (or have not) been resolved, the degree of bargaining power between the parties, and the nature of the agreement that has been reached. For these reasons, **negotiation** is defined here as:

> a process of dialogue through which the parties seek to reconcile their differences, with the aim of producing an agreement, whether formal or informal, by using elements of power, persuasion and argument.

Summary points

- Negotiation in employment relations is a process of exchange whereby the two parties seek to reconcile their differences.
- Unlike commercial or business negotiations, in employment relations the parties have expectations that each party can suffer harm at the hands of the other.
- Negotiation recognises that employees (or their unions) and managers have different and at times conflicting aims.
- Negotiation is no less an expression of conflict than industrial action, the difference being that the former uses the force of argument, whereas industrial action uses the argument of force.

Pause for reflection

Think of a situation in which you have experienced some domestic negotiation, either buying a car or requesting a student allowance from your parents. In that situation, what was your main objective, and how did you seek to persuade the other person to accept your point of view? In what way do you think your situation differs from negotiation in employment relations?

The theory of negotiation

Negotiation is a very dynamic process and no single set of negotiations is ever quite the same as another. Even in stable bargaining relationships, negotiations can vary quite considerably. The parties may choose to negotiate in either a *cooperative* or *distributive* manner, they may collaborate and seek a compromise, or they may decide not to negotiate at all. Often the process can take place over days, weeks or even months, rather than in a single session which lasts a few hours. In reality it consists of several processes, all of which are at work together. However, like all human interaction, it can take its tone from the context in which it takes place, and this can influence the character of a negotiation before it even starts. Therefore, before exploring the internal dynamics of negotiation, it is necessary to understand the importance of context.

The contexts of negotiation

In what follows it needs to be remembered that all the contextual factors interact with each other, and this means that it is always difficult to isolate the effect of one particular factor. In all probability, the importance of each factor varies over both time and space, from one organisation to another, and between different sets of negotiations even in the same enterprise. Consequently, they are only described separately for the sake of simplicity, and can be expressed as the four general groups shown in Fig. 10.1.

relative power of the parties (negotiations)
The capability to get the other side to change their view, which may or may not involve the use of sanctions.

The **relative power of the parties** is an important (many would argue the most important) contextual factor (Walton, 1969), and reflects the capability of one party to get the other side to change their view, which may, or may not, involve the use of sanctions. The important point here is not necessarily who actually has the most power, but rather what the parties *perceive* their power positions to be. Magenau and Pruitt (1979) argue that this is what most influences a negotiator's motivation to maintain and press home certain demands. In essence, each negotiator is likely to form a view as to what it will cost the other party to agree or disagree to certain demands, and in this lies their evaluation of the relative power of the parties. For example, if a trade union negotiator perceives that management's costs of not agreeing to the union's demands are much greater than the costs of agreeing to them, the union will evaluate their power position as much stronger than management's, and would therefore be prepared to press home the union's case. Clearly, the management negotiator will also have a view about his or her power position, and that of the trade union. Thus, it is perfectly possible for both sides to enter negotiations perceiving that they have a power advantage (or disadvantage). While the process of negotiation will refine these perceptions to some extent, those that the parties start with can have a huge influence on how matters evolve. Therefore, negotiation is not so much the use of power as the interpretation and use of potential (or latent) power (Morley, 1979).

It is for this reason that the threat of a sanction, either by implication or more openly, is a fundamental part of the process (Hawkins, 1979). This is, however, to portray negotiation as simply a matter of coercion, which it is not. Negotiation often involves the use of tactics and power to get the other side to re-evaluate their demands, claims and counter-claims. While having the capability to harm the other party is one source of power that can bring this about, it is not the only source of power, and in any event it can be a particularly expensive and risky strategy to adopt (Fisher and Ury, 1991).

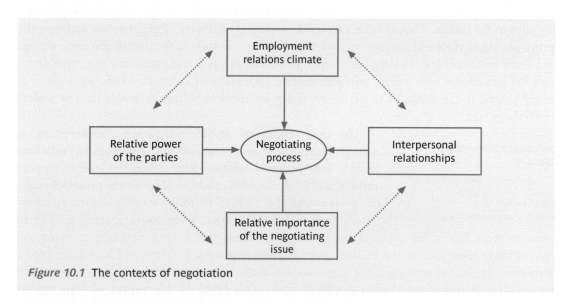

Figure 10.1 The contexts of negotiation

relative importance of a negotiating issue
The importance attached to a particular negotiating issue according to the constituent group the negotiator represents.

The **relative importance of a negotiating issue** is a second contextual factor. Negotiators are not free agents, but represent a constituency: for example, a trade union represents the interests of employees, and the employing organisation and its shareholders are represented by managers. While negotiators can exert some influence on their constituents, they are also subject to a great deal of pressure in return. Generally, the greater the importance of an issue to a constituent group, the greater is the pressure on the negotiator to achieve a particular outcome. The negotiator will be concerned to demonstrate publicly a strong commitment to achieving what the constituents want. In practice this often means taking a stand in negotiations, which in turn can mean that it takes longer to reach agreement. In most negotiations however, there are usually a number of issues on the table at the same time, and some of these are more important than others. The fact that there are multiple issues also tends to have a strong bearing on the tactics that negotiators are likely to use. For example, the least important of them can be sacrificed to achieve those that are paramount, and for this reason it is vital for a negotiator to know the *relative importance of a negotiating issue* in the eyes of the constituents that he or she represent. It is also important for the negotiator to have some idea of the significance of an issue to the opposing side. If, for example, a negotiator wrongly estimates this, it can become a major source of hostile interactions, crossed communications and misunderstandings during the negotiation (Bonham, 1971).

employment relations climate
A particular ethos or atmosphere that exists within an organisation at a given point in time, which is reflected in the way its members perceive, experience and react to the organisational context.

Employment relations climate is a particular ethos or atmosphere that exists within an organisation at a given point in time, which is reflected in the way its members perceive, experience and react to the organisational context (Rollinson, 2005). In negotiations this can be reflected in the way that the negotiators view the other side (Rim and Mannheim, 1979), and once these perceptions are formed, they can be extremely resistant to modification. Because each party treats the other one in a certain way, each tends to respond to this by behaving as expected (Lewicki *et al.*, 2004). In most organisations, large and small, there exists a set of sub-climates, each of which contributes to the overall employment relations climate. For example, Nicholson (1979) shows that memories of how past bargaining encounters have been handled affect how the parties relate to one another in the future. This, in turn, can set the tone and character of negotiations and how the principle negotiators will interact with one another. For example, if the overall climate is viewed as robust and capable of dealing with difficult issues in an open and pragmatic way, then negotiations can evolve into a joint problem-solving approach. In contrast, where the climate is more hostile, it can result in an extremely frosty atmosphere, where each side tries to undermine the other.

interpersonal relationship (negotiators)
The level of rapport and the degree of trust that can exist between the principal negotiators.

The final contextual factor, *interpersonal relationships*, is strongly connected with the overall employment relations climate. **Interpersonal relationships** reflect the level of rapport and the degree of trust that can exist between the principal negotiators (Lewicki *et al.*, 2004). In more trusting situations, negotiators tend to appreciate that their counterpart is subject to pressure from her or his constituents. Usually this means that an experienced negotiator will have a fairly good idea of the *relative power* of their opponent (Walton and McKersie, 1965). However, in labour–management negotiations, trust is not a simple or one-dimensional concept, but is multi-faceted and complex (Lewicki *et al.*, 2005). In this respect, separate negotiations are often interrelated exchanges, which can strengthen the on-going relationship between the two sides (O'Connor *et al.*, 2005).

A related aspect of interpersonal relations is whether a degree of *awareness* exists between negotiators (Morris, M. *et al.*, 1999). Awareness is something that enables negotiators to tune into what are often subtle clues and messages from one negotiator to the other. For example, should a manager comment during negotiations that points X, Y and Z will have to be explored in greater detail, and say nothing about points A, B, or C, this might convey an important message that the latter are agreeable, but such agreement is not explicit until movement or accommodation on points X, Y and Z. can be achieved. The outcome of this is that, irrespective of their constituents' demands, certain things are never said, and certain things are never asked for (Fisher and Ury, 1991). Moreover, while good interpersonal relationships on their own are not sufficient to result in a successful negotiation (Marsh, 1974), they can have a huge impact on the way the process is conducted, and the length of time it takes. Perhaps most important of all, good interpersonal relationships enable negotiators to 'get off the record' and explore potential solutions from outside the formal negotiating arena.

These then are the general contextual factors influencing negotiations, and it must be stressed again that they are all interconnected. An example will perhaps illustrate the point. The *importance of a particular issue*, say redundancy, will affect the *relative power position* of the parties, and this in turn will influence the way it is pursued. Thus the issue puts limits on the extent to which *interpersonal relationships* can emerge and develop between negotiators. In addition, the strength of *interpersonal relationships* amongst negotiators also plays a part in the way that they approach an issue, so there is some effect in the reverse direction.

Summary points

- The contexts to a given negotiating situation are important factors that can influence the way bargaining is conducted.

- There are four general contextual factors, which in reality all interact with each other to influence negotiating behaviours and outcomes. These include:
  - the perceived relative bargaining power of each party
  - the relative importance of a particular negotiating issue to a constituent group
  - the employment relations climate (and associated sub-climates)
  - the interpersonal relations that exist and develop over time between the principal negotiators.

Case study 10.1: **Negotiation and the signs of climate**

Consider the following statements made by managers and trade union officials in different situations.

1 *Manager*: We know how the union got into this firm; management was short-sighted and made a lot of mistakes, and if we had been on our toes it would never have happened. Now it's here we can't get rid of it, and the best we can do is to contain it by an intelligent and aggressive personnel policy.

▶

2 *Union Officer*. This company operates in a really difficult global market and managers have a tough time. While the members obviously all want security and better pay and conditions, they know you can't have a prosperous firm just by wishing for it. We have to work to make the company prosperous, but at the same time take care that the results of prosperity are fairly shared out.

3 *Union Officer*. If the company could find an excuse they would sack every steward in the place. The only reason they deal with us is that ten years ago we had a stand-up fight to get a decent pay deal, and this led to a long and bitter strike. Since then management deal with us because they have to, but they have never got over the bloody nose we gave them then.

4 *Manager*. Working in partnership with the union is not giving up control. In reality by working with them and enlisting their help in difficult times, management has more control over the future destiny of the firm than ever before.

5 *Manager*. In the past because we felt we were doing the right thing we fought the unions tooth and nail. Eventually, we saw that this was getting us nowhere. Bit by bit we have found that the union has a job to do, the same as we have. In a sense, by keeping management on its toes, the union has made most of us better managers.

6 *Union Officer*. Although the trade union should never try to take over management's job, we have a vested interest in working in partnership. I suppose you could say that we have stopped seeing management as the enemy; the real enemy is out there, and is globalisation. So far as getting the best of the real enemy is concerned, management and union are generally on the same side.

Questions for discussion

1 In each situation, what sort of employment relations climate or negotiating atmosphere do you feel the statement indicates?

2 In each situation, what do you feel that the aims and policies of management and union (or employees) would be with respect to each other?

The internal dynamics of negotiation

By far the most comprehensive and explicit analysis of the complexities of negotiation is that given by Walton and McKersie (1965). Indeed, not only has the original schema displayed remarkable endurance over time, it has also been shown to be capable of evaluating newer and more contemporary labour–management partnerships (Walton *et al.*, 1994). The Walton and McKersie scheme points out that negotiation consists of a number of activities rather than just one, and Fig. 10.2 gives some idea of the way in which the different activities link together. The actual interface where negotiators act on behalf of their respective constituency is classified as **inter-organisational bargaining**, and this can take place in one of two basic forms. The first is **distributive bargaining**, in which the issues are dealt with by attempting to reach agreement on how a fixed amount should be divided up, and is sometimes likened to dividing up a cake of a fixed size. The second form,

inter-organisational bargaining (negotiations)

The actual interface where negotiators negotiate on behalf of their respective constituency, which is the employing organisation for management, and employees who are union members for the trade union negotiators.

distributive bargaining (negotiations)

A zero-sum negotiation in which a gain to one side is a loss to the other party; likened to dividing up the slices of a cake.

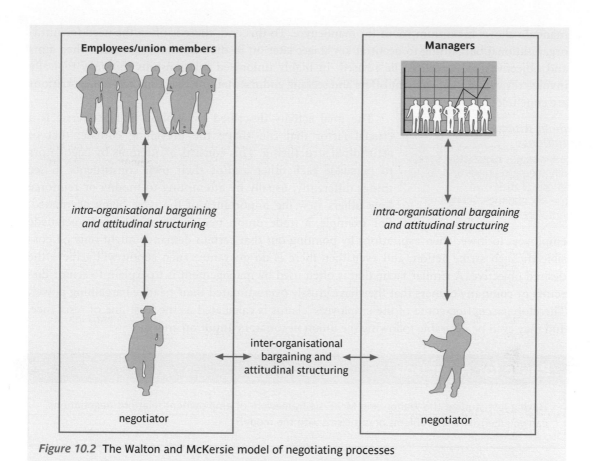

Figure 10.2 The Walton and McKersie model of negotiating processes

integrative bargaining (negotiations)

A positive-sum affair in which the parties engage in cooperative negotiation; likened to a joint effort to make the cake bigger.

mixed bargaining (negotiations)

The coexistence of both distributive and integrative bargaining activities.

intra-organisational bargaining (negotiations)

A process whereby negotiators negotiate with their own constituents in order to bring the expectations of the group they represent into line with their own expectations about what can realistically be achieved.

integrative bargaining, involves adopting a joint problem-solving approach, which is broadly a joint effort to make the cake bigger before dividing it up. In reality, negotiation often involves the coexistence of both integrative and distributive elements; a point acknowledged by Walton and McKersie when they allude to **mixed bargaining**; a style of negotiation that may have more contemporary relevance with those organisations pursuing a partnership relationship, or where negotiation occurs in some limited way through a non-union works council (Roche and Geary, 2002; Ackers *et al.*, 2005).

Another activity is **intra-organisational bargaining**. The groups that negotiators represent usually consist of sub-groups and individuals with divergent demands and objectives. Of particular significance is that employees are often far more optimistic than the negotiator about what can realistically be achieved (Rackham and Carlisle, 1978). Thus, before negotiators ever face each other across the bargaining table, they usually have to negotiate with their own constituents to try to bring the expectations of the group into line with their own assessment of what may be achievable. This can be a vitally important activity (Lewicki *et al.*, 2004). An effective negotiator will always try to ensure that his or her formal mandate allows maximum room for manoeuvre. To this end, there is often the need for intra-organisational bargaining to occur at key stages later on in the negotiating process, when aims and objectives may need to be revised. In highly unionised relationships this may typically involve reviewing management offers and seeking endorsement or rejection before negotiations are concluded.

attitudinal structuring (negotiations)

A process whereby negotiators seek to modify the perceptions and expectations of their own constituency, and those of the opponent negotiator.

The final activity described by Walton and McKersie is a crucial factor that can shape the prevailing climate: that of **attitudinal structuring**. This consists of attempts by negotiators to persuade each other and/or their own constituents to see things differently, usually by attempting to modify or reinforce how others view the importance of the issue being negotiated. For example, a trade union negotiator might try to persuade employees to lower their aspirations by pointing out that certain demands might only be possible through strike action, and even then there is no guarantee such action will achieve the desired objective. A similar tactic that is often used by management is to explain to senior directors or company owners that they have grossly overestimated their relative bargaining power. Therefore, accepting some of the employees' claims is calculated as the least line of resistance, and may even be desirable following the union negotiators' input on an issue.

Pause for reflection

Having just studied the Walton and McKersie framework of employment relations negotiations, can you identify any problems or criticisms with the model?

It must be noted however, that the Walton and McKersie scheme is not without its critics. Martin (1992), for example, criticises the overall model for being somewhat rigid in the way that it classifies different negotiation processes, while Burchill (1999) suggests that in industrial relations all negotiation is essentially distributive, and integrative bargaining can be viewed as a bargaining tactic to achieve what are essentially distributive objectives. The implication of this is that even within more cooperative or partnership relationships, negotiation is seldom concerned with anything other than dividing up a cake of a fixed size. Notwithstanding these points, because the aims and behaviours associated with integrative and distributive bargaining tend to influence the prevailing employment relations climate, the distinctions between them and the overall framework is still a useful one. Indeed, as Burchill (1999: 166) concludes:

> Unusually Walton and McKersie produce an inter-disciplinary text, with the disciplines woven into each part of the book and each used with considerable aplomb. There is nothing in the field which achieves such an approach with such assurance, and this is one of the main factors that has preserved its value and status. It is a unique piece of work.

In addition to its theoretical rigour, the Walton and McKersie framework also fits neatly with the reality of negotiation as a multi-stage process, and this will be described next.

Summary points

- Perhaps the most extensive framework that describes negotiating behaviour is that given by Walton and McKersie (1965).

- The model explains that negotiation is not a single process, but a series of related activities.

- These activities all interact with one another and influence the internal dynamics and behavioural outcomes of negotiations. The activities are:
  - inter-organisational bargaining, which can take the form of both integrative and distributive bargaining
  - where both integrative and distributive bargaining takes place, this is a sign of mixed bargaining
  - intra-organisational bargaining: an activity involving the principal negotiator and his or her constituent group
  - attitudinal restructuring: a process that seeks to modify the perceptions and expectations of a negotiators' own constituency, and those of the opponent.

- Critics of the Walton and McKersie scheme suggest that the model can be too rigid in the way that it classifies different negotiation processes.

Case study 10.2: Hillside District Council

Hillside District Council serves an expanding rural and urban area. The council is an extremely progressive one, which has expanded its activities and has been highly innovative in developing new services to the community. Although the council has reduced the size of its workforce because of various government initiatives such as compulsory competitive tendering and outsourcing, the council is now faced with further government plans that will force it to shed a number of its services. The Government's Audit Commission is to investigate Hillside's activities in the coming months, with a clearly stated objective to put as many services as possible out to private tender where it decides that these could be performed more cheaply.

Both the council and trade unions (UNISON, GMB and TGWU) believe they have already made significant savings from the previous outsourcing arrangements, although the Chief Executive is concerned the Audit Commission may produce an adverse report. To avoid this, management are seeking further reductions in the council's direct labour force. The plan proposes to reduce the Community Services department by 30 members of staff, and the Leisure Services department by about 50. If the council could avoid an adverse report, other departments would probably be allowed to remain unaltered.

The ruling political group on the council can be characterised as 'New Labour', and think of themselves as supportive of worker rights with a strong conviction in flexibility to meet changing demands and service provisions. They are very proud of the range of services provided by the council, and above all, have an ideological conviction that 'public–private partnerships' best serve the needs of the local community in terms of service provision and value for money.

The trade unions have also estimated that the same departments would be most at risk, and if the worst were to happen, this would pose problems for some members. Those most likely to be affected are specialists in their own fields, and are fairly well paid. Similar outsourcing activities among other local authorities would make it hard for them to find new jobs, and they would most

▶

certainly have to look to the private sector where pay and conditions are often inferior. Some would probably be prepared to go on enhanced early retirement, and a collective agreement which provides a scheme to give up to ten years' pensionable service exists. However, in the event of drastic cuts, the numbers opting for early retirement would be unlikely to be sufficient to meet the cutback levels expected. Accordingly, the membership can be expected to call for a strong resistance to any proposed cuts.

The distribution of the council and the result of its previous outsourcing are given in Table 10.1 below.

Department	Service provided	Staffing		
		Council staff	Outsourced/ agency staff	Agreed complement to provide effective service
Chief Executive	*Human resources* *Legal services* *Internal training*	66	17	87
Community Services	*Learning and skills training for employment*	35	6	60*
Finance and Administration	*Accounts*	119	0	135*
Housing	*Building maintenance*	35	112	147
Leisure and Community Services	*Parks, recreation centres, social services*	74	32	102
Operational Services	*Refuse collection, street cleaning, etc.*	2	64	66
Planning and Environmental Services	*Urban and rural planning, architects*	80	6	112*

Note
* Recruitment difficulties due to national shortage of qualified personnel.

Table 10.1 Hillside District Council

Questions

1 What do you feel will be the objectives of council and trade unions in this matter?

2 What type of negotiation between the employer and trade unions is likely to take place?

3 Can you identify an integrative solution to the difficulty? What is it, and how could it be proposed?

The practice of negotiation

Perhaps the easiest way to consider the practical aspects of negotiation is to view it as a process with three main stages: *preparation*, the *face-to-face negotiation*, and *post-negotiating activities*. In each of these however, there are usually a number of phases. To simplify matters a number of assumptions will be made in the following description of the stages. First, as is normal in employment relations, it is assumed that employees and management are each represented by a team of negotiators. The management side would probably consist of line managers and a human resource specialist, and the employees' team would be made up of representatives of the groups most affected by the issue. Second, each side has a spokesperson, who is referred to here as 'the negotiator'.

Stage 1 – Preparation for negotiation

Preparation is seldom something that can be done quickly, and to assemble the information to put forward a convincing case takes time. However, until the party raising the issue puts forward its claim or an opening proposal, the preparatory activities of the other side are limited. If a trade union presents a wage claim, there will be little negotiation at the first meeting. Management would probably hear the claim, ask questions to obtain clarification, and then the meeting would be adjourned. The adjournment might be for several weeks, in which time management would undertake its own detailed preparation. If management were the pro-active party, say in presenting a proposal for an extensive revision of working practices or a major reorganisation, then the trade union would listen and retire to commence preparation.

Clearly negotiators on both sides have to prepare their own case. They also have to be able to defend it, and if necessary launch a counter-attack if and when the opposition tries to undermine it (Lewicki *et al.*, 2004). Clearly, this means that a great deal of consideration has to be given to the opponent's likely position. However, it is just as essential for a negotiator to know the objectives, constraints and limits of manoeuvre imposed by her or his side. To this end, and before the first formal negotiating meeting, negotiators will probably take part in some initial skirmishing, both with those that they represent, and with the opposing side's negotiator.

Skirmishing with the opposing side often takes the form of preliminary meetings to set an agenda for formal negotiations. As well as settling procedural details, this initial skirmishing inevitably includes attempts to structure attitudes. Where negotiators have dealt with each other for a long time, these initial meetings often include an element of tacit negotiation, where negotiators communicate to each other about what they see as achievable and what is not.

In parallel with this, negotiators will also meet with their own side to prepare the case, and inevitably information gained in meetings with their opposite number will spill over into what takes place. In order to avoid being saddled with aims where only a fight will win the day, a negotiator is likely to bargain with her or his side to attempt to reshape their attitudes and aspirations. This shaping of aims is a fundamental part of working out bargaining positions and objectives. Often there will be multiple objectives, some of which are more important than others. A negotiator will try to get them ranked in order of importance to give some idea of the issues which can be conceded in the interests of reaching agreement (Kennedy, 1998). A crucial part of formulating these objectives is to establish the bargaining range for each one, and this involves estimating the likely bargaining range for the other side as well. The importance of the bargaining range can be explained with the simple diagram shown in Fig. 10.3 below.

bargaining range (negotiation)
A negotiating range for each party, depicting their lowest and highest points leading to a negotiated agreement.

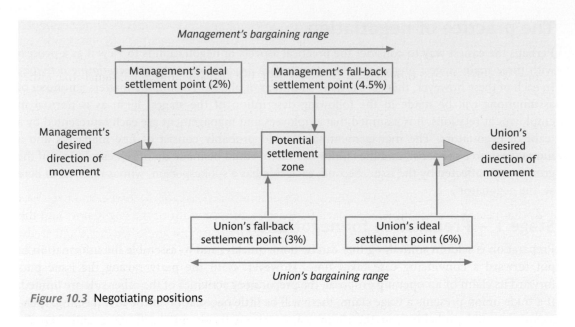

Figure 10.3 Negotiating positions

For every one of its bargaining objectives, each side will need to know what is its **ideal settlement**, and also the **fall-back point** below which an agreement would be considered unac-

___

ideal settlement (negotiation)
An ideal negotiating outcome on a particular issue for each party.

fall-back point (negotiation)
A negotiated minimum, below which agreement would be unacceptable for each of the parties.

potential zone of settlement (negotiation)
The potential for a negotiated settlement, without recourse to industrial action, within the range of each party's minimum fall-back position.

___

ceptable. For example, in Fig. 10.3, assume that a trade union has lodged a claim for a 6 per cent across-the-board pay increase. This is its ideal settlement point, but it has a fall-back position of 3 per cent, which is the minimum its members will accept: that is, they would be prepared to take industrial action to improve an offer of below 3 per cent. Thus, its bargaining range is somewhere between 3 and 6 per cent. Management would ideally like to settle for 2 per cent, but to avoid disruption, and if pressed hard enough, they would be prepared to go up to 4.5 per cent but no further: therefore, its bargaining range is somewhere between 2 and 4.5 per cent. The **potential zone of settlement** achievable by negotiation, and without recourse to industrial action, is somewhere between 3 and 4.5 per cent.

In reality, negotiation is more complicated than the above. For example, in addition to the union's ideal settlement of 6 per cent there could be additional items as part of the claim, such as increased holiday entitlement, a shorter working week or subsidies for child-minding. Indeed, management may be more willing to concede some of the other items, say holiday entitlements, than a higher percentage pay rise. On other issues man-

___

multiple bargaining objectives (negotiation)
The existence of a number of different negotiating issues, each with their own separate bargaining ranges and fall-back positions.

___

agement may not be prepared to concede at all. Thus, **multiple bargaining objectives** mean there are overlapping and separate bargaining ranges and fall-back positions, depending on the importance of particular issues to each side. For these reasons, effective negotiators are those who tend to build an element of flexibility into their strategy, and try to avoid having objectives which are so rigid that they are incapable of modification.

Preparation will also involve establishing a clear system of roles within each team, and this can be vital for ensuring there is a unified front. Usually the chief negotiator will already have been decided, and vital though this is, there are other important roles as well. If, for example, some things can be left to other team members, it enables the chief negotiator to concentrate on interacting with the other side. For this reason, it can be important to have someone who records what is said; not only its substantive content, but also any non-verbal signals that either reinforce or contradict a certain message. In complex negotiations, where several different groups could be affected by the outcome, it can also be vital to have members of the team who keep an eye open for the way in which developments can affect each group.

Stage 2 – Face-to-face negotiation

The second, face-to-face stage, often takes place in different phases. How long each phase lasts and what takes place within it, can depend crucially upon the skills of the negotiators and the issues under consideration. The required skills are multiple. At one level there are single skills, such as listening and communicating. At another level there are more complex composite skills that involve analytical judgements and knowing when best to press home a point (Cairns, 1996).

opening moves (negotiation)
The first phase of face-to-face negotiations, in which the proposing side will present its claim and supporting arguments.

The first phase tends to be one of **opening moves**. The proposing side will normally present its case, together with supporting arguments. If it is complex, and it often is, an adjournment is sometimes necessary to allow the receiving side the opportunity to study what has been proposed. This phase can be very formal, with each side attempting to convince the other of the justice of their case. In these opening moves, it can be very important that neither side conveys a 'take it or leave it' attitude (Fisher and Ury, 1991).

developing the case (negotiation)
The second phase of face-to-face negotiations, in which both sides argue the strength of their own case, and seek to reduce the validity of their opponent's arguments.

When the receiving side presents its response, negotiations are likely to move into the second phase: that of **developing the case**. Negotiators will attempt to argue the strength of their own proposals, and to reduce the validity of the opposing argument. It is a phase of thrust and parry, and argument and counter-argument. Negotiators will often try to reconnoitre the opponent's position and undermine it, and at the same time make their own case more legitimate. It is also the one in which the more subtle tactics of bargaining are most likely to be used. For example, experienced negotiators will use distributive bargaining tactics while simultaneously alluding to common integrative issues. In this way the negotiation process avoids being dominated by distributive bargaining alone, which can become counterproductive as the parties start to focus on their differences and miss the opportunity to identify what they have in common (Lewicki *et al.*, 2004). Thus, while negative tactics are useful in that they can divide the opposition or be used to intimidate them with lightly veiled threats, positive tactics are also likely to be used – for example, offering an olive branch to the other side in return for some concession. In a strange way, even hostile behaviour can actually have a positive purpose when looking at the negotiation process in its entirety.

Because new information is appearing fairly rapidly, in this phase it is quite likely that each side will occasionally wish to adjourn, in order to reconsider its position. During this phase it is common for negotiators to meet informally for off-the-record conversations – a process sometimes referred to in less complimentary terms as corridor bargaining. Overall, the phase is one of progressive refinement, in which those areas where agreement has been reached are put out of the way, to focus on those which will prove to be the crux of the final settlement.

seeking agreement (negotiation)
The third phase of face-to-face negotiations, in which one of the parties makes public definite and concrete proposals for agreement.

The third phase is that of formally **seeking agreement**. The previous phase was one where in public there was a high degree of polarisation, but in private a search for points of convergence tends to take place. This one, however, often contains more public signs that the parties are moving towards agreement, which sends messages to each constituent group who will be affected by the eventual outcome. Its opening can often be detected by one of the parties making concrete proposals for a settlement. In addition, the process tends to become more formal again, and negotiators step back more firmly into their representative roles.

concluding negotiations
The fourth and final phase of face-to-face negotiations, which is defined as the process of agreeing to what has been agreed.

The final phase is that of **concluding negotiations** to clarify what has been agreed. This phase can be quite tricky and is concerned with 'agreeing to what has been agreed' to avoid misunderstanding. The attitudinal structuring activities in the Walton and McKersie scheme may feature during this phase. It sometimes opens by one side offering in public what they have already agreed in private; perhaps by presenting it as a new concession, and asking for something in return that has also been conceded privately. On other occasions the phase will simply consist of a summary of what has been agreed in previous meetings. If and when the terms are formally accepted, it then remains to detail every point, and check that it is understood. This can be vital for two reasons. First, it is a public demonstration that an agreement has been reached, and that both sides have a common view about its terms. Second, in the relief of having come to the end of what can often be a stressful process, there is always a tendency for exhaustion to take over, and for details to be overlooked. Thus, a detailed review of everything can help reduce the possibility of future misunderstandings.

Before giving a description of the last stage it is important to make a final point about this one. Thus far negotiation has been portrayed as a process which leads to a negotiated agreement. But this is not always the case. For example, employees can take industrial action, and employers can withdraw from negotiations or impose change unilaterally. While it is important to note that this can happen, these matters are covered in the next chapter about conflict and protest behaviours, and so details are deferred until then.

failure to agree (negotiation)
A situation where both parties agree there is little likelihood of further concession or compromise, and agree to withdraw from the negotiating process to either seek third-party conciliation or engage in industrial action.

Perhaps the more interesting situation is where no agreement is reached, and the parties record a **failure to agree**. In essence this means that the negotiators recognise that there is little likelihood of further concession or compromise on either side, and mutually agree to withdraw from the process. What happens from then on, however, can depend a great deal on whether negotiating procedures allow for this contingency. The outcomes may vary from industrial action to the use of third-party intervention and/or arbitration, such as those services offered by ACAS. Suffice it to say that, if the parties have had the good sense to realise that an impasse has been reached, seeking help of an outside third party is not a sign of either incompetence or weakness. Indeed, because it can tend to take the heat out of matters, and can do much to safeguard the longer-term bargaining relationship, it is probably more a sign of wisdom than anything else. Otherwise one of the parties may resort to pressure tactics, and this can have repercussions on both future bargaining and the general employment relations climate, including the social and psychological exchange experienced by employees. Perhaps the most important point to make is that, if a withdrawal is necessary, both sides should agree the position they have already reached, and preferably set down in writing the remaining areas of disagreement. This way the task of conciliators, arbitrators or even higher-level negotiators is made much clearer.

Pause for reflection

Assume you have been involved in a process of negotiation that has now reached the concluding phase. Why do you think a third post-negotiation stage is still important?

Stage 3 – Post negotiation

When a satisfactory agreement has been reached there is a natural tendency to regard matters as having ended. However, no agreement in the world can deal with every possible contingency, and there is always the likelihood that minor points of detail will need to be sorted out. Sometimes these are not identified for days, or even weeks after agreement has been reached, and they are frequently left to the principal negotiators, or individual managers and shop stewards to resolve on an ad hoc basis. Indeed, there can be as much effort devoted to this tidying-up work as there was to reaching the agreement. It is not, however, a matter which can be neglected. Unless these issues are brought to light and resolved, the two sides have not achieved the clear understanding that they perhaps assume they have reached. Moreover, until these things are finally cleared up, it cannot really be said that the new agreement has been fully implemented.

Summary points

- The practice of negotiation is extremely complex and requires considerable skill and experience on the part of the principal negotiators.
- There are typically three stages: preparation, face-to-face negotiation, and post-negotiating activities.
- In addition, within each stage there are often a number of crucial phases that can affect the eventual outcome of a negotiated settlement.

Conclusions

This chapter has explained and reviewed a whole series of activities concerned with negotiation in employment relations. The topic of negotiation has a logical link to collective bargaining in the previous chapter, and in many ways it is connected to the topic of conflict and protest behaviour, which are considered in the chapter that follows. Moreover, employment relations negotiation is essentially a process of exchange between employees and management, where each side seeks to modify the expectations and perceptions of the other in order to facilitate a reconciliation of differences, at least in the short term. While the bulk of material concerning labour–management negotiations finds its strongest application in unionised relationships, informal bargaining and individual negotiation can and do occur in non-union settings; although, given the absence of an independent collective employee association, the balance of power in such situations is heavily skewed in management's favour. Crucially, and unlike negotiations in the wider business or commercial world, in employment relations the process of negotiation is an expression of conflict: that is, both employees and managers have different and at times directly conflicting aims, and they enter into negotiations knowing that the other side has the potential to inflict harm. As will be explained in the next chapter, in non-union organisations, given a lack of effective and formal negotiating structures, employees sometimes develop innovative and covert tactics to try and press home their point.

❓ Review and discussion questions

1 Why is negotiation in employment relations considered to be different from the process of negotiation in other commercial or business settings?

2 Briefly explain why the contexts surrounding negotiations can influence their outcome.

3 What is meant by the terms *inter*-organisational bargaining, and *intra*-organisational bargaining?

4 Explain why the activity of *attitudinal structuring* is considered important to negotiators.

5 Identify at least two criticisms of the Walton and McKersie framework for labour negotiations. Do you think these criticisms are valid?

6 The process of 'skirmishing' is considered extremely important in the initial stages of negotiation. Why?

7 Describe the phases associated with effective face-to-face negotiations.

8 Do you think post-negotiating activities are important? Why?

Further reading

Burchill, F. (1999) 'Review Essay: Walton and McKersie, a behavioural theory of labor negotiation', *Historical Studies in Industrial Relations*, Vol. 8, Autumn, pp. 137–168. A thoughtful and engaging debate that gives a critique of Walton and McKersie's book on labour negotiations.

Cairns, L. (1996) *Negotiation Skills in the Workplace: A Practical Handbook*, Pluto Press, London. Written from a trade unionist perspective, this book provides practical tips and skills for negotiators.

Fisher, R. and W. Ury (1991) *Getting to Yes: Negotiating an Agreement Without Giving In*, 2nd edn, Penguin, London. Although something of a 'how to do it' flavour is reflected in the book, it gives a very readable explanation of the principles which can be followed to try to develop negotiating skills.

Lewicki, R.J., D.M. Saunders, B. Barry and J.W. Minton (2004) *The Essentials of Negotiation*, 3rd edn, McGraw Hill, New York. An enjoyable read that explains in clear terms the psychology of negotiation and interpersonal conflict resolution. It also includes useful summaries and explanatory notes for students.

Walton, R.E. and R.B. McKersie (1965) *A Behavioural Theory of Labour Negotiations*, McGraw Hill, New York. A seminal work which gives a systematic examination of the strategies and tactics of negotiation. A book that is worth studying in its own right.

Walton, R.E, J.E. Cuther-Gershenfeld and R.B. McKersie (1994) *Strategic Negotiations: A Theory of Change in Labor–Management Relations*, Harvard Business School Press, Boston, Mass. A review of more contemporary developments in labour–management relations in the US, arguing that models of negotiation provide a strong theoretical lens with which to evaluate organisational changes and foster cooperative attitudes among organisational stakeholders.

Chapter **11**

Conflict and protest in employment relations

LEARNING OUTCOMES

After studying this chapter you should be able to:

☑ **explain** the nature of employment relations conflict

☑ **distinguish** between the different forms of conflict and protest, including strikes and non-strike action

☑ **describe** strike trends in Great Britain across the past four decades

☑ **describe** the process and causation of conflict and protest

☑ **explain** ways in which the law constrains the capabilities of the parties in employment relations to take conflict and protest action.

Introduction

As was explained in the previous two chapters, where an organisation has a mature negotiating or consultative process, it will usually be capable of resolving differences between managers and employees. However, there are occasions when agreement cannot be reached, and in an attempt to break the stalemate, one of the parties might take more visible action against the other. This is not inevitable, and seldom is it an end in itself, but rather a means to an end. Indeed, there are times when industrial action, or perhaps just the threat of it, seems to be a necessary prelude to finding a basis for agreement.

Conflict and protest in employment relations is an emotive and complex phenomenon, which is often misunderstood, if only because a minor episode of action can be exaggerated in importance by the media. Therefore, in order to place employment relations conflict within a wider context, the chapter commences with a brief examination of the conflict in organisations. Attention then turns to the subject of industrial action in Great Britain, and a number of essential definitions are given. The different forms of industrial action are then described, together with an explanation of the circumstances that constrain the use of each one. To illustrate some of the characteristic patterns of industrial action in Britain, strike trends are examined across the past four decades, and some of the factors that are said to prompt the use of strikes are examined. The focus then moves to the conduct of industrial action, and a model that explains some of the factors that can influence the decision to take action and the way it is conducted is explored. Finally, the chapter concludes with a short description of the legal implications of using industrial action.

Conflict: theories and perspectives

The coexistence of conflict and cooperation between an organisation and its employees is a constant feature of the employment relationship. Nevertheless, in some eyes conflict is considered to be unwarranted, and outside the bounds of reasonable behaviour (Hutt, 1973). However, it is just one of many forms of inter-group dynamics that occur in the workplace, and far from being exceptional, in one form or another it is very normal in organisations (Alderfer and Smith, 1982; Edwards, 1987). Indeed, the origins of these conflicts are virtually inbuilt in organisational life, in that most organisations are structured into departments and functions, with their own performance goals. Although these functions are interdependent, to achieve their goals they usually have to compete to obtain the necessary resources; a feature that on its own gives some potential for conflict. In addition to this, individuals and workgroups often pursue their own ends, and in so doing, use a range of political tactics to protect or advance their own interests (Pfeffer, 1992). The net result is that, while there is usually a great deal of conflict in organisations, most of it goes on beneath the surface.

However, because employment relations is often a highly visible activity, conflicts that do occur are almost impossible to conceal, and tend to assume a significance out of all proportion to their place in the wider scheme of things. Moreover, the view that employment relations conflict is unnatural is still the dominant one in organisations, and one reason for this could be the effect of other social processes and institutions in shaping attitudes. For instance, many of the important institutions in our society – the home, the church, etc. – are founded on the premise that harmony is the natural state of affairs in the world, and this has a powerful effect on the way conflict is regarded. Another and perhaps more influential reason is the prevalence of a unitarist ideology, which draws heavily on classical theories of management, such as those of Fayol (1949) and Urwick (1943). Together with more contemporary interpretations of people management and organisational performance (Pfeffer, 1998), these theories portray a well-managed organisation as one that has unity in goals and purposes, with all activities dovetailing into a master plan for goal achievement. The process of management is seen as an activity that makes things more predictable, with the energy of people being directed towards improved organisational effectiveness. An important implication of this view is that conflict absorbs energy, which could be more productively used for other ends. Accordingly, it is considered dysfunctional in any

dysfunctional conflict

Forms of conflict and protest behaviour that exist, but are associated with imperfect organisational functioning.

form, and comes to be seen as an aberration that is not only an exception to the norm, but is associated with imperfect organisational functioning.

An alternative and more realistic view, however, is that, while organisations are created to serve a purpose, they are also composed of people who are all different. Workers are placed into groups, who develop their own identities, norms and goals, which can be very different to those of management. Thus, conflict becomes an inevitable and integral part of the functioning of an organisation; it cannot be outlawed or eradicated, but is more appropriately handled by channelling it into non-destructive forms. In this way conflict can be highly **functional**, and serve positive outcomes. For example, it brings a diversity of opinions to the surface, and from this can flow a more creative range of solutions to problems.

functional conflict

Forms of conflict and protest behaviour that can be positive, allowing a diversity of opinions and solutions to problems to emerge.

Pause for reflection

Working with one of your colleagues, and drawing on your reading of material contained in Chapter 10, to what extent do you feel that when a trade union takes industrial action, this can legitimately be viewed as the negotiating process pursued in an alternative way?

Employment relations conflicts are probably the most disparaged of all forms of protest behaviour, and there are basically three reasons for this. First, they are vertical conflicts, and thus challenge the most fundamental building block of an organisation – the power in decision-making authority that is enshrined in its hierarchy. Conflicts of this type are a signal to a manager that the people over whom he or she has formal authority no longer accept this authority as legitimate. In a society that is nominally a meritocracy, where there is an assumption that those who rise to positions of authority are the best fitted to do so, this can be a powerful blow to a manager's self-esteem.

Second, political conflicts between groups or departments are mostly pursued beneath the surface in a way that makes them invisible to those not actually involved. However, in vertical conflicts those lower down in the hierarchy mobilise power to challenge those above, and this means that conflict often has to be pursued in a collective and highly visible way.

Third, there is a general misreading of the aims and purposes of industrial action, together with a widely held view that these episodes of conflict are highly irrational, prompted by 'troublemakers', and made worse because all conflicts should be capable of being solved by negotiation and compromise (Hanson and Mather, 1988). However, there is a huge flaw in this view. Although negotiation and consultation are able to resolve differences between the parties, they are both processes underpinned by power, and the motive to engage in them is that the opposing party can offer a less palatable alternative; it can inflict harm. Indeed, it has long been recognised that a prior reputation for militancy can sometimes have a highly positive effect in negotiations, in that a reputation for having used strikes successfully in the past can prompt employers to offer a more generous settlement (Cohn, 1993). Whether we like it or not, therefore, the collective bargaining relationship is a political one, which means that negotiation is likely to be a highly political process. For this reason industrial action occupies a similar role to the one occupied by the activity of war in the political processes used by nation-states to try to resolve their differences. War is seldom an end in itself, but a means to an end and a recognition that, at the present stage in the political process, the argument of force is likely to prove more persuasive than the force of argument. It is simply the pursuit of political ends by another means (Von Clauswitz, 1986) and, like war, industrial action is only ever intended to be a temporary state of affairs to achieve the end of bringing the other party back to the negotiating table in a more receptive frame of mind. Its use is seldom underpinned by a desire to apply pressure for its own sake, but rather to achieve the above end, and it is for this reason that the political process of dialogue and negotiation often continues while the battle is in progress (although it might well take place through an intermediary, such as ACAS, for example).

Employment relations conflict in Great Britain
Distinctions and definitions

Since conflict in employment relations can take many different forms, it is useful to start with a broad definition. The one adopted here is:

> the total range of behaviour and attitudes that express opposition and divergent orientations between owners and managers on one hand, and working people and their organisations on the other.
>
> (Kornhauser, 1954: 13)

Three important points are made in this definition, which the reader is asked to keep in mind:

1 Conflict in employment relations can manifest itself in a wide variety of ways.

2 The definition draws attention to the idea that an episode of conflict has its roots in a lack of agreement between owners and/or managers and employees.

3 By implication, this involves one party opposing the will of the other.

With these points in mind, and as a first step in exploring industrial action further, it is important to understand that the circumstances in which industrial action is initiated can have a significant effect on its perceived legitimacy, and this is considered next.

The status of industrial action

An important factor influencing the perceived legitimacy of action is whether it is constitutional or unconstitutional. **Constitutional action** is normally accepted as a legitimate part of the bargaining relationship, which means, for example, that it would only be used when all stages of a disputes procedure have been exhausted. Conversely, **unconstitutional action** might be used when negotiations are still taking place; something that can often have disastrous effects on the bargaining relationship itself. However, although this distinction is clear in theory, it is not always so clear in practice. For example, if either party has effectively stopped negotiating in good faith, but is using **stonewalling** tactics, it cannot truthfully be said that negotiation is still in progress. It is for this reason that Roy (1980) points out that the concept of 'bargaining in good faith' is a very slippery concept to pin down.

constitutional action
That which is initiated when all stages of a disputes procedure have been exhausted.

unconstitutional action
That which is initiated when negotiation is nominally still in progress.

stonewalling
Time wasting, or delaying tactics used to obstruct discussion.

official action

That which receives official trade union support or authorisation; normally after employees have been balloted beforehand, and indicated their willingness to support the action.

unofficial action

That which is initiated directly by employees without official trade union authorisation; sometimes as a spontaneous show of dissatisfaction, and sometimes as a revolt against the negotiating stance adopted by either of the two sides.

Another important distinction affecting the status of action is whether it is official or unofficial. Official action is that which has officially received trade union support, and these days it only happens if employees have been balloted beforehand. Unofficial action, however, is more commonly initiated by employees directly – sometimes as a spontaneous show of dissatisfaction with the bargaining situation, and sometimes as a revolt against a trade union's negotiating stance – and once again reality can be more complex. As noted above, industrial action is a political activity, used to exert pressure. It is not unknown for a trade union to secretly condone unofficial action, but for a number of reasons connected with the politics of negotiating, it will not want to be seen to give official or public endorsement. Thus, while unofficial action is officially unconstitutional, the underlying motives and reality can be quite complex in the real world.

The final distinction affecting the status of action is whether it is organised or unorganised. These days, both types of action are increasingly regarded as manifestations of employee dis-

organised action

A conscious attempt to bring about a change in the situation that has become a source of discontent; normally organised by an employee collective organisation, such as a trade union.

unorganised action

An individual reaction to having become discontented, which can take many forms that vary between absenteeism and sabotage.

content, but there is a huge difference between the forms they can take. In theory, organised action is a conscious attempt to bring about a change in the situation that has become a source of discontent (Hyman, 1989). Although this could occur by a spontaneous show of unofficial action, it normally involves using the offices of an employee collective organisation, such as a trade union, to organise matters. Conversely, the expression unorganised action has historically been used to describe a situation where an individual or group of individuals takes matters into their own hands, as a reaction to becoming discontented. In terms of the actions of individuals, it can take many forms that vary between absenteeism and sabotage. However, any explanation of unorganised conflict can be more complex, because the action is not always an attempt to change the situation, but can be more an attempt to find psychological escape from it: a reaction of 'flight' rather than 'fight'. There is also the added issue, which will be addressed later, that episodes of so-called 'unorganised' action can sometimes have a strong element of organisation.

Forms of industrial action

Management and employees (or their unions) both have ways of exerting pressure on each other, but with actions taken by management, the names used to describe them largely explain the nature of the action; the most obvious being the *lock-out*, which is management's direct equivalent to the strike. A milder step which management can take is in negotiations, where it can unilaterally impose a change, and threaten dismissal if employees do not comply. However, with action used by employees, there is such a wide variety of steps that can be taken that there can sometimes be confusion about the meanings of the terms used. Thus some clarification is required.

Case study 11.1: **Classifying the status of industrial action**

Classify the status of the following actions:

1 Negotiations have reached a deadlock, and as per the disputes procedure both trade union and management have agreed that the issue will be referred to external arbitration. Before this takes place the trade union ballots its members for strike action, and there is an overwhelming 'yes' vote. At this, management calls a special meeting of the negotiating committee and agrees to meet the trade union's claim.

2 In a company which uses assembly-line methods to manufacture high-tech components, union representatives protest to management about a speeding-up of the production line. Management admits that it has increased the speed of the line but states that this is unavoidable due to a backlog of orders, and refuses to reduce the speed back to its former setting. The matter is reported by the union convenor, who then meets with the Human Resource Manager and formally registers a dispute about the new speed of the line. She obtains an assurance of a return to the *status quo* pending the outcome of negotiations on the matter. Some days later the speed of the line has not been reduced, and the workers hold an impromptu meeting in their lunch break. A voice from the body of the meeting proposes that instead of returning to work they all walk out. This is put to the vote, carried, and the factory is idle from then on.

3 At the request of the members affected, the trade union, in protest at the downgrading of jobs in a reorganisation, boycotts new job posts. It places advertisements in newspapers telling its own members and the public what has happened. The advertisement advises people that existing staff should neither apply for nor occupy these posts, and that potential newcomers should do likewise.

4 Clerical workers employed by an airline refuse to do additional work, which involves handling cargo. This is work normally done by baggage handlers.

Organised forms of action

strike
A complete withdrawal of labour.

A **strike** is a complete withdrawal of labour, defined by Hyman (1989) as a temporary stoppage of work by a group to express a grievance, or to enforce a demand. Note that the stoppage is temporary – there is an intention to eventually return to work; and the action is collective in nature. Having said this, strikes can vary widely between an *indefinite strike*, which, in the case of the 1984 miners dispute, was effectively a *trial of strength*; and *demonstration stoppages*, in which labour is withdrawn for a short period to 'prove a point'. *Strategic stoppages* can involve small groups of key workers, whose absence has a serious and immediate impact on the running of the organisation, and in such situations those still at work can voluntarily make up the pay of those on strike. However, key workers are usually wary of being used to fight the battles of others, and in any event, management is seldom blind to the potential for their tactical use in this way. Thus, they are often highly rewarded to try to ensure a lack of militancy (Purcell *et al.*, 1978).

withdrawal of cooperation
Employees work strictly to formal operational procedures, refusing any flexibility or cooperation.

Withdrawal of cooperation occurs when employees work strictly to formal operational procedures, and refuse any flexibility or cooperation in the myriad day-to-day adjustments that are usually necessary to keep an organisation ticking over. The usefulness of this sanction usually depends upon the extent to which cooperative relationships have become normal and of value to management, and in some situations the loss of cooperation is highly disruptive (Batstone *et al.*, 1979). For example, professional groups such as teachers or healthcare professionals, whose work often involves a great deal of day-to-day adjustment, have successfully used this tactic (Edwards, 1983). Conversely where the work of employees has little discretionary content, the tactic has far less impact (Edwards and Scullion, 1982).

working to rule or to contract
A very strict refusal to step outside the duties laid down in job specifications, often accompanied by an insistence that management and supervision give clearly defined instructions on how duties shall be performed.

Working to rule or working to contract usually involves a very strict refusal to step outside the duties laid down in job specifications, and this is often accompanied by an insistence that management and supervision give clearly defined instructions on how duties shall be performed. Again the effect of this varies with the extent to which cooperation and initiative are needed by management, and its usefulness to employees is much the same as a withdrawal of cooperation.

overtime ban
A refusal to work beyond the strict contracted hours.

Overtime bans are a refusal to work beyond strict contracted hours. In some situations, usually where basic pay rates are low, employees customarily work well in excess of their basic hours on a day-to-day basis, and management can come to rely on this to meet operational requirements. For instance, in the public services such as the NHS this situation is widespread, and things can rapidly grind to a halt when an overtime ban is applied. Since the public as a whole is antagonistic to strike action (Edwards and Bain, 1988), particularly in areas such as the NHS, which is financed by public funds, the overtime ban can be used by workers to highlight their plight, but in a way that does not alienate the public. Indeed, it can sometimes actually enlist their sympathy, a case in point being its use by ambulance drivers in 1989 (Kerr and Sachdev, 1992), and during the fire fighters dispute of 2002.

go-slow
Working at lower than normal output levels, but not to the extent that a breach of contract occurs.

A **go-slow** involves working at lower than normal output levels – not, however, to the extent that a breach of contract occurs. In many manufacturing plants pay is made up of a basic element plus a bonus paid for higher levels of output, and manning levels are usually based on the assumption that employees will work at a pace that earns the bonus. A go-slow has an immediate impact on output, but without depriving the employees of all of their take-home pay.

work-in or sit-in
Employees occupy the workplace, usually as a form of protest when management proposes to close a plant or make workers redundant.

Work-ins and **sit-ins** occur when employees occupy the workplace. They are generally used as a form of protest; often when management proposes to close a plant, or make workers redundant. Interestingly they are an action that does not alienate the public unduly, and often they attract considerable sympathetic attention to the plight of employees. Moreover their impact on management is potentially very high. Being 'in control' is very high in the management value system, and there is probably no greater reminder that control has slipped away than when employees occupy a plant but are not under management's direction (Thomas, 1976).

Unorganised forms of action

Traditionally, unorganised forms of conflict have usually been viewed as individual reactions to the work situation. Thus, employees who feel the urge to give vent to their feelings in this way are limited only by their ingenuity in finding ways to hit back. Perhaps the most straightforward way is by **quitting**. A less dramatic alternative is to do something similar, but on a short-term basis, and engage in **absenteeism**. Judging by the current prevalence of so-called *absence management systems*, there is more than a suspicion in many firms that taking a day off without permission has reached epidemic proportions, although care is needed to avoid the assumption that all absence is a form of protest behaviour (Beaumont, 2005). Nevertheless, there is a considerable body of empirical evidence to show that absenteeism can be an effective way of challenging managerial plans or showing dissatisfaction (Edwards and Whitson, 1993; Edwards and Scullion, 1982). Perhaps more interesting is the idea that this form of protest can sometimes operate in a coordinated way, and is thus highly organised (see Exhibit 11.1). Therefore, taking the day off is, and will probably continue to be, one of the most favoured ways for employees who lack the collective muscle of a trade union to protest and even challenge management decisions.

Somewhat more seriously, because strictly speaking it constitutes an illegal act, is the practice of **pilfering**, or engaging in **fiddles**. Again care is needed here, because in some organisations *custom and practice* allow people to engage in activities such as helping themselves from the scrap bin. Nevertheless, people regularly oppose managerial interests by stealing, or cheating the employer in some way, and this is sometimes part of a counter-culture, in which people cover for each other to avoid detection. Where this is the case, it is questionable whether what occurs is genuinely unorganised conflict, rather than something that is organised, albeit in an unofficial way. Another significant practice is **sabotage**: a deliberate act of disruption designed to frustrate management's goals and objectives (Watson, 1995). While this is thought to be comparatively rare, it is by no means unknown, and can range from knowingly failing to pass on an urgent message, which subsequently has a dire outcome, to literally 'dropping a spanner in the works', to cause a machine breakdown.

quitting
Resignation from a position in an organisation.

absenteeism
Unauthorised absence (not to be confused with sickness absence).

pilfering and fiddles
Acts of minor theft.

sabotage
Deliberate acts of disruption designed to frustrate management's interests.

In May 1998 some 6800 individual members of the Irish police force, the *Garda Síochána*, were all absent from work, and reporting sick in support of a pay and productivity claim. About 95 per cent of all Gardai used uncertified sick leave *en masse* to stage *de facto* industrial action as away of getting around the legal bar on industrial action by members of the force. In effect, the non-union employee association, the Garda Representatives Association (GRA), had orchestrated a form of unofficial industrial action.

Exhibit 11.1 The 'Blue Flue' Epidemic
Source: adapted from Wallace *et al.*, 2004: 209; IRN, 1998.

Pause for reflection

Working with other students in your class, consider the following groups of employees and decide what type of action is likely to have the greatest tactical advantage to them.

1   Semi-skilled workers employed in a firm, which sells a mass-produced, highly perishable product in a competitive market. An example here could be bread.
2   Skilled workers in an organisation that produces custom-made products for a highly competitive market, but with very long production cycles. An example here could be aircraft manufacture.
3   Workers such as street cleaners, refuse collectors or security guards who are normally paid a very low basic rate, and often work additional hours.
4   An organisation manufactures a wide range of products and has rather erratic and unpredictable production schedules. To ensure a rapid response, maintenance craftsmen and salaried staff will, when necessary, do jobs on the production line. In addition, when maintenance workers are fully occupied, production workers will undertake minor maintenance work on their own machines.

The utility of different forms of action

Whether organised or unorganised, all the above forms of action are a suspension of normality, the impact of which is highly dependent upon the circumstances. Although a strike is very visible, it can sometimes result in far less pressure on management than other forms. In seasonal industries for example, where there are periods of overproduction and stockpiling, a strike might actually save management unwanted labour costs, whereas a work-to-rule would not. However, from a trade union point of view, while it is more difficult to obtain membership consent to a strike, when it is obtained, strike action can be much easier to control than other forms. There are few trade union members who would want to be seen to cross a picket line, particularly where a large majority voted 'yes' for the action. Moreover, picketing is comparatively economical in resources. Action short of a strike, however, is notoriously hard to sustain. Employees are at work, and they are susceptible to individual pressure from managers. Nevertheless, sustaining strike action also has its problems. Strikes are not popular with trade union members, and involve them in significant financial loss. Indeed, they might only take part because they assume that the action will be short lived (Gennard, 1981 and 1982). It is perhaps for this reason that there is an increasing tendency for strikes to be of the short, 'demonstration stoppage' variety. This raises the intriguing question of whether the different forms of action can be used in an exchangeable way, to which two theoretical answers have been suggested.

The first of these is *substitution theory*. Here Knowles (1962) suggests that workers have a reservoir of protest energy, and that the form of protest selected will depend primarily on a group's capability to mobilise for collective action. This suggests that strongly organised groups will use strikes; those who are less well organised will use action short of strike; and in the case of workers who are not organised at all, individual acts of unorganised conflict such as absenteeism will be more common. The competing *additive theory* (Bean, 1975) reasons that the different forms of action are complementary, and that groups with a tendency to use one type will show a predisposition to use others as well.

While there is no strong evidence to rule out either theory, one study has identified a weak correlation between the use of minor stoppages and other forms of action (Kelly and Nicholson, 1980a), which suggests a weak level of support for additive theory. In addition, there is work that shows that certain plants tend to use identifiable combinations of the different types of action (Brown, 1981; Edwards, 1983; Darlington, 2002). In these situations it is not unknown for a type of action to remain fairly constant, often with an embedded level of militancy among certain groups, such as fire fighters. On balance, therefore, the additive theory seems much more likely, although a lot depends on the particular industry and occupational group.

Notwithstanding these debates, there are seldom any hard-and-fast rules about industrial action. Each conflict episode has its own contextual circumstances, and it can be extremely hazardous to predict what will happen. For example, militant workgroups have been known to accept radical changes on management's terms, while less-organised workers sometimes adopt the hardest stance in negotiation. Thus, the complexity and detailed nuances associated with the decision to take action are something that is probably only fully understood by those involved. For that matter, even those involved might not fully understand it themselves, but embark on a course of action feeling that they have no other alternative when faced with an entrenched management position.

Summary points

- While the existence of employment relations conflict is real and important, care is needed as its magnitude is often overstated by the media.

- Conflict and protest behaviours are complex political activities and as such, can be an extension of (rather than a replacement for) the negotiating process.

- To define the nature and status of conflict, it is necessary to be precise in defining the conditions in which it occurs.

- It is also necessary to be precise about the different forms that conflict and protest action can take, the main distinctions being between: strike action; action short of strikes; and organised versus unorganised action.

Strike trends in Great Britain

The only industrial action on which records are consistently kept are strikes, and even these probably underestimate the real level of activity. Only strikes of over 10 employees are recorded, and unless it involves the loss of at least 100 working days, a strike lasting less than one day is not included. Thus, since 60 per cent of all strikes last less than one day, it has been argued that strike statistics probably only represent a quarter of what occurs (Brown, 1981). Moreover, since there is nothing to compel an employer to report a strike, it is likely that only two-thirds of those eligible to be included are actually counted (Edwards, 1983), so that official statistics give an imperfect basis on which to evaluate strike levels in Great Britain. More importantly, some highly significant and prolonged disputes are simply not recorded. For instance, from 1995 to 1997 there was a long dispute in the Liverpool Docks. This lasted nearly three years, and started with an unofficial strike. The employer, the Mersey Docks and Harbour Company, (legally) dismissed the strikers, and since this resulted in a situation where there was no longer an employment relationship between the employer and the dockworkers, statistics were not collected from this point onwards. Had this been done, however, it would have added a loss of a massive 420 000 working days to the strike statistics across the three years.

number of stoppages

A strike statistic that records the number of strikes that occur in each calendar year.

number of workers involved

A strike statistic that counts the number of workers involved, and gives some indication of the breadth of strikes.

number of working days lost

A strike statistic that counts the number of workers involved in a strike and also the duration of time for which the strike lasted.

Despite these shortfalls, strike statistics cannot be ignored, if only because they are the sole on-going indication of the level of industrial action in Great Britain. Moreover, the trends revealed by the statistics can be used to highlight some of the important characteristics of British strikes, and with this in mind Table 11.1 gives a year-by-year record of the three main indices of strike activity from 1975 to 2005, the last year for which full statistics are available. The indices given are for: the **number of stoppages**; the **numbers of workers involved**; and **working days lost**.

Pause for reflection

Given what has been said above about the limitations of strike statistics, what useful purposes do you feel they serve?

As can be seen, one noticeable feature of strikes in Great Britain is that the number fluctuates widely from year to year. Perhaps more important, there are some things that strike statistics cannot tell us. Since disputes involving action short of strike are not recorded, there is no attempt to give a comprehensive picture of the total level of industrial action in Great Britain, and this in itself is a serious omission. In addition, it should be remembered that a considerable number of organisations in Great Britain do not have a trade union presence, and so *organised protest* is largely blocked off in these firms. Since statistics do not make any attempt to record *unorganised forms of conflict*, this automatically creates an impression that these firms are 'conflict free', whereas the reality can be very different. For example, it has been reported that workers in non-union firms protest against management plans in less visible ways, either through absenteeism, or by semi-organised groups and teams deciding to resist or ignore managerially proposed changes (McKinlay and Taylor, 1996; Dundon and Rollinson, 2004).

Another shortfall is that official statistics make no distinction between a strike and a lockout. Both are recorded as the same thing: a stoppage. As such, we do not know who the initiating party is in a dispute, and if nothing else, this probably gives a rather biased picture. In the eyes of the popular press strikes are always newsworthy and because no distinction is made between strikes and lock-outs, the blame is almost always attributed to the workforce.

To explain strike trends and highlight some of the more obvious features, they will be discussed chronologically, as presented in Table 11.1. This will be followed by an explanation of some of the slightly less obvious and more contradictory tendencies in strike activity. Finally, by taking the whole period in five-year phases, some of the contextual factors that could have affected the general trends will be considered.

The first thing that can be noted is that in terms of *number of stoppages*, there was a steady decline in striking from 1975 onwards, followed by a much more significant decline since 1988. To illustrate one of the more important features, it can be noted that up to 1978 the number of *stoppages* was running at an average level of about 2300 per year, and the *numbers of workers*

Year	Number of stoppages	Workers involved (000s)	Working days lost (000s)
1975	2282	809	6012
1976	2016	668	3284
1977	2703	1166	10142
1978	2471	1041	9405
1979	2080	4608	29474
1980	1330	834	11964
1981	1338	1513	4266
1982	1528	2103	5313
1983	1352	574	3754
1984	1206	1464	27135
1985	903	791	6402
1986	1074	720	1920
1987	1016	887	3546
1988	781	790	3702
1989	701	727	4128
1990	630	298	1903
1991	369	176	761
1992	253	148	528
1993	211	385	649
1994	205	107	278
1995	235	174	415
1996	244	364	1303
1997	216	130	235
1998	166	93	282
1999	205	141	242
2000	212	183	499
2001	194	180	525
2002	146	943	1323
2003	133	151	499
2004	130	293	905
2005	116	93	157

Table 11.1 Strike trends for Great Britain, 1975 to 2005
Sources: *Employment Gazette*, 1999 and *Labour Market Trends*, 2006.

involved was only moderate, at about 900 000. This means that, on average, strikes were of comparatively short duration. The vast majority were in metal manufacturing, and this reflects what was then the nature of strike activity in British manufacturing industry – strikes of short duration, but involving a whole workforce.

In contrast, in other years patterns for *workers involved* and *working days lost* are somewhat different. For example, in 1979, while the number of *stoppages* was about the same as for earlier years, there were a large number of *workers involved*, and a high number of *working days lost*. A similar pattern appears in 1984, again in 1996, and most recently in 2002. This illustrates a major distinguishing feature of British strike patterns. In these years there were prominent strikes in the public sector: in 1979 the so-called 'Winter of Discontent'; in 1984 the miners' dispute, which lasted almost a complete year; in 1996 in transport and telecommunications industries; and in 2002 strikes involving fire fighters and other workers in the public sector. Because stoppages in this sector of the economy extend over a whole industry, public-sector strikes invariably involve very large numbers of workers. The 2002 strikes, incidentally, were said to have been prompted by a rising tide of militancy, and more effective union organisation in the public sector.

Commenting on Table 11.1 as a whole, the effects of various (contextual) factors can cannot be ignored. From 1975 to 1979, for example, the government of the day made a determined attempt to contain inflationary trends in pay settlements; for the most part by using incomes policies and other economic initiatives. However, this vanished in the so-called Winter of Discontent dispute, which effectively led to the fall of the Labour government. A Conservative government then took power and remained in office in one form or another until 1997. It quickly embarked on its legislative assault on trade union power, which is described in Chapters 2, 4 and 5, and also adopted laissez-faire economic policies to try to damp down economic expectations in the workforce. This brought about recessionary conditions, and although there were several serious attempts by trade unions to try to counter the effects of economic recession on their members, the employment relations laws passed by the government made it extremely difficult for unions to mobilise their members. In the private sector employers held firm in pay disputes, often with the aid of anti-union legislation and support from the State. Thus, by 1985 there was an increasing tendency on the part of trade unions to use 'cut-price' industrial action, such as overtime bans (Milner, 1993), and, if unions chose to strike, this often took the form of a 'token stoppage' lasting no more than a single day.

In 1985 the number of stoppages fell below 1000, for the first time in decades. They rose again in 1987, with major strikes in the public sector, fuelled to some extent by economic conditions and rising expectations among workers. However, from 1985 is perhaps the more significant year. Here, the miners failed to secure the guarantees they sought in a one-year strike, and by this time the Conservative government was firmly entrenched in its anti-union legislative programme, prominent in which was the introduction of compulsory strike balloting. However, there is some evidence that this turned out to be something of an 'own goal' for the government. For instance, although balloting was legally regulated and compulsory, unions were becoming more successful in securing a 'Yes' vote for strike action. Significantly, this did not lead to more strikes and according to Brown and Wadhawani (1990) it mostly led to a successful use of the *strike threat*. In other words, a successful ballot result provided unions with another bargaining tool for the process of negotiation.

From 1991 onwards the number of stoppages continued to decline and with the exception of 1996 and again in 2002, there were few large public-sector disputes. By now, of course, sizeable chunks of the public sector had either been privatised, or its bargaining mechanisms changed radically. Moreover, by the early 1990s industry was again in recession and, to some extent, workers had a tendency to 'keep their heads down'. One by-product of this was that disputes over redundancy became more frequent in the early 1990s, and another is that unions began to deploy other forms of industrial action given the excessively bureaucratic and legal constraints imposed by government legislation.

While aggregate statistics such as those in Table 11.1 can provide important clues about the nature and extent of strike activity in the economy, the major problem is that they mean that other contextual factors are obscured. For instance, strike rates are not the same everywhere, and can vary dramatically in different industries. One corrective is to examine 'action short of strike', and the Workplace Employment Relations (WERS) series provides some information on this, which is shown in Table 11.2.

As can be seen, not only did the percentages of union-recognising firms in all sectors experience less industrial action between 1980 and 2004, but the most dramatic decline was in both strike action and action short of a strike. As such, the decline is an absolute one, with no substitution effects. With these changes in mind it is now time to turn our attention to some of the explanations given for variations in strike activity.

Pause for reflection

Looking back over the past four decades, try to identify what you consider to be the most important influences that could explain the decline in industrial action in Great Britain.

Explanations of strike activity

The causes of strike activity have long fascinated researchers, and some of the main reasons for strike activity are given in the extract from national strike statistics for the years 1990 to 2005, which is shown in Table 11.3. This indicates that wages and earnings have been the main reasons for strike activity, whereas striking over working conditions or dismissals have featured less significantly.

While data such as these can be useful, they inevitably have some shortfalls of the type identified earlier when discussing aggregate strike trends. Therefore, the broadbrush survey approach is likely to have a limited utility in explaining what prompts the use of strikes, and it is necessary to examine other explanations, some of which are described in what follows.

Economic explanations

An early theory in this area was provided by Hansen (1921), who reasoned that in periods of falling profits, employers would try to reduce real wages, which would prompt employees to strike in retaliation. In addition, Hansen argued that in periods of rising prices, there would be higher strike levels, as employees tried to keep pace with the rising cost of living. Unemployment is, of course related to falling company profits, and somewhat later Creigh and Makeham (1982) showed that, when unemployment is high, employers are less willing to make

	Percentages				
	1980	1984	1990	1998	2004
No industrial action	75	69	80	96	89
Action short of strike only	10	8	4	2	4
Strike action only	9	11	11	2	7
Both strike and action short of strike	7	11	5	0	0

Table 11.2 Industrial action in workplaces having recognised trade unions: 1980 to 1998
Source: adapted from Millward *et al.* (2000). Figures for 2004 calculated by the WERS 2004 Information and Advice Service (www.wers2004.info).
Base: workplaces with 25 or more employees.

Cause	Years															
	1990	1991	1992	1993	1994	1995	1996	1997	1998	1999	2000	2001	2002	2003	2004	2005
Wage rates and earnings	1084	306	183	144	164	119	1028	103	147	159	375	141	1037	280	759	87
Extra wages and fringe benefits	14	3	14	5	6	75	34	24	19	8	8	3	137	139	3	7
Duration and patterns of hours worked	484	16	3	34	8	39	52	7	2	5	6	13	3	63	19	7
Redundancy questions	35	248	193	391	24	72	39	69	54	35	58	88	14	5	107	17
Trade union matters	32	4	10	4	1	3	6	2	2	2	0	6	5	0	11	6
Working conditions and supervision	59	66	49	3	2	1	91	8	14	13	11	172	110	3	0	9
Staffing and work allocation	145	62	52	62	67	88	35	18	16	6	23	79	10	7	5	22
Dismissal and other disciplinary matters	50	56	24	6	6	18	18	4	28	14	18	23	7	2	1	2
All causes	1903	761	528	649	278	415	1303	235	282	242	499	525	1323	499	905	157

Table 11.3 Strikes – working days lost (thousands) by main cause in all industries 1990–2005

Source: *Labour Market Trends*, December 2001, June 2006.

concessions than in more buoyant times, and for this reason, strikes tend to last longer. More recent work in this area has sought to link variations in strike activity with the 'Kondratieff' cycle of industrial output. This is a theory of long-wave economic cycles that predicts a period of sustained growth lasting 20 to 30 years, followed by an equally long period of stagnation. Increased strike activity is said to correspond to the early downturn phase in the cycle, because at this point workers' expectations are still rising, but employers are beginning to experience problems with profitability and, therefore, tend to resist large wage claims (Franzosi, 1995; Kelly, 1998). However, although economic cycles are acknowledged to have some impact on tendencies to strike, there is far less agreement about whether the effects are as straightforward as they seem. For instance, while there is little doubt that changes in the economic environment give rise to forces that could aggravate tendencies to strike, economic changes alone cannot explain everything, if only because different industries are affected to a different extent by the same economic conditions.

Social values explanations

One approach that explains why strike patterns could be higher in certain industries is given in Kerr and Seigal's (1954) attempt to link strike activity with social values. The theory argues that in certain occupations – for example, dockworkers and coal miners – jobs are tough and combative, which engenders a spirit of solidarity, and a high propensity to engage in conflict. Crucially, the type of job that these workers do tends to encourage close-knit communities – for example, among fire fighters there is a dependence on each other for safety on the job, and a shared camaraderie has been shown to be a particularly significant factor in their propensity to strike (Darlington, 1998). They are likely to be aware of commonly held grievances, and have a close emotional attachment to principles of working-class solidarity. However, while this explanation seemed highly plausible in the past, it has less relevance today, because many of the occupational communities on which the theory is based (e.g. coal mining) have largely disappeared (Turnbull et al., 1996).

Institutional explanations

One of the earliest studies in this area was reported in the work of Ross and Hartman (1960), which compared strike levels in 15 different countries between 1900 and 1956. In broad terms its findings were that strikes were far less likely to occur in industries that had mature, well-established procedures for negotiation, in which grievances could be quickly brought to the surface, and handled by negotiating machinery. Indeed, the authors were optimistic enough to forecast that if these mechanisms were to become more widely adopted, it would lead to an eventual 'withering away' of the strike. Although not couched in anywhere near such optimistic tones this, of course, is remarkably similar to the conclusions reached by the Donovan Commission on Trade Unions and Employers Associations (Donovan, 1968), the findings of which are described in Chapter 4. This line of thinking has been extremely influential, and subsequent work uncovered remarkably robust conclusions concerning the link between strike activity and bargaining structures (Britt and Galle, 1972 and 1974). However, useful as these studies are, they do not explain why firms within the same industry, or plants within the same firm, can have vastly different strike records. For instance, industry-wide surveys convincingly show that 5 per cent of plants account for 25 per cent of all strikes (Smith et al., 1978), which suggests that macro-level variables such as bargaining structures are not capable of giving anything more than a general explanation for strike levels. For this reason, attention then turned to conditions within organisations.

Technological explanations

There is a very long tradition in the social sciences of blaming technology for virtually everything, and drawing on a number of studies conducted in the 1950s and 1960s, there were attempts to establish links between high strike frequencies and the use of mass-production technologies. For instance, Chinoy (1955) and Walker and Guest (1957) both argue that repetitive, assembly-line work gives conditions ripe for conflict, and in a similar vein, Sayles (1958) pointed out that different types of technology influence the formation and nature of work groups, which in turn gives them different capabilities to use industrial action. In addition, Robert Blauner (1964) claimed to have uncovered a direct correlation between mass-production technologies and associated alienating conditions, which were said to result in extremely hostile employment relations climates between workers and managers. While there is probably a grain of truth in these explanations, they are now thought to be a gross overstatement, and have been much criticised for containing assertions that are far too sweeping about the outcomes of mass-production technology. Indeed, Hyman (1989) points out that Blauner's assumptions fail to account for the strike-prone nature of British car manufacturing, in comparison to the same industries in Japan and Germany (Gallie, 1978 and 1988).

Overall, while the many different approaches to explaining the causes of strikes all have some plausibility, each one only offers a partial explanation. For this reason, current ideas suggest that far greater account needs to be taken of the different ways in which employees view the work situation. For instance, employees in some situations could view striking as virtually an everyday event, while others would probably never dream of taking part in a strike. In addition, to some groups of workers conflict and protest is something that needs to be pursued collectively, and for others there may only be the opportunity for individual resistance because there is an absence of collective representation. Moreover, no matter how the action is taken, it should be remembered that workers are likely to have some aim in mind when protesting, and they take action in the anticipation that this aim is likely to be achieved. Therefore, their perceptions of the effects that the action will have on the other party can be a highly important influence on whether or not they take action, and if so, what form of action they use. Strikes are not the only form of industrial action, and might not even be the one that is perceived by employees to be the most useful. Thus, to explain the full range of conflict and protest behaviour, we need to view matters from the viewpoint of the protagonists. Subtle influences of this type are very hard to uncover in generalist explanations, and some recognition of this is given in the next section.

The processes of conflict and protest behaviour

Neither managers nor workers embark upon a course of industrial action lightly. Indeed, conflict is probably one of the most emotive features of employment relations. It is, therefore, important to understand the complexity of what is involved, if and when it occurs. Over the years, a number of leading scholars have sought to tease out the processes underpinning strikes and other forms of conflictual behaviour and some of these ideas have been noted earlier, when explaining theories of strike causation. However, it is also important to consider the matter of the processes at work when conflict and protest occurs in an organisation.

To this end it is interesting to note that some of these earlier ideas have now been revised and questioned by several scholars. For example, Kelly and Nicholson (1980b) provide valuable insights into strike processes and their internal dynamics, acknowledging that strike action takes place within a very specific context, and that many features of that context can be intangible. In addition, Edwards (1986) offers a scheme that describes different workplace arrangements, with each one having its own associated processes, according to the existence of militant or moderate work groups, and that these are likely to have a different impact depending on the nature of the relationships that exist between managers and workers. These different contributions all alert us to a very important point: that no two strikes are likely to be identical, and for this reason the social and behavioural processes that give rise to industrial action can be tremendously important. A more recent contribution in this area is that of social mobilisation theory, which is considered next.

Conflict and social mobilisation theory

Kelly (1998) has extended these earlier ideas on the processes underpinning conflict among workgroups, by drawing on a number of social movement theorists. Since the theory itself was more fully outlined in Chapter 4 (see Fig. 4.3) it will not be repeated here, other than to explain the key dimensions that aid our understanding of the processes underpinning conflict and protest behaviours.

Social mobilisation theory recognises that workers have the capacity to resist and challenge management, and crucially stresses that a conflictual climate can surface when workers are dissatisfied. For example, workers could believe they are being paid below the going rate in comparison to a similar workgroup elsewhere. However, dissatisfaction alone is probably not sufficient for conflict to emerge because, depending on the issue itself, workers could feel that while management action is unfair, it is also unavoidable: for instance, if management proposes restructuring the firm because it is faced with an impending financial crisis. For this reason, if conflict is to emerge, there also has to be a sense of *injustice* surrounding the dissatisfaction: that is, workers will need to believe it is 'wrong' or 'illegitimate' (Kelly, 1998: 27).

From this it follows that four critical processes are necessary to transform an individual's sense of injustice into a more collective climate of conflict. First, there has to be an *attribution* of blame to a specific agency (management) for injustice to be perceived. For example, workers have to identify who the offending party is, and believe that conflictual behaviour has a potential to redress the perceived injustice. The second process is that of *social identification*, which occurs when workers identify with one another for some reason, and form a collective group. For instance, aggrieved workers can more easily identify and empathise with colleagues who experience a similar grievance, and it is well known that craft, white-collar and unskilled workers see themselves as distinct work groups with their own sense of identity and trade union. Third, group identity and attribution can be articulated through effective *leadership*. For example, union stewards can act as a conduit for employee concerns by placing blame at management's door, rather than assuming the issue is a fait accompli prompted by some external market factor. Finally, workers evaluate the *costs and benefits* of engaging in some form of conflictual behaviour to try and redress their concerns. Here Kelly (1998: 34) explains that workers can be motivated into collective mobilisation for a variety of cost–benefit reasons, and these are often evaluated in subjective terms, such as individual self-interest, group interests, and social pressure.

It is important to note, however, that none of these distinct processes – *attribution*; *social identification*; *leadership*; and *cost–benefit calculations* – exists in a vacuum. Significantly, the role of leadership is an important one that links the different processes together, and can shape the direction or very existence of conflictual outcomes. For example, while union stewards can articulate employee concerns that facilitate conflictual action, managers can also invoke counter-mobilising strategies that seek to inhibit any potential action. However, attempts by management to undermine employee actions sometimes harden the resolve of workers, whereas opposition to strike action among employees has been found in situations where union negotiations have not fully exhausted all the procedural alternatives (Batstone *et al.*, 1978; Kelly, 1998).

The implications for strikes and other forms of 'organised' conflict

Social mobilisation theory predicts that, depending on the ways in which the above processes interact, some form of collective action can occur, but that types of action can vary considerably. For example, in Chapter 4 it was noted that one outcome could be that workers join trade unions as a way of making a protest to management. This could then be followed by the most extreme form of collective mobilisation: strike action. Here it is important to note what was said at the start of the chapter: industrial action is an extension of the negotiating process, and mainly occurs where agreement cannot be reached about the terms of the effort–reward bargain. This can also be said of all other forms of organised conflict that may flow from the processes of collective mobilisation, such as 'working to rule', 'go-slows' or 'overtime bans', the choice of which will depend on the context and circumstance in which workers find themselves at a given point in time.

Clearly there is a great deal of variation in the extent to which workers can pursue organised conflict, and social mobilisation theory alerts us to the fact that a decline in strike action is not the same as a complete eradication of conflictual behaviour. According to the circumstances in which workgroups find themselves, there is likely to be a huge degree of variation in the opportunities open to workers to pursue organised industrial action. For example, at one extreme, if there already exists a degree of control established by workers, and this prompts them to see conflict as just another way of maintaining control, then the 'threat' of strike action or some other form of conflict can be sufficient to press home certain demands at the bargaining table (Batstone *et al.*, 1978). However, when faced with a political and economic environment that restricts strike action, workers are often at a disadvantage compared to employers, who can avail themselves of a supportive legal framework (such as injunctions) to destabilise potential strike action. Organised conflict may present itself in ways other than a strike, and therefore the insights from social mobilisation theory can advance our understanding of organised forms of conflict.

The implications for 'unorganised' forms of conflict

Strike action is a particularly dramatic expression of industrial conflict, and while the decline in strike activity might suggest that there is now a level of trust or commitment between the parties to an employment relationship, it by no means indicates an absence of conflict. As Edwards (1995) has argued, the decline in strike activity might only demonstrate a fear of management, or an abuse of the managerial prerogative, especially in non-union organisations where the facility of trade union representation is absent. Indeed, in these circumstances there is rather more evidence to suggest that conflict and protest behaviours can take on elements of 'flight' as much as those of 'fight': that is, actions that are designed to 'hit back', as well as to try and exert a degree of 'control' over the job.

Therefore, social mobilisation theory also has implications for protest and conflict behaviours reported in studies of non-union organisations (McKinley and Taylor, 1996; Royle, 2000; Dundon and Rollinson, 2004). For example, *sabotage* as a way of 'hitting back' at the organisation (or its customers) is not unknown, and it can take the form of knowingly harming a machine to cause damage and disruption, or even be part of a workgroup strategy that seeks to ameliorate the worse conditions of a tedious or boring job. In this respect Bryman (2004) distinguishes between *passive protest* and *active protest* behaviour, which can be particularly illuminating in the growing number of service-sector occupations. **Passive protest** is when employees mentally 'switch off' from their work experiences, otherwise known as 'acting as a robot' or 'going on auto-pilot'. Examples include being polite to a customer, smiling at the appropriate time and place, but without any sincerity. Conversely, **active protest** could include consciously resisting an organisational rule or practice in some way, often by directing conflictual behaviours at customers. For example, Royle (2000) reports on the 'frying games' that workers at McDonald's deploy as way to 'get back' at the company: a game in which employees compete to see who can dispense the most amount of bodily sweat onto the company's food products, while they are being cooked. Similar forms of protest behaviour have been reported in many other service sector occupations, among supermarket checkout staff, restaurant waiters, Disney employees and call-centre operatives (see Exhibit 11.2).

passive protest
A form of protest in which employees mentally 'switch off' from their work.

active protest
A form of protest when employees consciously resist management or an organisational rule, often by directing their conflictual behaviours towards customers.

Active and passive protesting can also be found in acts of *pilfering* and the use of *fiddles*. In many occupations these are enshrined in custom and practice arrangements that have a degree of tacit connivance of supervisors. Perhaps the most widely used practice of all is *absenteeism*. In many organisations this form of protest can be an organised response in resistance to management, or as an unorganised action that acts as an escape valve that helps people accommodate to what can often be a very tedious job. Consequently, some of the so-called 'unorganised' conflict is probably nothing of the sort, but part and parcel of the social relations of a particular work system. Perhaps more important, it can often be semi-collective in nature, and therefore the processes of *social identification* and *attribution* described in social mobilisation theory have implications for passive and active forms of unorganised conflict.

Passive protest and conflict behaviours:
Workers seek to preserve some sense of individuality by mentally distancing themselves from their immediate work milieu. Examples include:

- switching off
- going on auto-pilot
- daydreaming
- going into a trance
- false or insincere customer service (a begrudging customer smile).

Active protest and conflict behaviours:
A series of activities which seek to 'hit back' at the company and/or its customers. Examples include the following:

- To be difficult or overbearing to a customer
- To make the customer wait unnecessarily, or suggest there is something wrong with their transaction (e.g. to go and check on their credit card)
- At McDonald's (and other restaurants) employees have been known to contaminate customer food, without customers knowing
- At Disney workers have been known to tighten the safety belt on a ride excessively, or to fasten the customer's safety belt in such a way that it 'inadvertently' slaps them
- Cutting off the heads of customers when taking their photographs.

Exhibit 11.2 Examples of passive and active conflict
Source: adapted from Royle, 2000; Noon and Blyton, 2002; Bryman, 2004.

There is also a growing body of evidence about the forms of employee resistance within non-union organisations, especially among the many small to medium-sized enterprises in Britain. For instance, Dundon and Rollinson (2004) show how workers in small non-union firms develop their own sense of group identity with distinctly different interests from those of management. In one particular case study workers displayed some signs of militancy with evidence of 'active' conflict. For instance, employees reacted to an arbitrary management decision that removed what was regarded as an established custom and practice: the use of company vehicles to travel to and from their place of work. In response, groups of employees arrived for work late in the full knowledge that this would disrupt customer delivery schedules, and blamed the act of lateness on inadequate public transport. The use of company vehicles was soon restored as an acceptable practice. Thus, far from being passive recipients of managerial actions, these non-unionised employees were able to exert a degree of power which altered (improved) the conditions of their employment. Moreover, the image that smaller (or non-union) firms are somehow characterised with harmonious and conflict-free employment relations is highly questionable, even though there are few reported strikes in such enterprises.

Overall, social mobilisation theory is capable of providing a dynamic and fluid explanation of conflict and protest behaviours in contemporary employment relations. It alerts us to the idea that the processes of *injustice, attribution, social identification* and *leadership* are key stages underpinning collective action of various types. Conflict is not always confined to its most visible form – a strike – but can manifest itself in passive and other subtle forms of protest. Significantly, this is all part and parcel of the nature of social relations in a particular enterprise, the type of occupations involved, and the relationships that exist between managers and workers.

It is important, however, to note that at the present time there are a number of caveats that need to be remembered about holding expectations that are too optimistic for social-mobilisation theory. First, its application to conflict and protest behaviours is in its infancy, and rather than being a fully tested model in its own right, it is mostly theoretical, with supporting evidence woven in from other studies. Second, some of its core dimensions, such as assumed cost–benefit calculations by employees, attribution and group identification, are very complicated cognitive processes, the evidence for which can be difficult to pin down empirically. Third, while it is acknowledged to be an important aspect, leadership itself is a very imprecisely defined attribute in the theory. Moreover, there is little acknowledgement that it is more difficult for leaders to emerge in non-union firms, unless they are prepared to face reprisals from management.

Pause for reflection

Drawing on what you have read in earlier chapters of the book, to what extent do you feel that legislation has an influence on workers and managers contemplating taking industrial action in Great Britain?

Industrial action and the law

There are several ways in which the law has a bearing on industrial action, but to simplify matters, attention will be focused on three areas: implications for the *individual*, in terms of his or her contract of employment; implications for the *trade union* that initiates an act of industrial action; and implications for the *conduct* of industrial action.

The individual (contractual) implications

In Great Britain there is no legal right to strike and, strictly speaking, in common law an employee who takes strike action has broken his or her contract of employment. While this is the position in Britain, it is not the case in other European countries where there is a well-established 'right to strike'; a principle upheld by the International Labour Organisation (Gernigon *et al.*, 1998). In Great Britain the Employment Relations Act (1999) moved some way towards this philosophy by establishing what can best be described as a 'protected' category of industrial action. The defining characteristics of this are that the action is *official*, and that it has been *organised lawfully*. Providing that these two provisos are observed, it would, for example, be automatically unfair to dismiss a striker during the first twelve weeks of a strike. This now gives a far greater degree of employment protection to workers than was previously the case, where as long as all striking employees were dismissed, and there was no attempt on the part of the employer to re-engage any of them selectively for a period of three months, the employer would not have been deemed to be acting in a discriminatory way. Having said this, and as was pointed out in Chapter 5, the Employment Acts of 1980, 1982 and 1988 are still on the statute book, and in a general way these severely limit the capacity for unions to organise strike action.

In the case of actions other than strikes, the contractual position is always less clear, and a great deal depends on what is custom and practice in the particular enterprise, or whether it can be demonstrated that non-strike action is contrary to the spirit of the implied terms of the contract of employment. For example, if a commonly accepted practice is that employees regularly work overtime, then refusing to do so while an overtime ban is in progress could be deemed to be a breach of contract. For the same reason, in certain circumstances working to rule can be considered to be a failure to observe the implied contractual terms of faithful and efficient service.

Implications for trade unions

Under the Trades Disputes Act (1906) unions have immunity in civil and criminal law from inducing workers to break their contracts of employment by taking industrial action. However, as explained in Chapter 5, a considerable amount of legislation enacted in the 1980s severely limits their scope to organise industrial action. For example the Employment Act (1980) removed trade union immunities in the case of most forms of secondary action, thus making it harder for trade unions to take supportive action, such as 'boycotting' goods from an employer whose workers are on strike. In addition, the Employment Act (1982) considerably narrowed what can be considered to be a bona fide trade dispute by confining it to one that is: (i) *between employees and their direct employer* (which excludes action in pursuit of general trade union policies such as opposing privatisation, or government policy) and (ii) *wholly or mainly related to very specific matters*, such as being confined to terms and conditions of employment, or related to the machinery for conducting negotiations (also see Exhibit 5.2, Chapter 5).

The Employment Act (1982) also made unions liable for their activities by defining many of them as unlawful actions, and this enabled employers to seek court injunctions to halt them, and to seek damages for what were now classified as illegal actions authorised by a trade union. In all probability employers were encouraged to use the law, and indeed, some showed an increased willingness to do so. Nevertheless, there were limits to how far employers were willing to go in this direction. Except for a few notable cases, employers seemed to have little desire to act punitively. Rather, their aims were more simply those of obtaining a court injunction to halt a particular action, and get the wheels of production rolling again (Evans, 1987). However, the

Trade Union Act (1984), which introduced balloting procedures, made it easier to obtain an injunction by removing immunity if there had not been a properly conducted ballot. The regulations for balloting were again tightened up with the passing of the Trade Union Reform and Employment Rights Act (1993), making it increasingly more difficult for a union to organise a strike (see Exhibit 11.3).

Further to this the Employment Act (1988) explicitly increased the rights of trade union members to hold their union to account if questions about the proper conduct of a ballot are raised. Perhaps the most controversial step of all was to introduce what has popularly become known as the 'scab's charter'. Even where a strike has been preceded by a properly conducted ballot, it makes it an offence for a trade union to discipline members who failed to abide by the ballot result, clearly making it much easier for employers to undermine action by putting pressure on individual employees to break the strike.

In addition to the above, the Employment Act (1990) outlawed all forms of secondary and unofficial action. Thus, the only way a trade union could avoid having its funds frozen or sequestrated, was to officially repudiate the actions of its members, and this of course, makes it much easier to dismiss shop stewards and trade union officials who are those who usually lead unofficial action. However, there are grave doubts about the extent to which employers made use of this legislation, even in the case of unofficial action. While a small number did, most of them did not, probably because it would have prejudiced constructive industrial relations climates that many of them had taken years to build up in their organisations (Dickens and Hall, 2003).

It is worth noting that, in some eyes, the provisions of the 1993 Act were considered as having gone too far; for example, in the requirement to provide an employer with the identities of employees balloted. Some of these were removed in the first legislation introduced by the Labour government, the Employment Relations Act (1999). Nevertheless, in principle, the introduction of balloting is widely perceived to have been a useful step. At present, approximately 90 per cent of the strike ballots held each year are won decisively by trade unions. This tends to give the decision to engage in strike action a far greater degree of legitimacy than prior methods such as a 'show of hands' at a mass meeting of employees in the factory car park, which was always open to accusations of manipulation.

The legal provisions stipulate that a properly conducted industrial action ballot is one which complies with the following:

- It must include all those who the trade union believed would be called upon to take action.
- It must be a secret ballot conducted by post.
- The trade union must provide the employer with written notice of the intention to hold a strike ballot at least seven days before the ballot takes place, and must provide the employer with a sample of the ballot paper.
- It must include a question on the ballot paper worded 'yes' or 'no' (to the action) and contain an explicit statement that a 'yes' vote could involve a breach of the individual contract of employment.
- After the ballot the employer must be provided with details of the ballot result, together with the names of employees balloted.
- It must obtain a straightforward majority in favour of the action, and acknowledge that an injunction to halt the action could result if all of the above provisions are not observed.
- It must provide the right for any individual who is deprived of goods or services as a result of unlawful action to bring proceedings to the High Court to restrain the action.

Exhibit 11.3 Summary of legal requirements for a properly conducted industrial action ballot
Source: Trade Union Reform and Employment Rights Act (1993).

Implications for the conduct of disputes

This is the one of the few areas in which criminal law comes into play in employment relations. The main acts applied are listed in Chapter 5, and will not, therefore, be repeated here. Since 1906 it has been regarded as intimidation to picket a person's home, and since the introduction of the Employment Act (1982) it has been unlawful for employees to picket anywhere other than their own place of work. It is also important to point out that, although picketing is a recognised strike activity, the law only recognises the right of pickets to *peacefully persuade* other employees to join or support a strike. Unfortunately, what is deemed to be reasonable and peaceful persuasion is often a matter of judgement, and if tempers get frayed on a picket line, it is not unknown for violence to occur. Perhaps because of the experience of mass picketing in the 1970s, a Code of Practice on picketing was introduced in 1980 (DOE 1980), and while this does not have the force of a law, it could well be taken into account in a court hearing. It suggests that a maximum of six pickets is all that is needed for peaceful persuasion at any one entrance, and also recommends that pickets should be clearly identifiable (perhaps by wearing armbands), and that they should be under the control of an experienced person who should preferably be a union official, and who also has a responsibility for maintaining close contact with the police.

Case study 11.2: **The law and industrial action**

1 During wage negotiations three workers refused to do overtime when asked. Although it was not in their contracts of employment that overtime was required, they were dismissed. Do you feel that they would have a case for unfair dismissal?

2 A strike is in progress on a building site. A union official holding a placard sees a lorry arriving to deliver materials. He walks into the middle of the road and holds up the placard. The lorry driver stops and listens, and then tries to manoeuvre around the official, who in return moves himself in front of the lorry – is this peaceful persuasion?

3 A union official is on picket duty outside a hospital in which management have brought in contract labour in an attempt to break the strike. The police form a cordon around a coach bringing in the contract workers, and refuse to let the union official speak to its passengers. If he attempted to push through and talk to them, what would you expect to be the result of his behaviour?

Summary points

■ In Great Britain national statistics going back for nearly half a century give a record of strike action.

■ While some indications of the causes of strikes can be obtained from national statistics, other explanations for strikes have also been derived, notably: economic explanations; explanations that hinge on social values; institutional explanations; and technological explanations.

■ A description of the internal dynamics of industrial action processes can be found in Kelly's model of the social mobilisation process.

■ Industrial action of all types is heavily affected by the law, mainly in terms of the constraints it places on the parties in terms of how they should behave towards each other.

Conclusions and overview

Because it is a way in which one of the parties to the collective bargaining relationship can exert pressure on the other, industrial action in its various forms should be seen as an extension of the tactics of negotiation. Action can be initiated by either management or employees, and although the strike is the most dramatic form used by employees, and the lock-out the most visible form used by managers, both sides have other methods which can be deployed to put pressure on the other side.

Each episode of industrial action takes place for a purpose, and this purpose is probably only fully understood by those taking part. For this reason, although general explanations of strike patterns say something about conditions that make the use of industrial action more likely, they cannot really explain why a particular incident takes place, nor why it is conducted in the way that it is. To some extent social mobilisation theory helps overcome these limitations by recognising that there are also deeper cognitive processes associated with conflict and protest behaviour, and in particular, the potential for workers to identify with one another as a cohesive group that blames management for a perceived injustice, and responds in a variety of organised and/or unorganised ways.

As in almost all areas of employment relations at the current time, there are legal implications and conceptual connections between various topics. For example, there is a very strong connection between the material covered in this chapter and the issue of State intervention and legislation covered in Chapter 5. Because organised conflict mostly requires a degree of cohesion and organisation in groups of employees, there are also connections to trade union membership and organisation covered in Chapter 4. Finally, it cannot be stressed too strongly that what has been covered here cannot be divorced from the topics of collective bargaining and negotiation, which were covered in the previous two chapters. Thus, all three should really be considered as one topic, which for convenience has been divided up to facilitate discussion. In a similar way certain aspects of conflict and protest have strong implications for the next chapter in the book: Chapter 12, which deals with control in employment relations.

? Review and discussion questions

1 Mintzberg (1985) once described organisations as 'arenas for conflict'. Why is it then that employment relations conflict comes in for so much criticism in organisations?

2 To what extent and why can industrial action be described as an extension of the negotiating process?

3 Distinguish between:
- constitutional and unconstitutional action
- official and unofficial action
- organised and unorganised action.

4 Define:
- a strike
- working to rule or to contract
- overtime ban
- go-slow
- work-in or sit-in
- lock-out.

5 Describe ways in which different forms of industrial action can have different advantages and disadvantages for workers in different circumstances.

6 To what extent do national strike statistics provide a comprehensive picture of industrial action in Great Britain?

7 Describe four different reasons that help explain the existence of strike action, and comment on their usefulness.

8 Name four pieces of British legislation that have each had a significant effect on the abilities of workers to take industrial action in Great Britain across the last quarter century, and explain the effects of the legislation.

Further reading

Darlington, R. (1998) 'Workplace union resilience in the Merseyside Fire Brigade', *Industrial Relations Journal*, Vol. 29 (1), pp. 58–74. A journal article that among other things, examines the nature of combative conflict and solidarity among fire fighters.

Edwards, P.K. and M. Scullion (1982) *The Social Organisation of Industrial Conflict: Control and Resistance in the Workplace*, Blackwell, Oxford. A very thorough investigation of all forms of conflict action, conducted in a cross-section of organisations. It demonstrates the effects of different contextual circumstances, and the way that these are interpreted by management and employees, to result in characteristic patterns of action.

Gernigon, B. and H. Guido (1998) 'ILO principles concerning the right to strike', *International Labour Review*, Vol. 137 (4), pp. 444–481. A useful paper that clearly sets out the ILO position with respect to the 'right to strike' in most European countries.

Hyman, R. (1989) *Strikes*, 4th edn, Fontana, London. A very readable examination of strikes and industrial conflict.

Jackson, M.P. (1987) *Strikes: Industrial Conflict in Britain, U.S.A. and Australia*, Wheatsheaf, Brighton. Despite its title the book contains relatively little in terms of international comparisons. However, it gives an excellent overview of the theoretical explanations of industrial conflict.

Kelly, J. (1998) *Rethinking Industrial Relations: Mobilisation, Collectivism and Long Waves*, Routledge, London. A thought-provoking analysis, which among other things, evaluates the extent of union militancy, with a prognosis for conflict and protest behaviour. There is also a chapter outlining social-mobilisation theory and long-wave analysis in terms of conflict.

Kelly, J. and N. Nicholson (1980) 'Strikes and other forms of industrial action', *Industrial Relations Journal*, Vol. 11 (5), pp. 20–31. An interesting paper that tests the evidence for substitution and additive theories of different forms of industrial action.

McKinlay, A. and P. Taylor (1996) 'Power, surveillance and resistance: inside that factory of the future', in *The New Workplace and Trade Unionism: Critical Perspectives on Work and Organisation*, P. Ackers, C. Smith and P. Smith (eds), Routledge, London. A book chapter that reports on empirical material which shows how even non-union employees can develop a strong sense of cohesion in resisting managerial plans, especially through teamworking.

Control in employment relations

Introduction

To ensure that goals and objectives are achieved it is necessary to coordinate a firm's activities, and this makes control an important process in any organisation. However, because this also involves exerting control over the behaviour of people, which can smack of coercion, manipulation or even exploitation, control can be a controversial activity.

To cover these issues the chapter incorporates different concepts and theories from the subjects of organisational behaviour, industrial sociology and critical management studies, all of which are prominent in exploring the matter of control. It starts by defining control and tracing its purpose in organisations. This is followed by an exploration of three contrasting perspectives on control, and in particular, on the control of human behaviour. The remainder of the chapter focuses more sharply on behavioural control: first, by describing some of the traditional ways of controlling employee behaviour in employment and, second, by explaining current developments in managerial control regimes. Resistance to control is then explored, and the chapter closes with a short overview section.

The purpose of organisational control

There are many definitions of control, but this chapter purposely opens with a broad one, which is:

> the regulation of organisational activities so that some targeted element of performance remains within acceptable limits.
>
> (Barney and Griffin, 1992: 329)

Organisations are brought into existence to achieve something, and this normally involves structuring human activity in an enterprise. The primary purpose of control is to coordinate different organisational activities in order to achieve the goals for a whole organisation. For this reason, control is normally applied at all organisational levels: the organisation as a whole has to be controlled in order to ensure that it adopts an appropriate stance vis-à-vis its environment and, at lower levels, control is applied to synchronise the activities of groups and individuals to ensure that they play their respective parts in achieving goals. Thus, control is not a 'one-off' activity, but an on-going process that involves monitoring what is achieved, and taking remedial action to ensure that discrepancies are corrected.

means–ends hierarchy
Goals at one organisational level are the means of achieving the goals of the organisational level immediately above.

Organisational objectives are thus crucial elements in the control process, and goals are normally arranged as a **means–ends hierarchy**, in which the goals at one level in the hierarchy are the means of achieving the goals at the level immediately above. For example, at the top level in a firm, to achieve a strategic goal of diversifying into a new market, it will be necessary to achieve lower-level goals of developing appropriate new products, acquiring sufficient capital to finance market development, and ensuring there is a sufficiently skilled workforce to perform any new job tasks. Therefore, from a purely management perspective, it is desirable that a control mechanism that monitors performance should exist for every goal that is set, and a great deal of effort is devoted to controlling organisational and employee activities. Indeed, it is not so much a matter of whether these control activities are necessary, but whether human beings would be capable of coping mentally with a situation in blissful ignorance of whether their plans and goals were successful in achieving the intended outcomes.

Pause for reflection

Carefully consider the department of the university or college in which you study, and answer the following:

1 What do you feel could be the goals or objectives for that department?
2 What control mechanisms does the department use to try to ensure that these goals are achieved?

Alternative views on organisational control

Although few people would question the idea that complex organisations need to be managed and coordinated, this can give a false impression that control is a harmless or neutral activity. Control exists for a number of reasons, and it can be exercised for a wide variety of motives in an equally wide variety of ways. There are a number of different schools of thought on the use of control, but for the sake of simplicity, discussion will be confined to three contrasting perspectives: *the managerialist perspective*, *the open systems perspective* and *the political perspective*. These are shown in Table 12.1.

The managerialist perspective on control

This represents a view that controlling others is a legitimate managerial activity – the so-called 'right to manage'. Its origins can be traced to the writings of classical management theorists and, in particular, Henri Fayol (1916), who set out what he defined as the five major functions of management: planning, organising, command, coordination and control. Since it goes to the very heart of achieving goals and objectives, many managers would argue that control is the most important of these.

Although it is not surprising that most managers feel this way, it is worth noting that it is also a view that is found in a number of academic texts. For instance, Barney and Griffin (1992) write about control as something akin to a management right, and Mullins (2002) goes even

	Assumptions underpinning the perspective	Major concerns of the perspective
Managerialist perspective	Control of resources (including the human resource) is a legitimate management activity. Therefore managers have the right to exercise control over the behaviour of subordinates	Identification of methods that can best be used by managers to exercise control
Systems perspective	Control mediates processes that transform inputs into outputs; for instance, budgetary control attempts to regulate financial resources used in the transformation process, and performance appraisal to achieve the most appropriate use of human resources. While control itself is neutral, it can have adverse consequences for employees	Modelling control systems for design, analysis and fault-finding purposes
Political perspective	Control is synonymous with the exploitation of human resources	Understanding the internal dynamics of control, e.g. how control is exercised and whether it gives rise to resistance or attempts at counter-control

Table 12.1 Three perspectives on control

further by suggesting that when an employee asks his or her manager 'how well am I doing?' the person is asking to be controlled, which comes close to portraying the control activity as a piece of managerial social work. Many managers, it can be noted, argue that what differentiates them from other employees is that they are allocated resources and made responsible for their efficient and effective utilisation. From this it is but a short step to laying claim to a right to command employee actions, which goes to the very heart of the employment relationship. This sort of tension exists for a number of reasons. First, as far as company law in Great Britain is concerned, the directors of a firm have a legal obligation placed on them to put shareholder interests before those of any other group, and this, among other things, implies that the resources of a firm must be used primarily to produce the best possible return for owners.

Second, the dominant view about corporate governance in Great Britain reinforces the 'right to manage' perspective, and significantly, this perspective is embedded in the prior education, training and development that many managers receive. On top of this there are powerful tendencies to view the manager's role as something which is not only different, but is somehow innately superior and confers almost omnipotent or god-like characteristics: witness the way that the popular press uses the two words 'manager' and 'leader' synonymously, without ever questioning what they mean.

Finally, as far as the relationship with employees is concerned, the concept of a 'contract of employment', which is the cornerstone of employment law, contains an assumption of an exchange of rewards for services. This in itself contains an implication that the role of the employee is a subordinate one that is under management control.

The open systems perspective

This perspective neither condemns nor endorses control. Instead, it takes the view that because of the size and complexity of organisations, control is inevitable and, indeed, has a number of benefits. For example: it can improve economic efficiency and help make the best use of scarce resources; it gives predictability, stability, order and reliability so that people know what they have to do, thus avoiding the ambiguities that many people can find disturbing.

However, the perspective also acknowledges that what makes control such a controversial matter is its application to people as well as machines. Control can be applied in inappropriate ways, or for suspect reasons, which can have a number of dysfunctional effects. For instance, employees can be subject to coercion and exploitation. As a consequence, employees can lose their individuality and self-esteem, innovation can be stifled, and they can end up by having little or no say in matters that affect them at work.

Nevertheless, the open systems perspective has a number of useful features, one of which is that it has given rise to a subject that effectively devotes its whole attention to the theoretical study of control processes in electrical, mechanical and biological systems, and this has important implications for employment relations. This subject is **cybernetics**, which although it can be highly mathematical, provides a very useful analytical tool: the **control model**. This model gives a symbolic representation of the components necessary for a system of control, their functions and how they should relate to each other. Moreover, the model is neutral in the sense that while it recognises the inevitable use of control in organisational life, it acknowledges that an effective control system (particularly one in which people

cybernetics
The theoretical study of control processes in electrical, mechanical and biological systems.

control model
A symbolic representation of the components necessary for a system of control, how they relate to each other and their functions.

are involved) is extremely difficult to construct. The model has two main uses: as a checklist for designing control systems; and as a diagnostic tool to pinpoint faults if a control system is not functioning correctly. The principles embodied in the model are explained in Exhibit 12.1, which can be applied at appropriate points throughout the chapter.

The political perspective

This perspective has become highly influential over the last two decades, and authors such as Willmott (1997) have long argued that control in organisations often goes well beyond the search for economic efficiency. Indeed, he argues that much management action has a strong focus on domination and exploitation, which is made relatively easy because managers control the distribution of rewards. This gives them the ability to obtain compliant behaviour, and allows the strong to manipulate and exploit the weak. For this reason, the political perspective on control has a strong emphasis on social control, in which compliance, conformity and obedience are achieved through processes that occur between groups and individuals. It has been observed, for example, that managers' activities tend to be far more concerned with controlling employees than simply coordinating their efforts, and that this results in on-going inequalities in the distribution of rewards, with a subsequent tendency for workers to resist control.

social control
Achieving compliance, conformity and obedience through interpersonal or intergroup processes.

The roots of the political approach can be traced to Marx's (1894/1974) analysis of the capitalist mode of production; something that has subsequently become known as the *labour process*, and is briefly covered in Chapter 1. There is, of course, a lot more to Marx's work than the examination of industry, and it is a theory that encompasses the whole structuring of society. However, Marx notes that, under capitalism, the relationship between employer and employee is essentially based on inequality and exploitation. For instance, only part of the surplus value created in transforming raw materials into saleable goods is returned to the worker in the form of wages; the rest is retained by the employer. As a result, the employer is said to have expropriated part of the just returns that are due to the worker, and the retained surplus is used to fuel the essential logic of capitalism: a continuous accumulation of wealth, which allows an on-going development of the production process to further reduce costs. For this reason the owner has an inbuilt incentive to maintain tight control of the labour process, and this inevitably means that the interests of those who own the means of production, and the workers who sell their labour power to the owners, will be opposed.

expropriate
To dispossess or remove property from someone.

Here it is worth noting that all of the so-called 'free-market economies' are capitalist, and so capitalism and its logic is now the norm throughout most of the world. Thus, Marx's analysis is equally relevant in explaining what occurs in the public sector and in service industries. Indeed, from the early 1980s onwards, the government in Great Britain has imposed mechanisms on the public sector that are designed to make it, if anything, more capitalist: for example, privatisation, cash limits, competitive tendering, and so on.

From the early 1970s onwards there was a rekindling of interest in the use of Marxist principles to analyse aspects of employment relations. This was prompted by a rediscovery of Marx's ideas by Braverman (1974), who argued that in the twentieth century work has been consciously de-skilled by employers in their systematic use of scientific management techniques to lower costs. However, there is an on-going debate about how widely Braverman's analysis can be applied, and whether Taylorist forms of control have been as absolute as Braverman suggested. Nevertheless, labour process theory has resulted in a very rich stream of work that seeks to explain the processes of managerial control and the attendant conflicts that occur in employment relations.

Summary points

- Organisational control systems do not exist in a vacuum. They are intended to make it more likely that formal goals are achieved.

- The managerialist perspective on control views it as something that managers exercise by right.

- The open systems perspective views control as something that is necessary in organisations, but which can have a number of adverse consequences.

- The political perspective on control focuses on the internal dynamics of the control of people in organisations, and argues that control can lead to exploitation, which in turn leads to employment relations conflicts and forms of resistance to control.

Since a clear understanding of this model is vital in understanding many of the points made in this chapter, you are recommended to read this exhibit thoroughly.

Control: the basic requirements

The starting point for the control model is that a process/activity exists that needs to be controlled. In its simplest form, this is shown in Fig. 12.1, and while the process has inputs and outputs, without exception it is the outputs that employers seek to control. The first requirement is to know something of the relationship between the inputs and the outputs. For instance, in an organisational process that produces goods or services, it is necessary to know:

- that the required quantity of labour with the appropriate skills is available
- that tools, machines and raw materials are available.

From here onwards it is then necessary to select between two basic control options:

- open-loop (feedforward) control
- closed-loop (feedback) control.

These are shown in Figs 12.2 and 12.3 respectively.

In essence, the only difference between the two options is that in closed-loop control a sensor exists on the output side of the process, and this is connected to a comparator by a feedback loop, the functions of which will be considered presently.

open-loop (feedforward) control

A method in which the inputs to a process or activity are carefully determined, but with no monitoring of outputs.

In **open-loop control** it is normally assumed that the workings of the process or activity are perfectly understood, which means the desired outputs will be obtained by simply feeding in the required inputs. In everyday life there are plenty of examples where open-loop methods are encountered. For instance, in convenience foods such as cake mixes and TV dinners, the ingredients all come pre-packaged and if the instructions are closely followed with respect to mixing, cooking times,

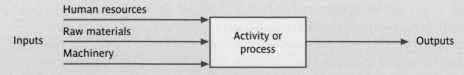

Figure 12.1 The process or activity to be controlled

Exhibit 12.1 The cybernetic model of control

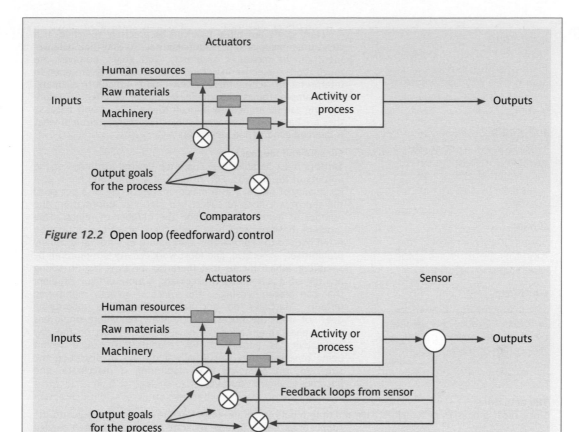

Figure 12.2 Open loop (feedforward) control

Figure 12.3 Closed loop (feedback) control

temperatures etc., a usable finished product is obtained. However, in many organisational activities, particularly those that rely on human inputs, the workings of the process are not precisely known, and it is not considered completely safe to rely on open-loop control.

closed-loop (feedback) control

A method in which the outputs of a process or activity are monitored and, if necessary, inputs are adjusted to achieve the desired outputs.

comparator

Something (or someone) that compares the desired attributes of the outputs of a process or activity with those actually achieved.

Exhibit 12.1 Continued

With **closed-loop control** the assumptions about complete understanding of the workings of the process are not made, and the basic sequence of activities is:

- The outputs of the process or activity are evaluated by a sensor.
- Information is fed back from the sensor to a comparator that compares the output goals for the process to those actually achieved.
- If there is a discrepancy between desired and actual outputs, information is fed to an actuator, which adjusts the inputs to the process or activity accordingly.

However, while this is very simple in principle, to work effectively the components of the control system must all be able to perform certain functions, and for this reason, it is necessary to consider each one in more detail.

Goals and comparator

Whether closed-loop or open-loop methods are used, it is necessary to be able to specify the output goals for the process, and here it is useful to distinguish between two types of goal: hard and soft.

hard goals

Those that can be precisely specified in an unambiguous and usually quantifiable way, and whose achievement can be measured accurately.

soft goals

Those that are more subjective and qualitative in nature, open to interpretation and whose achievement is more difficult to evaluate.

sensor

Something (or someone) that monitors the attributes of the output of a process or activity.

sampling

The characteristics of the total outputs of a process or activity is estimated by examining only a proportion of the output.

Hard goals are those that can be precisely specified in a clear, unambiguous and quantifiable way, so that their achievement can be measured accurately. **Soft goals**, however, are much more subjective in nature, and because they are open to interpretation, achievement is much more difficult to evaluate. For example, things like employee morale or effective team-working can be immensely difficult to evaluate, if only because they are based on a manager's subjective interpretation of what is deemed good or bad behaviour.

Sensors and feedback

Sensors must be able to evaluate the desired attributes of the outputs of the process. For instance, if a workgroup has a goal for quality of output (say a maximum reject rate of 3 per cent) the sensor will need to collect two pieces of information: the number of items produced, and the number of rejects. One problem that can occur here is the speed at which information is fed back to the comparator. Continuous monitoring is usually prohibitively expensive, and most work activity is monitored by **sampling**, which means that there can be time lags in taking any remedial action that is necessary. A more difficult problem that can plague sensing is the effect of actually monitoring outputs. Machines do not have feelings, and monitoring does not affect the process or the activity, but where employees are involved, monitoring can have a huge impact on the way an activity is performed. For example, if people resent being observed, they can usually find ways of distorting the situation, which means that monitoring is inaccurate, and becomes counterproductive.

The actuator

Since most processes or activities have multiple inputs, separate **actuators** are required to regulate the supply of each one. Indeed, separate actuators are often needed to regulate different attributes of an input. For instance, in the case of the workgroup described above, the actuator that adjusts the quantity of labour (number of people or hours worked) would need to be very different from the one that adjusts the skills of the workforce.

actuator

Something that adjusts the inputs to a process or activity.

While it is usually fairly easy to determine whether an actuator works properly in a mechanical system, this is not always the case with people in organisations. For instance, if jobs are designed according to Taylorist scientific management principles, payment is usually made contingent on the effort that people put into a job. This however, assumes that the main (if not only) thing that motivates people is money. Since we know that people also require a degree of intrinsic motivation, this is a half-truth, and it is now widely acknowledged that a host of **normative inputs**, such as values, attitudes, beliefs and motivations, are important inputs to any process that involves employee effort. These all come from within the person and, although managers might like to think that they can adjust them directly, this is nothing more than wishful thinking.

normative inputs

Human values, attitudes, beliefs and motivators.

The control model: an evaluation

As was pointed out earlier, the control model has two main uses. First, as a device to design control systems and second, as a tool to diagnose problems with existing systems of control. Although it can be a powerful instrument for either purpose, it is important to recognise that a number of criticisms of the model have been voiced, the most important of which are:

- It treats control as an engineering exercise, in which the properties of everything are well known, whereas some of the greatest difficulties arise in the use of highly variable human factors.

- Because it focuses exclusively on achieving goals that have already been decided, these are taken for granted, which ignores the possibility that the goals themselves could be inappropriate.

- It regards goals and goal setting as unproblematic, whereas goals are often compromises rather than statements of unassailable logic.

Exhibit 12.1 Continued

■ It tends to assume that links between cause and effect are perfectly understood, and in many cases this not a safe assumption.

■ It assumes that all the resources for a process or activity are readily available in sufficient quantities and qualities.

Although these criticisms can be perfectly valid, it should be remembered that the model is simply an analytical tool. Therefore, everything depends on how it is used. If suitable allowances are made for these points, it is far too valuable a model to discard out of hand, and it will be used at various points throughout the chapter to illustrate some of the problems that arise in managerial control regimes.

Exhibit 12.1 Continued

Behavioural control
Power and control

Control cannot be divorced from the use of power, if only because managers and supervisors usually have a degree of authority in organisations, and for this reason they are likely to assume that they have some right to control the behaviour of others. This can have a strong impact on the relationship between an organisation and its employees, and as Stewart (1991) points out, one of the dilemmas created by the desire to be 'in control' is that managers feel a need to obtain two different patterns of employee behaviour that are difficult to reconcile. On the one hand they want order and predictability in employees, which implies the need to tightly specify employee behaviour. On the other hand, they also want employees to be flexible, innovative, and to show initiative, which implies giving them a high degree of discretion. Paradoxically, these twin requirements are so different that an emphasis on one can lead to a near absence of the other. Thus, exerting control over employee behaviour involves a trade-off between order and flexibility, and Stewart illustrates this by contrasting three control strategies, which can be placed along the continuum shown in Fig. 12.4.

manager-directed control

Managers specify exactly how and what should be done, and then closely monitor employee behaviour.

Manager-directed control places a strong emphasis on the predictability of employee behaviour. Note that in control model

Case study 12.1: **Control of university learning**

Reflect carefully on the study activities that you undertake as a student at university or college. Focus on a particular module or subject that you study, and answer the questions below.

1 What standards of performance are set for you and who sets these standards?

2 What are the inputs to the process in which you learn the subject material?

3 Assuming that an important output of the learning process is that you understand (and can apply) the subject material, is this output monitored in some way, and if so, how is this done?

4 Is there any provision to compare this output (learning) with the standard of performance you identified in question 1? If so, who or what makes this comparison?

5 If a discrepancy was identified between your actual output and the targeted output you identified in question 1, what provision is there to adjust the inputs to the learning process? Who or what makes this adjustment?

6 Map your answers to questions 1–5 on an appropriate control model. In your view is the learning process controlled by open-loop or closed-loop methods?

7 In your view how effective is this control?

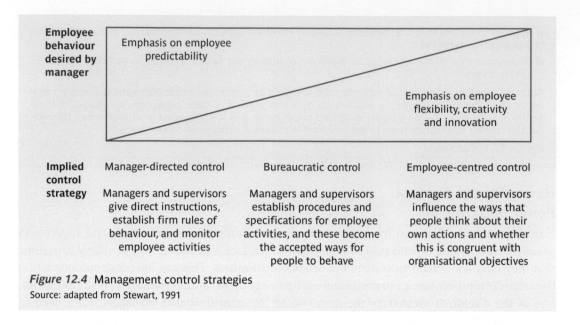

Figure 12.4 Management control strategies
Source: adapted from Stewart, 1991

terms, this equates to a strict application of closed-loop control. At the middle position on the continuum is **bureaucratic control**, in which limits are placed on employee discretion by clearly defining an employee's role with a tight job specification, and by using standard operating procedures to specify how things should be done. Although there would still be some monitoring of employees, this would probably consist of a somewhat looser application of closed-loop methods. **Employee-centred control** has a strong emphasis on obtaining a high degree of flexibility, creativity and innovation from employees. In theory, this means that employees exercise a high degree of self-control, and the task of management is to get employees to control themselves in a way that delivers the behaviour that managers want. Since this reduces the need for monitoring, control is much nearer to the use of open-loop methods.

bureaucratic control

The use of tight job specifications and standard operating procedures to specify employee behaviour, which then becomes the accepted way of doing things, to which employees conform.

employee-centred control

A strategy that involves influencing the way that employees think about themselves and what they do, so that they willingly subscribe to management's aims.

A move from left to right on this continuum represents what Friedman (1977) calls a shift from 'direct control' to 'responsible autonomy', using what Walton (1985) calls a 'commitment strategy'. Note, however, that all three options are equally control-orientated. Indeed, over 40 years ago Tannenbaum (1962) argued that by using employee participation to create an impression of shared decision making, managers can lower employee resentment at being controlled, and thus retain the major part of control to themselves. Similarly, Flanders (1970) added that for management to gain control, they must first 'learn how to share it'. Thus, management control strategies always involve the use of power, and it is not so much a question of whether power is used, but how it is used.

Summary points

- Since control is mainly exercised by supervisors and managers, who are given a degree of formal authority to direct the activities of employees, control cannot be divorced from the use of power.

- Supervisors and managers have control strategies which relate to their use of formal authority, and one way of classifying these control strategies is along a continuum, the extremes of which are manager-directed control and employee-centred control.

Pause for reflection

Within certain limits, all managers and employees have to comply with rules that constrain their behaviour. What type of control regime (manager-directed, bureaucratic control, or employee-centred) would you prefer to work under? What particular advantages would you see that this control regime could have for yourself, compared to alternative regimes?

Traditional methods of behavioural control

There are many ways in which managers can influence employee behaviour, and an exclusive focus on overt and visible forms of managerial power can give a misleading picture of control. For instance, Child (1984) argues that managers are quite adaptive in their use of control techniques, with many of them employing a **portfolio approach**, in which different control methods are applied to different groups of employees (or at different times) according to what managers hope to achieve. A number of the most commonly used methods will be described and we will return to how they are related at the end of the section.

portfolio approach (control)
The use of different strategies for controlling employee behaviour according to which one is seen to be the most applicable at the time.

Input control: recruitment, selection and socialisation

Although at first sight these activities do not look like a control mechanism, organisations usually try to employ people who can be relied upon to behave as required; those who are seen to 'fit in'. While there are anti-discrimination laws that regulate the recruitment practices of all organisations, management still has a great deal of freedom about whom they decide to employ. At the selection stage, which relies heavily on open-loop control, the process enables a line to be drawn between those allowed to become organisational members and those who are not. Interestingly, in a recent study by Callaghan and Thompson (2002), it was shown that even for quite junior positions, employers go to extraordinary lengths to obtain additional information about applicants to try to improve selection decisions, which in many cases included the results of extensive psychological testing.

Once people are admitted to an organisation, closed-loop methods then come into play in which they are subjected to a variety of pressures from peers and superiors to conform to established ways of doing things. In essence this *socialisation* process is a method of behavioural control in which attempts are made to ensure that those who have been recruited by the organisation are susceptible to other methods of control. However, while managers seem to have a great deal of faith in their abilities to select new employees, there is strong evidence that the selection process is not very effective in predicting future employee performance. This is mainly because there is a huge difference between performing well in selection, and performing well on the job. For this reason, it is often socialisation that plays a far bigger part in the process of control.

Pause for reflection

Think back to the time when you applied for a place on the course you are now following at university or college.

1 In what ways do you feel that the admissions process was a conscious attempt by the university to control the quality of students admitted to the course? What evidence do you use to support this idea?
2 To what extent do you feel that any induction process you received when first joining the university (including interaction with your peers and lecturers) was concerned with exercising control over your future behaviour at the university? What evidence do you use to support this idea?

Rewards and punishments

There are many ways in which rewards and punishments are used to try to bring employee behaviour under control. Although it is widely assumed by managers that *all* employees will expend effort in return for rewards, to rely completely on this happening of its own accord would mean relying on open-loop control. Thus, some degree of direct control over their efforts has traditionally been regarded as normal. With lower-level employees one way of doing this is to link rewards to effort by using incentive payments, and managers seem to have a sublime belief that incentive payments place them (the managers) firmly in control of the effort that people put into their work. Thus, to some extent there has been a use of open-loop control, with the anticipation of rewards being used to try and obtain employee compliance about the amount of effort expected (see Chapter 10). With salaried workers and more senior personnel however, it is near impossible to do this because incentives are usually vague and indeterminate: for example, merit payments, fringe benefits such as pensions and security, or the prospects of promotion. Moreover, most salary earners look upon themselves as distinctly different from those who earn wages, and it is often assumed that higher-level salaried workers have a degree of moral involvement with the organisation.

To some extent punishment – the reverse of reward – is also used to obtain compliance. However, trade unions have a vested interest in protecting their members from an arbitrary exercise of power by managers, and in any event the law tends to put limits on management's freedom of action in this matter (see Chapters 6 and 7).

Appraisal, training and development

Just as selection can be likened to a filter that admits only some of those who apply to join an organisation, appraisal, training and development are processes that can be used to reinforce the desired characteristics and behaviour of those who have been admitted. In appraisal an explicit link between performance and rewards is usually made, and for this reason it can become little more than a very crude form of psychological conditioning, in which employees learn to shape their behaviour into something that is personally acceptable to their superiors. Additionally, in most appraisal schemes managers evaluate employees, and decisions are made about whether some form of training or development will be provided. Thus, appraisal can influence access to future rewards that only come with promotion and/or conformance to the behaviour and attributes desired by management.

As a control mechanism, the main problems here relate to matters explained in Exhibit 12.1: the goals of the process; and how goal achievement is evaluated. For instance, although most guides to good practice for appraisal stress that it should primarily focus on measurable (or quantitative) achievements, it is common to find that employees have been assessed against very subjective (or qualitative) targets, such as 'improved attitudes or better customer relations'. These can be almost impossible to evaluate objectively, and any evaluation is at risk of being considered as nothing more than a 'matter of opinion'. Consequently, although appraisal schemes are one of management's most favoured methods of control, and having an appraisal scheme is regarded as the hallmark of enlightened human resource management, they very rarely deliver what they claim. For this reason the whole exercise can quickly degenerate into something in which appraisees try to 'please the boss' by showing that they take the exercise seriously, but quickly forget what has been said as soon as the annual appraisal interview is over.

Direct control

Employee monitoring by supervisors and managers is the oldest method of behavioural control, and to some extent everybody is subject to it. Nevertheless, the ways in which this occurs can vary considerably, as can the intensity with which control is applied. For instance, mild control might consist of giving instructions on what should be done, followed up by periodic checks to see that the instructions are observed. At the other extreme, very explicit instructions can be given about what is to be done and how it must be done, with almost continuous surveillance of employee actions and results, all of which is a variant of closed-loop control.

It is also worth noting that, in the past, variations in control methods tended to reflect the management styles of particular supervisors, most of whom had long service with an organisation. The expectations of acceptable behaviour in the firm were based on a detailed level of knowledge about organisational values, customs and practices and the types of workers being managed. These days, however, it is far more likely for there to be a degree of bland uniformity in terms of supervisory styles, and for this to be something that is imposed from above in the name of enlightened or sophisticated human resource management. Even so, research into some of these more modern control methods has clearly revealed that supervisors still have important control functions – either in circumventing or trying to make these newer methods work, or to exercise control where the newer methods fail to work as intended (Mulholland, 2002). Thus, the demise of direct control methods is almost certainly exaggerated (Thompson and Ackroyd, 1995).

Technology and job design

Technology generally denotes the means of accomplishing tasks. This is usually a management choice, and can have a huge effect on the ability to exercise control. For example, work on a mass-production assembly line is machine-paced, so that it is the speed at which the line moves that dictates how much effort employees are required to expend. The same is also evident in newer workplaces such as call centres, where technology dictates the pace of employee–customer interactions (Bain and Taylor, 2000). This makes it an issue with significant employment relations implications, and the speed of work tasks and management's use of technology can become a potential area of dispute.

Another way in which management can attempt to control the efficiency and effectiveness of employees is to design jobs with an eye to their motivational content. How to get the most willing work performance from employees has long been a concern of management, and across the years there have been many theories about what motivates employees, all of which imply that human behaviour can be brought under management's control (see Chapter 3). For a number of reasons, most of which are identified in Exhibit 12.1, this could be little more than wishful thinking on management's part. Although motivation plays some part in determining whether people work hard and willingly, motivation is a complex cognitive variable that is not

---

Case study 12.2: **Technology and job design at Tyreco**

Jerry is in his early thirties and is a tyre moulder at Tyreco. He services a bank of 40 presses; the final stage in the production of automobile tyres. The presses cure (a combination of heat and pressure) raw cases (the made-up tyre consisting of fabric and rubber) into the finished product. Curing time is pre-set and Jerry's task is to unload a cured tyre from a press when it opens, load an uncured tyre into the press, and then press a button to close the press and start the curing cycle. He does this continuously for an eight-hour shift, five days a week. The work is tedious and the building is extremely hot and noisy so that Jerry frequently feels near to the point of collapse at the end of a shift. He has two special mates in the shop: Alec, who works the line of presses backing on to those that Jerry operates, and Bill, who works back-to-back with Jerry. While there is little time for them to chat, which would be near impossible because of noise levels, they usually manage to take their meal breaks together. The work is very well paid but, since it is classified as semi-skilled, there are little or no prospects of advancement.

Jerry, Alec and Bill are all very similar in age and background, but have different approaches to work. Jerry dislikes his job and longs for a more interesting one. He is sometimes apprehensive about the future because he realises that when he gets older and slows down, he might find the present job too physically demanding. He has reconciled himself to reaching a point in life at which his earnings will decline, but since this is a while away yet, he just tries to get through the week and at the weekends, spends what he earns. Alec, who is a bit of a rebel, also feels that the job has no future. However, he quite enjoys his work and the social interactions with his mates. He takes a long-term view and saves every penny that he can, with the hope that he can put enough on one side to buy a small shop in a few years' time. To relieve the monotony of work, Alec sometimes makes a game out of the job by trying to beat his own output record. Bill, who is much more socially minded, also likes working at Tyreco and has been very active in the trade union for a number of years and he gets occasional relief from the drudgery of the production line to attend union meetings. In the long run he intends to rise in the union hierarchy and hopes within a few years to be elected to a full-time union position.

Questions

1 To what extent do you feel that the technological and job design conditions at Tyreco bring Jerry's behaviour under management's control?

2 Is this also the case for Alec and Bill?

3 What general conclusions can you draw from your analysis?

under management's control, any more than other cognitive traits such as commitment. Consequently, management's assumption about being in control of employee attitudes and behaviour rests on a huge self-deception.

Control through structure

Organisational structure and design, which are also covered in Chapter 3, usually result in a degree of specialisation of activities, together with a hierarchy of authority. A characteristic way of achieving control is through this hierarchy: for example, by specifying roles and rules that lay down the activities undertaken by role occupants. These details are often included in job descriptions, works rules and operational procedures, and are incorporated into the contract of employment, which gives a large measure of control over employee behaviour.

Needless to say, attempting to control employee behaviour through organisational structure also has distinct employment relations implications. The inclusion of certain duties on a job description, and the obligation to follow operational procedures establishes a reciprocal obligation to provide financial and other rewards in return. More important, perhaps, organisational hierarchies also shape behaviour in other, more subtle ways. Differences in authority not only map out the formal power of managers to reward some behaviour and punish those that are prohibited, differences in power also have psychological effects. They establish embedded rules of conduct that are taken for granted and which legitimise management power, so that those lower down the hierarchy cooperate in their own subjugation, and for many employees, adhering to management's will becomes organisational common sense to ameliorate the daily pressures that work throws at people (Weick, 2001).

Output control

As noted earlier, bureaucratic control focuses on two main aspects of a process or activity: *what* is done, and *how* it is done. A variant of this approach, which introduces an element of open-loop methods is **output control**. This consists of (i) specifying in advance the desired results (outputs) that should be obtained, usually by setting targets and time scales; (ii) holding the person concerned responsible for achieving these ends, but also granting a degree of discretion about how this is done; and (iii), reviewing achievement at a later date.

output control

Results to be achieved are specified (in advance) in terms of outputs, and a degree of discretion permitted in terms of how they are achieved, with outputs subsequently monitored.

This cycle is fundamental to most schemes of performance appraisal, and is widely used at middle management levels in systems of budgetary control, in which managers are set output and resource usage targets. For managers and other employees who have responsibilities that are not so easily translated into financial results, a similar way of introducing output control is to use a scheme of management by objectives (MBO), which is illustrated in outline in Fig. 12.5.

As can be seen this has a focus on achieving objectives and monitoring results at a later date. Since it also has a facility for an intermediate review of results, in control model terms it incorporates closed-loop principles. In general terms the following advantages are claimed for MBO:

- Because the employee is involved in selecting targets and defining what has to be done, he or she is said to be more highly motivated to perform well.

- The joint setting of targets also means that management gains a better understanding of the employee's problems and is able to assess what changes are needed to remove impediments to objectives being achieved.

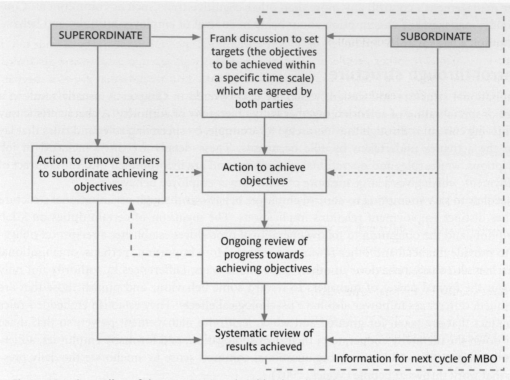

Figure 12.5 An outline of the management by objectives (MBO) process

- Information from the goal-setting and review stages can be valuable in identifying training needs, education and personal development programmes.
- Information from the MBO process can provide a thorough and systematic method of deciding whether individuals are ready for promotion.
- Since the same performance criteria are applied to everybody, in the case of promotion, this can demonstrate that decisions are fair.

Notwithstanding these points, it is important to stress that what is shown in Fig. 12.5 is MBO in theory; in practice things can be somewhat different. To start with, power is unequally distributed in all organisational hierarchies and this results in an ever-present danger that goals are imposed, rather than agreed. Second, unless jobs can, if necessary, be redesigned before using MBO so that an employee becomes responsible for a complete unit of output that is completely under his or her control, it is hard to see how meaningful goals can be derived. Indeed, if this is not the case, the whole cycle could be perceived as unfair, and may even result in resistance to control (Covaleski *et al.*, 1998). Finally, for some jobs the most important objectives require qualitative evaluations of performance, which makes it difficult to determine whether the most crucial goals have been achieved. For these reasons, it should not be taken for granted that MBO works effectively as a control mechanism in all situations and for all types of employees or line managers. Indeed, a poorly designed MBO system could well give rise to some thorny employment relations issues: for example, individual grievances.

Control by culture

A culture is a system of shared beliefs and values, which tells people about the behaviour that is accepted as normal by other people in a particular context, and since managers first discovered the topic in the 1980s, their interest has largely been focused on its potential use as a mechanism of control. For this reason, attempts to change cultures have become an essential element in recent developments in control regimes. These will be described presently, and in the meantime, traditional methods of behavioural control are summarised in Table 12.2.

Summary points

Traditional methods of behavioural control rely on a combination of:

- input control (recruitment, selection and socialisation)
- rewards and punishments
- appraisal, training and development
- direct control (personal supervision)
- technology and job design
- control through structure
- output control.

Recent developments in behavioural control

Over twenty years ago in reviewing the historic sequence of changes in control methods, Edwards (1979) predicted that some form of post-bureaucratic control was likely to emerge. He also forecast that this would most likely be based on more sophisticated monitoring techniques, utilising advanced information technology. Even before then, however, managers had long desired self-disciplined employees who do what managers want in a willing, productive and conscientious way, without the need for their efforts to be directly supervised. Electronic surveillance now offers the tantalising prospect of being able to obtain greater managerial control over employee effort. It also increases the possibility of introducing open-loop control methods, which are infinitely cheaper and more flexible than closed-loop control, the net result of which is a potentially 'self-correcting' work system. However, as was noted in Exhibit 12.1, open-loop control can only be used where two conditions are satisfied: first, where there is a perfect knowledge of cause–effect relationships in the processes to be controlled; and second, where inputs to the process are accurately regulated. With work systems this would mean in practice that:

- there is certain knowledge of the effects that different inputs have on each other
- the qualitative characteristics of these inputs are exactly known
- it is known for certain that all the required inputs are fed into the work system in the correct quantities.

With physical inputs such as machines and materials these things are not usually problematic, but people are more variable and complicated. They have feelings, emotions and minds of their own, and they react to situations in very different and unpredictable ways. Therefore, open-loop methods can only be used if control can be exercised over what employee 'think',

Designation and method	Aims	Components in control model and type of control	Most frequently used in conjunction with
Recruitment selection and socialisation	To control the quality of human resource inputs	The actuator in open or closed-loop control	All other methods
Appraisal, training and development	To set goals for individuals, monitor performance, and identify what is necessary to maintain/improve performance	Goals, monitoring, comparator and actuator in closed-loop control	All other methods
Direct control	To provide instruction and clarity about task performance and obtain compliant behaviour	Goals, monitoring, comparator and actuator in closed-loop control	All other methods
Technology and job design	To place constraints on employee behaviour by regulating what is done, how it is done and how much is done	The actuator, monitor and comparator in closed-loop control	Rewards and punishment structure
Rewards and punishments	To provide inducements to behave as required, and disincentives to unwanted behaviour	The actuator, monitor and comparator in closed-loop control	Appraisal, training and development
Structure (bureaucratic control)	To establish rules and procedures to limit discretion and make behaviour more consistent and predictable	The actuator, monitor and comparator in closed-loop control	Appraisal, training and development and sometimes as a substitute for direct control
Output control	To set goals for individuals, monitor performance, and adjust targets	Goals, monitoring, comparator, and actuator in closed-loop control	Appraisal, training and development, technology, job design and structure

Table 12.2 Comparison of traditional methods of behavioural control

so that they think in a way that managers want them to think, and this is a lot easier said than done. Because thoughts are invisible, we often have no idea of what people think until the results of their thoughts appear as visible actions.

Nevertheless, this does not stop managers yearning for self-regulating work systems. The current trend is to try to get as near as possible to open-loop conditions, and to do this some organisations are beginning to make use of control techniques that were relatively unknown in a prior era. Although one school of thought argues that this is a radical break with the past, the perspective adopted here is that recent systems of control use additional techniques that have been superimposed on older methods to give new and more intense control regimes (Casey, 1999). As yet no definitive model that describes these regimes has yet emerged, but Gabriel (1999) points out that they have some or all of the following features:

- The use of symbolic manipulation of meanings in a concerted attempt by managers to change employee cultures so that workers internalise the importance of service, quality, excellence, teamwork and loyalty

- Changes to structures and, in particular, the use of flatter hierarchies, flexible working practices, continuous benchmarking and performance measurement

- Changes in manufacturing techniques to introduce lean production, total quality management and just-in-time methods

- New methods of surveillance, including widespread use of electronic cameras, performance monitoring technologies, electronic tagging, and methods that enable identification of individuals who could be the source of operational problems.

An important characteristic of these features is that in theory, they are mutually reinforcing. This is shown in Fig. 12.6, and the ways in which they combine is explained in what follows.

Cultural control

While rudimentary attempts to manipulate organisational cultures have been attempted since the 1980s (with varying degrees of success) the cultural elements in new systems of control have more specific ends in mind. These are:

- to make new surveillance practices the norm, and more acceptable to employees

- to lead to greater effort on the part of employees

- to reduce levels of employee dissent or discontent, including any form of resistance or protest via trade unions (Casey, 1999; Purcell, 1993).

The objective of such cultural control is to win over the 'hearts and minds' of employees in supporting organisational goals, and to induce them to embrace a highly personalised relationship with the organisation, in which an individual's self-identity is largely derived from organisational membership (Jermier et al., 1994). The whole approach aims for an image of the firm as one big happy family, to which the employee has (or should have) a strong emotional and psychological attachment. The employee comes to accept that unswerving loyalty, intense effort and unquestioning obedience must be given to remain part of the family. In short, the aim is a system of total control that reflects managerial values, and any allegiances to other bodies, such as unions or occupational and professional associations, is abandoned (Willmott, 1993).

Cultural change is not easily accomplished and at best it can take years rather than months. The ways of trying to do this have been carefully examined in a number of research studies, and

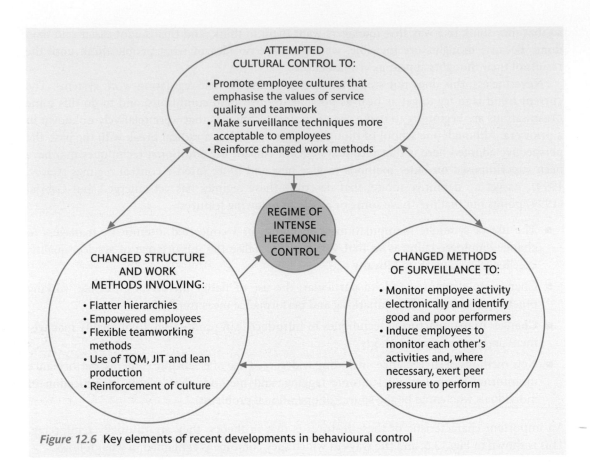

Figure 12.6 Key elements of recent developments in behavioural control

in almost all cases it has been shown that managers reinforce their ideas through a carefully chosen **discourse**. For instance, Knights and McCabe (2003) show that the discourse used to sell teamworking to employees is often concerned with appealing to their desires for a more enriched work experience. Similarly, Glover and Noon (2005) demonstrate how workers are induced to opt in to TQM initiatives, even though these will ultimately involve them in greater work effort. Here it is important to stress that the aim is to effect complete control over the hearts and minds of employees and, as Sewell (1998) notes, this is greatly facilitated if earlier forms of bureaucratic control can be replaced by **hegemonic control** (Rosen and Baroudi, 1992).

Bureaucratic control is really a rudimentary form of hegemonic control that extracts compliance in a very unobtrusive way, by using apparently neutral rules that employees perceive to be legitimate. However, true hegemonic control is much more personal, and it occurs when people come to believe that a source of authority is near-infallible. Thus, by using an appropriate discourse and language, managers set out to induce employees to adopt a unitarist ideology in which managers and workers are seen as being on the same side, and pulling in the same direction, towards the same common goals. If successful, this would result in managers being seen as leaders, whose instructions also represent the interests of the workforce, the net result of which is that there would no longer be a need for a set of

discourse

The idea that language is more than a useful tool of communication. Rather, what is said can convey what can seem to be the essential truth of how things are, which has the effect of disarming challenges to an argument that suppress alternative interpretations and supports particular interpretations and conclusions.

hegemonic control

Control exercised by an elite body whose power is accepted as supreme.

behavioural rules, because employees can deduce rules to fit any situation, simply by asking themselves 'what is it that the manager wants?'.

Structure and work methods

For a number of reasons that are largely economic, total quality management, just-in-time and lean production often feature strongly in current work systems. However, reaping the full advantages of these methods is acutely dependent on people working cooperatively. Consequently, they are usually accompanied by structural and work organisation changes, notably the introduction of teamworking and empowerment.

In popular management books teamworking tends to be presented as humanistic, and as something that frees workers from the drudgery of job designs based on scientific management principles (Katzenbach and Smith, 1993). In theory, this results in employees who are more committed, highly motivated and trustworthy because they have feelings of self-control, personal responsibility and autonomy (Tjosvold, 1991). However, teamworking often conceals the restrictions of scientific management behind a rhetoric of emancipation, and actually enhances managerial control (Sinclair, 1992; Barker, 1993). Moreover, because empowerment tends to be introduced after a workforce has been cut to the bare minimum, it becomes less of an opportunity for self-development, than an imperative for people to continually improve their performance to hold on to their jobs (Claydon and Doyle, 1996). While at first sight teamworking looks like a relaxation of control, in social and psychological terms, the reverse is true. Nevertheless, if people can be persuaded that they have really been empowered, and accept this idea within the culture outlined earlier, the result is likely to be highly significant. Employees will deliver the targets set by managers by making the decisions that management want them to make, and they will believe that they have made the decisions of their own free will; thus, a high degree of behavioural control is achieved in a near invisible way (Willmott, 1993).

Monitoring (surveillance)

Direct monitoring of employees is relatively expensive and contradicts the rhetoric of empowerment. Nevertheless, managers have a tendency to feel that they are not 'in control' unless employee behaviour is monitored in some way (Felstead et al., 2003), which poses the problem identified by Sewell (1998) – 'How do you achieve control without appearing to control?'. One possible answer to this lies in the way new surveillance technologies have been introduced in organisations. For example, Poster (1990) argues that technology has enabled highly sophisticated surveillance methods to emerge that are so unobtrusive that they tend to go unnoticed. Moreover, the facility for electronic monitoring of employee activities is advancing by leaps and bounds, and management's interest in remaining 'in control' is so strong that some of the latest advances are highly dubious in ethical terms. For instance, there is the reported case of a lecturer in cybernetics at Reading University who was approached by an American company to design a microchip that could be implanted under the skin of employees, to track their movements throughout the working day (Welch, 1999).

Sewell (1998) points out that many of the emerging work systems make use of teamworking, and these have been designed to incorporate two important forms of surveillance: **vertical surveillance** and **horizontal surveillance**.

vertical surveillance
Monitoring of a person's actions by someone located above the employee in the hierarchy, often by using electronic methods.

horizontal surveillance
Monitoring of a person's actions by people in the same workgroup, who then exert peer pressure on the individual to perform.

Horizontal surveillance is one of the most significant features of the new control regimes. Instead of monitoring the outputs of a work system, some monitoring is shifted to within the system itself, by having people observe the efforts of their colleagues (Barker, 1993). This is relatively cheap, and by introducing closed-loop methods at all the stages within a work system, the system as a whole is brought much nearer to being controlled by open-loop methods.

A number of authors have commented on the effect that this has on people who work under these conditions. Far from being the emancipated and self-actualising experience that is claimed for it, teamworking often turns out to be a highly stressful system that sets worker against worker (Parker and Slaughter, 1988; Taylor *et al.*, 2003). The whole process is made possible by attempting to manipulate cultures to promote the values of the organisation as though these are somehow the natural order of things. The reality is that workers are induced to police each other's actions. Thus, they are ultimately subject to an immensely tighter control regime: what Barker (1993) terms a 'concertive' form of control by peers and co-workers.

Summary points

- Current developments in control attempt to use a higher degree of open-loop control of work, by deploying mutually reinforcing techniques that result in more intense control regimes.

- One technique that is deployed is to attempt to change the culture of the workforce so that employees have values that result in them behaving as management desires.

- Another technique is to change structures and work methods so that employees work in teams which are empowered and held responsible for achieving results.

- Additional methods include the surveillance of employee behaviour by peers and co-workers through the use of increasingly sophisticated electronic means.

- These steps tend to result in more stressful and intense working environments.

Resistance to control

One of the things we should note about traditional methods of behavioural control used in organisations is that many of them have been in use for some time. While this does not mean that control is welcome, or that resistance does not exist, it suggests that many employees have either acclimatised themselves to control regimes, or have been able to shape management control into a form that they can 'live with'. Therefore, it is appropriate to start by re-examining what are said to be the underlying reasons for resistance.

As noted earlier, the political perspective on control argues that some degree of resistance is endemic, because workers are likely to resist control in order to avoid being exploited by managers. Although there is some evidence to this effect, it would be overstating the case to suggest that *all* resistance is for economic reasons. For example, a number of scholars have shown that resistance can have distinctly emotional roots, such as fear of change (Dent and Goldberg, 1999; George and Jones, 2001). In addition, because the opportunity to exercise valued skills is often central to a person's concept of self, and tight control can remove this opportunity, protection of self-identity is a powerful motive for resistance (Thomas and Davies, 2005; O'Doherty and Willmott, 2001). Moreover, since changed patterns of control can upset social relationships such as the structure of a workgroup (Bain and Taylor, 2000), it is also possible that people resist control as a way of protecting themselves from the effects of impending social changes. Finally, people who have a modicum of power and/or prestige can feel threatened by controls that might transfer this power into other hands (Mulholland, 2004). These, it can be noted, are all circumstances in which control could easily result in adverse emotional reactions. Thus, the political approach, which incorporates resistance to control with other forms of industrial action and workplace conflict, can present a somewhat oversimplified explanation that is limited in its capacity to encompass all the other reasons why resistance can occur.

Pause for reflection

Carefully reflect on the organisation for which you work, either full-time or part-time. If you have no experience of paid employment, use another organisation with which you are familiar or have been a member, and answer the questions below.

1 Are there any signs of resistance to control on your part or that of your colleagues?
2 Why do you feel that this resistance occurs? Is it for economic reasons, or as some form of emotional reaction?
3 What form does this resistance take?

Turning now to newer control regimes, there is no shortage of evidence to suggest that resistance continues to exist. However, as noted earlier, the cultural component in new methods of control is designed to remove employee resistance. While one school of thought argues that managers have been highly successful in doing this (see Casey, 1999), there are also arguments that when managers introduce new methods of control, employees find new avenues of resistance that remain hidden from managers. The middle view, which for the time being appears to be the most pragmatic, is that, while it is too soon to tell whether resistance has withered away, there is a body of evidence to show that it has taken on new forms (Thompson and Ackroyd, 1995). For example, Collinson (1994) points out that workplace resistance can manifest itself in two ways: **resistance through persistence**, in which employees go on the offensive; and **resistance through distance**, which is a defensive reaction in which people create their own physical and emotional space to opt out psychologically.

resistance through persistence
An aggressive or assertive way of resisting control.

resistance through distance
A defensive way of resisting control by psychologically opting out.

A number of authors point out that, as overt resistance has diminished among employees (see Chapter 11), in its place has emerged a more covert form of resisting control, in which employees seem to have found ways to undermine management's new control regimes. For example, Townsend (2005) shows that by seemingly adopting new electronic surveillance methods, call centre employees were able to turn them to their own advantage, and exert a degree of counter-control over management. Moreover, Bolton (2004) describes an interesting example of the ways in which NHS nurses were able to selectively re-interpret what managers stated they wanted, in order to deliver something that was much more in line with their own professional ethos. In addition to these examples, there are an increasing number of studies that seem to indicate that, far from being naive in their appreciation of what managers hope to achieve by using these new control regimes, employees are only too well aware of managerial intentions. Indeed, there is plenty of evidence to show that workers will, where necessary, find innovative and new ways of subverting managerial control methods (see Bain and Taylor, 2000; Geary and Dobbins, 2001; Knights and McCabe, 2000; Timmons, 2003). In particular, Jermier *et al.* (1994) identify the following as employee actions that can have this effect:

- Sabotage, pilfering and whistle-blowing
- Bloody-mindedness (being obstructive), legal retaliation and output restriction
- Developing counter-cultures, rumour mongering and refusal to accept autonomy and discretion.

With the exception of the first line, it can be noted that none of these is an overt act of defiance that would justify dismissal, and those in the two remaining lines are all what used to be called 'dumb insolence'. As many managers have found out to their cost, there is seldom a foolproof way of handling this. There are several employment relations implications that arise from these developments. First, it seems highly unlikely that resistance is completely dead. Instead, it has probably taken on a host of new forms to deal with new contingencies. Second, explaining why resistance still flourishes can often be found in the nature of the new control regimes. These days managers seem to be aware that, unless they take control of organisational culture, which has accurately been identified as 'the last frontier of control' (Ray, 1986), they have no chance whatsoever of exerting control over all the other aspects of organisational life. This is, however, a formidable task, and it would be an act of gross naivety for them to believe that employees are so gullible that they cannot spot an attempt to try and take over their hearts and minds. One of the few things that we can be sure of in this world is that a dislike of being under another person's control is a near-universal human attribute. Thus, people are likely to resent even more any attempt to manipulate their psyches. Therefore, new control regimes are virtually an invitation to resist the control that they seek to exercise. Finally, when resistance occurs, there are seldom any panaceas or recipes for removing it. Each case of resistance needs to be treated as unique, and an attempt made to understand why employees perceive that control has gone beyond the bounds of what is reasonable.

Summary points

- The political perspective on control argues that some resistance is inevitable because workers seek to avoid exploitation by managers.
- However, not all resistance occurs for economic reasons, and workers also resist control for a wide variety of emotionally based reasons, particularly in organisations that have adopted techniques associated with recent developments in behavioural control.
- Therefore, no matter how sophisticated the techniques it uses, the presence of a control system does not guarantee that control exists.
- Employees have their own ideas about the reasonableness of the boundaries of management's authority, and where these differ from management's ideas, resistance to control is almost inevitable.

Overview and conclusions

If large complex organisations are to achieve their goals and objectives, activities need to be coordinated and so control of some sort is inevitable. However, people tend to react to attempts to bring their behaviour under control, and have their own interpretations about what is acceptable and unacceptable control. Thus, even though control is often portrayed as a neutral activity, the reality and implications for employment relations can be very different.

Managerial control can be viewed from a number of different perspectives. Managers tend to believe that controlling the activities of others is a prerogative that comes with the job, while the political approach points out that control cannot be divorced from the use of power, and is often used for exploitative purposes. Between these two extremes lies the open-systems perspective, which views control as necessary, but also acknowledges that it can have unforeseen and exploitative consequences.

Many of the control strategies used in organisations attempt to regulate employee behaviour, and since control activities are normally in the hands of supervisors and managers, it cannot sensibly be divorced from the use of power. Traditionally, a wide range of practices have been developed to try to bring human behaviour under control, and these range from the recruitment, selection and socialisation of human resources, to the attempted manipulation of organisational cultures. However, people often have emotional reactions to attempted control, and there are arguments that a degree of resistance is virtually inevitable.

Recent developments in organisational control tend to result in more intensive control regimes. These attempt to use a number of mutually reinforcing elements that seek to obtain the ultimate degree of behavioural control – the control of employees' hearts and minds. Therefore, it is not surprising that some scholars argue that these can result in new forms of resistance that might ultimately turn out to be extremely difficult, if not impossible, to handle.

Review and discussion questions

1 Define what is meant by the word 'control' in an organisational context. What are the purposes of control in an organisation?

2 Compare and contrast the managerialist, open systems and political perspectives on control in organisations.

3 Explain the difference between open-loop and closed-loop control. What are the respective functions of the following components in closed-loop control: actuator, sensor, feedback path and comparator?

4 Explain the connection between power and organisational control. Why is it impossible to divorce power from control in an organisational context?

5 Describe seven methods that have traditionally been used to try to control employee behaviour. Which of these methods are most frequently used in combination?

6 Considering only traditional methods of behavioural control, what reasons could there be for this being resisted in an organisation?

7 Outline recent developments in behavioural control in organisations and explain why the use of these is likely to result in more intense control regimes.

8 Explain why resistance to recent developments of control might differ from the resistance found in traditional methods of behavioural control.

Further reading

Berry, A.J., J. Broadbent and D. Otley (1995) *Management Control: Themes, Issues and Practices*, Macmillan, London. A wide-ranging book written from what is basically a managerialist perspective, but which nevertheless gives good coverage of the topic.

Collinson, D.L. (1994) 'Strategies of resistance: power knowledge and subjectivity in the workplace', in *Resistance and Power in Organisations*, J.M. Jermier, D. Knights and W.R. Mond (eds), Routledge, London. A penetrating chapter, which deals with employee resistance to control in organisations.

Etzioni, A. (1975) *A Comparative Analysis of Complex Organizations: On Power, Involvement and their Correlates*, Free Press, New York. A revision by the author of his earlier (1961) text, in which he further develops the idea that an organisation's relationship with its employees is strongly influenced by the way power is used and the way that this engenders characteristic patterns of attachment by organisational members. A useful text that explains the underpinnings of control and resistance.

Hamilton, P. (2001) 'Rhetoric and employment relations', *British Journal of Industrial Relations*, Vol. 39 (3), pp. 433–449. An interesting paper that shows how organisational actors construct instrumental discourses aimed at moving the beliefs and behaviour of other people within an employment relations context.

Johnson, P. and J. Gill (1993) *Management Control and Organisational Behaviour*, Sage, London. The book has a focus on organisational structure, culture and power. It uses these to explore the use of formal control systems and behavioural control.

Mitchell, D. (1979) *Control without Bureaucracy*, McGraw-Hill, London. A useful text on industrial organisation that takes a humanistic stance on the matter of control.

Purcell, J. and R. Smith (eds) (1979) *The Control of Work*, Macmillan, London. A penetrating analysis of control from an industrial relations perspective.

Rosen, M. and J. Baroudi (1992) 'Computer based technology and the emergence of new forms of control', in *Skill and Consent: Contemporary Studies in the Labour Process*, A. Sturdy, D. Knights and H. Willmott (eds), Routledge, London. A penetrating chapter that fully explores emerging systems of behavioural control.

Integrating the effects of organisational processes

LEARNING OUTCOMES

After studying this chapter you should be able to:

☑ **describe** how interpersonal processes (discipline, grievance, dismissal and redundancy handling) can influence the organisational processes of employment relations (employee voice, collective bargaining and negotiation, conflict and protest, and control)

☑ **describe** the interconnections between organisational-level employment relations processes

☑ **explain** ways in which employee voice can have an impact on the employment relations climate of an organisation

☑ **explain** ways in which collective bargaining and negotiation can have an impact on the employment relations climate of an organisation

☑ **explain** ways in which conflict and protest can have an impact on the employment relations climate of an organisation

☑ **explain** ways in which control processes can have an impact on the employment relations climate of an organisation.

Introduction

This, the fourth and final integrative chapter in the book, has three aims. First, to show that there are interconnections between the interpersonal processes brought together in the previous integrative chapter (Integration 3) and the organisational processes described in the last five chapters. Second, to demonstrate that there are also strong interconnections between the processes covered in the previous five chapters. Third, to show that these processes not only affect each other, they also have an impact on the employment relations climate of an organisation.

Since employment relations climate was described in some detail in Integration 3, it is not necessary to repeat this here. The first matter to be covered is to extend the discussion given in Integration 3, by explaining how interpersonal processes (*discipline, grievance, dismissal* and *redundancy handling*) not only have effects on employment relations climates, they also have an impact on the organisational processes described in the last five chapters (*employee voice; collective bargaining and negotiation; conflict and protest;* and *control*). The chapter then identifies integrative links between organisational processes, and finally, it traces the all-important effect that these processes can have on the employment relations climate of an organisation.

The impact of interpersonal processes on organisational processes

As was noted in Integration 3, the way interpersonal processes are handled can result in either one or both of two climatic outcomes. The first, which arises out of an employee's experience of being subjected to one of these processes – say discipline – is referred to as a *psychological climate* (Koys and DeCotis, 1991). When a negative psychological climate of this type arises, the outcome is often that the relationship between the employee concerned and his or her manager seriously deteriorates. Ultimately, where there is a very serious deterioration, the employee can come to perceive that the terms of the *psychological contract* have been breached. There are a host of reasons why this could occur, and since these are documented in Integration 3, they will not be repeated here, except to note that in most cases they can be traced to poor or ineffective handling by management of the interpersonal processes that affect an employee's experience of their work situation.

The second outcome is probably more serious and arises from the social effects associated with the handling of one of these interpersonal processes. This comes about because workers share their interpretations of the treatment meted out to their colleague, which often leads to the group extending its moral and social support to an individual, and results in a more collectively orientated *employment relations climate* (Nicholson, 1979).

This second climatic effect has much wider implications. For instance, it is likely to colour employees' views and expectations about the likelihood of the same process being handled in the same way in the future. If social support has been extended to an individual because management was felt to have been unfair or unjust in its handling of the matter, social mobilisation theory (Kelly, 1998) tells us that workers have an agent (management) to whom they can attribute blame. In consequence, since they have begun to mobilise to give their support, mild attitudes of 'them and us' have probably already developed between employer and employee. However, matters do not necessarily stop here. There is always the possibility that workers will generalise their views and expectations about management's behaviour to a host of other processes connected with employment relations, including those matters normally conducted at an organisational level, such as the opportunity to have a voice or to bargain over certain issues.

Although it is unlikely that employees will use a single incident to draw conclusions about expected management behaviour, a series of small and single incidents can soon escalate into more serious issues, the net result being that processes designed to deal with matters at an interpersonal level can influence the climate at the organisational level. Moreover, there is also the possibility that organisational-level outcomes could travel in the reverse direction, and subsequently have an effect on interpersonal processes.

While this could theoretically occur with any of the organisational-level processes, the possibility of it happening could be particularly strong in the case of redundancy handling, which is an interpersonal process in which bargaining and negotiation have a central role. For instance, a chain of effects similar to the following could be produced:

- The handling of interpersonal processes (say a grievance case) could prompt an adverse employment relations climate.
- This climate spills over into collective bargaining and negotiation processes.
- Bargaining, negotiation and agreement seeking are central to redundancy handling, which is now also affected.
- A recursive cycle of poor climates is set up and that becomes a self-fulfilling prophecy at both interpersonal and organisational levels.

Organisational processes

This section of the chapter traces links between topics covered in the five preceding chapters, each of which deals with an organisational process that can have an important role in a firm's employment relations. It is important to note that these processes can all impact on each other. However, it is also important to stress that, in what follows, no attempt is made to imply a direction of causality. Rather the aim is to show that, if a firm has two processes that operate independently but are at the same time related – say employee voice and collective bargaining – their very existence will almost inevitably mean that they have an impact on each other.

For the sake of simplicity each process will be taken in the order in which it appears in a different chapter of the book and, to be comprehensive, all the processes will be covered. Nevertheless, it should be recognised that some of these processes are unlikely to exist in all firms. For example, some organisations might not have employee voice mechanisms and others, notably those that do not recognise trade unions, are unlikely to have formal arrangements for collective bargaining. Before embarking on this task however, it is important to make two preliminary observations. The first is that the processes considered in this chapter are all likely to be affected by the environment of the organisation. The second is that, in deciding to utilise these processes, it is vital for the organisation to try to ensure that arrangements for using them are compatible with each other. This might sound like an elementary design precaution, but it can be surprising how often it is neglected in practice, even when the processes have an obvious and evident linkage.

The impact of contexts on organisational processes

Perhaps the most obvious thing to note about all five processes is that they are conducted at what can most conveniently be called the 'strategic' level of an organisation. Here, top management, who normally manage the firm's interactions with its environment, have the task of reaching decisions about organisational policies and strategies. In the case of processes considered in this chapter, they are all concerned with establishing details of the relationship between a firm and its employees, and in most cases the process is strongly concerned with reaching decisions about the part that employees are intended (by management) to play in achieving business objectives. To express matters in what is admittedly a simple and stylised way, it can be argued that the different processes deal with the following:

1 *Employee voice* is concerned with *how* employees can contribute ideas towards the achievement of business objectives.

2 *Collective bargaining and negotiation* are concerned with sorting out the details of the *rewards* that employees will receive for their efforts.

3 *Conflict and protest* occur if management and employees *cannot reach agreement* about the terms of the reward–effort exchange.

4 *Control* is concerned with the methods that will be applied to persuade (or coerce) employees to perform in their agreed jobs.

In Chapter 2 of the book a model is given (see Fig. 2.1) which portrays the four contexts of an organisation: *political-legal*; *economic*; *socio-ideological*; and *technological*, and the text of the chapter gives a brief history of how changes emanating from these contexts have triggered changes within organisations. From the perspectives of both managers and employees, the most significant changes prompted by the environment have tended to be those that result in a perceived need for radical alteration of:

■ arrangements for the part that employees play in achieving business objectives

■ the process used for making decisions on this matter.

Changes of the first type can be prompted by changes in the circumstances posed by any of the contexts, and to give but a few of the many possible examples: the *economic* challenge of globalisation, the *socio-ideological* effects of changed labour-market composition, or the effects of new *technologies*. For the most part changes of the second type tend to arise because of a change that emanates from the *political-legal* context. For instance, the encouragement by government and the European Union for new information and consultation mechanisms (see Chapter 8), or provisions introduced for the statutory recognition of trade unions (see Chapters 4, 5 and 9). Note however, that seldom, if ever, is the environment completely static. Therefore, since organisations themselves are in constant interaction with their environments, most firms exist in a state of dynamic flux. Accordingly, there is a virtually continuous need for an ongoing use of the processes discussed in this chapter to handle changes and adjustments, and sometimes this extends to making necessary modifications to the processes themselves.

Compatibility between organisational processes

While it is not the intention to be prescriptive about the nature and content of the process that will be discussed, it is important to note that some of the most significant tensions that arise in employment relations occur because organisational processes are, in quite basic ways, incompatible with each other. Or to put matters more bluntly, it is often the *way* that management introduces new policies and practices that contradicts or sits uneasily with other existing processes, and this can occur for a number of reasons. For example, those responsible for drawing up the details of specific rules can have personal agendas for their use, and neglect the need for compatibility with other related processes. Similarly, management can be so eager to incorporate a much-needed change to deal with some impending crisis or market issue that they fail to realise that a change in one area contradicts processes serving other needs. In short, therefore, some processes have all the hallmarks of having evolved in splendid isolation from each other, and this is the case even when processes are intended to serve different purposes at different organisational levels. An example that illustrates this point is that of grievance. As was pointed out in Chapter 6, the word 'grievance' is often used in an imprecise way in employment relations, and there is often a failure to distinguish between grievance (individual matter) and dispute (collective matter). Nevertheless, it is not unusual for a considerable number of employees to have the same (or very similar) dissatisfaction. Thus, a well-constructed grievance procedure should ideally include a provision that enables what looks, at first sight, like an individual grievance to pass into the disputes procedures in an unimpeded way when it turns out to be a matter that needs to be pursued collectively.

However, there is another use for disputes procedures, and this is described in Chapter 10. If it has proved impossible to reach agreement in negotiations, it is sometimes convenient for the parties to collective bargaining to register a 'failure to agree', and move the matter into a 'disputes procedure' as a prelude to seeking third-party help in finding a resolution. For this reason, there is a clear need for the situation of being 'in dispute' to serve two purposes: first, to recognise the status of a group whose case has not yet been put to the test by being heard; and second, to recognise the existence of two parties whose case has been heard, but having failed to find a resolution, have agreed (for the time being) to suspend any hostilities. Needless to say, both purposes are equally important to those involved, and careful drafting of the integrative dimensions of both grievance and disputes procedures is needed.

Similar points can be made about links between many other processes. For instance, if voice mechanisms are to achieve their intended purpose, a degree of consensus is necessary about what these purposes are. If, for example, some topics are non-negotiable under a partnership approach, but these very same matters are negotiable under collective-bargaining arrangements, this needs to be sorted out well in advance so that the appropriate forum is used to raise an issue. Similarly, where the purpose of joint consultative arrangements is to communicate and nothing else, then any ambiguity about whether negotiation is allowed needs to be resolved. In summary, therefore, in whatever is said about the impact that different processes have on each other in what follows, there is always a caveat that attempts may be needed to ensure that these ambiguities do not exist, otherwise different processes are likely to be incompatible with each other before they are ever used.

Integrating organisational processes

Connections between employee voice and other organisational processes

Employee voice is very broadly defined in Chapter 8 as a whole variety of processes and structures that enable employees, either directly or indirectly, to contribute to decision making in a firm (Boxall and Purcell, 2003). The nature of employee voice is that it is something of a moveable feast that can have a wide range of purposes and perceived utilities to the parties to the employment relationship. At one extreme there are mechanisms that do little more than keep employees informed about decisions that have already been made, and at the other there are those that give them a relatively equal share in decisions that are yet to be reached. It is possible, therefore, to distinguish between voice mechanisms in terms of those that are *participative*, in which a relatively high level of influence is accorded to employees, with those that grant only *involvement*, where the aim of the practice is to bring about a degree of employee commitment, while still preserving management's exclusive right to make decisions unilaterally.

While there is now a degree of support by the British government for EU policy initiatives that promote employee voice (Ewing, 2003), it is also evident that many managers in Britain are less sympathetic to this form of regulation, and would prefer not to allow trade unions to be the main or exclusive channel of employee voice (Millward *et al.*, 2000). Indeed, in non-union firms it has been noted that so-called 'employee voice' schemes seem to be designed more to exclude the potential for union-centred forms of worker representation than anything else (Gall, 2004). Thus, managers have a preference for direct forms of voice that provide information to employees, with an emphasis on problem-solving activities. For this reason, although there is a connection between voice mechanisms and collective bargaining and negotiation processes, in terms of giving employees a real say on matters that affect them the connection is likely to be tenuous. Moreover, since bargaining and negotiation are 'at arm's-length' processes, in which the bond between employer and employees becomes more remote (Hyman, 2003), voice and collective bargaining may actually work in opposing directions: that is, although the former claims to integrate the interests of managers and employees, the latter more starkly illustrates matters about which there are divergent interests. While this does not mean that the aims of the two processes are always in opposition, it could mean that some forms of voice have a potential to cut across decisions reached in collective bargaining. Indeed, it may well be the intention of management to promote individualised forms of voice as a way to marginalise and ultimately exclude trade unions from organisational decisions.

In addition, it is important to note that, since there is some connection between voice and collective bargaining, by implication, conflict and protest behaviours, which are an extension of the negotiating process, are included in this connection. However, since conflict and protest only tend to come into play where highly visible and obvious disagreement exists between management and employees, its use is an even starker reminder that there are some matters in the employment relationship about which the parties are never likely to see eye-to-eye.

Finally, there are also likely to be strong connections between the voice mechanisms used in an organisation, and control in employment relations. Although many of the traditional ways of attempting to control workers have been in use for many years, two points can be made. First, although less controversial than newer methods, they should still be recognised for what they are: part of the management tool kit for attempting to bring human behaviour under control. Second, while newer control strategies might at first sight seem to offer employees a say in matters that affect them, their use is almost certainly underpinned by a management desire for a more effective control of employee actions (Tannenbaum, 1962). This could be particularly true with current developments in control, where cultural change programmes, job enlargement initiatives, the restructuring of work methods, and new surveillance techniques are all used in combination. Significantly, the use of these is often predicated on the idea that they operate in the employees' best interests, when in fact they primarily serve the aim of increased managerial control. Thus, by dressing up employee voice in the guise of a partnership approach, management seeks to convince employees that they both have identical interests, even though the eventual result is a more stringent control regime (Taylor and Ramsay, 1998).

Connections between collective bargaining, negotiation and other organisational processes

Because they are both complex processes, collective bargaining and negotiation have their own chapters in the book. Nonetheless, since collective bargaining is normally achieved through negotiation, they are virtually inseparable, especially in unionised settings. Of course, collective bargaining does not exist in anywhere near as many organisations as it did two decades ago. Indeed, de-collectivisation has occurred widely in British employment relations, and a firm might well decide to replace collective bargaining with an alternative voice mechanism of some sort. Furthermore, even where formal collective bargaining and union recognition is absent in a firm, this does not necessarily mean that negotiation is absent. For instance, grievances and dis-satisfactions can arise just as easily in non-union firms as in those that are unionised. As one of the most important functions of grievance handling is 'agreement clarification' (Briggs, 1981), this is likely to involve a considerable degree of negotiation, albeit at an individual level. In addition, with the increasing use of individualised employee-remuneration schemes, it seems likely that negotiation between individuals and their managers has become a frequent occur-rence in firms (Marsden and Belfield, 2005).

Perhaps more significantly, where the parties to a collective-bargaining relationship cannot reach agreement, conflict and protest can occur, which means that there is a clear connection between bargaining, negotiation and the use of different forms of conflict and protest behav-iours. Indeed, as is pointed out in Chapter 10, conflict and protest should more logically be regarded as an extension of the negotiating process rather than as something completely divorced from it.

Finally, there are also strong connections between collective bargaining and control processes, although control is such a 'taken-for-granted' term, that this connection is not always completely obvious. Because of the nature of their roles, it is perhaps only to be expected that managers will come to think of themselves as having both a right and a duty to control the activities of people in an organisation. Nevertheless, it is also fair to suggest that the desire to be 'in control' is sometimes viewed by a manager as such a fundamental part of his or her role that control regimes can sometimes exceed what is recognised in a firm as an acceptable frontier of control (Goodrich, 1975). When this happens, bargaining and negotiation, and sometimes con-flict processes, might be needed in order to reassert the previously agreed boundaries, or pos-sibly even readjust them for the future.

The implications for the employment relations climate

Just as interpersonal processes can have an impact on climate, so too can the processes at organ-isational level. Indeed, since organisational processes all tend to have effects on each other, the prevailing climate can result from the cumulative impact of several processes acting in tandem. The ways in which this can happen are many and varied, and it would be well beyond the scope of this chapter to try to detail them all. Therefore, only the most prominent will be identified, and to do this the processes will once again be taken in the order in which they are presented in the different chapters of the book.

Employee voice

As noted in Chapter 8, the phenomenon of a *representative gap* seems to have become evident in many organisations (Towers, 1997): that is, there is a noticeable difference between the amount of input that employees would like to have over certain matters, and the actual level of influence they have in reality. Indeed, this has been shown to be particularly true about such matters as terms and conditions of employment (Diamond and Freeman, 2001). Since these things are fundamental to the whole matter of the rewards–effort exchange, they could well have an adverse impact on the employment-relations climate. An even more pronounced effect could probably be predicted where voice opportunities have been 'sold' to employees as high-level *involvement* and *participation*, but in reality turn out to be nothing more that a shallow form of *communication*. In this situation employees are likely to have had their expectations aroused by believing they will participate, only to find that they have no real say in matters that affect them.

Several commentators also point out that partnership schemes can be weak and shallow, and can actually be used to weaken a trade union's participative role at an organisational level (Oxenbridge and Brown, 2004). Because this removes something that could well have been present in prior collective-bargaining arrangements, it could also result in a deteriorating climate.

Finally, there can sometimes be an adverse climatic effect that emanates from management. It is seldom the case that management introduce a voice mechanism without expecting something in return: for example, increased productivity, employee motivation or commitment. Perhaps more to the point, managers often have an unpleasant habit of wanting to see these returns almost immediately, and can be impatient for visible results. Unfortunately, measuring any improvement in these employee attributes is notoriously difficult, and as a result, management's enthusiasm for the initiative quickly wanes (Wilkinson *et al.*, 2004). Even worse, and to the confusion of employees, managers might then seek to withdraw their support for these voice mechanisms and turn to more arbitrary or coercive control methods.

Collective bargaining and negotiation

As noted in Chapter 9, in most cases where a collective bargaining relationship is retained in a firm, it can be a very effective (indirect) form of employee participation. In mature bargaining relationships, both parties will have learned that it is necessary to make concessions to each other, often by management ceding access to decision making to a trade union or other employee collective. For its part, the trade union will probably have adopted some responsibility for implementing decisions, rather than just acting as an opposition. It is well accepted that achieving this degree of maturity in the relationship takes time, and if there are attempts to rush the development process, this can be the fast route to a poor climate. Moreover, where other processes such as employee voice are required to act in concert, or side-by-side with collective bargaining, problems can be magnified considerably. For instance, great care is needed to ensure that the processes both have compatible degrees of scope and depth, and where this is not the case, decisions made in one process can cut across those reached in the other. As such there can be a considerable degree of frustration for those involved in the process, which in turn results in a worsened employment-relations climate. A case in point could well occur where a collective-bargaining process has hitherto had a relatively wide bargaining scope, allowing agreements to be reached about a wide range of topics, only to find that decision making on some of these has now been removed to a weaker and shallower voice process. This may well signal the *de facto* intention to marginalise or, worse still, to derecognise a trade union, and remove it from organisational decision making (Brown *et al.*, 1998).

While negotiation implies a willingness to compromise, both parties in employment relations enter the negotiating process knowing that either side can inflict harm on the other. Moreover, negotiation does not always lead to agreement, and there are occasions when one party might feel that it needs to put pressure on the other side, perhaps by threatening industrial action. While this action, or even the threat of it, is in force, there will almost inevitably be a worsening of climate, because the threatened party is effectively negotiating under duress. Furthermore, even when agreements are reached without this happening, one of the outputs (along with new substantive and procedural rules) is in any event a climatic one (Kelly and Nicholson, 1980b). Thus, if one of the parties has only been able to reach agreement by making large concessions, and has perhaps had to sacrifice some of its most cherished bargaining objectives, this can leave a bitter taste that has an impact on the climate long after the negotiation has been concluded. In an extreme case, for example, it can prompt the party to look for the opportunity to reopen the battle in order to recoup ground lost during a particular set of negotiations.

Conflict and protest

Although the collective bargaining process is usually conducted in an orderly way, if one of the parties feels it necessary to take industrial action this is not always instituted in a constitutional manner. For example, unofficial action might take place, or alternatively, a negotiator might feel that the opposing party needs a 'nudge', and proceed to ballot employees for industrial action while negotiations are still officially in progress. In either event, managers will probably feel that these steps are an attempt to force them to negotiate under duress, and this will almost certainly result in worse climate.

In addition, unorganised conflict can also result in a more adverse climate. For example, higher absenteeism, pilfering, fiddles or even sabotage can be an unpleasant reminder to managers that their control over the workforce is, at best, partial. Moreover, workers can sometimes be highly innovative in finding new ways of 'hitting back' at managers, and although steps of this nature are usually spontaneously taken by employees, managers can interpret them as a sign that a climate of 'them and us' exists, and respond in a heavy-handed manner.

Control

Some degree of control is necessary in most organisations, if only to ensure coordination of activities. Moreover, almost all organisations are structured in a hierarchical way, in which different levels in the hierarchy have increasingly greater authority. Control systems of some sort are a common feature in most organisations, and it is not surprising to find that managers lay claim to a right to exercise control over the activities of their subordinates. Indeed, we can hardly blame managers for feeling this way; it is what their education and training has taught them about the role of managing, and this means that 'being in control' is very high in the management value system. Having said this, and despite the fact that the whole concept of a contract of employment contains an assumption that it is an exchange of services for rewards (which in turn implies obedience), there are probably few matters in an organisation that have a greater potential to give rise to resentment and adverse climates than that of control.

The problem is that a dislike of being overtly under someone else's control is a near-universal characteristic of most people. For this reason, the right to control other people is usually circumscribed in organisations by fairly visible boundaries, some of which are enshrined in agreements between management and employees (or their unions). These agreements are intended to clearly indicate the respective 'frontiers of control' of the two parties, but this, of course, does not stop people wanting a greater degree of control. Indeed, the more absolute a manager's control over employees, the more that he or she is likely to perceive that it has become easier to do his or her job. Employees tend to have clear expectations about what are acceptable and legitimate forms of control, and that frontiers of control will be respected. However, from time to time someone in the organisation might decide that it would be personally advantageous to shift the boundaries of control in his or her favour. For the most part, both managers and employees recognise that this should not be attempted, at least not without adequate notice that allows the matter to be explained and negotiated. Unfortunately this sometimes fails to happen and when someone (manager or employee) decides to do this unilaterally, there is a huge potential for adverse climatic conditions to arise. For example, in situations where a manager seeks to extend his or her frontier of control, employees often 'hit back' in various ways, either by withdrawing their cooperation or finding an escape valve which enables them to disengage from management actions and the degradation of their work routine.

Conclusion

To summarise, this chapter has illustrated some of the ways in which the interpersonal processes covered in Integration 3 can have a climatic impact on the conduct of employment relations processes at the organisational level. It has also traced links between these organisational-level processes and shown that they can affect employment relations climates in various ways. These potential effects are summarised in Fig. I3, which, it will be noted, extends the scope of Fig. I2 from Integration 3, by integrating the possible interactions and effects of the material covered in this book.

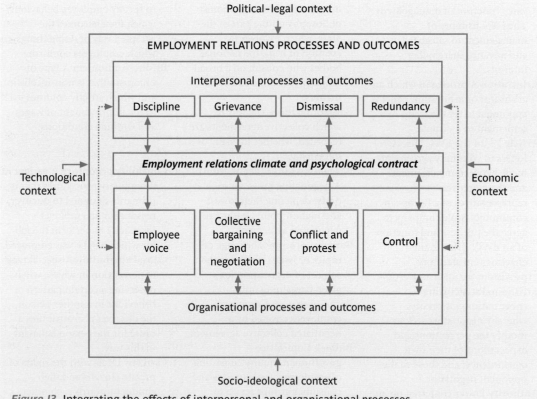

Figure I3 Integrating the effects of interpersonal and organisational processes

Glossary

A

Absenteeism Unauthorised absence (not to be confused with sickness absence).

Active protest A form of protest when employees consciously resist management or an organisational rule, often by directing their conflictual behaviours towards customers.

Actuator (control model) Something that adjusts the inputs to a process or activity.

Ad hoc approach (redundancy) There are no formally established arrangements for handling redundancy, and practice is varied according to the circumstances of each redundancy situation.

Agency function of management The responsibility of management to safeguard and advance shareholder interests.

Arbitration A process in which an arbitrator or arbitration panel is appointed to set the terms of a settlement to a dispute.

Article 13 (of the EWC Directive) Refers to voluntary agreements made between management and the employee representatives of a European community-scale company to agree the purpose and function of an EWC, prior to the enactment of statutory provisions for such an EWC.

Attitudinal structuring (negotiations) A process whereby negotiators seek to modify the perceptions and expectations of their own constituency, and those of the opponent negotiator.

Authority Power conferred on an individual or group as a legitimate part of the person or group's role.

Autonomous teamworking Employees working in groups who meet the criteria of: working alongside each another; taking responsibility for their job tasks; deciding how their tasks are to be accomplished; appointing their own team leader from among the members of the group.

B

Bargained corporatism A level of State intervention in employment relations synonymous with the existence of strong, autonomous trade unions and an interventionist philosophy on the part of the State, which involves the creation of tripartite national bodies who consult on a broad range of economic and social matters.

Bargaining form The way in which collective agreements are recorded, whether formally or informally.

Bargaining range (negotiation) A negotiating range for each party, depicting their lowest and highest points leading to a negotiated agreement.

Bargaining scope The range of topics or issues which are the subject of negotiation for a given bargaining unit.

Bargaining unit A group of employees covered by a negotiated collective agreement.

Bullock Committee A government inquiry consisting of employers, trade unions and consumer groups set up to identify how plans for worker directors could best be implemented in Britain.

Bullying and harassment procedures A procedure that enables an employee to formally complain about bullying or harassment to which he/she believes that he or she has been subjected.

Bumping (redundancy) For reasons of operational convenience, and with the consent of the two employees, a potential redundancy in one individual's role is transferred to another employee's role.

Bureaucratic control The use of tight job specifications and standard operating procedures to specify employee behaviour, which then becomes the accepted way of doing things, to which employees conform.

Business unionism A type of unionism that is non-idealistic and which strictly confines itself to the improvement of wages and working conditions.

C

Capability procedure A variant of disciplinary procedures that is primarily designed to uncover reasons for an employee's incapacity to perform the job for which he/she was employed.

Causal attribution A special type of perception in which, when observing a certain pattern of behaviour in another person, the observer also attributes a cause for the person behaving in this way.

Civil law Deals with the rights of private citizens and their conduct towards each other.

Closed shop An arrangement in

which union membership is a condition of employment.

Closed-loop (feedback) control A method in which the outputs of a process or activity are monitored and, if necessary, inputs are adjusted to achieve the desired outputs.

Co-determination A system based on legal rights for workers (at enterprise level) and unions (at national level) to participate in decision making.

Collective bargaining A process in which the representatives of recognised trade unions and employers negotiate, consult and communicate to agree the procedural and substantive terms and conditions of employment.

Collective bargaining coverage The proportion of employees in the economy as a whole whose pay is influenced by collective bargaining.

Collectivism A philosophical stance that recognises that some issues in the employment relationship are best dealt with on a collective basis.

Common law Laws that arise from legal decisions made in a court of law or an employment tribunal.

Comparator (control model) Something (or someone) that compares the desired attributes of the outputs of a process or activity with those actually achieved.

Compensation (unfair dismissal) A remedy which consists of the sum of four different awards.

Competency-related pay Pay is set at a level, either in whole or in part, according to a level of competence exhibited in carrying out certain job tasks.

Concession bargaining A practice used in America, where, because a negotiated contract is legally enforceable, the employer needs to engage in

bargaining with a trade union to be able to obtain concessions over matters such as wage rates in order to vary the contract during a recession.

Conciliation Advice and assistance to help resolve a collective or individual dispute.

Concluding negotiations The fourth and final phase of face-to-face negotiations, which is defined as the process of agreeing to what has been agreed.

Constitutional action That which is initiated when all stages of a disputes procedure have been exhausted.

Constructive dismissal A claim by an individual that he or she was forced to resign as a direct result of his or her employer's actions.

Contract of employment A legal agreement in which an offer of employment is made by an employer, and accepted by the employee.

Control model A symbolic representation of the components necessary for a system of control, how they relate to each other and their functions.

Convenor A lay officer of the workplace union appointed from among accredited shop stewards.

Corporate governance The enhancement of corporate performance via the supervision or monitoring of management performance to ensure the accountability of management to shareholders and other stakeholders (Keasey and Wright, 1997).

Corporatism A state of affairs in which centralised economic activity dominates society, trade unions are relatively weak and subordinated by State control.

Criminal case A legal prosecution brought to either the magistrates or crown court by

an agency of the State, such as the police or one of the various employment relations commissions.

Criminal law Deals with unlawful acts that are offences against the public at large.

Custom and practice Rules that result from an informal bargaining arrangement, which eventually become incorporated (implicitly) into the contract of employment.

Custom and practice arrangements Unwritten and informal workplace rules that regulate work and employment.

Cybernetics The theoretical study of control processes in electrical, mechanical and biological systems.

D

Decision-making function (collective bargaining) Analogous to a system of industrial democracy, in which employees, through their representatives, participate in decisions that affect their interests.

Delayering A reduction in the number of functional levels in an organisation's hierarchy, usually by removing one or more levels of supervision and/or middle management.

Demand side (economics) A macro-economic approach which seeks to stimulate the demand for goods in an economy, which is presumed to lead to an increase in employment and economic growth.

Depth (of employee voice) The extent to which employees (or their representatives) share in decision-making outcomes with management.

Deterrence approach (to discipline) The use of disciplinary action to provide an unpleasant consequence following a rule transgression, to deter an employee from future transgressions of the same nature.

Developing the case (negotiation) The second phase of face-to-face negotiations, in which both sides argue the strength of their own case, and seek to reduce the validity of their opponent's arguments.

Direct voice Where contact is between individuals or small groups of employees and their immediate manager.

Discipline Some action taken against an individual who fails to conform to the rules of an organisation of which he or she is a member.

Discourse The idea that language is more than a useful tool of communication. Rather, what is said can convey what can seem to be the essential truth of how things are, which has the effect of disarming challenges to an argument that suppress alternative interpretations and supports particular interpretations and conclusions.

Dismissal The termination of a contract of employment.

Dispute of interest A disagreement over the contents of a collective agreement, such as pay, pension entitlements or hours of work.

Dispute of right A disagreement over the interpretation of a collective agreement, such as the frequency of meetings for a negotiating committee or the facilities afforded to shop stewards to carry out their duties.

Distributive bargaining (negotiations) A zero-sum negotiation in which a gain to one side is a loss to the other party; likened to dividing up the slices of a cake.

Donovan Commission A Royal Commission (1965–1968) to review and make recommendations on the relations between trade unions

and employers associations in Great Britain.

Downsizing A reduction in the number of people employed by an organisation or in the scale of its activities, theoretically to attain the appropriate size for its volume of business.

Dysfunctional conflict Forms of conflict and protest behaviour that exist, but are associated with imperfect organisational functioning.

E

Economic context The overall state of the economy in which an organisation operates, for example whether it is buoyant or recessionary.

Economic function (collective bargaining) Sets the price at which labour power is bought and sold.

Economic regulation The trade union function of securing the highest possible real wages for its members.

Employee involvement The soliciting of employee views, opinions and ideas to harness the talents and cooperation of employees, but without the sharing of power in an eventual decision-making outcome.

Employee share ownership plans These schemes provide the opportunity for employees to either purchase company shares through a dedicated company savings scheme, or receive a certain number of free shares each year as part of the salary package.

Employee-centred control A strategy that involves influencing the way that employees think about themselves and what they do, so that they willingly subscribe to management's aims.

Employees and their associations Whether employees mobilise as a collective group, and the characteristics of that collective group.

Employer, paymaster and buyer of goods (the State) By virtue of its role as an employer, the State is able to intervene in employment relations in both public and private sectors of the economy by setting standards of responsible employment practice.

Employers and managers The roles and techniques used to manage employees in a firm.

Employers association An organisation of employers that exists for the purpose of regulating relations between employers and employees, or trade unions.

Employment appeals tribunal A higher legal court that deals with appeals from employment tribunals.

Employment regulation A set of rules and procedures governing the conduct of employment relations and the establishment of workers' rights that are determined by customs and/or legislation.

Employment relations – processes and outcomes The dynamic interactions between employees and an organisation that are concerned with the economic, social, psychological and legal exchanges associated with paid employment.

Employment relations climate A particular ethos or atmosphere that exists within an organisation at a given point in time, which is reflected in the way its members perceive, experience and react to the organisational context.

Employment tribunal A legal court that adjudicates on employment law cases.

Empowerment Giving people the authority to make decisions in their own area of operations, without the approval of senior management.

Enterprise union A union in which membership is restricted to employees of a particular firm.

Equal pay (for work of equal value) procedure A procedure that enables an employee to contest the pay grade for his/her job on the grounds that it entails duties and responsibilities equal to some other organisational role.

Equity The idea that people should be treated with parity to each other in terms of the personal costs they incur, and benefits they accrue from work.

European law Directives and regulations passed by the European Parliament, which are then transposed into British statute law.

European Social Policy A set of regulations that provide rights for workers which are comparable across EU member states, and which embrace rights on working hours, employee voice, redundancy, health and safety, and maternity and paternity leave.

European Trades Union Confederation (ETUC) A pan-European federal body to promote and coordinate the interests of trade unions across European countries.

European Works Council (EWC) An employee forum/committee for the purposes of sharing information and consulting with management on matters of interest in a European community-scale company.

Expropriate To dispossess or remove property from someone.

External attribution The cause of a person's behaviour is assumed to be connected with a factor in his/her environment.

External (third party) association An institution that articulates the concerns of employees to management and/or represents their interests in a court of law. One example are the Citizens Advice Bureaux (CAB).

F

Failure to agree (negotiation) A situation where both parties agree there is little likelihood of further concession or compromise, and agree to withdraw from the negotiating process to either seek third-party conciliation or engage in industrial action.

Fall-back point (negotiation) A negotiated minimum, below which agreement would be unacceptable for each of the parties.

Financial participation Mechanisms that allow employees to share in the financial success of their organisation.

Floor of rights concept The idea that individual rights established by law are no more than a fall-back position that can be resorted to if all else fails.

Form (of employee voice) The type of method used, which can be direct and/or indirect in nature.

Formal contract The formally agreed terms of the employment relationship, i.e. the legal concept as reflected in the contract of employment.

Frame of reference A 'world view' that influences how a specific state of affairs is perceived by its holder, and, by implication, how he/she reacts to the situation.

Free rider A person who receives the benefits of union membership, but who avoids any associated costs by not joining the union.

Frontiers of control A concept that describes the boundaries of either party's freedom of action to negotiate and bargain over certain issues.

Functional conflict Forms of conflict and protest behaviour that can be positive, allowing a diversity of opinions and solutions to problems to emerge.

Functional flexibility An organisation's capability to vary what is done and how it is done.

Functions of trade unions The means used by trade unions to achieve their aims.

G

Gainsharing A group-based incentive payment scheme that links employee effort to productivity improvements and/or cost savings made by a defined group or team of employees in an organisation.

Geographic federalism A form of union government which gives a degree of decision-making autonomy to districts or regions.

Geo-occupational federalism A more complex form of union government in which geographic and occupational autonomy exist together.

Gerontocracy Government by and respect for older people in society.

Globalisation A series of interrelated economic developments, in which organisations seek to produce goods and services for a one-world market economy.

Go-slow Working at lower than normal output levels, but not to the extent that a breach of contract occurs.

Government function (collective bargaining) Establishes a set of rules or a constitution which becomes the foundation for an on-going relationship between management and employees.

Grading appeals procedure A procedure that enables an employee to contest the pay grade for his/her role.

Grievance With respect to conditions of employment where a situation appears contrary to the provisions of collective agreements, the individual contract, work rules, laws or regulations or custom and practice.

Gross misconduct Transgression of one of the rules of employment established by the employer, which constitutes a serious breach of contractual terms and results in a fundamental breakdown in the employment relationship.

H

Hard goals (control) Those that can be precisely specified in an unambiguous and usually quantifiable way, and whose achievement can be measured accurately.

Hard HRM An approach focused on bottom-line considerations in which employees are viewed in much the same way as other resources that can be used or disposed of as necessary.

Health and safety representatives Union representatives at the workplace who have, among other things, the legal right to inspect the workplace on behalf of union members.

Hegemonic control Control exercised by an elite body whose power is accepted as supreme.

Horizontal differentiation The division of an organisation's overall task into different activities.

Horizontal surveillance (control) Monitoring of a person's actions by people in the same workgroup, who then exert peer pressure on the individual to perform.

Human resource information systems (HRIS) The use of a range of computer packages that store, manipulate and analyse information related to how people are managed in an organisation.

I

Ideal settlement (negotiation) An ideal negotiating outcome on a particular issue for each party.

Incentive payment system A system in which employee pay, either in whole or in part, is comprised of different monetary amounts determined by management evaluations of individual performance.

Incomes regulator (the State) An employment relations role adopted by the State, in which it seeks to control prices and wages, either through direct intervention or in its management of the economy.

Indirect voice Where contact is between management and an employee intermediary, such as a shop steward or other employee representative, who acts as the agent for a larger group of workers.

Individual performance-related pay (IPRP) A payment system designed to reward employees based on an evaluation of their whole job performance.

Individualism A philosophical stance that reflects the idea that each employee should be treated as an individual in the employment relationship.

Industrial union A trade union organised on the basis of representing all grades of workers in a particular industry.

Informal contract A less formal expression of the employment relationship that reflects a degree of give and take between the parties.

Integrative bargaining (negotiations) A positive-sum affair in which the parties engage in cooperative negotiation; likened to a joint effort to make the cake bigger.

Internal attribution The cause of a person's behaviour is assumed to be connected with his/her psychological characteristics, e.g. personality, etc.

Internal employee forum A management-initiated employee body, such as a company committee.

Inter-organisational bargaining (negotiations) The actual interface where negotiators negotiate on behalf of their respective constituency, which is the employing organisation for management, and employees who are union members for the trade union negotiators.

Interpersonal relationship (negotiators) The level of rapport and the degree of trust that can exist between the principal negotiators.

Intra-organisational bargaining (negotiations) A process whereby negotiators negotiate with their own constituents in order to bring the expectations of the group they represent into line with their own expectations about what can realistically be achieved.

Iron law of oligarchy A theory which predicts that union officials are likely to become incorporated into the ranks of management and further their own interests, rather than pursuing membership concerns.

J

Job regulation The trade union function of being one of the joint authors of the rules and procedures that govern employment in a firm.

Joint consultation A voice process that can be direct or indirect and one in which management and employees (or their representatives) discuss and consider each other's views prior to management making a final decision.

Joint regulation The agreement of substantive and procedural rules between employers and employee representatives, the authorship of which can be attributed equally to both parties.

Juridification The extent to which legislation influences employment relations processes and outcomes.

K

Keynesian (economics) A macro-economic theory which concentrates on managing the demand side of the economy through government fiscal policies, with the aim of achieving full employment, price stability and a balance of payments equilibrium.

L

Labour process theory A neo-Marxist perspective that focuses on employer attempts to control the labour process, and employee attempts to exercise counter-control in return.

Layoff An employee receives no pay at all for a period of time, although still technically an employee of the organisation.

Leader stewards Union stewards who tend to be politically and ideologically committed to trade union principles, and who seek to influence the opinions and actions of the membership accordingly.

Level of bargaining The organisational level at which bargaining normally takes place, which can exist at up to four levels: national, organisational, plant and workplace levels.

Level (of employee voice) The hierarchical level in an organisation at which a voice mechanism takes place.

Liberal collectivism A level of State intervention in employment relations synonymous with the emergence of stronger and more autonomous trade unions under a liberal capitalist philosophy, in which the outcome is a legislative framework that encourages the legitimate interests of both parties.

Line management Members of an organisation who normally have formal authority over other employees.

M

Management style A manager's preferred approach to handling employment relations matters with employees, which reflects the way that he/she exercises authority over subordinates.

Manager-directed control Managers specify exactly how and what should be done, and then closely monitor employee behaviour.

Managerial prerogative Rights or functions that managers assert are exclusively theirs.

Managing The activity of running an organisation (or part thereof), included in which is the responsibility for achieving one or more objectives.

Manpower manager (the State) An employment relations role adopted by the State, in which it promotes effective manpower utilisation.

Market individualism A level of State intervention in employment relations synonymous with weak, unregulated trade unions and laissez-faire economic philosophies, in which the State supports ruling-class interests and severely curtails trade union power.

Means–ends hierarchy Goals at one organisational level are the means of achieving the goals of the organisational level immediately above.

Mediation A process in which the mediator recommends a potential solution to a dispute for the parties to consider.

Meritocracy A social and economic system in which advancement is based on ability or achievement.

Minor misconduct Transgression of one of the rules of employment established by the employer.

Mixed bargaining (negotiations) The coexistence of both distributive and integrative bargaining activities.

Monetarism A right-wing economic theory which argues that self-regulation through market forces is the most efficient way to control inflation. In this trade unions are deemed to be a supply-side constraint, and so their activities need to be systematically weakened and curbed by the State.

Multi-employer bargaining An arrangement in which bargaining takes place between one or more trade unions and an employers' association for a whole industry, with the terms of the agreement covering the majority of firms (or employee groups) in that industry.

Multinational organisation One that is managed from the firm's country of origin, in which goods and services are produced in overseas subsidiaries to cater for the demands of overseas markets.

Multiple bargaining objectives (negotiation) The existence of a number of different negotiating issues, each with their own separate bargaining ranges and fall-back positions.

N

National delegate conference The supreme policy-making body of a trade union, which is comprised of lay representatives.

National minimum wage A statutory minimum rate of pay for all workers and trainees in Britain, which is changed periodically on recommendations from an independent Low Pay Commission.

Negotiation A process of dialogue through which the parties seek to reconcile their differences, with the aim of producing an agreement, whether formal or informal, by using elements of power, persuasion and argument.

Never-members Employees who have no experience of a unionised relationship.

Non-industrial civil courts Courts that deal with an array of other employment-related matters, such as claims of negligence against an employer or injunctions seeking to restrain union action.

Normative inputs (control) Human values, attitudes, beliefs and motivators.

Number of stoppages A strike statistic that records the number of strikes that occur in each calendar year.

Number of workers involved A strike statistic that counts the number of workers involved, and gives some indication of the breadth of strikes.

Number of working days lost A strike statistic that counts the number of workers involved in a strike and also the duration of time for which the strike lasted.

Numeric flexibility An organisation's capability to match the size of its workforce with its required output levels.

O

Occupational federalism A form of union government which gives a degree of decision-making autonomy to the union's different occupational groups.

Official action That which receives official trade union support or authorisation; normally after employees have been balloted beforehand, and indicated their willingness to support the action.

One-way communication A direct form of voice where information is disseminated from management to employees.

Opening moves (negotiation) The first phase of face-to-face negotiations, in which the proposing side will present its claim and supporting arguments.

Open-loop (feedforward) control A method in which the inputs to a process or activity are carefully determined, but with no monitoring of outputs.

Organisational culture A system of shared beliefs and deep-seated values, which are a prescription for the ways in which people behave.

Organised action A conscious attempt to bring about a change in the situation that has become a source of discontent; normally organised by an employee collective organisation, such as a trade union.

Organising unionism A type of trade unionism that focuses strongly on recruiting and training members, with the aim of leaving in place a strong, self-reliant cadre of workplace activists.

Output control Results to be achieved are specified (in advance) in terms of outputs, and a degree of discretion permitted in terms of how they are achieved, with outputs subsequently monitored.

Overtime ban A refusal to work beyond the strict contracted hours.

P

Paradigm An example or model, which is used as a standard and expresses the prevailing framework of theories and concepts.

Participation The sharing of power between employees (or their representatives) and management, in the making of joint decisions.

Partnership A concept that is normally taken to imply cooperation (usually between management and trade unions) based on the satisfaction of mutual as well as separate interests.

Passive protest A form of protest in which employees mentally 'switch off' from their work.

Payment by results A payment system in which employee pay is based on output and effort.

Pilfering and fiddles Acts of minor theft.

Pluralist perspective A frame of reference in which an organisation is seen as a collection of different groups, all with their own legitimate aims to pursue, and so a degree of conflict is a normal state of affairs.

Political-legal context The extent to which the government plays a role in employment relations, directly and/or indirectly.

Populist stewards Stewards who are content to let their constituents dictate how they act in representing member interests.

Portfolio approach (control) The use of different strategies for controlling employee behaviour according to which one is seen to be the most applicable at the time.

Position power The degree of freedom of action in a supervisor or manager's role.

Potential harms and benefits approach Defining stakeholders as anyone who potentially benefits or is potentially harmed by the activities of an organisation.

Potential zone of settlement (negotiation) The potential for a negotiated settlement, without recourse to industrial action, within the range of each party's minimum fall-back position.

Power The capacity of an individual or group to modify the conduct of other individuals or groups in a manner which they desire, without having to modify their own conduct in a manner which they do not desire.

Power holding The trade union function of acquiring power relative to management, so that it is capable of taking retaliatory action in pursuing its objectives.

Principal–agent (P–A) model A theory of corporate governance which explains the need to protect the organisation from the potentially harmful effects of the divorce of ownership from control.

Procedural rules The terms of a collective agreement that refers to the mechanisms to adjust substantive rules, such as when negotiations are conducted, and by whom.

Professional association A voluntary organisation which aims to improve professional practice by providing a qualification, controlling conduct, coordinating technical information and pressing for better conditions of employment.

Professional manager argument That management is a profession that has emerged as an occupational group which has a monopoly of the skills, knowledge and expertise necessary to conduct the affairs of an organisation.

Profit-related pay A scheme in which part of an employee's salary is based on company profits.

Property rights argument That managers are the agents of the ultimate owners of the business, and therefore have the delegated authority of the owners to make decisions on their behalf.

Protective award (redundancy) An award made to a group of employees in recognition of the fact that their employer failed to observe the statutory right for employees to be consulted about proposed redundancies.

Protector (the State) An employment relations role adopted by the State, in which it establishes and monitors minimum standards through its agencies.

Psychological contract An (unvoiced) set of expectations that the parties have of each other, together with the obligations that they feel towards each other.

Punishment approach (to discipline) An 'eye for an eye' and 'tooth for a tooth' philosophy, which emphasises taking retribution for having transgressed an organisational rule.

Q

Quality of working life (QWL) movement A campaign that concerns itself with measures to improve the experience of working life for American workers, often by placing emphasis on such matters as job design and the use of participative management techniques.

Quitting Resignation from a position in an organisation.

R

Radical perspective One that argues that employment relations mirrors the inequalities of social class, property ownership and political ideology in wider society.

Redundancy agreement Sets out a procedure that will be followed when redundancies need to be considered, with the contents of such a procedure being the subject of prior negotiation and agreement between trade union and management.

Redundancy policy Sets out the approach that will be adopted by management, if and when it is faced with having to make redundancies.

Re-engagement A remedy for unfair dismissal in which suitable alternative employment with the original employer is given, plus compensation for time spent unemployed.

Rehabilitation approach (to discipline) The use of the disciplinary process to show an employee that certain behaviour is unacceptable, with the aim that in the future she or he will voluntarily adopt patterns of behaviour that are acceptable.

Reification To treat an abstract idea as something that actually exists.

Reinstatement A remedy for unfair dismissal in which the employee gets his or her original job back, with all prior conditions restored, and with additional financial compensation to reflect any time spent out of work.

Relative deprivation Feelings of deprivation that arise when one individual or group feels that it has been unfairly treated in comparison to another individual or group.

Relative importance of a negotiating issue The importance attached to a particular negotiating issue according to the constituent group the negotiator represents.

Relative power of the parties (negotiations) The capability to get the other side to change their view, which may or may not involve the use of sanctions.

Representation gap The difference between how much influence employees say they have over management decisions, and how much influence they say they would like to have.

Resistance through distance (control) A defensive way of resisting control by psychologically opting out.

Resistance through persistence (control) An aggressive or assertive way of resisting control.

Reward system The total of pay and non-pecuniary rewards that make up an employee's remuneration package.

Rule maker (the State) An employment relations role adopted by the State, in which it enacts legislation to create auxiliary, restrictive and regulatory rules of conformity for the parties in employment relations.

S

Sabotage Deliberate acts of disruption designed to frustrate management's interests.

Sampling (control) The characteristics of the total outputs of a process or activity is estimated by examining only a proportion of the output.

Scope (of employee voice) The range of issues or matters on which employees (or their representatives) have a say.

Seeking agreement (negotiation) The third phase of face-to-face negotiations, in which one of the parties makes public definite and concrete proposals for agreement.

Sensor (control model) Something (or someone) that monitors the attributes of the output of a process or activity.

Servicing unionism The provision of a range of professional membership services by the parent union, such as the representation of members' interests and legal advice.

Shadow legal effect An indirect outcome of statutory trade union legislation, which has led employers and unions to agree new *voluntary* recognition arrangements.

Shop steward A general (but not universal) term used to describe a representative accredited with management by the trade union, who is elected by a specific group of members to represent their interests.

Short-time working An employee receives less than a week's pay for a particular week.

Single-table bargaining An arrangement in which an employer negotiates with several recognised trade unions simultaneously.

Single-union agreements An arrangement in which an employer recognises just one trade union for the purpose of collective bargaining, for all the different categories of workers in the employing organisation.

Skill-related pay Allocates a proportion of an employee's pay according to acquired skills and job qualifications.

Social control Achieving compliance, conformity and obedience through interpersonal or intergroup processes.

Social mobilisation theory A theory which argues that when people experience an injustice or grievance, they have a tendency to form into collective groups.

Socio-ideological context The behavioural norms and cultural values in a society which can influence the nature of the relationship between a firm and its employees.

Soft goals (control) Those that are more subjective and qualitative in nature, open to interpretation and whose achievement is more difficult to evaluate.

Soft HRM An approach that views

employees as valued assets, the appropriate use of which can lead to competitive advantage for an organisation.

Staff association A voluntary in-house collective association that caters for particular employees, mainly salaried staff, who all work for the same employer.

Staff management Those managers in specialist roles who advise line managers, or act on their behalf.

Stakeholder People or groups with an interest in the activities of an organisation and the outcomes of those activities . . . they are identified as people who have an interest in the organisation, whether or not the organisation has an interest in them.

Stakeholder management perspective Simultaneous attention to the legitimate interests of all appropriate stakeholders of an organisation.

Statute laws Laws that are passed by Parliament and have received royal assent.

Statutory instrument A device used by a minister of the government to change or update legislation that already exists.

Statutory minimum procedure (discipline) A set of stages that must be followed by all organisations which contemplate dismissing an employee, or imposing a disciplinary penalty that goes beyond suspension on full pay, or a warning.

Stonewalling Time wasting, or delaying tactics used to obstruct discussion.

Strike A complete withdrawal of labour.

Substantive rules The terms of a collective agreement that refers to the exchange of effort for reward, for example, pay and hours of work.

Substantive rules of behaviour Rules that are normally found in employee handbooks and disciplinary procedures that proscribe certain actions on the part of employees.

Supply side (economics) A set of macro-economic policies designed to eradicate presumed market constraints in managing prices, income, employment and economic growth.

T

Technological context The choices made by firms about the technology that they use in their activities, which affects employee job tasks, skills and competences.

The State The elected government of the day, together with all other agencies that carry out its will and implement its policies and legislation.

The 'Third Way' A political ideology in which government charts a path between state regulation and free-market forces. Its core values include support for competitive markets, innovation, skills, fairness and equity.

Trade dispute A dispute between workers and their employing organisation, which complies with Section 219(1)a of the TULRCA 1992 (i.e. the *Golden Formula*).

Trade union An organisation, whether permanent or temporary, which consists either wholly or mainly of workers whose principle purposes include the regulation of relations between workers and employers or employers' associations.

Trade union density The proportion of potential members who are actually in membership of trade unions.

Trade union government The internal management and decision-making processes of an individual trade union.

Trade union immunity A convention that protects a trade union from prosecution for inducing its members to breach their individual employment contracts when engaging in strike or other similar industrial action.

Trade union purpose To protect and improve the interests of union members, vis-à-vis those of management or the employing organisation.

Trade union recognition An arrangement in which an employer agrees that one or more trade unions will represent the interests of some or all of the employees in the organisation, for the purpose of collective bargaining.

Trade union structure The groups of workers represented by a particular union.

Trades councils Local bodies formed to coordinate union activities in cities throughout Britain.

Trades Union Congress A federal body for the coordination and cooperation of member unions in Britain.

Transnational organisation One that operates simultaneously in different international markets producing similar and different goods and services through independent subsidiaries.

Trigger mechanism (in ICE regulations) This sets out the initiation process to enact the legal rights for employees to be informed and consulted, which can occur either through a formal written request by employees, or by an employer notification to start the process and negotiate a new information and consultation agreement.

Two faces of justice concept That discipline and grievance are both processes that afford opportunities for the parties in employment relations (employer and employee) to obtain justice, ultimately by ensuring that the other party can be forced to observe the terms and conditions of the relationship.

Two-way communication A direct form of voice in which information is exchanged between management and employees.

U

Unconstitutional action That which is initiated when negotiation is nominally still in progress.

Unfair dismissal A claim by an individual that the circumstances of his or her dismissal fell short of reasonable treatment as laid down by the Employment Rights Act (1996).

Union learning representatives Union representatives at the workplace who have legal rights to advise union members on their training needs, and make representations to management.

Union substitution Non-union employment relations policies that seek to remove the demand for union membership among workers. Typical strategies include non-union voice and attractive remuneration packages.

Union suppression Aggressive and hostile managerial actions designed to resist possible union membership and recognition. Typical strategies include intimidation and discrimination.

Unitarist perspective A frame of reference in which an organisation is seen as one large family, all on the same side and pulling together in the same direction, and in which conflict is seen as deviant behaviour.

Unofficial action That which is initiated directly by employees without official trade union authorisation; sometimes as a spontaneous show of dissatisfaction, and sometimes as a revolt against the negotiating stance adopted by either of the two sides.

Unorganised action An individual reaction to having become discontented, which can take many forms that vary between absenteeism and sabotage.

Upward problem-solving Voice mechanisms that allow employees (either individually or in small groups) to suggest solutions to management about work and/or quality issues.

V

Vertical differentiation The establishment of a hierarchy of authority in an organisation.

Vertical surveillance (control) Monitoring of a person's actions by someone located above the employee in the hierarchy, often by using electronic methods.

Voice outcomes The potential organisational benefits arising from employees having a voice, which includes productivity measures, employee motivation and satisfaction levels, and lower labour turnover costs.

Voluntarist system A system of employment relations that operates with minimal legal intervention, where the parties determine for themselves the main terms and conditions of employment.

W

Whistle-blower procedure A procedure that enables an employee to formally complain (as per the provisions of the Public Interest Disclosure Act of 1998) about bullying or harassment to which the individual believes he or she has been subject, subsequent to having made public his/her concerns about unethical or unfair organisational practices.

Wider social change The trade union function that involves engaging in activities to bring about changes in wider society, often by political lobbying.

Withdrawal of cooperation Employees work strictly to formal operational procedures, refusing any flexibility or cooperation.

Work-in or Sit-in Employees occupy the workplace, usually as a form of protest when management proposes to close a plant or make workers redundant.

Working to rule or to contract A very strict refusal to step outside the duties laid down in job specifications, often accompanied by an insistence that management and supervision give clearly defined instructions on how duties shall be performed.

Works councils A joint council of workers and management, established in Germany under the Federal Works Constitution Acts (1952 and 1972) as a vehicle of co-determination.

Wrongful dismissal A claim by an individual that the way he or she was dismissed constitutes a breach of his/her contract of employment.

Bibliography

A

Abbott, B. (2004) 'Worker Representation through the Citizens' Advice Bureaux', in *The Future of Worker Representation*, G. Healy, E. Heery, P. Taylor and W. Brown (eds), Palgrave Macmillan, Basingstoke.

Abegglen, J.C. and G.J. Salk (1985) *Kaisha: The Japanese Corporation*, Basic Books, New York.

ACAS (2003a) Code of Practice 1: *Disciplinary and Grievance Procedures*, Advisory, Conciliation and Arbitration Service, London.

ACAS (2003b) *Pay Systems*, Advisory, Conciliation and Arbitration Service, London.

ACAS (2005a) *Advisory Booklet – Redundancy Handling*, Advisory, Conciliation and Arbitration Service, London.

ACAS (2005b) *Annual Report 2004–2005*, Advisory, Conciliation and Arbitration Service, London. (www.acas.org.ac).

Ackers, P. and J. Payne (1998) 'British trade unions and social partnership: rhetoric, reality and strategy', *International Journal of Human Resource Management*, Vol. 9 (3), pp. 529–550.

Ackers, P. and A. Wilkinson (eds) (2003) *Understanding Work and Employment: Industrial Relations in Transition*, Oxford University Press, Oxford.

Ackers, P., C. Smith and P. Smith (1996) 'Against all odds? British trade unions in the new workplace', in *The New Workplace and Trade Unionism: Critical Perspectives on Work and Organisation*, P. Ackers, C. Smith and P. Smith (eds), Routledge, London.

Ackers, P., M. Marchington, A. Wilkinson and T. Dundon (2005) 'Partnership and Voice, with or without trade unions: Changing UK management approaches to organisational participation', in *Partnership and Modernisation in Employment Relations*, M. Stuart and M. Martinez Lucio (eds), Routledge, London.

Addison, J., L. Bellman, C. Schnabel and W. Joachim (2004) 'The reform of the German Works Constitution Act: a critical assessment', *Industrial Relations*, 42 (2), pp. 292–420.

Alderfer, C. and K.J. Smith (1982) 'Studying intergroup relations embedded in organizations', *Administrative Science Quarterly*, Vol. 27, pp. 35–64.

Allen, T.D., D.M. Freeman, J.E.A. Russell, R.C. Reizenstein and J.O. Rentz (2001) 'Survivor reactions to organisational downsizing: does time ease the pain?', *Journal of Occupational and Organisational Psychology*, Vol. 74 (2), pp. 154–164.

Argyris, C. (1960) *Understanding Organisational Behaviour*, Homewood Ill., Dorsey.

Armstrong, E.A.G. (1969) *Industrial Relations*, Harrap, London.

Atkinson, J. (1984a) *Manning for Uncertainty: Some Emerging U.K. Work Patterns*, University of Sussex, Institute of Manpower Studies.

Atkinson, J. (1984b) 'Manpower strategies for flexible organisations', *Personnel Management*, August, pp. 28–31.

Atkinson, J. and N. Meager (1986) *Changing Work Practices: How Companies Achieve Flexibility to Meet New Needs*, National Economic Development Office, London.

B

Bacon, N. and J. Storey (1993) 'Individualization of the employment relationship and the implications for trade unions', *Employee Relations*, Vol. 15, pp. 5–18.

Bain, G.S. (1970) *The Growth of White Collar Unionism*, Oxford University Press, Oxford.

Bain, G.S. and H. Clegg (1974) 'A strategy for industrial relations research in Great Britain', *British Journal of Industrial Relations*, Vol. 12 (2), pp. 91–113.

Bain, G.S. and R. Price (1983) 'Union growth: dimensions, determinants and destiny', in *Industrial Relations in Britain*, G.S. Bain (ed.), Blackwell, Oxford.

Bain, G.S., D. Coats and V. Ellis (1973) *Social Stratification and Trade Unionism*, Heineman, Oxford.

Bain, P. and P. Taylor (2000) 'Entrapped by the electronic panopticon? Worker resistance in the call centre', *New Technology, Work and Employment*, Vol. 15 (1), pp. 2–18.

Baldry, C. (2003) 'Employment relations in the information society', in *Handbook of Employment Relations, Law and Practice*, 4th edn, B. Towers (ed.), London, Kogan Page.

Ball, G.A., L.K. Trevino and H.P. Sims (1994) 'Just and unjust punishment: influences on subordinate performance and citizenship', *Academy of Management Journal*, Vol. 32 (2), pp. 299–322.

Barbash, J. (1988) 'The new industrial relations in the United States: phase II', *Relations Industrielles*, 43 (1), pp. 32–42.

Barker, J. (1993) 'Tightening the iron cage: concertive control in self-managing teams', *Administrative Science Quarterly*, Vol. 38, pp. 408–437.

Barney, J.B. and R.W. Griffin (1992) *The Management of Organizations: Strategy, Structure, Behaviour*, Houghton Mifflin, Boston, MA.

Barrett-Howard, E. and T.R. Tyler (1986) 'Procedural justice as a criterion in allocation decisions', *Journal of Personality and Social Psychology*, Vol. 50 (2), pp. 296–304.

Batstone, E., I. Boraston and S. Frenkel (1978) *The Social Organisation of Strikes*, Blackwell, Oxford.

Batstone, E., I. Boraston and S. Frenkel (1979) *Shop Stewards in Action: The Organisation of Workplace Conflict and Accommodation*, Blackwell, Oxford.

Bean, R. (1975) 'Research note: the relationship between strikes and unorganised conflict in manufacturing industry', *British Journal of Industrial Relations*, Vol. 13 (1), pp. 98–101.

Beaumont, D. (2005) 'Absence minded', *People Management*, 14 July, pp. 36–38.

Beck, C.E. and E.A. Beck (1986) 'The manager's open door and communications climate', *Business Horizons*, January/February, pp. 15–19.

Bemmels, B. (1991) 'Attribution theory and discipline arbitration', *Industrial and Labor Relations Review*, Vol. 44 (3), pp. 548–561.

Bemmels, B., Y. Reshef and K. Stratton-Devine (1991) 'The roles of supervisors, employees and stewards in grievance initiation', *Industrial and Labor Relations Review*, Vol. 45 (1), pp. 15–30.

Bennett, R. (1997) *Employee Relations*, 2nd edn., London, Pitman.

Benson, J. and P. Debroux (2003) 'Flexible labour markets and individualised employment: the beginnings of a new Japanese HRM system?', *Asia Pacific Business Review*, 9 (4), pp. 55–75.

Berry, A.J., J. Broadbent and D. Otley (1995) *Management Control: Themes, Issues and Practices*, Macmillan, London.

Beyer, J.M. and H.M. Trice (1984) 'Managerial ideologies and the use of discipline', *Academy of Management Proceedings*, pp. 259–263.

Biasatti, L.L. and J.E. Martin (1979) 'A measure of the quality of union management relationships', *Journal of Applied Psychology*, Vol. 64 (4), pp. 387–390.

Blanden, J., S. Machin and J. Van Reenen (2005) *Have Unions Turned The Corner? New Evidence on Recent Trends in Union Recognition in UK Firms*, Centre for Economic Performance Discussion Paper No. 685, London School of Economics.

Blau, P. (1964) *Exchange and Power in Social Life*, Wiley, New York.

Blauner, R. (1964) *Alienation and Freedom*, Chicago University Press, Chicago Ill.

Blyton, P. and P. Turnbull (2004) *The Dynamics of Employee Relations*, 3rd edn, Palgrave Macmillan, London.

Bogg, A. (2005) 'Employment Relations Act 2004: another false dawn for collectivism?', *Industrial Law Journal*, Vol. 34 (1), pp. 72–82.

Böheim, R. and M. Taylor (2003) 'Actual and preferred working hours', *British Journal of Industrial Relations*, Vol. 41, pp. 149–166.

Bolton, S.C. (2004) 'A simple matter of control? NHS hospital nurses and new management', *Journal of Management Studies*, Vol. 41 (2), pp. 317–333.

Bonham, M.G. (1971) 'Simulating international disarmament negotiations', *Journal of Conflict Resolution*, Vol. 15, pp. 299–315.

Boraston, I., H.A. Clegg and M. Rimmer (1975) *Workplace and Union: A Study of Local Relationships in Fourteen Trade Unions*, Heinemann, Oxford.

Boroff, K.E. and D. Lewin (1997) 'Loyalty, voice and intent to exit a union firm: a conceptual and empirical analysis', *Industrial and Labour Relations Review*, Vol. 51 (1), pp. 50–63.

Boswell, W.R. and J.B. Olson-Buchanan (2004) 'Experiencing mistreatment at work: the role of grievance filling, nature of mistreatment and employee withdrawal', *Academy of Management Journal*, Vol. 47 (1) pp. 129–139.

Boxall, P. and J. Purcell (2003) *Strategy and Human Resource Management*, Palgrave Macmillan, Basingstoke.

Brannen, P. (1983) *Authority and Participation in Industry*, Batsford, London.

Braverman, H. (1974) *Labor and Monopoly Capital: The Degradation of Work in the Twentieth Century*, Monthly Review Press, New York.

Briggs, S. (1981) 'The grievance procedure and organisational health', *Personnel Journal*, June, pp. 471–474.

Britt, D. and O.R. Galle (1972) 'Industrial conflict and unionisation', *American Sociological Review*, Vol. 37, pp. 46–57.

Britt, D. and O.R. Galle (1974) 'Antecedents of the shape of strikes: a comparative analysis', *American Sociological Review*, Vol. 39, pp. 642–651.

Bronfenbrenner, K., S. Friedman, R. Hurd, R. Oswald and R. Seeber (eds) (1998) *Organizing to Win: New Research on Union Strategies*, Cornell University Press, Ithaca, NY.

Brown, W.A. (1972) 'A consideration of custom and practice', *British Journal of Industrial Relations*, Vol. 10 (1), pp. 42–61.

Brown, W.A. (1981) *The Changing Contours of British Industrial Relations: Survey of Manufacturing Industry*, Blackwell, Oxford.

Brown, W.A. and S. Wadhawani (1990) 'The economic effects of industrial relations legislation', *National Institute Economic Review*, Vol. 131, pp. 57–70.

Brown, W., S. Deakin, M. Hudson, C. Pratten and P. Ryan (1998) *The Individualisation of Employment Contracts in Britain*, Department of Trade and Industry Research Report No. 4, London.

Bryman, A. (2004) *The Disneyisation of Society*, Sage, London.

Bryson, A. and R. Gomez (2005) 'Why Have Workers Stopped Joining Unions? The Rise in Never-Membership in Britain', *British Journal of Industrial Relations*, Vol. 41 (1), pp. 67–92.

Budd, J.W. (2004) *Employment with a Human Face: Balancing Efficiency, Equity and Voice*, Cornell University Press, Ithaca, NY.

Bullock, A. (Lord) (1977) *Report of the Committee of Inquiry on Industrial Democracy*, Cmnd. 6706, HMSO, London.

Burchill, F. (1999) 'Review essay: Walton and McKersie, a behavioural theory of labour negotiation', *Historical Studies in Industrial Relations*, Vol. 8, Autumn, pp. 137–168.

C

CAC (2006) *CAC Annual Report 2005–06*, Central Arbitration Committee, London.

Cairns, L. (1996) *Negotiation Skills in the Workplace: A Practical Handbook*, Pluto Press, London.

Callaghan, G. and P. Thompson (2002) 'We recruit "attitude": the selection and shaping of routine call centre labour', *Journal of Management Studies*, Vol. 39 (2), pp. 233–254.

Callinicos, A. (2001) *Against the Third Way*, Polity Press, Cambridge.

Cameron, K.S. (1994) 'Investigating organisational downsizing – fundamental issues', *Human Resource Management*, Vol. 33 (2), pp. 183–188.

Cameron, S. (1987) 'Trade unions and productivity: theory and evidence', *Industrial Relations Journal*, Vol. 18 (3), pp. 170–176.

Campling, J. and P. Gollan (1999) *Bargained Out: Negotiating Without Unions in Australia*, The Federation Press, Sydney.

Cappelli, P., L. Bassi, H. Katz, D. Knoke, P. Osterman and M. Useem (1997) *Change at Work*, Oxford University Press, Oxford.

Carter, C., S. Clegg, J. Hogan and M. Kornberger (2003) 'The polyphonic spree: the case of the Liverpool Dockers', *Industrial Relations Journal*, Vol. 34 (4), pp. 290–304.

Casey, C. (1999) 'Come join our family: discipline and integration in corporate organisational culture', *Human Relations*, Vol. 52 (2), pp. 155–178.

Caulkin, S. (1995) 'Take your partners', *Management Today*, February, pp. 26–30.

Certification Officer (2005) Annual Reports 2004–2005, London, http://www.certoffice.org.

Chamberlain, N.W. and J.W. Kuhn (1965) *Collective Bargaining*, McGraw Hill, New York.

Charlwood, A. (2003) 'Willingness to unionize amongst non-union workers', in *Representing Workers, Trade Union Recognition and Membership in Britain*, H. Gospel and S. Wood (eds), Routledge, London.

Charlwood, A. (2004) 'Influences on Trade Union Organising Effectiveness in Britain', *British Journal of Industrial Relations*, Vol. 42 (1), pp. 69–93.

Child, J. (1972) 'Organizational structure, environment and performance', *Sociology*, Vol. 6, pp. 1–22.

Child, J. (1984) *Organization: A Guide to Problems and Practice*, Harper and Row, London.

Chinoy, E. (1955) *Automobile Workers and the American Dream*, Doubleday, New York.

Clark, I. (1994) 'The employment relationship and contractual regulation', in *Human Resource Management: A Contemporary Perspective*, I. Beardwell and L. Holden (eds), Pitman, London.

Claydon, T. and M. Doyle (1996) 'Trusting me, trusting you? The ethics of employee empowerment', *Personnel Review*, Vol. 25 (6), pp. 13–25.

Clegg, H.A. (1974) 'Trade unions as an opposition which can never become a government', in W.E. McCarthy (ed.), *Trade Unions*, pp. 74–86, Penguin, Harmondsworth.

Clegg, H.A. (1979) *The Changing System of Industrial Relations in Great Britain*, Blackwell, Oxford.

Coats, D. (2004) '*Speaking Up! Voice, Industrial Democracy and Organisational Performance*, The Work Foundation, London.

Coats, D. (2005) *Raising Lazarus: The Future of Organized Labour*, Fabian Society Pamphlet No. 618, London.

Cohen, G. (1988) *History, Labour and Freedom*, Clarendon Press, Oxford.

Cohn, S. (1993) *When Strikes Make Sense – And Why: Lessons From Third Republic French Coal Miners*, Plenum Press, New York.

Collins, H. (2001) 'Regulating the employment relationship for competitiveness', *Industrial Law Journal*, Vol. 30, pp. 17–47.

Collinson, D.L. (1994) 'Strategies of resistance: power, knowledge and subjectivity in the workplace', in *Resistance and Power in Organisations*, J.M. Jermier, D. Knights and W.R. Nord (eds), Routledge, London.

Colquitt, J.A., D.E. Conlon, M.J. Wesson, C.O.L. Porter and K.Y. Ng (2001) 'Justice at the millennium: a meta-analytic review of 25 years of organisational justice research', *Journal of Applied Psychology*, Vol. 86 (3), pp. 423–445.

Covaleski, M.A., M.W. Dirsmith, J.B. Heian and S. Samuel (1998) 'The calculated and the avowed: techniques of discipline and struggles over identity in the six big public accounting firms', *Administrative Science Quarterly*, Vol. 43 (2), pp. 293–327.

Cox, A., S. Zagelmeyer and M. Marchington (2006) 'Embedding employee involvement and participation at work', *Human Resource Management Journal*, Vol. 16 (3), pp. 250–267.

Creigh, S.W. and D. Makeham (1982) 'Strikes in industrial countries: an analysis', *Australian Bulletin of Labour*, Vol. 8 (3), pp. 139–149.

Crouch, C. (1982) *The Politics of Industrial Relations*, Fontana, London.

Cully, M., A. O'Reilly, S. Woodland and G. Dix (1999) *Britain at Work: As Depicted by the 1998 Workplace Employee Relations Survey*, Routledge, London.

Cunningham, I. and J. Hyman (1999) 'The poverty of empowerment? A critical case study', *Personnel Review*, Vol. 28 (3), pp. 192–207.

D

D'Art, D. and T. Turner (1999) 'An Attitudinal Revolution in Irish Industrial Relations: The End of 'Them and Us?', *British Journal of Industrial Relations*, Vol. 37 (1), pp. 101–116.

Dalton, D.R. and W.D. Todor (1981) 'Grievances filed and the role of the union stewards vs the rank and file member: an empirical test', *International Review of Applied Psychology*, Vol. 30, pp. 199–207.

Danford, A., M. Richardson, P. Stewart, S. Tailby and M. Upchurch (2004) 'Partnership, Mutuality and the High-performance Workplace: A Case Study of Union Strategy and Worker Experience in the Aircraft Industry', in *The Future of Worker Representation*, G. Healy, E. Heery, P. Taylor and W. Brown (eds), Palgrave Macmillan, Basingstoke.

Darlington, R. (1998) 'Workplace Union Resilience in the Merseyside Fire Brigade', *Industrial Relations Journal*, Vol. 29 (1), pp. 58–74.

Darlington, R. (2002) 'Shop Stewards' Leadership, Left-Wing Activism and Collective Workplace Union Organisation', *Capital and Class*, No. 76 (Spring), pp. 95–127.

Davis, P. and M. Freedland (eds) (1983) *Kahn-Freund's Labour and the Law*, Stevens, London.

Denison, D.R. (1996) 'What is the difference between organisational culture and organisational climate? A native's point of view on a decade of paradigm wars', *Academy of Management Review*, Vol. 21 (3), pp. 619–654.

Dent, E. and S. Goldberg (1999) 'Challenging resistance to change', *Journal of Applied Behavioural Science*, Vol. 35 (1), pp. 25–41.

Denton, A. (2005) 'Best to go by the book', *People Management*, 29 September, p. 21.

Diamond, W. and R. Freeman (2001) *What Workers Want from Workplace Organisations: Report to the TUCs Promoting Unionism Task Group*, Trades Union Congress, London.

Dickens, L. and M. Hall (2003) 'Labour law and industrial relations: a new settlement', in *Industrial Relations Theory and Practice*, 2nd edn, P.K. Edwards (ed.), Blackwell, Oxford.

Dickens, L., M. Hall and S. Wood (2005) 'Review of research into the impact of employment relations legislation', *Employment Relations Research Series No. 45*, Department of Trade and Industry, London.

Disability Discrimination Act (1997) HMSO, London.

DoE (1980) *Code of Practice, Picketing*, HMSO, London.

Donaldson, T. and L.E. Preston (1995) 'The stakeholder theory of the corporation: concepts, evidence and implications', *Academy of Management Review*, Vol. 20 (1), pp. 65–91.

Donovan (Lord) (chairperson) (1968) *Royal Commission on Trade Unions and Employers Associations Report*, Cmnd. 3623, HMSO, London.

Dore, R.P. (1973) *British Factory – Japanese Factory: The Origins of National Diversity in Industrial Relations*, Allen and Unwin, London.

DTI (1999) *The Unfair Dismissal and Statement of Reasons for Dismissal* (variation of qualifying period order 1999 – regulatory impact assessment), Department of Trade and Industry, London.

DTI (2002) *High Performance Workplaces: A Discussion Paper*, Department of Trade and Industry, London.

DTI (2003) *High Performance Workplaces: Informing and Consulting Employees*, Consultation Document, Department of Trade and Industry, London. (http://www.dti.gov.uk/er/consultation/perf_work.htm).

DTI (2004) *A survey of workers' experiences of the Working Time Regulations*, Employment Relations Research Series, No. 31, Department of Trade and Industry, London.

DTI (2005) *The Information and Consultation of Employees Regulations 2004: DTI Guidance*, January 2005, Department of Trade and Industry, London. (http://www.dti.gov.uk/er/consultation/i_c_regs_guidance.pdf).

DTI (2006) *Employment Rights on the Transfer of an Undertaking: A Guide to the 2006 TUPE Regulations for Employees, Employers and Representatives*, Department of Trade and Industry, London.

Duggan, M. (1999) *Unfair Dismissal: Law, Practice and Guidance*, CLT Professional Publishing, Welwyn Garden City.

Dundon, T. (1998) 'Post-Privatised Shop Steward Organisation and Union Renewal at Girobank', *Industrial Relations Journal*, Vol. 29 (2), pp. 126–136.

Dundon, T. (2002a) 'Employer opposition and union avoidance in the UK', *Industrial Relations Journal*, Vol. 33 (3), pp. 234–245.

Dundon, T. (2002b) 'Trade Union Recognition', in *The Informed Student Guide to Human Resource Management*, T. Redman and A. Wilkinson (eds), Thompson Learning, London.

Dundon, T. and D. Eva (1998) 'Trade Unions and Bargaining for Skills', *Employee Relations*, Vol. 20 (1), pp. 57–72.

Dundon, T. and D.J. Rollinson (2004) *Employment Relations in Non-Union Firms*. Routledge, London.

Dundon, T. and A. Wilkinson (2003) 'Employment relations in small firms', in *Handbook of Employment Relations, Law and Practice*, 4th edn, B. Towers (ed.), Kogan Page, London.

Dundon, T., A. Wilkinson, M. Marchington and P. Ackers (2004) 'The meanings and purpose of employee voice', *International Journal of Human Resource Management*, Vol. 15 (6), pp. 1150–1171.

Dundon, T., A. Wilkinson, M. Marchington and P. Ackers (2005) 'The Management of Voice in Non-Union Organisations: Managers' Perspectives', *Employee Relations*, Vol. 27 (3), pp. 307–319.

Dunlop, J. (1958) *Industrial Relations Systems*, Holt Press, New York.

Dworkin, J., S. Feldman, M. Brown and C. Hobson (1988) 'Workers' preferences in concession bargaining', *Industrial Relations*, 27 (1), pp. 7–20.

E

Earnshaw, J.M. (1997) 'Tribunals and tribulations', *People Management*, 21 May, pp. 34–36.

Eaton, J. (2000) *Comparative Employment Relations*, Polity Press, Cambridge.

Ebadan, G. and D. Winstanley (1997) 'Downsizing, delayering and careers – the survivor's perspective', *Human Resource Management Journal*, Vol. 7 (1), pp. 71–91.

Edwards, P.K. (1983) 'The pattern of collective action', in *Industrial Relations in Britain*, G.S. Bain (ed.), Blackwell, Oxford.

Edwards, P.K. (1986) *Conflict at Work: A Materialist Analysis of Workplace Relations*, Blackwell, Oxford.

Edwards, P.K. (1987) 'Industrial action 1980–84', *British Journal of Industrial Relations*, Vol. 13 (1), pp. 98–101.

Edwards, P.K. (ed.) (1995) *Industrial Relations: Theory and Practice in Britain*, Blackwell, Oxford.

Edwards, P.K. (2003) 'The Employment Relationship and the Field of Industrial Relations', in *Industrial Relations: Theory and Practice*, 2nd edn, P.K. Edwards (ed.), Blackwell, Oxford.

Edwards, P.K. and G.S. Bain (1988) 'Why are trade unions becoming more popular? Unions and public opinion in Britain', *British Journal of Industrial Relations*, Vol. 12 (3), pp. 311–326.

Edwards, P.K. and H. Scullion (1982) *The Social Organisation of Industrial Conflict: Control and Resistance in the Workplace*, Blackwell, Oxford.

Edwards, P.K. and C. Whitston (1993) *Attending to Work: The Management of Attendance and Shopfloor Order*, Blackwell, Oxford.

Edwards, R. (1979) *Contested Terrain: The Transformation of the Workplace in the Twentieth Century*, Heinemann, London.

Edwards, T. (2004) 'Corporate governance, industrial relations and trends in company-level restructuring in Europe: convergence towards the Anglo-American model?', *Industrial Relations Journal*, Vol. 35 (6), pp. 518–535.

EIRO (2006) *Employment relations in SMEs*, European Industrial Relations Observatory, April 2006, http://www.eiro.eurofound.eu.int/2006/02/study/tn0602101s.html.

Ellem, B. (2001) 'Trade unionism in 2000', *Journal of Industrial Relations*, Vol. 43 (2), pp. 196–218.

Employment Act (1980) HMSO, London.

Employment Act (1982) HMSO, London.

Employment Act (1988) HMSO, London.

Employment Act (1990) HMSO, London.

Employment Relations Act (1999) HMSO, London.

Employment Rights Act (1996) HMSO, London.

Etzioni, A. (1975) *A Comparative Analysis of Complex Organizations: On Power, Involvement and their Correlates*, rev. edn, Free Press, New York.

European Court of Justice (2005) *Irmtraub Junk v Wolfgang Kuhnel: Judgement Case Reference C – 188/03*, 27 January, Brussels, European Court of Justice, http://curia.europa.eu/.

Evans, J. (2003) 'Pay', in *Employment Relations*, 2nd edn, G. Hollinshead, P. Nichols and S. Tailby (eds), Financial Times/Prentice Hall, London.

Evans, S. (1987) 'The use of injunctions in industrial disputes, May 1984–April 1987', *British Journal of Industrial Relations*, Vol. 25 (3), pp. 419–435.

Evans, S. and M. Hudson (1993) *Standardised Packages Individually Wrapped? A Study of the Introduction and Operation of Personal Contracts in the Port Transport and Electricity Supply Industry*, Warwick Papers in Industrial Relations, No. 44, July, University of Warwick.

Ewing, K. (2003) 'Industrial relations and law', in *Understanding Work and Employment: Industrial Relations in Transition*, P. Ackers and A. Wilkinson (eds), Oxford University Press, Oxford.

F

Fairbrother, P. and C. Yates (2003) (eds) *Trade Unions in Renewal: A Comparative Study*, Routledge, London.

Farnham, D. and J. Pimlott (1987) *Understanding Industrial Relations*, Cassell, London.

Fayol, H. (1916) *General and Industrial Management*, trans. C. Storrs (1946), Pitman, London.

Fayol, H. (1949) *General and Industrial Management*, Pitman, London.

Felstead, A., N. Jewson and S. Walters (2003) 'Managerial control of employees working at home', *British Journal of Industrial Relations*, Vol. 41 (2), pp. 241–264.

Fenley, A. (1998) 'Models, styles and metaphors: understanding the management of discipline', *Employee Relations*, Vol. 20 (4), pp. 349–371.

Findlay, P. and A. McKinlay (2003) 'Surveillance, electronic communications technologies and regulation', *Industrial Relations Journal*, Vol. 34 (4), pp. 305–318.

Fiorito, J., C. Lowman and F. Nelson (1987) 'The impact of human resource policies on union organising', *Industrial Relations*, Vol. 26 (2), pp. 113–126.

Fisher, R. and W. Ury (1991) *Getting to Yes: Negotiating an Agreement Without Giving In*, 2nd edn, Penguin, London.

Flanders, A. (1965) *Industrial Relations: What is Wrong with the System?*, Faber, London.

Flanders, A. (1968) 'Collective bargaining: a theoretical analysis', *British Journal of Industrial Relations*, Vol. 6 (1), pp. 1–26.

Flanders, A. (1970) *Management and Unions: The Theory and Reform of Industrial Relations*, Faber and Faber, London.

Fletcher, B. and R. Hurd (1998) 'Beyond the organizing model: the transformation process in local unions', in *Organizing to Win: New Research on Union Strategies*, K. Bronfenbrenner, S. Friedman, R. Hurd, R. Oswald and R. Seeber (eds), Cornell University Press, Ithaca.

Fogler, R., D. Rosenfield and T. Robinson (1983) 'Relative deprivation and procedural justifications', *Journal of Personality and Social Psychology*, Vol. 45 (2), pp. 268–73.

Formbrun, C., N.M. Tichy and M.A. Devanna (1984) *Strategic Human Resource Management*, Wiley, New York.

Forth, J., H. Bewley and A. Bryson (2006) *Small and Medium-sized Enterprises: Findings from the 2004 Workplace Employment Relations Survey*, Department of Trade and Industry/Routledge, London.

Fox, A. (1966) *Industrial Sociology and Industrial Relations*, Donovan Commission Research Report No. 3, HMSO, London.

Fox, A. (1971) *A Sociology of Work in Industry*, Macmillan, London.

Fox, A. (1974) *Beyond Contract: Work, Power and Trust Relations*, Faber and Faber, London.

Fox A. (1975) 'Collective bargaining: Flanders and the Webbs', *British Journal of Industrial Relations*, Vol. 13 (2), pp. 151–174.

Fox, A. (1985) *Man Mismanagement*, 2nd edn, Hutchinson, London.

Franzosi, R. (1995) *The Puzzle of Strikes: Class and State Strategy in Postwar Italy*, Cambridge University Press, Cambridge.

Freeman, R. and J. Medoff (1984) *What do Unions do?*, Basic Books, New York.

Friedman, A. (1977) *Industry and Labour*, Macmillan, London.

Frone, M.R. (2000) 'Interpersonal conflict at work and psychological outcomes: testing a model among young workers', *Journal of Occupational Health Psychology*, Vol. 5 (3), pp. 246–255.

G

Gabriel, Y. (1999) 'Beyond happy families: a critical re-evaluation of the control–resistance–identity triangle', *Human Relations*, Vol. 52 (2), pp. 179–203.

Gall, G. (1998) 'Resisting the Rise of Non-unionism: the Case of the Press Workers in the Newspaper Industry', *Capital and Class*, Vol. 64, pp. 43–61.

Gall, G. (2004) 'British employer resistance to trade union recognition', *Human Resource Management Journal*, Vol. 14 (2), pp. 36–53.

Gall, G. (2005) 'Happy Anniversary: Union Leglisation', *People Management*, Vol. 11 (11), pp. 30–33.

Gallie, D. (1978) *In Search of the New Working Class: Automation and Social Integration in the Capitalist Enterprise*, Cambridge University Press, Cambridge.

Gallie, D. (1988) *Employment in Britain*, Blackwell, Oxford.

Gallie, D., M. White, Y. Cheng and M. Tomlinson (1998) *Restructuring the Employment Relationship*, Clarendon Press, Oxford.

Gartrell, C.D. (1982) 'On the visibility of wage referents', *Canadian Journal of Sociology*, Vol. 7 (2), pp. 117–143.

Geary, J. (2003) 'New Forms of Work Organisation: Still Limited, Still Controlled, but Still Welcome?', in *Industrial Relations: Theory and Practice*, 2nd edn, P.K. Edwards (ed.), Blackwell, Oxford.

Geary, J. and A. Dobbins (2001) 'Teamworking: a new dynamic in the pursuit of management control', *Human Resource Management Journal*, Vol. 11 (1), pp. 3–23.

Geary, J. and W. Roche (2003) 'Workplace partnership and the displaced activist thesis', *Industrial Relations Journal*, Vol. 34 (1), pp. 32–51.

Gennard, J. (1981) 'The effects of strike activity on households', *British Journal of Industrial Relations*, Vol. 19 (3), pp. 327–344.

Gennard, J. (1982) 'The financial costs and returns of strikes', *British Journal of Industrial Relations*, Vol. 20 (2), pp. 247–256.

Gennard, J. (2002) 'Employee relations and public policy developments 1997–2001: a break with the past?', *Employee Relations*, Vol. 24 (6), pp. 581–594.

George, J. and G. Jones (2001) 'Towards a process model of individual change in organisations', *Human Relations*, Vol. 54 (4), pp. 419–444.

Gernigon, B., A. Odero and H. Guido (1998) 'ILO principles concerning the right to strike', *International Labour Review*, Vol. 137 (4), pp. 441–481.

Ghoshal, S. (2005) 'Bad management theories are destroying good management practices', *Academy of Management Learning and Education*, Vol. 4 (1), pp. 75–91.

Giddens, A. (2000) *The Third Way and Its Critics*, Polity Press, Cambridge.

Giles, A. (2000) 'Globalisation and industrial relations theory', *Journal of Industrial Relations*, Vol. 42 (2), pp. 173–194.

Glover, L. and M. Noon (2005) 'Shop-floor workers' responses to quality management initiatives: broadening the disciplined worker thesis', *Work, Employment and Society*, Vol. 19 (4), pp. 727–745.

Godfrey, G. and M. Marchington (1996) 'Shop stewards in the 1990s: a research note', *Industrial Relations Journal*, Vol. 27 (4), pp. 339–344.

Goldthorpe, J.H., D. Lockwood, F. Bechofer and J. Platt (1968) *The Affluent Worker: Industrial Attitudes and Behaviour*, Cambridge University Press, Cambridge.

Gollan, P. (2002) 'So what's the news? Management strategies towards non-union employee representation at News International', *Industrial Relations Journal*, Vol. 33 (4), pp. 316–331.

Goodrich, C.L. (1975) *The Frontier of Control*, Pluto Press, London.

Gordon, M.E. and R.L. Bowlby (1985) 'Propositions about grievance settlements: finally, consultation with grievants', *Personnel Psychology*, Vol. 41 (1), pp. 107–123.

Gospel, H. and G. Palmer (1993) *British Industrial Relations*, 2nd edn, Routledge, London.

Grahl, J. and P. Teague (2004) 'The German model in danger', *Industrial Relations Journal*, 35 (6), pp. 557–573.

Grainger, H. and H. Holt (2005) *Trade Union Membership 2004*, Employment Market Analysis and Research, Department of Trade and Industry, London. (http://www.dti.gov.uk/er/emar/trade.htm).

Green, R. (2001) 'Social Europe and the Third Way: The "New Labour" challenge to European social policy', *Kurwechsel*, Vol. 3, pp. 43–56.

Greene, A.M. (2003) 'Editorial to Special Issue', *Industrial Relations Journal*, Vol. 34 (4), pp. 280–281.

Greer, C.R. and C.E. Labig (1987) 'Employee reactions to disciplinary action', *Human Relations*, Vol. 40 (8), pp. 507–542.

Gregg, P. and J. Wadsworth (1995) 'A short history of labour turnover, job tenure and job security, 1975–1993', *Oxford Review of Economic Policy*, Vol. 11 (1), pp. 73–90.

Grimshaw, D. and J. Rubery (2003) *The Organisation of Employment: An International Perspective*, Palgrave Macmillan, London.

Grimshaw, D., M. Marchington, J. Rubery and H. Willmott (2004) 'Introduction: Fragmenting Work Across Organisational Boundaries', in *Fragmenting Work: Blurring Organisational Boundaries and Disordering Hierarchies*, M. Marchington, D. Grimshaw, J. Rubery and H. Willmott (eds), Oxford University Press, Oxford.

Guest, D. (1995) 'Human Resource management, industrial relations and trade unions', in *Human Resource Management: A Critical Text*, J. Storey (ed.), Routledge, London.

Guest, D. and N. Conway (1997) 'Employee motivation and the psychological contract', *Issues in People Management No. 21,* Institute of Personnel and Development, Wimbledon.

Guest, D. and N. Conway (1999) 'Peering into the black hole: the downside of the new employment relations in the UK', *British Journal of Industrial Relations*, Vol. 37 (3), pp. 367–389.

Guest, D. and N. Conway (2002) 'Communicating the psychological contract: an employer perspective', *Human Resource Management Journal*, Vol. 12 (2), pp. 22–38.

Guest, D. and N. Conway (2004) 'Exploring the paradox of unionised worker dissatisfactions', *Industrial Relations Journal*, Vol. 35 (2), pp. 102–121.

Guest, D. and K. Hoque (1994) 'The good, the bad and the ugly: employment relations in new non-union workplaces', *Human Resource Management Journal*, Vol. 5 (1), pp. 1–14.

Guest, D. and R. Peccei (2001) 'Partnership at Work: mutuality and the balance of advantage', *British Journal of Industrial Relations*, Vol. 39 (2), pp. 207–236.

Guest, D., N. Conway, N. Briner, and M. Dickman, M. (1996) 'The state of the psychological contract', *Issues in People Management No. 16,* Institute of Personnel and Development, Wimbledon.

Gunnigle, P., S. MacCurtain and M. Morley (2001) 'Dismantling pluralism: industrial relations in Irish greenfield sites', *Personnel Review*, Vol. 30 (3), pp. 263–279.

H

Hall, M. and M. Terry (2004) 'The Emerging System of Statutory Worker Representation', in *The Future of Worker Representation*, G. Healy, E. Heery, P. Taylor and W. Brown (eds), Palgrave Macmillan, Basingstoke.

Hamilton, P. (2001) 'Rhetoric and employment relations', *British Journal of Industrial Relations*, Vol. 39 (3), pp. 433–449.

Hansen, A.H. (1921) 'Cycles of strikes', *American Economic Review*, Vol. 11 (4), pp. 618–630.

Hanson, C.G. and G. Mather (1988) *Striking Out Strikes: Changing Employment Relations in the British Market*, Hobart Paper No. 110, Institute of Economic Affairs, London.

Harbison, F. and J. Coleman (1951) *Goals and Strategy in Collective Bargaining*, Harper, New York.

Harney, B. and T. Dundon (2006) 'Capturing Complexity: developing an integrated approach to analysing HRM in SMEs', *Human Resource Management Journal*, Vol. 16 (1), pp. 48–73.

Hawkins, K. (1979) *A Handbook of Industrial Relations Practice*, Kogan Page, London.

Hawkins, K. (1981) *Trade Unions*, Hutchinson, London.

Haynes, P. and M. Allen (2001) 'Partnership as union strategy: a preliminary evaluation', *Employee Relations*, Vol. 23 (2), pp. 164–187.

Heery, E. (1998) 'The Relaunch of the Trades Union Congress', *British Journal of Industrial Relations*, Vol. 36 (2), pp. 339–356.

Heery, E. (2000a) 'Trade unions and the management of reward', in *Reward Management: A Critical Text*, G. White and J. Druker (eds), Routledge, London.

Heery, E. (2000b) *Research Bulletin No 8: New Unionism Research Project*, Cardiff University: Mimeo.

Heery, E., G. Healy, and P. Taylor (2004) 'Representation at work: themes and issues', in *The Future of Worker Representation*, G. Healy, E. Heery, P. Taylor and W. Brown (eds), Palgrave Macmillan, Basingstoke.

Heery, E., M. Simms, D. Simpson, R. Delbridge and J. Salmon (2000) 'Organising unionism comes to the UK', *Employee Relations*, Vol. 22 (1), pp. 38–57.

Hendry, C. and A. Pettigrew (1990) 'Human resource management: an agenda for research', *International Journal of Human Resource Management*, Vol. 1 (1), pp. 17–43.

Henry, S. (1987) 'Disciplinary pluralism: four models of private justice in the workplace', *Sociological Review*, Vol. 35 (2), pp. 279–319.

Hepple, B. (1983) 'Individual labour law', in *Industrial Relations in Britain*, G.S. Bain (ed.), Blackwell, Oxford.

Herzberg, F. (1966) *Work and the Nature of Man*, World Publishing Company, New York.

Hirschman, A. (1970) *Exit, Voice and Loyalty: Responses to Decline in Firms, Organisations and States*, Harvard University Press, Cambridge Mass.

Hirst, P. and G. Thompson (1996) *Globalisation in Question*, Polity Press, London.

Hofstede, G. (2001) *Cultures Consequences: Comparing Values, Behaviours, Institutions and Organisations*, 2nd edn, Thousand Oaks, Sage, CA.

Hogan, J. and R. Hogan (1989) 'How to measure employee reliability', *Journal of Applied Psychology*, Vol. 74 (2), pp. 273–279.

Homans, G.C. (1950) *The Human Group*, Harcourt Brace and World, New York.

Honeyball, S. (1989) 'Employment law and the primacy of contract', *Industrial Law Journal*, Vol. 18 (2), pp. 97–108.

Hook, C.M., D.J. Rollinson, M. Foot and J. Handley (1996) 'Supervisor and manager styles in handling discipline and grievance: part one – comparing styles in handling discipline and grievance', *Personnel Review*, Vol. 25 (3), pp. 20–34.

Houston, D. and G. Marks (2003) 'The role of planning and workplace support in returning to work after maternity leave', *British Journal of Industrial Relations*, Vol. 41 (2), pp. 197–214.

Huselid, M. (1995) 'The impact of human resource management practices on turnover, production and corporate financial performance', *Academy of Management Journal*, Vol. 38 (3), pp. 635–672.

Hutt, W.N. (1973) *The Strike Threat System*, Arlington House, London.

Huzzard, T. (2004) 'Boxing and Dancing – Trade Union Strategic Choices', in *Strategic Unionism and Partnership: Boxing or Dancing?*, T. Huzzard, D. Gregory and R. Scott (eds), Palgrave Macmillan, Basingstoke.

Hyman, R. (1975) *Industrial Relations: A Marxist Introduction*, Macmillan, London.

Hyman, R. (1989) *Strikes*, 4th edn, Macmillan, London.

Hyman, R. (2001) *Understanding European Trade Unionism: between market, class and society*, Sage, London.

Hyman, R. (2003) 'The historical evolution of British industrial relations', in *Industrial Relations: Theory and Practice in Britain*, 2nd edn, P. Edwards (ed.), Blackwell, Oxford.

I

IDS (2005) *Managing Redundancy*, Human Resource Studies Plus No. 797, *Income Data Services*, May.

ILO (1965) 'Examination of grievances and communications within the undertaking', in *International Labour Conference Report No. 7*, pp. 7–9, International Labour Office, Geneva.

IPA (undated), *Key Themes: Partnership*, Involvement and Participation Association, www. partnership-at-work.com.

IRN (1998) 'Taoiseach's move designed to ensure Gardai play by the rules', *Industrial Relations News*, Issue 24 (18 June 1998).

J

Jackson, M. (1982) *Trade Unions*, Longman, London.

Jackson, M.P. (1987) *Strikes: Industrial Conflict in Britain, U.S.A. and Australia*, Wheatsheaf, Brighton.

Jacoby, S.M. (2005) *The Embedded Corporation: Corporate Governance and Employment Relations in Japan and the United States*, Princeton University Press, Princeton NJ.

James, L.R. and A.P. Jones (1974) 'Organisational climate: a review of theory and research', *Psychological Bulletin*, Vol. 83 (8), pp. 1096–1112.

Jensen, M. and W.H. Meckling (1976) 'Theory of the firm: managerial behaviour, agency costs and ownership structure', *Journal of Financial Economics*, Vol. 3 (2), pp. 305–360.

Jermier, J.M., D. Knights and W.R. Nord (1994) *Resistance and Power in Organisations*, Routledge, London.

Johnson, N. and P. Jarley (2004) 'Justice and union participation: an extension and test of mobilisation theory', *British Journal of Industrial Relations*, Vol. 42 (3), pp. 543–562.

Johnson, P. and J. Gill (1993) *Management Control and Organisational Behaviour*, Sage, London.

Jones, A.P. and L.R. James (1979) 'Psychological climate dimensions and relationships of individual and aggregated work environment perceptions', *Organisational Behaviour and Human Performance*, Vol. 23 (2), pp. 201–250.

K

Kadzin, A.E. (1986) *Behaviour Modification in Applied Settings*, Dorsey, New York.

Kahn-Freund, O. (1965) 'Industrial relations and the law: retrospect and prospect', *British Journal of Industrial Relations*, Vol. 7, pp. 301–316.

Kahn-Freund, O. (1967) 'A note on status and contract in British labour law', *Modern Law Review*, Vol. 30, pp. 635–644.

Kahn-Freund, O. (1977) *Labour and the Law*, Stevens, London.

Katzenbach, J.R. and D.K. Smith (1993) *The Wisdom of Teams: Creating the High Performance Organisation*, Harvard Business School Press, Boston, MA.

Kavanagh, M.J., H. Gueutal and S. Tannenbaum (1990) *Human Resource Information Systems: Development and Application*, Kent Publishing Company, Boston Mass.

Keasey, K. and M. Wright (eds) (1997) *Corporate Governance: Responsibilities, Risks and Remuneration*, Wiley, Chichester.

Keegan, W. (1984) *Mrs. Thatcher's Economic Experiment*, Penguin, London.

Keegan, W. (1991) 'Europe and the decade of disillusionment', *The Observer*, 8 December.

Kelly, J. (1998) *Rethinking Industrial Relations: Mobilisation, Collectivism and Long Waves*, Routledge, London.

Kelly, J. (2005) 'Social Partnership Agreements in Britain', in *Partnership and Modernisation in Employment Relations*, M. Stuart and M. Martinez Lucio (eds), Routledge, London.

Kelly, J. and C. Kelly (1991) 'Them and us: social psychology and the new industrial relations', *British Journal of Industrial Relations*, Vol. 29 (1), pp. 25–48.

Kelly, J. and N. Nicholson (1980a) 'Strikes and other forms of industrial action', *Industrial Relations Journal*, Vol. 11 (5), pp. 20–31.

Kelly, J. and N. Nicholson (1980b) 'The causation of strikes: a review of theoretical approaches and the potential contribution of social psychology', *Human Relations*, Vol. 33 (12), pp. 853–883.

Kelly, J. and P. Willman (2004) *Union Organisation and Activity*, Routledge, London.

Kennedy, G. (1998) *The New Negotiating Edge: A Behavioural Approach for Results and Relationships*, Brearly Publishing, London.

Kerckhofs, P. and I. Pas (2004) *European Works Councils Database*, European Trade Union Institute, Brussels. (http://etui.etuc.org/etui/databases/default.cfm).

Kerr, A. and S. Sachdev (1992) 'Third among equals: an analysis of the 1989 ambulance dispute', *British Journal of Industrial Relations*, Vol. 30 (1), pp. 127–143.

Kerr, C. and A. Seigal (1954) 'The inter-industry propensity to strike', in *Industrial Conflict*, A. Kornhauser, R. Dubin and A. Ross (eds), McGraw-Hill, New York.

Kersley, B., C. Alpin, J. Forth, A. Bryson, H. Bewley, J. Dix, and S. Oxenbridge (2005) *Inside the Workplace: First Findings from the 2004 Workplace Employment Relations Survey*, Department of Trade and Industry/Routledge, London.

Kersley, B., C. Alpin, J. Forth, A. Bryson, H. Bewley, J. Dix, and S. Oxenbridge (2006) *Inside the Workplace: Findings from the 2004 Workplace Employment Relations Survey*, Routledge, London.

Kessler, S. and F. Bayliss (1998) *Contemporary British Employment Relations*, 3rd edn, Macmillan, Basingstoke.

Kessler, I. and J. Purcell (2003) 'Individualism and collectivism', in *Industrial Relations: Theory and Practice in Britain*, 2nd edn, P. Edwards (ed.), Blackwell, Oxford.

Kets de Vries, M.F.R. and K. Balazs (1997) 'The downside of downsizing', *Human Relations*, Vol. 50 (1), pp. 11–50.

Kirkpatrick, I. and K. Hoque, K. (2005) 'The decentralisation of employment relations in the British public sector', *Industrial Relations Journal*, Vol. 36 (1), pp. 100–121.

Klass, B.S. and A.S. De Nisi (1989) 'Managerial reactions to employee dissent: the impact of grievance activity on performance ratings', *Academy of Management Journal*, Vol. 32 (4), pp. 705–717.

Klass, B.S. and H.H. Wheeler (1990) 'Managerial decision making about employee discipline: a policy capturing approach', *Personnel Psychology*, Vol. 43 (1), pp. 117–134.

Klass, B.S., T.W. Gainey and G.G. Dell'Omo (1999) 'The determinants of disciplinary system effectiveness: a line management perspective', *Industrial Relations*, Vol. 38 (4), pp. 542–553.

Knights, D. and D. McCabe (2000) 'Ain't misbehavin'? Opportunities for resistance under new forms of quality management', *Sociology*, Vol. 34 (3), pp. 421–436.

Knights, D. and D. McCabe (2003) 'Governing through teamwork: reconstituting subjectivity in a call centre', *Journal of Management Studies*, Vol. 40 (7), pp. 1587–1619.

Knowles, K.G.K. (1962) *Strikes*, Oxford University Press, Oxford.

Kochan, T., H. Katz and R. McKersie (1986) *The Transformation of American Industrial Relations*, Basic Books, New York.

Kornhauser, A. (1954) 'Human motivations underlying industrial conflict', in *Industrial Conflict*, A. Kornhauser, R. Dubin and A. Ross (eds), McGraw-Hill, New York.

Koys, D.J. and T.A. DeCotis (1991) 'Inductive measures of psychological climate', *Human Relations*, Vol. 44 (3), pp. 265–285.

Kozlowski, S.W.J. and M. Doherty (1989) 'Integration of climate and leadership: examination of a neglected issue', *Journal of Applied Psychology*, Vol. 74 (5), pp. 546–553.

Kuwahara, Y. (1987) 'Japanese industrial relations', in G. Bamber and R. Lansbury (eds), *International and Comparative Industrial Relations*, Allen and Unwin, London.

L

Labour Market Trends (2003) *Labour Market Trends Bulletin*, Office for National Statistics, Cardiff.

Labour Market Trends (2004) *Labour Market Update 112*, Issue No 7, Office for National Statistics, London. (www.statistics.gov.uk/).

Lansbury, R. and N. Wailes (2004) 'Employment Relations in Australia', in *International and Comparative Employment Relations: Globalisation and the developed market economies*, 4th edn, G. Bamber, R. Lansbury and N. Wailes (eds), Sage, London.

Larwood, L., P. Rand and A. Der Hovanessian (1979) 'Sex differences in response to simulated employee disciplinary cases', *Personnel Psychology*, Vol. 32 (3), pp. 529–550.

Lawler, E.E. (1975) 'Measuring the psychological quality of working life', in L. Davis and A. Cherns (eds), *The Quality of Working Life*, Free Press, New York.

Lawler, E.E. (2000) *Rewarding Excellence: Pay Strategies in the New Economy*, Jossey Publishing, New York.

Lawler, J.J. (1990) *Unionisation and Deunionisation: Strategy, Tactics and Outcomes*, University of South Carolina Press, Columbia, SC.

Lawrence, P.R. and Lorsch, J.W. (1967) *Organization and Environment*, Harvard University Press, Harvard, Mass.

Lewicki, R.J., D.M. Saunders and B. Barry (2005) *Negotiation*, 5th edn, McGraw-Hill, New York.

Lewicki, R.J., D.M. Saunders, B. Barry and J.W. Minton (2004) *The Essentials of Negotiation*, 3rd edn, McGraw-Hill, New York.

Lewin, D. and K.E. Boroff (1996) 'The role of exit in loyalty and voice', in *Advances in Industrial and Labour Relations*, D. Lewin, B.E. Kaufman and D.S. Sockell (eds), JAI Press, Greenwich, CT.

Lewin, D. and R.B. Peterson (1999) 'Behavioural outcomes of grievance activity', *Industrial Relations*, Vol. 38 (4), pp. 554–576.

Lewis, D. and M. Sargeant (2004) *Essentials of Employment Law*, 8th edn, CIPD Publishing, London.

Lewis, P. (1981) 'An analysis of why legislation has failed to provide employment protection for unfairly dismissed employees', *British Journal of Industrial Relations*, Vol. 19 (3), pp. 316–328.

Lewis, P., A. Thornhill and M. Saunders (2003) *Employee Relations: Understanding the Employment Relationship*, Prentice Hall, Harlow.

Lindsay, C. (2003) 'A century of labour market change: 1900–2000', *Labour Market Trends (Special Feature)*, Office for National Statistics, London.

Lloyd, C. (2001) 'What do employee councils do? The impact of non-union forms of representation on trade union organisation', *Industrial Relations Journal*, Vol. 32 (4), pp. 313–327.

Logan, J. (2001) 'Is statutory recognition bad news for British unions? Evidence from the history of North American industrial relations', *Historical Studies in Industrial Relations*, Vol. 11 (Spring), pp. 63–108.

LPC (2005) *The Low Pay Commission's Pay Report 2005*, Cmnd. 6475, Low Pay Commission, HMSO, Norwich.

LRD (1985a) *Fall in company funds to the Tories*, Labour Research Department, London, August.

LRD (1985b) *Company Cash for the Liberals*, Labour Research Department, London, May.

Lubatkin, M.H., P.J. Lane, S.O. Collin and P. Very (2005) 'Origins of corporate governance in the USA, Sweden and France', *Organization Studies*, Vol. 26 (6), pp. 867–888.

M

Magenau, J.M. and D.G. Pruitt (1979) 'The social psychology of bargaining', in *Industrial Relations: A Social Psychological Approach*, G.M. Stephenson and C.J. Brotherton (eds), Wiley, Chichester.

Marchington, M. (2005) 'Employee involvement: patterns and explanations', in *Participation and Democracy at Work: Essays in Honour of Harvie Ramsay*, B. Harley, J. Hyman and P. Thompson (eds), Palgrave Macmillan, Basingstoke.

Marchington, M. and P. Parker (1990) *Changing Patterns of Employee Relations*, Harvester Wheatsheaf, Hemel Hempstead.

Marchington, M. and A. Wilkinson (2005a) *Human Resource Management at Work: People Management and Development*, 3rd edn, CIPD Publishing, London.

Marchington, M. and A. Wilkinson (2005b) 'Direct Participation', in *Personnel Management: A Comprehensive Guide to Theory and Practice*, 4th edition, S. Bach (ed.), Blackwell, Oxford.

Marchington, M., J. Goodman, A. Wilkinson, and P. Ackers, (1992) *New Developments in Employee Involvement*, Employment Department Research Paper No 2, London.

Marchington, M., D. Grimshaw, J. Rubery and H. Willmott (eds) (2004) *Fragmenting Work: Blurring Organisational Boundaries and Disordering Hierarchies*, Oxford University Press, Oxford.

Marchington, M., A. Wilkinson, P. Ackers and T. Dundon (2001) *Management Choice and Employee Voice*, CIPD Publishing, London.

Marsden, D. and R. Belfield (2005) 'Unions and performance related pay: what chance of a procedural role?', in *Trade Unions: Resurgence or Demise?*, S. Fernie and D. Metcalf (eds), Routledge, London.

Marsden, D., S. French and K. Kubo (2000) *Why Does Performance Pay De-motivate?*, Centre for Economic Performance Discussion Paper, London School of Economics, London.

Marsh, A. (1966) 'Disputes procedures in British industry', *Royal Commission on Trade Unions and Employers' Associations. Research Papers 2*, HMSO, London.

Marsh, A. (1974) *Contract Negotiation Handbook*, Gower, Aldershot.

Martin, R. (1992) *Bargaining Power*, Clarendon Press, Oxford.

Martinez Lucio, M. and M. Stuart (2005) 'Where next for partnership?', in *Partnership and Modernisation in Employment Relations*, M. Stuart and M. Martinez Lucio (eds), Routledge, London.

Marx, K. (1894/1974) *Capital, Vols. 1 and 3*, Lawrence Wishart, London.

Maslow, A. (1970) *Motivation and Personality*, 3rd edn, Harper and Row, New York.

Masterson, S.S., K. Lewis, B.M. Goldman and M.S. Taylor (2000) 'Integrating justice and social exchange: the differing effects of fair procedures and treatment on work relationships', *Academy of Management Journal*, Vol. 43 (3), pp. 738–748.

Matsuura, K., M. Pollitt, R. Takada and S. Tanaka (2003) 'Institutional restructuring in the Japanese economy since 1985', *Journal of Economic Issues*, Vol. 37 (4), pp. 999–1022.

McClelland, D.C. (1961) *The Achieving Society*, Free Press, New York.

McGregor, D. (1960) *The Human Side of Enterprise*, McGraw-Hill, New York.

McIlroy, J. (1995) *Trade Unions in Britain Today*, Manchester University Press, Manchester.

McKinlay, A. and P. Taylor (1996) 'Power, surveillance and resistance: inside the factory of the future', in *The New Workplace and Trade Unionism: Critical Perspectives on Work and Organisation*, P. Ackers, C. Smith and P. Smith (eds), Routledge, London.

McLoughlin, I. and S. Gourlay (1994) *Enterprise Without Unions: Industrial Relations in the Non-union Firm*, Open University Press, Buckingham.

Mercer Human Resource Consulting (2005) http//www.mercerhr.com/pressrelease/details.jhtml/dynamic/idContent/1187220.

Metcalf, D. (1999) 'The British national minimum wage', *British Journal of Industrial Relations*, Vol. 37, pp. 171–201.

Metcalf, D. (2005) *British Unions: Resurgence or Perdition?*, Provocation Series, Vol. 1 (1), The Work Foundation, London.

Michels, R. (1915) *Political Parties: A Sociological Study of the Oligarchical Tendencies in Modern Democracy*, Free Press, London.

Milkman, R. (ed.) (2000) *Organizing Immigrants: The Challenge for Unions in Contemporary California*, Cornell University Press, Ithaca.

Millerson, G. (1964) *The Qualifying Associations*, Routledge, London.

Millward, N., A. Bryson and J. Forth (2000) *All change at work: British employment relations 1980–1998 as portrayed by the Workplace Industrial Relations Survey Series*, Routledge, London.

Milner, S. (1993) 'Overtime bans and strikes: evidence on relative incidence', *Industrial Relations Journal*, Vol. 24 (3), pp. 201–210.

Mitchell, D. (1979) *Control without Bureaucracy*, McGraw-Hill, London.

Mitchell, R.K., B.R. Angle and D.J. Wood (1997) 'Towards a theory of stakeholder identification and salience: defining the principles of who and what really counts', *Academy of Management Review*, Vol. 22 (4), pp. 853–886.

Mitchell, T.R. and R.E. Wood (1980) 'Subordinate poor performance: a test of an attributional model', *Organisational Behaviour and Human Performance*, Vol. 25 (2), pp. 123–138.

Moody, K (1988) *An Injury to All: The Decline of American Unionism*, Verso, New York.

Moore, R.J. (1980) 'The motivation to become a shop steward', *British Journal of Industrial Relations*, Vol. 18 (1), pp. 91–98.

Moore, S., S. McKay and H. Bewley (2005) *The Content of New Voluntary Trade Union Recognition Agreements 1998–2002: Volume II – findings from the survey of employers*, Employment Relations Research Series No 43, Department of Trade and Industry, London.

Morley, I.E. (1979) 'Behavioural studies of industrial bargaining', in *Industrial Relations: A Social Psychological Approach*, G.M. Stephenson and C.J. Brotherton (eds), Wiley, Chichester.

Morrell, K. and J. Smith (1971) 'The white collar split', *Industrial Society*, August, pp. 7–10.

Morris, J.R., W.F. Cascio and C.E. Young (1999) 'Downsizing after all these years: questions and answers about who did it, how many did it and who benefited from it', *Organisational Dynamics*, Winter, pp. 78–87.

Morris, M., R. Larrick, and S. Su (1999) 'Misperceiving negotiation counterparts: when situationally determined bargaining behaviours are attributed to personality traits', *Journal of Personality and Social Psychology*, Vol. 77 (1), pp. 52–68.

Mulholland, K. (2002) 'Gender, emotional labour and teamworking in a call centre', *Personnel Review*, Vol. 31 (3), pp. 283–303.

Mulholland, K. (2004) 'Workplace resistance in an Irish call centre: slammin, scammin, smoking and leaving', *Work, Employment and Society*, Vol. 15 (1), pp. 709–724.

Mullins, L.J. (2002) *Management and Organisational Behaviour*, 6th edn, Financial Times, Harlow.

Mumford, P. (1975) *Redundancy and Security of Employment*, Gower Press, Aldershot.

N

Nicholson, N. (1979) 'Industrial relations climate: a case study approach', *Personnel Review*, Vol. 8 (3), pp. 20–25.

Nolan, P. and P. Marginson (1988) 'Skating on Thin Ice?: David Metcalf on trade unions and productivity', *Warwick Papers on Industrial Relations, No. 22*, University of Warwick, Coventry.

Noon, M. and P. Blyton (2002), *The Realities of Work*, 2nd edn, Palgrave, London.

Norsworthy, J.R. and C.A. Zabala (1985) 'Worker attitudes, worker behaviour, and productivity in the U.S. automobile industry, 1959–76', *Industrial and Labour Relations Review*, Vol. 38 (4), pp. 544–547.

O

O'Connor, K.M., J.A. Arnold and E.R. Burris (2005) 'Negotiators' bargaining histories and their effects on future negotiation performance', *Journal of Applied Psychology*, Vol. 90 (2), pp. 350–563.

O'Doherty, D. and H. Willmott (2001) 'The question of subjectivity and the labour process', *International Studies of Management and Organisation*, Vol. 30 (4), pp. 112–132.

Office for National Statistics (2003) *Social Capital*, London, (www.statistics.gov.uk/cci/nugget.asp).

Office for National Statistics (2004) *Inland Revenue: Personal Wealth*, London, (www.statistics.gov.uk/cci/nugget.asp).

Office for National Statistics (2005) *Public Sector Employment*, London, (www.statistics.gov.uk/cci/nuggest.asp).

Ogden, S.G. (1981) 'The reform of collective bargaining: a managerial revolution?', *Industrial Relations Journal*, Vol. 12 (5), pp. 30–42.

Olson, M. (1965) *The Logic of Collective Action: Public Goods and the Theory of Groups*, Harvard University Press, Harvard Mass.

Olson-Buchanan, J.B. (1996) 'Voicing discontent: what happens to the grievance filer after grievance?' *Journal of Applied Psychology*, Vol. 81 (1), pp. 52–63.

Ornatowski, G.K. (1998) 'The end of Japanese-style human resource management?', *Sloan Management Review*, Vol. 39 (3), pp. 73–84.

Osterman, P., T. Kochan, R.M. Locke and M.J. Piore (2001) *Working In America: A Blueprint For The New Labour Market*, MIT Press, Cambridge, Mass.

Oxenbridge, S. and W. Brown (2002) 'The two faces of partnership and cooperative employer and trade union relationship', *Employee Relations*, Vol. 24 (3), pp. 262–277.

Oxenbridge, S. and W. Brown (2004) 'A Poisoned Chalice? Trade Union Representatives in Partnership and Co-operative Employer-Union Relationships', in *The Future of Worker Representation*, G. Healy, E. Heery, P. Taylor and W. Brown (eds), Palgrave Macmillan, Basingstoke.

P

Parker, M. and J. Slaughter (1988) 'Management by stress', *Technology Review*, October, pp. 27–31.

Pateman, C. (1970) *Participation and Democratic Theory*, Cambridge University Press, Cambridge.

Pedler, M.J. (1973) 'Shop stewards as leaders', *Industrial Relations Journal*, Vol. 3 (1), pp. 43–60.

Peetz, D. (2002) 'Decollectivist strategies in Oceania', *Relations Industrielles*, Vol. 57 (2), pp. 5–18.

Pelling, H. (1987) *A History of British Trade Unionism*, 4th edn, Pelican, Harmondsworth.

Pendleton, A. (2000) *Employee Ownership, Participation and Governance: A Study of ESOPs in the UK*, Routledge, London.

Pfeffer, J. (1992) *Managing with Power: Politics and Influence in Organisations*, Harvard Business School Press, Boston, Mass.

Pfeffer, J. (1998) *The Human Equation: Building Profitability by Putting People First*, Harvard Business School Press, Boston, Mass.

Phelps Brown, H. (1990) 'The Counter-Revolution of Our Time', *Industrial Relations Journal*, Vol. 29 (1), pp. 1–14.

Pickard, J. (2005) 'Richmond Mirrors', *People Management*, Vol. 11 (11), p. 33.

Poole, M., R. Mansfield, J. Gould-Williams and P. Mendes (2005) 'British managers' attitudes and behaviour in industrial relations: a twenty-year study', *British Journal of Industrial Relations*, Vol. 43 (1), pp. 117–134.

Poster, M. (1990) *The Mode of Information: Poststructuralism and Social Context*, Polity Press, Cambridge.

Prandy, K., A. Stewart and R.M. Blackburn (1983) *White-Collar Unionism*, Macmillan, London.

Proctor, S. and S. Ackroyd (2006) 'Flexibility', in *Contemporary Human Resource Management: Text and Cases*, 2nd edn, T. Redman and A. Wilkinson (eds), Prentice Hall, London.

Purcell, J. (1979) 'The lessons of the commission on industrial relations: attempts to reform British workplace industrial relations', *Industrial Relations Journal*, Vol. 10 (2), pp. 9–22.

Purcell, J. (1993) 'The end of institutional industrial relations', *British Journal of Industrial Relations*, Vol. 31 (1), pp. 6–23.

Purcell, J. (1999) 'The search for best practice and best fit in human resource management: chimera or cul-de-sac?' *Human Resource Management Journal*, Vol. 9 (3), pp. 26–41.

Purcell, J. and B. Ahlstrand (1993) *Strategy and Style in Employee Relations*, Oxford University Press, Oxford.

Purcell, J. and K. Sisson (1983) 'Strategies and practice in industrial relations', in *Industrial Relations in Britain*, G.S. Bain (ed.), Blackwell, Oxford.

Purcell, J. and R. Smith (eds) (1979) *The Control of Work*, Macmillan, London.

Purcell, J., L. Dalgleish, J. Harrison, I. Lonsdale, I. McConaghy and A. Robertson (1978) 'Power from technology: computer staff and industrial relations', *Personnel Review*, Vol. 7 (1), pp. 31–39.

R

Rackham, N. and J. Carlisle (1978) 'The effective negotiator – part 2: planning for negotiations', *Journal of European Industrial Training*, Vol. 2, pp. 2–5.

Ram, M. (1994) *Managing to Survive: Working Lives in Small Firms*, Blackwell, Oxford.

Ramsay, H. (1977) 'Cycles of control: worker participation in sociological and historical perspective', *Sociology*, Vol. II, pp. 481–506.

Ray, C.A. (1986) 'Corporate culture: the last frontier of control', *Journal of Management Studies*, Vol. 23 (3), pp. 287–297.

Reddish, H. (1967) 'From Memoranda of Evidence', submitted by Sir Halford Reddish, F.C.A. (Chairman and Managing Director, The Rugby Portland Cement Co. Ltd.), in advance of the Oral Hearing. *Royal Commission on Trade Unions and Employers Associations*, Commission Reference WE/383.

Redeker, J. (1983) *Discipline: Policies and Procedures*, Bureau of National Affairs, Washington, DC.

Redundancy Payments Act (1965) HMSO, London.

Rees, W.D. (1997) 'The disciplinary pyramid and its importance', *Industrial and Commercial Training*, Vol. 29 (1), pp. 4–9.

Rim, Y. and B.F. Mannheim (1979) 'Factors relating to attitudes of management and union representatives', *Personnel Psychology*, Vol. 64 (4), pp. 387–390.

Robinson, A. and N. Wilson (2006) 'Employee financial participation and productivity: An empirical reappraisal', *British Journal of Industrial Relations*, Vol. 44 (1), pp. 31–50.

Roche, W. and J. Geary (2002) 'Advocates, critics and union involvement in workplace partnership: Irish airports', *British Journal of Industrial Relations*, Vol. 40 (4), pp. 659–688.

Roethlisberger, F.J. and W.J. Dixon (1939) *Management and the Worker*, Harvard University Press, Harvard Mass.

Rogers, J. and W. Streeck (eds) (1995) *Works Councils: Consultation, Representation and Cooperation in Industrial Relations*, University of Chicago Press, Chicago, Ill.

Rollinson, D.J. (1992) 'Individual issues in industrial relations: an examination of discipline and an agenda for research', *Personnel Review*, Vol. 21 (1), pp. 46–57.

Rollinson, D.J. (1997) 'More than a rap on the knuckles', *Croner Reference Book Employers Magazine*, June, pp. 10–13.

Rollinson, D.J. (2000) 'Supervisor and manager approaches to handling discipline and grievance: a follow-up study', *Personnel Review*, Vol. 29 (5/6), pp. 743–768.

Rollinson, D.J. (2005) *Organisational Behaviour and Analysis: An Integrated Approach*, 3rd edn, Prentice Hall, Harlow.

Rollinson, D.J., J. Handley, C. Hook and M. Foot (1997) 'The disciplinary experience and its effects on behaviour: an exploratory study', *Work, Employment and Society*, Vol. 11 (2), pp. 283–311.

Rose, E. (2004) *Employment Relations*, 2nd edn, Prentice Hall, Harlow.

Rosen, M. and J. Baroudi (1992) 'Computer-based technology and the emergence of new forms of control', in *Skill and Consent: Contemporary Studies in the Labour Process*, A. Sturdy, D. Knights and H. Willmott (eds), Routledge, London.

Ross, A.M. and P.T. Hartman (1960) *Changing Patterns of Industrial Conflict*, Wiley, Chichester.

Rousseau, D. (1995) *Psychological Contracts in Organisations: Understanding the Written and Unwritten Agreements*, Sage, London.

Roy, D. (1980) 'Repression and incorporation. Fear stuff, sweet stuff, and evil stuff: management's defences against unionisation in the south', in *Capital and Labour: A Marxist Primer*, T. Nichols (ed.), Fontana, Glasgow.

Royle, T. (2000) *Working for McDonald's: The Unequal Struggle*, Routledge, London.

RSA (1995) *Tomorrow's Company*, Royal Society for the Encouragement of Arts, Manufactures and Commerce, London.

Rubery, J., J. Earnshaw and M. Marchington (2004) 'Blurring the Boundaries to the Employment Relationship: From Single to Multi-Employer Relationships', in *Fragmenting Work: Blurring Organisational Boundaries and Disordering Hierarchies*, M. Marchington, D. Grimshaw, J. Rubery and H. Willmott (eds), Oxford University Press, Oxford.

Rubery, J., J. Earnshaw, M. Marchington, F. Lee-Cooke, and S. Vincent (2001) 'Changing organisational forms and the employment relationship', *The Future of Work, Working Paper No. 4*, ESRC, London.

S

Salamon, M. (2000) *Industrial Relations: Theory and Practice*, 4th edn, Prentice Hall, London.

Sayles, L.R. (1958) *Behaviour of Work Groups*, Wiley, New York.

Schaede, U. (2004) 'What happened to the Japanese model?', *Review of International Economics*, Vol. 12 (2), pp. 277–294.

Schein, E.H. (1980) *Organisational Psychology*, 3rd edn, Prentice Hall, Englewood Cliffs.

Schneider, B. (1983) 'Work climates: an interactionist perspective', in *Environmental Psychology: Directions and Perspectives*, N.W. Feimer and E.S. Geller (eds), Praeger, New York.

Seifert, R. and M. Ironside (2001) *Facing Up to Thatcherism: The History of NALGO 1979–1993*, Oxford University Press, Oxford.

Sewell, G. (1998) 'The discipline of teams: the control of team-based industrial work through electronic and peer surveillance', *Administrative Science Quarterly*, Vol. 43 (4), pp. 397–428.

Sinclair, A. (1992) 'The tyranny of a team ideology', *Organisation Studies*, Vol. 13 (4), pp. 611–626.

Sisson, K. (1993) 'In search of HRM', *British Journal of Industrial Relations*, Vol. 31 (2), pp. 201–210.

Sisson, K. (2002) 'The Information and Consultation Directive: unnecessary "regulation" or an opportunity to promote "partnership"?', *Warwick Papers in Industrial Relations*, No. 67, Industrial Relations Research Unit (IRRU), Warwick University, Coventry.

Sisson, K. and P. Marginson (2003) 'Management: Systems, Structure and Strategy', in *Industrial Relations: Theory and Practice in Britain*, 2nd edn, P. Edwards (ed.), Blackwell, Oxford.

Sisson, K. and J. Storey (2000) *The Realities of Human Resource Management*, Open University Press, Buckingham.

Smith, C.T.B., R. Clifton, P. Makeham, S.W. Creigh and R.V. Burn (1978) 'Strikes in Britain', *Department of Employment, Manpower Paper No. 15*, HMSO, London.

Smith, P. and G. Morton (2001) 'New Labour's reform of Britain's employment law: the devil is not only in the detail but in the values and policy too', *British Journal of Employment Relations*, Vol. 30 (1), pp. 119–138.

Stewart, R. (1991) *Managing Today and Tomorrow*, Macmillan, London.

Storey, J. (1983) *Managerial Prerogative and the Question of Control*, Routledge, London.

Storey, J. (2001) *Human Resource Management: A Critical Text*, Thompson, London.

Strauss, G. (1998) 'Participation Works – If Conditions are Appropriate', in *Organizational*

Participation: Myth and Reality, F. Heller, E. Pusic, G. Strauss and B. Wilpert (eds), Oxford University Press, Oxford.

Summerfield, C. and B. Gill (2005) *Social Trends, No. 35*, Palgrave Macmillan, London.

Swann, J.P. (1981) 'Formal grievance procedures and non-union plants: do they really work?', *Personnel Administrator*, August, pp. 66–70.

T

Tannenbaum, R. (1962) 'Control in organisations: individual adjustment and performance', *Administrative Science Quarterly*, Vol. 7 (2), pp. 236–257.

Taylor, F.W. (1911) *Scientific Management*, Wiley, New York.

Taylor, P. and H. Ramsay (1998) 'Union, Partnership, and HRM: sleeping with the enemy?', *International Journal of Employment Studies*, Vol. 6 (2), pp. 115–143.

Taylor, P., C. Baldry, P. Bain and V. Ellis (2003) 'A unique working environment: health, sickness and absence management in UK call centres', *Work, Employment and Society*, Vol. 17 (3), pp. 435–450.

Terry, M. (1977) 'The inevitable growth of informality', *British Journal of Industrial Relations*, Vol. 15 (1), pp. 75–90.

Terry, M. (2003) 'Can "partnership" reverse the decline of British trade unions?', *Work Employment and Society*, Vol. 17 (3), pp. 459–472.

Terryn, B. (1999) 'Redundancies in the UK', *Labour Market Trends*, May, pp. 251–261.

Thomas, C. (1976) 'Strategy for a sit-in', *Personnel Management*, January, pp. 32–35.

Thomas, G.N. and R. Kumar (1987) 'The Social Psychology of Crisis Bargaining: towards a contingency Model', *Columbia Journal of World Business*, Vol. 22 (1), pp. 23–32.

Thomas, R. and A. Davies (2005) 'Theorising the micro-politics of resistance: new public management and managerial identities in the UK public services', *Organisation Studies*, Vol. 26 (5), pp. 683–706.

Thompson, M. and D.G. Taras (2004) 'Employment Relations in Canada', in *International and Comparative Employment Relations: Globalisation and the Developed Market Economies*, 4th edn, G. Bamber, R. Lansbury and N. Wailes (eds), Sage, London.

Thompson, P. and S. Ackroyd (1995) 'All quiet on the workplace front? A critique of recent trends in British industrial sociology', *Sociology*, Vol. 29 (4), pp. 615–633.

Thomson, A. and P.B. Beaumont (1978) *Public Sector Bargaining: A Study of Relative Gain*, Saxon House, Farnborough.

Thomson, A.W.J. and V.V. Murray (1976) *Grievance Procedures*, Saxon House, Farnborough.

Thornhill, A., M.H.K. Saunders and J. Stead (1997) 'Downsizing, delayering – but where's the commitment?', *Personnel Review*, Vol. 26 (1/2), pp. 81–98.

Timmons, S. (2003) 'A failed panopticon: surveillance of nursing practice via new technology', *New Technology, Work and Employment*, Vol. 18 (2), pp. 143–153.

Tjosvold, D. (1991) *Team Organisation: An Enduring Competitive Advantage*, Wiley, London.

Torrington, D., L. Hall and S. Taylor (2002) *Human Resource Management*, 5th edn, Prentice-Hall, London.

Towers, B. (1997) *The Representation Gap: Change and Reform in the British and American Workplace*, Oxford University Press, Oxford.

Towers, B. (2003) 'Overview: The changing employment relationship', in *Handbook of Employment Relations, Law and Practice*, 4th edn, B. Towers (ed.), Kogan Page, London.

Townsend, K. (2005) 'Electronic surveillance and cohesive teams: room for resistance in an Australian call centre?' *New Technology, Work and Employment*, Vol. 20 (1), pp. 47–59.

Trade Union Act (1984) HMSO, London.

Trade Union and Labour Relations (Consolidation) Act (1992), HMSO, London.

Trade Union Reform and Employment Rights Act (1993) HMSO, London.

Trades Disputes Act (1906) HMSO, London.

Trevino, L.K. (1992) 'The social effects of punishment in organisations: a justice perspective', *Academy of Management Review*, Vol. 17 (3), pp. 647–676.

Truss, C., L. Gratton, V. Hope-Hailey, P. McGovern, and P. Stiles (1997) 'Soft and hard models of human resource management: a reappraisal', *Journal of Management Studies*, Vol. 34 (1), pp. 53–73.

TUC (2001) *Partners for Progress*, Trades Union Congress, London.

Turnbull, P., J. Morris and D. Sapsford (1996) 'Persistent Militants and Quiescent Comrades: Intra-Industrial Strike Activity on the Docks, 1947–89', *Sociological Review*, Vol. 44 (4), pp. 710–745.

Turner, J.T. and J.W. Robinson (1972) 'A pilot study of the validity of grievance settlement as a predictor of union management relationships', *Journal of Industrial Relations*, Vol. 14, pp. 314–322.

Turner, T. and D. D'Art (eds) (2002) *Industrial Relations in the New Economy*, Blackhall Press, Dublin.

Tuselman, H. and A. Heise (2000) 'The German model of industrial relations at the crossroads: past present and future', *Industrial Relations Journal*, Vol. 31 (3), pp. 162–176.

U

Urwick, L. (1943) *The Elements of Administration*, Harper, New York.

V

Visser, J. and J. van Ruysseveldt (1996) 'Robust corporatism still? Industrial relations in Germany', in *Industrial Relations in Europe: Traditions and Transitions*, J. van Russeveldt and J. Visser (eds), Sage, London.

Von Clauswitz, C. (1986) *On War*, English translation, Penguin, Harmondsworth.

Vroom, V.H. (1964) *Work and Motivation*, Wiley, New York.

W

Waddington, J. and C. Whitston (1997) 'Why do people join unions in a period of membership decline?', *British Journal of Industrial Relations*, Vol. 35 (4), pp. 515–546.

Walker, C.R. and R.H. Guest (1957) *Man on the Assembly Line*, Yale University Press, New Haven.

Wallace, J., P. Gunnigle and G. McMahon (2004) *Industrial Relations in Ireland*, 3rd edn, Gill and Macmillan, Dublin.

Walton, R.E. (1969) *Interpersonal Peacemaking: Consultations and Third Party Consultation*, Addison Wesley, Reading, Mass.

Walton, R.E. (1985) 'From control to commitment in the workplace', *Harvard Business Review*, March–April, pp. 77–84.

Walton, R.E. and R.B. McKersie (1965) *A Behavioural Theory of Labour Negotiations*, McGraw-Hill, New York.

Walton, R.E., J.E. Cuther-Gershenfeld and R.B. McKersie (1994) *Strategic Negotiations: A Theory of Change in Labor-Management Relations*, Harvard Business School Press, Boston Mass.

Warhurst, C. and P. Thompson (1998) 'Hands, hearts and minds: changing work and workers at the end of the century', in *Workplaces of the Future*, P. Thompson and C. Warhurst (eds), Macmillan Business, Basingstoke.

Watson, T.J. (1995) *Sociology, Work and Industry*, Routledge, London.

Webb, S. and B. Webb (1897) *Industrial Democracy*, Longman, London.

Weber, M. (1919) 'Politics as a vocation', in *From Max Weber*, H. Girth and C. Wright Mills (eds), Routledge, London.

Weber, M. (1976) *The Protestant Ethic and the Spirit of Capitalism*, 2nd edn, Allen and Unwin, London.

Wedderburn, K.W. (Lord) (1980) 'Industrial relations and the courts', *Industrial Law Journal*, Vol. 9, pp. 65–94.

Wedderburn, Lord (1986) *The Worker and the Law*, 3rd edn, Penguin, Harmondsworth.

Wedderburn, Lord (2001) 'Collective bargaining or legal enactment: the 1999 Act and union recognition', *Industrial Law Journal*, Vol. 29, pp. 1–42.

Weekes, B., M. Mellish, L. Dickens and J. Lloyd (1975) *Industrial Relations and the Limits of the Law: the Industrial Effects of the Industrial Relations Act 1971*, Blackwell, Oxford.

Weick, K.E. (2001) *Making Sense of the Organisation*, Blackwell, Oxford.

Welch, J. (1999) 'ROM with a view', *People Management*, 17 June, pp. 34–40.

Wheeler, H. (1987) 'Management – labour relations in the U.S.A', in *International and Comparative Industrial Relations*, G. Bamber and R. Lansbury (eds), Allen and Unwin, London.

Wheeler, H.M. (1976) 'Punishment theory and industrial discipline', *Industrial Relations*, Vol. 15 (2), pp. 235–243.

White, G. and J. Druker (eds) (2000) *Reward Management: A Critical Text*, Routledge, London.

Whittaker, D.H. (1990) 'The end of Japanese-style employment?', *Work, Employment and Society*, Vol. 4 (3), pp. 340–353.

Wickens, P. (1987) *The Road to Nissan*, Macmillan, London.

Wilkinson, A. (1999) 'Employment relations in SMEs', *Employee Relations*, Vol. 22 (3), pp. 206–217.

Wilkinson, A., T. Dundon, M. Marchington and P. Ackers (2004) 'Changing patterns of employee voice, *Journal of Industrial Relations*, Vol. 46, (3), pp. 298–322.

Willmott, H. (1993) 'Strength is ignorance: slavery is freedom: managing culture in modern organisation', *Journal of Management Studies*, Vol. 30 (4), pp. 515–551.

Willmott, H. (1997) 'Rethinking managerial work: capitalism, control and subjectivity', *Human Relations*, Vol. 50 (11), pp. 1329–1359.

Wills, J. (1999) 'European works councils in British firms', *Human Resource Management Journal*, Vol. 9 (4), pp. 19–38.

Wilson, J.G. (1966) 'Innovation in organizations: notes towards a theory', in *Approaches to Organizational Design*, J.D. Thompson (ed.), University of Pittsburg Press, Pittsburg Pa.

Winchester, D. (1983) 'Industrial relations in the public sector', in *Industrial Relations in Britain*, G.S. Bain (ed.), Blackwell, Oxford.

Wood, S., S. Moore and K. Ewing (2003) 'The impact of trade union recognition under the Employment Relations Act 2000–2002', in *Representing Workers: Trade Union Recognition and Membership in Britain*, H. Gospel and S. Wood, (eds), Routledge, London.

Z

Zand, D.E. (1972) 'Trust and managerial problem solving', *Administrative Science Quarterly*, Vol. 17 (2), pp. 229–239.

Index